SPINOZA
ISSUES AND DIRECTIONS

BRILL'S STUDIES
IN
INTELLECTUAL HISTORY

SPINOZA

ISSUES AND DIRECTIONS

The Proceedings of the Chicago Spinoza Conference

Edited by

Edwin Curley and Pierre-François Moreau

E.J. BRILL

LEIDEN · NEW YORK · KØBENHAVN · KÖLN

1990

The paper in this book meets the guidelines for performance and durability of the Committee on Production Guidelines for Book Longevity of the Council on Library Resources.

Library of Congress Cataloging-in-Publication Data

Chicago Spinoza Conference (1986: Chicago, Ill.)
 Spinoza: issues and directions: the proceedings of the Chicago Spinoza Conference/edited by Edwin Curley and Pierre-François Moreau.
 p.   cm.—(Brill's studies in intellectual history, ISSN 0920-8607: v. 14)
 Contributions in English and French.
 Includes indexes.
 ISBN 90-04-09334-6
 1. Spinoza, Benedictus de, 1632-1677—Congresses. I. Curley, E. M. (Edwin M.), 1937-   . II. Moreau, Pierre-François, 1948-
III. Title. IV. Series.
B3950.C35   1986
199'.492—dc20   90-49020
                                                        CIP

ISSN   0920-8607
ISBN   90 04 09334 6

PRINTED IN THE NETHERLANDS

CONTENTS

PREFACE

This volume contains the texts of the papers presented at the conference on Spinoza held over a period of six days in Chicago in September 1986, with support from the University of Illinois at Chicago, the National Endowment for the Humanities, the Department of Philosophy at Northwestern University, and the Italian Cultural Institute of Chicago. For a long time the climate of opinion in American philosophy was not favorable to the history of philosophy or to the kind of metaphysical system-building of which Spinoza is one of the outstanding historical examples. But in the past twenty years or so there has been renewed interest both in the history of philosophy and in metaphysical systems. This change of climate has brought with it a flood of work re-interpreting and re-evaluating the philosophy of Spinoza. One major purpose of the conference was to reflect collectively on recent work on Spinoza, and to identify the major issues in current Spinoza studies and the lines of work most likely to be fruitful in the future.

But the conference was also intended to bring together the two worlds of Spinoza scholarship. One feature characteristic of post-war philosophy has been the split between the styles of philosophy popular in the U. S. and on the Continent. This has made communication difficult between philosophers educated in the different traditions. To help improve communication we invited a broad cross-section of scholars from all over the world. About half of the 31 speakers came from the U.S., but the remainder came from England, France, Germany, Italy, Holland, Belgium, Israel and Australia. To the best of my knowledge, this was the first time that a conference on Spinoza of this scope has been held in the United States.

The reader will see that this did indeed result in a variety of approaches. One characteristic of American scholarship, it seems, is a tendency to focus on the traditional problems of Spinoza's metaphysics and philosophy of mind, treated with particular emphasis on Spinoza's masterwork, the *Ethics*: the interpretation of the arguments for the existence of God (Doncy), the status of the attributes (Eisenberg, Ariew), the concept of infinity (Ariew), the doctrine of the eternity of the mind (Matson, Allison), the status of teleology (Curley, Bennett), the nature of ideas and their relation to judgment and error (Donagan, Lloyd). It is more characteristic of Continental scholars, on the other hand, to encompass the whole range of Spinoza's writings, focussing particularly on problems in ethics, social and political philosophy, and philosophy of history. Thus we have Matheron writing on the evolution of Spinoza's political thought from the *Theological-Political Treatise* to the *Political Treatise*, Moreau on the role of *fortuna* in history, Macherey and Tosel on questions of development and progress in history, Giancotti on the problem of freedom in Spinoza.

Various of our authors, of course, escape these generalizations: e.g., Balibar treats central problems in Spinoza's metaphysics, causality and individuality; Garrett focuses on the problem of reconciling the claim that the free man never acts deceptively with the foundation of Spinoza's ethical theory in the principle of self-preservation; and all of the essays dealing with topics in Spinoza's theory of knowledge come from authors who are more or less in the Continental tradition (Klever, Mignini, Yovel, and DeDijn).   And the geographical base of the author is by no means a reliable guide to the style of treatment (cf., e.g., the essay by Rorty).   But surely one result of the confrontation of the two worlds of Spinoza scholarship is a broader sense of the range of problems which might attract an interpreter.

It is also encouraging to see the extent to which American scholars are attending to the work of such masters of the Continental tradition as Gueroult (e.g., Doney, Donagan, Eisenberg, Ariew, Matson) and Matheron (Rice, Matson), and Continental scholars to the work of Bennett (Balibar, Yovel). Some of our articles devote themselves explicitly to giving an account of important scholarly works which, given our various cultural preoccupations, might otherwise escape attention: e.g., Walther on Negri, and Kline on Macherey.   And the late Professor Hubbeling, who died only a few weeks after our conference and who will be very much missed, has provided us with a splendidly illuminating survey of work on Spinoza in the Netherlands since the end of the Second World War.

The relation between Spinoza and other philosophers is a frequent theme in these papers.   Thus we have Beyssade, Wilson, Rorty, Ariew, Donagan, and Lloyd all dealing with the relation between Spinoza and Descartes; Macherey, Harris, and Kline all dealing with the relation between Spinoza and Hegel (and in Harris' case, with the German idealists generally); Ariew again on Spinoza in relation to the scholastics; Benardete on Spinoza's relation to Freud; and finally, Popkin on Spinoza's relation to an underground critique of religion, *The Three Imposters*.

This conference was, we believe, an important event in the history of Spinoza scholarship and we are pleased to present this record of it here.   The papers have been arranged, however, according to their subject matter, and not according to the order in which they were presented at the conference. Between the time of the conference and the time of the publication of the proceedings one of the papers (that of Amélie Rorty) has been published in the *Review of Metaphysics*.   We reprint it here with their permission.   Edwin Curley has been responsible for editing the papers written in English and Pierre-François Moreau for those written in French.   We are both enormously indebted, however, to others for their help: Jacqueline Lagrée, who assisted with getting the French papers on disk; Lee Rice and Mike Friedman, who helped us to deal with papers which had been written in alien wordprocessing systems and had to be converted to WordPerfect; the support staff at WordPerfect, who provided at great deal of assistance in learning the ins and outs of their program; and the National Endowment for the Humanities, whose funding supported the year of research at the National Humanities Center where the ms. finally was completed.

But the person we are most indebted to is Ruth Curley.   Not only did she do a great deal to make the conference itself run smoothly, but at the critical moment she volunteered to see the ms. through the laborious process from copy-editing to the production of camera-ready copy. This cost her what must have seemed endless hours of painstaking effort, learning the mysteries of desktop publishing, trying to make sure that the final disk versions of the mss. corresponded to the intentions of the thirty-one different authors, and at the same time trying to preserve a reasonably uniform style of citation. This was service beyond any call of wifely duty. Without her determination and persistence this book would never have appeared.

The standard edition of Spinoza's works in their original languages is that edited by Carl Gebhardt, *Spinoza Opera*, Heidelberg: Carl Winter, 1925, 4 vols. References to this edition will be abbreviated as follows: G II/37/5-9 = volume II, page 37, lines 5 through 9 of the Gebhardt edition. Some scholars still find it convenient to use the editions of J. van Vloten and J. P. N. Land: Spinoza, *Opera quotquot reperta sunt*, The Hague, 1st edition, 2 vols., 1895, 2nd edition, 3 vols., 1914. References to these editions will be abbreviated: VVL(1) and VVL(2).

The English language edition of Spinoza's works most commonly used by contributors to this volume is that edited by Edwin Curley, *The Collected Works of Spinoza*, Princeton: Princeton UP, 1985, vol. 1, abbreviated: Curley (1985). Though this edition is incomplete (the political works and the bulk of the correspondence being reserved for vol. 2, which is yet to appear), it has the advantage of giving the Gebhardt pagination in the margins. For the political works the most commonly used edition is that of A. G. Wernham, Benedict de Spinoza, *The Political Works*, Oxford: Clarendon Press, 1965, abbreviated: Wernham. For the correspondence, the edition of A. Wolf is frequently cited: *The Correspondence of Spinoza*, New York: Dial Press, n.d., abbreviated: Wolf.

There are two French language editions of Spinoza's works in common use by French scholars, that of Charles Appuhn, *Oeuvres de Spinoza*, Paris: Garnier, 1965, 4 vols. (abbreviated: Appuhn) and that of Roland Caillois, Madeleine Francès, and Robert Misrahi, *Oeuvres complètes de Spinoza*, Paris: Gallimard, 1954 (abbreviated: Pléiade).

Usually it is possible to make a fairly specific textual reference which is independent of the particular edition used. For that purpose the following system of abbreviations is employed:

E = the *Ethics*

KV = the *Short Treatise on God, Man and his Well-Being*

TdIE = the *Treatise on the Emendation of the Intellect*

PP = Descartes' *"Principles of Philosophy"*

CM = the *Metaphysical Thoughts*

Ep = the correspondence

TTP = the *Theological-Political Treatise*

TP = The *Political Treatise*

I, II, III, etc., refer to parts of the work cited if it is divided into parts (e.g., E, KV, PP, CM) and to chapters if they form the major principle of division (e.g., TTP, TP).

1, 2, 3, etc., refer to axioms, definitions, propositions, etc. in the case of works organized geometrically (E, PP), to chapters if the main division of the work is into parts and the work is not geometrical (KV, CM), and to section numbers if the main division of the work is into chapters (TTP, TP).

A = axiom

D (following a roman numeral) = definition

P = proposition

D (following an arabic numeral) = the demonstration of the proposition cited

C = Corollary

S = Scholium

Post = Postulate

L = Lemma (in the *Ethics* these occur after IIP13)

Exp = Explanation

Pref = Preface

App = Appendix

DefAff = the definitions of the affects at the end of E III.

So "E ID1" refers to the first definition of Part I of the *Ethics*, "KV I, 2" refers to the second chapter of Part I of the *Short Treatise*, "TP I, 5" refers to chapter I, section 5 of the *Political Treatise*, etc.

Because of the important influence of Descartes on Spinoza, contributors to this volume frequently cite his works in the standard edition of Charles Adam and Paul Tannery, *Oeuvres de Descartes*, Paris: Vrin, 1974-86, 11 vols., abbreviated: AT. The works of Leibniz are cited in the edition of C. I. Gerhardt, *Die philosophischen Schriften von Gottfried Wilhelm Leibniz*, Hildesheim: Olms, 1978, abbreviated: Gerhardt.

Some of the more recent works of scholarship are cited frequently enough in these essays to make it sensible to use the following system of shortened references:

Alquié (1981) = Alquié, F. *Le rationalisme de Spinoza.* Paris: Presses Universitaires de France, 1981.

Bennett, (1984) = Bennett, Jonathan. *A Study of Spinoza's Ethics.* Indianapolis: Hackett, 1984.

Blackwell (1985) = Blackwell, Kenneth. *The Spinozistic Ethics of Bertrand Russell.* London: Allen & Unwin, 1985.

Curley (1988) = Curley. E. M. *Behind the Geometrical Method.* Princeton: Princeton University Press, 1988.

Curley (1969) = Curley, E. M. *Spinoza's Metaphysics: an Essay in Interpretation.* Cambridge: Harvard University Press, 1969.

DeDeugd (1984) = *Spinoza's Political and Theological Thought.* Ed. C. DeDeugd. Amsterdam: North Holland, 1984.

Deleuze (1968) = Deleuze, Gilles. *Spinoza et le problème de l'expression.* Paris: Les éditions de minuit, 1968.

Den Uyl (1983) = Den Uyl, Douglas. *Power, State, and Freedom: An Interpretation of Spinoza's Political Philosophy.* Assen: Van Gorcum, 1983.

Giancotti (1985) = *Proceedings of the First Italian International Congress on Spinoza.* Ed. Emilia Giancotti. Naples: Bibliopolis, 1985.

Grene (1973) = *Spinoza: A Collection of Critical Essays.* Ed. Majorie Grene. Garden City, N.J.: Doubleday, 1973.

Gueroult (1968, 1974) = Gueroult, Martial. *Spinoza.* Hildesheim: Georg

Olms Verlag, Tome I 1968, Tome II 1974.

Hardin (1978) = Hardin, C. L. "Spinoza on Immortality and Time." *Spinoza: New Perspectives.* Norman: University of Oklahoma, 1978.

Hampshire (1962) = Hampshire, Stuart. *Spinoza.* Baltimore: Penguin, 1962.

Hessing (1977) = *Speculum Spinozanum.* Ed. Siegfried Hessing. London: Routledge & Kegan Paul, 1977.

Joachim (1901) = Joachim, M.M. *A Study of the Ethics of Spinoza.* Oxford: Clarendon Press, 1901.

Kashap (1972) = *Studies in Spinoza.* Ed. S. P. Kashap. Berkeley: University of California Press, 1972.

Kennington (1980) = *The Philosophy of Baruch Spinoza.* Ed. R. Kennington. Washington, D. C.: The Catholic University of America Press, 1980.

Kline (1977) = Kline, George L. "On the Infinity of Spinoza's Attributes." In Hessing (1977).

Macherey (1979) = Macherey, Pierre. *Hegel ou Spinoza.* Paris: François Maspero, 1979.

Mandelbaum and Freeman (1975) = *Spinoza: Essays in Interpretation.* Ed. M. Mandelbaum and Eugene Freeman. LaSalle: Open Court, 1975.

Matheron (1971) = Matheron, Alexandre. *Le Christ et le Salut des Ignorants chez Spinoza.* Paris: Aubier Montaigne, 1971.

Matheron (1969) = Matheron, Alexandre. *Individu et Communauté chez Spinoza.* Paris: Les éditions de minuit, 1969.

McKeon (1928) = McKeon, Richard. *The Philosophy of Spinoza.* N.Y.: Longmans, 1928.

Negri (1981) = Negri, Antonio. *L'anomalia Selvaggia: Saggio su potere e potenza in Baruch Spinoza.* Milano: Feltrinelli, 1981.

Rice (1985) = Rice, Lee C. "Spinoza, Bennett, and Teleology." *Southern Journal of Philosophy* XXIII (1985), 241-254.

Shahan and Biro (1978) = *Spinoza: New Perspectives.* Ed. R. W. Shahan and J. J. Biro. Norman:University of Oklahoma Press, 1978.

Walther (1971) = Walther, Manfred. *Metaphysik als Antitheologie: Die Philosophie Spinozas im Zusammenhang der religionsphilosophischen Problematik.* Hamburg: Meiner, 1971.

Wolfson (1969) = Wolfson, Harry Austryn. *The Philosophy of Spinoza.* 2 vols. New York: Schocken Books, 1969.

ON THE ATTRIBUTES AND THEIR ALLEGED INDEPENDENCE OF ONE ANOTHER: A COMMENTARY ON SPINOZA'S *ETHICS* IP10

PAUL EISENBERG
Indiana University

P10: *Unumquodque unius substantiae attributum per se concipi debet.*
Dem.: Attributum enim est id, quod intellectus de substantia percipit tanquam ejus essentiam constituens (*per Defin. 4.*); adeoque (*per Defin. 3.*) per se concipi debet. *Q.E.D.*
P10: *Each attribute of a substance must be conceived through itself.*
Dem.: For an attribute is what the intellect perceives concerning a substance, as constituting its essence (by D4); so (by D3) it must be conceived through itself, q.e.d.[1]

Coming upon this proposition, the interpreter of Spinoza is most pointedly confronted by the question of the ontological status of the attributes and, more particularly, by the question whether any subjectivistic interpretation of their status does not run counter to the present proposition's insistence that "each attribute... must be conceived through itself." By the phrase 'any subjectivistic interpretation' I mean to refer both to what I shall call the extreme or strong subjectivism advocated, e.g., by Wolfson (1969), according to which any attribute is an "invention" of the finite human intellect, and the more moderate position which, apparently somewhat unfashionably now, I am inclined to favor, the position according to which any attribute is a product of the workings of intellect as such, whether the intellect in question be finite or infinite.[2]

But is that interpretation correct? Are the attributes indeed mind- or intellect-dependent? More generally, is it or is it not the case that substance is identical *formaliter* with the attributes? Three types of answer have been proposed to that question - the objective, the subjective, and the linguistic - and each of them does have, *prima facie*, some textual support, even as each of them has its special difficulties. Not to make matters too complicated, however, I shall discuss in the body of this paper only the two leading types of interpretation, viz., the subjective and the objective. In the Scholium, however, I discuss variants of the linguistic interpretation, including the recent and radical version offered by Bennett.

Although I do not have the space to argue this point in proper detail here, I think that the bulk of the evidence weighs against the objective interpretation. For example, it seems to me to be very difficult, if not impossible, to interpret along objectivist lines Spinoza's explanation in Ep.9:

> By substance I understand what is in itself and is conceived through itself, i.e., whose concept does not involve the concept of another thing. I understand the same by attribute, except that it is called attribute in relation to the intellect, which attributes such and such a definite nature to substance (IV/46/20-23).

That Spinoza does *not* add "a nature (e.g., Extension) which *it* cannot but suppose to be different from such and such another nature (e.g., Thought) which it also attributes to substance" - i.e., that he does not assert what, according to some objectivists, is the distinctive thesis of subjectivism - is in fact of no help to them. What he does assert unambiguously is that the intellect "attributes such and such a definite nature to substance." I take that to mean, to imply, that apart from this activity of intellect substance would not have *that* definite nature (*certam naturam*), even though, presumably, it would then still have (and have necessarily) *some* nature - i.e., I take Spinoza to mean that the intellect does not discover that definite nature in substance but, rather, renders that nature definite for itself via the attributes.[3] Moreover, it surely seems to be the case that Spinoza's claim in, e.g., IP4D that "outside the intellect there is nothing except substances and their affections" is meant to imply that in some sense or in some way the attributes exist only *in* the intellect. Again, the view, implied, e.g., by IP20D or by IP10S itself, that any attribute actually *constitutes* the essence of God cannot be taken as clear-cut support for the objectivist interpretation since, as will be indicated below, 'constitutes' seems to be synonymous in such contexts with 'manifests,' 'expresses,' or 'explains'- words which, however, are much more strongly suggestive than is 'constitutes' itself of something's *appearing* so-and-so to some perceiving/conceiving subject(s). And Spinoza's talk in, e.g., IP25C about the modes of God's attributes may well be taken as a somewhat elliptical way of talking about the modes insofar as they are conceived under or in terms of this or that attribute.[4]

On the other hand, one need not and cannot accept the full-blown subjectivist position as it has been stated by Wolfson. In particular, Wolfson himself (I, p. 146) contrasts the objectivist interpretation as holding that the attributes are *discovered* by the mind with his own subjectivist interpretation, according to which the attributes are *invented* by the mind. But to say that the attributes are mind-dependent need not be taken to imply that they are somehow invented by the mind, any more than to say, as do Descartes and Spinoza, that the so-called secondary qualities of objects (e.g., colors) are mind-dependent is to say or imply that they are invented by the mind. Or to take another (but this time a post-Spinozistic) example: for Kant to say that the categories of the understanding do not represent features of things in themselves that can be discovered by human beings is not tantamount to his saying that they are so many *inventions* of human beings. What all human beings - indeed, on Spinoza's view, all intellects - *always* do cannot sensibly or truly be said to be something invented by them.

Of course, if one thinks, as does Wolfson, that only the finite human intellect perceives substance and its modes *sub specie attributorum* but that the infinite intellect does not do so, it becomes easier for one to say that the finite human intellect invents the attributes and to suggest that they are so many means which the human intellect employs in its *futile* attempt to know the nature of substance. One must, however, give heed to the suggestion that the reference in D4 to "the intellect" may well be meant to include the infinite intellect as well as all finite intellects (cf. IP30).[5]

It certainly appears, however, that even the moderate form of subjectivism cannot plausibly be maintained in the face of the present proposition. How, after all, can an attribute be "conceived through itself" if, according to the very definition of attribute (ID4), an attribute is what "intellect perceives of...substance, as constituting its essence"[6] but intellect turns out, according to IP31D, to be merely a mode - indeed, a mode of what Spinoza there calls "absolute thought," i.e., Thought *per se*, Thought *qua* unmodified? Actually, however, that question leads back to the yet more general - and the yet more troublesome - problem: Whatever the ontological status of the attributes, how can Spinoza consistently maintain that "each attribute... must be conceived through itself" and yet introduce a reference to intellect in the very definition of attribute? Obviously, the objectivist (like Curley (1969) or Gueroult (1968, 1974)), who wishes to identify substance with its attributes, owes us at this point an account of how the alleged conceivability through itself of any attribute is to be squared with Spinoza's own definition of attribute.

Perhaps, however, the objectivist will respond in some such fashion as this: D4 is misleadingly stated. What Spinoza means to be saying, fundamentally, is that an attribute *constitutes* the essence of a substance. Secondarily, however, he means to be informing us that intellect can apprehend attributes and thus is able to have real knowledge of *what substance is.* Given the further suppositions that (i) 'constitutes' in such a context is synonymous with 'is identical to' and that (ii) the essence of a thing (more exactly, a substance) and the thing itself are for Spinoza *essentially* (!) identical, one can indeed proceed to infer, apparently validly, from the very definition of substance as "what is in itself and is conceived through itself" that an attribute of substance must also be conceived through itself - in fact, must also be *in* itself. (Actually, I shall later be suggesting that Spinoza's sought-for proof does not go through thus neatly even if one were to grant the two presuppositions just indicated.) But these two presuppositions are in fact more or less problematic. The less problematic of the two is the former, but even here the problems are not insignificant. There is, after all, textual evidence within the *Ethics* itself which indicates that Spinoza was prepared to employ *explicare* ('to explain') as a synonym for *constituere* ('to constitute'): cf. IP20D, "the same attributes of God which (by D4) explain God's eternal essence at the same time explain his eternal existence, i.e., that itself which constitutes God's essence at the same time constitutes his existence." But 'explain' is, rather more obviously than 'constitute,' an incomplete predicate or, better, a relational verb: to explain is to explain something *to* someone. Hence, if indeed Spinoza is prepared to use *explicare* interchangeably with *constituere*, it seems reasonable to conclude that the latter should also be treated as a relational verb in fact (however elliptical most of Spinoza's uses of it may be), so that one should understand him as meaning that an attribute constitutes an/the essence of substance to or for someone or something. Indeed, the someone or something in this case appears to be intellect itself or, if you prefer, anyone or anything insofar as it possesses and employs intellect. But if so, then there is always an at least implicit, as sometimes there is an explicit, reference to intellect built into Spinoza's account of attributes, a point which (if correct) certainly undercuts the objectivist reading of that account.[7]

Even more problematic, however, is the second of the above-mentioned presuppositions, namely, that an attribute of substance, as "constituting" the essence of substance, is identical to substance as it essentially is. Here we do come up against the very grave problem insisted upon, for example, by Gram [5]: If (e.g.) Thought, as an attribute of God, is supposed to be identical to the essence of substance but also Extension is identical to the essence of substance, then two things which, according to Spinoza himself, are supposed to be irreducibly different from one another (namely, Thought and Extension) turn out to be identical to one and the same thing and, hence, identical to one another - a manifest contradiction.[8]

It will hardly do to escape from *that* objectivist mess by arguing, as does Gueroult, that God's essence consists of infinitely many elements, each of which is a substance constituted by a single attribute. Gueroult has to argue at length that in God, the *ens realissimum*, these diverse "substances" unite to form one absolutely infinite substance - i.e., that the diversity of substances disappears in God while the infinity of attributes remains. If I have so far represented Gueroult's position accurately, however, it is very difficult to see that he really can reconcile his view that Spinoza's *one* really existing substance is constituted by or consists of infinitely many attributes with his further view that *each* attribute satisfies the definition of substance and, therefore, is a substantial being in its own right. Admittedly, however, a subjectivist interpretation of the attributes is not without its problems, too. On the very face of it, it is odd - not to say paradoxical - that all the attributes or, even for that matter, that one of them (namely, Thought itself) should turn out to be dependent in any way on what is, *qua* intellect, only a mode of Thought itself. Since, however, there is no interpretation of the status of the attributes known to me which is problem-free, I prefer to keep to a view which is merely odd than accept one which (I believe) turns out to be self-contradictory.[9] But the oddity of the subjectivist position seems to turn all too quickly to a contradiction, too - if, that is, one construes the attributes' dependence upon intellect as being at once logical (conceptual) and ontological. For according to Spinoza's very definition of mode, a mode is precisely that which is both conceptually and ontologically dependent upon something else. It seems to follow, then, that on the subjectivistic interpretation the attributes turn out to be *modes* (which they cannot be).

Here, however, there are *prima facie* several ways out.[10] Thus one might insist that for Spinoza whatever is thus doubly dependent on any other thing, whatever that other thing itself turns out to be, must be a mode; but one might seek to argue that the attributes' dependence upon intellect is not thus a double dependence. Since, clearly, the subjectivistic account is precisely the account of the attributes which makes their *ontological* status to be dependent upon the workings of intellect (*inter alia*), one would have to maintain that Spinoza does *not* also think of the attributes as conceptually dependent upon intellect. That is, one would have to maintain that for him the concept of (something's being an) attribute does not depend upon (that is, does not logically presuppose) the concept of intellect. That, however, raises the very problem with which we began this discussion of P10: how can the very definition of attribute make reference to intellect without its being the case that the former notion depends somehow upon the latter? Maybe there is no good answer to that question - that is, maybe the best one can do is to insist that Spinoza meant to deny any logical dependence of attributes upon intellect, but that he quite failed to indicate how that denial is to be reconciled with his own definition of attribute.

Leaving that question deliberately unanswered, let us return to the examination of P10, continuing to investigate it on the supposition that *somehow* for Spinoza an attribute is (at most) *ontologically* dependent upon intellect. Or, rather, let us now turn our attention to the demonstration of P10. I am not at all sure that the demonstration of this proposition, so brief and apparently so straightforward, really works. Even if it does, it remains unclear whether the only things ever specified by Spinoza as attributes - namely, Thought and Extension - really are such. At first, one might think that one could argue (*against* Spinoza) thus:

While it is, in the context of Spinoza's philosophy, true by definition (D3) that substance is to be conceived through itself and also true by definition (D4) that an attribute is that which the intellect conceives of substance as constituting its essence, it does not clearly follow that any one attribute so-called by Spinoza must therefore be conceived as *logically independent* of any and all other attributes. For to conceive of substance through itself is, negatively, *not* to conceive of it by reference to any (of its) modes or by reference to any other substance (should there be any such) and, positively, it is to conceive of substance in some one or more of its attributes, as *res (substantia) extensa, res (substantia) cogitans*, etc. But what Spinoza is presently arguing or implying is, *inter alia*, that Thought cannot truly be conceived as in any way dependent upon Matter (= Extension), contrary to materialism and to so-called epiphenomenalism, and equally that Extension (= Matter) cannot be truly conceived as in any way dependent upon Thought, contrary to metaphysical idealism. The alleged necessity of conceiving substance through itself does not, however, clearly carry over to the case of the attributes.

To be sure, if substance is for intellect constituted by its attributes, it follows that no "given" attribute can truly be conceived as in some way *logically* dependent upon some mode(s), including modes of that attribute itself. Yet to conceive of Matter *per se* as logically derivative from Thought *per se*, or conversely, seems to be compatible with conceiving of either of them through the concept of substance. Granted, Spinoza could have made the following stipulation: as soon as one does conceive some *alleged* attribute by reference to another, the former turns out to be no genuine attribute, but only a mode of the latter attribute. Spinoza, however, is not seeking to define attribute in that way. He is seeking, rather, to prove that any attribute, defined as he has already defined it (D4), must be logically independent of any other attribute. And *that*, I am suggesting, he does not prove.

What Spinoza is requiring is that for intellect - whatever (if anything) may be true of substance *per se* - the essence of substance be completely unstructured at the "level" of the attributes themselves. There can, therefore, be no reason, even in principle - at least none which can be known - for God's manifesting Himself both as Matter (if it is an attribute) and as Thought (if it is another). Spinoza is, perhaps, correct in that point. Maybe it just is and, finally, has to be recognized to be a brute fact that Extension is one kind of "thing" and Thought another; but so far as I can see, Spinoza has not argued persuasively here or later in the *Ethics* for there being no more than that bare difference between them. (Indeed, the admission of a "brute fact" in *this* case hardly squares with Spinoza's regular adherence to what Bennett has termed his "explanatory rationalism"; see (1984) 29). More generally, even if we agree with Spinoza's implicit view that if something - in this case, substance - has an essence at all, it has *exactly one* essence and even if we remember that for him *the* essence of substance is (as if) constituted by any one of its attributes, we may still believe that some attributes are somehow more basic than others, i.e., that some attributes reveal to us the one essence of God more perspicuously than do others.

To argue that God must be, even for Spinoza, as for the prior religious traditions out of which his thought grew, essentially simple and, hence, not in reality structured internally, is to forget that Spinoza's God, as identical with Nature, must be the sole source of the infinite complexity of the world. But if the *modal* complexity of Nature, a complexity which requires us, according to Spinoza, to view one mode as the cause of another, is compatible with God's unity or unicity, it seems reasonable to believe that the oneness of the essence of God may be preserved compatibly with an insistence upon the attributional complexity of substance, which would at least permit us to view one attribute as the logical foundation, the "cause," of some other(s) among the attributes. This attributional complexity of Spinoza's one and indivisible God is, however, much easier to understand on a subjectivistic interpretation of the status of the attributes than it is on any objectivistic account.

There is need, however, for a final turn of the dialectical screw: *Given* Spinoza's belief in the perfect parallelism, if not indeed the identity, between the order of Thought and the order of (material) things (cf. IIP7), it seems to follow that what is logically grounded upon something else is also ontologically grounded or dependent upon something else. If so, then there is open to him no way of distinguishing between i) a logically derivative "attribute" of substance and ii) a mode of substance. For, as we have already seen, that which is both ontologically and logically dependent or derivative is a mode of substance and, therefore, cannot be either substance itself or one of its attributes. It appears, therefore, that a logically derivative "attribute," being also (on the subjectivistic view, of course) ontologically derivative, can be no genuine attribute at all but only a mode. Q.E.D.?

The immediately preceding argument still leaves it open whether both Extension and Thought are attributes or, indeed, whether either of them is. In fact, there is a real question whether there can be any attributes. The question arises if one takes it to have been Spinoza's own doctrine that all attributes depend upon intellect, which, we remember, he took to be a mode of Thought.[11] The question is this: if that subjectivistic interpretation of Spinoza is correct, and if it is also correct to hold that he maintains a sameness (unity) between the order of logic and the order of what is, i.e., between the realm of logic and the realm of ontology, then the ontological dependence of all attributes upon intellect carries with it their logical dependence upon it and therefore destroys their claim to be attributes, not modes.

We do seem entitled to conclude with the subjectivist that all the attributes are *ontologically* dependent upon intellect - but also to conclude, by the preceding reasoning, that they are *logically* dependent upon intellect. Yet what is both ontologically dependent upon something else, that is, is "in another thing" and logically dependent upon that other thing, that is, "through which it is also conceived" is, by definition (D5), a mode. We seem, therefore, so far to have located no attributes at all and to be incapable of finding any. The fault would not be ours, however, but Spinoza's: his very doctrine of attributes would be incoherent, if all of the foregoing is correct.

Thus consideration of the suggestion that no attribute can be logically derivative from another because logical derivability carries with it, on Spinoza's view, ontological derivability and because that double derivability or dependence shows the thing in question to be a mode rather than an attribute turns out to lead Spinoza's philosophy into contradiction. Perhaps, however, I have misinterpreted his doctrine of the relation of attributes to intellect, as non-subjectivists will certainly think. *More plausibly*, as it seems to me, it may be that Spinoza's ambiguous doctrine concerning the relation between the order of thought and the order of things is not to be taken as I have taken it here. Perhaps, that is, he did consistently envisage something's being logically but not also ontologically dependent upon something else, or something's being ontologically but not also logically dependent upon something else. If he allowed for the latter, what I take to have been his general insistence on (divine) attributes as being intellect-dependent is saved; for attributes would not then collapse into modes. If, however, he allowed also for the former, his particular insistence, here in P10, on the conceptual ultimacy of each attribute would fail, for the reasons that I have indicated.[12]

Scholium: On So-Called Linguistic Interpretations of the Status of the Attributes and on the Debate concerning the Attributes as Constituting a Pseudo-Problem

One form of the linguistic interpretation, a form according to which the difference for Spinoza between substance and attribute is merely the difference between senses of two terms (i.e., 'substance' and 'attribute') the referent of which is identical, is strongly suggested by Spinoza himself in his response, in Ep.9, to De Vries's question.

> ... I say that this definition explains clearly enough what I wish to understand by substance, *or* attribute.
> Nevertheless, you want me to explain how one and the same thing can be

designated by two names (though this is not necessary at all). Not to seem niggardly, I offer two: (i) I say that by Israel I understand the third patriarch; I understand the same by Jacob, the name which was given him because he had seized his brother's heel; (ii) by flat I mean what reflects all rays of light without any change; I understand the same by white, except that it is called white in relation to a man looking at the flat [surface].

Especially the first example here suggests that the referent of 'substance' is identical *formaliter* with the referent of 'attribute' (and, hence, of 'extension,' 'thought,' etc.) and that the difference consists only in the fact that the *sense* of the name (or, designating expression) 'substance' is not the same as the *sense* of the name 'attribute.'

In my opinion, however, this version of the linguistic interpretation seems to be, not an alternative interpretation to the modified subjectivistic view which I am defending, but only an alternative formulation of that same view. To be sure, Spinoza's own first example in Ep.9 of how "one and the same thing can be designated by two names" does nothing to suggest that the difference between substance and attribute is the difference between a thing conceived without reference to any (possible) perception of it and that same thing so far as it is "colored" by perception. But Spinoza's own second example seems to be much more apt: the difference between substance and attribute is like the difference between a two-dimensional surface (of a physical object) and a white patch (which is seen as part of the surface of a physical object).[13] It should be added that on Spinoza's view, as on Descartes' or Locke's, the color of physical objects is not invented by (human) percipients of them, at least not by any of those percipients with "normal" color vision; but neither do physical objects, on their view, possess colors independently of being perceived. (It would, I think, be pointless or foolish to push this example very hard; for it is by no means clear that Spinoza designed it to be, or hoped it to be, a *perfect* analogue to the relation which on his view obtains between substance and its attributes.)

Recently, however, Bennett has revived the linguistic interpretation or, more exactly, he has offered what may be regarded as a new and radical version of it, a version according to which there is for Spinoza no real difference between substance and attribute, not even, apparently, a difference in senses of the corresponding terms. Rather, the alleged difference is *merely* linguistic or, as Bennett prefers to say, "a bit of formal apparatus" to which no real difference (in content) attaches. In effect, Bennett is dismissing the very question whether an objectivist or a subjectivist reading of Spinoza on the status of the attributes is preferable. He thinks that both in D4 and in Ep.9 Spinoza is saying (or, at any rate, is trying to say) "that substance differs from attribute only by the difference between a substantival and an adjectival presentation of the very same content... he [Spinoza] is rejecting the view that a property bearer [i.e., a substance] is an item whose nature qualifies it to have properties, in favour of the view that the notion of a property bearer... is a bit of formal apparatus, something which organizes conceptual content without adding to it" (Bennett (1984), pp. 62-63). This is a position, however, which - although it may represent good philosophy in itself - lacks textual warrant and so seems to be untenable as an interpretation of Spinoza. Surely *the* central notion in Spinoza's metaphysics is the notion of substance. While, on the one hand, it is perfectly true that Spinoza's understanding of substance focusses primarily on the concept of substance as an or the independent being as against the concept of substance as the (in itself unknowable?) subject of "predicates" - on that much I certainly agree with Bennett or, for that matter, with Curley (1985), p. 404), yet, on the other hand, it is hard (for me) to see why Spinoza gives the emphasis he does to the notion of substance if in fact he believes that it has the same content as does the notion of attribute(s). Further, there are, according to Spinoza, infinitely many attributes of that one substance (namely, God) which, he thinks, exists (and by existing precludes the existence of any other substance). Spinoza's insistence on the unity of substance despite the infinite multiplicity of attributes cannot, I think, be intelligibly interpreted by anyone who thinks that the only difference here is that "between a substantival and an adjectival presentation of the very same content." Finally, Bennett's refusal to take the reference to *intellectus* seriously in D4 or in comparable passages in the *Ethics* or in the letters - that is, his insistence that Spinoza is *not* making an ontological-epistemological point (viz., about how we or, for that matter, about how any entity insofar as it is using its intellect apprehends substance) but, instead, is making a "logical" one (viz., the point about the notion of a property bearer as just "a bit of formal apparatus") - arises (p. 62) all too quickly from his claim there that "in fact Spinoza often uses psychological language to make logical or conceptual points," a claim about Spinoza which Bennett previously elaborated in sec.14. While I think Bennett is (or may well be) correct in this latter claim, by itself that claim or acceptance of it does little to show that *in this particular context* a logical point is being made, albeit misleadingly, in Spinoza's talk about what *intellectus* apprehends/perceives of substance.

In a somewhat different way from Bennett's, Arthur W. Collins has also recently suggested [2] that the perennial debate about whether the attributes have an objective status in substance (are there independently of the action of the intellect) or, instead, a subjective status of some sort (are projected by the intellect onto substance, *or* are only manifestations to an intellect of what substance is *per se*) may itself be misplaced, indeed may be a kind of pseudo-question. He thinks so, not because Spinoza seems to him to say one thing on this subject in one passage or set of passages and another in another, but because he holds that Spinoza does not want to view this matter in terms of an "either/or" and is thinking, instead, of a "both/and." Consider, e.g., the following brief but very provocative passage from IP8S2 (Collins himself provides no direct textual evidence in support of this part of his interpretation): "the truth of substances is not outside the intellect unless it is in themselves, because they are conceived through themselves" - or, in the variant provided by the *Nagelate Schriften*, "the object of a true idea of substances can be nothing other than the substances themselves...," etc. Spinoza does indeed seem to be saying here that the only way in which anyone can form a true idea of a substance is to conceive the substance or something about it just as the latter is in itself, objectively. But if, moreover, as D4 has already indicated, an intellect conceives an/the essence of substance via some attribute(s), it should follow that the only way by which a true idea of that essence under such-and-such an attribute can be present *in* the intellect is for that same essence, under that same attribute, to be present objectively *in* substance itself.

Unfortunately, however, while this inference is certainly plausible and while, perhaps, it is even correct (who knows?), it is not indubitably correct. Certainly we do not find Spinoza *saying*, here or elsewhere, that attributes exist in the intellect as true ideas of substance only because they also exist *extra intellectum*, in substance itself. In particular, let us notice the exact context of the present passage: Spinoza's claim about "the truth [i.e., a true idea] of substances" is meant to contrast with the immediately preceding claim about "true ideas of modifications which do not exist." Concerning such non-existent modifications Spinoza says that, though (by hypothesis) "they do not actually exist outside the intellect" (they do not because if, *per impossibile*, they did exist "outside the intellect" they would be objectively real, contrary to the present hypothesis), "nevertheless their essences are comprehended in another [sc.: real thing] in such a way that they can be conceived through it." This very passage, obscure as it is, is sufficient to allow us to see already that Spinoza's developed theory of truth cannot be a (simple) correspondence theory, à la that allegedly held by Meinong. That is, the agreement between a true idea and its object (what Spinoza calls its '*ideatum*'), the agreement spoken of in IA6, cannot be construed as a relation or "tie" which can obtain only between existing things - or, more particularly, between something, the *idea vera* or true idea which exists *in* the intellect, and its object or *ideatum* which exists *extra intellectum*. Now, to be sure, Spinoza does proceed immediately to contrast what he has just said about the true ideas of certain modes with what he wants to say about substance, and *that* might lead us (as, perhaps, it led Collins) to conclude that, in the case of substance, Spinoza does want to say that our true ideas via attributes concerning it must capture wholly objective features of substance itself. Unfortunately, one does not know *exactly* how to take the contrast. One does know that Spinoza is here committed to the view that there may be a true idea in some intellect the *ideatum* of which is not, *per se*, any objectively existing real thing. *Perhaps*, then, what Spinoza does mean to say about true ideas of substance is that, while the true idea must indeed "correspond" to something objective which is, roughly speaking, part of the essence of substance, nonetheless that essence, or (what comes to the same thing for Spinoza) the true idea of it, existing *in intellectu* may have, so to speak, an intellectual coloration which does not match an objective feature of substance itself. In short, while Spinoza does think that we can and, indeed, *must* have true ideas about substance and while he does think that fundamentally any such ideas must be the mental equivalents of the essence of substance, no one of *those* ideas need itself be the idea of (an) attribute. Rather, the attribute may simply be the way in which that essence of substance presents itself in or to the mind itself: no objective attribute need correspond to the attribute which is in the mind.

References

1. Bennett, J. "A Note on Descartes and Spinoza," *Philosophical Review* 74 (1965), 379-380.

2. Collins, A. W. *Thought and Nature: Studies in Rationalist Philosophy* (Notre Dame (In.): Notre Dame Press, 1985).

3. Curley, E. "Recent Work on 17th Century Continental Philosophy," *American Philosophical Quarterly*, 11 (1974), 235-255.

4. Donagan, A. "A Note on Spinoza, *Ethics*, I, 10," *Philosophical Review* 75 (1966), 380-382.

5. Gram, M. "Spinoza, Substance, and Predication," *Theoria* 34 (1968), 222-244.

6. Haserot, F. S. "Spinoza and the Status of Universals," *Philosophical Review* 59 (1950). Reprinted in S. P. Kashap, (1972), 43-67.

7. Leibniz, G. W. *Philosophical Papers and Letters*, ed. L. E. Loemker, 2d ed. (Dordrecht: D. Reidel, 1969).

1. Unless otherwise indicated, all translations in this paper from Spinoza are those of Curley (1985).

2. Unlike Curley (1985), e.g., I do *not* understand the subjectivist thesis to be the view "according to which the differences between the attributes are illusory" (p. 409). To claim, as I would wish to do, that (a) the attributes "have no real existence in the essence of God" ([3], 240) need not imply that (b) they have no real existence at all (except as inventions of the mind or illusions generated by it). I take subjectivism to be a thesis about the locus of the attributes rather than about their status as "real." Nonetheless, it has to be admitted that the strong form of subjectivism advocated by Wolfson runs together, or, at least, involves commitment to, both (a) and (b).

The (core of the) view which I personally favor amounts to the following, which I offer here, in this note, merely in the form of a sketch and without supporting argumentation: I take Spinoza (in IP16 and elsewhere) to mean, à la Plotinus, that from the necessity of the divine nature there follows or emanates an infinite Intellect, which in some sense serves as an "intermediary" between God as substance (*Natura naturans*) and all other modes, be they finite or infinite, so that without this mode no other mode could be. Moreover, it is this Intellect which, by its activity, brings it about that everything, including that mode which it itself is, can be seen to follow from God "in infinite ways" - i.e., it is it which "first" views all things *sub specie attributorum* so that without this mode no other mode (nor, it seems, the essence of substance itself) could be conceived. But according to Spinoza - and here he makes a radical break with both pagan and Judaeo-Christian Neo-Platonism - this mode, which I have been describing as the infinite *Intellect* of God, is also what Spinoza terms *Motion and Rest*, i.e., the immediate infinite mode under the attribute of Extension. In other words, this mode, which, *qua* Intellect, is the "source" of the attributes, is perceived by itself "in infinite ways" and is perceived (i.e., conceived) by us who have, or are, finite intellects in two ways or under two attributes, namely, Thought and Extension. "In itself" the mode in question is *no more* an Intellect, a mode of Thought, than it is a mode of Extension or indeed of any other attribute. I hasten to add, however, that the view which I have been sketching here is not explicitly formulated anywhere by Spinoza himself, and that it has proceeded on the principle, which may not have been held unambiguously by Spinoza, that the attributes are intellect-dependent and, hence, dependent *primarily* upon that very mode which, conceiving itself under the attribute of Thought, appears to itself as the infinite intellect of God.

In this paper I am not much concerned with the direct defense of subjectivism of the second subtype which I have distinguished above, a defense which would certainly require close and detailed examination of (many of) the passages, both in the *Ethics* and in others of Spinoza's works, including especially various of his epistles, in which Spinoza talks about the attributes. I am concerned - *inter alia* - merely with the or an indirect defense for such subjectivism, a defense which consists in my attempting to prove that that interpretation does not lead to manifest contradiction and, in particular, to the contradictory conclusion that Spinoza's so-called attributes turn out to be mere modes. Admittedly, I do not feel entirely comfortable with my own favored interpretation; but then, I think, one cannot be entirely comfortable with any one interpretation of the attributes, given the apparently conflicting texts on that subject which Spinoza himself offers to us his readers.

3. Granted, in this very passage Spinoza also says that he "understand[s] the same" by 'attribute' as he understands by the term 'substance'; and he goes on immediately to add, "this definition explains clearly enough what I wish to understand by substance, *or* [*sive*] attribute." All this seems to suggest, indeed, that on Spinoza's view there can be no *ontological* difference whatsoever between substance and attribute (although at the same time there is some difference in sense or connotation between the one term and the other). Leaving aside the possibility, on which one should not lay much emphasis, that what we now have as EID4 (along with other passages in EI concerning the attributes and their status) represents a somewhat different doctrine from that advanced by Spinoza in his letter of 1663 (a letter which antedates the final form of EI by *at least* two years), one might suggest that Spinoza means to be saying that the only (clear) concept of substance which we can form (indeed, which can be formed) is due to intellect, so that there is no point in making much of the distinction between substance *per se*, the very notion of which is "intellectual," and attribute; for any conception of substance which intellect forms is a conception of substance as possessing such and such attributes.

4. If the (moderate) subjectivist interpretation of the status of the attributes is indeed correct, then others of Spinoza's phrases in the *Ethics* must also be read as elliptical, including his occasional declaration (e.g., in the very statement of D6) that substance does consist of its attributes, or that that substance which is God consists of infinitely many attributes. (*Per Deum intelligo ens absolute infinitum, hoc est, substantiam constantem infinitis attributis*...). On that interpretation such an assertion should be taken as short for the longer and far more cumbersome claim that substance is constituted for intellect or manifests itself to intellect via its attributes, so that the attributes are not "in" the substance, strictly speaking. On that interpretation there can be no problem of how substance's indivisible unity (cf. P12) is to be reconciled with its consisting of so-and-so many attributes.

5. Wolfson's assertion - or is it an argument? - to the contrary has simply to be dismissed. I refer to his remarks in I, p. 153, fn. 2:

> By the term "intellect" in this definition [D4] Spinoza means the finite human intellect. When he says in...[IIP7S], that "we have already demonstrated, that everything which can be perceived by the *infinite intellect* as constituting the essence of substance pertains entirely to one substance, and consequently that substance thinking and substance extended are one and the same substance...," it is not to be inferred that an attribute of substance is that which can be conceived only by the "infinite intellect." What the passage means to say is that "*everything* which can be conceived of by the *infinite intellect* as constituting the essence of substance" - and the infinite intellect can conceive of an infinite number of things as constituting the essence of substance - is only an attribute of substance... and consequently extension and thought, which alone can be conceived by the finite human intellect as constituting the essence of substance, are only attributes of substance and not substances themselves.

But this very explanation of Wolfson's does nothing to support his claim that in the original definition of attribute the intellect referred to is only the finite human intellect. Indeed, Wolfson himself seems to imply that what the infinite intellect perceives or conceives "as constituting the essence of substance" is only (infinitely many) attributes; hence, he seems to imply that intellect as such, finite or infinite, perceives God or substance only through attributes. If so, there is obviously much less warrant than Wolfson supposes for holding that (the finite human) intellect fails to apprehend the divine essence, for it knows in the same basic way as does the infinite intellect itself, namely, via attributes. Could it be maintained that the divine intellect, like the human, is inadequate to the task of knowing the divine essence? One tends to think not. Yet the divine intellect, like any intellect, is only a mode of substance, and it might be claimed that Spinoza wants to say, as some of his predecessors (I mean Neo-Platonists) did say, that no mode or emanation of substance can understand substance itself. It is doubtful, however, that that arch-rationalist Spinoza held such a doctrine.

6. As is well-known to Spinoza scholars, the Latin *tanquam* may be translated either 'as' or 'as if.' The suggestion, emphasized elsewhere in this paper, that even God's own infinite intellect apprehends the divine substance *sub specie attributorum* makes it plausible to suppose that *tanquam* here and in similar contexts in the *Ethics* is to be translated merely by 'as.' On the other hand, problems about the translation of *constituens* and other forms of the verb *constituere* or, at least, about the proper interpretation of forms of that verb as they figure in the *Ethics* may lead one to think that Spinoza is employing the verb in a somewhat unusual sense which he wishes to signal here, the first occurrence of a form of that verb in the Latin text of the *Ethics*, by explicitly introducing *constituens* with *tanquam*, meaning indeed 'as if.' Nothing in my interpretation of EIP10 hangs on a decision as to which translation of *tanquam* in D4 is preferable.

7. This matter is more complicated than I have indicated so far, nor do I have space to explore it adequately in this paper. On the one hand, close examination of the *Ethics* reveals that Spinoza there uses (in the relevant contexts) *exprimere* as synonymous with *explicare* and, hence, as yet another synonym for *constituere*. Taking *exprimere* as 'express,' as Curley himself does, at the least does not rule out, if it does not actually suggest, a relation to intellect: the attributes express the essence of substance to or for something, namely, intellect. On the other hand, one should not entirely ignore the root meanings of *explicare* and *exprimere* - namely, 'to unfold' and 'to press out,' both of which suggest that Spinoza has in mind a process or quasi-process which occurs or may occur quite independently of the operations of intellect. Yet one must be wary of any such interpretation, lest *explicare* and *exprimere* be amalgamated to or construed in terms of the relation of flowing or following, i.e., the relation or tie by which Spinoza designates the dependence of all *modes* upon the intellect. Whatever the relation between attributes and substance, it cannot be the same as that obtaining between the modes and substance.

8. In fact, however, Spinoza does not say that substance is identical to, e.g., Extension and to Thought despite the fact that neither of these is identical to the other. Rather, he says that substance is identical *in* each of its attributes, which is to say that *the* extended thing (*res extensa*) is identical to *the* thinking thing (*res cogitans*) - i.e., that it is one and the same substance which is to be conceived both as extended and as thinking. The failure to draw precisely that distinction between 'identical with (or, to)' and 'identical in' is largely responsible for the puzzles which Gram claimed to find in Spinoza's doctrine of substance and its attributes. As it seems to me, however, objectivism is committed to the view that the "constitutive" relationship between an attribute and (the essence of) substance is or is tantamount to any attribute's being in fact identical *to* the essence of substance.

9. The preceding claim is deliberately polemical. More guardedly, I should want to say merely that, even if the *prima facie* contradiction(s) of the objectivist interpretation can be satisfactorily removed, so can the *prima facie* contradiction(s) involved in modified subjectivism and that, moreover, there is at least as much textual support for the latter interpretation of Spinoza as there is for the former.

10. One way is to construe Spinoza's definition (ID5) of mode, "that which is in another [sc.: 'thing'] through which it is also conceived," as meaning by 'another,' not just *any* other, but in fact that other which is substance itself. In other words, Spinoza would be defining mode as that which is ontologically and conceptually dependent upon *substance*. Leaving aside other considerations in favor of that construal, one may note that the phrase "that which is in another through which it is also conceived" is explicitly offered by Spinoza in D5 as a paraphrase for "the affections of a substance," a point which indeed suggests that the "another" of the second phrase should be taken to refer merely to substance. But if so, then even the admission that the attributes are doubly dependent - i.e., both ontologically and conceptually dependent - upon intellect is not tantamount to the discovery that the so-called attributes are themselves merely modes. On further reflection, however, this alternative may seem not to offer a genuine way out of the present difficulty. For given that Spinoza is explicit that for him any intellect, be it finite or infinite, is merely a mode, an attribute's double dependence upon intellect, although *directly* only a dependence upon another which is not itself substance, is *indirectly* a dependence upon substance itself (since any mode is, by the present construal of D5, dependent upon substance).

11. The proof text, if one is needed for the claim that Spinoza construes intellect as being only a mode of Thought, is IP31D. P31 itself indicates explicitly that this modal nature of intellect, its falling within *Natura naturata* rather than *Natura naturans*, holds whether the actual intellect be finite or infinite.

12. (A) The upshot of my protracted investigation of EP10D leaves me in agreement with Bennett, who, however, goes through no such elaborate investigation himself. His all too brief comment on that demonstration ((1984), 61) can now be seen to be essentially correct. He says simply, "I am suspicious of the argument he [Spinoza] gives for this and prefer to see it [i.e., the thesis enunciated in P10] as following directly from his intention to use the term 'attribute' to mean something like 'basic and irreducible way of being'...or the like." Of course, it needs to be added that Spinoza does not actually define attribute as "a basic and irreducible way of being" or as "that which the intellect construes as a basic and irreducible way of being"; and that if he did, he would, presumably, not need to *prove* or seek to *prove* that "each attribute of a substance must be conceived through itself."

(B) Curley ((1969), 15-16) has argued that existence *in se* implies logical (conceptual) independence of other things and conversely. From that, of course, it follows that what is ontologically dependent (as, I wish to claim, the attributes are for Spinoza) is also conceptually dependent. It is only by interpreting the attributes objectively that Curley himself avoids the conclusion that the so-called attributes, being thus doubly dependent, have in fact the status of modes in Spinoza's ontology. (Incidentally, it might be mentioned, quite as Curley himself does, that Leibniz took these two notions not to imply one another and insisted that "the contrary seems rather to be true, that there are some things which are in themselves though they are not conceived through themselves" ([7],p. 196).)

I shall not claim in response either that Spinoza himself, on whose behalf Curley constructs his argument, would not have accepted it, or that through acceptance of it Spinoza's doctrine of attributes versus modes becomes inherently self-contradictory. Rather, what needs to be pointed out is that Curley's argument, although (I think) valid, is not completely general. That is, it works with, and only with, the notions in terms of which Spinoza defines or characterizes substance and its modes; thus it has nothing to say directly about the attributes. More specifically, it employs the ideas of (i) "external cause" (vs. "cause of itself") and of

(ii) the knowledge (including the very concept) of what has an external cause as dependent upon the knowledge (hence, the concept) of that external cause. Admittedly, for Spinoza what has an external cause (and so is, in that way, ontologically dependent) is also conceptually and epistemologically dependent upon that external cause. I do not take Spinoza to have meant, however, that intellect is the external cause of the attributes' existence. Curley himself wishes to say, in response to Leibniz's objection - namely, that "an attribute is perceived by the understanding as belonging to substance and as constituting its essence [and that t]herefore the concept of the attribute is necessary to form the concept of the substance" ([7], *ibid*.) - that for Spinoza an attribute is not another thing than is substance itself (since, says Curley, Spinoza identifies substance with the totality of its attributes). Similarly, I wish to suggest, in response to the present difficulty, that for Spinoza an attribute is not another thing than its modes, i.e., I take it that Spinoza wishes to identify an attribute with the totality of its modes or, more exactly, with the totality of all the modes insofar as they are conceived in terms of that attribute. Thus on my reading of Spinoza Extension, e.g., is the totality of all bodies and Thought the totality of all ideas.

This interpretation is, of course, not itself uncontroversial. In particular, it seems not to reckon with the fact that, e.g., in IP21 Spinoza distinguishes between the "absolute nature of any of God's attributes" and all "the things which follow" from that absolute nature - i.e., all of that attribute's modes. (More exactly, he distinguishes there between the "absolute nature" of some attribute and the eternal and infinite mode(s) which follow immediately from it; he then goes on to distinguish an immediate infinite mode from the further modes which follow, directly or indirectly, from it.) It is by no means clear, however, that the distinction is more than verbal or formal. Rather, it is by no means clear that Spinoza's story of the emanation of the modes from some absolute attribute of God is not best taken as a tale which, although employing a Neo-Platonic schema, is in fact designed to show that the notion of such an attribute, like the corresponding notion of absolute substance, is only a philosophical construction or abstraction, and that in reality substance (or what from the point of view of intellect comes to the same thing - viz., an attribute) cannot exist except in and through the totality of "its" modes. Clearly, however, I do not have the space in this paper, much less in this note, to develop this response adequately. The foregoing has to be construed, therefore, as the mere sketch of a response to Curley on the point in question.

13. Wolf in his comment on this part of the letter notes (p. 393): "The idea that a plane... which reflects all the rays of light incident upon it is white...appears to have been put forward by Democritus... The idea prevailed more or less up to the time of Spinoza. It is to be found in Boyle's *Experiments and Considerations touching Colours* (1664)..."

THE INFINITE IN SPINOZA'S PHILOSOPHY

ROGER ARIEW
Virginia Polytechnic Institute
and State University

I wish to develop and offer evidence for an interpretation of Spinoza's doctrine of the infinite. To accomplish this, I attempt, in part 1, to establish that Spinoza knew well and rejected Descartes' doctrine of the infinite, except for a nonsystematic element Spinoza made his own. I then argue that Spinoza's own doctrine is a synthesis of medieval theories and the above Cartesian element. In part 2, I accept Wolfson's thesis that Spinoza was familiar with theories of 12th- to 14th-century Jewish (and Arabic) thinkers, but I suggest that the medieval theories with which Spinoza constructed his synthesis included those of 14th-century Christian Scholastics. With this as background, I attempt to evaluate, in part 3, the various contemporary solutions to the problem of God's infinite attributes. I conclude that a thinker familiar with 14th-century Scholastic theories of infinity could not have accepted unconditionally an equivalence between "absolutely infinite attributes" and "all attributes, without exception" - the basis of the Wolf-Kline solution to the problem of God's infinite attributes. So, I further conclude that one should accept the solutions of Gueroult and Curley, that unknown attributes are indeed a part of Spinoza's later philosophy, and that these unknown attributes do not entail that God is incomprehensible.

1. Descartes and Spinoza on Infinity

In Meditation III, Descartes considers the idea of God and whether there is something in it that cannot have originated from himself. The answer he gives is that since the idea of the infinite cannot originate from something finite,[1] it has to have been placed in him by something truly infinite. As part of the argument Descartes considers whether he might be something greater than he himself understands. He investigates whether he might have potentially all the perfections he attributes to God, that is, whether it is possible that his faculties might be perfectible indefinitely (AT VII, 46; IX, 37). But he argues that even if he were able to perfect himself indefinitely he could not become infinite (or perfect). True infinity implies absolutely no potentiality; therefore, nothing increasing indefinitely will ever be actually infinite (AT VII, 47; IX, 37). For Descartes, God is the only being in whose perfections we notice no limits (*Principles* I, 27, AT VIII, 37); he is the only being we positively "intellect" as infinite (*To More*, 5 February 1649, AT V, 274). But we can see that he is greater than the world (*To More*, 15 April 1649, AT V, 345), so that the world cannot be called infinite (*To Chanut*, 6 June 1647, AT V, 52). However, it conflicts with our conception, or it involves a contradiction, that the world should be finite or bounded (*To More*, April 1649, AT V, 345). Hence we call it indefinite;[2] we can say a thing is indefinitely large, provided we have no arguments to prove that it has bounds (*To Chanut*, 6 June 1647, AT V, 51 and *Principles* I, 27). But that is not the same as knowing that it has no bounds: "I cannot deny that there may be some reasons [for the finiteness of the world] which are known to God though incomprehensible to me."[3]

Descartes' indefinite is therefore to be understood as an epistemic notion, stemming from a limitation of our understanding, and not as a metaphysical notion, arising from the nature of things; our intellectual relations to the finite, indefinite, and infinite reflect this. For Descartes, the infinite is "incomprehensible."[4] Since God is infinite, God is also incomprehensible: "As I have insisted in several places, when God or infinity is in question, we must consider not what we can comprehend - we know that they are beyond comprehension."[5] And since the infinite is incomprehensible, Descartes rejects all disputes about it: "I have never written about the infinite except to submit myself to it and not to determine what it is or what it is not."[6] But we must be able to receive the idea of God in some way, so that we must be able to stand in some intellectual relation to God. Although we cannot comprehend God's infinity and he is properly inconceivable (*To Mersenne*, 27 May 1630, AT I, 152), we can know and perceive that God is infinite (*To Mersenne*, 27 May 1630, AT I, 152; AT IX, 210) and we can have an idea of him (*To Mersenne*, July 1641, AT III, 393; *To Regius*, 24 May 1640, AT III, 64).

Spinoza knows Descartes' doctrine well and expounds it fully. Initially he seems to accept many of its elements; ultimately he rejects the doctrine. The doctrine he finally formulates echoes the discussions of the medievals on infinity,[7] but it is inserted into a framework Spinoza might have considered as genuinely Cartesian. In his exposition of Descartes' *Principles of Philosophy*, Spinoza refers to the traditional puzzles against actual infinity: "if an infinite is not greater than another, quantity A will be equal to its double, which is absurd," and "whether half an infinite number is also infinite, whether it is even or odd, and the like."[8] He also refers to the traditional argument against potential infinity, that because of God's omnipotence, the impossibility of actual infinity entails the impossibility of potential infinity: "If two quantities, A and its double, are divisible to infinity, they will also be able to be actually divided into infinitely many parts by the power of God."[9] In this exposition, Spinoza answers such problems as would Descartes, namely, that there are things which "exceed our intellect, or grasp, and that we therefore perceive only quite inadequately" (G I/191). This is the case with respect to the infinite and its properties. "For this reason Descartes considers those things in which we do not perceive any limits - like the extension of the world or the divisibility of matter - as indefinite."[10] That is to understand Descartes' doctrine very well.

In the previously written *Short Treatise*, Spinoza had endorsed for himself various portions of Descartes' doctrine, including "that a finite intellect cannot comprehend the infinite" (G I/16) and that man, being imperfect, cannot produce the idea of God (G I/18). But there is a movement in Spinoza's philosophy that draws him away from Descartes' doctrine, toward the complete comprehensibility of God and infinity.[11] Even in the exposition of Descartes'

Principles, where Spinoza attempts to develop Descartes' doctrines (and not necessarily his own), he demonstrates an inclination to discuss what Descartes had excommunicated as incomprehensible.[12] Spinoza makes sure that Meyer, in his editorial preface to Spinoza's exposition of Descartes' *Principles*, warns his readers that "what is found in some places - viz. *that this or that surpasses the human understanding...* is said only on behalf of Descartes. For it must not be thought that our author offers this as his own opinion" (G I/132).

What Spinoza does offer as his own opinion is revealed in the *Letter on the Infinite* of 20 April 1663 (written to Meyer in the same year as Spinoza's exposition of Descartes' *Principles*). Spinoza already hints at this opinion in his exposition of the *Principles*; given Descartes' persistent finitism it would be difficult to overlook Spinoza's reference in the *Principles* to Descartes' having refuted one of Zeno's paradoxes,[13] a refutation Spinoza seems to accept as his own. In fact, it is clear that the doctrine Spinoza has in mind is consistent with his treatment of Zeno's paradoxes in his exposition of the *Principles* (and his treatment of the puzzles about infinity in the *Letter on the Infinite* and in E IP15S). What is not clear is whether Descartes' treatment of Zeno's paradoxes is fully consistent with other Cartesian doctrines (at least when it is given Spinoza's interpretation).

There is nothing terribly uncharacteristic of Descartes in his *Letter to Clerselier* about Zeno's paradoxes. Essentially Descartes does little more than to demonstrate his consistent finitism about the world. He treats the series $1/10 + 1/10^2 + 1/10^3 + ... + 1/10^n$ as *equal to*, instead of as *tending toward* $1/9$.[14] But he asserts that the cause of the paradox is that people *imagine* that this $1/9$ is an infinite quantity, because it is divided *by the imagination* into infinite parts (*To Clerselier*, June or July 1646, AT IV, 447). Now, that cannot be taken too literally as a Cartesian doctrine. After all, the same faculty of imagination, at the beginning of Meditation VI, is said to be incapable of representing a chiliagon (AT VII, 72-73); we are presently insisting that it allows us to imagine the infinite parts of $1/9$ of a league. Descartes must be using "imagination" untechnically here, as roughly equivalent to false understanding.[15] And, of course, it is this nonsystematic Cartesian element that Spinoza makes his own. It is likely that Spinoza adopts it because it fits well with his consistent infinitism and the other aspects of the doctrine he is formulating, a synthesis of the above "Cartesian" element and medieval infinitism.

In the *Letter to Meyer*, Spinoza distinguishes between three kinds of infinites. (i) What is infinite because of its nature and cannot in any way be conceived as finite;[16] it cannot be equated with any number - it exceeds every number that can be given (G IV/59); it cannot be divided into parts without contradiction (G IV/61); it is the infinite as substance (and eternity), understood by the intellect alone (G IV/54, 56-57). (ii) What is infinite, in the sense that it has no bounds, because of its cause (G IV/53); it can be conceived abstractly (or superficially) as finite (G IV/61), that is, it can be divided into parts and therefore numbered by the imagination with the aid of the senses (G IV/56, 61); it is infinite as the affections of substance or as mode (and duration) (G IV/54,

57). And (iii) what is infinite, in the sense that it cannot be expressed by any particular number, though it is determined - it has a maximum and minimum (G IV/53, 59-60, 61); it can be called indefinite.[17]

Spinoza's distinctions allow him to solve such traditional puzzles as what kind of infinite can or cannot be divided into parts and what kind of infinite can or cannot be conceived to be greater than another. The infinite as comprehended by the understanding cannot be divided into parts or conceived to be greater than another. The infinites attended to in the imagination can be so divided or so conceived (G IV/56-61). This strategy of dealing with the puzzles of infinity is clearly reminiscent of Descartes'. Spinoza agrees with Descartes that we only imagine infinite quantities in 1/9 of a league and would even agree with Descartes that there is no absurdity in an infinity being greater than another.[18] What he rejects is Descartes' insistence that the infinite is incomprehensible. Spinoza's critique of Descartes is that Descartes makes the infinite incomprehensible by making number into an idea of the understanding.[19] Spinoza asserts that number, time, and measure are beings of reason, or creatures of the imagination;[20] hence he is able to conclude that the infinite is not imagined or numbered, but comprehended by the understanding.

The negative Cartesian strategy of dissolving puzzles by referring them to the imagination must therefore be supplemented by a positive Spinozistic strategy of resolving paradoxes by showing that they rest on a false conception of infinity. That is what Spinoza tries to accomplish when he discusses Zeno's paradoxes. Instead of accepting the paradox as evidence of the incomprehensibility of the subject matter, he attempts to reject it by showing that it rests on such contradictory concepts as greatest speed (or slowest speed). And, of course, that greatest speed is contradictory does not entail that the infinite is contradictory. So Zeno's paradox, that the greatest speed does not differ from rest, relies on a false conception of infinity, infinite as greatest, or "that bodies can be conceived to move so quickly that they cannot move more quickly" (G I/193). But "we can never conceive a motion so fast that we do not at the same time conceive a faster one" (Ibid.). Infinity cannot be numbered or an infinite is greater than any number no matter how great:

> Hence it is clear why many who confused [number, measure, and time] with the things themselves, because they were ignorant of the true nature of things, denied an actual infinite. But let the mathematicians judge how wretchedly these people have reasoned - such arguments have never deterred the mathematicians from the things they perceived clearly and distinctly. For not only have they discovered many things which cannot be explained by any number - which makes plain the inability of numbers to determine all things - they also know many things which cannot be equated with any number, but exceed any number that can be given. Still they do not infer that such things exceed every number because of the multiplicity of their parts, but because the nature of the thing cannot admit a number without manifest contradiction.[21]

Spinoza's two-fold strategy also agrees well with some medieval treatments of infinity.

2. The Medievals and Spinoza on Infinity

H. A. Wolfson and others have already established numerous connections
between the doctrines of Spinoza and medieval Jewish thinkers; the links between
the doctrines of Hasdai Crescas and Spinoza on infinity seem particularly
strong.[22] Spinoza even refers to Crescas by name when he paraphrases Crescas'
revised form of the cosmological argument (To Meyer, 20 April 1663, G IV/62),
and some of Spinoza's puzzles of infinity and their solutions (in E IP15S and
in the Letter to Meyer) reflect those of Crescas. But there is no need to retrace
Wolfson's steps. I will discuss below just one of these puzzles and its solution,
in the light of medieval discussions; these puzzles (and the discussion of Zeno's
paradoxes in Spinoza's exposition of Descartes' Principles) seem also to reflect
knowledge of medieval doctrines not contained in the Jewish and Arabic
doctrines Wolfson discusses, Crescas in particular.[23] For example, Spinoza's
reference to mathematicians who "know many things [among these being actual
infinity] which cannot be equated with any number, but exceed any number that
can be given" (G IV/59), cannot have been received from Crescas. Crescas
does not think of actual infinity as that which exceeds any number, no matter
how great. Similarly, the concepts of minimum and maximum, which Spinoza
discusses in the Letter to Meyer,[24] cannot have been derived from Crescas, who
does not seem to have developed those concepts.

However, the above conception of the actual infinite (or the categorematic
infinite) and the concepts of maximum and minimum are standard elements of
14th-century Scholastic discussions of infinity - Gregory of Rimini, John Buridan,
and Albert of Saxony, for example.[25] In his Commentary on the Sentences,
Gregory of Rimini criticizes what he takes to be the standard definition of the
categorematic infinite, as given in Peter of Spain's Logic: "A quantity so large
that there is, and can be, no larger; referring to distinct objects, one defines it
as, a multitude so considerable that there can be no greater."[26] He insists that
the categorematic infinite should be defined as larger than any finite quantity,
however large, and greater than any finite multitude, however numerous:

> Hence others give a better definition of the [categorematic] infinite by stating, with
> reference to continuous quantities, that it is larger than one foot, two feet, three feet,
> and any given magnitude - with reference to a collection of distinct objects that it is
> more numerous than two, three, four, and any finite multitude. One can state that
> the infinite, taken in this sense, with respect to continuous magnitudes, can be defined
> by the following phrase, it is larger than any given finite quantity, however large. With
> respect to a multitude of distinct objects, it can be characterized by the phrase, it is
> greater than any finite multitude, however numerous.[27]

In the same commentary one can find exemplary discussions of maxima and
minima, and the same doctrine can be read in the works of John Buridan and
Albert of Saxony. The discussions of maximum and minimum normally begin
with Zeno's paradox, "Achilles and the Tortoise" (discussed by Descartes and
Spinoza). The process of a division which is forever pursued without end -

dividing a continuum into two equal parts, dividing one of the halves into two other parts, the fourth thus obtained into eighths, etc. - is called dividing a continuum into proportional parts. Gregory of Rimini, John Buridan, and Albert of Saxony all recognize that the series of parts thus produced is potentially infinite (or syncategorematically infinite) but that it has an upper limit, a maximum, which is not part of the series.[28] Gregory of Rimini uses division into proportional parts to explain how a quantity being divisible to infinity entails that it can be actually divided to infinity by the power of God. (We should recall that this puzzle is referred to by Spinoza, though without a resolution.) The example is particularly interesting because it transforms a puzzle about endless continuation (like the endless continuation of a line) into one concerning an endless, yet bounded series (like the division of a line into proportional parts):

> God could have created a stone measuring a cubic foot each day and united it with a previously created stone; it is not doubtful that this infinite multitude of stones each measuring a cubic foot would form an infinite magnitude... If it is certain that God could have created a stone and acted as above, it is also certain that he could have created a stone in each of the proportional parts forming an hour and continued as above; since the multitude of these proportional parts is infinite, by the end of the hour there will result an infinite stone.[29]

The above examples provide some evidence that, directly or indirectly, Spinoza was acquainted with the doctrines of 14th-century Scholastics on infinity. The puzzles Spinoza discusses and his solutions of them, while supporting Wolfson's thesis that Spinoza was influenced by Crescas' work, also provide evidence that Spinoza was acquainted with the doctrines of other medievals.

The puzzle I wish to discuss, as formulated by Spinoza, is "if corporeal substance is infinite, they say, let us conceive it to be divided into two parts. Each part will be either finite or infinite. If the former, then an infinite is composed of two finite parts, which is absurd. If the latter [NS: i.e., if each part is infinite], then there is one infinite twice as large as another, which is also absurd" (E IP15S, G II/57). Spinoza's formulation echoes some of the elements of Crescas' formulation of the puzzle about the impossibility of the infinite as incorporeal substance (though Spinoza's puzzle concerns corporeal substance):

> Again, that incorporeal substance would inevitably have to be either divisible or indivisible. If it be divisible, since it is also incorporeal, simple and homoeomerous, it would follow that the definition of any of its parts would be identical with that of the whole, and since the whole is assumed to be infinite, any part thereof would likewise have to be infinite. But it is of the utmost absurdity that the whole and a part of the whole should be alike [in infinity].[30]

And Crescas' formulation, as these things generally are, is merely a restatement of the problem as written by Averroes, commenting upon a proposition of Aristotle. Again, there are some similarities between the formulations of Spinoza and those of Aristotle and Averroes, but again they are with respect to different puzzles.[31]   On the other hand, Spinoza's formulation is almost identical to, and used for the same purpose as, the standard formulas of 14th-century Scholastics, like John of Bassols':

> From an actual infinite magnitude, it is possible, at least by means of God's power, to detach a first part of one foot, for example, or of two feet; I ask then, if the remaining part is finite or infinite. One cannot say that it is infinite, for, since the whole is greater than its parts, and since an actual infinity is thus given, another thing of the same kind could be greater - which is false and absurd. One cannot say that it is finite either, for with two finite magnitudes, one cannot form an infinite [magnitude].[32]

Moreover, Bassols' solution, which immediately follows the puzzle, is:

> When you say, an infinite would therefore be greater than another infinite of the same kind, I reply that there is no difficulty with that unless it concerns infinity considered as absolute, which is infinite in all ways and respects; it is thus that a line having no eastward or westward termination would be greater than a line unbounded on its eastward side, but having a termination on its westward side (*Ibid.*, fol. 213, col. c).

Crescas uses a similar example of a comparison between two lines which are infinite in only one direction as the solution to the puzzle about the alleged impossibility of an infinite being greater than another. Crescas' solution does not immediately follow the puzzle about the relation holding between the part and the whole of an infinite magnitude; it is formulated in response to another argument, which he calls Altabrizi's argument of application:[33]

> ... one infinite [being] greater than another is true only with respect to measurability, that is to say, when we use the term greater in the sense of being greater by a certain measure, and that is indeed impossible because an infinite is immeasurable. In this sense, to be sure, the first one-side infinite line cannot be greater than the second one-side infinite line, inasmuch as neither of them is measurable in its totality. Thus indeed the former line is not greater than the latter, even though it extends beyond the latter on the side which is finite... The case of time... must be conceived in the same way, that is to say, it must be conceived as capable of increase on the side on which it is limited, even though it is infinite on the other side (Crescas, p. 191. See also Wolfson's note on p. 423).

We have recaptured Spinoza's solution to the puzzle of how an infinite can be greater than another. As Crescas says, it is only in our conception, only with respect to measurability, when we use the term greater by a certain measure, that one infinite is greater than another; and Spinoza echoes: it is only in our imagination, only with respect to number and measure that one infinite is greater than another.[34] But the example Spinoza gives with respect to an infinite being greater than another is not Altabrizi's lines which are infinite in only one direction; it is the example of the two circles and all the inequalities of the space between them, all the variations exceeding every number, though they are contained within a minimum and maximum.   The example reflects the transformation of such problems into problems of maxima and minima, which the 14th-century Scholastics accomplished.[35]

Perhaps a skeptical audience will not be convinced about the claim that Spinoza was acquainted with the 14th-century doctrines about infinity. But there is little more one can do, except to repeat Wolfson's historiographical pronouncement about such matters:

> the views [from the various sources] under discussion are a common philosophical heritage. Before quoting a passage from a certain book we do not stop to ask ourselves whether that book was known to Spinoza. In several instances we rather suspect that the book in question was unknown to him. But that makes no difference to us. Provided the idea expressed in the passage under consideration is not uncommon, we assume that it was known to Spinoza, even though for the time being we do not know the immediate literary source of his knowledge. In such instances, only one who would arrogate to himself divine omniscience could assert with certainty that the idea could not be found in any source available to Spinoza. The burden of proof is always upon the negative. (Wolfson (1969) I, 14-15)

In this case, I must agree with Wolfson's strategy (given that Descartes cannot be the literary source of the complete doctrine). I would like to apply the strategy to the problem of the infinity of God's attributes, giving a reading of the problem which assumes the 14th-century discussions of infinity as part of the context of the discussion.

3. The Problem of the Infinity of God's Attributes

There seems to an opposition between late Spinozistic metaphysics and epistemology. Spinoza's assertion, in *Ethics* I, that God is "a substance consisting of an infinity of attributes, each of which expresses an eternal and infinite essence" (E ID6), causes a conflict with such propositions of *Ethics* II as the proposition "that the human mind has an adequate knowledge of God's eternal and infinite essence" (E IIP47). If so, and if we know only[36] the attributes of extension and thought, then there seems to be something about God's eternal and infinite essence which is inaccessible to our minds. Spinoza was well aware of the problem. Tschirnhaus posed it to him, though in another fashion, by emphasizing E IIP7S (G II/89-90): if the order and connection of causes is the same under the attribute of extension, or under the attribute of thought, or under any other attribute, then we should be able to perceive not only the modifications expressed through extension, but also the modifications expressed through the other attributes.[37] Spinoza's answer to Tschirnhaus is brief and unsatisfactory.[38] The likely answer is that the problem of God's infinite attributes is an unresolvable puzzle in Spinoza's philosophy. That is, as Spinoza moves away from Cartesian epistemology, from Descartes' doctrine of the incomprehensibility of God, he would also have to move away from residual elements of Cartesian metaphysics, from the various Cartesian notions of infinite being and substance and the traditional concepts of God as having infinite attributes.[39] And that movement might not have reached its terminus.

A number of contemporary interpreters have given readings of Spinoza that attempt to resolve the problem. They divide into two camps, with Martial Gueroult and Edwin Curley on the one side, limiting the epistemology in favor of the metaphysics, and A. Wolf and George Kline on the other, limiting the metaphysics. Gueroult, relying on the evidence of the early *Short Treatise* (G I/16-18 and 45-47) maintains that Spinoza's doctrine is: through the intermediary of the idea of God, we know that there are unknown attributes, but we do not know what these unknown attributes are (Gueroult I, 54; see also Gueroult I, 11-12 and 50-4, and II, 44-5 and 91-2). Gueroult denies that this introduces any incomprehensibility into God's nature: "we know a priori that everything happens in the same way, according to the same necessity, and according to the same laws, in the unknown attributes and the modes they produce, as in the known attributes."[40] Even if one accepts that answer, one also has to rid oneself of the traditional view of the attributes and accept that the attribute of mind somehow extends more widely than the rest of the attributes.[41]

All this would appear baroque to Wolf and Kline,[42] since neither of them thinks that Spinoza intends "infinite," in infinite attributes to mean "countless or indefinitely many" attributes, but simply "all" the attributes.[43] Given that thought and extension may be all the attributes, they conclude that Spinoza does not have to worry about any unknown attributes, if he does not want to.

The Wolf-Kline thesis might look paradoxical (i.e., infinite, therefore two), but Kline's argument is as convincing as his evidence is thorough. He distinguishes many senses of infinite in Spinoza, some systematic, some nonsystematic,[44] and he argues that there is no simple way of distinguishing them: "We are left to distinguish between systematic and nonsystematic senses of the key terms *infinitum* and *absolutum* either from the philosophical context, by philosophical intuition, or through some combination of the two." [45] Of these systematic and nonsystematic senses, the only one that interests us is *infinita II*, which Kline says is an emphatic form of all: "all conceivable," as well as, "all without exception." Kline's evidence for this view are passages in which Spinoza conjoins *infinita* and *omnia*.[46]

I am willing to accept almost everything Kline asserts about the infinite in Spinoza's philosophy, but still I wish to reject his conclusion. The difficulty is that the conjunction of one of the senses of "infinite" with "all" is not original with Spinoza, but traditional in the history of philosophy. Therefore, our philosophical intuitions about what Spinoza might have meant by "infinite" should be guided by the appropriate historical background. Wolf, Kline, *et al.*, avoid the anachronism of attributing a post-Cantorian theory of infinity to Spinoza, but they do not ask whether there are appropriate pre-Cantorian theories that Spinoza might be drawing upon.

For example, Aristotle in *Physics* III (iv-viii, 202b-208a) frequently associates the infinite with the All. But he recognizes that there may be a problem with that association. He argues that, since infinite is such that we can always take a part outside what has already been taken, and since that from which something is absent is not all, then Parmenides must be thought to have spoken better than Melissus. "For to connect the infinite with the all and the whole is not like joining two pieces of string" *(Physics* III, vi, 207a). Hence, Aristotle agrees with Parmenides that the All is not infinite. These passages were commented upon extensively.

The medieval distinction between categorematic and syncategorematic infinites is partly motivated by the problem of "infinite" entailing "all" and "all" entailing "infinite." The syncategorematic infinite is defined as Aristotle defined "infinite" - as incomplete or "a quantity such that there is always some part left to be taken" - so that "syncategorematic infinite" does not entail "all."[47] However, the categorematic infinite is not incomplete, and can be all. A consensus seems to have been reached, in the 14th century, that "categorematic infinite magnitude or multitude," in the appropriate sense of "greater than any magnitude no matter how great," or "greater than any multitude, no matter how numerous," entails "all without exception." For example, John Buridan argues that since all the proportional parts of a line are not all the parts of the line, the proportional parts of a line are not a categorematic infinity - i.e., "if not all, then not categorematic infinite"; or "if categorematic infinite, then all."[48] But we can also see Gregory of Rimini reject "infinite" in the sense of "so great that there can be no greater," because "if all, then categorematic infinite" would then be false: "The manner of expositing the notion of categorematic infinite does not seem suitable. According to the Philosopher, the ultimate heaven, or at least the universe, is a body so great that there is no, and can be no greater. However, it is not an infinite body."[49] For Aristotle, the universe is all and all that can be, but it is not infinite; the eight, nine, or fifty-five spheres are all and all that can be, but they are not an infinite multitude.[50]

Similarly, for Spinoza, "absolutely infinite" can entail "all without exception." That would explain Kline's conjunctions of "infinite" and "all." Spinoza would agree that if not all without exception, then not absolutely infinite, but he would add that that all or infinite is greater than any number, no matter how great; "all" would not entail "absolutely infinite" if the all were simply "greatest number" or "a quantity so great that there is no greater." Assuming that Spinoza thought that "infinite" and "all" are interchangeable, under the proviso that infinite is "greater than any number, no matter how great," what can be concluded? Surely, not that two attributes might be all the attributes there are and all there can be, but that the multitude of attributes is greater than two, greater than three, and so on for all the rest. Interestingly, a common medieval sophism was "infinitely many, therefore two."[51] Its resolution was that the "inference does not hold good, just as 'more than two therefore two'" does not hold good, since infinitely many means "*more than* two, [more than three], and so on with respect to the others" *(Ibid.).*

Therefore, the problem of the unknown attributes remains. One can decide that it is a genuine problem that must remain unsolved in Spinoza or one can adopt Gueroult's and Curley's partial solutions.

1. AT VII, 45; IX, 36. Infinite is, in some sense, prior to finite: *To Regius,* 24 May 1640, AT III, 64; *To Hyperaspistes,* August 1641, AT III, 426-7; *To Clerselier,* 23 April 1649, AT V, 356.

2. *Ibid.*; cf. also *Principles* II, 21, AT VIII, 74 and AT XI, 656. For the extension of matter called indefinite, see: *To More*, 5 February 1649, AT V, 274-75 and AT VII, 112-114 (AT IX, 89-90).

3. *To Chanut*, 6 June 1647, AT V, 52. Cf. also *To More*, 5 February 1649, AT V, 274-75 and the French version of *Principles* I, 27.

4. *To Mersenne*, 15 April 1630, AT I, 146; 11 October 1638, AT II, 383; 11 November 1640, AT III, 233-34; 31 December 1640, AT III, 273-74; 28 January 1641, AT III, 293-94; *Meditations* AT VII, 134 (AT IX, 85); *Principles* I, 26, AT VIII, 37; AT XI, 656.

5. *To Hyperaspistes*, August 1641, AT III, 430; cf. also *To Mersenne*, 6 May 1630, AT I, 150; 21 January 1641, AT III, 283; *Meditations* AT VII, 141 (AT IX, 87-8); *Principles* I, 19, AT VIII, 33.

6. *To Mersenne*, 28 January 1641, AT III, 293. See also "avoiding disputes about the infinite" in 27 May 1638, AT II, 138; *To Mesland*, 2 May 1644, AT IV, 112-13; *Principles* I, 26, 27; AT VIII, 14-15; the prudential language of "necessary caution" in *To More*, 5 February 1649, AT V, 274-5; and "not daring to call the world "infinite" in *To More*, 15 April 1649, AT V, 345. See also "reserving the name 'infinite' to God alone" in *Principles* I, 27; AT VIII, 15, and "honoring God by representing his works as very great," *To Chanut*, 6 June 1647, AT V, 51.

7. The medievals I have in mind include 12th- to 14th-century Jewish thinkers like Maimonides, Levi ben Gerson, and Hasdai Crescas, Arabic thinkers like Avicenna and Averroes, and Christian Scholastics, like Thomas Aquinas, but also such great 14th-century thinkers as Gregory of Rimini, John Buridan, and Albert of Saxony. Although Descartes probably knew the doctrines of the Christian thinkers well - at least indirectly, through the commentaries of the University of Coimbra or Collegio Romano Jesuits - his doctrine does not seem to be much influenced by them. Descartes' doctrine does have philosophical antecedents, however, since it is practically identical with Nicholas of Cusa's doctrine from *On Learned Ignorance*. On the other hand, there is little evidence that Descartes knew Cusa's doctrine well. On this issue and Descartes' doctrine about infinity generally, see Roger Ariew, "The Infinite in Descartes' Conversation with Burman," *Archiv für Geschichte der Philosophie*, 69 (1987), 140-63.

8. Gebhardt I, 190; unless otherwise indicated, all translations of Spinoza are from Curley (1985). See also Spinoza's discussions of Zeno's paradoxes, in the same work, G I/192-196. For the claim that these are traditional arguments, see Hasdai Crescas' *Or Adonai*, in H. A. Wolfson's *Crescas' Critique of Aristotle* (Cambridge, MA: Harvard University Press, 1929), p. 149, for "an infinite cannot be greater than another," and pp. 151, 219-223, for "whether an infinite is odd or even."

9. G I/190. For the claim that this is a traditional argument, see Pierre Duhem, *Medieval Cosmology: Theories of Infinity, Place, Time, Void, and The Plurality of Worlds*, ed. and trans. Roger Ariew (Chicago: U of Chicago P, 1985), ch. 1-3, especially p. 99.

10. *Ibid.* Spinoza refers his reader to Descartes' discussion of the matter in *Principles* I, 26.

11. Cf., for example, the later works: "An actual intellect, whether finite or infinite, must comprehend God's attributes and God's affections, and nothing else" (E IP30); "The human mind has an adequate knowledge of God's eternal and infinite essence" (E IIP47); and Letter LVI To Boxel, G IV/261 "To your question whether I have as clear an idea of God as I have of a triangle, I answer in the affirmative." The change seems to occur between the *Metaphysical Thoughts*, in which Spinoza asserts that "God's knowledge agrees no more with human knowledge than the dog that is a heavenly constellation agrees with the dog that is a barking animal" (G I/274), and E IP17S (G II/62-3), in which Spinoza uses the same image polemically: "If will and understanding pertain to the eternal essence of God ... the will and intellect which would constitute God's essence would have to differ entirely

from our intellect and will, and could not agree with them in anything except the name. They would not agree with one another any more than do the dog that is a heavenly constellation and the dog that is a barking animal." See also Martial Gueroult (1968), ch. 10, especially pp. 277-78n, and App 3.

12. Among other things, one can point to the proof in G I/178 depending on the absurdity of God's conceiving himself as not existing; it is likely that Descartes would have shied away from giving such a proof. Similarly, Descartes would not have given extended discussions of Zeno's paradoxes.

13. G I/195: "In addition to these two, still another argument of Zeno's is commonly mentioned. This can be read, together with its refutation in the next to the last of Descartes' Letters, Volume one [that is, *To Clerselier*, June or July 1646, AT IV, 442-7]." Spinoza's reference is to the only one of Descartes' letters in which there is an extended discussion of Zeno's paradoxes, a topic which does not seem to have interested Descartes.

14. For a more extensive analysis of Descartes' finitism, see Y. Belaval, *Leibniz critique de Descartes* (Paris: Gallimard, 1960), ch. 4.

15. Belaval points out that Descartes is not always consistent in his usage of "imagination," that he sometimes uses it in places where we would expect "understanding." The example he gives is from *To Mersenne*, 15 April 1630 (AT I, 146): "In general we can assert that God can do everything that we can comprehend but not that he cannot do what we cannot comprehend. It would be rash to think that our imagination reaches as far as his power."

16. *To Meyer*, 20 April 1663, G IV/53, 61. Gueroult's generally excellent analysis of this topic (I, App 9, 500-28) seems overly complex; surely his six cases can be reduced to three kinds of infinites.

17. *Ibid.*, G IV, 61. This indefinite is similar to, but not the same as Descartes' indefinite (see Gueroult I, 503-8).

18. *To Mersenne*, 15 April 1630, AT I, 146-7. Descartes asserts that there is no absurdity in an infinity being greater than another because we have no reason to judge the matter one way or another.

19. Number is said to belong to the class of simple and universal things in Meditation I, AT VII, 20. See also Gueroult I, 521.

20. *To Meyer*, 20 April 1663, G IV/57-8. That is why Gueroult talks of a "chute foudroyante du nombre," I, 518. It is also Ferdinand Alquié's conclusion in ch. 7 of *Le rationalisme de Spinoza* (Paris: PUF, 1981).

21. *To Meyer*, 20 April 1663, G IV/59. The question arises, who are the "mathematicians" referred to by Spinoza? The answer is not obvious. Those we would refer to as mathematicians - Gregory of Saint-Vincent, Francois Viète, Simon Stevin, Pierre de Fermat, Gilles de Roberval, et al. - form a separate, insular mathematical tradition; although these mathematicians do use infinitesimals and discuss maxima and minima, with the exception of Fermat they do so as finitists, and they do not discuss their questions in the terms referred to by Spinoza, terms that seem to echo the discussions of Late Scholastics (that is, of a different tradition, which these early modern mathematicians do not seem to know). Oddly, that is true even for the mathematical work of Christopher Clavius, a mathematician who is clearly familiar with the late-Scholastic doctrines.

22. See, for example, H. A. Wolfson, *Crescas' Critique of Aristotle*, 36-37, 120, 393-4, 423, and 466, or Wolfson (1969) I, 14-20 and 262-295 (see also Wolfson's references to the prior work of M. Joel, M. Schreiner, I. Efros, and M. Waxman, on p. 264).

23. Crescas seems to be at the end of a progression, both temporally and in sophistication, and his discussion of infinity is particularly thorough.

24. It is also discussed by Spinoza in the *Letter to Tschirnhaus*, 5 May 1676, G IV/332, and, in another context, in G I/198-200.

25. There is, of course, no direct evidence that Spinoza knew the works of any medievals. We have little knowledge of his actual sources. Still, the works of the three 14th-century thinkers were available in printed editions throughout the sixteenth century, in the same editions still reproduced as facsimiles during this century: e.g., Gregorius de Arimino, *Super Primum et Secundum Sententiarum* (Venice, 1522), Johannes Buridanus, *Subtilissima questiones super octo physicorum libros Aristotelis* (Paris, 1509), and Albertus de Saxonia, *Quaestiones super libros de Physica auscultatione Aristotelis* (Rome, 1516). I argue that Spinoza is acquainted with some of the 14th-century doctrines of infinity. But it is not likely that one could understand the 14th-century doctrines about infinity indirectly, that is, by reading others who report them. The 17th-century textbook discussions of these doctrines make little sense of them - see, e.g., Eustachius of Sancto Paulo's confused discussion of categorematic and syncategorematic infinites in his *Summa philosophica quadripartita* (Cambridge, 1648), pp. 149-54. (The same may be said for the reports of such late 14th- and early 15th-century thinkers as Marsilius of Inghen and Paul of Venice; see Pierre Duhem, *Medieval Cosmology*, ch. 1-3.) On the other hand, a reasonable source might be Franciscus Toletus, a Collegio Romano professor Descartes refers to - cf. Toletus, *Commentaria una cum quaestionibus in octo libros Aristotelis De Physica Auscultatione* (Venice, 1589). Toletus ably treats such topics as the categorematic infinite, division into proportional parts, and whether a body can be actually infinite, in lib. III, quaest. v to vii (fol. 100, col. a, to fol. 103, col. d); but he does so in order to affirm a generally conservative 13th-century doctrine on infinity. On the other hand, Toletus does refer his readers to Albert of Saxony's discussions of infinity: "Alber. Saxo. hoc lib.q.9." (p 103, col.a). (Roughly the same may be said about the commentaries of the Jesuits of Coimbra, the Conimbricences; see the *Commentariorum Collegii conimbricensis societatis Iesu, in octo libros physicorum Aristotelis Stagiritae* (Coloniae, 1596) vol. I, col. 509-540, especially col. 524.) Another standard textbook, Abra de Raconis' *Summa philosophica quadripartita*, while also maintaining a conservative Thomist line about the possibility of a categorematic infinite in actuality, gives accurate citations to Gregory's doctrine: "Prior est Ochami in 2. qu. 8 & quodlibeto 2. q. 5. Greg. Ariminensis in 1. dist. 43. q. 4. & aliorum per divinam potentiam infinitum actu categorematicum posse creari," (2nd ed., Paris, 1651) pars III, 194.
26. Gregory of Rimini, *Commentary on the Sentences* II, fol. 35, col. b.
27. *Ibid*. Buridan defines the categorematic infinite in a similar fashion; he also states that "the word taken categorematically has numerous properties... the first is that it is opposed to the finite as privation, in the same manner that the nonlimited is opposed to the limited and having no termination is opposed to having a termination," *Questions on Aristotle's Physics*, fol. 61, col. d.
28. See Duhem, *Medieval Cosmology*, ch. 2. Unlike John Buridan and Albert of Saxony, Gregory of Rimini thinks that a categorematic infinite can be produced in this way.
29. Gregory of Rimini, *Commentary on the Sentences* II, fol. 14, col. c and d. John Buridan and Albert of Saxony discuss this and similar examples. See John Buridan, *Questions on Aristotle's Physics*, lib. III, quaest. XVI, fol. 58, col. b, to fol. 61, col. b, and Albert of Saxony, *Questions on Aristotle's Physics*, lib. III, quaest. XII, fol. 39, col. c, to fol. 40, col. d.
30. Crescas, in Wolfson, 137. Crescas' first argument against infinite corporeal magnitude resembles Spinoza's first puzzle even less: "If there existed an infinite tangible body, it would have to be simple or composite. In either case, and however that simple or composite body is conceived to be, one of its elements would have to be infinite in magnitude, inasmuch as it has been demonstrated in the first book of the *Physics* that an infinite number of elements is impossible. This element, infinite in magnitude, if it were so, and being also tangible and endowed with qualities, would in the course of time bring change and corruption to other elements..." *Ibid.*, 151.

31. Aristotle, *Physics* 204a20-27: "It is plain, too, that the infinite cannot be an actual thing and a substance, and principle. For any part of it that is taken will be infinite, if it has parts... Hence it will be either indivisible, or divisible into infinites. But the same thing cannot be many infinites." Averroes, *Commentary on the Physics* 204a20-27 (in Wolfson, 331): "If it [immaterial substance] be divisible, then the definition of the part and the whole of it will be the same in this respect, as must necessarily be the case in homoeomerous things. But if this be so, then part of the infinite will be infinite." As these examples make clear, the gist of these arguments does not revolve about the nature of the infinite, whether it can be greater than another, but about the relation of part to whole, whether they can have different natures. Spinoza would not reject the argument if it is given this reading, since he himself uses it in E IP13D: "if it [a substance which is absolutely infinite] were divisible, the parts into which it would be divided will either retain the nature of an absolutely infinite substance or they will not. If the first, then there will be a number of substances of the same nature, which (by P5) is absurd..."

32. Joannes de Bassolis, *In quattuor sententiarum libros* I, fol. 213, col. b, of his *Opera* (Paris, 1516). Bassols' formulation seems even neater than Spinoza's, since it does not need an infinity to be divisible into two equal parts.

33. Crescas, p. 149: "Suppose we have a line infinite in only one direction. To this line we apply an infinite line, having the finite end of the second line fall on some point near the finite end of the first line. It would then follow that one infinite would be greater than another. But this is impossible, for it is well known that an infinite cannot be greater than another."

34. *To Meyer*, 20 April 1663, G IV/59. I should note that, in part 2 of this paper, I argued that Spinoza could have derived part of this doctrine by reading Descartes' *Letter to Clerselier*. My speculation is that he might have accepted Descartes' uncharacteristic analysis because it fit so well with what he read in Crescas and other medievals.

35. *Ibid.*, G IV/59-60 and elsewhere. Spinoza's example is an improvement over those of the 14th-century Scholastics, because it concerns both a minimum and a maximum. Aside from this nicety, the example is isomorphic with Gregory of Rimini's example of line segments divided into proportional parts or John Buridan's *linea gyrativa*, a spiral line winding tighter and tighter, in relation to the proportional parts of the cylinder on whose surface it is inscribed.

36. Perhaps I should add "and can know only two attributes." But it should not make any difference how many attributes we know and how many attributes we can know, since, however many we do know and can know, there should still be infinitely many left to know. (We can paraphrase Descartes: true infinity implies no potentiality.)

37. "... it seems to follow that the modification which constitutes my mind, and the modification which expresses my body, although it is one and the same modification, is nevertheless expressed in infinite ways - one way through thought, in another through extension, in a third through an attribute of God unknown to me, so on to infinity. For there are infinite attributes of God, and the order and connections of modifications seems to be the same in all. Hence, there now arises the question, why the mind, which represents a certain modification, the same modification being expressed not only in extension but in infinite other ways, perceives only that modification expressed through extension, that is, the human body, and no other expressions through other attributes," *To Spinoza*, 12 August 1675, G IV/279.

38. "I say that although each thing is expressed in infinite ways in the intellect of God, nevertheless, those infinite ideas by which it is expressed cannot constitute one and the same mind of a singular thing, but infinitely many minds. For each of the infinitely many ideas has no connection with the other..." *To Tschirnhaus*, 18 August 1675, G IV/280.

39. Since the traditional doctrine concerns the infinity of attributes (not in Spinoza's sense, but in Descartes' sense, what Spinoza calls *Propria*), it might seem that Spinoza can dispense with that element.

40. *Ibid.*, p. 11. See also Pierre Macherey, *Hegel ou Spinoza*, (Paris: Francois Maspero, 1979), pp. 158-75.

41. That is Curley's position in Curley (1969), 144-53; see also Gueroult II, 91. The answer takes the response to Tschirnhaus seriously, but it also relies on the suspect evidence of the *Short Treatise*: "Therefore, the essence of the soul consists only in the being of an Idea, or objective essence, in the thinking attribute, arising from the essence of an object which in fact exists in Nature. I say *of an object that really exists*, etc., without further particulars, in order to include here not only the modes of extension, but also the modes of all the infinite attributes, which have a soul just as those of extension do," G I/119. A puzzle still remains: how can this reading of a different soul connected with each attribute allow for a creature with three attributes, a live possibility from the Letter to Schuller, IV/278; Curley's option 2, from p. 146, seems to require pairs of attributes (actually, 1, 2, 4, 6, 8...) This puzzle might force us to the less satisfactory option 1, which is also more consistent with the response to Tschirnhaus. (Unless I am mistaken, that is Curley's latest position, in Curley (1988).)

42. A. Wolf (ed.), *The Correspondence of Spinoza*, 462-3, and "Spinoza's Conception of the Attributes of Substance," in Kashap (1972), 16-27; and George L. Kline, "On the Infinity of Spinoza's Attributes," in Hessing (1977), 333-352. The Wolf-Kline thesis has been accepted lately by such able interpreters of Spinoza's thought as Alan Donagan, in "Spinoza's Dualism," in Kennington (1980), 93-4, and Jonathan Bennett, in Bennett (1984), 75-9. Kline claims Joachimas a predecessor, calling the interpretation the Joachim-Wolf-Kline line. In Joachim (1901), Joachim does assert that the true infinite cannot have its nature expressed in number and that substance is infinite in the sense of complete, all-inclusive, and self-contained. But the evidence for his being counted is not complete and unambiguous.

43. There are some minor differences among the four principal interpreters who have adopted that line. Wolf: "Spinoza did not posit innumerable attributes at all... He posited 'infinite or all the attributes,'... There *may be*, but there need not be more than two Attributes," p. 26 of "Spinoza's Conception of the Attributes of Substance." Kline: "the appropriate systematic sense [of infinite, in infinite attributes, is] *infinita* II ('all without exception'). Two attributes might perfectly well be 'all the attributes [there are] without exception,'" p. 352. Donagan: "What Spinoza says about the number of the divine attributes [is that] they *all* belong to the infinite substance, and not merely some finite sub-set of them. Hence, depending on whether the number of attributes that express the essence of an infinite substance is one... or, say, three or nineteen, or aleph-null, E IP11 entails that the number of divine attributes is one, or three, or nineteen, or aleph-null. How many attributes did Spinoza think infinite substance to have? The only certain answer that may be deduced from the *Ethics* is 'at least two,'" p 94. Bennett: "Spinoza used 'infinite' as a virtual synonym for 'all [possible]'... When Spinoza says that God has infinite attributes, he means only that God exists in every possible basic way. This does not entail that God exists other than as extended and as thinking, i.e., that there are more than two attributes." p. 76.

44. I agree that there is a problem with nonsystematic uses of the infinite in the 17th century. In fact, one can even find such informal phrases as "une infinité de passages de la divine écriture," in the writings of normally careful writers (Leibniz, Gerhardt IV, 429). Galileo got into trouble for talking about the infinite illumination of stars. He has an amusing reply in the *Assayer*, pp. 242-3 of *Discoveries and Opinions of Galileo*, ed. and trans. S. Drake (New York: Anchor, 1957), including a Biblical quotation, "Stultorum infinitus est numerus."

45. Kline, 337. Kline distinguishes among the systematic senses of infinite as (i) supremely perfect and (ii) complete, without exception, and its nonsystematic sense of countless or indefinitely many. I will discuss (ii) below. It seems to me that what I will say about (ii) can also be said about (i), namely that the sense of supremely perfect would be more accurately reflected by "more perfect than any, no matter how perfect." That is what Spinoza implies in the following, from the Letter to Boxel, September 1674, G IV/354: "Between the finite and the infinite there is no proportion: so that the difference between the greatest and most excellent creature and God is the same as the difference which exists between God and the least creature."

46. Kline, 343-45. The evidence includes a couple of passages from the *Short Treatise* in which Spinoza conjoins infinite and all (G I/19 and 19n); we should also mention Spinoza's reference to "the All" (*ibid.*). The *Short Treatise*, of course, is the work in which Spinoza gives the fullest treatment of infinite attributes as more than the two we know.

47. A similar point can be made about the earlier distinction between the infinite *in actu* and the infinite *in fieri*.

48. "I would agree with this [syncategorematic] proposition: along all the parts, a spiral line is drawn; and I would not agree with this [categorematic] proposition: a spiral line is drawn along all the parts. Moreover, even though there is a spiral line circling a hundred proportional parts, or a thousand, or any number of parts whatever, there is none drawn along an infinity of parts, for there are no parts which are an infinity of parts, and there are no parts which are all the parts, whether we take the word *all* in its collective sense or in its distributive sense," *Questions on the Physics*, fol. 59, col. c. Gregory of Rimini would agree that the proportional parts are not all the parts, "all" taken distributively, but would disagree that they are not all the parts, "all" taken collectively (*Commentary on the Sentences*, fol. 175, col. b).

49. *Commentary on the Sentences*, fol. 35, col. b. It is important to note that Gregory of Rimini himself does not think the universe is all that it can be, since he thinks that God can create more matter.

50. So, "categorematic infinite" cannot mean "so great that there can be no greater." For Buridan and Gregory of Rimini, "categorematic infinite" means "greater than any number, no matter how great"; with that as a proviso, it can be used as equivalent to "all."

51. William of Sherwood *Treatise on Syncategorematic Words*, trans. by N. Kretzmann (Minneapolis: U of Minnesota P, 1968) p. 42. A similar sophism can be found in Peter of Spain's *Logic*; cf. *Tractatus*, ed. by L. M. De Rijk (Assen: Van Gorcum, 1972), pp. 230-2.

GUEROULT ON SPINOZA'S PROOF OF GOD'S EXISTENCE

WILLIS DONEY
Dartmouth College

My discussion is more limited than the title suggests, for I am concerned, not with Gueroult's accounts of all of Spinoza's arguments for God's existence, but with his account of the first 'official' proof of IP11.[1] In my estimation his account of that proof contains important insights. But there are also mistakes that tend to obscure these insights. My aim is to salvage the insights and offer an emended interpretation on the lines of Gueroult's.

IP11 is: "God, or a substance consisting of infinite attributes, each of which expresses eternal and infinite essence, necessarily exists." About the sentences immediately following the statement of this Proposition - sentences in which Spinoza's official demonstration is ostensibly stated - Gueroult makes two points of great importance.

(a) Distinguishing two parts of the definition (D6) embedded in P11, namely, that God is a substance and that God is a being constituted by an infinity of attributes, he points out two ways in which an apriori or ontological argument might proceed from the definition: one from the notion of God as substance, and the other from the notion of God as a being constituted by an infinity of attributes (p. 182). An argument of the latter sort is located in the Geometrical Appendix of the *Short Treatise*.[2] But that, Gueroult maintains, is not Spinoza's way in the *Ethics* (p.183ff). The argument in the *Ethics* is based on the notion of God as substance and is - to use Gueroult's expression - a proof by way of substantiality. That this is so is evident from the citation of IP7 in the sentences following P11. P7 is: "It pertains to the nature of a substance to exist," which is clearly not a proposition about an attribute or an infinity of attributes, but about what, according to Spinoza, is an important and relevant characteristic of a substance.

This first point, though it may seem obvious, is worth making. For one thing, it calls attention to a distinctive (perhaps unique) feature of Spinoza's ontological proof. Unlike Descartes's arguments from perfection and omnipotence[3] or Malebranche's from infinity[4] or Leibniz's from the idea of a necessary being (Gerhardt IV, 405-406), Spinoza's argument is based on the conception of God as substance. Moreover, this point has not been universally acknowledged. According to Wolfson (1969, I, 183), Spinoza's first proof in the *Ethics* is based on "the idea of self-causality." This is not a minor or negligible inaccuracy on Wolfson's part, for it is difficult to see how, on Spinoza's view, an argument containing the premise "God is self-caused" could fail to be a flagrantly question-begging argument.[5] Finally, the point is important because it makes explicit an implicit first premise of Spinoza's argument, namely, "God is a substance."

(b) The second noteworthy feature of Gueroult's interpretation consists in his treatment of the *reductio* in the sentences following P11:

If you deny this, conceive, if you can, that God does not exist. Therefore, (by A7) his essence does not involve existence. But this (by P7) is absurd. Therefore God exists, q.e.d.

Gueroult maintains that the *reductio* is an *ad hominem* argument intended for the less than clear-sighted reader who fails to grasp the evidence of P11 and that it is not an argument that Spinoza used to demonstrate God's existence.[6] There is, however, an "unformulated positive" argument (p. 181) that can be derived from the statement of the *reductio*, and it is this unformulated argument that he takes to comprise Spinoza's first proof of God's existence.

The derivation of the positive argument proceeds as follows. In the *reductio*, Spinoza attempts to show that a consequence of denying God's existence, namely, the consequence that God's essence does not involve existence, is necessarily false. The argument to show that is not stated. But IP7 is cited, and a premise of the argument intended is, in terms that Spinoza indicates in the Demonstra- tion of P7 can be used to formulate P7: the "essence [of a substance] necessarily involves existence." Recasting this premise and making explicit an implicit premise, Gueroult comes up with the following premises: "God is a substance" and "Every substance exists necessarily through itself" (p. 181). And these premises are taken to yield the conclusion "God exists necessarily."

The argument attributed to Spinoza can, I believe, be simplified. Since it is supposed to be a proof of God's existence and not, or not just, of the kind of existence that God enjoys,[7] "necessarily" and "through itself" can be eliminated. Moreover, though, it might be argued - and I believe Gueroult holds[8] - that P7 is intended to have existential import, at least part of what is asserted in P7 can be stated hypothetically: "Necessarily, if something is a substance, it exists." Since this hypothetical proposition is sufficient to get from "God is a substance" to "God exists," a pared down version of the argument ascribed to Spinoza is: "God is a substance; Necessarily, if something is a substance, it exists; Therefore, God exists." And it seems to me that, in imputing this argument to Spinoza, Gueroult hits the nail on the head.

*   *   *

There are two objections to be considered. (a) The first concerns the initial premise "God is a substance." It can be objected that, on Spinoza's view, it follows immediately from D3 that, if something is a substance, it exists in itself and a fortiori that, if something is a substance, it exists. But, if it follows immediately from the definition of "substance" that, if something is a substance, it exists, to say that God is a substance is to say or imply that God exists. Hence, the question at issue would be begged with the first premise, and the additional premise is idle. What appears, therefore, to be an argument is in reality no argument at all.

This objection seems to me to be based on a mistake. Although it is true that, on Spinoza's view, it follows immediately from D3 that, if something is a substance, it exists in itself, it is false that, on his view, it follows immediately from D3 that, if something is a substance, it exists. That is a proposition that, on my interpretation, is proved in P7D, and P7D does not rely exclusively on D3. Accordingly, to say that God or infinite substance exists in itself is to specify the kind of existence that God or infinite substance would have to have, namely, existence in itself and not in another - it is not to say or imply that such a being *has* that kind of existence. The short answer I have given to this objection can be questioned in light of what Spinoza says in IP8S2 and in Letter 12 to Meyer (1663),[9] but an examination of these seemingly contrary passages would take me too far afield from my main concern, which is a problem arising from an objection that Gueroult raises against the second premise.[10]

(b) The second objection is that the Demonstration of IP7 proves only or at most that it pertains to the nature of a substance constituted by a single attribute to exist and not the general proposition that existence pertains to the nature of any substance no matter the number of attributes (pp. 124, 182ff.). It can be argued that, since P7 depends on P6 and P6 in turn depends on P5 and P5 is a thesis restricted to single-attribute substances, P7, too, is a thesis restricted to single attribute substances.[11] If this is correct, in P11D Spinoza must be convicted of a rather obvious, indeed too obvious, blunder. If the second premise is taken to be "A substance constituted by one attribute alone necessarily exists," the premise cannot be used to prove that God, i.e., a substance having infinite attributes, necessarily exists. But if the second premise is, as is evidently required, the general, unrestricted proposition, the argument - so the objection goes - contains a premise that has not been demonstrated to be true.

To answer the objection, Gueroult qualifies his well-known thesis that PP1-8 are about single-attribute substances and contends that P7 contains "two truths" (p. 186). The first, in line with his unqualified thesis, is: "Every substance constituted by a single attribute necessarily exists through itself." There is also - and he thinks this has to be shown - a second "more general" truth: "*Every* substance [without restriction] exists through itself" (my emphasis). To show that the general truth is also contained in P7, he refers to P6CD2 and to the contention already cited in P8S2 (pp. 185-186). P6C is, to quote Gueroult, the "pillar" of P7, and the second "easier" demonstration of P6C proceeds by way of D3 and A4 and, unlike the demonstration proper of P6, does not cite P5. From these facts it is concluded that Spinoza provides us with a way of proving the general truth independently of P5, and so the general truth, as well as the more particular truth about single-attribute substances, can be said to be implicit in P7. The general truth, Gueroult adds, is made explicit in P8S2 when Spinoza observes that "if men would attend to the nature of substance, they would have no doubt at all of the truth of P7" and P7 "would be an axiom for everyone, and would be numbered among the common notions." If P7 can be known independently of any proof, it seems it is not - to use Gueroult's expression - "conditioned" by P6 and in turn the suspect P5. Granting, then, that the more general truth is implicit in P7, Gueroult can maintain that Spinoza's proof by way of substantiality is not subject to the objection raised.

*   *   *

There is, I believe, a more obvious way of attacking the argument on which the objection is based. Instead of trying to show that P7 is not dependent on P6 and so on P5, the premise that P5 is restricted to single-attribute substances can be questioned. Such a restriction is indeed not explicit in the formulation of P5, which is, "In nature there cannot be two or more substances of the same nature or attribute," and not "In nature there cannot be two or more substances having only one attribute of the same nature or attribute."[12] Nor is what I shall call the single attribute thesis -that a substance has at most one attribute - stated anywhere in the *Ethics*. But it can be argued that, at a crucial juncture in the *reductio* in support of P5, the thesis is presupposed. One premise is that two or more putative substances having the same attribute could not be distinguished by a difference of attributes. No citation is given for this premise, yet it seems to invite a very powerful objection - an objection that Gueroult ascribes to Leibniz (p. 120). Why could there not be a universe consisting of two substances S1 and S2, S1 having attributes p and q, S2 attributes p and r? In the envisaged universe, S1 and S2 would have the same attribute p but they would be distinguishable by way of attributes q and r, which they do not share.

In view of this objection, an important and neglected question to which Gueroult's interpretation gives rise is why, in P5D, Spinoza is content to leave a controvertible premise undefended. I believe Gueroult - and also Curley (1985, p. 410, n.8) - provides the wrong answer, namely, that Spinoza bases his argument on the single-attribute thesis. There are some difficulties that attend Gueroult's answer. It is, of course, somewhat paradoxical to say that Spinoza presupposes here a thesis that he thinks is false. God, after all, has an infinity of attributes. Moreover, if he makes this assumption here and P5 is restricted in the way indicated, P14D ("Except God, no substance can be nor be conceived") fails. One step in the argument is: "If there were any substance except God, it would have to be explained through some attribute of God, and so two substances of the same attribute would exist, which (by P5) is absurd." If Gueroult's interpretation of P5 is correct, it has not been shown that there cannot be an attribute in common in the case of a substance having infinite attributes and some other substance. Finally, in view of the antecedent definition of "God" as a "substance consisting of an infinity of attributes..." (D6), it seems unlikely that, even for the sake of argument, Spinoza would presuppose here - or would ask his reader to assume - a thesis that has already been questioned. But Gueroult thinks he can take account of such objections to his interpretation.

*   *   *

Exposition - let alone criticism - of Gueroult's labyrinthine answer to these questions is beyond the compass of my discussion. Instead, I want to propose an alternative explanation of why, in P5D, Spinoza is content to leave a controvertible premise without support. Part of the explanation is that he thinks he has precluded the possibility envisaged in the objection in his proof of P2.

P2 is: "Two substances having different attributes have nothing in common with each other." From this it follows that, if putative substances S1 and S2 have attributes q and r respectively, they cannot have p in common.[13] But this is only part of the explanation, for, though Spinoza says that P2 is evident from the definition of substance, that is not in fact the case, and it can be argued that the single-attribute thesis is assumed here (Curley, 1985, p. 410, n.8).

To show that it is not, I shall construct two arguments that do not depend on that thesis and are consonant with Spinoza's citation of D3. The first seems to be suggested by what he says, all too briefly, in P2D:

> This is also evident from D3, for each [substance] must be in itself and be conceived through itself, or the concept of the one does not involve the concept of the other.

The clause "or the concept of the one does not involve the concept of the other" seems to suggest that P2 is supposed to follow from the second part of D3 (substance is "what...is conceived through itself..."). And an argument based on that part of the definition would be that, if putative substances S1 and S2 having attributes q and r respectively are supposed to share a common attribute p, they could not be conceived independently. To spell out the argument: the conception of S1 would involve the conception of p; but the conception of p involves the conception of S2;[14] hence, S1 could not be conceived independently of S2. Similarly, for S2. It would follow that the conception of one involves the conception of the other and, according to the second part of D3, neither could be a substance. There is, however, a strong reason for not attributing the argument suggested to Spinoza, namely, that it is rather obviously fallacious: it is clear that S1 could be conceived by way of p *or* q, and so the conception of S1 does not involve or require the conception of p nor in turn the conception of S2. Similarly, for S2.[15]

There is, fortunately, a less objectionable argument that can be based on the first part of D3 (substance is "what is in itself") along with a proposition that I believe follows from ID4 and IID2. That proposition is: if a substance were *per impossibile* to cease to exist, an attribute or the attributes of the substance would cease to exist, and, if an attribute or attributes of a substance were to cease to exist, the substance having the attribute or those attributes would also cease to exist. From this proposition, it follows that, if S1 were to cease to exist, S2 would cease to exist. Hence, S2 would be existentially dependent on S1 and, according to the first part of D3, it could not be a substance. And, similarly, for S1.[16]

*   *   *

Against this interpretation of P2D, it can be objected that the premises ascribed to Spinoza would prove too much. From these premises, it would follow that substances cannot have a common attribute. Yet that is precisely what is asserted in P5, and the *reductio* following P5 does not contain these premises. Why, if my interpretation is correct, does Spinoza offer a different argument?

And why is he not content to restate, or rather state a variant of, the argument implicit in P2D? It is, I believe, appropriate to note that Spinoza has (among others) Descartes in mind here. Though I believe he is not, as Curley suggests, arguing within the confines of Descartes' view that a substance has only one (principal) attribute, he is trying to preclude a possibility suggested by Descartes that substances having a common attribute could nonetheless be distinguished by modes.[17] That substances having a common attribute cannot be distinguished by attributes has already been shown and a new argument is proposed in order to take cognizance of, and explicitly reject, the Cartesian view that substances with a common attribute can be distinguished by their modes.

What that enigmatic argument is has been variously conjectured. I shall end by proposing another *reductio* that is at any rate consonant with the citations in this part of the argument for P5.[18] Assume that putative substances S1 and S2 having common attribute p and different modes m1 and m2 are distinguished by the modes m1 and m2. For S1 and S2 to be distinguished, the conception of S1 must differ from the conception of S2 and conversely. Since the two conceptions cannot differ with respect to attribute p, the only way they can differ is by the inclusion of modes m1 and m2 in the conceptions, the conception of S1 including the conception of m1 and the conception of S2 involving the conception of m2. But it is absurd to suppose that the conception of a substance, i.e., of what is conceived through itself, includes the conception of a mode; and so the assumption of the *reductio* - that two substances having a common attribute can be distinguished by modes - must be false.

1. By "official proof" I mean the argument stated or implied in the sentences immediately following the enunciation of a Proposition and headed *Demonstratio*. References to Martial Gueroult are all to Gueroult (1968) and are given by page numbers in the text. I have used E. M. Curley's admirable translation, Curley (1985).
2. In AppI P4 and C. (In Curley (1985), 151-152). I am inclined to question Gueroult's suggestion (p. 178) that, in these passages, the necessary existence of Nature and, through the identification of God and Nature, the necessary existence of God is based on the necessary existence of attributes rather than the necessary existence of substance.
3. An argument from perfection can be found in Meditation V and the argument from omnipotence in "Replies to the First Set of Objections," AT VII, 65ff. and 118-119.
4. As in *Entretiens sur la métaphysique et sur la religion*, II in *Malebranche: Oeuvres Complètes*, ed. by A. Robinet, (Paris: Vrin, 1965), Vol XI, pp. 49ff.
5. On my understanding of Spinoza's conception of self-causation or -- its equivalent (D1) - - essence-involving-existence, the "minor premise" in Wolfson's formulation of the proof ("God's essence involves existence") asserts or implies God's existence and the "major premise" is otiose.
6. This important point is made on pp. 179-181 (though it is somewhat obscured by Gueroult's further contention that God's existence (an *évidence première*) is, strictly speaking, indemonstrable): *Pour les contraindre à ouvrir les yeux, il faut donc leur faire toucher du doigt l'absurdité de la négotiation où les entraîne leur aveuglement.*" That Spinoza would accept any *reductio* as a demonstration of an affirmative truth is highly doubtful in view of Letter 64, G IV/278, and TdIE, GII/19ff.

7. This is contested by some commentators, for instance, by Henry E. Allison, *Benedict de Spinoza*, (Boston: G. K. Hall & Co., 1975), 65ff., but not by Gueroult (v. p. 179). It is beyond the scope of my discussion to defend what I say here, but a line of defense is indicated in my "Spinoza's Ontological Proof" in *The Philosophy of Baruch Spinoza*, ed. by Richard Kennington (Washington: Catholic U of America P, 1980), pp. 35-51.

8. The argument is, he says, *une première version de la preuve ontologique*; and the existential proposition is, presumably, that there necessarily exists a substance or substances *constituées d'un seul attribut* (pp. 123-126).

9. In IP8S2: "But if men would attend to the nature of a substance, they would have no doubt at all of the truth of P7. Indeed, this proposition would be an axiom for everyone, and would be numbered among the common notions," and, in Letter 12 to Meyer (1663), Spinoza says of substance "that existence pertains to its essence, i.e., that from its essence alone and definition it follows that it exists...". (G IV/54).

10. Two brief remarks about the seemingly contrary passages. About P8S2: even if P7 is taken to be an axiom, it would nonetheless be an *axiom* and not a proposition that is supposed to be deducible from D3. (It would, of course, be wrong to attribute to Spinoza the view that axioms are "true by definition.") The second passage is more troublesome. After claiming that existence follows from the essence alone or definition of substance, Spinoza adds, "...if my memory does not deceive me, I have previously *demonstrated* this to you in conversation without the aid of any other Propositions..." (my italics). This is puzzling, for how could this claim about substance be true by virtue of a definition yet also be "demonstrated"? In this early letter, Spinoza does not say what the "other Propositions" are, and, according to an earlier letter from Oldenburg (3, G IV/11), what is later in the *Ethics* a proposition, i.e., P2, is here an axiom. A reconciliation I suggest is that, though the demonstration did not invoke those "other propositions," it did involve other truths, perhaps axioms. How else could there have been a demonstration?

11. According to Gueroult, PP1-8 are about single-attribute substances. An examination of all the reasons he gives to support his famous thesis exceeds the compass of my paper. I shall consider only this one, which relates to P7 in particular.

12. It might be argued that the restriction is implicit in the expression *natura sive attributum*, *natura* signifying any possible attribute of a substance and *attributum* -- singular -- indicating that there is supposed to be but one. For reasons I go on to give, what seems to be the strongest reason for this conclusion is not a good reason.

13. This might be questioned on the ground that P2 is to be read, "Two substances having totally different attributes have nothing in common with one another."

14. There is an assumption here that the conception of an attribute involves the conception of any substance of which it is an attribute, but there seems to me to be no reason to suppose that Spinoza would not have made that assumption.

15. It has been suggested that, according to Spinoza, the attributes of putative substance S1 could not be conceived independently. But for Spinoza, as in P10S, there is a real distinction between attributes and one attribute *can* be conceived apart from another.

16. These arguments undermine Spinoza's unsupported assumption at the beginning of the *Ethics* that what can be conceived independently and what can exist independently must be the same.

17. Descartes does not make this assertion with respect, say, to two minds, but it seems that he is committed to the view.

18. P1, D3, and A6.

ON BENNETT'S SPINOZA: THE ISSUE OF TELEOLOGY

EDWIN CURLEY
University of Illinois
Chicago, Illinois

The dust jacket of Bennett's *Study of Spinoza's Ethics* bears a quotation from G.H.R. Parkinson praising it as "the most exciting book on Spinoza that I have read for a long time... written with great intelligence, lucidity and verve... a stimulating book, which will make its readers think." Let me say right away that I believe Parkinson's praise is amply justified. I would add that I think much of what Bennett says in this exciting book is true. And even where I am inclined to disagree, I think Bennett asks a lot of hard questions which needed to be asked, questions which are hard not merely in the sense that they are intellectually difficult to answer, but also in the sense that they force those of us who sympathize with Spinoza's philosophy to examine our consciences, and to ask ourselves whether the philosophy to whose study we have devoted so much time was worth our pains.

Bennett's study of Spinoza will no doubt be characterized as a piece of "analytic history of philosophy." To the extent that that (often deprecatory) label is justified, what justifies it is not that Bennett's work is dominated by commitment to some distinctively 20th Century philosophical program - to some view, say, that the proper task of philosophy is the analysis of language, or that metaphysics is impossible. What justifies it is that Bennett insists on asking whether Spinoza gives us any rational grounds for accepting the conclusions he reaches, that he asks over and over again: "Does this demonstration really work?" And if the answer is "no," as it very frequently is, then "Are there any suggestions in Spinoza of an alternative argument, from plausible and genuinely Spinozistic assumptions, and reaching the same (or a very similar) conclusion by valid means?" Some lovers of Spinoza may find this kind of inquiry, as pursued by Bennett, offensive. He does not give Spinoza high marks for deductive rigor. Sometimes, I think, he reaches a negative conclusion too quickly. But we would do no honor to Spinoza's memory if we did not recognize that Bennett is approaching Spinoza in the spirit in which he would have wished to be approached. Spinoza would have had no patience with anyone who rejected the propriety of the kind of logical questions Bennett raises.

I begin with these words of praise for Bennett's book, because most of what I shall have to say will be critical. I do not want anyone to mistake my overall evaluation of the book. I think it is an excellent piece of work. But I also think it is wrong about many things, and my main task tonight will be to explore a few of those things.[1] It would not be very interesting to spend much time on issues where Bennett and I agree. I shall concentrate on the topic of teleology, which is central to Bennett's analysis of Parts III-V of the *Ethics*.

One of Bennett's most striking conclusions is his claim that Spinoza denies all teleology: not only does Bennett's Spinoza maintain that God never acts for the sake of an end, he does not think that *any* being does, including man.

According to Bennett, Spinoza rejects all final causes, and if we do not see this, we "miss most of what is interesting in Part 3," the attempt to develop a nonteleological theory of human motivation (§51.1). But Bennett thinks this attempt is a failure and a persistent source of trouble for Spinoza in the latter parts of the *Ethics*, since he cannot consistently adhere to his psychological program, and cannot, within the confines of that program, give a satisfactory account of what it is to act from the guidance of reason. So the problem which first arises in his philosophical psychology spreads, striking at one of the fundamental concepts of his moral philosophy. (§68.3)

Now I am not persuaded that it is Spinoza's intention to offer a non-teleological theory of human motivation. So I don't agree that Spinoza is being inconsistent, when, later in the *Ethics*, he interprets his conatus principle in a teleological way. And I do not think there is any reason in principle why he cannot give a satisfactory account of what it is to act from the guidance of reason. But it's certainly not obvious that Bennett is wrong in these matters. There are passages which tend to support his reading, even if they are not, in my opinion, sufficient to show that he is right to read Spinoza as he does. So the textual situation is at least confused.[2]

Let's begin by looking at a passage Bennett cites in support of his reading. In the Appendix to Part I, the first of the two main texts in which Spinoza discusses final causes, he writes:

> Not many words will be required now to show that Nature has no end set before it, and that *all final causes are nothing but human fictions*. For I believe I have already established this, both by the foundations and causes from which I have shown this prejudice to have had its origin, and also by P16, P32C1 and C2, and all those [arguments] by which I have shown that all things proceed by a certain eternal necessity of nature, and with the greatest perfection (II/80/3-9).

The clause I have italicised for emphasis certainly does seem, taken in isolation, to express an unqualified rejection of final causes.

But I think it is not intended to, and that read in context, it does not involve such a rejection. The immediately preceding clause, after all, proclaims that Spinoza's object is to show that *Nature* has no end set before it. So I would read the italicised clause as saying that *all final causes we are apt to ascribe to (God or) Nature are nothing but human fictions*. And I would note that the propositions and corollaries Spinoza goes on to cite, as having already established this, all have to do with divine causality.

Those are considerations about the immediate context. But the larger context confirms this reading. The Appendix is an extended attack on one prejudice which Spinoza says underlies all the prejudices he has undertaken to expose in Part I of the *Ethics*:

> men commonly suppose that all natural things act *as they themselves do*, on account of an end; indeed, they maintain as certain that God himself directs all things to some certain end; for they say that God has made all things on account of man, and has

made man that he might worship him [i.e., has made man to worship God]. (II/78/2-6, my emphasis)

The rest of the Appendix discusses, first, the reasons why men have this prejudice (from II/78/12 to 80/1), second, the reasons why it is false (from II/80/2 to 81/24), and finally, the other prejudices which have arisen from this one (from II/81/25 to 83/32). Now I would have thought that the passage just quoted makes it quite clear that Spinoza does not deny purposive action to man: the prejudice Spinoza is exploring in this preface is precisely the attribution to natural things of *a form of activity characteristic of men,* viz. action for the sake of an end.

Moreover, Spinoza reiterates his assumption that men act purposively when he undertakes to explain why men have this prejudice: men know that they themselves do everything for the sake of an end, viz. their own advantage; they know that explaining their own behavior involves ascribing to themselves desires, i.e., conscious appetites; but although they are conscious of the appetites by which they explain their own behavior, they are not conscious of the causes of those appetites; and because those appetites are internal to themselves, they imagine that if their appetites did have a cause, they would know what that cause was; so they come to think of their own purposes as providing them with a model of an uncaused cause, something which can be invoked, satisfactorily, to explain activity, without itself being susceptible to explanation; so when they come to try to explain the activities of *other* things, they find purposive explanations more satisfying than explanations in terms of efficient causes, which always seem to admit, and hence to require, an explanation in terms of some prior cause; explanations in terms of efficient causes generate an infinite regress which will be terminated only by our ignorance, by our inability, as finite human beings, to trace the causal chain any further back, not by our having discovered a cause which does not admit, and hence does not require, any further explanation.[3]

Now Bennett is well aware of the passages I have been citing against him. He quotes one himself when he is trying to explain why people have interpreted the Appendix to Part I as an attack only on divine teleology:

This more drastic attack is easy to overlook in 1 Appendix, because it is well buried in a discussion of God's purposes and also because Spinoza there seems at times to concede that men do have purposes which explain their behaviour (§51.1).

And he offers two explanations for these "seeming concessions of human teleology":

We shall see in §52 that he offers a partial rescue of that sort of talk: his concept of 'appetite,' which is free of the supposedly noxious elements in teleological concepts, might have seemed to him to underpin such remarks as 'Men always act on account of an end, namely on account of their advantage, which they want' (1 Appendix at 78/21). Or perhaps the seeming concessions of human teleology in 1 Appendix may be due to Spinoza's having written most of his polemic against divine teleology before his case against all teleology occurred to him, and neglecting to revise the text when that discovery was at last made. (§51.1)

Now I don't think we can do much with the second of these explanations. It requires us to suppose one of two things: either that at some stage of his development Spinoza *discovered* an argument against all teleology and incorporated it in his previous attack on divine teleology, *without recognizing* that it required a rewriting of that attack; or that at some stage of his development Spinoza *discovered* that an argument he had previously used against divine teleology applied equally well to human teleology, but *failed to see* that this required a rewriting of his previous attack on divine teleology.

But neither of these alternatives is at all plausible. The assumption that men act for the sake of an end is too central to the argument of the Appendix to Part I for Spinoza to have consciously made any such discoveries without at the same time noticing that accepting such arguments would require extensive revision of the Appendix. The "seeming concessions" are not, as Bennett suggests, remarks made in passing, but either crucial and explicit assumptions in his argument or else essential elements in his statement of his main conclusion. Only if we fall back on the first explanation- i.e., only if we assume that Spinoza thought his talk of human teleology could be understood in an acceptable way- is his failure to make the revisions credible.

Before we can deal adequately with the first explanation, however, we need to see why, according to Bennett's Spinoza, talk of human teleology is not all right as it stands. We must ask: "what are the noxious elements from which teleological concepts need to be freed?" To ask this is to ask: "what are the arguments against teleology which apply, with equal strength, both to human and to divine teleology?" This is a vital question in any case. For Bennett attributes a radical rejection of all teleology to Spinoza, not so much because he has a text in which he sees Spinoza saying, explicitly, that all purposive explanation is a fiction,[4] as because he thinks that

> mixed in with the attack on divine purpose there are two arguments which, if they are any good at all,[5] count against any kind of teleology- against "He raised his hand so as to shade his eyes" as well as against "Elbows are formed like that so that men can raise their hands". (§51.1)

What are those arguments?

The first, discussed in §51.2 and supported mainly by the passage from II/80/3 cited above on p. 40, might be put as follows: Spinoza has shown in Part I that (i) all things proceed by "a certain eternal necessity of Nature"; (ii) but things which are to be explained by final causes cannot occur by a necessity of Nature; (iii) for to explain something by a final cause is to explain it in terms of the uncaused volitions of the person whose purposes are invoked; (iv) what occurs because of an uncaused volition is ultimately contingent;[6] since (v) nothing is ultimately contingent, (vi) nothing is to be explained by final causes.

In stating this argument I haven't put it in quite the way that Bennett does, because I would like to avoid certain interpretive issues which I think it inessential to resolve. But I don't think that matters. Bennett does not lay much stress on the argument and I shall not either. Bennett objects to the argument that the "link between teleology and radical freedom is a mistake." I agree. And I think Spinoza would agree also. I think he really views the argument as an *ad hominem* one, directed against an opponent who holds that teleology and indeterminism are linked. I take it that he would reject both step (ii) and step (iii), though (iii) would be all right if the word "uncaused" were deleted. More of this anon.

In stating the second argument I propose to stick closely to Bennett's own way of putting things, because more is at stake here. Let me quote, first, a whole paragraph:

> Spinoza also objects against teleological explanations that they purport to explain events by reference to their effects. A stone is thrown at me, and I raise my hand in time to deflect it: the event Raise causes the event Deflect. But if we purport to explain Raise by saying that it was performed 'so as to deflect the stone,' we are using Deflect to explain Raise. Spinoza protests: 'This doctrine concerning the end turns Nature completely upside down. For what is really a cause, it considers an effect, and conversely. What by nature comes before it puts after.' (1 Appendix at 80/10) He thinks one cannot explain an item by reference to something which it causes. (§51.3)

Now clearly Spinoza does object to some teleological explanations on the ground that they treat the effect as the cause of its cause, and so reverse the order of nature. But the passage Bennett quotes from Spinoza is really quite vague about what form of teleological explanation is at issue here. Spinoza simply refers to "this doctrine concerning the end." By embedding the quotation in the kind of example he does, Bennett suggests that the doctrine concerning the end is a doctrine the contentious point of which is that human actions can be explained by final causes. But someone who came upon this phrase immediately after reading the earlier parts of the Appendix might more naturally take it to be the doctrine that everything which happens in Nature happens, as human actions do, as the result of a final cause. That is, he would take it to be a doctrine the contentious point of which is that things other than human actions can be explained by final causes.

When we're in doubt about what Spinoza means by a phrase, it's a good policy to look at the kinds of illustration he uses. So it's worth noting that when he chooses, in this section (viz. II/80/2-81/24), to illustrate the kind of thing he thinks it inappropriate to explain in terms of final causes, he never picks anything like a human action. His examples are either of biological phenomena ("the structure of the human body") or of events involving objects we would characterize as inanimate ("a stone has fallen from a roof onto someone's head and killed him"). He never uses the kind of example Bennett does.

But, you might say, even if Spinoza doesn't illustrate the kind of explanation he's opposed to by selecting examples of human actions, doesn't his objection apply to them with as much force as it does to the examples he selects? When we say that I raised my hand to deflect the stone, aren't we explaining the cause by its effect just as much as we would be doing if we said that the stone fell from the roof so as to kill the man?

On the face of it, the answer to this is "no," for reasons Bennett explains very cogently:

> In a teleological explanation the event is usually explained by reference not directly to an effect of it but rather to an antecedent thought about an effect of it. In saying 'He raised his hand so as to deflect the stone' we are saying that Raise happened because he thought it would cause the stone's being deflected. What is there in that for Spinoza to object to? Why can he not just accept it, saying that the subsequent event enters the story only as something represented in an antecedent thought, so that 'the [thought] of the "final cause" functions as "efficient cause"'? (§51.4)

Now I think that's precisely what Spinoza does say. But before I come to the passage in which I think he says it, I want to note a peculiarity of the first sentence of the passage just quoted. Bennett speaks of the way events are *usually* explained in teleological explanations. Perhaps he is right about the form teleological explanations usually take *now*. But surely he is not right about the form they usually took *in the 17th Century*. The passage just quoted betrays a lack of historical perspective which becomes acute as the passage continues.

Bennett does not think Spinoza can, consistently with his deepest thoughts about human action, accept the common sense analysis of the teleological explanations we usually offer of such actions:

> Spinoza does himself explain actions by reference to the agent's thought about the future, as we shall see; which suggests that he has no case against such explanations. I shall maintain, on the contrary, that he objects to them strenuously, and that he is caught in an inconsistency- explaining actions in a manner he ought to condemn. If his attack on teleology were intended only to condemn explaining Raise with help from Deflect, and to allow the explanation of Raise in terms of a thought about a deflection, then it is a noisy assault on a miniscule target. Spinoza is hunting bigger game than that. (§51.4)

In a moment we'll come to the reasons why Bennett thinks Spinoza would object strenuously to our explaining human actions, not in terms of their consequences, but in terms of our anticipation of those consequences. What I want to do first is to call attention to the way we are being manoeuvred into regarding alternative interpretations as unworthy of consideration.

I repeat, and isolate for special attention, the critical step in Bennett's argument:

> If his attack on teleology were intended only to condemn explaining Raise with help from Deflect, and to allow the explanation of Raise in terms of a thought about a deflection, then it is a noisy assault on a miniscule target.

Now, of course, there's a sense in which that's exactly right. No one who thinks human actions can be explained in terms of their purposes really wants to explain my raising my arm by the simple fact that my doing so deflected a stone. Anyone, if pressed, will say: "Of course what I mean is that my anticipation that raising my arm would deflect the stone is (part of) what explains my raising my arm." If Spinoza were attacking only the former kind of explanation, it would indeed be a noisy attack on a miniscule target.

But by posing the alternatives in this way Bennett is neglecting an Aristotelian tradition of teleological explanation which in the 17th Century was still very much alive, to judge from the examples of final causation Spinoza gives. In calling this tradition "Aristotelian" I don't mean to suggest that Aristotle originated it. His doctrine of the four causes is meant to be an account of the various ways in which he has found the concept of cause to be used by his predecessors, and the concept of a final cause is certainly anticipated in Plato.[7] Nor do I mean to suggest that Aristotle himself held a doctrine of final causation of the kind Spinoza attacks. For one thing, he evidently does not think that *everything* which happens in nature has a final cause. The rain does not fall in order to make the corn grow, but of necessity.[8] More importantly, for our purposes, Aristotle himself does not think that when things in nature happen for the sake of some end, this is because a divine craftsman has so ordered things. The God of Book Lambda of the *Metaphysics* is not one which takes any thought for things other than itself.[9] So if we say that the camel has extra stomachs in order to cope with its thorny diet, we will not be true to Aristotle himself if we elaborate on our explanation by adverting to God's plan for his creation.

Nevertheless, that's essentially what certain medieval followers of Aristotle did. Like some modern students of Aristotle,[10] they could not make any sense of the idea of an unconscious teleology in nature. But believing, as they did, in a rather different kind of God, they felt that they could explain teleology in nature better than the master had. Here's Maimonides:

> What is the cause that has particularized one stretch [of the heavens] in such a way that ten stars should be found in it and has particularized another stretch in such a way that no star should be found in it?... All this... would be very unlikely, or rather would come near to being impossible, if it should be believed that all this proceeded obligatorily and of necessity from the deity, as is the opinion of Aristotle. If, however, it is believed that all this came about in virtue of the purpose of one who purposed, who made this thus, that opinion would not be accompanied by a feeling of astonishment and would not be at all unlikely... All this has been produced for an object that we do not know and is not an aimless and fortuitous act... You know that the veins and nerves of any individual dog or ass have not happened fortuitously ... There is no doubt that all of these things are necessary according to the purposes of one who purposes.[11]

This, I suggest, is the way phenomena were *usually* explained teleologically by the 17th Century followers of Aristotle whom Spinoza mainly had in mind. They found a great many phenomena in nature which, it seemed, could only be adequately explained by calling attention to the ends they served. Not finding authentic Aristotelian teleological explanation intelligible, they invoked a theological teleology which was not authentically Aristotelian. And Spinoza undertook to show that that theological alternative was not, in the end, any more satisfactory. In the 17th Century this was not a miniscule target, and I imagine that even in the 20th Century there are some circles in which Spinoza's lessons have not been learned.

Now I'm sure that Bennett knows all this, or enough of it so that the difference doesn't matter. And I'm sure he will not be impressed by it, because he thinks Spinoza does, on his own principles, have a strong case against teleological explanations, even when they are understood in the way common sense, as opposed to speculative theology, understands them. Why might Spinoza object to our explaining my raising my arm by appeal to my thought that to do so would deflect an impending stone?

Bennett does not give the obvious answer. That is, he does not think such an explanation is flatly ruled out by the impossibility of any interaction between modes of thought and modes of extension. It's true that if we said simply that my thought causes my arm to move, we would violate IIP6. But the doctrine of parallelism implies that corresponding to my thought there is a contemporaneous state of my brain which is the direct object of my thought. And that state of my brain is certainly available to be a cause of the future state of my arm which is the indirect object of my thought. There's nothing in IIP6 to rule out that transaction.

The problem, according to Bennett, is that none of the causal powers of that state of my brain

> depend on its being the counterpart of a thought with such and such a content, i.e., the counterpart of something which is an idea indirectly of a so-and-so. The physical theory inserted between 2p13 and 14 firmly assumes that physical events are to be explained purely in terms of the shapes, sizes, positions, velocities etc. of particles of matter. There is no work to be done by representative features. (§51.5)

The fact that my brain state is the object of an idea with a certain content, viz. the (direct) object of an idea which is (indirectly) an idea of my deflecting the stone, is as irrelevant to its causal powers as the fact that the movement of my arm resembles one Olivier made in a film is to the causal powers of that movement.

Now I think there are a number of things we might say about this. But I'll relegate most of them to the notes.[12] What I chiefly want to emphasize is that Bennett offers virtually no direct textual evidence for this claim. In the paragraphs in which he is setting out this argument (¶¶s 3-7 of §51.5) the only textual reference is the one occurring in the passage I have just quoted, and all that says is that the physical theory of Part II limits the causally relevant aspects of physical objects to the kinds of features which were acknowledged as causally relevant by 17th Century mechanists. This leaves out representative features, i.e., the fact a certain state of my brain is the direct object of an idea which is indirectly of some future physical event.

But suppose my brain's being in a certain state (defined in terms of the shapes, sizes, positions, velocities etc. of its component particles) just *is* its being the object of an idea indirectly of a certain future state of my body. To conceive it in the first way is to conceive it under the attribute of extension; to conceive it in the second way is to conceive it under the attribute of thought. The mind-body identity theory of IIP7S surely implies that anything occurring in the mental realm, such as an idea of a possible future physical event, will be identical with something occurring in the physical realm. If we take that identity seriously, why should we say that the representative features are being given no work to do? Bennett's idea seems to be that, so long as our explanation of the future physical event is conducted in purely physical terms, i.e., so long as we conceive the cause of the movement of my arm under the attribute of extension, we are leaving out something essential to the explanation of that event, or at any rate, something a genuine believer in human teleology would regard as essential.

But I take it that this is precisely the kind of dualistic claim Spinoza was protesting against in IIIP2S:

> They will say, of course, that it cannot happen that the causes of buildings, of paintings, and of things of this kind, which are made only by human skill, should be able to be deduced from the laws of nature alone, insofar as it is considered to be only corporeal; nor would the human body be able to build a temple, if it were not determined and guided by the mind. But I have already shown that they do not know what the body can do, or what can be deduced from the consideration of its nature alone, and that they know from experience that a great many things happen from the laws of nature alone which they never would have believed could happen without the direction of the mind... (II/142/34-143/7)

One purpose which the theory of mind-body identity serves in Spinoza is to let him have his cake (posit the possibility of a completely physicalistic explanation of all physical events) and eat it too (allow for teleology at the level of human action).

Earlier I promised to cite a passage in which Spinoza gave the common sense answer to the question how an end can explain the things people do to attain that end, a passage in which he says that

> the subsequent event enters the story only as something represented in an antecedent thought, so that 'the [thought] of the "final cause" functions as "efficient cause."'

The passage occurs in Spinoza's second main treatment of the topic of final causes, the Preface to Part IV:

> As [God *or* Nature] exists for the sake of no end, he also acts for the sake of no end. Rather, as he has no principle or end of existing, so he also has none of acting. What is called a final cause is nothing but a human appetite insofar as it is considered as a principle, *or* primary cause, of some thing. For example, when we say that habitation was the final cause of this or that house, surely we understand nothing but that a man, because he imagined the conveniences of domestic life, had an appetite to build a house. So habitation, insofar as it is considered as a final cause, is nothing more than

this singular appetite. It is really an efficient cause, which is considered as a first cause, because men are commonly ignorant of the causes of their appetites. (II/206/27-207/12)

Spinoza has a way of making talk of final causes acceptable, but it is precisely the way Bennett says he would reject: when it appears that something is being explained by a subsequent result, what is really happening, if the explanation is legitimate at all, is that we are explaining a human action by appealing to the person's anticipation of the consequences to be expected from that action, his desire for those consequences, and his resultant desire to perform the action.[13]

Now according to Bennett, it is legitimate for Spinoza to identify final causes, properly understood, with antecedent appetites, but inconsistent of him to bring an imagination of the future into the account of the appetite referred to here.[14] Bennett takes it that the concept of appetite introduced in IIIP9S deliberately does not mention any thoughts about the future. That is what makes it free of the noxious elements involved in ordinary teleological concepts, and a suitable foundation for building a genuinely Spinozistic psychology.

I think there is enough truth in this to be interesting, but not enough to support the conclusions Bennett seeks to draw from his account of Spinoza's supposedly nonteleological theory of motivation. Let's begin, not with the concept of appetite, but with the closely related concept of the striving for self-preservation which Spinoza introduces in IIIP6:

Each thing, as far as it can by its own power, strives to persevere in its being.

"To strive to" is my favored term for *conari*; Bennett prefers "to try to"; but whatever term we use, it is important to recognize that the *conatus ad motum* was a central technical concept in Cartesian physics, where it referred to a tendency of bodies to persist either in a state of rest or, if they were in motion, in uniform motion in a straight line, unless acted on by external bodies. Both Descartes and Spinoza use *conatus* in that context *in spite of*, rather than because of, its psychological connotations. Descartes certainly doesn't think that the bodies to which he ascribes this *conatus* have any awareness of where they're going, or desire to reach that goal. This is part of *his* attack on Aristotelian teleology. And in spite of his "panpsychism," I don't think Spinoza does either. He thinks the *conatus* to persevere in one's being is an absolutely universal principle, possessed even by the simplest bodies. And whatever the proper interpretation of IIP13S, I'm sure he doesn't think that very simple moving bodies have any idea where they're going, or any desire to get there. All this is grist for Bennett's mill, though he curiously doesn't make any use of it.[15]

IIIP7 tells us that "the striving by which each thing strives to persevere in its being is nothing but the actual essence of the thing." And IIIP9S connects the concept of striving with those of appetite and desire:

When [this striving] is related to the mind and body together, it is called appetite. This appetite, therefore, is nothing but the very essence of man, from whose nature there necessarily follow those things which promote his preservation. And so man is determined to do those things. Between appetite and desire there is no difference, except that desire is generally related to men insofar as they are conscious of their appetite. (II/147/28-148/3)

When Spinoza reprises this passage at the end of Part III, he relies on this identity to substitute the term "desire" for the term "appetite":

Desire is man's very essence, insofar as it is conceived to be determined, from any given affection of it, to do something.

I find these passages very puzzling, and would be grateful for any light Bennett could shed on them. Here is what Bennett offers us as a gloss:

To have an appetite for x is just to be so constituted that you will behave in ways which increase the probability of your getting x; or, in a shorthand which I find convenient, to be so constituted that you will 'move towards' x... The thesis, pretty clearly, is that 'appetite for x' is to be analysed in terms of 'intrinsic state which causes one to move toward x.' (§52.1)

So far this seems reasonable enough. I suppose I have appetites for many things which I am nevertheless not disposed to move towards, all things considered. But if that's a problem, it's as much a problem for Spinoza as for Bennett.

The specification that what causes the movement toward the thing desired should be an *intrinsic state* of the person who has the desire also seems a plausible guess as to what Spinoza might have in mind by saying that an appetite or desire is an affection of the thing's essence. But I find that when Bennett glosses his gloss I begin to have problems:

In this account, a desire or appetite is identified with some aspects of the essence or nature of a person, something which could be fully described without mentioning any subsequent state of affairs... The plain man thinks that an action can be caused or explained by a desire which essentially involves the future... Spinoza replaces that concept of desire by one which he thinks covers roughly the same territory without implying that anything involving the future helps to explain the present. (§52.2)

Now it's true that Spinoza's official definition of appetite or desire does not require that this affect should involve the future in any way. Neither does it explicitly exclude the possibility that the affect should involve a representation of the future. *If* the requirement that the state should be intrinsic excludes the possibility of its involving the future by representation, and *if* the requirement that the state should be intrinsic, so understood, is the right interpretation of Spinoza's reference to an affection of the person's essence, then Bennett's gloss must be right.

But that's enough "ifs" to leave room for a doubt or two. Perhaps Spinoza doesn't mention any representation of the future in his analysis of appetite/desire because he wants to allow for a generalized concept of appetite/desire which will apply both to humans and to less complex entities, all the way down to the simplest bodies. Perhaps he thinks that at the very simplest level "appetite" does not involve any conception of the future, but that at some point on the continuum from *corpora simplicissima* to humans "appetite" does involve such a conception.[16] That might make it easier to reconcile this definition with IIA3. And it might make it easier to understand why Spinoza no sooner introduces his nonteleological concept of appetite than he abandons it by giving the conatus principle a teleological interpretation (Cf. Bennett, §57.4-5). According to Bennett, from IIIP12 on Spinoza is regularly inconsistent with one of his most interesting claims. Perhaps, rather than ascribe such massive inconsistency to Spinoza, we should take a harder look at the evidence for interpreting his definition of appetite as reflecting a deliberate decision to advance a nonteleological theory of motivation.

1. Elsewhere I have discussed other aspects of Bennett's work: "On Bennett's Interpretation of Spinoza's Monism," forthcoming in the proceedings of the Jerusalem Spinoza conference of March 1987; "Le corps et l'esprit: Du *Court traité* à l'*Ethique*," *Archives de philosophie*, 51(1988): 5-14; and Curley (1988), passim.
2. We might note that Lee Rice is already in print with an interesting article in which he accepts Bennett's central point. See "Spinoza, Bennett, and Teleology," *The Southern Journal of Philosophy*, 23 (1985): 241-253.
3. Here I paraphrase, very freely, the passage from II/78/12 to II/78/28. I take it that it is this passage which Bennett is trying to explain in §50.2. In attempting to understand what is going on there, both of us need to bring in a later passage in the Appendix, the famous "sanctuary of ignorance" passage (II/80/35-81/11). But Bennett, if he is indeed trying, in §50.2, to explain what is going on in my passage, does so without ever invoking the doctrine that men act always for the sake of an end, or the doctrine that they are conscious of their appetites without being conscious of the causes of those appetites. Perhaps this is why he finds it so difficult to locate a satisfactory argument in Spinoza at this point. (In §51.3 he remarks that he does not fully understand this passage and suspects it of a muddle.) He asks why anyone should be "embarrassed by having to say, a short distance along the backwards explanatory chain, that he doesn't know what the earlier items in the chain are?" The point, I think, is not that people are embarrassed by their ignorance, but that they find efficient causal explanation unsatisfactory, because they believe themselves to be familiar with a different kind of explanation in which the cause is an explainer which needs no explanation, viz., the kind of explanation they give of their own behavior.

   Let me take this opportunity to correct a mistake in my translation of this passage (Curley (1985), 440). For "so they necessarily judge the temperament of other men from their own temperament," read: "so they necessarily judge the temperament of the other from their own temperament."
4. Though I think he would count II/80/3-4 as such a text. That is the passage discussed above on p. 40.
5. I don't think Bennett means to suggest that Spinoza has *no* good arguments against divine teleology in particular which do not count equally against teleology in general. But I do think he tends to undervalue the attack on divine teleology in particular. E.g., he writes in §50.1 that it is "nothing like as important and instructive as" the attack on teleology in general. I conjecture that part of the reason Bennett thinks it less important is that he

does not think divine teleology is any longer a theory which non-Catholic philosophers need to take seriously. But if this is so, it is because philosophers like Spinoza developed arguments against divine teleology which led subsequent philosophers to feel that they could disregard it. If the arguments aren't good, the disregard is inappropriate. If the arguments are good, and Spinoza is one of the first people responsible for stating them persuasively, he should be given full credit for doing so.

In §50.3 Bennett approves the argument against divine teleology in IP33S2 (II/76/24-34), but devotes only two sentences to it. His emphasis is on an argument of which he does not approve:

> Less good is the argument in 1 Appendix that it is impious to attribute purposes to God because 'If God acts for the sake of an end, he must want something which he lacks.' (80/22) That reflects the widespread assumption that purposive activity is unintelligible unless directed to a future which is preferred to the present: as Locke said, in effect: 'Why should I act unless I am discontented with the *status quo*?' There are many answers to that. The crucial point is this: if someone acts, he prefers a certain possible future- not to the present, but to other possible futures.

To this Spinoza might reply as follows: you assume that for God there might really be two possible futures, one of which is preferable to the other; but that cannot be reconciled with the assumption that God is a supremely perfect being; if God is supremely perfect, then the only future really possible for him is the one which is most preferable; again, the distinction between preferring a possible future to the present and preferring it to another possible future cannot apply to God, who is supposed to be immutable; to say that he prefers one possible future to another, but not to the present, is to say that there is a possible future for him which is different from his present; this cannot be in a supremely perfect being; it is not a question of piety here, but of remaining consistent with the only conception of God which gives us any reason for believing in the existence of God.

6. By "ultimately contingent" I here mean "neither absolutely nor relatively necessary," in the sense in which those terms are explained in ch. 3 of Curley (1969).

7. See, for example, *Metaphysics*, I, vii: "Of those who speak about about principle and cause no one has mentioned any principle except those which have been distinguished in our book on nature, but all evidently have some inkling of them, though only vaguely." As regards the distinction between efficient and final causes, this seems a bit unfair to Plato. Cf. *Timaeus* 46C-47C.

8. See *Physics* II, viii, 198b17, and W. Wieland, "The Problem of Teleology," in *Articles on Aristotle*, vol. I, *Science*, ed. by J. Barnes, M. Schofield, and Richard Sorabji, Duckworth, 1975. Note here the assumption (central to the argument summarized at the bottom of p. 42) that what happens of necessity does not happen as a result of a final cause.

9. See *Metaphysics* XII, ix, and Ross, *Aristotle*, Meridian, 1959, pp. 181-2.

10. E.g., Ross, *op. cit.*, p. 182: "The notion of unconscious teleology is ... unsatisfactory. If we are to view action not merely as producing a result, but as being aimed at producing it, we must view the agent either as imagining the result and aiming at reaching it, or as the tool of some other intelligence which through it is realising its conscious purposes." For a dissenting view, see R. Sorabji, *Necessity, Cause and Blame*, Cornell UP, 1980, p. 164.

11. *The Guide for the Perplexed*, II, 19, quoted from the translation by Shlomo Pines, U of Chicago P, 1963, II, 310.

12. Bennett himself calls attention to a couple of problems. E.g., his argument depends on treating events (concrete particulars, which may have a multitude of unstated features) as causes, rather than facts (abstract entities, which have no unstated properties). He acknowledges that Spinoza's causal rationalism is easier to make plausible when causality is treated as a relation between facts rather than events. But though he thinks Spinoza

did tend to prefer facts to events as causes, he thinks this was only a tendency, and that Spinoza's thought about final causes exhibits contrary tendencies.

More seriously, perhaps, Bennett thinks Spinoza is required by the doctrine of parallelism to hold that, just as the fact that a mode of extension is the correlate of an idea having certain representative features has no effects at the physical level, so the representative features of the thoughts themselves are causally impotent even in the mental realm: the fact that a thought has a certain content (is the idea of a certain possible future event, for example) makes no contribution to its causal powers. (See, p.220, ¶1) He seems to think that if he is right about Spinoza's reasons for rejecting teleology, Spinoza would be forced to such a conclusion, and that he would not shrink from it. I suggest that the unpalatability of this consequence should have provided Bennett with a sufficient reason to give up the whole line of interpretation. How could Spinoza have reconciled any such doctrine with his fundamental insight that affects like love and desire depend on our having a conception of the object loved or desired. (IIA3) Bennett recognizes the importance of cognitive elements in Spinoza's theory of the emotions in §62, and acknowledges Spinoza's superiority to both Descartes and Hume in this regard in §63. But his account of the causal impotence of representation in §51.5 undermines that whole aspect of Spinoza's philosophical psychology.

13. This is why I said above (p.6, ¶1) that step (iii) of the argument under discussion there would be all right if the word "uncaused" were deleted.

14. See his remarks on the passage just quoted in §52.3 (final ¶). His attempts to explain this passage away do not seem to me convincing. He treats it as if it were a casual remark, and hence not carefully considered, whereas it seems to me a passage in which Spinoza brings to a conclusion the attack on divine teleology begun in the Appendix to Part I, and hence one to which Spinoza must have attached considerable theoretical importance.

15. What Bennett *says* is just this: "The verb 'try', in its ordinary meaning, is teleological ... Spinoza ought, in using this term, to see a need to detoxify it by showing that it does not really involve explaining items in terms of their effects ... " (§57.3) This makes it sound as though Spinoza wrote in English. What Bennett *ought to have said* is: "The English terms Spinoza's translators use to render *conatus* have inappropriately teleological connotations. We need to remember, if we fall in with their usage, that Spinoza's own term had a use in which it did not imply any anticipation of a state to be reached." Of course, if Bennett did say that, he would have to take back part of §57.5.

For references supporting the lexicographical claims made in this ¶, see the Glossary-Index in my Spinoza edition, under "striving."

16. It's worth noting that, whereas the striving referred to in IIIP6-7 had been one which *each thing* was supposed to have, the striving which is identified with appetite/desire in P9S is one which constitutes the essence of *man*.

SPINOZA AND TELEOLOGY: A REPLY TO CURLEY

JONATHAN BENNETT
Syracuse University

A Retraction

Curley is right: Spinoza's opposition to cosmic teleology was at the time a large matter, not a small one; when I brushed it aside as minor, I wasn't thinking historically. But since I was taking a view about what Spinoza himself actually thought about teleology, historical thinking would have been appropriate.

Curley is also persuasive in suggesting that the line between human and cosmic teleology might plausibly be thought to correspond to the line between teleology that does involve and teleology that does not involve causation by a *thought*. When I was writing my book I don't think that this idea crossed my mind. It should have.

Putting those two points together, and adding to them the fact that Spinoza undoubtedly does - as I acknowledged in my book - sometimes openly attribute thoughtful teleology to human beings, I ought to have considered patiently and seriously the possibility that Curley puts before us and thinks to be actual: namely that Spinoza really did want to attribute thoughtful teleology to humans, and denied it only for items - such as the universe - that don't have thoughts about the future. I have now considered it, and am inclined to accept that Spinoza did in a way, and up to a point, and sometimes, think of teleology in that way rather than in the comprehensively rejecting way that I attribute to him.

Spinoza's Difficulty With Thoughtful Teleology

I have reasons for those grudging qualifiers. The text does not clearly, explicitly and consistently go Curley's way. Spinoza never says outright that in thoughtful teleology the order of nature is not reversed because what causes the action is an earlier *thought about* the future; and that is just one negative sign of something that I still believe to be the case, namely that Spinoza's acceptance of thoughtful teleology is, at its strongest, a notably half-hearted affair. *And so it ought to have been.* Given the rest of Spinoza's views, the human teleology that he did allow (in a way, up to a point, etc.) could not consistently contain the feature that is ordinarily taken to lie at the core of teleology, namely that what happens at one time is causally explained in a way that essentially, operatively, non-idly mentions some future time. I shall now explain why.

The order and connexion of ideas is the same as the order and connexion of things: Spinoza held that the physicalistic explanation of why my arm goes up is paralleled by a mentalistic explanation of what happens in my mind when my arm goes up. Now, the mentalistic antecedents may well include a thought of my raised arm's deflecting a stone that I see being thrown towards me; that thought cannot of course help to explain the physical event, the raising of the arm (Curley and I agree about that), but it helps to explain the mental counterpart of that physical event, just as the physical counterpart of the thought explains the arm's going up. Curley adds, in effect: "But according to Spinoza, the mental antecedent *just is* the physical antecedent, so in Spinoza's scheme of things the mental antecedent does after all have a role in the causation of the physical movement of my arm."

Now, we all know that this sort of reasoning must be handled cautiously where Spinoza is in question. He does assert an identity across the mental/physical divide, but he also insists, firmly and clearly, that no causal explanations can cross the divide, and he ties causation to explanation. So I don't think that that move of Curley's can be right.

The main point I want to make, however, is entirely additional to that. Granted that Spinoza thinks that mentalistic causal chains have a structure that mirrors the structure of physicalistic causal chains, so that causal explanations under one attribute map onto causal explanations under the other, it is a further question whether that isomorphism brings in any of the *representative* aspects of mental states and events.

A strong current of thought in contemporary philosophy of mind says that the representative features of mental states, though they figure in rough-and-ready laymen's explanations of behavior, have no place in any disciplined, scientific account of how the mind does its work; the reason being that very same intrinsic state might count for one person as the thought that P, and for another as the thought that Q, where P and Q are entirely different. Whether a mental item with a certain intrinsic nature counts as having this or that *content* or *representative* aspect depends upon when the animal got it, in what circumstances, in association with what other mental items, and so on. One (extreme) upshot of this is that the following could happen: animals x and y are now intrinsically exactly like one another and unlike z, whereas x and z are exactly alike in their mental contents and in that respect unlike y.

I think that this is probably correct, but I can't embark on a defence of it here.[1] Anyway, whether or not it is true, this thesis can be found in the pages of Spinoza's *Ethics*.

There is more than a hint of it in IIP16 and its corollaries, where Spinoza first introduces the notion of a mental item as representing something other than a bodily state of its owner. What he says there clearly implies that what makes an idea of mine count as being "of" your body is not *what the idea is intrinsically like* but rather *how it is caused*. This clearly makes room for the possibility that your idea of x and mine are intrinsically quite different, and that the very same intrinsic mental state might be in you an idea of x and in me an idea of y.

(Spinoza says that he has explained *this* through many examples in 1 Appendix; but he hasn't. The only way of making *any* significant link between IIP16C2 and I App is by means of the position I am now expounding: namely that Spinoza held that the representative features of ideas do not map onto their intrinsic features and thus have no serious explanatory role, this being relevant to his views on thoughtful teleology.)

There is a further indication in IIP40S1, where Spinoza talks about "imagination." This includes most mental content that represents particular things outside oneself, and thus most of the thoughts that might come into a teleological account of behavior. Explaining why it is such a limited cognitive instrument, he says that our "imaginative" ideas are not formed by all men in the same way, but vary according to what the body has more often been affected by, and so on. This clearly implies that two mental states that are unalike in their representative content may be alike in their intrinsic natures and thus in what their physical counterparts are. There are other indications as well.

Summing up this part of my argument, I submit: (1) It is not credible that intrinsic states of mind that are isomorphic with states of the brain should also be systematically connected with the representative content of states of mind. For the representative content of a person's state of mind - the "of x" and "that P" aspect of his thought - depends upon *relational* features of that state, e.g. on the person's past history of being in that state, what else was going on at the time, and so on. (2) This truth can be derived from Spinoza's doctrines, and is indicated in his pages clearly enough to make it ungenerous to deny him the credit for having seen it himself. (3) To the extent that he did see it, he must have thought that when my arm's going up has a physical cause whose mental counterpart is a mental event that is (among other things) the thought of my arm's deflecting a stone, *that* fact about the mental item has no part in the serious causal explanation of the mental counterpart of the arm's going up. So there was some place in Spinoza's mind for the view that even in thoughtful teleology the notion of the future is causally idle: something is being caused by a thought about the future, but its being about the future - and indeed its entire content, its whole representative nature - is irrelevant to its causal powers.

Spinoza's Struggle to Exclude Thoughtful Teleology

That would explain two puzzling aspects of the text of the *Essay*.

(1) Spinoza repeatedly says that "desire is man's very essence, insofar as it is conceived to be determined... to do something." Curley agrees that this is puzzling, and that I have a prima facie possible explanation of it, namely: Spinoza means that desire (or the underlying phenomenon of appetite) is to be understood as causally potent only when construed in intrinsic rather than representational terms, and that our notion of desire or appetite *for* x in the future is just the notion of an intrinsic state that does in fact tend to lead its owner to achieve x. This fits in with my present theme, because it implies that when I raise my arm "so as to deflect the stone," the notion of the stone's subsequently being deflected is relevant to the effects of my arm's going up but not to its causes; which is just to say that real teleology, final *causation*, is excluded.

Curley says he has "a doubt or two" about my explanation; so do I. But I have tried in these remarks to go a bit further than I did in my book in explaining why I think that Spinoza *ought* to have held - and probably at some level of his mind *did* hold - that the representative features of thoughts are irrelevant to their causal powers. As long as that is right, I don't see much room for doubt about my treatment of the "desire is the man's essence" passages.

(2) Up to IIIP12 Spinoza deploys his conatus doctrine in conditionals to the effect that

> If x does A, it is helpful to x to do A,

and from there on he quietly switches to the converse, that is, to conditionals to the effect that

> If it would help x to do A, x does A,

That this switch occurs is beyond dispute: it is minutely documented in my book. Nor can there be any doubt that the two conditionals are quite different, and that neither follows from the other.

The switch has an enormous effect on the work.   The post-switch conditional can be used to predict and explain someone's *doing A*, whereas the pre-switch conditional, in which "x does A" occurs in the antecedent but not in the consequent, can only explain or predict someone's *not doing A*. So Spinoza's show of having a richly explanatory theory of behavior depends on his use of the post-switch conditional.   Yet his attempted proof of the conatus doctrine is addressed exclusively to the pre-switch conditional, not to the one he eventually wants and employs.

This could be made to look like mere blundering incompetence, but I see it differently. I think it is Spinoza's attempt to deal with a terrific problem that is created by his insight that there is a difficulty about teleological explanation, even the thoughtful kind.

The crucial point is that the post-switch conditional lies at the core of teleology, properly understood; or so it is alleged by the only plausible theory of teleology that we have.[2]   I conjecture that Spinoza had some awareness of that conceptual fact, and that this warned him off the post-switch conditional when he was at the stage of consciously trying to keep teleology out. To do that, he had to avoid implying that any causal explanation of behavior could essentially involve anything that happens subsequently to the behavior, yet that is just what the post-switch conditional does; so he couldn't have it, and had to settle for its pre-switch converse. But later on he moved from abstract causal theory down into the thick of the human condition, wanting to use his conatus doctrine to explain various patterns of behavior. For this he needed behavior not in the antecedent but in the consequent; he needed not the pre-switch but the post-switch conditional; he needed not his official conatus doctrine but outright teleology. Thoughtful teleology would have sufficed. If Spinoza had had no problem about that, wouldn't he have devised some way of introducing it at the outset and sparing himself any need for the IIIP12 switch from one conditional to its converse?

1. For defences, see Stephen Stich, "Autonomous Psychology and the Belief-Desire Thesis", *The Monist* (1978), 573-591; Jerry A. Fodor, "Methodological Solipsism Considered as a Research Strategy in Cognitive Psychology", *Behavioral and Brain Sciences* (1980), 63-73.
2. I didn't invent it, but it is defended at length in the early chapters of my *Linguistic Behaviour* (Cambridge: Cambridge University Press, 1976).

INDIVIDUALITÉ, CAUSALITÉ, SUBSTANCE: RÉFLEXIONS SUR L'ONTOLOGIE DE SPINOZA

ÉTIENNE BALIBAR
Université de Paris - I

L'énigme de l'ontologie spinoziste, aujourd'hui encore, ce n'est pas seulement son *sens* doctrinal (ce à quoi elle tend, en matière de théologie, de sagesse ou de politique), mais *l'objet* dont elle nous parle, qu'elle se propose de saisir dans le réseau de ses propositions, du moins si nous ne nous tenons pas pour satisfaits d'une tautologie: l'objet d'une ontologie de la substance, c'est l'être dénommé substance. D'ailleurs, sous prétexte que la substance spinoziste n'est manifestement pas "sujet" (au sens psychologique, transcendantal ou dialectique), peut-on dire qu'elle est un "objet"? C'est toute la question. Pourtant, quel que soit le mot dont nous nous servons (nous pourrions parler de "référence") nous ne pouvons éluder ce type d'interrogation. De l'ontologie classique, Spinoza parle apparemment le langage, mais l'extrémisme de ses énoncés menace à chaque instant d'en faire éclater les catégories. Faut-il alors considérer sa philosophie comme la première grande entreprise de critique radicale de cette ontologie, pratiquement contemporaine de sa constitution, au moment où se forme également la nouvelle "conception du monde" liée à l'émergence de la science classique? La difficulté surgit du fait que Spinoza, manifestement, ne se propose pas seulement de critiquer, mais de connaître quelque chose, en constituant une véritable analytique de la substance, sans aucune discontinuité depuis l'identification initiale de son "essence" et de sa "puissance," jusqu'à la description minutieuse du *conatus* individuel et à la dynamique des affects qui en représente le déploiement complet. Peut-être la meilleure formulation serait-elle alors celle-ci: l'objet de l'ontologie spinoziste est l'individuation, ou *la différence de l'activité et de la passivité comme telle*. Mais cette différence, qui n'est que le mouvement de la propre production, est tout aussi bien une unité originaire. Elle est immédiatement "pratique." Pourtant elle doit être pensée comme intégralement "naturelle."

Spinoza pouvait-il (autrement que par métonymie) fixer dans les mots la singularité de cet objet? pouvait-il la rattacher à l'idée d'une ontologie, sous laquelle nous en sommes venus à la penser? La création même du terme précède d'assez peu son oeuvre. Or, qu'il l'ait connu ou non, il devait être inacceptable pour lui, dans la mesure où il impliquait à la fois l'établissement d'une distance entre le général et le spécial (ou le régional), et le dualisme des ontologies "spécialisées." Dans E IIP40S1, Spinoza caractérise "les termes appelés *Transcendantaux*, tels que Etre, Chose, Quelque chose" comme des imaginations confuses nées de l'incapacité du corps humain à distinguer une multiplicité d'images. Il les range dans le même genre de connaissance (ou plutôt de méconnaissance) que les notions générales (par exemple, la notion d'Homme) et leur oppose les "notions communes" qui "sont également dans la partie et dans le tout" (E IIP38). D'ou vient alors que ses lecteurs n'aient cessé de se représenter à nouveau la substance comme un genre suprême ou un fondement? Il faut voir ici une divergence originaire, mais aussi une difficulté inhérente au système. Peut-être Spinoza n'a-t-il disposé en fait d'aucun terme univoque pour désigner "son" objet et le distinguer d'autres objets d'analyse ou de spéculation. Cette diffficulté devient manifeste lorsque le texte spinoziste est contraint de se confronter à d'autres discours qui, en apparence, figurent dans le même espace historique ou théorique. Les conflits et les malentendus qui surgissent alors en éclairent indirectement les enjeux.

Spinoza croit pouvoir affirmer que toute la philosophie avant lui (à l'exception peut-être de celle de Démocrite, Epicure et Lucrèce) a, d'une façon ou d'une autre, succombé à l'illusion du finalisme, à laquelle il se propose d'opposer une causalité rigoureusement exclusive de toute téléologie. D'un bout à l'autre de l'*Ethique* se déploie l'idée que toutes les philosophies, en dépit de leurs différences et de leurs affrontements, relèvent d'une seule "doctrine des causes finales." Qu'est-ce qui supporte cette affirmation brutale, historiquement très surprenante? C'est avant tout l'identification de la métaphysique aristotélicienne et de la métaphysique cartésienne. Autrement dit, c'est l'idée paradoxale qu'on peut rattacher à une même problématique sous-jacente l'ontologie naturaliste des "formes substantielles," ouvertement liée au primat de la cause finale, et l'ontologie créationniste des "natures simples," commandée par les dualismes théologiques et anthropologiques de la substance étendue et de la substance pensante, de l'entendement et de la volonté, de la cause éminente et de la cause formelle.

Discuter cette idée pour elle-même serait ici hors de portée. Je me propose d'en tirer une hypothèse qui prendra d'abord une forme négative. Alors que les ontologies d'Aristote et de Descartes sont d'emblée des *métaphysiques* de la substance, ce qui veut dire qu'elles entretiennent un rapport permanent et privilégié de fondation et d'imitation avec une représentation de la "phusis" (d'ou procèdent leurs conceptions antithétiques de l'individualité), l'ontologie spinoziste n'est pas, elle, une métaphysique en ce sens. Autrement dit, ce qu'il y a effectivement de "commun" à l'aristotélisme et au cartésianisme, par delà les représentations totalement divergentes de la nature qu'ils construisent, est précisément ce qui les oppose ensemble au spinozisme, dont la *Natura*, au bout du compte, ne se laisse penser ni comme hiérarchie de formes sensibles, ni comme extension de processus mécaniques quantifiables, c'est-à-dire comme champ d'expérience physique en aucun des deux grands sens historiquement constitués. On conçoit facilement qu'une telle différence (à vrai dire déjà enregistrée sous la forme équivoque d'un nom, dans le titre général qui présente l'ontologie comme une "Ethique") ne soit pas très simple, ni à imaginer, ni à expliquer. D'autant qu'elle ne signifie nullement, à l'évidence, que la philosophie spinoziste n'ait rien à énoncer sur la *phusis* et n'entretienne aucun rapport avec elle. On ne peut faire abstraction du fait que toute la théorie des affects, qui conduit finalement à l'analytique de l'activité et de la passivité, se fonde sur une théorie du mode de constitution des *corps* comme "affections" de la *res extensa* et de la puissance propre à "l'idée du corps." Et on ne peut s'en tirer avec l'idée que la théorie des corps est une "physique imaginaire," ce qui ne résoud rien puisque les physiques d'Aristote et de Descartes nous apparaissent également comme des physiques imaginaires. Le fond de la question doit résider dans la conception même du rapport entre "cause," "individu" et "substance." C'est ici qu'il peut être instructif de découvrir chez Spinoza l'aveu d'une aporie qui montre que le problème de la physique forme, d'une certaine façon, une frontière épistémologique du système lui-même.

Les aveux de la Correspondance de Spinoza et l'aporie de la Physique

J'emprunte cette indication à deux moments de la correspondance de Spinoza qui se situent de part et d'autre de l'élaboration de l'*Ethique*, et dont on peut suppposer - sans que cette supposition soit indispensable - qu'ils sont séparés par une "refondation" du système.

En premier lieu, examinons la confrontation des années 1661-1665 entre Spinoza et Boyle par l'intermédiaire d'Oldenburg. Les propositions avancées par Spinoza face à la "doctine enfantine et ridicule des formes substantielles" (lettres 11 et 13) et à l'atomisme de Boyle, à propos de la composition des corps ou espèces chimiques, sont à première vue d'inspiration cartésienne: insistance sur la distinction des qualités premières et des qualités secondes, affirmation que les propriétés sensibles de la matière doivent s'expliquer à partir des configurations et mouvements de l'étendue géométrique (lettre 6). Pourtant, si jamais Spinoza a totalement adopté le cartésianisme en matière de physique, on peut penser que cette discussion aura finalement contribué à l'en éloigner, préparant la thèse de E IPP8-15 qui renvoie à l'imagination, en tant qu'elle confond l'essence de la substance avec celle des modes, la distinction numérique des individus et l'alternative de la divisibilité ou de l'indivisibilité à l'infini de la matière. L'échange d'arguments ne cesse de buter sur l'équivoque de la notion même d'*individu*, qui dans la tradition philosophique désigne tantôt une "chose" absolument simple, irréductible en idée ou en pratique à des éléments préalables (d'ou le paradoxe des indiscernables), tantôt une "chose" qui est un tout, irréductible à la juxtaposition de ses parties et susceptible de se conserver par lui-même (d'ou le dilemme des explications mécanistes et finalistes de l'être vivant).

C'est précisément sur la question des "parties" de la matière et de leur réunion en corps caractérisés par des propriétés spécifiques, que s'achève la confrontation (lettres 30 à 33). Spinoza nous avertit qu'il "n'a pas cette connaissance" qui permettrait de "savoir absolument en quelle manière les choses se lient les unes aux autres (*cohaerent*) et comment chaque partie de la Nature s'accorde (*conveniat*) avec son "tout," étant donné qu'une telle connaissance devrait envelopper "la Nature entière et toutes ses parties." Il s'engage pourtant dans la tentative d'en formuler le principe, et il le fait dans l'intention précise d'opposer l'idée adéquate du "tout" de la Nature à l'imagination d'un *ordre* cosmique (*me Naturae non tribuere pulchritudinem, deformitatem, ordinem, neque confusionem*).

L'exemple proposé par Spinoza (la composition du sang) illustre le caractère essentiellement relatif des notions de "tout" et de "partie": non pas au sens subjectif, mais au sens d'un ordre de grandeur objectif, qui correspond à la distinction de "causes extérieures" et de "causes intérieures" soumises à un même "rapport de mouvements." On peut évidemment se demander si cette explication n'est pas tautologique, puisque l'ordre de grandeur d'une combinaison donnée (les "parties" du sang, le sang lui-même, l'homme, le "milieu" de l'homme, etc.), caractérisé par une intériorité (le contrôle des variations de certaines causes: *quae leges naturae sanguinis certo modo moderantur*) et une extériorité (l'indépendance de certaines autres) équivaut déjà à la donnée d'une individualité. Spinoza ne s'y arrête pas, et il étend ce modèle à l'Univers, c'est-à-dire à une "nature absolument infinie."

Ici, l'argumentation se divise, dans une juxtaposition troublante. D'un côté, l'unité des parties de l'Univers peut être conçue comme une réciprocité d'action entre toutes ces parties: *omnia enim corpora ab aliis circumcinguuntur, et ab invicem determinantur ad existendum et operandum certa ac determinata ratione.* La condition qui permet de penser une telle action réciproque, c'est que "le mouvement et le repos conservent toujours dans l'Univers entier une même proportion." Proposition presque littéralement empruntée à Descartes (*Principes* II, 36) à ceci près que cette conservation n'est pas attribué à l'action constante de la toute puissance de Dieu. De l'autre côté, Spinoza ajoute qu'il conçoit, *ratione substantiae* (c'est-à-dire à cause de la substance, ou sous le rapport de la substance) une union "encore plus étroite" (*arctiorem*) entre chaque partie et son tout. Comment comprendre cette précision? Nous pouvons y voir la contrepartie positive de l'omission du Dieu de la création continuée. Mais elle pourrait être interprétée soit comme posant une "unité de substance" qui serait *plus* (et autre chose) *qu'un tout*, soit comme posant que *la totalité véritable* (non relative, donc infinie) ne peut être conçue que comme substance indivisible, c'est-à-dire sans "parties" au sens propre. Sans développer ce point, Spinoza conclut qu'on peut sur ces bases comprendre en quoi le corps humain et l'âme humaine sont l'un et l'autre des "parties de la nature" - plus précisément de la "substance corporelle" (*substantia corporea*) et de la "puissance infinie de penser" qu'elle contient l'un et l'autre.

La réponse d'Oldenburg est du plus grand intérêt: "je ne comprends pas très bien comment nous pouvons [sc. dans ces conditions] exclure de la Nature, comme tu sembles [vouloir] le faire, l'ordre et la symétrie; ne reconnais-tu pas toi-même que tous les corps qui la composent s'entourent les uns les autres et se déterminent réciproquement tant à exister qu'à agir dans un rapport déterminé et invariant (*certa et constanti ratione*), le même rapport du mouvement au repos étant conservé à chaque instant entre eux tous (*eadem semper in omnibus simul motus ad quietem ratione servata*)? Ce qui semble bien constituer exactement la raison formelle de l'ordre véritable (*ipsissima veri ordinis ratio formalis esse videtur*)."

En d'autres termes Oldenburg, soit par naiveté soit par malice (il poursuit immédiatement en redemandant à Spinoza de s'expliquer sur les règles du mouvement que Descartes pensait pouvoir déduire de son principe) élève l'objection la plus forte qui soit. Elle revient à dire que, même sans référence à la création divine, un principe comme celui de la "conservation du mouvement et du repos dans la nature" reste un principe téléologique. Et plus généralement que tout énoncé portant sur la "raison du tout" est l'équivalent d'un principe d'ordre et de symétrie.

Nous ne pouvons ignorer cette objection. Non seulement parce que Spinoza, dans la "physique" qu'il incluera dans son systéme (ou dans ce qui, à la IIème partie de l'*Ethique*, peut se lire comme l'esquisse d'une physique), continuera de se référer, il est vrai assez hypothétiquement, à ce principe à propos du "tout de la nature conçu comme un seul Individu" (IIL7S, II/102).[1] Mais surtout parce que, dans l'*Ethique*, après avoir disqualifié le concept d'ordre comme typique de l'imagination finaliste, il ne cessera pourtant de l'utiliser lui-même, à la fois dans la formule même qui développe sa définition de la cause (*ordo et connexio rerum*), et dans sa référence constante à "l'ordre de la Nature," conformément auquel il s'agit de penser l'enchainement des choses singulières et de leurs idées, sans oublier "l'ordre géométrique" et l'ordre de l'intellect" (ou l'ordre "conforme à l'intellect").[2] Il y a donc au moins *deux* notions d'ordre, homonymes et cependant antithétiques. On peut tout de suite remarquer - différence en effet essentielle - que l'une exige la notion corrélative de désordre, ce qui n'est à aucun degré le cas de l'autre, pas plus que la notion de perfection entendue comme réalité n'appelle comme corrélat l'imperfection. Mais il n'est nullement évident qu'elles n'impliquent pas l'une et l'autre une finalité. Il ne suffit pas de le dire. D'ailleurs Spinoza, s'il pratique constamment la différence de ces deux notions, ne s'en explique nulle part, ne donnant pas ce qu'on pourrait appeler une définition adéquate de l'ordre.

Or l'objection d'Oldenburg touche un point central de la philosophie de la Physique. Ce qui marque la "coupure" entre les physiques antiques (à commencer par celle d'Aristote) et la physique moderne (telle qu'on la voit se constituer avec Galilée justifiant la "simplicité" du copernicanisme et des lois du mouvement, et se réfléchir pour la première fois avec la définition cartésienne des "lois de la Nature") ce n'est pas le fait que les unes se référeraient à la notion d'ordre ou de symétrie et pas l'autre. C'est le fait que les premières appliquent des principes mécanistes ou finalistes à l'explication du visible, des formes symétriques directement observables dans la Nature, tandis que la seconde recherche *la symétrie des lois* mathématiques elles-mêmes (ce qu'on définira plus tard comme leur invariance pour certains groupes de transformations). La symétrie des lois n'exclut pas le désordre apparent, c'est-à-dire la complexité irrégulière ou l'évolution divergente des phénomènes (qui dépend des "conditions initiales").[3] L'énoncé cartésien (d'ou se déduisent les "lois de la Nature" ou "lois du mouvement") est bien, malgré son imprécision, le prototype des principes d'apparence téléologique qui assurent la cohérence et la "simplicité" de la théorie physique, et qui prendront la forme de lois de conservation ou de principes d'invariance. Sans symétrie en ce sens, la possibilité même d'une explication causale resterait indéterminée. Ce n'est donc pas solliciter abusivement la réplique d'Oldenburg que d'y lire rétrospectivement l'alternative suivante: *ou bien* une science de la Nature doit être guidée dans la recherche des causes et leur détermination (mathématique) par des principes d'ordre; *ou bien* elle en dénie la nécessité et prétend s'en passer radicalement pour n'avoir affaire qu'à la causalité "pure." Mais alors elle ne sera jamais *une science* au sens de la théorie physique (ce qui en effet semble bien être le cas de la théorie spinoziste des corps, à la différence cette fois de la physique de Descartes lui-même, malgré toutes ses erreurs, pour ne pas parler de celles de Leibniz ou de Newton).⁴

Mais inversement, il n'est pas interdit de rechercher chez Spinoza les éléments d'une interrogation adressée à la physique (ou à la philosophie de la physique). Quels critères distinguent *a priori* un concept scientifique d'ordre, de "simplicité" ou de symétrie d'une notion théologique ou métaphysique du même nom, suspendue à des postulats tels que "la nature ne fait rien pour rien," à la croyance dans une création ou dans une harmonie préétablie? Et dans quelle mesure la déduction des lois de la nature opérée par le physicien à partir de tels principes (si bien vérifiés qu'ils soient expérimentalement) correspond-elle en fait à une abstraction, ce qui revient à dire que le physicien ne connnaît pas *les choses* elles-mêmes, mais seulement une "nature" théorique, par hypothèse simplifiée de façon à coïncider avec le domaine des régularités universelles, ou des situations d'expérience dans lesquelles ces régularités se réalisent approximativement? Qu'est-ce qu'une "chose" si ce n'est pas l'objet d'une expérience organisé d'après l'idée d'un ordre qui la rend possible? On le voit, à l'horizon de cette discussion et de son inachèvement, ce n'est rien moins que la question du "principe de raison" qui se profile.

Tournons-nous maintenant vers les ultimes lettres échangées en 1674-1676 entre Spinoza, le médecin Schuller et son ami Tschirnhaus (lui aussi philosophe-savant, correspondant de la Royal Society et de Leibniz), qui avaient entrepris ensemble de lire l'*Ethique*. En dépit de son apparent désordre, cette discussion se concentre autour de trois points vraiment névralgiques, qui s'avèrent étroitement liés:

1. Quelle est la nature de la définition d'une "chose réelle," exprimant l'*essence* de la chose, ou la "cause efficiente" de toutes ses propriétés (par opposition à l'énoncé d'une simple propriété caractéristique)? (Lettres 59, 60, 82, 83)

2. En quoi consiste la "correspondance" entre la Pensée et l'Etendue, et plus généralement entre la Pensée et "tout autre" attribut, qu'énonce E IIP7? Tschirnhaus relève à ce propos deux paradoxes au moins apparents: d'une part la Pensée, comprenant toutes les idées adéquates de toutes les choses dont l'essence suit de *tous* les attributs, semble ainsi dotée "d'une extension bien plus grande que tous les autres attributs"; d'autre part les choses singulières, en tant que modes de la substance, semblent devoir "être exprimées d'une infinité de manières" (c'est-à-dire dériver simultanément d'une infinité d'attributs), alors que la définition de l'individu humain centrée sur l'âme "idée du corps" semble, elle, signifier que l'essence d'une chose singulière comprend seulement un mode

de la pensée et un mode d'*un* autre attribut déterminé. (Lettres 63, 64, 65, 70, 72)

3. Enfin comment s'effectue à partir du (seul) attribut de l'étendue infinie la déduction (et, corrélativement, la production) de *l'existence* des choses singulières, conçues comme des "parties" de la matière ou des "corps," ayant une figure et un mouvement déterminés? (Lettres 69, 70, 80 à 83)

Toutes ces questions ont en commun d'impliquer à nouveau les rapports entre *l'infini* (de la substance, de chaque attribut, des effets qui suivent d'une cause ou d'une essence), *la causalité* (de la substance, de l'étendue infinie en elle-même, des modes entre eux, voire - c'est le "contre-sens" de Tschirnhaus - de l'objet d'une idée sur cette idée), enfin *la singularité* réelle (des essences et des existences). Elles traduisent aussi l'embarras du lecteur de Spinoza devant le renversement qu'il fait subir à la représentation traditionnelle du "possible" et du "réel," inscrivant toute pensée d'un possible dans l'ordre du réel au lieu d'en faire, soit l'anticipation de son actualisation, soit l'univers logique dont il tirerait les conditions de son existence.

Or deux apories ne peuvent manquer de nous frapper dans cet échange d'arguments (lui aussi interrompu, mais par la mort). Quand Spinoza est sollicité de clarifier la façon dont, de la définition causale d'*une chose réelle*, découlent une infinité de propriétés ou de conséquences, il donne comme "exemple" *la définition de Dieu*, alors que le point de la difficulté réside manifestement dans les *choses singulières* (lettre 83). Surtout, quand il est sollicité par Tschirnhaus (qui a cru trouver dans la IIème partie de l'*Ethique* l'ébauche prometteuse d'une physique) d'expliquer comment l'existence des modes étendus se déduit (ou se construit) à partir de l'essence de leur attribut, Spinoza commence par déplacer la question en réitérant sa critique de la conception cartésienne "géométrique" de l'étendue-matière, à la fois quantitative et inerte. Mais il avoue finalement que sur cette question il n'a "pas réussi jusqu'à présent à disposer quoi que ce soit avec ordre": bref il n'a rien réussi à démontrer (lettres 81 et 83).

Devons-nous craindre de solliciter cet aveu? Dans l'alternative classique d'un mécanisme géométrique à la Descartes et d'un dynamisme à la Leibniz (auquel font penser les voies explorées par Tschirnhaus, tenté de retrouver dans chaque mode ou individualité réelle une infinité expressive qui, implicitement, l'identifie à nouveau à une substance), Spinoza semble à la recherche d'une troisième voie ou d'un dépassement. Mais, dans ce contexte au moins, il ne parvient pas à s'en expliquer autrement que de façon générale. On retrouve ici l'aporie de la physique spinoziste (et de sa philosophie comme méta-physique), telle que la faisaient pressentir les lettres à Boyle-Oldenburg, avant l'élaboration de l'*Ethique*. On retrouve la difficulté que représente la multiplicité des choses existantes, susceptibles de se "composer" ou de se "convenir" en formant des "touts" et des "parties" réels (dont la "configuration de l'univers entier": *facies totius universi*), bien que leurs essences n'expriment que des modes de la substance unique. On découvre, de plus, qu'elle peut se lire simultanément à deux niveaux. Elle porte sur l'individualité des choses singulières, conçue à la fois comme une *essence* et comme un *effet* de la "connexion" causale universelle. Et elle porte sur le sens et la fonction épistémologique de la notion d'attribut, puisque celle-ci représente à la fois une essence à partir de laquelle une infinité d'autres essences peuvent être déduites, et une existence constituée par l'enchainement infini de toutes les existences données qui peuvent s'affecter réciproquement.

Le dilemme est ainsi reconduit: ou bien une ontologie cohérente en elle-même, mais qui ne "convient" pas à la fondation d'une physique, ou bien une juxtaposition énigmatique entre l'ontologie et la théorie des corps, qu'on retrouve peut-être, en effet, à chaque grand tournant du système. Cette interprétation est celle de Gueroult, qui considère que " l'*Ethique* doit se fonder sur la physique autant que sur la métaphysique" (Gueroult (1974), 145), mais qui conclut par ailleurs à la persistance d'un problème dans l'unification des différents concepts de "cause" par l'immanence spinoziste (Gueroult (1968), 409-412). Ce qui le conduit à considérer qu'il y a chez Spinoza *deux* "physiques": l'une serait "abstraite," "purement relationnelle," étudierait la constitution des Individus comme modes de l'étendue, et serait en fait une variante du mécanisme excluant toute finalité; l'autre serait "concrète," exprimant un "substratum métaphysique," et nous ferait passer "dans l'intérieur des choses," où leur *conatus* communique directement avec l'unité de la substance - la nécessité de ce passage étant signalée par l'impossibilité d'appliquer à "l'Individu suprême, à savoir l'Univers entier" le schème de la presssion des ambiants (Gueroult (1974), 145-189). A l'inverse Negri (*L'anomalie sauvage, puissance et pouvoir chez Spinoza*, tr. fr. Paris 1982, p. 95-96) considère que l'être spinoziste, d'abord déterminé comme univoque sur le terrain de l'ontologie, "se présente comme être équivoque sur le terrain de la connaissance": c'est pourquoi "la tension qui se libère ici ne peut être résolue que sur le terrain de la pratique." Il voit le système évoluer d'une utopie de l'être comme plénitude vers une "ontologie de la constitution" pratique du réel, dans laquelle "l'infini n'est pas organisé comme objet, mais comme sujet" (p. 263), c'est-à-dire comme puissance de la multitude et multiplicité des puissances, des "forces productives" s'organisant collectivement en tendant vers leur libération (p. 283 sv.). Dans l'*Ethique*, nous aurions le passage l'une métaphysique à une autre, l'indice du passage étant constitué par "l'extinction" progessive de la notion d'*attribut*, ultime trace des métaphysiques de l'émanation (p. 110, 118-123, 291, 322, etc.).

Essayons de rouvrir cette question, *sans* admettre comme évidents les termes de "physique" et de "métaphysique."

Les deux voies de production
des choses singulières et la pluralité des "Mondes"

La correspondance avec Tschirnhaus, en dépit des incompréhensions de l'un des interlocuteurs et du retrait de l'autre, manifeste la possibilité de comprendre le rapport de la substance, des attributs et des modes selon deux schémas antithétiques, dont chacun représente l'amorce d'une ontologie tout-à-fait différente.

Ou bien - c'est ce que j'appellerai la voie A - le concept de la substance est "distribué" sur une infinité d'attributs distincts, qui en expriment l'essence chacun à sa façon, c'est-à-dire que tous sont également substantiels. Et ce sont ces attributs qui sont *ensuite* affectés de modifications finies ou infinies, d'où résultent en dernière analyse les "choses singulières," à la fois quant à leur esssence et quant à leur existence. Les choses singulières sont alors produites à partir de la substance *par la médiation* des attributs, selon l'essence et la causalité propre de chacun. On se représentera alors que les choses singulières sont "dans" (ou "de") la substance par la médiation d'attributs qui sont eux-mêmes déjà "dans" (ou "de") la substance, et que nous ne pouvons pas contourner, car ils n'ont rien de "commun," si ce n'est la substance même qu'ils expriment et que nous connaissons par eux. Les choses singulières ont alors en quelque sorte une "double" singularité: en tant qu'elles se distinguent entre elles "modalement" (ce qui ne veut pas dire abstraitement ou fictivement), et en tant qu'elles se distinguent des modes de tous les autres attributs. Par exemple une idée se distingue d'une autre idée *et* elle se distingue d'un corps. Ou bien un rapport déterminé de mouvement et de repos, caractéristique d'un individu corporel, se distingue d'un autre rapport également déterminé, *et* il se distingue de n'importe quelle idée (y compris l'idée *de ce* corps qu'il forme, autrement dit de son "âme").

Mais une médiation est aussi une séparation: la différence modale, redoublée par la différence attributive (par l'assignation des choses dans le "champ" d'un attribut déterminé: pensée, étendue ou autre), assure la différence de tous les modes (y compris, bien entendu, les modes infinis) et de la substance elle-même, elle sépare l'essence et de l'existence des modes de l'essence et de l'existence de la substance, l'être causé de l'être causant.

Si nous renversons cette proposition, nous obtenons ce que j'appellerai la voie B: les choses singulières doivent être pensées comme *des modes de la substance*, sans aucun "intermédiaire," car il n'y a pas d'autre puissance productive de modes que la substance elle-même, pas de différence ontologique entre l'être des modes et l'être de la substance (qui est *leur* être). Ce qui revient à dire que la tension entre l'un et le multiple, l'indivisible et le divisible, l'immuable et le changeant, l'infini et le fini, est tout entière contenue dans cette dérivation ou ce "passage" de la substance à ses modes tel qu'il s'effectue "à l'intérieur" de la substance elle-même. Alors que, nous le verrons, il est dans le logique de la voie A de privilégier les modes infinis pour en faire une médiation supplémentaire entre la substance "spécifiée" par ses attributs et les choses singulières ou les individus, il est dans la logique de la voie B de considérer que *les modes finis* sont les "véritables" modes, ceux dont l'inhérence à la substance manifeste le mieux l'originalité du spinozisme, par opposition à toute doctrine qui fait du fini une dégradation de l'infini, voire une réalité "intermédiaire entre l'infini et le néant" (comme Descartes est amené à l'écrire). C'est pourquoi la façon dont chaque mode fini "enveloppe" l'infini est ici le problème décisif de l'ontologie.

Dans ces conditions, que signifie le concept d'attribut, ou plutôt à quoi sert-il? Précisément à rendre ce passage *immédiatement* intelligible, tout en posant qu'il peut être compris d'une infinité de façons. Chaque attribut constitue une façon, elle-même singulière, d'appréhender l'inhérence des modes à la substance. En d'autres termes il est une façon de penser la (dé) multiplication de l'indivisible et, corrélativement, l'essence commune d'une multiplicité d'essences absolument distinctes. L'attribut, en se "concevant par soi" (E IP10), tout comme la substance elle-même, en "exprimant une essence éternelle et infinie" (E IP11), *nie* donc pour nous, par là même, toute distance entre les modes et la substance. Pour parler un autre langage, il ne s'apparente pas à une médiation, mais à une *unité de contraires* immédiatement donnée. Ainsi l'étendue infinie (ou l'infini d'étendue) permet de penser l'unité d'une infinité de choses singulières en tant que "corps" convenant ou disconvenant avec d'autres corps; la pensée infinie (ou l'infini de pensée) permet de penser l'unité substantielle d'une infinité de choses singulières en tant qu'"idées" enchaînées à d'autres idées qui les affirment ou les nient. Mais la différence des attributs *ne s'ajoute* pas à la différence des modes: dire qu'une idée "diffère" d'une autre idée et dire au même sens qu'elle "diffère" d'un corps - si abstraitement ou transcendantalement qu'on l'entende - serait une absurdité. Ce qui nous conduit effectivement à penser que les choses singulières, chacune définie par son essence ou sa cause, doivent, exactement comme la substance elle-même et parce qu'elles ne sont que ses effets, être pensées selon l'infinité des attributs (l'infinité des "infinis").

Dans la compréhension que notre entendement peut en avoir, à toute chose conçue comme un corps doit être unie une idée de la même chose, autrement dit "son âme" (*omnia sunt animata*). Mais cette compréhension ne saurait épuiser ni l'infinité de la substance ni celle des modes. Dans cette perspective, la "finitude" de l'individu humain se marquerait d'abord par le fait qu'il ne perçoit jamais qu'une partie des attributs de la substance, c'est-à-dire qu'il ne perçoit les choses singulières que sous certains attributs (en fait deux). On ne saurait toutefois en conclure que toute connaissance adéquate des choses lui est interdite, ni même qu'il "manque" ainsi de quoi que ce soit, puisque la connaissance des choses n'est rien d'autre que la connaissance des causes et que celle-ci est adéquate dans n'importe quel attribut.

Réciproquement, il nous faut supposer que toute idée est essentiellement l'âme de quelque chose, qui peut être conçu comme un corps, ou autrement. C'est pourtant ce que, semble-t-il, Spinoza refuse explicitement dans la lettre 66 à Tschirnhaus, mais pour introduire l'idée difficile d'une *infinité d'âmes*, "expressions" de chaque chose dans l'entendement infini de Dieu, qu'on ne retrouve pas dans l'*Ethique* (du moins je ne l'y ai pas trouvée).[5]

Cette alternative a-t-elle un sens spinoziste? Rien n'est moins sûr. Il est clair pourtant, que, sous cette forme ou d'autres voisines, elle est à l'oeuvre dans les lectures divergentes de Spinoza, dont l'incompatibilité mutuelle ne cesse nous étonner. La voie A semble se prêter particulièrement bien à une lecture mécaniste, dans laquelle chaque attribut représente une multiplicité infinie en son genre, suffisante pour expliciter un type d'enchaînement des causes ou des raisons. Par exemple l'ordre et la connexion des choses en tant qu'elles sont les modes de l'étendue ou des corps est entièrement intelligible comme une composition "extérieure" de mouvements, une "pression des ambiants" (Gueroult), etc.[6] Analogiquement, l'ordre et la connexion des idées en tant qu'elles sont des modes de la pensée serait intelligible comme un "espace logique" de leurs relations de composition. A l'inverse, la voie B suggère inévitablement que la réalité des choses est *encore au-delà* de ce qu'exprime chaque multiplicité numérique, donc qu'elle correspond à une infinité "intérieure." Elle se prête tout naturellement à une lecture vitaliste ou énergétiste. Qui prétendrait que l'interprétation du *conatus* des essences, notamment, a jamais échappé à ces dilemmes?

Chacune des deux voies induit en effet sa propre lignée d'interprétation des catégories fondamentales. Elle fait ressortir, par les obstacles auxquels elle se heurte, la fonction statégique de certains énoncés de Spinoza, mais aussi la difficulté de les concilier en première lecture.

Dans la voie A, la substance n'agit en fait que par ses attributs. D'où la tentation de "substantialiser" ceux-ci. Spinoza n'emploie-t-il pas des expressions comme "chaque être doit être conçu sous un certain attribut" (E IP10S1), "les modes de tel attribut" (avant tout IP25C et IIP6; mais également IPP21-23; IP28D; IIP5D; IIP7D), "la substance corporelle" (à vrai dire, uniquement dans la partie introductive de l'*Ethique*[7]: IP13C; IP15S, et dans la correspondance)? Dans la définition complète de Dieu, qui en fait la substance "consistant en une infinité d'attributs dont chacun exprime une essence éternelle et infinie," ce qui devient premier, essentiel, c'est alors l'infinité (comme puissance infinie) *de chaque attribut*. Quant au fait que la substance (Dieu) "possède" une infinité d'attributs, ou plutôt consiste en attributs infinis d'une infinité de manières (pensons à la difficulté classique de traduction du mot *constans*: "constituée par" ou "consistant en"), il est difficile de ne pas le percevoir comme secondaire, surajouté à l'idée principale. Celle-ci serait déjà clairement exprimée avec la distinction des deux attributs que nous pouvons nommer: c'est-à-dire justement le minimum requis pour formuler une telle idée. A moins que nous soyons tentés d'en faire la forme sous laquelle se perpétuerait chez Spinoza l'idée théologique d'une éminente perfection divine, d'un être "infiniment plus réel" que celui dont notre entendement fini peut avoir l'idée.

Ce n'est plus alors l'attribut dont la fonction peut sembler évanescente ou formelle. C'est la substance elle-même. A quoi sert-elle? On croit le voir cependant, en passant d'un point de vue épistémologique à un point de vue ontologique. L'autonomie des attributs pose le problème de leur "correspondance," sans laquelle aucune connaissance objectivement vraie ne serait possible. IIP7 affirmera à son tour la réalité de cette correspondance, sous la forme d'une stricte réciprocité. Et la substance sera alors le "fondement" de cette correspondance, au sens d'une garantie toujours déjà acquise. Mais aussi, il faut bien le dire, d'un mystère. Pour que la substance assure la correspondance de deux attributs donnés, il faut en effet qu'elle les "comprenne" dans une réalité supérieure, qui les "précède." C'est ici que l'infinité d'infinis qui définit la substance (presque une contradiction dans les termes!) devient opérante. Mais cette infinité d'infinis est pour nous un mystère: paradoxe, puisque c'est elle qui fonde la possibilité de la connaissance. On imagine trop bien quelque adversaire retournant alors contre Spinoza l'expression d'"asile de l'ignorance." D'ailleurs cela n'a pas manqué.

On découvrirait ainsi chez Spinoza une surprenante analogie à la fois avec Descartes et avec Kant. Avec Descartes, puisque la garantie de l'objectivité des idées passerait de la véracité divine à la productivité de la substance, de la "création des vérités éternelles" à l'unité substantielle des attributs, mais sans se dégager, en fait, de son arbitraire: au contraire, celui-ci ne concernerait plus seulement notre compréhension de la garantie divine, mais serait le propre du Dieu-substance, toujours en retrait de ses expressions. Avec Kant également, dans la mesure où le "schématisme de l'imagination transcendantale," fondement de la correspondance entre les conditions de possibilité de l'expérience et celles des objets de l'expérience eux-mêmes, demeure chez lui un "art caché." Mais ce qui ne fait pas problème chez Kant (puisqu'il s'agit justement d'établir l'impossibilité d'une connaissance des choses en soi et la limitation intrinsèque de la raison pure) soulèverait une grave difficulté chez Spinoza, qui n'a cessé (contre Descartes) de soutenir que faire de l'infini un inconnaissable rendrait toute connaissance humaine impossible.

Tout ceci peut se dire autrement. Spinoza pense la "correspondance" entre les attributs comme identité *des connexions* causales dans chacun des attributs. Dans la perspective de la voie A, cette identité se construira de proche en proche, par une descente toujours conforme à la nature des attributs. Le premier moment, décisif, sera la "correspondance" entre *les modes infinis* des différents attributs (E IPP21-23; lettre 64). D'abord entre les modes infinis immédiats: universalité du mouvement d'une part, idée de Dieu dans son propre entendement infini d'autre part, c'est-à-dire correspondance entre deux systèmes de "vérités éternelles," qu'on peut interpréter l'un comme celui des "lois de la nature" (étendue), l'autre comme celui des "lois de la pensée." Puis, franchissant une nouvelle étape, correspondance entre les modes infinis médiats: la *facies totius universi*, et l'ensemble de toutes les idées, qui font l'un et l'autre partie de la "nature naturée." Enfin, dernière étape, correspondance entre des "parties" de l'univers étendu et des "parties" de l'ensemble des idées (ou des complexes d'idées), jusqu'aux choses singulières. La structure complète de cette correspondance exprimerait l'identité de l'ordre causal des choses et de l'ordre rationnel des idées.

Mais à cet enchainement il faut à son tour une cause. Si la substance est cette cause, elle sera la "cause des causes." Ce qui est compatible avec l'idée de Dieu "absolument cause première" (IP16C3). Mais peu compatible avec l'idée de Dieu "cause immanente, non transitive, de toutes les choses ... qui sont en lui-même" (IP18). Et moins encore avec l'idée que "au même sens (*eo sensu*) où Dieu est dit cause de soi, il doit être dit aussi cause de toutes choses" (IP25&S) et que "Dieu ne peut pas être dit proprement cause éloignée (*remota*) des choses singulières" (IP28&S), autrement dit qu'il n'y a pas de différence de réalité entre les effets de la causalité divine, qu'ils soient infinis ou finis. Comme on pouvait s'y attendre, la représentation de la substance comme cause des attributs, eux-mêmes cause des modes (ou des attributs comme des super-modes de la substance, eux-mêmes faisant l'objet d'une modification "seconde") est l'impasse de la voie A.[8]

Revenons alors à notre voie B. Ici les modes sont modes de la substance elle-même, sans intermédiaires, et, à la différence de tout-à-l'heure, *l'infinité des attributs* va révêtir une importance fondamentale, qui l'emporte d'abord sur le fait que chaque attribut soit lui-même "infini en son genre," ou plutôt qui ne peut en être dissociée. D'emblée cette infinité exclut, comme inadéquat à l'essence de la substance, le dénombrement des attributs, et même leur dénomination par des termes exclusifs qui ne peut représenter, au mieux, qu'un "auxiliaire de l'imagination" (lettre 12). Mais qu'est ce, positivement, que l'infinité des attributs, s'il ne s'agit pas d'un mystère mais d'un concept ou d'une essence?

Relisons IPP16-18, qui parlent explicitement de l'infinité des attributs: "De la nécessité de la nature divine doivent suivre en une infinité de modes une infinité de choses (*infinita infinitis modis*), c'est-à-dire tout ce qui peut tomber sous un entendement infini." Donc "rien ne peut être hors de lui [= de Dieu], par quoi il soit déterminé à agir ou contraint d'agir." Donc Dieu "est cause immanente mais non transitive de toutes choses," c'est-à-dire qu'il est cause "par les seules lois de sa nature" de "choses qui sont en lui-même," et réciproquement, "en dehors de Dieu nulle chose qui soit en elle-mêmes, ne peut être donnée." Propositions quasi axiomatiques (IP16 "doit être évidente pour chacun"), qui signifient que la puissance divine ne comporte aucune limitation (pas même au sens d'une "auto-limitation," recours habituel des théologies de l'émanation), donc *aucune extériorité*. Elle agit entièrement en elle-même. Bref, l'idée de l'infinité des attributs enveloppe d'abord la thèse de l'immanence, avec sa dissymétrie fondamentale: l'essence des modes est autre que celle de la substance (puisqu'ils ne sont pas infiniment infinis), mais la substance n'existe pas ailleurs que ses modes. Ni dans un "autre lieu" physique ou intellectuel, ni, comme chez les mystiques, dans un retrait de l'Etre, un néant primordial, "autre" absolu de tous les étants.

Pourtant, si la substance n'agit *qu'en elle-même*, sans jamais s'extérioriser, elle *agit* nécessairement en elle-même. La difficulté est de penser effectivement, d'une façon conceptuelle ou déterminée, cette action ou cette production d'effets dont résultent les choses finies et toutes leurs actions mutuelles ("transitives"), *en tant* que réalisation de la puissance divine infinie. Tel est précisément l'objet de la fameuse IIP7 (*ordo et connexio idearum idem est ac ordo et connnexio rerum*), à condition de l'interpréter du point de vue de l'infinité des attributs.

A nouveau, Spinoza lui-même le souligne, il s'agit d'un énoncé quasi-axiomatique. La tradition le présente comme posant un "parallélisme" des attributs (terme dont Spinoza ne s'est jamais servi). En réalité IIP7 ne vient pas, après-coup, conférer une propriété épistémologiquement remarquable à des attributs *déjà donnés*. Elle ne suit pas de leur distinction, mais elle en règle l'usage. Si l'on croit y lire la désignation de deux attributs exemplaires, c'est par une illusion rétrospective, prisonnière de dualismes métaphysiques et épistémologiques que Spinoza, en ce point précis, se propose de supprimer une fois pour toutes. On ne prête pas suffisamment attention au fait que, dans cet énoncé, il n'est pas question d'étendue, ni d'attributs juxtaposés, mais de "choses" qui peuvent être pensées sous n'importe quel attribut (*y compris* la pensée infinie elle-même) et d'"'idées," autrement dit de l'adéquation intrinsèque des idées des choses, à condition que les unes et les autres soient pensées *comme des causes* (ce qu'indique d'ailleurs la variante *ordo et connexio causarum* IIP7S.)

Mais cette adéquation nous reconduit immédiatement à l'infinité de la substance. Entre "l'ordre et la connexion des choses" et "l'ordre et la connexion des idées," il ne saurait être question de *correspondance*, au sens où les "élements" de deux ensembles ("choses," "idées") se correspondraient terme à terme et soutiendraient entre eux des relations homologues. Il ne s'agit pas en effet d'appliquer un tableau des idées sur un tableau des choses, pour représenter la causalité des unes par celle des autres. Ce que dit exactement IIP7, c'est qu'il y a identité d'ordre-et-connexion, que "c'est le même" (*idem*) et non pas autre chose (le différent voire le différant), autrement dit qu'il y a une *seule réalité* à penser comme "ordre-et-connexion." Réciproquement le même, l'identique, ne peut être pensé dans sa réalité que comme "ordre-et-connexion" (et non pas comme évènement isolé). Cette réalité ne peut donc être que *la substance elle-même, en tant qu'elle est identique à la cause.* L'expression pratiquement indécomposable "*ordo et connexio*" (qu'on peut ici suggérer de traduire par "ordre *de* connexion," en exploitant une figure classique de la grammaire latine), signifie l'essence de la substance. Non pas cependant, comme le faisait la définition initiale (cause de soi, existant par soi et conçue par soi), de façon encore nominale et abstraite. Mais synthétiquement, telle que l'exposition de la Ière partie parvenue à son terme permet maintenant de la comprendre: comme l'identité de *tous* les sens du concept de "cause" dans l'activité immanente à la puissance infinie, ou, ce qui zeisent au même, comme la complexité interne de la cause. C'est pourquoi IIP7D peut être présentée par Spinoza comme une *autre formulation* de IA4: "la connaissance de l'effet dépend de la connaissance de la cause et l'enveloppe elle-même (*eamdem involvit*)."

Cette autre formulation permet de lever l'équivoque de l'expression *causa sui*, qui risquait toujours d'être comprise comme l'application "à elle-même" d'une notion transitive de causalité (ou comme réflexivité d'une "relation" x R y, en posant x = y), et d'aboutir à singulariser une cause première ou à l'extraire du complexe des causes. Mais elle exclut tout aussi bien que les choses singulières nous apparaissent comme le simple phénomène d'une chose en soi. L'infinité des attributs exprime *positivement* cette double négation. Elle pose l'identité à elle-même de la connexion nécessaire d'une infinité de singularités ou de différences. La substance apparait ainsi comme puissance d'individuation, cause productrice de *ses* modes parce qu'elle *se* cause en *les* causant d'une façon unique comme causes *les uns des autres*.

Or de cette puissance il existe une idée adéquate. "Les attributs expriment l'essence de la substance"; chacun d'eux "exprime la réalité ou l'être (*realitatem sive esse*) de la substance" (IP10S1): sans qu'il soit besoin de le comparer avec d'autres, il réalise l'ordre de connexion de *tous* les modes de la substance. Mais chacun d'eux exprime par là-même, dans sa propre infinité, l'infinité de tous les autres. Aucune idée adéquate (se réalisant elle-même commme ordre de connexion, c'est-à-dire produisant nécessairement la série de ses propres effets) ne saurait donc introduire un écart dans la réalité, une coupure de principe entre la connaissance et son objet. Si, par une hypothèse qui est une fiction, les "choses" n'étaient pas des "causes" réalisant la causalité même de la substance, elles ne seraient pas connaissables selon la causalité des idées. Inversement, dans les choses il n'y a rien d'autre à connaitre que les singularités déterminées d'une puissance unique de causer et d'être causé.

Est-ce à dire que la voie B, telle que nous venons de l'esquisser, ne comporte aucune difficulté? Evidemment pas. La première, c'est que dans cette perspective, au lieu de substantialiser les attributs, nous pourrions être tentés de les "irréaliser," en les considérant comme de simples "points de vue" conceptuels sur la substance. A la limite - autre façon de lire Kant dans Spinoza - les attributs seraient comme des formes transcendantales délimitant les conditions *a priori* sous lesquelles l'essence causale de la substance et de ses modes peut être conçue par un sujet. Cette tentation se heurte à l'affirmation liminaire de Spinoza selon laquelle l'essence de la substance est d'être "conçue par soi." Et surtout elle contredit ce que nous venons de poser: que l'infinité de chaque attribut est indissociable de l'infinité collective des attributs et lui est même en un sens identique. Elle ne saurait donc constituer un point de vue ou une limitation.

Mais si l'identité d'une infinité d'attributs exprime le fait que la même nécessité causale, comprise dans l'essence de la substance, produit les "choses" et les "idées," une autre difficulté surgit. Dans l'ontologie spinoziste, les choses et les idées (qui sont elles-mêmes des choses) doivent être conçues immédiatement comme des causes. Pourtant Spinoza maintient une distinction entre les *essences* et les *existences* (sauf précisément pour la substance elle-même). Il semble alors que la scission entre les choses et les idées va se trouver reportée au niveau de la différence entre les essences et les existences. Nous savons en effet que les essences sont absolument positives, et ne peuvent se nier entre elles. C'est pourquoi, notamment, le faux et le vrai ne se détruisent pas réciproquement: "Rien de ce qu'une idée fausse a de positif n'est ôté par la présence du vrai" en tant qu'elles expriment adéquatement quelque essence, c'est-à-dire qu'elles sont l'idée d'une modification de la puissance divine. Par contre certaines existences sont compatibles entre elles, tandis que d'autres se détruisent mutuellement, ce qui fait qu'elles ne peuvent "être dans un même sujet" (IIIPP4,5). C'est pourquoi Spinoza ignore toute problématique des "compossibles" ou de la "compatibilité des essences," et transfère le principe de contradiction du domaine des essences dans celui *des existences*.[9]

Pour rendre compte de cette différence, qui risque fort de se transformer en un abîme, il semble que nous devions "dédoubler" à nouveau la nécessité causale. La notion d'attribut peut-elle, sans équivocité, nous faire passer de la causalité des essences, qui inscrit les choses singulières dans une série infinie d'essences également positives, à l'ordre des existences, dans lequel s'établissent des "rapports de forces," entre des causes particulières *à la puissance inégale*, agissant les unes sur les autres pour se conserver, se faire varier ou se détruire? Ne serons-nous pas obligés d'invoquer ici l'irrationalité pure et simple d'un fait? Tel pourrait être le sens de l'axiome (unique) de la IVe partie (qui bien entendu doit s'appliquer dans tous les attributs, y compris si la "chose" dont il parle est une idée existante), axiome fondamental pour l'éthique, dans lequel nous passons de la puissance comme cause à la puissance comme droit naturel: "Il n'est donné dans la nature aucune chose singulière qu'il n'en soit donné une autre plus puissante et plus forte. Mais si une chose quelconque est donnée, une autre plus puissante, par laquelle la première peut être détruite, est donnée."

Cependant la positivité des essences et la conflictualité des existences sont l'une et l'autre requises pour penser la puissance propre aux choses singulières, ou le *conatus* par lequel elles "s'efforcent" de persévérer dans leur être. Chaque chose singulière, ou mieux chaque individu réel est donc conçu comme un point (ou moment) d'identification de l'ordre des essences et de l'ordre des existences. D'autre part, dans la *totalité* de chaque attribut infini, et même dans la totalité des modes pensés sous cet attribut (par exemple la *facies totius universi*, qui est elle aussi un individu, éternellement identique à lui-même), les rapports de puissance coïncident avec une intériorité essentielle, entendue "du point de vue de l'éternité" (*sub specie aeterni*). A ces deux niveaux nous retrouvons quelque chose comme la présence immédiate de la substance. Mais, comme le sentait Tschirnhaus, nous resterons fort embarrassés pour expliquer ce qui rattache chaque individu à cette totalité infinie comme une de ses "parties" propres.

En somme, l'indication des deux voies nous permet de mettre en évidence un noeud de difficultés interdépendantes. Y a-t-il chez Spinoza un concept totalement unifié de la causalité, englobant de façon intelligible la production même des choses singulières et leurs interactions, susceptible d'être exprimé de façon équivalente en termes de "lois de la nature" et de "lois de la pensée?" Ou bien faut-il supposer que la causalité réelle n'est pensable que spécifique selon les différents "genres d'existence" que représenteraient les attributs - leur commune inhérence à la substance étant alors chargée à la fois de rendre compte de la nécessité de tous les enchaînements causals et de l'égalité qui existe entre eux (en sorte qu'aucune forme de nécessité causale ne peut être considérée comme le "modèle" des autres)?

D'autre part, l'individualité des choses est-elle en quelque sorte le "sous-produit" de leur existence modale, toujours déjà pensée *sous* des attributs déterminés, la difficulté étant alors de comprendre ce qui confère une *essence* singulière à chaque individu, et non pas simplement une *forme* naturelle, relativement stable sous certaines conditions? Ou bien faut-il considérer la singularité des modes comme une expression directe de la puissance divine (qui, nous l'avons vu, peut être pensée au sens le plus fort comme puissance d'individuation), la difficulté étant alors de ne pas conférer aux essences individuelles le statut d'archétypes, et corrélativement aux existences celui d'une participation aux essences, dont les attributs fourniraient en quelque sorte la "matière"?

Formellement, ces questions retrouvent des dilemmes classiques de la philosophie. Elles obligent à se demander si ce sont les concepts spinozistes de substance, d'attribut et de mode qui prètent indéfiniment à équivoque, ou si, au contraire, leur articulation étrange n'est pas la "solution" trouvée par Spinoza aux antinomies de la métaphysique, une solution qui paradoxalement, dans les mots mêmes de la métaphysique, exige que nous en sortions. L'impression d'une équivoque viendrait alors tout simplement de ce que, désarticulant la démonstration spinoziste, nous ne cessons de projeter à nouveau sur ses concepts les présupposés que Spinoza considère comme imaginaires et qu'il veut dépasser: soit ceux d'une anthropologie (dont la trace persistante apparait dans le problème de la "correspondance" des attributs), soit ceux d'une théologie (qui nous pousse toujours à renverser la positivité de la substance en négativité d'un principe qui n'est rien de ce qu'il détermine).

Pour saisir ce que Spinoza veut dire, trois conditions au moins semblent requises.

La première, c'est de ne pas rétablir subrepticement la distinction du *possible* et du *réel*, et l'antécédence du premier sur le second. Les "deux voies," séparées l'une de l'autre, sont toutes deux des entreprises de ce genre, l'une à partir de la distinction de l'infini et du fini, l'autre à patir de la distinction de l'essence et de l'existence. Du moins on peut les tirer en ce sens.

La seconde, c'est, comme l'a souligné fortement Macherey dans un livre récent,[10] de prendre au sérieux la thèse de l'infinité des attributs eux-mêmes infinis, c'est-à-dire d'éviter de la réinscrire dans l'espace d'une multiplicité numérique, y compris en comprenant la thèse de l'*unicité* de la substance comme un prédicat numérique, c'est-à-dire comme la négation d'une pluralité. Comment ne pas penser ici à la proposition de Wittgenstein: "Die logische Formen sind zahl*los*. Darum gibt es in der Logik keine ausgezeichneten Zahlen und darum gibt es keinen philosophischen Monismus oder Dualismus" etc. (*Tractatus*, 4.128)?   Le "nombre" des attributs n'a pas de signification essentielle; ou plutôt, "dépassant tout nombre," il signifie immédiatement que, s'il nous faut à moins de contradiction poser que la substance est *une*, nous ne saurions comprendre par là qu'elle n'est *rien qu'une*. Si difficilement applicable qu'elle soit en pratique (comment inscrire *l'un* dans la discursivité d'une démonstration, et tout simplement dans une logique, sans le réduire au *rien qu'un*?) cette thèse doit constituer la butée incontournable de notre lecture.

La troisième condition, c'est d'appliquer une interprétation analogue à l'*individualité* des choses singulières. Aux antipodes des idées de *species infima*, d'atome ou de substance individuelle, qui font corps avec des classifications et des hiérarchies cosmologiques, la singularité des individus spinozistes ne signifie ni l'irréductibilité dans une comparaison avec d'autres choses, ni l'intériorité par opposition à l'extériorité, mais l'adéquation d'une chose à sa propre essence, la puissance d'agir ou d'être cause. C'est pourquoi elle ne peut s'opposer à l'idée de "notions communes," bien qu'elle s'oppose à leur utilisation comme des abstractions. C'est le paradoxe d'un "nominalisme," celui de Spinoza, qui affirme l'idée de connexion nécessaire au lieu de la dissoudre.

Ces conditions sont problématiques. Mais elles font ressortir les enjeux du problème. Au fond les embarras de Tschirnhaus en étaient déjà un très bon indice. Tantôt il supposait qu'il "existe autant de mondes que d'attributs de Dieu" (lettre 63), autrement dit un monde de l'étendue, *plus* un monde de la pensée, *plus* d'autre mondes encore à l'infini. Tantôt il supposait que "le monde est unique" (lettre 65), d'où il concluait qu'il doit exister "une infinité d'expressions différentes d'une seule et même modification qui sont comme autant de points de vue sur la réalité de la chose. L'apparence des deux voies (l'équivocité de la substance), on le voit bien ici, est liée à *notre* besoin de nous représenter la nature comme un "monde" de choses (qui peuvent être aussi des personnes, des Etats plus ou moins stables, etc.) et les choses comme des choses pour un "monde," leur existence comme un "être au monde," qu'il s'agisse d'un monde pour l'homme, ou d'un monde pour Dieu.

Réciproquement, si la pensée de Spinoza (aux prises avec ses propres notions de "Nature entière formant un seul Individu," d'"ordre de la Nature," mais aussi de l'homme comme "partie de la Nature") ne correspond exactement ni à l'une ni à l'autre de ces voies, n'est ce pas qu'elle représente une tentative pour penser une Nature qui ne soit pas un Monde - même un Monde infini - échappant ainsi à toute "conception du monde"? Il nous faudrait cette fois donner tort à Wittgenstein ("Die Anschauung der Welt sub specie aeterni ist ihre Anschauung als - begrenztes - Ganzes. Das Gefühl der Welt als begrenztes Ganzes ist das Mystische," *Tractatus*, 6.45), et rejoindre plutôt l'indication d'Althusser: l'effort pour penser "une causalité qui rendît compte de l'efficace du Tout sur ses parties, et de l'action des parties dans le Tout" fait de Spinoza le "premier et presque unique témoin" de la pensée "d'un Tout sans clôture" (*Eléments d'autocritique*, Paris 1974, p. 81).

1. Dans ses propres *Principes de la philosophie de Descartes* (IIPP12,13,15, Spinoza résume la position de Descartes, qui fait de Dieu la (seule) cause de la création et de la conservation de la "quantité de mouvement et de repos." On peut toutefois remarquer: A) qu'il omet de spécifier que cette quantité se conserve, comme dit Descartes, "en l'univers"; B) que cette exposition (avec IA10, auquel elle renvoie, et donc aussi IP7) donne lieu de sa part au maximum d'interrogation et d'objection "théologiques." Ce point serait à examiner de près dans la perspective d'une lecture des *Principes de la philosophie de Descartes* comme laboratoire d'une critique du cartésianisme. Gueroult discute l'attitude de Spinoza par rapport au principe cartésien, et il conclut: "par là est posé le problème de la cohérence interne de la physique spinoziste," et plus loin: "on doit admettre que Spinoza a laissé voisiner dans sa physique des doctrines incompatibles." (Gueroult (1974), 179-181, 563-569).

2. N'oublions pas, ce qui n'arrange rien, que cette formule est de Saint Thomas, chez qui elle joue un rôle essentiel dans la définition de la vérité à partir de la "science de Dieu": "*Unde unaquaeque res dicitur vera absolute secundum ordinem ad intellectum a quo dependet*" (*Summa Theologica*, I, Quaest. XVI, art.1).

3. Cf. par exemple Eugene P. Wigner, *Symmetries and Reflections*, Ox Bow Press, Woodbridge 1979. Lorsque Newton doit rendre compte de la remarquable simplicité des lois de Kepler, c'est-à-dire de l'harmonie *visible* du système solaire, il lui faut supposer des conditions initiales spécialement créées par Dieu, logiquement indépendantes des lois physiques elles-mêmes. Idée difficile à discerner de celle de miracle.

4. Il y aurait lieu, évidemment, de se demander dans quelle mesure ce dilemme se reproduit lorsque Spinoza lui-même se propose de constituer (dans le *Traité politique*) une "science" ou théorie des individus politiques, c'est-à-dire des causes de la fluctuation des Etats et de leur mode de "régulation."

5. L'énigme est donc la suivante: Dieu pense chaque chose (ou il y a en Dieu une idée de chaque chose) selon une infinité d'attributs alors que "nous" la pensons seulement selon deux attributs. Mais ce faisant Dieu ne pense "rien de plus" que nous, dès lors que nous avons une idée adéquate.

Il est surprenant que Gueroult n'examine pas la lettre 66 lorsqu'il discute "une objection au premier abord insurmontable, contre l'affirmation selon laquelle il y a autant d'âmes différentes que de modes corrélatifs du Corps (*sic*) dans l'infinité des autres attributs" (*op. cit.*, II, p. 255-256). De son côté, Negri (*op. cit.*, p. 291 et note 24) écrit: "sans doute, au fil de son débat avec Tschirnhaus ... Spinoza parvient-il à rendre claire sa critique de l'attribut et de toute tentative de lire son système comme une philosophie de l'émanation ... Ces lettres contiennent toutefois encore de nombreuses ambiguïtés au sujet de la théorie de l'attribut. Il y a comme une fidélité de Spinoza à la totalité de son systéme "écrit," à la totalité de son oeuvre, qui persiste alors même qu'il s'achemine vers de tout autres solutions."

6. Il me parait douteux qu'à cet égard la possibilité de découvrir chez Spinoza l'anticipation d'une physique des "champs" de forces (cf. Bennett (1984), p. 88 sv.) change quelque chose au problème, d'autant qu'elle s'accompagne de la thèse explicite selon laquelle *il n'y a que deux attributs* de la substance qui comptent vraiment.

7. C'est-à dire dans le processus de construction de la substance indivisible, qui est en même temps le processus de déconstruction de la dualité cartésienne des substances, dont sa terminologie porte nécessairement la trace.

8. Notons que Descartes pose explicitement "modes" et "attributs" comme les espèces d'un même genre logique, qui est, conformément à la tradition aristotélicienne, l'attribution de propriétés à un sujet: le nom d'attributs est réservé aux propriétés premières, essentielles; celui de modes (= modes de modes ou attributs d'attributs) aux propriétés secondes, contingentes (*Principes* I,56).

9. Cf. Deleuze (1968), p. 174 sv.; et Macherey (1979), p. 208 sv.

10. Ouvr. *cit.*, p. 118 sv.

SPINOZA'S WORLDS:
REFLECTIONS ON BALIBAR ON SPINOZA

DANIEL GARBER
University of Chicago

Etienne Balibar is concerned with one of the central (and most difficult) questions in Spinoza's metaphysics: what is the *object* of Spinoza's metaphysics? What is this substance, these attributes, these modes that Spinoza is trying to snare in the dense network of words that constitutes the opening parts of the *Ethics?*

Balibar approaches this question with caution, care and sophistication. He begins by outlining two exchanges that Spinoza had with correspondents, exchanges which, Balibar argues, reveal certain tensions in Spinoza's views. The first exchange involves Spinoza, Boyle, and Oldenburg, and took place between 1661 and 1665. For Balibar, the importance of this exchange is the tension it shows between Spinoza's metaphysical views, and his conception of the physical world. On the one hand, Spinoza wants to eliminate all final causality from nature, and with it, all beauty and deformity, order and confusion.[1] But at the same time, in discussing the individuation of bodies in the physical world, Spinoza allows himself to appeal to something very like Descartes' law of the conservation of quantity of motion, "the prototype of principles teleological in appearance, which assure the coherence and 'simplicity' of physical theory," as Balibar characterizes it. (Balibar, pp. 62-63). The tension, pointed out by Oldenburg, is obvious, and continues into the *Ethics* itself, Balibar claims, where despite the tirade against final causes in nature (E IApp), Spinoza continues to appeal to the conservation law and, more generally, to the order of nature. The second exchange involves Spinoza, Schuller, and Tschirnhaus, and took place roughly a decade after the first, between 1674 and 1676. Of the many issues in play in the correspondence, Balibar emphasizes the difficulties Spinoza had articulating his conception of the (finite) individual, the way in which its properties flow from its nature, and the way in which the existence of individual modes of infinite extension follow from the attribute extension. Here, as with the earlier exchange, Balibar sees a certain tension between Spinoza's abstract metaphysical thought, and his conception of the physical world. Paraphrasing Gueroult with apparent approval, he notes that for Spinoza, it seems, we can have "either an ontology coherent in itself, but which does not 'cohere' with the foundations of a physics, or we can have an enigmatic juxtaposition between the ontology and the theory of bodies..." (*Ibid.*, p. 65).

Balibar sees in the tensions revealed in these two exchanges the reflection of a deeper tension, two "schémas antithétiques" by which we can represent two importantly different conceptions of the relations between substance, attribute, and mode. According to conception A ("la voie A"), the concept of Spinoza's unique substance is "distributed" among an infinity of distinct attributes, including thought and extension. On this view, modes of substance are modifications not of substance *per se*, but of each of its attributes. Individual things, modes, are produced through the mediation of attributes, in accordance with the essence and causality that pertains to the individual attributes. And so, on conception A, there is no notion of causality or individuality that transcends attributes. On conception B ("la voie B"), on the other hand, individual things are modes of substance directly, and without the intermediation of attributes. On this view, attributes are necessary only to make substance and its modes *intelligible* to us; each attribute constitutes a way of apprehending the inherence of modes in substance. But, strictly speaking, on conception B, the notion of an individual and its (causal) connection to substance transcends the attributes.[2]

Conception A is, presumably, what underlies our intuitions about the physical world; conception B is, presumably, what corresponds to Spinoza's more purely metaphysical thought. Balibar, though, hesitates to attribute these divergent conceptions to Spinoza himself (*Ibid.*, pp. 67-68). The fact that Spinoza seems to lead us in these two divergent ways suggests to Balibar that Spinoza is grasping at something else, something that stands outside the usual list of metaphysical options. In connection with the Spinoza-Schuller-Tschirnhaus exchange, Balibar characterizes the view as follows: "To the classical alternative between a geometrical mechanism, as in Descartes, and a dynamism, as in Leibniz... Spinoza seems to be seeking a third way or a way of going beyond" (*Ibid.*, p. 64). At the end of his paper, Balibar puts the point more generally and more suggestively: "...if Spinoza's thought... does not correspond exactly to either of these conceptions [i.e., conceptions A and B], is it not because it represents an attempt to think of a nature which is not a world - even an infinite world - thus escaping every 'conception of the world'" (*Ibid.*, p. 75; cf. p. 74)? It is this - the nature that is not a world - that, presumably, constitutes the object of Spinoza's metaphysics.

We will, of course, have to return to this conclusion of Balibar's and examine it with some care. But before doing this I would like briefly to examine one detail in Balibar's picture. Balibar naturally enough associates the notion of order in the physical world with teleology and final causality; in particular, he sees in Descartes' conservation law "the prototype of principles teleological in appearance" (*Ibid.*, p. 62). But however teleological the law may appear, it should be emphasized that Descartes did not see matters in that way.

Though he may not always have been consistent in this, Descartes professed opposition to final causes much as Spinoza was later to do. In the *Principia Philosophiae*, for example, Descartes argues that we should not seek to find God's ends. Rather, he urges, "considering him [i.e. God] as the efficient cause of everything, we should see what we must conclude by the light of reason he gave us from those of his attributes which he wants us to have knowledge of, concerning those effects which are apparent to the senses."[3] And this is precisely how Descartes derives his principles of order for the material world, his laws of motion. In II,36, of the *Principia*, where Descartes presents his conservation law, he begins by introducing the "universal and primary [cause of motion], which is the general cause of all motions in the world," God. God, Descartes tells us, "is not only in himself immutable, but he also acts in as constant and immutable a way as possible." And so, when he sustains the world, as he must for it to continue to endure beyond its initial creation, he preserves the same amount of motion as he originally created there, Descartes argues. Descartes thus derives the conservation law from God's immutability, one of his attributes, and from the claim that God must be the efficient cause of the world's continuing to exist; final causes, God's ends, never enter in at all. However, it is not clear to me that either Oldenburg or Spinoza recognized this point. Discussion of final causality is curiously missing from Spinoza's 1663 exposition of Descartes' *Principles*, and while Spinoza gives a reasonably faithful rendering of the conservation law and Descartes' argument for it (G I/200-1) he does not broach the question of order and final causality in that connection.

With this aside I would like to turn back to the main thread of Balibar's essay. Balibar's ultimate conclusion is that Spinoza was attempting to step beyond traditional metaphysics, and present a nature that is not a world. What does this mean? In the beginning of his essay, Balibar contrasts the metaphysics of Descartes and Aristotle with that of Spinoza. For Descartes and Aristotle, Balibar claims, metaphysics "maintains a permanent and privileged relation of foundation and imitation with regard to a representation of 'phusis'" (Balibar, p. 59). I take it that what Balibar means here is that for both Aristotle and Descartes, the basic categories of their ontologies link more or less directly into nature, that Aristotle's substances and Descartes' minds and bodies are intended as recognizable components of our experience of nature. But, Balibar claims, "the Spinozist ontology is not a metaphysics in this sense." For Spinoza, "nature, in the end, does not allow itself to be thought of either as a hierarchy of sensible forms, or as the extension of a quantifiable mechanical process, that is, as a field of physical experience in either of these two great historically constituted senses" (*Ibid.*, p. 59). It is this, I think, Balibar has in mind when he says that the object of Spinoza's ontology is a nature that is not a world; it is a nature that is not a world in the sense in which Aristotle's and Descartes' natures *are* worlds, attempts to make metaphysically orderly and precise the objects of our experience, taken broadly. Spinoza's metaphysics, as Balibar interprets it, attempts to go beyond the field of our experience, and attempts to characterize an object - substance and its modes - that stands outside that field. It is nature (*Deus sive natura*), but it is not a world in which we live, unlike the worlds of Aristotle and Descartes.

This, I take it, is Balibar's main claim. But is it correct? In a sense. The very abstract treatment of substance, attribute, and mode in part I of the *Ethics* certainly fits Balibar's account. There Spinoza treats substance, its infinity of infinite attributes, and the modes, infinite and finite that pertain to substance in a way that is very distant from any of the "worlds" Balibar sees in Aristotle or Descartes. But there is another way of viewing Spinoza's metaphysics. Although we can prove general theorems about substance, its uniqueness, its multiplicity of attributes, and so on, it is only through its attributes that we can comprehend its essence: "by attribute I understand what the intellect perceives of a substance, as constituting its essence" (E ID4). And, of course, the two attributes we have access to, the two ways in which we can comprehend the essence of the substance that is God or nature are thought and extension (cf. IIP1, IIP2). And so, Spinoza concludes, since modes of substance must be conceived through substance (IA4, P15), the modes of substance, bodies and any other singular things, must be conceived through one of God's attributes (IIP45). God or nature is thus a thinking thing, an extended thing, and an infinity of other things beyond our ken, as is each of its modes. In the often quoted words of IIP7S: "...[T]he thinking substance and the extended substance are one and the same substance, which is now comprehended under this attribute, now under that. So also a mode of extension and the idea of that mode are one and the same thing, but expressed in two ways." Now, substance conceived through the attribute extension and substance conceived through the attribute thought would certainly seem to be 'worlds' in the sense in which Balibar wants to use the term. And so it seems to me that while one *can* say that Spinoza's nature is not a world, one can equally well say that it is at very least *two* worlds, and perhaps an infinity of other worlds. Or, to put it another way, Spinoza's nature is not *a* world, not because it is *no* world, but because it is *many* worlds. Understood in this way, Spinoza's point is *not* that nature stands *outside* of the worlds in which we live, but that the worlds in which we live, the world of thoughts and the world of bodies are really two alternative but equally definitive ways of comprehending nature, which is one.

Spinoza attempts to make a unity out of a multiplicity of worlds by grounding the multiplicity, a multiplicity of attributes, in a unique God with a unique essence. It is not surprising that such a project leads to some apparent contradictions or, at least, to some real tensions. Emphasize the multiplicity and mutual independence of the words unified, and one naturally falls into Balibar's conception A; emphasize the unity of the worlds, and we are attracted toward conception B. But, as Balibar acknowledges, these two divergent conceptions represent more divergent interpretive strategies than they do genuine contradictions in Spinoza's thought. Though his commentators may have inclinations toward one or both of these conceptions, the Spinoza of the *Ethics* seems to steer a middle course between the two. As conception A emphasizes, modes are, in an important sense, radically distinct, and must be comprehended through the appropriate attribute. But as in conception B, there is is only one substance and *one* world of modes, and though in an important sense distinct, the mode of thought that constitutes the idea of a given body is strictly speaking identical with the body of which it is an idea. Though complex and difficult to comprehend, it is not inconsistent, so far as I can see.

This is not to say that Spinoza is always clear about things. The difficulties Balibar displayed in the Spinoza-Schuller-Tschirnhaus correspondence show that Spinoza had some trouble going from the abstract metaphysical picture of substance, attribute, and mode to the concrete worlds of bodies and thoughts. I also don't mean to suggest that there is not something *very* paradoxical about a single thing that is an element of both the world of thought and the world of extension. Though Spinoza's view may be formally consistent, his attempt to forge a unity out of a diversity of attributes is an idea that continues to give commentators monumental headaches, and may, indeed, border on the unthinkable.

It may sometimes be useful to think of Spinoza's ontology as Balibar does, a nature that is not a world, a metaphysics that stands outside of our experience of the world. But it is wrong to see Spinoza as abandoning the world of the mechanical philosophy for an unworldly metaphysics. Balibar is happy to admit that Spinoza's metaphysics does bear some relation to the world of physics, and has something to contribute to it (*Ibid.*, p. 60). But I would put the point more strongly. Spinoza's point is *not* that nature properly conceived is *not* the world of bodies as we experience them; it *is*. But it is also something more, it is a world of thought and an infinite number of other worlds, as many potential worlds as there are attributes. His intention is not to deny or subordinate the world of physics, but to show that that world is far richer than any of us imagined. The world of bodies and the world of thoughts thus remain firmly within Spinoza's ontology.

1. (G IV/170, quoted by Balibar, p. 61).
2. For Balibar's full account of these two conceptions, see *Ibid.*, p. 66.
3. *Principia Philosophiae* I 28. (See also the discussion in *Meditatio* IV, AT VII, 55.)

BODY ESSENCE AND MIND ETERNITY IN SPINOZA

WALLACE MATSON
University of California,
Berkeley, California

Spinoza says at the end of VP20S: "So now it is time for me to proceed to those things that pertain to the duration of the mind without relation to the body." Obviously he intended the remainder of the *Ethics* to be a superlatively upbeat ending. This is where at last we are to be told how to discover and attain what will enable us to enjoy continuous, supreme, and unending happiness, which he says (in TdIE) he sought. *Literally* continuous, *literally* supreme, *literally* unending, *literal* happiness.

No one who reads these dozen pages can fail to perceive that they are, in their author's eye, the joyous capstone to his chief work. *Even if* the mind perished utterly with the body, the life of reason would still be the best life, as has been shown; but how much more there is besides! (VP41 - exactly parallel to Plato's *Republic* 621 to end.) The wise man "never ceases to be" (*nunquam esse desinit*) "but always (*semper*) possesses true contentment of the soul (*vera animi acquiescentia*)" (VP42S fifth sentence from end of the book).

Few of his commentators have shared Spinoza's euphoria. For what is said here seems to stand in glaring contradiction to the sovran teaching of IIP7 that the human mind and the human body are "one and the same thing" (though "expressed in two ways"). Attempts to deal with this embarrassment take three main forms, which, crudely put, are the contentions that Spinoza meant what he said (and so contradicted himself); that he meant what he said, but didn't say all that he meant; and that he didn't mean what he said.

The first of these, the simple and straightforward reading of Spinoza as claiming that not the whole mind, but an important part of it, survives bodily death intact - that for example part of Spinoza's mind was still around in 1678, and is today - has been adopted in recent times, most notably by Jonathan Bennett, who faces, indeed emphasizes, the consequence - as it appears to him - that at the end of his chief work Spinoza, for unfathomable reasons, abandoned his hitherto so carefully crafted philosophy and began to write "pretty certainly worthless" "nonsense," "rubbish which causes others to write rubbish" (Bennett (1984), 372 ff.). And many Spinozists must have felt that such shocking strictures are not to be gainsaid *if* Spinoza indeed meant what he said, reading Latin words such as *semper*, *remanet*, and *ante* in their usual senses; which is why they have striven to interpret the passages in other ways.

I think, however, that if we attend carefully to what Spinoza said, a reading will emerge that is consistent with what has gone before - perhaps is even entailed by it - and that presents an intelligible and non-trivial doctrine, which I shall attempt to expound. Whether it is true or plausible is another matter, which I shall not ponder in this paper.

The Doctrine

The remainder of the *Ethics*, about six percent of the whole, consists of twenty-two propositions, twelve scholia, and four corollaries. I venture to summarize this doctrine concerning the duration of the mind without relation to the body as follows:

1. Imagination (which includes sensation) and memory do not survive the body (VP21).
2. But, since there is in God an idea expressing the essence of the body under form of eternity (VP22), the mind is not absolutely destroyed when the body is; something of it remains (*remanet*) that is eternal. This is the idea of the essence of the body; it pertains to the essence of the mind (VP23).
3. We do not remember that we existed before the body. Nevertheless we "feel and experience" (*sentimus experimurque*) that we are eternal (VP23S).
4. The formal cause of the third kind of knowledge (viz. *scientia intuitiva*) is the mind "in so far as the mind is eternal" (VP31).
5. Intellectual love of God, arising from the third kind of knowledge, is eternal (VP33), i.e., without beginning, as well as without end (VP33S).
6. Passive affects, on the other hand, exist only while the body endures (VP34). Therefore intellectual love of God ("gladness accompanied by the idea of God as cause, that is, the love of God not insofar as we imagine him as present but insofar as we understand God to be eternal" - VP32C) is the only eternal love (VP34S).
7. This intellectual love is "part of the infinite love wherewith God loves himself." (VP36) It is our "salvation or blessedness or freedom, ... called glory in the Holy Scriptures, and rightly so" (VP36S). It is indestructible (VP37).
8. "The greater the number of things the mind knows by the second and third kinds of knowledge, the greater is the part of it that survives" (VP38).
9. "He whose body is capable of the greatest amount of activity has a mind whose greatest part is eternal" (VP39).
10. We endeavor to arrange things in this life so that "everything relating to memory or imagination should be of scarcely any importance in comparison with the intellect" (VP39S).
11. The part of the mind that survives - viz. the intellect - is more perfect than the rest (VP40S).
12. All the intellects together "constitute the eternal and infinite intellect of God" (VP40S).
13. Salvation is a goal that is difficult but not impossible of attainment (VP42S).

In a nutshell, only while the body exists can we imagine (have sensations) and remember. But both before birth and after death a part of the mind, viz. the intellect, exists eternally. The contents of the intellect are rational and intuitive knowledge and the intellectual love of God. The repertoire of the intellect can be augmented while the body exists; thereby salvation, which involves eternal joy, is attainable.

I shall now expound, in the same order, what I take to be Spinoza's meaning.

Duration and Eternity

Spinoza says (VP29S) that things are conceived as actual (*actuales*) in two ways: (1) as existing in relation to a certain time and place, (2) as contained in God and following from the necessity of the divine nature. It is clear that the part of the mind declared to "remain" is conceived as actual in the second way; the other part, memory and "imagination" (including sense perception and everything to do with words), is actual in the first way, and ceases to be at the destruction of the body (VP21). The second way of being actual is necessary being or *aeternitas*, defined (ID8) as "following solely from the definition of the eternal thing." This, the *Explicatio* adds, "cannot be explicated through duration or time (*durationem aut tempus*)," even if the duration has neither beginning nor end. The question has been raised whether Spinoza held that what is actual in the second way, i.e. eternal, is also actual - *a fortiori* as it were - at all times: "sempiternal." I shall call the affirmative answer "Knealeism," after the philosopher best known for its defense, and the negative "Hardinism" - which holds, not that it is false, but that it is meaningless to assert of an eternal thing that it is actual at time *t*, whatever *t* may be.

The title of my summary comes from the final sentence of VP20S. Spinoza uses the word *duratio* there, and in VP23 says that after the destruction of the body something of the mind "remains" (*remanet*). In VP23S his explanation of why it is impossible for us to remember that we (sc. part of our mind) existed before (*ante*) the body implies that nevertheless we did so exist. In VP38D we are again told of part of the mind that "remains" after bodily death, for which reason (VP38S) death is less hurtful (*noxia*). The part that remains is again mentioned in VP40C. Finally, VP42S, the wise man is declared never to cease to be (*nunquam esse desinit*).

All this, read with words retaining their normal meanings, favors Knealeism. But *prima facie* Hardinism can be found also. The principal texts are (1) the declaration (ID8) that eternity cannot be "explicated" through duration or time, which is repeated in VP23S and strengthened by the addition "nor can [eternity] be in any way related to time", and (2) IP33S2, "...the eternal does not admit of 'when' or 'before' or 'after'..."

For purposes of this paper it is not required to take sides in this controversy. Nevertheless, not to appear cowardly, I plump for Knealeism. The insistence that eternity "cannot be explicated by" duration is hardly an embarrassment, for - despite Aristotle and etymology - necessity (whatever it is) may be something more than sempiternity. Spinoza's stronger claim that there cannot be *any* relation between eternity and duration is harder to dismiss. But a Knealeist can view it as a harmless exaggeration, pointing to (e.g.) IIIP39S as a parallel: "I have omitted ... tremor, pallor, sobbing, laughter, etc. because they are referred to the Body without any relation to the Mind." (Of course *nothing* in the Body has *no* relation to the Mind: IIP7, 12, etc.). As for the IP33S2 passage, its context shows that it is limited to ruling out any order of temporal priority within eternal things, and has no bearing on the Kneale vs. Hardin issue. But the principal reason for being a Knealeist, as far as I can see, is simply that there is no intelligible alternative. If the principle of inertia is an eternal truth (as Spinoza believed, IIL3C), how can it be denied that it holds (is in effect, is real, is actual) *today*? No one would want to say that it does *not* hold, so Hardinists must claim that it is "meaningless" to say either that it does or it doesn't. But evidently it is *not* meaningless: one uses it in solving problems today, quite on a par with non-eternal truths, such as the formulas for conversion from English to metric units.

To be sure, our question is not whether Knealeism is true, but whether Spinoza was a Knealeist. However, if the alternative is incoherent, then it should not be foisted onto Spinoza unless the textual evidence is incontrovertible, which it is not. Hardinists on their part are obliged to explain away such things as Spinoza's announcement (VP20S *ad fin*) that he is going on to consider "the things that pertain to the duration of the mind without relation to the body." Even if *durationem* is a slip of the pen - and if it isn't, Kneale's case is proved - it shows at any rate the cast of Spinoza's mind. If he really was committed to the (alleged) meaninglessness of saying that eternal truths are true now, it is hard to conceive how he could make such a slip. I shall therefore take it as given - assume, if you prefer - that Spinozist eternity of the intellect is a condition that obtains before, during, and after the bodily career.

Essence

Spinoza's demonstration of the eternity of part of the mind hinges on the notion of "essence of the human body." What is this?

What, indeed, is an essence? Bennett complains (61) that although Spinoza uses the term freely from the first line of the   *Ethics* on, he does not "condescend to define it" until IID2. But that is not quite right: he *never* defines it. The definiendum of IID2 is "to pertain to the essence of any thing," *ad essentiam alicujus rei pertinere*, and that is not the same thing. (Saffron pertains to the essence of Spanish cookery, but saffron is not the essence of Spanish cookery, *tout court*.) No other of Spinoza's fourscore formally explicit definitions is framed in a similar way. Spinoza tells us, IIP10S, that his purpose in IIP2 was to avoid having to say that the nature of God pertains to the essence of each singular thing - which would be the case if whatever is a necessary condition for the being of *x* pertains to the essence of *x*. So he adds the proviso that in order for *y* to qualify as pertaining to the essence of *x*, it must also be the case that *y* can neither be nor be conceived without *x*. He supposes that this fills his bill, since, while singular things can neither be nor be conceived without God, it is not the case that God can neither be nor be conceived without singular things (cf. IP1, IIA1).

According to the first part of IID2, "there pertains to the essence of a thing that which, when granted, the thing is necessarily posited, and by the annulling of which the thing is necessarily annulled." Bennett (61) holds that literally read this implies that the essence of *x* is *x*, "so that 'the essence of' means nothing." I do not see why this is necessarily so. Let "the thing" be a circle, and let "that which" be having the minimum perimeter for given area. Then if what you have before you is a figure such that no other figure of the same perimeter has a larger area, what you have before you is a circle; and if not, not. Perimetric minimality pertains to the essence of the circle, without being conceptually identical to circularity; it is at least a distinct description. It also pertains to the essence of the circle to be produced by a point moving at a fixed distance from a given point (Spinoza's preferred definition of circle). This property is trivially deduced from the definition; Spinoza seems to have supposed that a property such as perimetric minimality was also deducible from the definition, but Tschirnhaus corrected him (Letter 82) - you need further geometric apparatus. Nevertheless, that property is entailed by "the nature of the circle," as it is embedded in the whole structure of Euclidean geometry.

Traditionally the definition of a thing is supposed to state the essence or nature of the thing; and Spinoza agrees (e.g. at IIIP4D). However, his preferred form of definition is not Aristotelian, but "genetic" (see Matheron (1969), 11; Wolfson (1969), II, 143). The definition should state the "proximate cause," it should enable us to understand the process whereby the thing defined comes into being. For to understand is to be able - at least in thought - to produce.

Now we can answer the question, Why did Spinoza define "pertaining to essence" rather than just "essence"? - Because a proper definition of 'essence' would present the essence of essence; it would provide a test that we could apply to a candidate for essence of x, pass or fail, and conclude whether a given string of words is or is not a statement of the *whole* essence of x. Spinoza wisely refused to commit himself to the feasibility, or even possibility in principle, of ever succeeding in such an endeavor, when the essence sought is that of a natural object, not a mere entity of reason such as the circle. We can know whether a formula states something that "pertains to" the essence of x, or even "is perceived by the mind as constituting" the essence of x (ID4 e.g.); but we can never know that the account is complete. Statements of "proximate cause" are (in *our* vocabulary) scientific theories; and Spinoza was aware that interesting theories are open-ended. He was thus more optimistic about the possibility of knowing real essences than were Locke and Hume, but far from being the complete dogmatist some historians paint him as.

When Spinoza speaks of the essence of "the human body" in VP23D it is clear he means the individual, not the species. So I have an essence, which is, moreover, eternal. Could it be "all the non-relational facts" (Bennett (1984), 233) about me?

Indeed, could it be just all the facts about me, relational and nonrelational? That is to ask, Could Spinoza's essence of the body be an anticipation of Leibniz's "complete concept?" No, for essence is created by God (IP25) - directly, without (IP28) the cooperation of the common order of nature that exists durationally - and it is what is known "under form of eternity" (VP29S; cf. IIP45D,S). It is not known under form of eternity that my body has ten toes and mass of 76kg. These are accidental consequences of my strange eventful history. All that is known about me under form of eternity is that this creature is the sort of thing that, *given a certain placement in the order of nature* is capable of manifesting these traits.

To know the essence of a thing is to know how that thing fits into the divine plan, that is to say, how it follows from the infinite modes. Only possible things have essences, and what is possible - in itself - is just what accords with the divine nature.

IIP8C,S are the key to Spinoza's doctrine of essence. (What I shall have to say here owes much to Gueroult's masterful exegesis: (1974), II, 93ff). The Corollary has to do with the somewhat perplexing notion of "individual things that do not exist except insofar as they are comprehended in the attributes of God," and the Scholium tries to clarify the Corollary by the example of the equal rectangles, drawn or not, contained in a circle.

Now, Extension is an attribute of God. How can anything be "comprehended in Extension" without actually *being* extended, i.e., existing as an extended thing? The answer becomes apparent when we remind ourselves that strictly speaking there is no such thing as Extension (a universal, a mere aid to imagination), there is only Extended Substance = God = *Natura naturans*, from which follows the immediate infinite mode Motion-and-Rest = all the laws of Physics, which are eternal. That is to say, from the nature (essence) of Extended Substance, as expressed in Motion-and-Rest, all the essences of all individual extended things (modes) follow. So there are eternally "contained in extension" an infinity of essences of individual things that will exist in duration at one time or other, depending on when in the common order of nature their causes turn up. By the parallelism, there are eternally, in the attribute of Thought, ideas of these individual things; ideas, however, do not "affirm the existence" of the things unless the things exist in duration. Spinoza illustrates this in the Scholium by the near analogue of the infinity of (undrawn but possible-to-draw) equal rectangles "contained in a circle" which itself exists (= has been actually drawn), contrasting these undrawn rectangles with two which, being actually drawn, are the objects of ideas "distinguished from the other ideas of the other rectangles." From the nature of the circle it follows that the rectangles formed by intersecting chords within it will all be equal in area; in other words, the nature (the geometry) of the circle excludes the possibility of unequal rectangles thus formed. Just so, the nature of Extension permits the existence of some things and excludes others: there can be hydrogen sulfide, there cannot be helium sulfide - because (to simplify somewhat, but not to lose the essential point) chemical compounds are aggregates of molecules in which dissimilar atoms are united by the sharing of valence electrons; each hydrogen atom has a single valence electron, so that two atoms can supply the two-electron deficiency of a sulfur atom to bring its orbitals to the stable condition of the next noble gas (argon); while helium, being already a noble gas, has no valence electron, thus cannot enter into compounds. These facts follow - deductively - from the essences of hydrogen, helium, and sulfur, namely that they are elements nos. 1, 2, and 16. The necessary and sufficient condition for being sulfur is being Element No. 16; the idea that this designation symbolizes is adequate, representing the (vertical, nomological) "proximate cause" of sulfur.

Being Element No. 16 "pertains to the essence" of sulfur, as being yellow and smelly do not; although those properties too follow from the essence. One can sense, "imagine" sulfur by its color or odor; but only by articulating it into the Attribute, as the atomic number does, can one understand it. From the essence follows (together with the essences of other things) the truth of such hypotheticals as that if there is hydrogen around, then sulfur will combine with it; if chlorine, no; if there are fleas in contact, they will be discommoded; and an infinity of others.

The Periodic Law was not foreseen by Spinoza; all the same, his conceptual scheme has a place for it. One can hardly read Spinoza without feeling that this man of the time of Newton and Huyghens enjoyed prescience of the fundamental character of the world picture at which physics would eventually arrive. Almost alone of the ghosts of departed metaphysicians, Spinoza's is entitled to materialize at a 20th century congress of theoretical physicists and intone "I told you so." But I do not wish to "afford material for the superstitious;" this is neither supernatural nor yet a matter of lucky guessing, but rather (in my view) a vindication of a priori method in science, even of what Bennett (29f.) abhors as "causal rationalism": sit in the armchair and think hard enough about what things must be like if the universe is a real unity, and you are bound to come up with Spinozism or something close to it.

Spinoza held that bodies differ from one another in respect of "motion and rest" (E IIP13L1-3), which vague phrase is his stand-in for a detailed physical theory in his time not yet worked out (see Matson, 404, Bennett, 232). 'Element No. 16,' together with the comprehensive theory in which this conception is embedded, is a specification of "motion and rest," indicating, in fact, that particular, unique "proportion of motion and rest" that is the necessary and sufficient condition for being sulfur.

Sulfur is a stuff, and 'sulfur' is a mass term, whereas Spinozistic essences are of individual things. But there is no Spinozistic identity of indiscernibles; strictly speaking, 'being Element No. 16' is the essence of an individual sulfur atom - but all the other sulfur atoms share the same essence. Composite bodies, such as kitchen matches, then have different complex essences (Def. after IIA2, II/99-100).

Are essences possibilia? In a way, yes: relative to duration, they are in Donagan's phrase (249) "intrinsically possible," that is, they will come upon the durational stage when other finite modes, their causes in the common order of nature, determine them to do so (IP28). (Let us dismiss the odd mention in IP33S1 of a thing whose *essentia seu definitio contradictionem involvit* as a momentary aberration). These conditions for existence are among the hypotheticals mentioned above. Sulfur came into existence relatively early; plutonium, equally an intrinsic possibility, had to wait a long time for the presence of a peculiar combination of bodies whose ideas comprised both a lot of knowledge of the second kind (and possibly third) and hatred. It is of crucial importance for the eternity of the mind, however, that for Spinoza the essences of "non-existent things" are perfectly real, actual items (VP29S). Spinoza has no truck with *mere* possibilities.

Let us now return to the essence of the human body. It differs only in complication from that of sulfur.

Spinoza uses the word *essentia* synonymously with *natura* (IIIP57D, IVP19D, e.g.) and *forma* (IV Pref, II/208/26); *definitio* is what expresses all of them. Now in IVP39S the form of the body (*forma corporis*) is declared to be the body's particular proportion of motion and rest (Cf. IIP24D, first sentence). This amounts to what we may call the dynamic physiognomy of the body ('dynamic' because in the passage cited Spinoza admits the possibility of the same body's having now one form and later another on account of change in "proportion of motion and rest"). People differ from one another according to their different particular essences (forms, natures), each person having his or her own proportion of motion and rest, a natural signature as it were. Usually it is unique, but not necessarily; Spinoza allowed for twins and clones (IP17S, II/63/18).

If it is right to think of atomic numbers as the specifications of proportions of motion and rest for certain stuffs, in the case of the human being (or any living creature) the obvious analogue is the genetic code, the formula for the structure of the individual's (quasi-)unique DNA molecule. Viewed Spinozistically, as helped by Bennett's "field" interpretation of the substance-mode relation, the nature of extension has from eternity contained the essence of my body, that is, the laws of physics do not rule out the existence of a being of my particular constitution. Eternally I have been intrinsically possible. Certain actual modes having in due course cooperated to determine the actuality in duration of an instantiation of this formula, here I am.

That is how from eternity the formal essence of the until recently non-existent W. M. body was (and, of course, still is) contained in the attribute Extension. The body essence is the license (from the nature of Extension) for there to come to be an organism of a certain sort. When it comes into existence, there is no guarantee that it will develop into exactly the kind of thing that the DNA blueprint specifies. For to come into existence is to become subject to buffeting from the other modes, some of which will help, others hinder development according to the plan in the essence. My DNA provides for ten fingers, but there are chain saws and alligators lurking. One thing is certain, though: I will at any rate *try* to develop in the manner specified. The form of my body is not dumb symbols on a blackboard; it *is* the *conatus* to preserve myself (IIIP7).

IIP8 tells us that it is obvious from the parallelism (IIP7) that corresponding to the formal essence of the body an idea of that essence has also been contained from eternity in the attribute Thought. Since the mind is identical to the idea of the body, is "one and the same thing expressed in another way" (IIP7S), the idea of this formula expresses the possibility of the mind correlated with the (possible) body. It expresses the *way of thinking* that goes with the way of being extended that the genetic code expresses. Now, that way of being extended is, before my birth, only a possibility; and correspondingly the idea of it is only the idea of a possible way of thinking. But, as Donagan has pointed out (254f.), an idea of a merely possible thing is nevertheless an *actual* idea. (This, I fear, is contrary to Bennett's dictum [360] that modal status, like all logical relations, is preserved across the attributes.) According to IIP8 this idea is "comprehended in the infinite idea of God," which is certainly an actual thing. Hence there is *actually*, eternally, what I shall call my proto-mind. It is a mind, for by definition a (human) mind is the idea of a (human) body. From all eternity it has existed, as part of God's infinite mind, and of course it will go on after my body ceases to be.

This, however, is far from the whole, or the most interesting part, of Spinozistic mind eternity.

The Eternity Experience

The claim that "we feel and experience that we are eternal" (VP23S) is curious. Commentators have had little to say about this passage.

"We" means people in general, with no restriction to Spinoza and his coterie, nor even to those who have read the demonstrations in the *Ethics* and been convinced by them. Spinoza never uses the first person plural in such senses. Further, he states explicitly (VP34S) that people in general "are conscious (*conscios*) of the eternity of the mind," although they "confuse it with duration and assign it to imagination or to memory."

Sentio occurs forty times in the *Ethics*, and though 'think' is sometimes a good translation, it is always in the sense 'feel,' 'judge,' 'sense,' 'estimate' - it never designates or even includes the drawing of an inference by a formal process of reasoning. The nearest it comes is at IVP18S, where Spinoza tells us he is going to set out briefly "what I think (*ea, quae sentio*)" about the dictates of reason. *Experior*, 15 occurrences, always means 'try,' 'learn,' or 'find by experience.' So unless Spinoza in this passage is departing sharply from his usage everywhere else, he is asserting that we know *by experience*, indeed by experience common to everyone, that we are eternal. This is strange, for knowing by experience is "the first kind of knowledge" and usually deprecated as unreliable.

A sort of argument is given for this proposition, but it is hardly more than a metaphor (though one of the most famous in the *Ethics*). Spinoza says: "For the mind senses (*sentit*) those things that it conceives by its understanding just as much as those which it has in its memory. For the eyes of the mind, by which it sees and observes things, are demonstrations themselves (*ipsae demonstrationes*)."

I take this to be a reference to the 'click' or 'aha! experience' when we (as we say) 'see' the cogency of a demonstration. This kind of apprehension signals the onset of an item of knowledge of the second or third kind, which thereupon *becomes part of the intellect*, as the bodily sighting of the cat on the mat is stored in the memory, the repository for knowledge of the first kind. The click *is* an *experience*, and common enough so that "we" can be said to be familiar with it, just because we are human minds. Let us recall, too, that in the seventeenth century people made a big fuss about this, e.g., Hobbes when in the "gentleman's library" he happened upon the Pythagorean theorem (Aubrey 150).

But why can having this experience be said to be "feeling and experiencing" that we are eternal? Well, this is our contact in experience with what eternity, by Spinoza's definition, is: "existence itself insofar as it is conceived to follow necessarily from the definition of the eternal thing." That is to say, this is our contact with the kind of reality that "cannot be explicated by duration."

To say this is to change the subject (a modern objector will complain). That the three angles of a triangle = two right angles, is an eternal truth, OK. But what has that to do with the alleged eternity of the mind that becomes aware of the truth?

The Spinozistic answer - in a tradition going all the way back to Parmenides' pronouncement that "thought and being are the same" - is that the mind is *constituted* by ideas; insofar, therefore, as these ideas are eternal, so is the mind! (Plato held a weaker form of this thesis: for him the mind was not to be identified with the Ideas, but in order to be able to grasp them it had to be "like" them - another basic metaphysical notion that surfaces in Spinoza as IA5 and IP3: Things with nothing in common cannot stand in either logical or causal relations.)

The Proto-Mind's Knowledge

The proto-mind, being the idea corresponding to the eternal essence of the body (the genetic code, or whatever is its eternal pattern), is (to speak in yet another way of it) the core of the mind. It is not "affected by the idea of any other body" and consequently is not passive nor subject to passion. Therefore (IIIP3) the idea that constitutes it is adequate. To say this is to imply further that whatever it conceives, it does so "under the form of eternity," that is, rationally, and without reference to duration.

Intellectual Love of God

Intellectual, of course, since it has nothing to do with memory or imagination. Love, because (so Spinoza maintains) it is "gladness with con-comitant idea of God as cause." But what - if it is proper to ask - does it *feel* like? Bertrand Russell equated it to the pleasure of scientific discovery; and why not? If it is right to talk about the 'click' in this context, Russell's notion seems to express the same thing.

However, VP33 presents a difficulty inasmuch as Spinoza claims that the intellectual love of God is "eternal" - that is to say, without a beginning as well as without an end. It can't be something that *happens*. No, but like any eternal item in thought, say, the equality of the angles of a triangle to two right angles, the intellectual love of God can (as we shall see) be something that the individual mind connects up with, incorporates into its being, in the course of its (durational) development. The proto-mind does not know (i.e. does not have as a constituent of itself) the truth about the angles; nevertheless it is essentially the sort of thing that can, of itself (actively, not passively) unite that truth to itself. (I am putting this in tentative metaphors; I hope they are right, but with limited confidence, as Spinoza never vouchsafes details about how the mind acquires knowledge of the second and third kinds - or even what it is to do so.)

How the Eternal Part of the Mind Grows

In E V *passim*, most clearly in VP39S and VP42S (the last sentences of the *Ethics*), it is implied that we can *do* something, while existing in duration, to increase the extent of that part of the mind that is eternal, and thus attain blessedness. Many commentators take this teaching to imply that according to Spinoza there is something that is both eternal and capable of increase, a doctrine they find "completely unintelligible" (Curley (1969), 143; cf. Bennett, 362). Gueroult in the last footnote of his monumental study (II 538) said that the question would be "examined in Volume III of the present work." Alas.

I suggest that the difficulty vanishes once we give up the assumption that the eternal part of the mind is identical with - neither more nor less than - the idea of the essence of the human body, which idea has already existed from eternity: what I have called the 'proto-mind'. Although it is only the proto-mind that is explicitly proved to be eternal in VP23, we cannot infer that no *more* remains. It is sufficient for Spinoza's purpose at the stage he has reached in VP23 to prove simply this much. What else remains, he tells us in the sequel. And note that in VP23, just as in IID2, he speaks not of the essence *simpliciter* of the mind, but only of what "pertains to the essence."

The proto-mind, the idea of the genetic code or what you will, is the idea of a body which *can* develop in various ways so as to have and exercise various capacities. It is the idea, therefore, of a body with which is associated a mind that *can* think various ideas. Some of the ideas, corresponding to interactions of the body with other bodies, will be the first kind of knowledge, in which the mind is (at least partly) passive: sense perception and memory, ceasing at death. But other ideas will be the results of the mind's activity: from being *able* to form them, the mind will advance to doing so in act (IIIP1). These are the adequate ideas, knowledge of the second and third kinds, the understanding of things *sub specie aeternitatis*. They are the making explicit of what is implicit in the proto-mind, a fact that Spinoza expresses somewhat obscurely in VP29 as "Whatever the Mind understands *sub specie aeternitatis*, it understands not from conceiving the present actual existence of the Body, but from conceiving the essence of the Body *sub specie aeternitatis*."

The proto-mind, which is eternal and incapable of change, is constituted of few or no developed ideas. It is, however, sufficient to establish individuality, for it *is* an individual. The adequate ideas that in the course of life "we" so assiduously cultivate (VP39S) are likewise eternal and changeless. But the intellect, the part of the mind that is the repository of these ideas, grows by accretion. The mind is "not simple, but composed of very many ideas" (IIP15). There is nothing contradictory in the notion of one eternal entity's serving as a magnet, so to speak, capable of attracting other eternal entities into an indissoluble unity. Once there - since they are there as the result of the mind's *activity* exclusively - they *constitute* the intellect, and remain even after the destruction of the body.

We now need not be astonished (as Curley was, *loc. cit.*) by the suggestion of VP39 that improving the fitness of the body is a means to increase the eternal part of the mind. The point is obvious, given the mind-body parallelism. The key word is 'activity,' which is, as always in Spinoza, to be contrasted with being affected from outside. Bodily activity, especially of the brain, is the correlate of mental activity, which is the acquisition of knowledge of the second and third kinds, which is the augmentation of the eternal part of the mind.

Summary of this Interpretation

1. The laws of physics (i.e. the infinite mode motion-and-rest) of themselves imply the intrinsic possibility of certain human bodies - just as they imply the intrinsic possibility of certain edifices (cf. TdIE) and rule out others. If a body is possible, then it is eternally possible. The structural specification of one such possibility is the essence of one human body. And it is eternally part of the infinite idea of God.

2. By the mind-body parallelism, the idea of that essence is - not the mere possibility but the actuality of - the correlated mind. So every *possible* human body is correlated to an *actual* human mind! Such minds, however, if they go no farther, are unendowed with memory and sensation, which can arise only from *inter*action with other minds - which is precluded by the fact that these entities are not (yet) connected with the "common order of nature." That is why we do not remember existing before birth: "there can be no traces of this in the body nor can eternity be defined by time."

3. Of the intrinsically possible bodies some few become actual "as related to a fixed time and place" (VP29S). The proto-mind of such a body, as I call the idea of the essence of the body, which before birth expresses nothing but this essence, can then begin to be augmented with other ideas. Some of them are ideas of modifications of the body by impingement of other bodies: these ideas are imaginations, memories, and passive emotions. But other ideas that coalesce in the mind are expressions of the active nature of the mind. These are adequate ideas, knowledge of the second and third kinds. They are eternal.

4. When the body is destroyed, then, all those ideas that (as Spinoza puts it) "affirm the existence of the body" are destroyed with it. But as we have seen, those are not all the ideas that constitute the mind. Indeed, if one has been diligent, they may constitute only a vanishing small proportion of the totality. The rest go on eternally, in liaison with the proto-mind. As the latter is unique to the individual, the eternal part of the mind is in a certain sense personal, even though its only reality is its being comprised in God's infinite intellect (which = the totality of such eternal individual minds) (VP40S). (However, it is not personal by Spinoza's Spanish-poet test (IVP39S), which makes continuity of memory the criterion of personal identity.)

But Wherefore the Joy?

A problem for any interpretation of the last part of E V is this: How could it be that Spinoza was so excited and enthusiastic about so highbrow and esoteric a kind of immortality? How could it be a consolation, how could it quiet putative fear of extinction? The difficulty is most acute for those accounts that reduce the doctrine of the mind's eternity to the triviality that my essence or definition, like *any* essence, is an eternal truth; or that find in it merely a misleading way of saying that my *having* existed makes - eternally - a difference to the universe. If I am right, Spinozistic mind survival is a little more full bodied (you should pardon the expression) than that: if I have been diligent in my stretch of duration, I shall eternally *know*, e.g., the Periodic Law (if that may be taken as an example of an adequate idea), though I can nevermore smell sulfur or be burned by kitchen matches or remember the chemistry lab with the big oilcloth chart above the blackboard. This is beatitude?

Since, despite the reassurance of VP23S, I can form no conception of the kind of being envisaged, I am at a loss to imagine(!) its attractions. But perhaps an inkling of a more satisfactory response can be inferred from the fact that Bertrand Russell, no less, got consolation from the "impersonal self-enlargement" that is the consequence of (at any rate his conception of) "the intellectual love of God." (See Blackwell (1985)). It was for him the escape route from "the prison of the self." He took quite seriously the notion of identifying oneself with the universe at large (or, at least, all humanity) until in the end personal concerns virtually vanished, as Spinoza promised. Russell, like Spinoza, held that it is only passive emotions that separate people, Reason being the same for all.

In fact, being a dead Spinozist rationalist is very much like being a Rawlsian behind the 'veil of ignorance.' Spinoza would not like that label, but he would probably approve of the concept of that status in which at last our "true self" is revealed. (For the Rawlsian Spinoza see IVPP35-7, 40, 62, 65-6).

A Concluding Speculation

Unless I am mistaken, the theory of intellectual eternity can be squared with the rest of Spinoza's philosophy. (Whether it follows rigorously seems to turn on epistemologico-pedagogical issues that the philosopher left unresolved.) Yet to me there seems something strange and unnatural about the union.

We know that Spinoza changed his mind on this topic between the *Short Treatise* (which teaches only an impersonal survival of the active intellect, *à la* Aristotle and Averroes) and the personal immortality of the *Ethics*. And the biographers tell us that Spinoza's rejection of personal immortality was a principal reason for his excommunication.

Why did he change his mind?

Wolfson (II,323ff) says that Spinoza's theory of immortality was directed against the Averroism of Uriel Acosta. But as we have seen, Spinoza in his twenties upheld that very theory!

Surely the *Short Treatise* view is more consonant with the general outlook of the *Ethics* than are VPP21-40. More than that: personal immortality, for an entity that is not capable of memory (VP21) blatantly *contradicts* the criterion of personal identity laid down in the Spanish poet case (IVP39S). (Fortunately for the logical soundness of the *Ethics*, this criterion is an *obiter dictum*).

I have pointed out elsewhere (in "Death and Destruction in Spinoza's *Ethics*,") certain passages in the *Ethics* suggesting that Spinoza was obsessed by the idea of suicide and was tempted to commit it - like Acosta. Thus one motivation for his philosophy may well have been a desire to find a basis for overcoming this temptation. Along these lines, one might suppose that his acceptance of and 'proof' of personal immortality was part of his exorcism of the ghost of Acosta.[1]

References

Aubrey, John, *Brief Lives*, ed. Dick. London: Secker & Warburg.
Donagan, Alan, "Spinoza's Proof of Immortality," in Grene (1973).
Hardin, C.L., "Spinoza on Immortality and Time," in Shahan & Biro (1978).
Kneale, Martha, "Eternity and Sempiternity," in Grene (1973).
Matson, Wallace, "Death and Destruction in Spinoza's *Ethics*," *Inquiry* 20, 403-17.

1. "How to Make Yourself More or Less Eternal," an earlier draft of this paper, was presented to the Pacific Division of the American Philosophical Association in March 1986. If any transition to a greater perfection is here discernible, the proximate causes are the acute comments of Jonathan Bennett and Charles Jarrett.

THE ETERNITY OF MIND:
COMMENTS ON MATSON ON SPINOZA

HENRY E. ALLISON
University of California
San Diego, California

In "Body Essence and Mind Eternity in Spinoza," Wallace Matson has made an insightful and suggestive but, in my judgment, unsuccessful attempt to defend a literal reading of Spinoza's doctrine of the eternity of the mind. Spinoza, according to Matson, means just what he says when he claims that "The human Mind cannot be absolutely destroyed with the Body, but something of it remains which is eternal" (VP23). Indeed, if Matson is correct, Spinoza means even more than he says in this famous proposition because we need not limit the eternal part of the mind to the portion corresponding to the essence of the body. In what follows, I shall first indicate what I take to be valuable in Matson's account and then state where (and why) I think he goes wrong. Finally, I shall sketch my own interpretation of Spinoza's doctrine of the eternity of the mind, which I call the "epistemological interpretation."

The most valuable aspect of Matson's account is his discussion of *essence* in Spinoza. In brief, his view, with which I am in substantial agreement, is that the essence of a particular thing is its intrinsic nature or structure considered as a pure possibility, in abstraction from its concrete realization in the order of nature. Thus, translating Spinoza's doctrine into contemporary terms, the essence of a human body becomes its genetic code and the essence of the corresponding mind becomes the way of thinking that is functionally correlated with that code. Although I cannot pursue the topic here, I think that this conception of essence provides the key to the answer to many of Bennett's criticisms of Spinoza's use of that slippery notion, particularly insofar as they concern the *conatus* doctrine.[1] For present purposes, it must suffice to note that, on this interpretation, both the essence of every finite mode (including a human body) and the idea in God corresponding to this essence are clearly eternal. Moreover, this follows whether one construes Spinozistic eternity in "Knealeist" or "Hardinist" terms.

So far so good. But, as Bennett has pointed out, the real issue regarding Spinoza's proof concerns the move from the idea in God to the human mind (in Matson's terms the particular "way of thinking" or "proto-mind" correlated with a particular genetic code). In the language of VP23, the crucial and problematic step is the claim that the idea in God "pertains to the essence of the human mind."[2] Spinoza, of course, bases this move on his conception of the mind as the idea of the body (IIP13), and Matson seems to follow him at this point. Given this conception, together with the eternality of the idea in God, it certainly follows that something pertaining to the essence of the human mind is eternal. And since whatever pertains to the essence of the mind obviously pertains to the mind itself, it likewise follows that part of the mind is eternal.

Such an interpretation of Spinoza's proof is admittedly the most natural one. Unfortunately, however, it trades on a notorious ambiguity in Spinoza's conception of idea. Following Bennett, the ambiguity can be brought out by distinguishing between the logical and psychological senses of *idea*.[3] Construed logically, ideas are propositions; construed psychologically, they are mental episodes, believings or cognitions. It is generally recognized that Spinoza uses *idea* in both senses, and it is frequently thought that at crucial points in the *Ethics*, e.g. IIP7 and IIP13 and, of course, VP23, he slides from the logical to the psychological sense.

How, then, does Matson stand with respect to the distinction? The answer, I fear, is that he not only construes *idea* in both senses, but that, without any explanation, he moves from one sense to the other, as if it were non-problematic.

For example, he states that it follows from the parallelism that "corresponding to the formal essence of the body an idea of that essence has also been contained from eternity in the attribute of thought" (p.89). This is good Spinozistic doctrine; but it requires a logical reading, that is, it requires us to take Spinoza to be claiming that in the attribute of thought (or in God) there is from eternity a true proposition or set thereof regarding the essence of the body (indeed, of all possible modes in all the attributes). Appealing to the same parallelism, however, he also claims that this idea "expresses the way of thinking that goes with the way of being extended that the genetic code expresses" (p.89). This way of characterizing the mind is likewise good Spinozistic doctrine (perspicaciously expressed in twentieth century terms); but it makes sense only if *idea* is taken in the psychological sense.

Put simply, a way of thinking that goes with a way of being extended is one thing and a set of true propositions about this way of being extended (or way of thinking) quite another. But the whole argument, on Matson's interpretation, seems to turn on their conflation. Thus, rather than avoiding the "howler" that Bennett and many others have attributed to Spinoza, Matson merely repeats it in slightly different terms.

The same conflation is also operative in Matson's use of Donagan's claim that "an idea of a merely possible thing is nevertheless an *actual* idea," since, according to IIP8, "this idea is comprehended in the infinite idea of God, which is certainly an actual thing" (p.90). Once again, this makes perfectly good sense on the logical reading. So construed, the claim is that there are true propositions in the infinite intellect of God regarding the essence of unrealized possibilities in extension (and all of the other attributes, including thought). It does not follow from this, however, that there are actual "ways of thinking" or minds corresponding to these unrealized possibilities. Otherwise, to use Delahunty's example, which is intended as a *reductio* of Donagan, Spinoza would be committed to the eternal existence of the mind of the eldest son of the Duke and Duchess of Windsor, and of an infinite number of other unrealized possibilities.[4]

Is Spinoza's argument itself then "rubbish," as Bennett suggests, and in trying to make sense of it are we merely adding to the rubbish? I think not, although the reading that I find plausible is rather bland compared to Matson's and not strikingly original. Nevertheless, the doctrine that it attributes to Spinoza is non-trivial and in accord with the basic tenets of the *Ethics*. Moreover, the conception of eternity with which it operates is unabashedly "Hardinist."

In order to appreciate the motivation for the epistemological interpretation, it is important to realize that there is no problem with the soundness of Spinoza's reasoning if one consistently construes *idea* in the logical sense. The point is simply that if the idea that Spinoza identifies with the human mind just is the complete set of true propositions about a corresponding body, then, presumably, the essence of the mind must consist in the subset of true propositions concerning the essence of the body. Since this essence is unchangeable, the corresponding propositions will be eternally true, and since, *ex hypothesi*, the essence of the human mind is identical with these propositions, it too will be eternal.

The obvious problem with this reading is that it saves Spinoza's reasoning by trivializing his doctrine. Thus, it fails to explain why Spinoza should have regarded it (as he certainly did) as the culmination of the *Ethics*. Since, according to Spinoza, there must be in God a set of eternally true propositions about the essence of everything in nature, it follows that human beings (one can no longer speak of minds on this interpretation) have no greater share of eternity than other finite modes. But, although this consequence is clearly unacceptable, it does, together with the distinction between the logical and the psychological senses of *idea*, serve to define the parameters of a successful interpretation: namely, it must steer a course between the Scylla of trivialization and the Charybdis of conflation. Matson, to my mind, certainly avoids the first but falls victim to the second.

The heart of my proposed solution consists in the rejection of the assumption that, in VP23, Spinoza is literally identifying the human mind (or its essence) with the idea in God of the essence of the body. I claim instead that the statement that this idea "pertains to the essence of the mind" should be taken to mean merely that the human mind has the capacity to comprehend it, that is, that it can form an adequate idea of the essence of its body and of itself. Since to have an adequate idea of something is to conceive it under a "species of eternity," this is equivalent to participating in the infinite intellect of God. This is, however, a matter of epistemological accomplishment, not of ontological identification. But since it refers to an actual capacity in the mind rather than to certain propositions about its object or *ideatum*, the eternality claim is non-trivial. Nevertheless, it does not imply sempiternal existence, since the mind cannot retain this capacity any longer than it itself endures, which is no longer than the duration of the body of which it is an idea.

Clearly, if such a revisionary interpretation is to be at all convincing, it must be possible to reconcile it with the passages, duly emphasized by Matson, in which Spinoza appears to affirm an endless duaration for part of the human mind. Although I have nothing very original to say on this score, I do think that reasonable alternatives to a literal reading of these passages are already prevalent in the literature. My only real addition to this topic is to suggest that these non-literal readings become more plausible if one keeps in mind the work that needs to be done by the final propositions of the *Ethics*. Before turning to that, however, it should be noted that there is considerable textual support for the epistemological interpretation.

To begin with, there are the "Hardinist" passages in which Spinoza appears to deny that the mind's eternity has anything to do with duration. These include the claim that "we do not attribute duration to it except while the body endures" (VP23D) which Matson ignores; the remark that the eternity of the mind "cannot be defined by time or explained through duration" (VP23S) which Matson implausibly dismisses as a "harmless exaggeration" (p. 84); and the reflection that, although human beings are conscious of the mind's eternity, they nevertheless "confuse it with duration, and attribute it to the imagination or memory, which they believe remains after death" (VP34CS), which Matson likewise ignores.

More directly relevant to the epistemological interpretation of the mind's eternity is VP31S. After maintaining in the proposition that "The third kind of knowledge depends on the Mind itself... insofar as the mind is eternal," which itself suggests a close connection between the mind's eternity and its intellectual capacity, he states explicitly in the scholium that "the mind is eternal insofar as it conceives things under a species of eternity."

Finally, it seems obvious that Spinoza's mysterious claims that minds differ in the extent to which they are eternal (this difference being a function of their adequate ideas) and that minds can increase their eternal portion in this life through an increase in their stock of adequate ideas strongly suggest the epistemological interpretation. Indeed, it is noteworthy that, in order to reconcile these claims with his own interpretation of the mind's eternity, Matson is forced to maintain that the eternal part of the mind can literally grow beyond the original "proto-mind" through the aquisition of knowledge of the second and third kinds. Now, it certainly makes sense to suggest that a mind can increase its intellectual capacities beyond those contained in its initial "core" or essence. What is difficult to understand, however, is how, as Matson assumes, the whole complex (core plus acquired knowledge) can be eternal in the same sense, particularly when eternity is construed as existence "without beginning, as well as without end" (p. 83). To put the problem somewhat differently, perhaps, as Kneale suggests, it does make sense to claim that eternal truths are true today and will be true tomorrow; but does it make sense to suggest that more of me is eternal today than was at birth and less than shall be tomorrow?

Admittedly, all is not clear sailing for the epistemological, or, indeed, any interpretation of Spinoza's doctrine of the mind's eternity. Thus, in apparent conflict with such a non-literal reading of the text is Spinoza's enigmatic statement that "With this I have completed everything which concerns the present life... so it is now time to pass to those things which pertain to the Mind's duration without relation to the body" (VP20S), which sets the agenda for the

last twenty-two propositions. In addition, there is the claim that something of
the mind "remains" (*remanet*) after the destruction of the body (VP23), as well
as the other references to part of the mind "remaining," noted by Matson.
Finally, there is the claim, also noted by Matson, that the wise man "never ceases
to be" (*numquam esse desinit*) (VP42S).

As I have already indicated, I believe that the first step in dealing with
these passages is to determine what work remains to be done in the final
propositions. The operative assumption here, and, indeed, in any interpretation
that does not dismiss these propositions as "rubbish," is that they must advance
the overall argument of the *Ethics* in a significant way. Now, after contrasting
the life of freedom, lived under the guidance of reason, with the life of bondage
to the passions in the fourth part, in the first twenty propositions of the fifth
part Spinoza provides some remedies against the passions, all of which involve
knowledge of the second and third kinds. Accordingly, knowledge, including the
intuitive knowledge of God, is considered in these propositions merely as a force
for controlling the passions. Clearly, however, Spinoza must demonstrate not
merely that knowledge provides the only means to escape from bondage, but
also, and primarily, that human perfection, or "blessedness," consists in
intellectual activity. In short, Spinoza must move from a consideration of reason
(construed in a broad sense to include both the second and third kinds of
knowledge) as a force for controlling the passions to a consideration of the life
of reason as an end in itself.

If this is correct, then it is not surprising that Spinoza uses traditional
religious language to indicate his shift of concern. To begin with, as Joachim
has noted, by "the present life," with the concern for which Spinoza claims to
be finished, we need understand nothing more than the life of conflict with the
passions.[5] Moreover, since the conflict is between the mind's adequate ideas
and the inadequate ideas corresponding to the bodily appetites, it can certainly
be said to concern the mind as it is "in relation to the body." Thus, in moving
from a consideration of reason as a weapon in the struggle with the passions
to a consideration of rational activity as constitutive of intrinsic and ultimate
satisfaction (blessedness), Spinoza is, indeed, in a certain sense both turning
from all that "concerns the present life" and considering the mind as it is
"without relation to the body."

But what of the *duration* of the mind so considered? Following Joachim,
Matson acknowledges the possibility that it might be a slip of the pen, but
suggests that, if it is not, then "Kneale's case is proved" (p.4). My own view
is that there are other, more reasonable, alternatives. For example, one can take
the reference to the mind's "duration" ironically; the point of the irony being
that the result of considering the mind "without relation to the body" is the
realization that, so considered, it does not have any duration. As for the claim
that "the wise man never cease to be" (VP42S), to which Matson seems to attach
considerable significance, it must suffice to note that Spinoza carefully qualifies
this to concern the wise man "insofar as he is considered as such."

Finally, as many others have already noted, the Latin term *remanet* can
be taken as equivalent to 'remainder' in arithmetic or 'residue' in chemistry.[6]

Thus, the troublesome claim that something of the mind "remains which is eternal" can be taken merely to indicate that there is some "eternal" aspect to the mind that has not yet been considered. Presumably the other appearances of the term in the last propositions can be dealt with in a similar fashion.

I do not wish to insist on any of this here, however, and I certainly do not intend to suggest that these are the only plausible alternatives to a literal reading. My point is only that the literal interpretation of these passages raises insuperable difficulties, and that there is plenty of room for a non-literal interpretation of them that neither is inconsistent with the uncompromisingly naturalistic program of the *Ethic* nor trivializes its last propositions.

1. Bennett (1984), esp. 231-237. I discuss this topic in *Benedict de Spinoza: An Introduction.* (New Haven: Yale University Press, Rev. ed. 1987), 131-136.
2. *Ibid.,* 359-363.
3. *Ibid.,* 50-54, 128-131. Bennett actually emphasizes the contrast between the logical and psychological conceptions of the attribute of thought, but the distinction applies to ideas, the contents of that attribute, as well.
4. R. J. Delahunty, *Spinoza,* (London: Routledge & Kegan Paul, 1985), 299-300.
5. Joachim (1901), 296.
6. See E. Harris, "Spinoza's Theory of Human Immortality," in Mandelbaum & Freeman (1975), 250; C. L. Hardin, "Spinoza on Immortality and Time", in Shahan and Biro (1978), 310; and Delahunty, *Spinoza,* 293.

HOMO COGITAT:
SPINOZA'S DOCTRINE AND SOME RECENT COMMENTATORS

ALAN DONAGAN
California Institute of Technology

1. Cogitatio in Spinoza's Axioms and Definitions.

What can be learned from Spinoza's definitions and axioms about what he took to be the activity he describes by the verb *'cogitare'* and its cognate noun *'cogitatio'*? The second axiom of Part II of the Ethics, "Homo cogitat," is followed by another about the modes of *cogitatio*: it lays down (i) that there can be no *modus cogitandi* (such as love, desire, or whatever is designated by the word *'affectus animi'*), unless in the individual who has it there is an *idea* of the thing it is about, and (ii) that there can be an *idea* without any other *modus cogitandi* (EIIA3). This directs attention to the definition of *"idea"*: namely,

> Per ideam intelligo Mentis conceptum, quem Mens format, propterea quod res est cogitans (EIID3).

An *'explicatio'* is attached to it:

> Dico potius conceptum, quam perceptionem, quia perceptionis nomen indicare videtur, Mentem ab objecto pati. At conceptus actionem mentis exprimere videtur.

And that prompts one to ask: What is the *conceptus* a mind forms, simply because it is a *res cogitans*?

Still, we have learned something. We have not learned what 'ideas' are (Spinoza's Latin word *'idea'* cannot be better rendered into English than by adoption) but we have learned something about their function in thinking. The most elementary exercise of thinking is forming an idea; and forming an idea is an action, not something caused *ab objecto*. This presupposes that ideas have objects. And that should remind us of EIA6, that a true idea must agree with its object. That does not strictly presuppose that all ideas are true or false, but it strongly suggests it; and, as we shall see, Spinoza believes it (EIIP49D). So, from the definitions and axioms of *Ethics* I and II, we are entitled to infer: (1) that merely forming an idea is thinking, and all thinking involves forming ideas; (2a) that ideas have objects, and (2b) are true or false; (3) that if they are true they agree with their objects; and (4) that their objects do not cause them to be formed.

Since forming an idea is sufficient and necessary for thinking, and since all the definitions and axioms tell us about the internal character of ideas, as distinct from what does or does not cause them, is contained in (2a), (2b), and (3), we must begin with them. What is it for an idea to be true or false? What is it for something to be the object of an idea - to have a relation to an idea usually signified in Latin by putting the noun or noun phrase standing for the object in the genitive case as qualifying the noun or noun phrase standing for the idea? And what is it for an idea to 'agree' ('*convenire*') with its object?

2. Forming Ideas: the Propositional Interpretation.

Since philosophers today for the most part think 'true' and 'false' in their fundamental senses refer to the truth and falsity of propositions expressed by sentences, it is natural for them to assume that the truth or falsity of ideas Spinoza speaks of is propositional truth or falsity, and hence that ideas are propositions. *Modi cogitandi* such as love and desire will then be what Bertrand Russell called 'propositional attitudes'; an idea's agreeing with its object will be a proposition's being true of its object. Edwin Curley develops an interpretation of 'idea' on these lines in his pioneering *Spinoza's Metaphysics,* where ideas are regarded as propositions, and their objects, on the lines of Wittgenstein's *Tractatus*, as facts which they depict (Curley (1969), 53-55, 123-6).

There is direct textual evidence for such a propositional interpretation. In some of Spinoza's examples, ideas are expressed by sentences: thus in E IIP40S1 his specimens of the confused ideas of imagination usually called 'universal notions' are presented in the form of sentences: "that man is an animal capable of laughter, or a featherless biped, or a rational animal." This has led Jonathan Bennett, to declare that "[m]uch of the time Spinoza takes ideas to be propositionally structured, i.e., to be of the form 'that p,' where 'p' stands for a sentence" (Bennett (1984), 51).

To the evidence of the verbal form in which Spinoza expresses a number of his examples, Curley has recently added an argument from the best explanation (Curley (1975), 169-70, 173-74). Spinoza goes on to reject Descartes's distinction between forming an idea and affirming something; and Curley has suggested that the best explanation of his doing so is that he rejects Descartes's doctrine that ideas are in us *quasi imagines* and he conceives them instead as propositions. I shall examine this suggestion in its place; but, for the moment, I shall confine myself to showing that the textual evidence for Curley's contention that "[m]uch of the time, Spinoza takes ideas to be propositionally structured" (Bennett (1984), 51) is weak. That evidence is that Spinoza frequently expresses ideas in sentences. It is inconclusive, because, as nobody disputes, he also expresses ideas by nouns and noun phrases. The variation in the forms in which he expresses ideas linguistically would be natural if, like Descartes, he did not think of any linguistic expression of ideas as prototypical.

That he does not is supported both by what what he says about the relation of words to thought and what he does not say. First, he does not say that ideas are propositionally structured and nobody is likely to embrace the doctrine that they are in a fit of absence of mind. If Spinoza had embraced it, and especially if he was led to differ from Descartes because he did, why did he not explicitly say so? No answer to this question is plausible.

Secondly, he *does* say that it is dangerous to confuse ideas with their verbal expressions. Propositional theorists characteristically find the relation of language to the world to be relatively unproblematic, and that of Cartesian thought to the world relatively problematic, because the one is public and open to scientific investigation, and the other is neither. They therefore conclude that thought is not Cartesian, but propositional, and that the problem of its relation to the world should be dissolved by identifying thinking with an activity characteristically expressible in language. What Spinoza says in at least one place about the relation of thought to language is the opposite of this.

In the scholium to E IIP49C, denouncing the "prejudice" of those who "confuse words with the idea" as a fruitful source of error, he offers a remedy: it is "easily... put aside by anyone who attends to the nature of thought, which does not at all involve the concept of extension," because "the essence of words ... is constituted only by corporeal motions, which do not at all involve the concept of thought" (G II/132/13-21). This amounts to saying that the relation of words (corporeal phenomena) to the world cannot elucidate the concept of thought at all; and that so far as words express thoughts it must be because they are associated with non-corporeal ideas. In other words, it is the exact reverse of the truth to imagine that the relation of ideas to the world is problematic, while that of linguistically expressible activities to the world is not.

3. Forming Ideas: Spinoza as a Post-Cartesian.

In describing thought as an activity involving ideas, Spinoza followed Descartes, whose description of thinking about things as having ideas of them before his mind had perplexed both Caterus and Hobbes in preparing their Objections to the third *Meditation* (AT VII, 35; 92-94; 179-80). In replying to Hobbes, Descartes protested that he had made it clear that he was "taking the word *'idea'* to refer to whatever is immediately perceived by the mind," and revealingly added, as Curley has pointed out, (Curley (1985), 640) that he "used the word 'idea' because it was the standard philosophical term used to refer to the forms of perception belonging to the divine mind" (AT VII, 181). It is presumably not questioned that it is the nature of ideas in the divine mind both to be immediate to God and to represent things in the world. And that being their nature, no further explanation of either fact is called for. Of course, Descartes did not think that ideas in human minds are more than analogous to ideas in God's, but Spinoza developed his comparison as he did not, and ultimately concluded that human ideas are God's.

Given this Cartesian setting, Spinoza's definitions and axioms about *cogitatio* are readily interpreted non-propositionally as amounting to four theses:

(i) Ideas are Immediate Objects of Thinking.

> In thinking of something, a thinker is not related to it directly, as his body is when he touches it, but indirectly, through the mediation of an immediate object to which he is related directly: all such immediate objects are of the same kind, and they are what Descartes called ideas.

> As Gueroult points out, Spinoza presupposes this in E IIP3D, when he offers "God can think (*cogitare*) infinite things in infinite ways" and "[God] can form an idea

(*ideam... formare*) of his essence and of all that necessarily follows from it" as two ways
of saying the same thing (Gueroult (1974), 26, n.28). Assuming that this would be
a commonplace to his readers, Spinoza could assume that E IID3, would remind them
that, despite the heterogeneity of the things thinkers think of, the immediate objects
through which they do so are all of the same kind, and so would convey to them that
in using the word 'idea' he meant an object of that kind.

(ii) Ideas Represent What is Thought of.
Ideas are representations of the things a thinker thinks of through them, their *ideata*.
Neither Descartes nor Spinoza offers any account of how ideas represent; but both
presuppose that representation pertains to their essence.

(iii) Ideas have a Double Esse.
Descartes analysed the representativeness of ideas as the medieval Aristotelians did,
by ascribing two kinds of *esse* to them: *esse formale*, the being they have as individual
modes of substance under the attribute *cogitatio* (which corresponds to the medievals'
esse naturale), and *esse objectivum*, the being they have as being *of* something - as
representing something (which corresponds to the medievals' *esse intentionale*) (cf.
AT VII, 41-47). As E IIP8C and P48S[NS] show, Spinoza accepted this Cartesian
distinction as sound, and was willing to make express use of it (cf. Gueroult (1974),
26-28).

(iv) Ideas Explain How Words Express Thoughts, and Not Vice Versa.
Human speech and writing express thoughts to the extent that they stand for ideas.
The thoughts they express are elucidated by reference to ideas, and not vice versa.
It does not follow, because sentences have certain structural features, that the ideas
they express must have parallel features.

These four theses are common to Descartes and Spinoza, and to most
seventeenth and early eighteenth century post-Cartesians.

As Ian Hacking has forcibly argued, in discussing recent interpretations of
what Locke called 'the new way of ideas,' Descartes and his immediate successors
regarded the immediacy and representativeness of ideas as something utterly
familiar and unproblematic. That is why the authors of the *Port Royal Logic*
dismissed the suggestion that 'idea' can be usefully defined. "Some words are
so clear," they write, "that they cannot be explained by others, for none are more
clear and more simple. 'Idea' is such a word."[1] For them, as Hacking observes,
"Ideas ... form no artificial class of disparate entities. *Idea* is the most elemental
kind of entity imaginable, beyond possibility of definition" (Hacking, 28). And
so it was for Spinoza.

It is natural that those who interpret forming ideas as forming propositions
should complain, as Bennett does, that Spinoza treats ideas in two different and
incompatible ways: psychologically, as mental episodes, distinguished from
physical ones by the attribute through which they are conceived; and logically,
as something like Fregean *Gedanke* - that is, as objects or 'contents' of those
mental episodes, belonging neither to the physical nor to the psychological realm.
While for the most part Spinoza uses *'idea'* psychologically, Bennett declares,
"from time to time he makes his psychology double as a logic as well, taking

the term 'idea' to stand indifferently for a mental item and for a concept or proposition" (Bennett (1984), 52).

Spinoza would have replied, I think, that such complaints arise from the delusion that a Fregean third realm must be postulated. There is no need to postulate logical entities linking linguistic utterances to the world, because the ideas they are associated with do that. And ideas are necessarily spoken about in two ways, because as 'mental items' they have a double *esse*: *esse formale* as finite individual modes under the attribute of *cogitatio*, and *esse objectivum* as representing *ideata*. As having *esse formale* they are neither true nor false, nor have they any other logical properties; as having *esse objectivum* they are true or false (Descartes would say 'materially true or false'), and stand in other logical relations. But this does not imply that the word 'idea' stands now for one thing and now for another. If ideas have a double *esse*, there can be no objection to describing them in two different ways: sometimes psychologically, with respect to their *esse formale*; and sometimes logically, with respect to their *esse objectivum*. It may be that the theory of a double *esse* is objectionable; but if it is, let it be objected to. As it stands, it explains the double character of the properties with which ideas are credited.

4. Ideas as Quasi Imagines: Spinoza's Departure from Descartes.

Descartes's theses that ideas, while non-propositional, are immediate to the mind and representative, explains both why he describes them in the *Meditations* as "*quasi imagines*" (AT VII, 42), and why he goes on in *Resp. Obj.* II to insist that they are not counterparts in the imagination of physical drawings or sculptures. Descartes recognizes that some ideas have such counterparts, namely, images in the corporeal imagination; but he denies that such images are ideas at all, except in so far as they give form to the mind itself, when it is directed to the relevant part of the brain (AT VII, 160-61). The force of saying that ideas are "*quasi imagines*" is that they represent the things they do, not by some mental equivalent of saying how they are, but by depicting them, although they do not depict them as material pictures depict what they are of.

In E IIP49S, Spinoza repeats Descartes's distinction between ideas and images in the corporeal imagination, and insists that ideas are not like "mute pictures on a panel." And at the same time he denounces the error of confusing ideas with words, tracing both errors to the same source: mistaking ideas for "corporeal motions, which do not at all involve the concept of *cogitatio*." It has been suggested that here Spinoza is criticizing Descartes; but he does not say so, and if he is, he is mistaken - Descartes denies that ideas are corporeal *imagines* as unmistakably as Spinoza does.

Should not both Descartes and Spinoza have been embarrassed by their inability to describe how ideas depict what they do? I think that they would be surprised by the question. For, as Hacking has pointed out, what they consider problematic is not how ideas depict, but how words and material pictures do (cf. Hacking, ch. 3). Like twentieth century philosophers, they explain the problematic by the unproblematic: words represent because they are conventionally associated with ideas which *naturally* depict what they represent; and material pictures *artificially* depict because seeing them in some ways resembles seeing what they depict, and so prompts their viewers to form ideas both of what they depict and of them as artificial depictions. The problematic representativeness of words and pictures is explained by what is taken to be the unproblematic representativeness of ideas.

I do not deny that the new way of ideas which Descartes introduced is open to objection, or that the revolt against it in the nineteenth and twentieth centuries is justified. I agree that Cartesian ideas no more exist than the luminiferous ether. But we cannot understand Spinoza's writings unless we recognize that he accepted not only Descartes's doctrine that thinking is an activity necessarily involving ideas, but also his chief theses about what ideas are. Would it then be better to misunderstand Spinoza's writings: to ask ourselves what they have to teach us on the assumption that in them human thinking is treated as something explained by linguistic communication in human societies? No: it would be as perverse as to propose that we treat the work of Huygens and his successors as presupposing that there is no luminiferous ether. Just as the work of Huygens can only be corrected and incorporated into quantum electrodynamics by studying it as it is, so the work of Spinoza can only be corrected and incorporated into philosophy today by studying it as it is. And if it is objected that no philosophy that contains an error so gross as the theory of ideas can be anything but a tissue of nonsense, one can only reply that that remains to be seen. The scientific parallels suggest otherwise.

Although Spinoza implicitly accepts Descartes' doctrine that ideas are in us *quasi imagines*, but non-corporeal ones, he utterly repudiates a subordinate thesis on which his theory of knowledge depends. Descartes's position is as follows. Ideas, *quasi imagines*, are 'materially' true or false in that what they depict either exists as they depict it, or is a mere nonentity. Hence a materially true idea is not a true belief, nor a materially false one a false belief. You have neither a true belief nor a false one until you advance from having an idea to making a 'judgement' about it: that is, to affirming or denying its material truth. It is because judgements are acts of will, not of intellect, that the doctrine of divine veracity which grounds human knowledge can be reconciled with the fact of human error. God's veracity is not impugned by the fact that human beings are caused, in the course of nature, to have numerous materially false ideas, because their materially false ideas do not, as such, involve any judgements at all. It would be impugned only if the ideas that cause them to make judgements - their clear and distinct ideas, and their ideas of sensation as a class - were materially false. But no clear and distinct idea is materially false; nor are ideas of sensation materially false as a class, although they are individually.

Spinoza rejected any such distinction between idea and judgement. All ideas are affirmations or Cartesian judgements. That is, they both represent and affirm that they are, as representations, what Descartes called materially true. Not that you affirm the material truth of every idea that you have, any more than every sentence you utter purports to be true. Just as false sentences can enter into true truth-functional compounds, so false ideas can combine with others into

complexes that are true as wholes. A false judgement is simply an idea
representing something that does not in fact exist, unaccompanied "by an idea
that excludes the existence" of what it represents (cf. E IIP17CS - G/II/11-15).
This distinction between what an idea affirms by itself, and its contribution to
what a complex idea of which it forms a part affirms, is the foundation of
Spinoza's theory of error.

5.0. Why does Spinoza Maintain that All Ideas are Affirmations?

Before going into the implications of Spinoza's doctrine that all ideas are
affirmations, it is necessary to understand why he held it. He nowhere
demonstrates it. Rather, in the course of demonstrating E IIP49,

> In mente nulla datur volitio, sive affirmatio et negatio, praeter illam, quam idea,
> quatenus idea est, involvit,

he employs an arbitrary instance of it as a step:

> Porro haec trianguli idea, hanc eandem affirmationem involvere debet, nempe, quod
> tres eius anguli aequentur duobus rectis -

that is, "this idea of a triangle must involve the affirmation that its three angles
equal two right angles." Interpreted in the light of my analysis of Spinoza's
conception of an idea as non-propositional, this is equivalent to: the idea of a
plane figure bounded by straight lines with three interior angles must both
affirm its own material truth (that something existent corresponds to it), and
exclude the idea of such a figure without interior angles equalling two right
angles. This step, however, as Curley has pointed out, "is not justified by the
citation of anything that has gone before" (Curley (1975), 169). If he is entitled
to assert it, his proof of IIP49 is sound. But is he?

5.1. Curley's Answer: the Propositional Theory Reconsidered.

In simply asserting, in his demonstration of E IIP49, that an arbitrary idea
can neither be nor be conceived except as affirming its own (material) truth,
Spinoza unquestionably departs from the *ordo geometricus* he professes to follow,
which forbids the making of any assertion that does not immediately follow from
a definition, an axiom, or a proposition already demonstrated. But is his
departure venial? Could he have proved that every idea as such involves an
affirmation? Or is he entitled to assert it as an axiom?

One reason for treating it as venial has already been acknowledged. If ideas
are propositions, some would say that they must be affirmations too. So
Spinoza's failure to justify his assertion that they are affirmations can be made
part of an argument from the best explanation that, discarding Descartes's
conception of ideas as *quasi imagines*, he conceives them as propositions. In
the form Curley gives it, that argument is a powerful one.

In at least one important use of the term 'idea' [he writes], an idea is supposed to be a representative entity which can be affirmed or denied. Now an image or a picture can represent an object as having certain characteristics simply by being a good likeness of the object. When we spiritualize our representative entity and deprive it of all the characteristics of a material object, it is hard to know what to make of this notion of a resemblance between the idea and its object. We can do something with the notion if we regard the idea as the sort of thought which might be expressed by a proposition. But if we do that, then we can no longer say that the idea in itself involves neither an affirmation nor denial and is neither true nor false.[2]

Yet although this is persuasive, two objections to it seem to me decisive. First, it is implausible that Spinoza believed that Descartes confused ideas with corporeal images. He could not have been ignorant that, although he said that ideas are in us "*quasi imagines*," he was at pains to deny that they are corporeal. It is significant that, in observing that those who confuse ideas with corporeal images do not see that they are affirmations (E IIP49S - G/II/132/5-12), Spinoza does not name Descartes as one who did so; for when a doctrine he criticizes is, by common agreement, Descartes's, he usually says so. Secondly, while it may be hard for twentieth century readers to make head or tail of the notion of a spiritualized quasi-image depicting a physical object while having no physical resemblance to it, there is ample evidence that many seventeenth century philosophers thought that notion to be so simple and clear that no further explanation of it was needed. Whatever was Spinoza's reason for asserting that ideas are affirmations, it is most unlikely that it was that the representative character of ideas would be unintelligible if they were not propositions.

5.2. Gueroult's Answer: the Presuppositions of Spinoza's Theology.

Without alluding to the formal flaw in Spinoza's demonstration, Gueroult offers an alternative informal justification of the ungrounded step (Gueroult, 498). However, for direct textual evidence that Spinoza would have endorsed it, he goes, not to the *Ethics*, but to ch. 4 of the *Tractatus Theologico-Politicus*, where, with respect to God's understanding of the nature of the triangle, Spinoza asserts that

> Dei voluntas et Dei intellectus in se revera unum et idem sunt, nec distinguuntur nisi respectu nostrarum cogitationum quas de Dei intellectu formamus (G III/62/30-32).

God's intellect is an infinitely complex idea, comprising both the infinite modes of God under the attribute *cogitatio*, and also the totality of finite modes under that same attribute, but if the divine intellect is not really distinct from the divine will, and if affirmation is a variety of willing, then, since the ideas in the divine mind are true and the whole truth, and since God wills to affirm all that is true, for God to have the ideas he has is the same thing as for him to affirm them.

This line of thought takes seriously Spinoza's departure from Descartes in holding that the ideas constituting human minds are fragments of the complex infinite idea constituting the divine mind. This is how Gueroult develops it.

> To separate the necessity of the properties contained in the nature of things from the act by which we necessarily affirm them returns to dissociating God's understanding and will, in arbitrarily disjoining the necessity conceived by our notions from divine necessity. And that leads to misunderstanding necessity as it is in itself; for, in itself, it is nothing other than the productive power of God. It is because the eternal truths are necessary by the nature of their notions that one places them in God's understanding; and it is because they are necessary by God's nature that one makes them depend on the decree of his will. But the divine decree and the nature of things are but one thing in the same necessity of God. In God, will is nothing but the power of the understanding, which is God himself produced necessarily by himself. That is why the necessity of ideas is in me only as their necessary affirmation (Gueroult, 498).

Although Gueroult's exposition makes complete sense of the text of *Ethics* II, it indirectly implies that Spinoza's exposition of his thought is flawed. He has not made clear to his readers that, in saying that thinking is forming ideas, he means that *cogitatio*, as an attribute expressing the eternal infinite essence of substance, is to be analysed without remainder in terms of the ideas formed by God as *natura naturans* under that attribute. The *Dei infinita idea* cannot be supposed merely to represent the infinite substance and its modes with complete material truth, without also affirming that it does so. But in that case, neither can any fragment of that idea (and there every idea other than it is a fragment of it) merely represent: it must also affirm its own material truth.

How might Spinoza have corrected his exposition? One way (I do not say that it would have been the best) would have been to enlarge the *expositio* of E IID3 so that it would have read: "But concept seems to express an action of the mind; and ideas not only are not caused by their *ideata*, but are affirmations of the formal being of their *ideata*." It would also have been well if, citing, for demonstration, the enlarged *expositio* of IID3, he had added a second corollary to IIP7, to the effect that God's actual power of thinking is not only the power to represent all that is truly, but also to affirm the formal being of what it represents. If he had done so, then in IIP49D, instead of asserting without support that the idea of an arbitrary object (a triangle) cannot be conceived except as affirming all that it involves, he could have cited the enlarged IID3 and the additional corollary of IIP7. That he remained committed to his position in the *Tractatus Theologico-Politicus* is evident from EIIP49 itself.

6. How is Error Possible?

Spinoza's doctrine of what Gueroult calls extra-cogitative parallelism, the paralleism between ideas and 'things,' makes the phenomenon of error perplexing. For if the infinite complex idea that is the divine mind and the finite complex idea that is God as constituting the essence of a given human mind differ only as a whole differs from one of its parts, it appears to follow that the latter can be no more than ignorant. And Spinoza himself acknowledges that "to be ignorant and to err are different" (IIP35D).

The problem is insoluble if ideas are conceived as propositions. If somebody believes only one proposition about snow, and that proposition, say, 'Snow is white,' is true, then there is much about snow of which he is ignorant; but he is not in error about it. Propositional ignorance is not believing some true proposition, and propositional error is believing some false one. If Spinoza thinks of ideas as propositions, then Bennett would be right when he says:

> Spinoza, although he can accommodate ignorance, has no room for error. He can say that I am ignorant of an event in the outside world if it fails to cause any change in my body, but what can he say about error. What he *does* say is that it is a kind of ignorance. His arguments for this are amazingly stubborn and ingenious, but they are complete failures, as they are bound to be since their conclusion is completely false (Bennett (1983), 51; cf. Bennett (1984), 167-71).

Would this objection stand if Spinoza did not think of ideas as propositions? I do not think it would. But in this paper I can do no more than show how the nonpropositional conception of ideas I have ascribed to Spinoza allows him to accommodate the fact of error while denying that there is anything positive in ideas by virtue if which they are false.

If the propositions we believe are as it were shadows of our ideas, and if ideas are non-propositional and non-corporeal representations, as it were *imagines*, that affirm their own material truth, would somebody whose idea of snow is simply an idea of white stuff be merely ignorant and not in error? The analogy of corporeal images is valid here. A child is invited to make a picture of snow in a space on a blackboard, and colours the space a uniform white. When asked, 'Is that really what you picture snow as?' he replies that it is. If he understands the question and speaks the truth, then his picture is materially false; for it depicts snow as indistinguishable from any uniform white expanse. And if he affirms that it is materially true, he is in error.

Why do both *imagines* and ideas, which are *quasi imagines*, differ from propositions in this respect? I submit that it is because a set of propositions that are each true of an object (that snow is white, that snow is cold, etc.) each contribute to the whole truth about that object by being true of it in their own right. But two fragments that would be a true *imago* of something if put together in the right way are not each true *imagines* of it in their own right. The proposition that snow is white does not purport to be as it were an *imago* of snow: it says only what its colour is, and it says truly. But an idea of snow as white, if that is the whole of of it, would represent snow as white and nothing more, and so would represent it falsely. It would not agree with its *ideatum*, though what is positive in it would be part of the true idea of snow.

Spinoza's theory of error rests on four theses: (i) that every idea is an affirmation in the sense that it is a given mind's total representation at a given time of what there is, or is a fragment of such a representation; (ii) that every idea is a representation of an ideatum, which may be either what there is, or part of it; (iii) that an idea is a false representation of its ideatum if it does not agree with it, that is, if there is anything essential to the ideatum that it fails to represent; and (iv) that every idea affirms its own truth unless it is part of a total complex idea which represents it as not agreeing with its ideatum. Given these theses, he can consistently maintain that human beings can have false ideas (ideas that do not agree with their ideata) that are not false affirmations (because they are parts of total complex ideas that do not represent them as false). This enables him to distinguish ignorance from error: ignorance is having a false idea that is not itself an affirmation, because it forms part of a total complex idea that represents it as false; error is having a false idea that is itself an affirmation, either because it is a total complex idea, or because the total complex idea of which it forms a part does not represent it as false. Spinoza's examples of error in IIP17CDS and IIP49CDS can, I believe, be elucidated along these lines.

References

(1) References to Spinoza's works are either to the Gebhardt edition or to Curley (1985). I adopt Curley's renderings in quoting from Spinoza in English, with occasional departures in the direction of literalness.

(2) Other works referred to (apart from those given in the list of frequently cited sources at the beginning of this volume) are:

Bennett (1983). Bennett, Jonathan. 'Glimpses of Spinoza' *The Syracuse Scholar* 4 (1983), pp. 42-56.

Curley (1975). Curley, Edwin M. 'Descartes, Spinoza, and the Ethics of Belief,' in Mandelbaum and Freeman (1975).

Hacking, Ian. *Why does Language Matter to Philosophy?* (Cambridge: Cambridge University Press, 1975).

1. Hacking quotes this from James Dickoff's and Patricia James's translation, *The Art of Thinking: the Port Royal Logic* (Indianapolis: Bobbs-Merrill, 1964), p. 31.
2. Curley (1975), 173. In a note to this passage, Curley draws attention to Descartes's distinction between the truth and falsity of judgments and the material truth and falsity of ideas, but dismisses it as a desperate attempt to escape the difficulty. He should, I think, also notice that speech act theorists distinguish between propositions and assertions, and deny that entertaining a proposition is the same thing as affirming it.

SPINOZA ON THE DISTINCTION BETWEEN INTELLECT AND WILL

GENEVIEVE LLOYD
University of New South Wales

Spinoza's arguments, in Part Two of the *Ethics*, against the Cartesian account of judgment and the distinction between will and understanding, are notoriously inadequate for the conclusions he wishes to draw. He argues that ideas, in so far as they are ideas, carry affirmation with them; that they cannot be in the mind without being affirmed or negated; that the mind cannot, by an act of the will, suspend judgment; and, more generally, that there is in the mind no "absolute or free" will (IIP49C,S).[1] What is usually taken as at stake between Spinoza and Descartes here is the possibility of what we now call an "ethics of belief," concerned with the conditions under which it is right or reasonable to give our assent in judgment. It is not surprising, against the background of post-Kantian epistemological pre-occupations, that what is salient about these passages should be how Spinoza's rejection of free will bears on the avoidance of error and the gaining of certainty. And, in the context of those epistemological aspects of skepticism, Spinoza's arguments against the Cartesian distinction between intellect and will do seem to leave a lot to be desired.

Those concerns are certainly there. Spinoza is trying to undermine the Cartesian program for attaining certainty through attending to criteria of truth and withholding judgment where we lack clear and distinct perception. But there is more at stake between Descartes and Spinoza than rival theories of knowledge. The rejection of the will is supposed to tranquillize our spirits and show us our highest happiness and virtue. The passages on the will's role in judgment point forward in the text to Spinoza's version - a very different one from Descartes' - of Reason's power over the passions. And they also point back to the discussion, in Part One, of the contrasts between the human mind and the divine will and intellect - on which, again, Spinoza's position is very different from Descartes'. If we take into account how Spinoza's rejection of the will's role in judgment is positioned in the text, we get a rather different picture of his treatment of judgment from the one usually offered. Descartes and Spinoza represent two different stances on the ethical significance of truth, as distinct from the cluster of epistemological issues we now label the "ethics of belief."

Descartes was of course concerned to secure the foundations of scientific knowledge against skeptical doubt. But in recommending that we suspend judgment where we lack clear and distinct perception, he appropriates to the search for certainty some more ancient concerns which skepticism had shared with stoicism and epicureanism - concern with the right attitude to necessity, with whether or not we can control our destiny, with how to attain tranquillity and reconcile ourselves to mortality. Descartes' and Spinoza's discussions of the suspending of judgment are framed by a shared concern with those issues. In rejecting the will and insisting that the sole power of the mind resides in understanding, Spinoza assigns judgment to the realm of necessity, over which we have no control.   For Descartes, in contrast, there was an element in judgment which did lie under human control, and this was the mark of human exemption from the realm of necessity.   I want in this paper to put Spinoza's discussion of the Cartesian "ethics of belief" back into this wider context of shared concerns with issues which have largely receded from contemporary theory of knowledge.   This will not of itself remedy all that is unconvincing in Spinoza's attack on the distinction between will and intellect.   But it may show the differences between Descartes and Spinoza to be more complex and more interesting than they do if we ignore their textual and historical context.

Descartes' linking of judgment and volition, as Jonathan Bennett remarks with some puzzlement in *A Study of Spinoza's Ethics* ((1984), 159), cuts across the traditional distinction between cognitive and conative states.   Philosophers traditionally distinguish cognition - knowing, believing, understanding - from conation -   disliking, wanting, intending, trying.   Descartes, in contrast, as Bennett points out, puts sensing, imagining and abstract thought into one category; disliking, affirming and denying into another.   In repudiating the role of the will in judgment, Spinoza does not reaffirm the traditional dichotomy between the cognitive and the conative.   Rather, in identifying will and understanding, he transforms the concept of understanding, so that it become conative.   And he does this, here as in other parts of the *Ethics*, by pushing further points which Descartes had already stressed.

For Descartes the capacity to choose is the essence of the will; and this capacity is manifested in the "liberty to abstain" from judgment, from giving or withholding assent, which we discover in ourselves through enacting the method of doubt.   This capacity, he says in the *Principles*, is the greatest human perfection (I, 37) and in the *Passions of the Soul*, he presents it as the feature of the human mind wherein it most resembles God (III, 152).   In the fourth Meditation, he suggests that in fact the human will, considered in itself, is of no less stature than the divine will, the superiority of which arises solely from the greater knowledge and power conjoined with it.   It is the combination of the infinite, active faculty of the will with the finite, passive faculty of understanding which is the source of our errors; and we avoid error by schooling the will to assent only in the presence of ideas which are clear and distinct.

But there are for Descartes restraints on this power of autonomous choice; and Spinoza exploits them to collapse the Cartesian distinction between will and intellect into his own doctrine that the power of the mind resides in understanding only - an understanding which is itself subject to the necessities that govern the rest of nature.   In the lack of accompanying will, however, understanding does not remain a bare cognitive state.   It becomes conative, though not in a way that could be summed up in Descartes' idea of the will as wishing or shunning, seeking or avoiding.   The essence of Spinoza's conative understanding becomes not a choice but acquiescence.   And this is at the center of his differences with Descartes.

For Descartes the freedom of the will is inconsistent with subjection to external causes.   It is manifested in the fact that, in affirming or denying, seeking or avoiding what is placed before us by the understanding, we act without being conscious that any outside force constrains us. But clear and distinct ideas, as well as God's grace, determine the will without interfering with its freedom as "external" causes would. To be free, he says in Meditation Four, and in Part One of the *Principles*, it is not necessary to be indifferent as to the choice between two contraries. The indifference we feel when we are not swayed to one side by reason is in fact the lowest grade of liberty, showing a lack in knowledge rather than a perfection of will. If we always recognized clearly what was true or good we should have no trouble in deliberating as to what judgment or choice we should make, but be entirely free without ever being indifferent. The most striking illustration of this absence of indifference is of course Descartes' certainty of his own existence. He cannot prevent himself from believing that a thing so clearly conceived is true, not because he finds himself compelled to do so by some external cause, but simply because from great clearness in his mind there follows a great inclination of his will. He believes in his own existence, he says, with so much greater freedom or spontaneity as he possesses the less indifference towards it. In relation to other matters, and especially in relation to matter, the will lacks a compelling reason to assent; and the appropriate course is to withhold judgment. If he abstains from assenting when he does not perceive with sufficient clearness and distinctness, he acts rightly. But if he determines to deny or affirm, he no longer uses his free will as he should.

On this picture, Spinoza performs a devastatingly simple conceptual manoeuver. The belief in the will, grounded for Descartes in the lack of knowledge of external causes, becomes for Spinoza just that lack - ignorance of the external causes which govern our minds and their operations, along with the rest of nature. In the mind there is, he says, no free will, but the mind is determined to wish this or that by a cause, which has also been determined by another cause, and so on to infinity (IIP48). Even more ingenious, though to us rather less accessible, is the way Spinoza exploits Descartes' other crucial point - that the highest grade of freedom is the mind's "free" assent in the presence of clear and distinct perception. And he exploits it by following through the implications of what for Descartes was the antithesis of freedom in the mind - the mind's inclusion in a totality of finite causes.

The thought that human minds and their ideas should be, along with everything else, determined by external causes does not easily co-exist with our sense of freedom - imbued as we are with the spirit of Descartes', and later Kant's, commitment to the autonomous rational will. But for Spinoza the mind's subjection to external causes follows from the claim, which Descartes would have had difficulty rejecting, that strictly God is the only "free cause," able to act safely by the laws of his own nature (IP17C2). And it is a further consequence of God's being the only free cause that our minds and their ideas are included in a totality of thought, in which truth is affirmed freely, though necessarily, in a way that echoes and incorporates Descartes' "highest grade of liberty." The mind's subjection to external causes is rendered harmless by being accommodated into the "mind of God" which affirms the material universe. Spinoza's account of human judgment is framed by his treatment of the human mind as part of the infinite intellect of God. And that in turn is related to his discussion of divine will and understanding in Part One. But before turning to that I want to look briefly at what Descartes had to say about the will of God.

For Descartes our capacity to suspend judgment manifests the separation of human will and intellect, whereas in God's case they are inseparable. Having senses, he says in the *Principles*, involves passivity, which indicates dependence. Hence it cannot be supposed that God has senses, but only that he understands and wills. "And even his understanding and willing does not happen, as in our case, by means of operations that are in a certain sense distinct from one another; we must rather suppose that there is always a single identical and perfectly simple act by means of which he simultaneously understands, wills and accomplishes everything" (I, 37). The unity of divine intellect and will, as Descartes himself saw, suggests that everything happens of necessity, that God makes real everything of which he can form the idea, so that all things possible must come to be. But, as Leibniz later complained, Descartes drew back from the full consequences of that idea, which were made explicit by Spinoza.[2] One of the restraints for Descartes here was, of course, the freedom of the human will, in which we resemble God. If our wills are free, their results must remain indeterminate, although we cannot comprehend, he says in the *Principles*, how God leaves them indeterminate. In a familiar Cartesian move in response to the appearance of contradiction, he urges us not to try to think both free will and God's pre-ordaining at the same time (I, 40).

Descartes hankers strongly after necessities, although that conflicts with his other strong conviction - the freedom of the human will. His version of the mind's tranquillity is poised uneasily between the acceptance of necessity and the self-esteem that comes of our sense of control over our lives. In the *Passions of the Soul*, he speaks of the folly of vain desires, of wanting to change the things that cannot be changed. The remedy lies in schooling our desires to accord with true judgments, the proper arms of the soul. Desire is always good when it conforms to true knowledge, and cannot fail to be bad when it is founded on error. When we err in relation to desire it is because we do not sufficiently distinguish the things which depend entirely on us from those which do not so depend. Things which depend on us alone, that is on our own free will, cannot be too ardently desired, and we should always receive from them all the satisfaction we expected (II, 144).

For Descartes, then, we avoid vain desire through self-reliance, by retreating to what depends on us alone. All that lies beyond our control should be assigned to the inscrutable wisdom of providence. In a passage which seems to anticipate Spinoza, Descartes urges us to reflect that it is impossible that anything should happen in any other way than as it has been determined by providence from all eternity. The appearance that things happen by chance is founded only on the fact that we do not know all the causes that contribute to each effect (II, 145). The eternal decree of providence is so infallible and immutable that, apart from the things it has willed to leave dependent on our own free will, nothing happens to us which is not necessary and "as it were by fate," so that we should not desire that it happen otherwise. But because most of our desires extend to things which do not depend entirely on us, nor entirely on others, we ought to distinguish in them what does depend only on us, in order to limit our desire to that alone (II, 146).

Descartes' concept of the will amounts to this idea of what depends only on us. The will is the mind's principal activity, in which it exerts its freedom, expresses its autonomous selfhood. Yet what happens, he also thinks, is absolutely decreed by fate and immutable. We should nonetheless endeavour to choose by reason, not because we can have any confidence that it will affect the outcome, but because it strengthens and cultivates the "internal emotions" which the soul excites in itself. Following after virtue does not ensure a good outcome, as far as external events are concerned. The area of what depends only on us, it emerges, is really an inward zone of contentment. None of the troubles that come from elsewhere have any power to harm the soul. They serve rather to increase its joy, for in seeing that it cannot be harmed by them, the soul is more sensible of its perfection.

> And in order that our soul should have the means of happiness, it needs only to pursue virtue diligently. For if anyone lives in such a way that his conscience cannot reproach him for ever failing to do something he judges to be the best (which is what I here call 'pursuing virtue,' he will receive from this a satisfaction which has such power to make him happy that the most violent assaults of the passions will never have sufficient power to disturb the tranquillity of his soul. (*Passions of the Soul* II, 148)

To follow after virtue is to exercise the will aright. We can then rest content in our self-esteem, secure in the knowledge that the onslaught of external causes has no power to harm our true selves. In recommending that we suspend judgment in the lack of clear and distinct perception, Descartes accommodates judgment into this general account of following after virtue. Such judgments belong in the domain of what lies within our control. So human judgment escapes the dreaded state of subjection to external causes. Either it is elicited from us in a spontaneous and in the highest sense "free" response to clear and distinct perception, or, where it is lacking, it remains under the control of a free will, in the exercise of which we rightly esteem ourselves as superior to the rest of nature. This, then, is the ethical dimension of Descartes' redrawing of the boundaries between the cognitive and the conative. We avoid error through a virtuous exercise of free will. The practice of Cartesian method becomes an occasion for moral self-esteem, an expression of our superiority over the rest of nature, bound as it is by necessity. The foundations of knowledge are thus secured through an exercise of virtue.

That, then, is the ethical rationale of Descartes' account of judgment. The Spinozistic picture is of course very different. For him there is no providence. God acts solely by the laws of his own nature, without ends or purposes. He acts, as he says at IIP3, by the same necessity as that by which he understands himself. All that can be thought must be. It is a stronger version of the unity of divine intellect and will than Descartes ambivalently affirmed. There is no area of indeterminacy in which the human will might affect the course of events.

That God acts by necessity means too that any sense of intellect or will that would apply to him can provide no model for a human will, no respect in which we might find our minds to be god-like. The divine mind, precisely because it does produce everything that is thinkable, must, Spinoza says, be as different from ours, in respect of both intellect and will, as the dog in the heavens from the dog that barks - a resemblance in name only (IP17S).

Those who have asserted that God's intellect, God's will and God's power are one and the same, he suggests, have dimly grasped this truth. What it means is that the concept of will is subsumed into the idea of an understanding which is of it nature productive. Intellect, in any sense in which it could be applied to God, could not be, as our intellect is generally thought to be, "posterior to or simultaneous with" the things understood. God, by reason of his status as "free cause," is prior to all things. Whereas our intellect follows the truth, God's intellect precedes it. The truth is as it is because it exists objectively in the intellect of God. The relations of priority and posteriority here are of course not meant to be temporal ones. The point is that whereas our intellects must match themselves to an independent truth, the truth depends on God's intellect. And, given the kind of relationship that holds between Spinozistic attributes -each expressing completely all that can be - whatever material modes exist do not exist because God has had representations of them in thought. Spinoza's God, unlike the God of Leibniz, does not make things to accord with exemplars inhabiting his understanding, awaiting the exercise of creative will. Whatever is thinkable exists, but not because it has first been thought.

> ... the formal being of things which are not modes of thinking does not follow from the divine nature because [God] has first known the things; rather the objects of ideas follow and are inferred from their attributes in the same way and by the same necessity as that with which we have shown ideas to follow from the attribute of Thought (IIP6C).

God's power of thinking is equal to his realized power of action. So "whatever follows formally from God's infinite nature follows objectively in God from his idea in the same order and with the same connection" (IIP7C). All this is a consequence of Spinoza's version of substance: "... the thinking substance and the extended substance are one and the same substance, which is now comprehended under this attribute, now under that," a truth which was seen "as if through a cloud," by some of the Hebrews, when they maintained that "God, God's intellect, and the things understood by him are one and the same" (IIP7S).

So much for the divine intellect and will. What bearing does all that have on Spinoza's distinction between human will and intellect in Part Two? Our intellect and will, as he has stressed in Part One, must be utterly different in kind from any sense of intellect or will that could be applied to substance. We cannot look to the divine intellect or will to provide a model for our own. But our minds, though utterly different in kind from God, conceived as free cause, as *Natura Naturans*, are nonetheless part of the mind of God which is the realization of the total power of Substance under the attribute of thought. Wherever we are dealing with a mode of thought, it has to be referred not to *Natura Naturans* but to *Natura Naturata* (IP31). The mind of God, of which our minds are part, is the totality of all that follows, under the attribute of thought, from the power of substance. We are not part of the "dog in the heavens" intellect, but of the "dog that barks" version. But, with that proviso, we are part of the infinite intellect of God. When we say that the human mind perceives something, what that really means is that God has the idea, insofar as he is manifested through the nature of the human mind, although, insofar as the idea is adequately understood only in conjunction with other ideas outside the mind, the human mind perceives it only inadequately (IIP11C). This encompassing of the human mind and its subsidiary ideas in the infinite intellect of God, as Spinoza himself acknowledges, can be expected to bring his readers to a halt in comprehension - a mind-stopping suspension of judgment, as Descartes would have it. But if we do, as he urges, persist a little with this strange, but tantalizing suggestion, and try to see it in the context of his earlier discussion of the concepts of intellect and will, we get some insight into what is going on in his repudiation of Cartesian will.

Let us turn now to those notoriously inadequate considerations which Spinoza advances to justify his rejection of the Cartesian distinction between human will and intellect (IIP49C,S). There is in the mind, he says, no affirmation and negation, save that which an idea, in as much as it is an idea, involves. The mind's affirmation involves the idea which is affirmed; and, less obviously, the idea involves the affirmation. Spinoza gets to this conclusion by taking what seems an unreasonably favorable case: the affirmation that the three angles of a triangle are equal to two right angles can neither be nor be conceived without the idea of a triangle; and conversely, he says, the idea can neither be nor be conceived without the affirmation. Therefore the affirmation belongs to the essence of the idea of a triangle, and is nothing besides. What we have said of this volition, he continues, "inasmuch as we have selected it at random," may be said of any other volition, namely that it is nothing but an idea. The obvious rejoinder, of course, is that the example has not been taken at random. The flow-on from idea to affirmation, which does hold here, does not apply to what we would see as non-necessary truths.

It is certainly true that Spinoza has not chosen his example at random. But he has not chosen it merely out of a desire to trade on the peculiar features of a favorable case. It is an example which he used in Part One to illustrate the point that all things flow of necessity from the power of God.

> ... from God's supreme power, *or* infinite nature, infinitely many things in infinitely many modes, i.e., all things, have necessarily flowed, or always follow, by the same necessity and in the same way as from the nature of a triangle it follows, from eternity and to eternity, that its three angles are equal to two right angles. So God's omnipotence has been actual from eternity and will remain in the same actuality to eternity. And in this way, at least in my opinion, God's omnipotence is maintained far more perfectly. (IP17S)

From the perspective of an individual human mind, there is of course a world of difference between the idea of the triangle, in relation to the sum of its angles, and contingent truths in relation to their subjects. Spinoza does not deny that there is a distinction here. But for him it holds precisely because of the limited position held by an individual mind as part of the totality of thought. The necessity of the truth about the triangle rests on "common notions," which are equally present in the part and in the whole, and hence not subject to the error which results from our fragmentary awareness. About triangles, it is possible to have adequate knowledge, even if for any one of us there is a great deal about their properties we do not know. That is to say, in Spinoza's terminology, the adequate idea of the triangle can occur in God in so far as he constitutes an individual human mind. But there are other ideas which are not adequate in our minds - ideas, that is which are in God only in so far as he "has the idea of another thing together with the human Mind" (IIP11).

There is for us a very real distinction between the kind of knowledge we can have of triangles and our knowledge of contingent truths. Spinoza does not wish to deny that distinction. What he does want to say is that the distinction drops out within the total context of all the ideas in the mind of God. In relation to the totality of thought, there is for Spinoza no distinction of the kind Leibniz invokes between those truths which depend only on God's understanding and those that depend on his will. The belief in contingency in general, as in the particular case of belief in human free will, just amounts to our ignorance of causes. "In nature there is nothing contingent, but all things have been determined from the necessity of the divine nature to exist and produce an effect in a certain way" (IP29).

The adequacy which is lacking within the limits of my mind is supplied in wider contexts of which my mind is a part. To say that all things flow from God's nature with the same necessity as the sum of its angles flows from the nature of a triangle is to say that in the infinite intellect of God all truths are necessary. But their affirmation is not always encompassed in our minds. Ideas are always accompanied by affirmation, but the affirmation is not always "ours" in Descartes' sense. But is not this to admit that what in the intellect of God is affirmed is, in our mind, present without affirmation - that the idea which is affirmed in the mind of God is in our mind merely entertained? And is not that to admit that for the human mind, unlike the mind of God, we do need a distinction after all between will and intellect? But we can make that objection only if we detach the idea from the affirmation, which is precisely what Spinoza will not allow us to do. To continue the spatial metaphors, wherever an idea is, there the affirmation must be. To think that one and the same idea could be present, unaffirmed, in a human mind and, affirmed, in the mind of God, is to think, again, in terms of the Cartesian picture - of ideas as laid out like passive pictures on a panel, as Spinoza puts it, with the affirmation added from elsewhere.

Still, we may say, something must be able to be present, unaffirmed, in the human mind, or the whole problem would not arise. Spinoza's discussion of this in the illustration of the boy imagining a winged horse is not at first sight helpful in countering our Cartesian prejudices. Spinoza grants that the boy can imagine the horse without being in error, but denies that in the act of perception he does not make any affirmation. If the boy does have just the idea of the winged horse, he insists, then it is affirmed. "For what is perceiving a winged horse other than affirming wings of the horse" (IIP49S)? His mind may be in error, but again, that is not because of a misuse of free will, but just through the fragmentation involved in being part of a whole. We can explain the error, Spinoza thinks, without having to suppose that an idea lies unaffirmed in the mind. But what of the cases where the boy imagines the horse without affirming its existence, either because he judges correctly that it does not exist or because he does not judge one way or the other? Surely in those cases Spinoza must admit that there is in the mind an idea which is not affirmed? This is another of those points in the text where Spinoza's argumentation seems all too swift. What we want to see as an unaffirmed idea, he transforms into a different affirmed one - of the non-existence of the horse, or at any rate, an affirmation of something inconsistent with its existence. And what we want to see as the presence in the mind of an idea in the lack of any propositional attitude, he transforms into a perception of inadequacy. Suspension of judgment, he says, is strictly speaking a perception and not an exercise of free will. When we say that someone suspends judgment we are saying only that he does not perceive the matter in question adequately.

But surely we must be able to consider the original idea of the horse before we arrive at any of these outcomes? Spinoza's treatment of these cases is all too brief. But he means it to be taken in conjunction with a remark he makes in the preamble to his replies to the Cartesian position, where he warns of the need to have an accurate distinction between ideas, on the one hand, and words and images on the other. An idea, being a mode of thinking, does not, he says, consist in the image of anything, nor in words. Words and images are constituted by bodily motions, which do not at all involve the conception of thought (IIP49S). For Spinoza, images, which Descartes treated as confused ideas, present in the mind through the causal influence of body, are not ideas at all. The boy's "image" of the horse in so far as it does not involve affirmation is not an idea either. That ideas are not images but modes of thinking means that they do not mediate between judgment and an external material reality. Judgment involves the affirmation of something real, not the affirmation that something real corresponds to a mental representation. There are layerings of ideas of ideas, superimposed endlessly on the most fundamental level of knowledge. But Spinozistic ideas, to appropriate Wittgenstein's comment on language in the *Tractatus*, "reach right out to reality," articulating it, affirming it. What exactly is involved in this unmediated relationship between ideas and reality is by no means clear. But it is clear that the removal of the passive pictures involved in Cartesian judgment makes for a very different view of the act of judging.

Bennett, in his *Study of Spinoza's Ethics* (Bennett, 162-7), criticizes Spinoza's account of judgment as involving the implausible claim that all ideas come before the mind as beliefs. But this interpretation rests, I think, on construing the affirmation involved in a Spinozistic idea as if it were akin to the assent component in a Cartesian judgment. Spinoza is not saying that we believe compulsively whatever comes before the mind. That is mistaken in the same way as Leibniz's account of the implications of Spinoza's rejection of the distinction between divine will and intellect. Spinoza's God does not compulsively make real all the possibilities that occur to him. Rather, in the lack of a distinction between will and intellect, there is no array of possibles waiting to be made real. Leibniz's own treatment of the divine will choosing freely but without indifference the best, in the face of compelling reason, echoes Descartes' treatment of human judgment, choosing the truth. For Spinoza, in contrast, the human mind does not exert rational will in choosing the truth in the presence of compelling reason. And it is also misleading to present it as compulsively believing image-like ideas which come before it for judgment. The array of passive ideas awaiting the mind's choice disappears. It is true that the mind is aware of images. But they are bodily traces, affections of body - part of the totality of material modes which correspond to the totality of thought.

Where does all this leave skepticism? If everything happens as a necessary expression in thought or matter of the full power of substance, the supposed problem of skepticism as an issue of which ideas our minds should affirm disappears. What remains of skepticism is the tranquillity which the ancient skeptics thought would ensue from the suspension of judgment. But there is no suggestion that the existence of the world is open to doubt, or that the wise mind should withdraw to contemplate its own contents. The infinite intellect of God, the total expression in thought of the power of substance, affirms in an intellectual love the corresponding order of material things, whose existence is not at issue. And the human mind participates in that, however inadequate and partial may be its understanding of its place in it.

Love, on Descartes' account of it in the *Passions of the Soul* (II, 79, 80) is the mind's voluntary uniting of itself with the loved object, an act of the will. For Spinoza the wish to unite with the loved object cannot be a free decision of the mind. For he has, he thinks, shown that to be fictitious. It becomes instead "a Satisfaction in the lover on account of the presence of the thing loved, by which the lover's Joy is strengthened or at least encouraged" (III Def.Aff. 6). Applied to the love of wisdom, the point becomes this. We do not, as Descartes thought, "choose the truth" as a free response to a compelling reason in the form of clear and distinct perception. Nor do we follow virtue by training a faculty of will to withhold judgment where that compelling reason is lacking. Judgment is not a matter of wishing or avoiding. That is not to say it is compulsive. Nor is it to say it is a bare cognitive act, devoid of conative force. There is no choice here. But we do find a contentment in knowledge. In terms of Descartes' distinction, that contentment comes not from self-satisfaction in the right exercise of a god-like will, but from an affirmation of necessity. For Descartes the key to all the virtues and the remedy for the disorder of the passions is reflection on our free will (*Passions of the Soul*, III, 152, 153). For Spinoza, in the lack of the will, that role shifts to intellect, now construed as an intellectual love, a conative understanding. The mind rests content in affirmation of and acquiescence in body, the awareness of which defines its being, although it knows its understanding of body is inevitably partial and confused.

All this amounts to a richer view of our intellectual lives than the disagreeable picture of our minds as compulsive yea-sayers, to which Bennett reduces Spinoza's account of judgment. But it involves, of course, a view of mind and world which is in many ways alien to us, influenced, as we are, by Cartesian theory of knowledge.

1. Descartes quotations are from *The Philosophical Writings of Descartes*, tr. by J. Cottingham, R. Stoothoff, D. Murdoch (Cambridge: Cambridge University Press, 1985). Spinoza quotations are from Curley (1985).
2. Leibniz, Letter to Philipp, end of January, 1680; Gerhardt, IV, 283-4; in L. E. Loemker, Leibniz: *Philosophical Papers and Letters*, 2nd ed. (Dordrecht, Holland: Reidel, 1969), 273.

ANTI-FALSIFICATIONISM: SPINOZA'S THEORY OF EXPERIENCE AND EXPERIMENTS

WIM KLEVER
Erasmus University, Rotterdam

Spinoza has no place in books on history of chemistry, like his opponent in the discussion on saltpetre, Robert Boyle. Neither is his name mentioned in books on the history of physics and optics like the name of his contemporaries, Christiaan Huygens, Descartes and Leibniz. He discussed in his correspondence the hot items of mathematics and natural science and did experimental work on various fields. He studied a lot of books on anatomy, astronomy and mathematics. But his name as a natural scientist, mathematician or experimental "philosopher" is virtually non-existent.

Still Spinoza *loved experiments* and tried to arrange them wherever possible. This becomes clear not only from his research report Ep. 6 & 13, but also from his endeavour to find out the structure of gold (Ep. 40 to J. Jelles), performed in the presence of many other people,[1] and from his effort to create an experimental situation for the measuring of hydrostatic laws. [2] Again he did work with other people: *Eramus tres adeo, ac quidem possibile erat occupati...* and came to a conclusion on the ground of his experimental work (*Re ergo hisque experimentis perpensis cogor concludere...*) His work in optics was likewise built on experimental discoveries: the discussions with Hudde (Ep. 36), Jelles (Ep. 39, 40), Leibniz (Ep. 46) and Tschirnhaus (Ep. 83) reveal that optics was for Spinoza not only a theoretical but also a practical business.

In general *experience has a place of paramount importance* in Spinoza's scientific practice and in his theory of science. On the first page of his *Tractatus Politicus* he rejects the speculative and mainly satirical writings of the philosophers in favour of the theories of the practical politicians, because these have learnt lessons from experience: *Docuit nimirum eosdem experientia, vitia fore, donec homines... Nam quoniam experientiam magistram habuerunt, nihil docuerunt, quod ab usu remotum esset.* Experience has to be our teacher.

The whole *Ethics* is a theoretical, but nevertheless also an *empirical work,* comparable with modern psychological and sociological sciences which have an empirical bias. It is without any doubt Spinoza's intention to present an exact description of the visible relationships between things or passions and to discard by those positivistic descriptions the usual fictions about reality. I cannot agree with Bennett's assertion that the "*Ethics* is noted for playing down experience in favour of reasoning" (Bennett (1984), 23). It would be better to say, that the *Ethics* is a strongly rationalistic work, in which the reasoning is not detrimental to the experience but draws upon it. In Spinoza's view it is impossible that there is an opposition between reason and experience. It is only fiction or imagination which may be in conflict with experience.

Let us have a look at some passages in which experience is invoked. I quote this time from Shirley's translation:

And although daily experience cried out against this and showed by any number of examples that blessings and disasters befall the godly and the ungodly alike without discrimination, they did not on that account abandon their ingrained prejudice.[3]

Prejudicia are refuted by the *infinita exempla* of the *experientia in dies*:

Yet I do not think that I am far from the truth, since all the postulates that I have assumed contain scarcely anything inconsistent with experience; and after demonstrating that the human body exists just as we sense it (IIP13C), we may not doubt experience (IIP17S p. 78).

Spinoza claims that his six basic postulates (after IIP13) are a general formulation of what is established by experience (*quod constat experientia*); the truth-value of experience (*de qua nobis non licet dubitare*) was already demonstrated in IIP13C: "that human body exists according as we sense it." Experience is certainty about or consciousness of what happens in our body. Science has to respect and to integrate experiential knowledge, which is surely not fully possible in the most comprehensive postulates.[4]

Yet although the matter admits of no shadow of doubt, I can scarcely believe, without the confirmation of experience, that men can be induced to examine this view without prejudice, so strongly are they convinced that at the mere bidding of the mind the body can now be set in motion, now be brought to rest, and can perform any number of actions...

'But,' they will say, 'Whether or not we know by what means the mind moves the body, experience tells us, that unless the mind is in a fit state to exercise thought, the body remains inert...' Now as to the first point, I ask, does not experience also tell them that if, on the other hand, the body is inert, the mind likewise is not capable of thinking? (IIIP2S).

Rem experientia comprobavero - Experientia etiam docet. Experience is an authority for Spinoza; and he tries to convince his readers by an appeal to this authority.

What we have just demonstrated is also confirmed by daily experience with so many convincing examples as to give rise to the common saying: 'Man is a God to man.' Yet it is rarely the case that men live by the guidance of reason (IVP35S).

Experientia... testatur... testimoniis. Experience is the chief witness in the trial in which we, reasoning and arguing, try to find out the laws of human individual and social life.

I have no reason to hold that a body does not die unless it turns into a corpse; indeed, experience seems to teach otherwise. (*Aliud suadere videtur*) (IVP39S).

Experience is our *advisor*.

The more this knowledge (namely, that things are governed by necessity) is applied to particular things which we imagine more distinctly and more vividly, the greater is the power of the mind over the emotions, as is testified by experience. For we see... (VP6S).

According to Spinoza *experience testifies* to his most paradoxical laws. It all depends on one's understanding, as is most ingenuously explained in VP23S:

Nevertheless, we feel and experience that we are eternal. For the mind senses those things that it conceives by its understanding just as much as those which it has in its memory. Logical proofs are the eyes of the mind, whereby it sees and observes things. (*Mentis enim oculi, quibus res videt observatque, sunt ipsae demonstrationes*).

There is no difference between this Spinozistic standpoint and that of Wittgenstein: *Während des Beweises wird unsere Anschauung geändert ... Unsere Anschauung wird umgemodelt... Der Beweis leitet unsere Erfahrungen sozusagen in bestimmte Kanäle.*[5] *In einem andern Gedankenraum - möchte man sagen - schaut das Ding anders aus.*[6]   The way we understand things and their relationships by means of a rational (re-)construction and *concatenatio* is decisive for the way we look at them and the results of this observation.

Our promenade through the five parts of the Ethics has brought us to the conviction that Spinoza not only laid high value on the evidence of experience, but moreover that he realised that the language of experience is different according to the level of intelligence. Whoever is drowned in fictions and prejudice will find experiential confirmation of his irrational belief just as the scientist or mathematician whose eyes are enlightened by reason sees around him everywhere the confirmation of his paradoxical propositions about the necessary structure of reality. *That means that the evidence of experience can never be considered an independent and unambiguous proof.*

Perhaps we are now prepared to give serious attention to some passages in which Spinoza seems to row against the current of his time and of our age. Spinoza, the experimenter, who devoured all literature of the new physical science (cf. the list of his library), expresses in these texts an apparently anti-empirical attitude.

Spinoza writes in Ep. 10 (to the very learned young man Simon de Vries) the following disconcerting lines:

You ask me whether we need experience to know whether the Definition of any thing is true. To this I reply, that we need experience only for those things which cannot be inferred from the definition of the thing, as, for example, the existence of Modes (for this cannot be inferred from the definition of the thing); but not for those things whose existence is not distinguished from their essence, and therefore is inferred from their definition. *Indeed no experience will ever be able to teach us this, for experience does not teach any essences of things.* The most it can do is to determine our mind to think only of certain essences of things. So since the existence of the attributes does not differ from their essence, we will not be able to grasp it by any experience (Curley (1985), 196).

The hard and perhaps bitter kernel of this letter is the stiff thesis: *experientia nullas rerum essentias docet.* You cannot learn anything about the essence of things, about their necessary and lawlike structure by experience. Nobody today and in those days of the quickly developing empirical science does believe in the truth of this rationalistic idiosyncracy. Again, as in so many other fields, Spinoza is completely abnormal, anomalous. By his reading, his practical work, his frequent contacts with many excellent scientists (besides the already mentioned persons also: Kerckrinck, Bontekoe, Velthuysen, Stensen, Pufendorf, Helvetius, etc.) he was an active and respected member of the scientific community of his days; but, in his philosophical interpretation of the scientific praxis, he stays alone.

But let us be careful before we indulge in our inclination to condemn such a stranger in our Jerusalem. If Curley's definition of rationalism is correct, Spinoza cannot be caught under this rubrique. "Experience, for the rationalist, plays no fundamental role, either in the discovery or in the verification of scientific truth."[7] In Spinoza's just quoted statement a *twofold* role (instead of none) is awarded to experience:

1. Experience is the only possible way to get some (if not scientific) knowledge about the existence of modes. From our meteorological knowledge we cannot deduce that we will have sunshine or rain tomorrow in Chicago; we will know that by experience; the weather forecast is not safe enough.

2. Experience compels us (*mentem nostram determinat*) to form thoughts about (*ut cogitet circa...*) the essential structure of things. It induces the mind to conceive the world of changing and seemingly incoherent things in a certain way, because we cannot be content with complete casuality, inconsistency and impredictability.

I don't exaggerate, it seems to me, if I claim that this second function of experience is very important in the eyes of Spinoza and that science could not be generated without this necessitating pushing power from below, which forces the mind to think. Experience is the way we are acquainted with the world as far as it works on our body, without knowing how everything comes about. The unrelated, confused and swerving ideas produced don't reveal the definition, but do suggest something. Is it far fetched,then, to say - in the words of Curley - that they play a "fundamental role... in the discovery... of scientific truth?" In the second part of Ep. 10 Spinoza explains that not only attributes as such but also finite "things and their affections" can become object of science (in his terminology *aeternae veritates*). Well, their existence (that was the first role) can only be known by experience, so that also for this reason experience cannot be missed.

There is another disconcerting passage in Spinoza's work on our subject, which is not notorious because nobody reads *Descartes' Principles of Philosophy*, pretending that only Descartes' philosophy can be found in it. In the second part of this work, after the sixth proposition ("Matter is indefinitely extended and the matter of the heavens is one and the same as that of the earth"), which is demonstrated with the axiom that extension cannot be perceived by the human intellect under any limits, we find a very long scholium, in which Spinoza himself (he is not expounding Descartes now) refutes the objections of Zeno against the possiblility of local motion. In Cartesian physics - and Spinoza agrees with this point[8] - local motion is the only possible motion, "since we clearly and distinctly understand that extension is not capable of any motion except local motion nor can we even imagine any other motion" (Curley (1985), 270). Therefore, Spinoza takes up not only Zeno, but also Diogenes, who thought to refute Zeno experimentally.

> Zeno, they say, denied local motion, because of various arguments, which were refuted by Diogenes the Cynic in his fashion, i.e. by walking about the School in which Zeno was teaching these doctrines and thus disturbing those who were listening to Zeno... Someone who is deceived by Zeno's argument might think that the senses show us something (viz. motion) which the intellect finds absolutely contradictory, so that the mind would be deceived even about those things that it perceives clearly and distinctly with the aid of the intellect. To prevent any such confusion, I shall set out here Zeno's main arguments and show that they rest only on false prejudices, because he did not have a true concept of matter (Curley (1985), 270).

From this introduction it is already clear that according to Spinoza the senses are not able to demonstrate something (*ostendere*) against our rational expectations. He does not accept the validity of Diogenes' empirical falsification of Zeno's peculiar theories. This was his way of refuting Zeno (*suo more*), not Spinoza's *mos geometricus*. Whoever "has learnt the elements of mathematics" (*qui elementa matheseos tantum didicit*, PPA9 Exp) knows about infinity and continuity of matter. After having pulverized Zeno's sophisms with the help of AA9,10, and PP3,5, Spinoza rounds off his scholium with a *personal remark about epistemology*:

> But here I should like my Readers to note, that I have opposed my reasonings to Zeno's reasonings (*rationibus... rationes*), and therefore that I have *refuted him by reason* (*ratione redarguisse*), not by the senses, as Diogenes did. For *the senses* cannot *provide* (*suggerere*) anything else to one who is seeking the truth except *the phenomena of nature, by which he is determined to investigate their causes* (*quibus determinatur ad illorum causas investigandas*). *They can never show him that something is false* (*non autem umquam quid... falsum esse ostendere*) that the intellect has clearly and distinctly found to be true. For so we judge. And therefore, this is *our Method*: to demonstrate the things we put forward by reasons perceived clearly and distinctly by the intellect, and to regard as negligible whatever the senses say that seems contrary to those reasons. As we have said, the *senses* can only determine the intellect to inquire into this matter rather than that one. *They cannot convict it of falsity* (*non autem falsitatis... arguere*), when it has perceived something clearly and distinctly (Curley (1985), 273).

Not only does this interesting quote confirm the twofold function of experience as we read it in Ep. 10, namely, 1. to suggest what is apparently the case, and 2. to put us on the way of discovery and research, it provides us also with an unambiguous rejection of its capacity to falsify our eventual clear understanding of causal relationships.

In these texts Spinoza travels on the highest tops of the mountains, far above the low grounds of Popperianism or positivism. Of course, observed facts can falsify and refute other... opinions, conjectures, hypothetical semi-rational constructions. Spinoza does not deny this sort of "elimination": *imaginationes... evanescunt... quia aliae occurrunt iis fortiores quae rerum quas imaginamur, prasesentem existentiam secludunt* (IVP15). What he maintains, however - and that is far more interesting - is that mathematical theorems (*or* "eternal truths" *or* "adequate ideas") are unattainable and invulnerable for contrary experiential evidence or data of the simple, unenlightened observation.

Above the clouds *Spinoza is not alone* but in companionship with other philosophers and scientists of different times. *Es winken sich die Groszen aller Zeiten über den Wolken* (K. Jaspers). *Protagoras* was a forerunner with his "Man is the measure" - proposition; *Plato* also, who states in his *Phaedo* (75d) that with the concepts is sealed what there is. Most obvious is the agreement between the mathematical natural science of *Galileo* and Spinoza's attitude in these epistemological matters. In case of conflict, they both prefer the guidance of mathematical reason above the suggestions of experience, which they, therefore, don't allow to refute or falsify the insights of reason. I quote the famous passage in the *Dialogue concerning the two chief world systems* where Galileo exclaims:

> Nor can I ever sufficiently admire the outstanding acumen of those who have taken hold of this opinion and accepted it as true; they have *through sheer force of intellect done such violence to their own senses as to prefer what reason told them over that which sensible experience plainly showed them to the contrary...* There is no limit to my astonishment when I reflect that Aristarchus and Copernicus were able to make reason so conquer sense, that, in defiance of the latter,the former became mistress of their belief."[9]

Verification or falsification of ideas can only be performed by other ideas. *Cogitatio alia cogitatione terminatur. At corpus non terminatur cogitatione, nec cogitatio corpore* (E ID2Exp). *Ideae non ipsa ideata sive res perceptas pro causa efficiente agnoscunt* (IIP5). Spinoza joins *G. Bachelard, J. Cavaillès* and *L. Wittgenstein* in their common rejection of empirical falsification of theories. A theory becomes stronger or weaker to the degree to which it can or cannot be integrated in the totality of our beliefs, without the tribunal of sense experience (against Quine). The adequate ideas are themselves the measure, the tribunal of "reality" and truth. Proof and disproof in science is a purely conceptual process.[10]

Coming back to Spinoza with less mistrust and conceit than before, we'll now pay some attention to the discussion which he, through the mediator Oldenburg, had with Robert Boyle. A. Rupert and Marie Boas Hall have written a fascinating paper on this discussion: "Philosophy and natural philosophy: Boyle and Spinoza."[11] They stress the historical and systematic relevance of this discussion: "In fact the central issue at stake beween rationalism and empiricism emerges more clearly in Boyle's debate with Spinoza than it does in any of Newton's controversies concerning scientific method" (*Op. cit.*, p. 242). They show that the fact that Boyle was roughly speaking right and Spinoza wrong in precise chemical questions is only of minor significance against the background of Spinoza's superior interpretation of chemical experiments and theory. "To Spinoza empiricism as a philosophy of science was either useless or misleading. The best guarantee of truth was offered by formal systems of reasoning" (*Op. cit.*, p. 244). Experiments don't have the power of proving the necessary structure of reality. What can they achieve, then? This aspect of the discussion is neglected by the Halls. It is, again, very instructive, to have a close look on the relevant texts. But I shall confine my selection and commentary to the epistemological headline and leave other things out.

> He (Boyle) infers from his experiment concerning the reconstitution of Niter that Niter is something heterogeneous, consisting of fixed and volatile parts, whose nature (so far as the Phenomena are concerned, at least) is nonetheless very different from the nature of the parts of which it is composed, though it arises solely from the mixture of these parts. But I would say that for this conclusion to be regarded as valid (*bona*), a further experiment seems to be required, which would show that Spirit of Niter is not really Niter and cannot be solidified or crystallized without the aid of the alkaline salt (Curley (1985), 173-174).

Videtur mihi adhuc requiri aliquod experimentum. No contempt of experiments on the side of Spinoza; on the contrary, he positively appreciates their role in the discussion.

What is more, Spinoza has set up some experiments himself in the barn of the Spinoza-house in Rijnsburg and is proud of the results:

> To make this clear, I shall set out briefly what occurs to me as the simplest explanation of this phenomenon of the reconstitution of Niter, and at the same time add two or three quite easy experiments which to some extent confirm (*confirmatur*) this explanation (Curley (1985), 174).

The message of these experiments is related in a consistent and very cautious language:

> - pergam iam ad experimenta, quae hanc explicationem comprobare *videntur* ...
> - secundum experimentum, et quod ostendere *videtur* partes fixas non nisi faeces nitri esse...
> - tertium experimentum quod indicare *videtur*...

Spinoza reproaches Boyle for his endeavour to prove something by artifcial experiments which is evident by reason and can be seen much more clearly in natural phenomena than by any experiment:

> In par. 13-18 the Distinguished Gentleman tries to show that all the tangible qualities depend only on motion, shape, and the remaining mechanical affections. Since he

does not present these demonstrations as mathematical, it is not necessary to examine whether they are completely convincing. But meanwhile, I don't know why the Distinguished Gentleman strives so anxiously to infer this from his experiment (*colligere ex suo experimento*), since it has already been more than adequately demonstrated by Bacon and later by Descartes. Nor do I see that this experiment offers us more illuminating evidence[12] than other experiments which are obvious enough.[13] For as far as heat is concerned, is the same (conclusion) not just as clear from the fact that if two pieces of wood are rubbed together, though they are cold, they produce a flame simply from that motion? Or that if lime is sprinkled with water, it becomes hot? As for sound, I do not see that anything more remarkable is to be found in this experiment, than in the boiling of ordinary water and in many other things. Regarding the Color, to restrict myself to things which are probable,[14] I shall say only that we see all green plants changing into so many and such different colors. Again, if bodies that give off a foul smell are shaken, they give off a still more offensive smell particularly if they become somewhat warm. Finally, sweet wine is changed into vinegar, and similarly with many other things. (Curley (1985), 179).

Spinoza does not disagree with Boyle's assertion that natural phenomena have to be explained mechanically. This is mathematically demonstrated by other physicists and becomes apparent from daily experience which has, in his eyes, no less worth than artificial experiments. He challenges, however, the pretention, that experiments (or experience) can be employed to prove or demonstrate something convincingly (*an prorsus convincant*). And he does not concede that Boyle's specific point is made probable by his experiment and daily experience. It is not up to me to decide on this last point, who is right or wrong. At stake is the question whether Spinoza is right in stating his general thesis, that experience does never definitely decide the truth or falsehood of an opinion. On occasion of another remark of Boyle in that direction, Spinoza makes the quite bold statement: *Nunquam chymicis neque aliis experimentis nisi demonstratione et computatione aliquis id comprobare poterit*. It seems that here Curley's translation for this crucial sentence is slightly misleading: "No one will ever be able to 'confirm' (WK: no, to 'prove') this by Chemical experiments, nor by any others, but only by demonstration and computation." According to my understanding of the English language, "confirmation" is weaker than "proof" or "verification," which excludes definitely the possibility of falsehood. *Comprobare* is one of Spinoza's words for mathematical demonstration. Later on in this discussion we will find a confirmation of the weak sense of *confirmare*.[15]

Why does Spinoza disagree with Boyle's opinion that experiments can prove that something is the case? He without delay provides us with a statement that must be considered as an argument:

For it is by reasoning and calculation that we divide bodies to infinity, and consequently also the forces required to move them. But we can never prove this by experiments.

Innumerable and *endless are the bodies and the forces, which together are responsible for a phenomenon.* A phenomenon cannot be looked upon as the product of a finite number of causes. The mathematical concept of the infinite extension of matter forbids us to accept an end point for the process of dividing matter.[16] Of course, this endless quantity of causes can never be grasped or made visible by experiments, which would be, however, necessary to get an adequate proof of the constitutive elements and sufficient causes of a phenomenon. There cannot be any proportion between the infinity of forces and the few factors which can be confirmed by artificial experiments. How would it be possible to show infinite bodies and forces and in this way prove something to be the effect of them?

Boyle's reaction is told by Oldenburg in Ep. 11. Boyle is not disconcerted by Spinoza's objections against the content of his physiological essays. He is polite, but stays with his theory. "He adds that he had shown that the thing occurs thus (*se ostendisse rem ita se habere*), but has not discussed how it occurs, which seems to be the subject of your conjecture." Further, he blames Spinoza for having argued from a gratuitous hypothesis, which has no experiential basis at all: "Nor does our Author see that the necessity of that very fine matter, which you also allege is proved from any phenomena. Rather it is assumed simply from the Hypothesis that a vacuum is impossible." Leaving aside this interesting aspect of the physics of both learned natural scientists, I turn to an interpretative remark of the mediator Boyle, which gives a new impulse to the discussion by hitting the real issue:

> Our Boyle is one of those whose trust in reason is not so great that they have no need for the Phenomena to agree with their reason (*cum ratione convenire phaenomena*) (Curley (1985), 199).

Although Spinoza complains in Ep. 13 that Boyle has only superficially answered his objections (*obiter et quasi aliud agendo*), one can discover in this letter that he is inspired by the remark about the scientists longing for the agreement between phenonema and reason. He makes a clarifying distinction to explain in what sense he accepts and rejects this position.

> I pass now to the experiments I offered to confirm my explanation - not absolutely, but as I expressly said, to some extent (*experimenta quae attuli, non ut absolute, sed... aliquo modo meam explicationem confirmarem*)...

After six lines already he repeats the same formula with a slight variation:

> For as I expressly said, I did not offer these experiments that they might confirm absolutely what I said (*ut iis ea quae dixi, prorsus confirmarem*). It was only that these experiments, which I had said and *showed to agree with reason, seemed* to confirm those thing to some extent (Curley (1985), 210).

Even the partial confirmation can at most be seeming or apparent. Experiments can at best bring to light a certain aspect of the endless complicated network of causal relationships. As an experimental philosopher Boyle cannot boast of something which is extraordinary or new. Also Bacon and Descartes (and Spinoza himself) have strived for the correspondence between the phenomena and their reason (*ipsos etiam voluisse, ut cum eorum ratione convenirent phaenomena*).   And they all have (just like Boyle) tried to discover the mechanical laws which produce the phenomena.   They have failed sometimes. How these mechanical laws exactly work, cannot be incontrovertibly proven (*non evincitur*) by experiments.   Neither in spontaneous experience nor in artificial experiments do we know all the things which are in the game.   In this aspect the acceptance of a *magnum discrimen* (as Boyle wants) is unjustifiable to Spinoza.   In the one case as in the other our acquaintance remains very abstract:

> Again, I do not know why the Distinguished Gentleman is *bold enough to maintain that he knows what Nature contributes* (*quae natura adferat*) in the matter we are speaking of.   By what reasoning, I ask, will he be able to show us (*ostendere*) that that heat has not arisen from some very fine matter?   Was it perhaps because so little of the original weight was lacking?   But even if none was lacking, one could, in my judgment at least, infer nothing.   For we see how easily a thing can be imbued with a color from a very small quantity of matter and not on that account become sensibly heavier or lighter.   *So it is not without reason that I can doubt whether perhaps certain things have concurred, which could not have been observed by any sense perception...* (Curley (1985), 211).

As a mathematician Spinoza had a clear idea of the disproportion between the infinity of causes, responsible for a phenomenon, and the finite number of causes, which can be shown at work in it.   This (and no anti-experimental attitude) was the deeper reason of his maintaining the thesis, that experiments and/or experience can never prove or disprove definitely that something is or is not (necessarily) the case.   It was his mathematical genius (the expression is from the pen of Oldenburg)[17] that saved him, so to say, from the naive empiricist standpoint.   The experience which is not determined by the intellect (*quae non determinatur ab intellectu*, TdIE, §19) can never reach certainty.   It always hits on "accidents" (TdIE 26-27) and must necessarily remain *vagus*, i.e. "swerving" or "wandering."[18]

In a footnote to this place Spinoza remarks, that he is referring to "empiricorum et recentium philosophorum procedendi methodum," which is a clear hint that not only Bacon but also Boyle is included.

Coming to the end of my paper, I must confess that I don't find much support for my defense of Spinoza's theory of science in the available literature. "Spinoza's doctrine of reason - as it is expounded in the Treatise - is confused. It does not seem to be consistently thought out," writes Edwin Curley.[19]   The Halls speak about "a weakness in Spinoza to evade Boyle's empiricism by hypotheses."[20]   In a recent article,[21] E. Yakira, who considers the controversy between Boyle and Spinoza as *un épisode secondaire*, tries to explain *le refus de Spinoza d'accorder un rôle essentiel à l'expérience dans la confirmation de la philosophie mécanique, qui l'empêche de voir juste et qui l'amène à critiquer Boyle.* Spinoza would be *très inattentif à la vraie nature de l'expérience scientifique - ce qui est quand même remarquable après Galilée.*   In the appendix to his translaton and edition of the spurious treatises *Algebraic calculation of the Rainbow* and *Calculation of Chances,*[22] Petry tells us that "the difficulties he (Spinoza) creates for himself by modelling his basic philosophical position exclusively on pure mathematics and so excluding himself (! w.k.) from any easy dialogue with the empirical sciences, are by no means typical of the period" (p.141). The new volume on *Spinoza and the sciences* (Reidel 1986) which is still in print could not yet be explored for this paper.[23] But... I remain hopefull that some day some other people will see, with me, that Spinoza was right, after all.

1. *Diversi quoque alii domini, tum temporis praesentes, hoc ita sese habere experti sunt.* See also Ep. 72 to Schuller, *in fine.*
2. *...curavi ut mihi fabricaretur tubus ligneus* - Ep. 41.
3. E IApp. *Spinoza: The Ethics and selected letters.* (Hackett, 1982), p. 58.
4. Cf. PP III: "quamvis sic orta non fuisse probe sciaimus," I/227/22.
5. *Bemerkungen über die Grundlagen der Mathematik III*, 30-31, Suhrkamp Ed. VI, 240.
6. *Bemerkungen über die Philosophie der Psychologie*, Oxford, I (1980), 98.
7. E. M. Curley, "Experience in Spinoza's theory of knowledge," in Grene (1973), 25.
8. Cf. A. Lécrivain: "Spinoza et la physique cartésienne," *Cahiers Spinoza* (1977-78) I, 235-236, II, 93-206; P. van der Hoeven, *De cartésiaanse fysica in het denken van Spinoza*, Leiden, 1973.
9. S. Drake, Berkeley, (1953), 328.
10. Cf. Bachelard, *L'activité rationaliste de la physique contemporaine* (PUF, 1951); J. Cavaillès, *Sur la théorie et logique du science*, Paris, 1976; L. Wittgenstein, *Über Gewissheit*, (Harper Torchbooks, 1969); G.G. Granger, "Jean Cavaillès: Ou la montée vers Spinoza," *Etudes Philosophiques* (1947), 271-279; H. Sinacoeur, "L'épistemologie de Jean Cavaillès," *Critique* (1985), 975-988.
11. In *Mélanges Alexandre Koyré. L'aventure de l'esprit.* Tome II (Paris: Hermann, 1964).
12. *luculentiora nobis praebere indicia.*
13. *alia satis obvia experimenta*; Curley translates wrongly: 'which are readily enough available'). [Editor's note: I took *obvia* to have the sense of *commonplace* and I still think that is right. (EMC)]
14. *ut tantum probabilia adferam*; Curley is also wrong in translating 'provable' instead of 'probable'). [Editor's note: *Provable* is one classical meaning of *probabilis* and that translation is confirmed by the NS (*bewijsbar*). Had Spinoza meant *probable* he probably would have used *verisimilis*. It is suggestive that he should regard these ordinary experiences as proofs. (EMC)]
15. [Editor's note: There's no real disagreement here. As my entry in the Glossary-Index (p.630) was meant to convey, I think that in the quotation from Boyle (IV/29/12) *comprobare* means *confirm*, whereas in Spinoza's comment on that passage (IV/29/14,17) it means *prove*. That is why "confirm" appears in single quotes in Spinoza's comment. (EMC)]
16. Cf. PP IIPP3,5; Ep. 32: *et quoniam natura universi non est ... limitata sed absolute universa, ideo ab hac infinitae potentiae natura eius partes infinitis modis moderantur et infinitas variationes pati coguntur*; VP65: *Mens res omnes necessarias esse intelligit et infinito causarum nexu determinari ad existendum et operandum.*
17. Ep. 16: "mathematici tui ingenii acumine."
18. Cf. my "Remarques sur le *Tractatus de Intellectus Emendatione* (experientia vaga, paradoxa, ideae fictae)." *Revue des sciences philosophiques et theologiques* 71 (1987) 101-115.
19. "Experience in Spinoza's Theory of Knowledge," p. 49.
20. "Philosophy and Natural Philosophy: Boyle and Spinoza," p. 256.
21. "Boyle et Spinoza," *Archives de Philosophie* 51 (1988), 107-124.

22. Dordrecht 1985. On the basis of a newly discovered document J. de Vet had already made it sure that these anonymously published treatises cannot be from the hand of Spinoza. See his "Was Spinoza de auteur van 'Stelkonstige Reeckening van den Regenboog' en van 'Reeckening van Kanssen'? *Tijdschrift voor Filosofie*, 45 (1983), 602-639; W.N.A. Klever, "Nieuwe argumenten tegen de toeschrijving van het auteurschap van de SRR en RK aan Spinoza," *ibid.* 47 (1983), 493-502. Petry's loose argumentation, in which, by means of a series of "might-be's," he sticks to the traditional ascription to Spinoza against historical and philological evidence, is analysed and refuted by De Vet in *Studia Spinozana*, 2 (1986), 267-309.

23. I have done it after the congress in my review of this book in *Studia Spinozana*, III (1988).

IN ORDER TO INTERPRET SPINOZA'S THEORY OF THE THIRD KIND OF KNOWLEDGE: SHOULD INTUITIVE SCIENCE BE CONSIDERED *PER CAUSAM PROXIMAM* KNOWLEDGE?

FILIPPO MIGNINI
Université de Macerata

The third kind of knowledge, or intuitive science, is considered by Spinoza to be the highest form of knowledge and the expression of the maximum perfection which can be attained by man. It is surprising, therefore, that it has not been studied with the same methodology and interest with which the doctrine of the imagination was examined, for example, or to a lesser extent, that of reason. I do not intend discussing the reasons behind the different treatment meted out to the three kinds of knowledge by Spinoza scholars: I merely want to point out that the following analysis can be regarded as a provisional chapter toward a much broader study which will require further historical and philological research and a more complex critical articulation.

I should also state that the logical order in which I will examine the works pertaining to this study (*Tractatus de intellectus emendatione, Korte Verhandeling, Ethica*) implies, in my opinion, a corresponding chronological order, as I have tried to demonstrate elsewhere.[1] The following analysis, therefore, with its various assumptions and conclusions, constitutes a moment and a standard of judgement in this new hypothesis concerning the chronological order of the early writings of Spinoza.

1. The twofold form of adequate knowledge in the *Tractatus de intellectus emendatione (TdIE)*.

The concise definition of adequate knowledge is expounded in the fourth formulation of the various *modi percipiendi: Denique perceptio est, ubi res percipitur per solam suam essentiam, vel per cognitionem suae proximae causae* (G II/10/20-21). Note the difference in the formula used to indicate the two sources of adequate knowledge: why is it that the author does not say in the first phrase, as in the second: *per cognitionem suae solae essentiae*? or in the second, as in the first: *per suam proximam causam*?

In the first instance, the *perceptio* of the fourth kind would appear to be constituted through the immediate relationship between the mind and the essence of the thing perceived; in the second instance, the *perceptio* would *not* imply an immediate relationship with the proximate cause of the thing, but with an idea, or knowledge of the cause. Is there an actual difference here, or is it merely an illusion? I think that the difference between the two formulae is both illusory and real. Since the term *perceptio (Denique perceptio est)* indicates - just as in the three preceding cases - a form of knowledge which presupposes a knowledge in act, it is evident that in both cases the *perceptio* refers (as in the previous modes) to actual knowledge of the thing's essence or of the proximate cause of its existence. Therefore, if the *percipere* of the definition is assumed, as is necessary, in the meaning of a state or mode of knowledge, the *ubi percipitur* does not add an active or dynamic valency to *denique perceptio est*, since it, too, refers to a knowledge which makes perception possible. Spinoza could have said, therefore: *Denique perceptio est, ubi res percipitur per cognitionem suae solae essentiae*, assimilating the second formula to the first one.

But if we consider the structural difference between the two types of knowledge which would together constitute the fourth kind, the diversity of the expository formula seems to be justified, somehow. The perception of the thing through its essence coincides with the immediate perception of the thing itself, since between *thing* and *essence* no distinction is made. If there was a difference, then the perception of the *essence* of the thing would not necessarily imply perception of the thing itself.

But since the proximate cause of the thing differs from the thing itself and from its essence, its knowledge does not coincide with the knowledge of the thing, neither in regard to its essence nor its existence. One could suppose that perhaps the author differentiates the two formulae because, while perception of the thing by means of its essence coincides perfectly with the perception of such essences and both perceptions (of the thing and of its essence), it is one single operation; in the second case, perception of the thing would not coincide with the perception of its proximate cause, while necessarily seeking it.

However, even if this were not the reason for the different formulation of the two kinds of knowledge comprising the fourth mode, there remains, doubtless, their structural epistemological diversity, springing from the ontological difference of their object. In this regard, toward the end of the treatise, the author gives the following clarification:

> *si res sit in se, sive ut vulgo dicitur, causa sui, tum per solam suam essentiam debebit intelligi; si vero res non sit in se, sed requirat causam, ut existat, tum per proximam suam causam debet intelligi: nam revera cognitio effectus nihil aliud est, quam perfectiorem causae cognitionem acquirere* (G II/34/10-15).

The identification of the prime object of knowledge (aside from all considerations relating to its nature and the possibility of knowing it) does not present particular difficulties; it is the most perfect Being, subsistent and uncreated, primary cause of Nature and of all things which are found in it, that is to say, of God.[2] Since this being is one alone and infinite, and since outside of it there is no other being, its idea will be, of necessity, clear and distinct (G II/29/9-18). Besides, since the essence and the existence of this being have no external cause, we can therefore state that the *perceptio per solam essentiam* is a form of immediate knowledge.

We come across greater difficulty, however, regarding the interpretation of the second kind of object, that is, objects whose existence is not derived from their essence, but from an external cause. Spinoza states that clear and distinct knowledge of a thing coincides with the definition of its own particular affirmative essence (G II/34/18-20); but he adds that in order to explain the intimate essence of something created, the definition must *comprehendere causam proximam*. We will see what Spinoza means by *causam proximam* in this work and the difficulties to which this notion gives rise: in the meantime, it is sufficient to emphasize that such knowledge, formulated *per aliam rem*, is not immediate but mediate.

Spinoza couples the two forms of knowledge into one single kind now described *(per essentiam, per causam proximam)*, since he considers both of them to be adequate: *solus quartus modus comprehendit essentiam rei adaequatam, et absque erroris periculo* (G II/13/11-12). The adequacy of the second kind of knowledge derives, as has just been recalled, from the particular, affirmative definition of the proximate cause of an object; this knowledge, however, still consists in the deduction of the essence of one thing from another, just as occurs with the third kind of knowledge. This, however, is inadequate since it proceeds from the knowledge of the effect to that of the cause, or purports to deduce the essence of a particular thing for a general notion (10/16-19). The knowledge of that which does not exist by its essence must therefore imply or *comprehendere* the knowledge of the cause - not vice versa - and precisely that of the proximate cause. But what is the semantic meaning and value of this *comprehendere*? How is it possible to deduce the essence of a particular thing from its proximate cause, if this is such in relation to the existence, and not in relation to the essence, of that particular thing? If the proximate cause of the existence of a particular thing were to be identified with the essence of this thing, then the existence of such a thing would derive from its essence and it would not be regarded as created, but as uncreated.

Also, while Spinoza affirms that the definition of a thing must explain its essence, he does not identify the proximate cause with the essence, but limits himself to stating - with an ambiguous formula - that the definition of a thing must *comprehendere* the proximate cause. What is meant by *proximate cause* in the TdIE?

It is stated in the treatise that the essence of singular, changeable things cannot be deduced from the essence of other changeable things, nor from a sequence of their existences; so it is not there that we must look for their proximate cause. This is to be found in fixed and external things from which the changing things depend

> *adeo intime atque essentialiter (ut sic dicam)... ut sine iis nec esse, nec concipi possint. Unde haec fixa, et aeterna, quamvis sint singularia, tamen ob eorum ubique praesentiam, ac latissimam potentiam erunt nobis, tanquam universalia sive genera definitionum rerum singularium mutabilium, & causae proximae omnium rerum* (G II/36/20-37/9).

Leaving aside, at this point, any analytical examination of this text, which I will refer to in a broader discussion of it which has developed in Spinoza's historiography and also to a writing of mine on this subject,[3] I will limit myself here to dealing with two considerations.

1) Note that Spinoza had to use the mediation of that definition to understand singular fixed and eternal things as *causae proximae* of those singular

and changeable things. Since fixed and eternal things can be considered as universal or forms of the definition of changeable things, they will also be (for us) the proximate cause of their existence. In other words, since it is not evident, *per se*, why each fixed and eternal thing would be the proximate cause of a multiplicity of singular and changeable things, Spinoza, assuming the existence of these things, presumes that they can be defined in relation to the former, as being specific and individual, in respect of a genus; but if that is the logical relationship presumed between these entities, he concludes that their ontological relationship must also be identical. He used the mediation of a logical relation to found an ontological one.

2) Note also that Spinoza gives us no indication in the TdIE which permits us to determine the nature of the singular fixed and eternal things. The fundamental articulations and terms of ontology, present in the KV and the E, are missing in the TdIE, so that it is difficult to understand, in the sense just determined, the strength and depth of the notion of proximate cause. Moreover, the author himself recognizes this difficulty. Immediately following the above-quoted text, he goes on to say *sed, cum hoc ita sit, non parum difficultatis videtur subesse, ut ad horum singularium cognitionem pervenire possimus...* (G II/37/10-11).

Our difficulty has increased and is perhaps insurmountable, due to the fact that the series of conditions which Spinoza considers necessary for obtaining that knowledge are not fulfilled, due to the interruption of the treatise. In order to know the essence of the singular changeable things, it is necessary, first of all, to know the fixed and eternal things; but since they are eternal, their essences cannot explain *per se* the essences of changeable things; it is therefore necessary, Spinoza goes on to say, to look for other means besides those used for the knowledge of eternal things, and thus build up a science of sensibility. To this, however, must be prefixed the study on eternal things which, in turn, presupposes the study regarding nature and the property of the intellect (G II/37/13-18/12). But the treatise comes to a halt when this last-mentioned enquiry gets underway. I do not intend to discuss the reasons for the interruption, but will merely observe that this fact, and the difficulties which are intrinsic to it, directly influences this doctrine of the fourth kind of knowledge, in particular in relation to its second form - that is to say, regarding knowledge of something through its proximate cause. This doctrine cannot, therefore, be considered to be founded in the TdIE; we will see what foundation it receives in the other two works under examination.

2. The doctrine of the intellect, or immediate knowledge of God, in the **Korte Verhandeling** (KV).

The doctrine of the intellect, understood as knowledge of the third kind, is notably clarified in the KV and from its definition the second source of the TdIE is eliminated, at least formally speaking, i.e. the possibility of having adequate knowledge by proximate cause.

In the first two chapters of the second part, it is defined as a clear and distinct knowledge (II, i; ii, 2) which derives from "a feeling and enjoying of the thing itself" and greatly outweighs the other two forms of knowledge. "True and pure love with all its effects" is derived from it (II, ii, 3). The disappearance of the formula "through the knowledge of the proximate cause" does not mean that the KV renounces, generally speaking, the fundamental principle according to which real knowledge is *per causam*. We clearly read, in the treatise, that "it is necessary to know things in their causes" (II, v, 11). This principle, taken in its entirety, can also be maintained with regard to the knowledge of God, because now - unlike in the TdIE in which only a negative connotation of the *causa sui* exists - God is conceived as *causa sui* in the positive sense. Since God is his own cause, *he can* be conceived through himself (I, i, 10). But God also *must* be known through himself because, being the cause of all other things, he precedes all other things in being and in knowledge (II, v, 11). Therefore, God is known immediately through himself (II, xxii, 3) and it can be said that he is the cause of the knowledge that we have of him (II, xxiv, 12), or that the intellect is an immediate and immanent effect of God. And since it is an immediate and immanent effect, it is also immortal - that is, it lasts as long as its cause, which is eternal (I, Dial. 2, 11; II, xxvi, 8, #2). The intellect is so united to God that without God it cannot exist nor be conceived (II, xxiv, 11).

It would be an error to interpret these texts, as has often occurred in the past, as being the expression of a mystical phase in Spinoza's thinking. These texts, and especially the notion of *God*, must be read and interpreted in the light of other pages which confer on them their real meaning, robbing them of all mystical connotations which the formulae and traditional language used might possibly suggest. A "demystification"[4] plan is already present in the KV, in fact, and, in certain aspects, in a more explicit manner than in *Ethics*.

If, then, we consider that the God in the KV - unlike that in the TdIE - is already the unique Nature or Substance constituted by infinite attributes, each one of which is infinite and perfect in its kind (I, ii, 1; ii, 12; App.1, P4C), the doctrine of the immediate and immanent production of the intellect on the part of God must be interpreted in the light of the particular and specific categories of the new Spinozan philosophy. Now, if the intellect knows things in their essence, in a clear and distinct manner, since God-Nature's own essence is composed of its attributes, then the intellect will have immediate knowledge of the attributes of God and because of the constant identity between God and its attributes, it will have immediate knowledge of God. If the intellect is conceived as infinite, it constitutes the immediate and infinite mode of the attribute of thought, it is pure and eternal activity of understanding accompanied by immutable joy and has for its object all the other attributes of God and all its modes (I, ix, 3). If the intellect is considered as a finite mode, that is to say, as the third kind of which we are speaking, it has for its object only two of the infinite attributes of God, thought and extension, in other words, those attributes of which man is a mode, a finite being.

In what sense, then, can one talk about the intellect as *immediate knowledge* of the essence of things, as a "feeling and enjoying of the thing itself?" Besides, what things does it mean: only those which are infinite, that is, attributes of a God and/or *their* immediate modes, or else those which are finite, particular and specific modes?

In reply to the first question, one can say that with regard to the attribute of thought, since the activity of understanding is unique and infinite - that is, the intellect considered as an immediate, eternal and infinite mode of that attribute - all activity of understanding which is considered as determined and finite (no matter what its reality or the legitimacy of its demonstration) appears as a moment or a part, specific and finite, of that same infinite activity. And since that activity has for its object the infinite attributes of God and all that proceeds form it, infinite and finite modes, even the activity of understanding of a finite intellect is referred to the same objects. But what is the difference between finite and infinite intellect?

In the second dialogue, Theophilus states that to produce an idea of God in us (that is to say, intellect) you merely need "a body in Nature, the idea of which is necessary in order to show God immediately" (I, Dial.2, 12). One can argue whether that "body" of which the idea is considered necessary, is an ordinary finite and specific body, or that "infinite body" constituting the attribute of extension itself. At any rate, it is certain that since the human mind is an idea of the human body and gets its first being from it (II, xxii, 3-5), the idea of God - that is, of its infinite attributes - is not constituted apart from the idea of the body, be it finite or infinite. The idea of God does not coincide with the idea of the body (finite or infinite), but the existence in act of an idea of the body is the condition which permits the idea of God to be constituted, like the opening of a window allowing the light to illuminate the room. It is the light of the sun which directly illuminates the room; but it is the opening of the window which makes it possible for the light to immediately illuminate the room (I, Dial.2, 12). Since the mind is a mode of infinite thought and of its infinite activity of understanding, it is therefore capable of participating immediately in such knowledge and knowing according to truth.

We have also answered the second question now, regarding the objects of the intellect. The intellect is not only an idea of God and of his attributes, but also of the body and other bodies, besides ideas of those bodies. In II, iii, 10, it says that "this real knowledge varies according to the objects presented to it"; in II, xxvi, 8 it is implicitly assumed that the intellect may know external objects. By the doctrine of union *through Nature*, between the idea of God and God himself, expounded in II, xxiv, 5, one can state that the primary object of intuitive knowledge is God, understood as the substantial unity of its attributes and of the modifications of these; but since the idea of God is understood as a substantial relationship of its modes, it necessarily implies the idea of these - as the idea of the proportion of numbers implies the idea of the numbers themselves - and the mind which knows God does not cease to be the idea of the body, so even the modes constitute an object of intuitive knowledge.

The essence of God is therefore the object of the intellect constituted by the attributes - and the essence of the modes, that is, of the singular and determined things.

But how is it possible to know the essence of the finite modes? What is the meaning of, or, in the words of the TdIE, what must be "comprehended" by the definition of that essence? In the preface to the second part, Spinoza criticizes the traditional definition of "what belongs to the nature of a thing," just as he had criticized, in the previous part, the doctrine of the definition by means of the proximate genus and specific differences (I, vii, 6-9). The traditional definition states that it "belongs to the nature of a thing, without which the thing cannot exist nor be recognized." Spinoza maintains this definition while adding a reciprocal condition, that is, that "the predicate cannot even exist, nor be conceived, without the thing." The author explains the reason for this addition: since things cannot exist or be conceived without God, if you kept only the first part of the definition, you would arrive at the conclusion that the essence of God and of his attributes belongs to the nature of things. And that is impossible since the essence of God is infinite and that of things finite. It follows thus: 1) that the essence of God or his attributes does not constitute the essence of singular, finite things; 2) that the definition of this essence implies the definition of the thing, in that it exists (see, later on, what difficulties arise from this); 3) that the definition of the essence of things implies at all events the idea of the attributes of God as their cause, since without them those things do not exist (first condition of the definition of that which belongs to the nature of a thing); 4) that the definition of the existence of the thing also implies the definition of another thing regarded as the proximate cause of that existence, since the essence could not be considered as such.

The final two consequences propose again the question of the cause and in particular, that of the proximate cause. In the classification of the modes of the efficient cause (I, iii, 2) Spinoza states that God is the *"proximate cause"* of infinite and unchangeable things which we say to be immediately created by him. He adds that God is the *causa ultima* or, more precisely, as you can read in the second dialogue, that he is the *causa remota*, but only "in a certain sense" of all particular things (I, Dial.2, 12). The specification of this *sense* is to be found again in the second dialogue: God cannot be considered the remote cause of particular things in the absolute sense, because the causes on which these immediately depend - that is to say, the mediate causes - do not exist and cannot act without God, as would happen if God were the remote cause. Therefore God can be said to be the remote cause only "in a certain sense" because in order to produce particular things, he does not make use of his existence alone (§2) or of his attributes alone (§10), but he needs some other modification or reality outside that of attributes (§12) which acts as a "subsidiary instrumental cause" of divine action (I, iii, 2,5). That reality cannot be an infinite mode; it, too, is a finite mode. However, in that case, the problem is only displaced; how is the mediate finite cause produced, through which the other finite things will be produced? How does one proceed from the infinite to the finite?

In the light of the preceding considerations, neither God nor his attributes can be considered a proximate cause of finite things; nor can finite modes be so either, since they are the immediate cause only of existence, not of the essence of things. On the other hand, neither can the notion of proximate cause *in suo genere* - a denomination which Spinoza never uses, either in the KV or in the E - resolve the problem of deducing the mediate cause which God must use to produce particular things (I, iii, #5).

Let us come therefore to the final question: in what does the difference between the infinite intellect and the finite intellect consist? Is it simply a quantitative difference or is there also a difference in cognitive procedure? This is what we will try to discover in the *Ethics*.

3. The doctrine of intuitive science in the **Ethics** (E)

The greater number of interpreters hold that the doctrine of the fourth kind of knowledge expounded by Spinoza in the TdIE was set out in a substantially similar way in E IIP40S2:

> *Praeter haec duo cognitionis genera datur, ut in sequentibus ostendam, aliud tertium, quod scientiam intuitivam vocabimus. Atque hoc cognoscendi genus procedit ab adaequata idea essentiae formalis quorundam Dei attributorum ad adaequatam cognitionem essentiae rerum"* (G II/122/15-19).

Whether one accepts that opinion or refutes it, a decision must be based on the interpretation of the given definition. In particular, we must know what is the meaning of the words *procedit ab... ad...* For M. Gueroult there is no doubt whatever: intuitive science is defined as a deductive process which goes from the idea of God to the knowledge of the essence of things (Gueroult (1974), 447). Moreover, on this point, as also with regard to the notion of essence, the E contrasts with the TdIE (*Ibid.*, p. 449 and App. 16). Gueroult (like other interpreters) presupposes two conditions: 1) that the essence of some attributes of God are to be considered as the proximate cause of the essence of things; 2) that the essence of things should not be conceived as a singular essence of an existing thing in act, but as a specific, universal essence of singular things. In fact, Gueroult maintains that *le probleme de savoir par quel moyen de telles essences* (that is to say, singular essences of singular things) *peuvent etre adequatement connues, parait insoluble* (*Ibid.*, App.16, 607-608). To understand, therefore, the meaning of *procedit ab... ad...* it is necessary, above all, to know what is meant by *essentiae rerum*. The second definition is well-known (in the second part) and substantially repeats what has been said in the KV, indicating that which belongs to the essence of a thing:

> Ad essentiam alicujus rei id pertinere dico, quo dato res necessario ponitur, & quo sublato res necessario tollitur; vel id, sine quo res, & vice versa quod sine re nec esse nec concipi potest.

1) This definition is simultaneously founded on the affirmation of the distinction of essence from existence and on the negation of their ontological separation.

In other words: the essence of the thing and the thing itself are seen as really distinct in the sense that they are not identifiable one with the other because, if this were the case, the essence of things would not be distinguished from the things themselves and this definition would be absurd, as well as superfluous.

However, it is also stated that what belongs to the essence or simply the essence, does not exist, *per se*, separately from the thing, but can exist and be conceived only through the thing. In what way can this second condition be understood without identifying the essence with the thing? Spinoza doesn't explain this and omissions such as this certainly constitute one of the principal problems of his philosophy, with particular regard to the interpretation of Part V of the *Ethics*. However, in one sense, the text must certainly be accepted: the actual existence of the thing is a necessary condition of the determinate existence and intelligibility of the essence. The essence of things does not really exist separately from the actual existence of the thing (KV, App.2, 11; E IIP8CS).

2) That this is so is demonstrated by Spinoza's reason for adding to the traditional definition of the essence of a thing: to eliminate the possibility that the essence of God or of its attributes should be considered to be the essence of singular things which, without them, could neither exist, nor be conceived (E IIP10S2). Since the essence of God and of its attributes exists and is conceived *per se*, without the need for the existence of singular things, it cannot constitute their essence. But if so, then in E IID2 by *essence of things*, one means the essence of the singular things, that is, of all those realities which are "finite and have a determinate existence" (E IID7), which have their cause in infinite things. In that sense, therefore, the formula *essentiae rerum* which recurs in the definition of the third kind of knowledge, must be assumed. It can thus be integrated: intuitive knowledge *procedit ab adaequata idea essentiae formalis quorundam Dei attributorum ad adaequatam cognitionem essentiae (formalis) rerum (singularium)*. In what sense is *procedit* meant to be understood? In the sense that it would be possible to deduce, analytically, the singular essence of singular things from the essence of the attributes of God? Does one support the possibility of an intuitive knowledge as a concrete deduction, founding it on the assumption of the essence of an attribute of God as a *proximate cause in its kind* of all bodies existing in act, so as to make possible deductive knowledge of the specific essence of a single thing (*Ibid., p. 447*).

Leaving aside the discussion as to whether God can be considered as the *proximate cause in its kind* of singular and finite things, I repeat that Spinoza never uses such a denomination, either in E IP28S (where the nomenclature of the scholastic tradition is referred to) or elsewhere, and I note that such a denomination should be used only with some qualification, at least ("according to a certain sense"), that is, to distinguish between the immediate cause of the infinite modes and the mediate cause of finite modes.

There is a reason which has probably influenced Spinoza's decision to renounce the terminology of "proximate cause in its kind" and which, while leaving aside the problem of denomination, should be remembered. In I PP21-23, Spinoza demonstrates that only infinite modifications can follow from the absolute nature of God's attributes. In an analytical sense, only the infinite can be deduced from the infinite. In P29 and in its demonstration, this theory is clearly repeated: what is finite and has a determinate existence cannot have been produced either from the absolute nature of an attribute of God or from one of his attributes, insofar as that is affected by an eternal and infinite modification; but it had to follow from some attribute insofar as it is modified by a finite and determinate modification. However, Spinoza did not offer in these definitions, nor does he do so later on, any demonstration as to *why* and *how* an infinite attribute of God can be "modified" by an infinite series of finite modes. This is equivalent to saying that the philosopher has not offered any deductive reason for the passage or process of the infinite to the finite, since he considered this to be impossible. He has simply limited himself to stating the *de facto* existence of the finite without giving a specific deduction of the finite and the determinate - since this was made impossible by the initial suppositions.

But if this is really so, if Spinoza is lacking, *de facto* and *de iure*, a deduction of the finite from the infinite, how is it possible that adequate knowledge of things has a deductive nature or the form of real deduction? How can we interpret the verb *procedit ab..ad..?* This definition recurs in the same terms in E VP25D, while the verb *procedere* appears several other times in E; six times in association with the noun *demonstratio (Hujus propositionis demonstratio procedit eodem modo ac demonstratio...)* and in the sense of *going on, carrying out;*[5] it then appears in E IApp simultaneously in the sense of *sequi* and *operare* (see P16 and P32C1 and 2): *ostendi omnia Naturae aeterna quadam necessitate summaque perfectione procedere* (80/5-9). As in this case, why could the *procedere* in the definition of the third kind of knowledge not be understood according to two simultaneous meanings, both different and complementary? In conformity with the context and descriptions of the preceding modes of knowledge, the first and partial sense in which *procedit* is understood, in the first part of the definition, is that of *deriving, coming forth, arising.* In the same way, *notiones universales* are formed *ex singularibus, ex signis, ex eo, quod notiones communes... habemus;* thus the third kind of knowledge derives and is formed *ab adaequata idea essentiae formalis quorundam Dei attributum.* However, this sense is accompanied and integrated by another one which embraces both aspects of the definition and which is extensively confirmed in the lexicons:[6] *hoc genus procedit,* that is, *is extended from ... to...,* taking its own particular origin and source from the adequate idea of God.

In the third kind of knowledge, these two characteristics are fulfilled: intuitive knowledge of the nature of God and *also* intuitive knowledge of the essence of singular things. This two-fold intuition is not presented as something which is separate and unrelated - it is both related and reciprocally implicative. It is not possible to discover clearly and distinctly the nature of God without discovering the necessity which infinite objects derive from him in infinite modes; but neither is it possible to discover the essence of singular things without this implying the idea of God as the cause. Therefore, in E VP24, Spinoza can state as an immediate consequence to E IP25, that "the more we understand singular things, the more we understand God." In E VP25D, he states: the more we come to know things with the third kind of knowledge, the more we know God, which would also be legitimate. We arrive at knowledge of God, therefore, through knowledge of the body, as was pointed out in the KV; but since knowledge of the body implies the attribute of which it is the mode, then knowledge of the body is the essence of God to be known immediately, just as the opening of the window permitted the light to illuminate the room, according to the example quoted in the KV.

From what has been said, we can therefore conclude that the logical situation stated in the *processio* in the third kind of knowledge can be considered equal to that expressed in a formula which is rather diffused in E, that is, *concomitante idea*. The third kind of knowledge immediately concerns the essence of God *concomitante idea rerum singularium* as its determined and necessary modes. But it is also, at the same time, an idea of the essence of singular things *concomitante idea Dei, tanquam causa*. One sees that the notion of cause is a being of reason which expresses a relation in general and does not explain in a determinate manner, why and how the infinite causes a finite effect, even through mediation. As has been seen, nothing finite is deduced from the infinite. Besides, it must be observed that a finite intellect, unlike the infinite one, is not capable of analytically deducing (or as others prefer to say, synthetically) the essence of things in a determinate manner, aside from the relation which they have with their actual existence. Therefore, it is necessary that one has a somewhat immediate and intuitive idea of the actual existence of finite things, in order to also have an idea of their determinate essence. In intuitive knowledge, imagination and reason are both presupposed and maintained in a form which surpasses, however, their particular and determinate constitution. Analysis of such an implication constitutes a further fundamental chapter in the interpretation of intuitive science. But it is a chapter which we will have to postpone for another occasion.

1. "Per la datazione e l'interpretazione del *Tractatus de intellectus emendatione* di Spinoza," *La Cultura*, 17 (1979), 87-160; *Introduzione a Spinoza*, Bari, Laterza 1983, ch. 1-2.

2. There is no explicit mention in the TdIE of God as being identified with Nature, but there are various passages in which He is formally considered the *causa* of Nature, Nature being one of his effects: GII/17/3-7; 19/2-5; 28/32-29/18; 34/4-7; and above all 34/13-15 and 34-35.

3. "Nuovi contributi per la datazione e l'interpretazione del *Tractatus de intellectus emendatione*," in *Spinoza nel 350th anniversario della nascita*, ed. by E. Giancotti, (Naples: Bibliopolis, 1985), 515-525.

4. For this matter, refer to my comment in B. de Spinoza, *Korte Verhandeling van God, de mensch en deszelvs welstand*, intr., ed., tr. and comment by F. Mignini. (L'Aquilla-Roma: Japadre Editore, 1986), 709-719, 751.

5. E IP22D; IIP2D; IIIP39D; IIIP44D; IIIP59S; VP40D.

6. See for example *Lexicon totius latinitatis, s.v. procedo, ad* 4; *Oxford Latin Dictionary, s.v., ad* 7.

WISDOM AND THEORETICAL KNOWLEDGE IN SPINOZA

HERMAN DE DIJN
Katholieke Universiteit Leuven

1. Spinoza's philosophy can be interpreted as a peculiar reaction to the crisis brought about by the advent of the new physical sciences (this advent itself being related to broader cultural and economico-political changes).[1] From then onwards, and up to this day, the problem of the good and meaningful life, which had always occupied people, took the form of a confrontation of morality and religiosity with the new view of Nature and of man's place in it. This new view on nature and man was *disenchanting* and meant in the eyes of many a serious threat to morality and religion. Accordingly, the task of philosophy was (and is) often seen as the elaboration of a new synthesis which aimed at containment of the impact of the new view either by imposing certain limits on it, or by playing down its disenchanting nature.

Even if one is only slightly familiar with Spinoza's thinking, it is obvious that the problem of the good and meaningful life is at the core of his philosophy (although not unrelated to other problems, as e.g. the problem of the good State and how to bring it about). Spinoza, like all modern men, is confronted with what Alquié calls *le problème de la valeur morale du rationalisme* (Alquié (1981), 240). According to E. Renan, Spinoza understood that a completely unedited synthesis was necessary which negated neither the new scientific spirit nor the religious spirit.[2] Indeed, what is paradoxical in Spinoza is that he tries to deal with the problem of the good and meaningful life not by attempting to contain the new view, but through the very adoption of the rational view of nature and man.[3] For Spinoza the solution to the problem of the good and meaningful life precisely requires the rejection of an anthropomorphic and anthropocentric view of things, and the adoption of a neutral, purely objective view - at least this is so for the philosophically minded person (as is well-known, Spinoza does recognize the possibility of a kind of "salvation" for the ordinary man in a sort of purified Judaeo-Christian religiosity).

Spinoza has not been the only thinker to come to such a paradoxical solution for this problem of the clash between science and religiosity. In our century, another Jewish thinker and scientist, Albert Einstein, expressed opinions concerning the relationship between science and religion in many ways comparable to those of Spinoza. According to Einstein, science can lead to the decay of existing morality and religion in so far as it can bring about a detachment from the level of the immediate experience of meaning (e.g. the scientific attitude transcends the level of ordinary human concerns - even those of good and evil).[4] This detachment is produced by adopting the objectifying attitude of science which seems to make the everyday experience of meaning impossible.[5] Yet the very scientific spirit which thus leads to disenchantment vis-à-vis the old values can lead to a new, special form of enchantment, to a purified religiosity bereft of all anthropomorphic notions about God.[6] As a human activity, science has for Einstein a moral-religious significance: it is an activity capable of constituting the ultimate meaning and worth of the lives of certain people, who in this very activity of the search for truth, are capable of transcending themselves (Einstein, *op. cit.*, 23).

In Spinoza there is a similar transcendence of ordinary concerns and views through rational cognition. Reason leads to a repudiation of our usual anthropomorphic views of Nature and man. It teaches us that our human activities, including those thought to follow from free acts of the will, are to be grasped in the same way as when we are dealing with lines, planes and bodies (E IIIPref.); that nothing is *in se* good or bad, orderly or confused, beautiful or ugly... (E IApp.; E IVPref.); and so on. Nevertheless it is precisely *through* this rational activity that we can arrive at true freedom and even wisdom.

Yet, both in Einstein and in Spinoza, it is not the scientific or rational insight on its own which constitutes the new religiosity. Something more seems to be needed: a "cosmic religious feeling," according to Einstein (*op. cit.*, pp. 48, 50); some special kind of knowledge (intuition) combined with an "intellectual love of God," according to Spinoza. This leads to the question of the exact nature of the relationship between - in Spinoza's terms - rational knowledge and intuitive knowledge, and how the one can lead to the other. To study this relationship in Spinoza's case is not easy, because it is not absolutely clear from Spinoza's definitions what these two kinds of knowledge are. Commentators disagree, e.g., as to whether the knowledge of the second kind contains knowledge of God, and therefore whether the *Ethics* itself belongs to the second or the third kind of knowledge. In an attempt to understand the nature of Spinozistic religiosity or wisdom, we will first recapitulate some of Spinoza's most fundamental theses concerning the relationship between reason and intuition.

2. Knowledge of the third kind or intuitive knowledge is in a crucial sense knowledge of singular things,[7] more precisely of singular essences grasped in relation to (certain attributes of) God. An example of such a singular essence is the essence of the idea that expresses the essence of *this or that* body (e.g. the essence of my mind) (E VP22). These singular essences must be grasped "under the species of eternity"; this means as contained in God with eternal necessity (E VP22). The singularity of the eternal essences should not be confused with the singularity of things as existing in time and space (E VP29S), though this does not necessarily mean that eternity and time are in no way related.[8] Intuitive knowledge is not opposed to deduction: knowledge of the third kind "*proceeds* from an adequate idea of the formal essence of certain attributes of God to the adequate knowledge of the (formal) essence of things" (E IIP40S2). But this definition seems compatible with the proposition that the idea of a singular (eternal) essence necessarily involves knowledge of God (E VP30).

Intuitive knowledge differs from *reason* or knowledge of the second kind in so far as the latter is "universal" knowledge, i.e., knowledge of things based on "common notions" and adequate ideas of the properties of things (E IIP40S2 and VP36S). As an example of such "universal" knowledge Spinoza gives the proposition that all things, and consequently also the human mind, depend on God both for their essence and their existence (E VP36S). Although this seems as close as can be gotten to knowledge of a thing (the human mind) in relation to God, still it is not really intuitive knowledge. In order to have intuitive knowledge, what is needed is the grasping of the singular (eternal) essence of the thing in its intimate dependence on God (*ibid.*).

This intuitive knowledge is said to give rise to the greatest possible satisfaction (E VP27), and to lead to the intellectual love of God (E VP32C). These propositions incidentally show that there are links between eternity and time.

The "ontological" possibility-condition of intuitive knowledge is the human mind insofar as it is itself eternal, and gifted with adequate knowledge of God (E VP31). Yet Spinoza insists that man can *desire* to know things by the third kind of knowledge, and while this desire cannot arise from the first kind of knowledge (knowledge based on sense-perception combined with language), it can indeed arise from the second kind (E VP28). P28 is established by means of the following premises: a desire is a particular striving, dependent on some "affection" (ultimately an idea) of man's essence, and the desire to know intuitively (= adequately) can only arise from an "affection," i.e., an idea which is itself adequate (E VP28D). Unfortunately, this does not tell us *how exactly* this desire depends on knowledge of the second kind or reason. Can the origination of intuitive knowledge be understood simply on the basis of the *tendency* of the rational knower to derive further conclusions from established premises? and what then are these premises (are they propositions like those contained in *Ethics I*)? *Or* should we understand the relationship rather in this way: that intuitive knowledge is obtained through the *application* of a general truth (e.g. the dependence of all things, and therefore also of the human mind, on God) on to a particular case (my mind)? But this would still only be the *application* of a general truth, and does not seem to yield the grasping of a singular essence (see E VP36S).[9] Although Spinoza gives the impression that the transition from reason to intuition is a transition from certain adequate information to other adequate information, it is unlikely that we can understand the origination of intuition in this way (through simple deduction, or through application of a general truth).

Suppose we know everything about God and human nature as explained in the *Ethics* I-IV. Would this constitute knowledge of the third kind? It is doubtful. It is in any case significant that Spinoza's most explicit and extensive treatment of intuitive knowledge is found in the second half of *Ethics V* (21-40), which deals with the eternity of the human mind, which is the eternity of the idea, expressing the essence of *this or that* body immediately conceived through the essence of God (as Extension) (E VP22). There can be no knowledge of the third kind, except on the basis of an understanding of *ourselves* as involved in God (E VP29 and VP39S). All knowledge of the third kind seems to imply knowledge of one's *own* eternal essence as conceived through God. Do we get this knowledge of our eternal essence in a logical deduction from God, or in an application of knowledge about human nature (as understood through God) upon ourselves? The first seems impossible; the second does not seem to yield real intuitive knowledge: to get an idea of our eternal essence does not seem to be reducible to metaphysical and physical knowledge about humans in general, as applied to ourselves. (Which is not to say that to get such an intuitive idea does not presuppose such knowledge). What could it possibly mean to have the idea of one's own singular eternal essence as contained in God? Spinoza says at the same time that it is a question of experience (*Sentimus, experimurque, nos aeternos esse*) *and* that it is a question of insight through demonstrations (E VP22S). But how can the experience of eternity be the same as an insight acquired through demonstration?[10] Or should we rather say that demonstrative insight should *go together* with a certain experience. I can only make sense of the second possibility (which, I confess, requires some reconstruction of what Spinoza says). The question then becomes: what sort of experience and which demonstrations?

3. The rational pursuit of objective knowledge of things is an activity in which we can *experience* ourselves as powerful (active, free, as Spinoza calls it) (e.g., E IVP68D). This experience of power is not unrelated to an experience of transcending the level of ordinary ideas and concerns:[11] we now see things as they *really* are, a world very different from the ordinary "anthropomorphic" world we usually construct for ourselves. Physics on its own, as a body of truths about the world, does not necessarily lead to a new life. The same is true even of a metaphysics which has taken to heart the lessons of physics and conceives of the relationship between whole and parts in a deterministic, naturalistic way: is it not possible to understand it all, and yet have one's life not really be changed? But is it not almost inevitable that there will be produced in people who have made great progress in physical-metaphysical knowledge, the *experiences* of self-transcendence and of power (to which Spinoza undoubtedly refers at the beginning of the *Tractatus de Intellectus Emendatione*)? One might even relate this to Spinoza's rationalistic conception of man as fundamentally a knower, or an intellect: it would not be astonishing that a being, whose nature is primarily to understand, feels a deep satisfaction when it can work out its nature unhindered. It is tempting in this context to try and understand the relationship between reason and intuition as a relationship not of a purely epistemic nature, but rather as follows: the joyful *experience* of rational knowing leads to a desire for new experiences of power and self-transcendence in the intellectual pursuit. It is also tempting to stop one's interpretation here, and to simply equate knowledge of the third kind with this experience of the growing power of the self as intellect. Yet too much remains unaccounted for in this way, especially the relationship between knowledge of the third kind and an awareness of our eternal essence as involved in God (and leading to "intellectual love" of God).

It is interesting to note that Russell at one point identified Spinoza's intellectual love of God with the emotional state accompanying intellectual discovery (See Blackwell (1985), 118). But Russell came to see that this could not be the whole story: in order to understand Spinoza's intuitive knowledge and intellectual love of God, we have to understand the relationship between the joy of intellectual discovery *and* a certain metaphysical view of Nature (Blackwell (1985), 149).

4. The insight into our *own* eternal essence (as being *in* God), which is an essential element in intuitive knowledge, can hardly be a purely theoretical insight acquired through demonstrations. It must be more a kind of *experience,* not unrelated however to demonstrations of truths about finite essence applicable to ourselves as instances of such essences (E VP23S). At the same time knowledge of the third kind must originate in knowledge of the second kind. All these elements can be pieced together to produce a picture of something approaching a certain kind of "religious" experience.

In the very pursuit of our meta-physical knowledge we produce an *experience* of ourselves as power, self-transcendence, in which we escape our ordinary concerns: this is a *"personal"* experience of an activity which seems to belong to our "purest" self. *But,* at the same time, *within* this activity we come to *know* in an *objective* way that everything is radically determined by God: everything is a necessary modification of the essence of the divine Substance or Nature, which does not act with any end in view.

On their own, these insights are "simply" *insights,* which are the object of rational discussion and argumentation, which can be transmitted to others, without these insights necessarily "changing our lives." But in combination with the self-experience of the rational knower, these insights can produce a sort of "cosmic religious emotion."[12]   In the joy of adequate knowing, the rational knower experiences himself as transcending his ordinary concerns in the pursuit of a purely scientific, objectifying view of things. But he can also envisage himself and his experience as part of the impersonal, non-goal-directed whole. At this moment, in this "envisaging," something other than a purely intellectual process takes place: the knower relates *himself* as a singular entity to the whole, now envisaged as all-encompassing God or Nature of which the individual can *feel* himself to be an eternal part. Something like this is probably also expressed in Einstein's "cosmic religious feeling": the whole of nature which one is studying in physics can become something to which one can also relate "personally," something which then appears as Mystery, as Beauty (or even as Rationality - although as I will show this name is misleading); it appears like this in a moment of contemplation which is different from purely theoretical insight, rather of the kind of "knowledge of" than "knowledge that," although it is not unrelated to the preceding "knowledge that."

Russell describes this kind of knowledge as "a form of union of Self and non-Self."[13]   This characterization can be accepted as very appropriate if the union is not meant to exclude *contrast,* which seems to be an essential element in the contemplative experience. The experience of rapture in contact with God-Nature, of transcendent contact with something infinitely surpassing us, is probably due to the experience of the contrast between our self-awareness (as powerful intellect) and the impersonal, infinite God-Nature of which we feel ourselves to be a part: a form of union of Self and non-Self which, so to speak, shocks us out of ourselves. Russell thought that even a materialistic metaphysics can produce intellectual love of God (Blackwell (1985), 119).

According to Einstein the "cosmic religious feeling" is not just *any* religious feeling: it is a religious feeling co-determined by the peculiar metaphysical insights which make it impossible to envisage God-Nature as something personal, as something resembling the judaeo-christian God.

The *same* object which occupies our intellectual search and curiosity can also *affect* us, if we relate to it in a non-purely cognitive way: it can become something which makes us pause in wonderment. But here confusion is possible: what is interesting from the point of view of the search for knowledge (reality as what lies always ahead of us) should not be confused with what is interesting from the point of view of individual meaningfulness (reality as something in the light of which ordinary things lose their importance, in relation to which we escape the bondage of our passions because it appears to us as what surpasses us, as Mystery, as Glory). What appears as a perhaps extremely complicated puzzle from the point of view of the knowledge-search, can also appear as *Mystery,* but only from the point of view of the individual relationship with the Whole. Implied in the notion of mystery is that it will never be solved (it can only disappear: if we lose interest, if we are no longer affected), whereas a puzzle is (at least in principle) solvable. (To call the Mystery Rationality - as Einstein does - is confusing because it expresses a tendency to conflate puzzlement and sensitivity to mystery).

If we were pure knowers, if we did not have other concerns and experiences (e.g., experience of ourselves as singular selves; attitudes and feelings with respect to ourselves as singular individuals affectively relating to other individual things and wider contexts), we would never produce in ourselves "intuitive knowledge," i.e., the feeling that we are eternal parts of God-Nature. But that we experience ourselves *like this* is co-determined by specific physical-metaphysical insights. So, far from the insights into the eternity of our singular essence being deducible from God, an *experience* of ourselves (as powerful in knowing) is required, and it is this experience which, in combination with a general metaphysical truth, leads to intuitive "knowledge" of the inherence of *ourselves* as an eternal essence in God.

5. This peculiar combination of a certain experience of ourselves and certain metaphysical ideas leading to a kind of "religious emotion" can even explain some of the characteristics of Spinozistic religiosity. As has been suggested by some commentators, Spinozistic religiosity seems to be characterized by a reverence for "the terrifying side of nature" (See Sprigge, *o.c.*, 158). In connection with the "atmosphere" of Spinoza's wisdom, Renan spoke of *l'air du glacier* (Renan, *o.c.*, 13), which was peculiar to the Spinozistic mode of living. The specific character of Spinozistic religiosity (or wisdom) is undoubtedly related to the sort of metaphysical insights which "inform" this religiosity: they are anti-anthropomorphic insights, which introduce us to a Nature to which we of course belong, of which we are an expression (as power of autonomous intellectual thinking), but which, though immanent in us, is not there for us, but infinitely transcends all our concerns. Strange though it may sound, it seems possible that in relating *personally* to such a "God," we are not overpowered by terror,[14] but come to feel joy in the awareness of our immersion in such a "God," and even come to "love" "God or Nature," although it is so unlike a personal being. That the affective relationship between the Spinozistic knower and the impersonal

God or Nature is one of joy and love, and not one of terror, is probably explicable in terms of a kind of "feedback" of the "positive" self-experience of the knower (as enjoying his knowing-activity), on the basis of which he situates himself within the context of Nature.

Spinoza is not the only one to have spoken about personal feelings towards something impersonal (Heidegger, e.g., talks about gratitude towards Being, which is certainly not personal; Nietzsche speaks about *amor fati,* alluding perhaps to Spinoza).[15]   Spinoza is also not the last representative of what I called the Spinozistic religiosity. In a poem quoted by Russell (in translation) in *The Impact of Science on Society,*[16] the famous Italian poet Leopardi writes:

> But as I sit and gaze, my thought conceives
> Interminable vastnesses of space
> Beyond it, and earthly silences,
> And profoundest calm: whereat my heart almost
> Becomes dismayed. And as I hear the wind
> Blustering through these branches, I find myself
> Comparing with this sound that infinite silence;
> And then I call to mind eternity,
> And the ages that are dead, and this that now
> Is living, and the noise of it. And so
> In this immensity my thought sinks drowned:
> And sweet it seems to shipwreck in this sea.

In his *Prisons,* Russell himself describes Spinozistic contemplation as follows: ... the contemplative vision: partly sad, partly filled with a solemn joy, wholly beautiful, wholly great: the vision of all the ages of the earth, the depths of space, and the hierarchy of the eternal truths, met and mirrored in one mind whose being ends almost as soon as its knowledge has come to exist" (Quoted in Blackwell, 142).

The way in which I understand the coming about of Spinoza's intuitive knowledge may seem far-fetched, but that a special *effect* (of experience) can be produced by the combination of personal feelings or experiences and certain pieces of information is undeniable. Information, even theoretical information, can have other effects on us than addition to or completion of knowledge; it *can* in appropriate circumstances produce "new experiences." There are plenty of examples of this in ordinary life and literature. Our relationship with things we love or admire *can,* when confronted with the truth that all things must disappear, lead to a special experience which can enhance our love or admiration, or better perhaps, give these feelings a special flavour (mixed now with a greater tenderness for example).

Once we interpret Spinoza's knowledge of the third kind in this way, we can also give a new interpretation to a couple of related ideas which have always puzzled commentators. What is "eternity," what is it to conceive one's own *singular* essence "under the species of eternity"? Eternity has nothing to do with time, yet is it not unrelated to time? We can perhaps understand a little bit better this strange relationship between time and eternity, if we relate it to the "cosmic religious emotion." In intuitive "knowledge" we are "shocked out of ourselves" when we, *while* experiencing ourselves as powerful in thinking, at the same time realize that we are part of a Nature which is just there, for no reason. In this "religious experience," we have transcended ourselves: *in* time we experience ourselves *momentarily* as outside time, as having nothing to do any more with any of the ordinary concerns; death is totally irrelevant (E VP38S), we are simply a part of Nature's play, and we completely accept this. Why shouldn't this be eternity?[17]

Spinoza also says that the *more* we understand singular things, the more we understand God (E VP24). But how can this be: either we understand him or we don't? Once we interpret intuitive knowledge not as some kind of enlargement of the body of information, but as a form of "knowledge of," we can more easily give meaning to this proposition. Each singular essence we come to experience as "eternally in God," indeed "tells us more" about God, in the sense that we come to have a new, unedited "cosmic religious emotion." It is comparable to the experience of beauty: each new experience of beauty leads in a way to a better "understanding of beauty," in the sense that each experience is something unedited, a way of experiencing beauty which is unique, as determined by this occasion (this peculiar combination of words in this poem for example).

Intuitive knowledge is a *"personal"* relationship with God-Nature, requiring a certain experience of ourselves and of other things (as "eternal essences"). This means that intuitive knowledge of God cannot exist, except as an experience of the whole of Nature *in* our experience of ourselves and of other *singular* things; and vice versa: there is no intuitive knowledge of singular essences, except in so far as they are experienced as "situated" in "something surpassing," or as "expressing" something which is "transcendent" and yet at the same time strangely immanent in the particulars ("strangely" immanent, because the transcendent is not there for the particular). Again, an important "truth" seems to be expressed here, which many people have been aware of, and which is expressed again in many forms, also in literature: that "religiosity" is not a direct relationship with ultimate meaning, but a relationship which is necessarily "mediated" by our experience of one or another particular thing, of something or other which is mortal and yet an expression of the a-human Immortal. In the relationship with the finite expression of the Infinite, with the mortal expression of the Immortal, the mortal is not mistaken for the Immortal, but mortality is made acceptable in a momentary reconciliation. As Vladimir Nabokov puts it in his *Speak, Memory*:

the highest enjoyment of timelessness - in a landscape selected at random - is when I stand among rare butterflies and their food plants. This is ecstacy, and behind the ecstacy is something else, which is hard to explain. It is like a momentary vacuum into which rushes all that I love. A sense of oneness with sun and stone. A thrill of gratitude to whom it may concern - to the contrapuntal genius of human fate or to tender ghosts humoring a lucky mortal (Nabokov, *o.c.*, 109-110).

Why not understand in a similar way Spinoza's "intellectual love" for a God without a face: as a love "to whom it may concern," even though we can expect no love in return (E VP19); what happens to us in such moments of intuition and love can even be experienced as if it were a gratuitous gift of Nature's spontaneous and purposeless activity which in us takes the form of an "intellectual love of God-Nature."[18]

1. See e.g., Walther (1971), *Einleitung*. For English translations of Spinoza's works, I use Curley (1985).

2. Renan, *Spinoza (Discours...)*, (La Haye: Nijhoff, 1877), p. 25: *Malheur à qui prétend que le temps des religions est passé! Malheur à qui s'imagine qu'on peut réussir à donner aux vieux symboles la force qu'ils avaient quand ils s'appuyaient sur l'imperturbable dogmatisme d'autrefois.*

3. Delbos, *Le Spinozisme* (Paris: Vrin, 1983), p. 173: *Ce que son système contient de plus audacieux, et sans doute de plus discutable, c'est, en éliminant par principe tout ce qui porte le manque de la subjectivité humaine, de prétendre contenter le désir le plus essentiel de l'homme, qui est le désir de vivre, et de vivre heureux.*

4. Einstein, *Ideas and Opinions* (New York: Dell Publishing Co, fifth Laurel Print, 1983), p. 48-49.

5. Einstein, *Autobiographical Notes*, in P. A. Schilpp (ed.), *Albert Einstein: Philosopher-scientist*, The Library of Living Philosophers, VII (La Salle (Ill.): Open Court-London: Cambridge University Press, 1970), 3-5.

6. Einstein, *Ideas and Opinions*, pp. 47-48, 57.

7. See E. Leroux, "Qu'est vraiment la science intuitive de Spinoza," in *Travaux du 2me Congrès de Sociétés de Philosophie Française et de Langue Française*, (Lyon: 1939), 39-42.

8. Concerning the relationship between eternity and necessity, and eternity and time, see the interesting papers of Martha Kneale and Alan Donagan in Grene (1973).

9. See also what Spinoza says in *The Emendation of the Intellect*, p. 14 concerning the requirements of grasping particular essences (which I suspect still hold in the *Ethics*).

10. See Alquié (1981), 230: *Il demeure malaisé de joindre et de confondre un sentiment de jouissance et la compréhension intellectuele d'une démonstration, et de voir en tout cela une intuition.*

11. See the beginning of Spinoza's *The Emendation of the Intellect*, where the *experience* of rational, cool thinking about his own situation leads Spinoza to the realization that in reason itself may be found the solution for his desperate search for "the real good."11.

12. Blackwell (1985), 119: "If we are to make sense of Russell's later interpretation of the 'intellectual love of God,' we may have to see in it an implicit recognition or a continuous though subdued appreciation of the necessary order of the universe. Looking at events in this light and in the light of the whole, or at least in a larger context, does, according to Russell, 'enlarge the eternal part of you.'"

13. This expression is applied to Spinoza by Sprigge, *Theories of Existence* (Harmondsworth: Penguin Books, 1984), 158 (ch. on Spinoza).

14. As is not impossible in certain experiences of nature, see, Nabokov's short story entitled "Terror" in Nabokov, *Tyrants Destroyed and Other Stories* (Harmondsworth: Penguin Books, 1981).

15. See Würzer, *Nietzsche und Spinoza* (Meisenheim am Glan: Hain, 1975), 80-86.

16. Russell, *The Impact of Science on Society* (London: Allen & Unwin, 1976, 1952), 91.

17. Borges begins his famous short story, *The Aleph*, with two quotes, the second of which is from Hobbes's *Leviathan* IV, 46: "But they will teach us that Eternity is the Standing still of the Present Time, a *Nunc-stans* (as the Schools call it); which neither they, nor any else understand, no more than they would a *Hic-stans* for an Infinite greatnesse of Place." Borges's story is precisely about such a *Hic-stans*. It is clear that Borges is not relating a super-scientific report, he is evoking a possible human experience which has been "understood" better by mystics and poets, than by philosophers. Cf. Nabokov, *Speak, Memory*, (Harmondsworth: Penguin Books, reprint 1982) 169: "... to try to express one's position in regard to the universe embraced by consciousness, is an immemorial urge. The arms of consciousness reach out and grope, and the longer they are the better. Tentacles, not wings, are Apollo's natural members. Vivian Bloodmark (=V.N.), a philosophical friend of mine, in later years, used to say that while the scientist sees everything that happens in one point of space, the poet feels everything that happens in one point of time. Lost in thought, he taps his knee with his wandlike pencil, and at the same instant a car (New York licence plate) passes along the road, a child bangs the screen door of a neighbouring porch, an old man yawns in a misty Turkestan orchard, a granule of cinder-gray sand is rolled by the wind on Venus, a Docteur Jacques Hirsch in Grenoble puts on his reading glasses, and trillions of other such trifles occur - all forming an instantaneous and transparent organism of events, of which the poet (sitting in a lawn chair, at Ithaca, N.Y.) is the nucleus."

18. We allude here to the difficult problem of the relationship between E VP19 and P35 which seem to contradict each other. On this point (and for a very interesting discussion of intuitive knowledge in general, staying very close to Spinoza's texts), see the interesting paper by W. Bartuschat, "Selbstsein und Absolutes," in *Neue Hefte für Philosophie*, Heft 12, Spinoza 1677-1977, 54.

THE THIRD KIND OF KNOWLEDGE
AS ALTERNATIVE SALVATION

YIRMIYAHU YOVEL
The Hebrew University
Jerusalem

My aim in this paper is to put together the elements for a new interpretation of Spinoza's mature notion of "knowledge of the third kind" as it stands in the *Ethics*. I do not insist that Spinoza held this view explicitly (although I think it probable) but that his texts suggest this reading as a plausible reconstruction. And since my reconstruction depends in large measure on the way I interpret *other* issues in Spinoza's system, I shall have to mention them, too, in brief.

As a by-product, I hope the paper will also illustrate the "Marrano of reason" dimension in Spinoza and how it can provide a context for understanding systematic problems as well. So prior to the reconstruction, let me briefly introduce this context.

I. *Marranos and Alternative Salvation*

Salvation does not lie in Jesus, but in the Law of Moses: this, as the files of the Inquisition insistently tell us, was the invariable claim of Judaizing Marranos, the common secret which made them an esoteric fraternity holding in its possession no less than the greatest prize their culture treasures. Only they, a persecuted minority, possess the key to salvation; they alone can attain what others, the ruling Christian establishment, have always distorted and misrepresented and therefore inevitably missed.

As Georg Simmel suggests, the sharing of such a hidden and exclusive possession can foster a secret group's identity and reinforce the individual's devotion to it even where other sociological indicators may show dispersion, discord, or poor communication. Marranos, however, did not only share a metaphysical secret but also a common "impure blood." This is what made them a "nation" (as indeed they were called) rather than merely a secret sect. But at least the Judaizers among this "nation" had also the traits of a secret religious fraternity, neither Christian nor actually Jewish, and bound by a road to salvation which rivals that of the ruling tradition around them.

Spinoza, too, retained an analogous Marrano feature,[1] translated into rational and secular terms. He, too, believed he held the key to true salvation which only a select group can attain, and which rivals that of the established tradition. But whereas Judaizing Marranos replaced Christ by Moses within historical religion, Spinoza rejected all historical religion and cult as superstitious. Salvation lies neither in Christ nor in the Law of Moses, but in the laws of reason leading to the "third kind of knowledge." Reason thereby yields the same elevated results which religion and mysticism have claimed to attain but have always distorted because of their irrational ways. Spinoza thus offers a *religion* of reason over and above ordinary rationality, the one which expresses itself in science and in practical ethics. Rationality has two forms, discursive and intuitive, fragmentary and synoptic, emotionally dull and emotionally explosive; and through the higher form of rationality - which, as we shall see, *presupposes the former and cannot be attained by a direct leap* - reason alone can lead in Spinoza to an immanent, this-worldly form of salvation, in which eternity penetrates temporal life, finitude is redeemed, the passions are turned into free, positive emotions and vigor, which transform one's whole life to the point of a "new birth" and the individual realizes his or her unity with God (= the deified universe) through knowledge and intellectual love.

The vehicle of this kind of salvation, the "third kind of knowledge," is not only one of the most difficult and controversial issues in Spinoza, but the *Ethics* is notoriously parsimonious in speaking of it. Worse, part of what the *Ethics* does say on the third kind of knowledge is confusing, if not downright wrong from Spinoza's own mature standpoint. I refer particularly to a famous example, carried over from Spinoza's earliest and less mature works (the essay *On the Emendation of the Intellect* (TdIE) and the *Short Treatise* (KV), where Spinoza explains intuitive knowledge by the manner in which a mathematician may grasp the nature of proportion in a single flash (E IIP40S2, reiterating TdIE and KV). If all there is to the third kind of knowledge is an ordinary mathematical intuition which, as Spinoza adds, "no one" (*nemo*) would fail to achieve, then we should not ponder much about it and may let the issue die of sheer banality. No one would dream of using this commonplace as a lever for mental emancipation - let alone salvation.[2]

The third kind of knowledge, however, is clearly a matter for the happy few. It is the road Spinoza offers to secular salvation - a rival road, rational and unmediated by any historical creed, to the same exalted goal which, as Spinoza believes, traditional religion and mysticism have sought in vain to achieve through irrational faith and acts. That Spinoza's philosophical effort was ultimately aimed at this goal is made unmistakably clear from the first known lines he wrote to the concluding phrase of the *Ethics*.

Spinoza starts to philosophize (in the TdIE) by setting up an ethical goal, the "highest good" to which all human endeavor should be subordinated. He seeks a radically new kind of life, in which his existence will attach to what is permanent and eternal. The same perspective later dominates Spinoza's mature thought; it also explains why he chose to entitle his major work the *Ethics*, even though the book deals mainly with metaphysics, the theory of knowledge and the psychology of the emotions. These branches of knowledge, along with the physical sciences, are to serve an ethical goal, first on the lower level of *ratio* (discursive rationality) and then, for the select few, leading to salvation through the third kind of knowledge.

Some modern readers may find this pervasive goal annoying or its elaboration incoherent; but as a recent example has proven again,[3] one can dismiss this dimension of Spinoza's thought only at the risk of losing much of his philosophical meaning. Spinoza without the third kind of knowledge would be as lame throughout as Plato would be without the Ideas. In both cases we shall be unable to form an adequate notion of the *rest* of the system without considering where it is meant (and construed) to lead.

The scant information which the *Ethics* supplies about the third kind of knowledge revolves around the following definition, which occurs twice in the book :

> The third kind of knowledge proceeds from an adequate idea of [the formal essence of] certain attributes of God to an adequate knowledge of the essence of things (IIP40S2; VP25D; in the latter the bracketed phrase is omitted).

Adding the idea of "one glance" or synopsis, we understand that the third kind of knowledge grasps at a single glance what in itself is a multiple chain of derivations, *by which the essence of a particular thing follows from God through one of his attributes.* The latter part is crucial, since the third kind of knowledge is defined not by its mode of cognition only but also by the kind of object which is thereby formed and revealed. When the third kind of knowledge takes place, a plurality of items of knowledge is *synthesized in a new way* so as to form a new cognitive object, which is proper to this mode of cognition. What is this object, and what further knowledge, or insight, do we gain by it?

For the moment I set aside the moral and existential gains which the third kind of knowledge is said to produce. My first question is whether it is supposed to add anything new to our *knowledge*. Does it represent a net cognitive advance over the second kind of knowledge? Is it meant to enrich us cognitively even before it provokes its alleged salutary effects?

Let me from the outset indicate the answer I intend to give. It will be No and Yes. No, there is no additional *information* gained through the third kind of knowledge. All the information we need and can possess of the object of our inquiry has already been supplied by *ratio*, the scientific investigation which subjects the object to a network of mechanistic natural laws. But yes, there is a distinct cognitive gain involved here, because what we already know of the object by external causality is now *interiorized*,[4] to produce a grasp of its *particular essence* and, thereby, also of the immanent-logical way in which it derives from the nature-God and inheres in it.

This is a change of perspective which, without addition or subtraction, provides us with a deeper insight of the *same* thing through a new processing, or synthesis, of the same informative ingredients. Formerly we had only external causes and universal laws by which to understand the particular thing - or rather, the way this thing instantiates a set of abstract common properties. Now, however, all the former information coalesces to produce a singular item, the *particular essence* of this thing as it follows immanently from one of God's attributes according to a logical principle of particularization.

It is characteristic of Spinoza that he sees both approaches as expressing the same fundamental information and as having a single ontological reference. The higher form of rationality (*scientia intuitiva*) does not abolish its ordinary form (*ratio*) but is taken to express the same metaphysical truth in a complementary, and also deeper way. Moreover, according to Spinoza's mature position, the internal viewpoint *depends upon the external as a necessary condition*. This is a crucial novelty introduced in the *Ethics*. There is no direct access to immanent essences. First we must explicate the object externally, by the intersection of mechanistic causal laws, and only when we have achieved a point of saturation, when a network of law-like explanations has, so to speak, closed in on the object from all relevant angles, can we expect the third kind of knowledge to also take place, so that, by an intuitive flash, all the causal information is re-processed in a new synthesis which lays bare the particular essence of the thing and the inherent way in which it flows by logical necessity from one of nature's attributes.[5]

This account of the third kind of knowledge is far less mystical than the one given by the *Short Treatise*. In so far as a semi-mystical element does remain here, it is reminiscent of the passage in Plato from *dianoia* to *nous*, from the account of the world through discursive sciences to the vision of eternal essences. And as in Plato, intuitive reason presupposes in Spinoza the work of scientific knowledge as a necessary condition.

Needless to say, this interpretation of the third kind of knowledge presupposes Spinoza's metaphysics, which views all things as immanently derived from the divine substance according to a logical principle (IP16, IP18, IP25 & C), and which, as I see it, admits particular essences in addition to natural laws as two adequate ways of explaining the same entity.

There are further background issues which provide the context for my reading of the third kind of knowledge. I refer specifically to what Spinoza scholars (following Curley and others) call the "vertical" and the "horizontal" types of causation; to the logic of complementarity which dominates Spinoza's system; and to his view of natural laws and of particular essences. I shall briefly discuss each of these matters before summarizing the cognitive import of the third kind of knowledge. Then, in the last part of this paper, I shall consider its role as secular salvation.

II. Vertical and Horizontal (Immanent and Transitive) Causality

Given a particular thing, there are two ways in Spinoza to account for it. According to IP28, the thing is produced by other finite things in an endless chain of external causation. This is the "horizontal" line, expressing the universe from the viewpoint of mechanism and finitude. However far we may regress or progress in the line of causes, we shall always remain in the realm of finite modes and external determination.

On the other hand, according to IP16 (and its extensions in IP18 through IP25), particular things are derived from God as their *immanent* cause, following a *logical* principle of particularization. This is the "vertical" line of causation. It goes from the substance through an attribute to a series of infinite modes (direct and mediated), until it is said to reach and determine the particular individual.

I interpret the infinite modes as the locus of natural laws in Spinoza. Natural laws are individual entities transmitting the power and necessity of God through one of the attributes. Thereby they serve as intermediary agents in engendering particulars. Spinoza conceives of natural laws as real powers, the actual *causes* of the particular things falling under them. Laws do not merely describe how a finite thing will behave but *make* it behave in that way.

Spinoza evidently sees the horizontal and the vertical lines of causation as expressing the same process - that of cosmic particularization. But how is their relation to be construed?

The answer, I think, is that the horizontal causality realizes the vertical one, by translating its inner logical character into external mechanistic terms. This realization applies especially to the crucial last step in the vertical line, when it passes from the narrowest law or infinite mode to the finite particular. How does a law determine particular things? Not directly, Spinoza answers, but in that it determines how *other* particular things will act and affect it. Suppose that A is determined by B, C, and D as its mechanistic causes, and that these causes operate in accordance with law L: we may say that L determines A in that it determines how B, C, D, will act upon A. And if we are ready, as Spinoza is, to view as equivalent the following two statements:

(1) A is determined by the logical necessity of the law L;
(2) A is determined by the mechanistic causes B, C, & D, whose action obeys and instantiates the law L,

then we have acknowledged the equivalence, or complementarity, of the vertical and horizontal views of causation.

This dual perspective implies that *we must distinguish between what causes a law to exist, and what causes a particular thing to exist under that law.* The law is generated in nature by immanent logical derivation. But the particular thing is produced under that law by other particular things, transmitting external causality to each other in endless chains.

Let us elaborate on the former example. When a car is moving on the road, it is "vertically" determined by a system of mechanical laws anchored in the supreme law of motion and rest. This law is the "infinite mode" in the world of extension, which assigns a fixed proportion of motion and rest to the universe at large; thereby (1) it determines the rule which binds all changes in the universe and (2) it shapes the universe itself as a single individual. The laws of nature are the permanent features of this global individual; their network is, so to speak, inscribed upon the universe as its immutable "face," and is duly dubbed *facies totius universi* ("the face of the whole universe").[6]

These laws, or a cross-section of them, also determine the car moving on the road. But how? In that they determine, both generally and with reference to this particular instance, how gasoline burns, gears are shifted, power is transmitted, metals resist pressure - that is, how the "horizontal" factors will behave which actually engender the car and produce its movement.

Thus the laws determine the particular thing vertically by the mediation of other particulars which affect it horizontally. And this is also how Spinoza supposes IP28 to translate and realize the logical principle implied in IP16, and why he thinks of the vertical and horizontal systems as equivalent.

III. The Logic of Complementary Systems

This complementarity is not an ad hoc device, but Spinoza's characteristic way of handling dualities which amounts to a philosophical logic of his own. In order to maintain his radical monism while avoiding Parmenides' results or Hegelian-like dialectics, Spinoza handled the fundamental dualities in the universe by declaring them to be complementary aspects of the same. This logic of equivalence is more prevalent in Spinoza than meets the eye. Officially it is said to obtain between extension and thought, body and mind, the order and connexion of things and the order and connexion of ideas; but it also applies in the relation of *natura naturans* to *natura naturata* (that is, of the infinite and finite aspects of nature, nature as totality and nature as a plurality of finite things: this distinction replaces in Spinoza the traditional dualism of the creator and the things he creates); of perceptions to their accompanying affects; of God's "intellect" to his "will" - and also to the relation between logical derivation and mechanistic causation. These are two parallel, or equivalent, ways of construing the *same* universe and the *same* process of particularization within it.

A similar logic had been admitted before Spinoza - but with reference to the God only, not to nature and finite things. God was so different from the world that he had an ontology of his own, and it has been frequently said, e.g., that knowledge, will and creation are in God one and the same. Spinoza eliminates God's transcendence and transfers to nature the radical unity of God - and the special ontology which comes along with it.

Two minor points should be added to avoid misunderstanding. Equivalences in Spinoza are not necessarily dualities. They do not always work in pairs, as we see in the case of the attributes, which are numerous. Even the pair we discussed, logical derivation and mechanistic causation, may well have a third member - cosmic love; but we cannot do justice here to this somewhat obscure issue.

Also, I admit the analogy with the attributes is incomplete.[7] But what counts more than the differences in detail is the common methodological thrust, the logic of complementarity which marks Spinoza's thinking throughout.

Finally - and at some greater length - let me point out that finite modes in Spinoza are as eternal as the substance itself from which they derive. The line of causality we called vertical should be understood not as a process of "creation" or "emanation" but as ontological dependence or support. Seen through their essences (or *sub specie aeternitatis*), finite things are just as eternal and primordial as their sustaining substance. The difference is that the essence of finite things does not imply existence, but requires the essence of the substance in order to exist; but this dependence too is eternal; it is a logical, timeless relation by which the modes, seen as particular essences, presuppose God. They inhere in God as their ontological support, they are implications of God's essence, but they are there eternally, like God himself.

Generation and destruction occur in Spinoza as particular essences become translated into concrete things in the domain of duration and external causality. Here horizontal causality takes over from the vertical one, and a time-dimension is added to being. This is *natura naturata*, the world of dependent things, seen (and existing) *sub specie durationis*. But the same system of finitude exists and can be seen also *sub specie aeternitatis*, and in this case the particular things in it are grasped as having neither beginning nor end.

Thus the eternity (and sempiternity: existence in all times) of the world of particulars can be interpreted in two ways: (a) the sub-system of *natura naturata* is eternal, although particular modes within it are generated and destroyed; (b) particular things, too, are eternal when seen through their essences, although their span within *duratio* is necessarily limited.

In conclusion, both *natura naturans* and *natura naturata* are simultaneously eternal systems existing irrespective of beginning or end. The system comprising the substance, the attributes, and the infinite modes, provides the finite things with ontological support and with their nature and laws; it does not so much *engender* them (in time) as it *constitutes* them (timelessly). For such a thing, entering into time translates the vertical relation into a horizontal one which is conceived as another facet of the same system. Thus eternity and duration are also, eventually, a dual pair understood in terms of the logic of equivalence.

This interpretation is made both possible and inevitable by the fact that particular things have eternal essences which are logically (and thus simultaneously) implied in God's essence.

IV. Infinite Modes, Laws, and Particular Essences

To complete this picture we must consider a little more closely the status of natural laws and essences in Spinoza. Earlier I have interpreted natural laws as infinite modes and as the causes of the particulars which they govern. In Spinoza's metaphoric language, the laws of nature embody God's immutable "will" or "decrees"[8] - that is, they express his necessity to be and to operate in certain modes. If by inner necessity God must particularize himself, then the immutable patterns in which this particularization takes place mediate between God as One and God as Many, between *natura naturans* and *natura naturata*. They express the unity and infinity of God in a variety of hierarchically-ordered patterns, and transmit his power and necessity "downward" to the world of finite modes.

In calling laws "infinite," Spinoza means that, like the attribute, laws are uniformly present in an infinite range of phenomena falling within their domain. Just as the attribute of extension is present in all extended bodies, so these bodies are all uniformly subject to the laws of motion, from the supre me law (the direct infinite mode) to the more specific laws which derive from it.

Infinity has, however, also a second sense, in which laws are distinguished from the attribute.   Laws are permanent and immutable in the sense of *duration*. They are sempiternal (= existing in all times) and belong to *natura naturata*, the world seen as a plurality of modes. The attribute is eternal in the sense of timelessness and belongs to *natura naturans*, the world seen from the standpoint of totality.

The use of natural laws instead of genera and species is one of the characteristics of the New Science of which Spinoza was a part.   Scientific explanation since ancient times has been understood as requiring the subsumption of a particular item under some principle of universality.   Plato had spoken of independent universal essences, whereas Aristotelian science placed these essences in the actual individuals as their inherent generic forms. Explanation was by and large a matter of essential classification, the referring of a particular thing to its genus and species, understood also as the thing's ideal perfection.   This gave science a teleological orientation and a marked qualitative character.

The scientific revolution of the 17th century replaced species with natural laws as the universal principle by which science proceeds. Laws are indifferent to genus and species; they cut through qualitatively different domains and allow only unilateral effective causes as valid.   Hence they lend themselves to a mechanistic and quantifiable explanation of nature, barring purposes, ideal models, and *universal* essences.

Spinoza was a proponent of the New Science in that in him, too, the causal, mechanistic laws of nature have replaced genera and species as the universal principles by which science proceeds.   This abolished universal essences - but not the concept of essence altogether. Along with the modern category of natural law Spinoza went on adhering to the older category of essence as a valid, even as a deeper, scientific category - but he substituted particular essences for the universal ones.

Universal essence is a fiction, an empty word.   But essences do exist - as *particular* essences. Each individual thing in the universe has its own essence, by which its specificity is constituted. The essence of a particular thing is the unique place it occupies in reality; it is, so to speak, the logical or metaphysical "point" which belongs exclusively to it in the overall map of being. Of course, this specific point is determined by the other items and coordinates of the map - that is, by everything which determines the thing to exist and to act in the way proper to it.   And this establishes a logical link - to Spinoza, even an equivalence - between what the thing is and the causal network which makes it be what it is.   In other words, a thing's particular essence is ontologically equivalent to the process of its determination (an idea which Spinoza had conceived and was groping for already in the TdIE).[9]

Particular essences exist actually (*formaliter*) in God and are presented as ideas in the "infinite intellect." According to IP16 and its corollaries (including a distant but crucial corollary in VP29S), God particularizes himself into an infinitely diverse system of particular things, or existing ("formal," in 17th century jargon) essences, each of which, when seen vertically, is as eternal and necessary as God himself. In this sense, particular essences take on in Spinoza a status which is partly similar to the Platonic ideas. They are pure and immutable, even eternal in a supra-temporal sense, yet each refers to one particular thing only. Existing as separate items in the attribute of thought (or in God's "infinite intellect"), they are objective metaphysical definitions which assign to each thing its specific place in being or, what amounts to the same, by which the uniqueness of each thing is immanently constituted and engendered in God. (This uniqueness may imply the career or biography peculiar to it: essences are generic in nature and may involve complex stories and processes; but each of these will amount to the necessarry and sufficient account of one single entity, and all will be a apriori, contained timelessly in one of God's attributes (or in God's infinite intellect) from which they derive.) A few quotations:

> If God had created all men like Adam... then he would have created only Adam, and not Peter and Paul. But God's true perfection is that he gives all [individual] things their essence, from the last to the greatest... (KV I/43, Curley (1985), 87).

> Things must agree with their particular ideas, whose being must be a perfect essence, and not with universal ones, because then they would not exist. (KV I/49, Curley (1985), 92).

> Peter must agree with the idea of Peter... and not with the idea of Man. (ibid)

This selection from the *Short Treatise* (KV) may be complemented by quotes from *Metaphysical Thoughts* (CM)[10] and the *Ethics*. In the latter work, particular essence is defined (IID2) as what constitutes a thing's individuality, and the definition lends itself to explication both in terms of logical essences and of complete mechanistic determination.[11]

Since essences lay bare the internal design of nature and its occupants, they offer, on the basis of the same body of information, a deeper view into the world. Herein lies the cognitive advantage of the third kind of knowledge. We can also see from this that Spinoza, although a nominalist, is not a positivist, since he attributes a metaphysical interior to things and makes it accessible through the third kind of knowledge. Grasping this interior is not a direct mystical revelation. It is based upon a discursive, mechanistic science which it supplements not with new informative ingredients, but with a new synthesis of the old ones.

A final remark concerning essences. Spinoza's adherence both to essences and to mechanistic causality may indicate his position between antiquity and the modern era as two scientific cultures, a position which his theory of wisdom and intellectual salvation highlights even more. On the matter of essences, however, Spinoza is not quite beyond the frontiers of his Zeitgeist. Other philosophers made an attempt to reconcile a mechanistic science with entities having an interior essence (Leibniz) or residing eternally in God (Malebranche), and they, too, described the eternal essences as unfolding themselves in their things' career (Leibniz again). Contrary to Leibniz, however, Spinoza refuses to see these essences as *substances*; to him they are individual crystallizations of the causal processes themselves. In that he comes closer, I think, to the modern outlook. In addition, there may be a certain affinity between Spinoza's way of thinking and some contemporary theories about how things can be individuated by means of the causal processes that lead to (or from) them. In Spinoza, however, this takes place in a *single* world - the idea of many possible worlds being self-contradictory.

Given the background issues we discussed so far, we may now return to the third kind of knowledge and summarize the way it is supposed to work.

V. The Third Kind of Knowledge Resumed

In principle the third kind of knowledge can apply to any particular thing; but because he offers this kind of knowledge as an alternative kind of salvation, Spinoza makes no secret that he has a privileged object for it: the philosopher himself, his body, mind, and environment. The third kind of knowledge is preferably, though not exclusively, a form of self-knowledge. But it is the opposite of direct self-awareness. It is not a subjective mode of *cogito*, not an immediate grasp of ourselves, but a most elaborate form of *mediated* self-knowledge. The intuitive element is added at the end only, to crown an effort of scientific objectification.

What in direct awareness I feel to be my "innermost self" is but a distorted idea of my body being affected by external causes. Therefore, to achieve self-knowledge of the third kind I must not develop my direct self-awareness (as in yoga and mystical experiences), but rather *expel* it as a form of *imaginatio*. True self-knowledge starts with overcoming the illusion of pure subjectivity and objectifying the *cogito*, by referring it to the body and by referring them both to the causal order of nature at large. To do this I have to engage in an arduous scientific investigation (of my body, my mind, my situation) in which I approach myself "from the outside," through the mechanistic laws of nature and other natural entities which determine my own being in the world.

This may seem to entail a form of self-alienation, but only apparently so. Objectification may often be painful and hard to perform, but it is not necessarily alienation, because what I approach in this objectified way is my true being rather than a feigned, illusory self. For in Spinoza's ontology I am, in both body and mind, the product of an impersonal substance-God which has no human-like features and may not be anthropomorphized; in other words, the natural processes which produce me bear no resemblance to my own subjectivity: they do not work by intention and purpose, have no privileged affinity to human affairs and allow no room or special laws for history as distinguished from the rest of nature. Recognizing this, I may well become emancipated from religious and metaphysical illusions, but also lose their soothing comforts.[12] This hard element in liberation - what I call "dark enlightenment" - is what attracted Nietzsche to Spinoza and invoked Hegel's criticism.[13] It is also part of the reason why true philosophy - even at the level of *ratio* - is never for Spinoza a matter for the multitude.

Equally painful to accept, for many people, may be the idea that their dear and most intimately felt self is but a confused idea. Yet as long as nothing makes them objectify and externalize their view of themselves, they will not be able to attain true self-knowledge, neither in the external mode of *ratio* nor in the intuitive mode which recurs in the third kind of knowledge; for the latter is based upon the former as a necessary prerequisite.

In the stage of *ratio* (the ordinary rational mode), the philosopher studies himself through the general, mechanistic processes of nature. He understands his bodily existence as determined by all the causal processes explained by physics and its corrolaries - chemistry, biology, medicine (and, as we may add today: genetics, neurophysiology, biochemistry etc.). Equally, he studies his mind by the help of psychology and its various derivatives, including sociology, linguistics, and politics (today we may add psychotherapy and the study of the unconscious). Each of the two branches of study is independent and irreducible to the others, yet both express one and the same ontological entity. Moreover, investigations in both branches of knowledge are conducted in conformity with the mechanistic paradigm of explanation which Spinoza believes applies to all sciences. Everything occurs by external, transitive causes obeying the laws of nature.

This scientific knowledge is supplemented, or rather supported, by a basic metaphysical framework. The philosopher understands nature as a single substance equivalent to God, in which we all inhere as a modes. This is, roughly speaking, the contents of Book I of the *Ethics*, which is here grasped in the *second* mode of knowledge. It already gives metaphysical (and even a semi-theo-logical) interpretation to the body of scientific knowledge, but it fails to turn this interpretation into a living experience.

However, as I gather more scientific knowledge of my body and of my mind, as I close in, so to speak, on myself from all relevant causal angles, the ground is set for the third kind of knowledge. The network of transitive causes has placed and defined my body as it stands uniquely within nature at large. Now, in a flash of intuition, all this causal information is synthesized in a new way, which produces its epistemic counterpart: my particular essence. Nothing new is added to the scientific information we already possess, yet all its ingredients coalesce in the formation (or reproduction) of this essence as a new synthesis, which lays bare the metaphysical "interior" of the thing I am and the way in which I derive immediately (or "vertically") from God as my *immanent* logical cause.

Therefore, the third kind of knowledge represents a net cognitive gain over the second kind, since it allows me to gain a new and deeper perspective of myself and the world, although it uses exactly the same materials as before. The second kind of knowledge has given me only a partial account of reality. It drew the law-like ways in which transitive causes produce their effects in an endless chain. Thereby it served as an adequate explication of IP28, *but not of the crucial IP16.* What it lacked, and the third kind of knowledge supplies, is the grasp of things according to their particular essences as they immanently issue from God. This changes not only the mental quality of our perception but the *categories* embedded in it. Things are understood by their particular essences, not their universal laws merely, and the causes which determine them are understood as logical and immanent, not as mechanical and transitive causes; and this now allows the philosopher to penetrate into nature's *interior design* where formerly he had its external facet only.

It is essential to see that the same occurs *in the other direction as well.* I do not only grasp myself now as I exist in and through God; I also grasp God, the totality, through some concrete particular (myself) and no longer as an abstract concept or entity. This is a crucial change with respect to my former metaphysical knowledge. I had an adequate idea of God, or the totality of nature, before as well; but it was general and abstract. I knew that individuals are, in principle, in God and that God, in principle, must be particularized and expressed as particulars. But all this knowledge remained abstract for me, I did not realize it as an actual awareness. Now, in *scientia intuitiva*, direct awareness comes back to the fore, no longer a first and overall stage but the *last* stage in a long rational and demonstrative process. It is only after I have investigated how exactly my particular essence is determined by the universe at large that I can also interiorize this knowledge and become aware in one grasp that and how I exist in God just as God necessarily exists and expresses himself in me. This is a powerful realization, redeeming, liberating, and engulfing all, not in the diffuse manner of romantic pantheism but controlled by rational comprehension - which is why the love for the universe which flows from here is described as "intellectual love." And it is the *content* of this realization, not only its intuitive manner, which gives it the powerful affective response it has.

We may also say that it is through Part V of the *Ethics* that the student comes back again to Part I and understands it in its true and deeper light. *Our metaphysical comprehension, too, has passed into the phase of scientia intuitiva.* What we had known before as an external abstraction we now experience as a full realization. Again, nothing has changed in the material ingredients of this knowledge; if we were to verbalize them, they would yield exactly the same statements. But it is not any more the same cognitive object and experience.[14]

This deeper insight into the totality (and the place of the actual particular within it) cannot be attained in the merely discursive stage of *ratio*. This is why Part I of the *Ethics* is grasped in full only when revisited from the standpoint of Part V. Spinoza's book, no less than his system, has this tacit circular (or spiral) form which overshadows its apparent linearity. The linear progression is a necessary condition for attaining the third kind of knowledge but is transformed and superseded in its new, holistic and intuitive grasp.

VI. The Third Kind of Knowledge as Secular Salvation

So far I have concentrated on the cognitive gain involved in the third kind of knowledge. Let me now refer in brief to the *ethical effects* which make it count as salvation.

These salvational effects are of two kinds, psychological and metaphysical: (a) psychologically, the third kind of knowledge is supposed to produce vigor, joy, love, and an intense sense of liberation capable of transforming the whole personality to the point of "rebirth"; and (b) metaphysically it is said to overcome the mind's finitude and endow it with immortality - or rather (to express Spinoza's meaning more accurately), with eternity. Let me comment briefly on these two aspects.

(a) Salvation as Mental Transformation

Cognitions are affective events in Spinoza. Every idea has a corresponding affective response, and the two are not separate entities but the same thing seen from different angles. (This is another of Spinoza's equivalences.) That the third kind of knowledge is supposed to provoke, or come along with, the most potent affect, which has power to overcome all the others, is made plausible by Spinoza both by the mode of this experience and by its content (though primarily, I think, by the latter.)

In mode, the third kind of knowledge is an intensive intuition, in which a great many items of discursive knowledge are compressed into a single cognitive object and grasped at one glance. Such concentration can plausibly make the experience highly potent and intense, regardless of what it contains.

And yet, the content of the third kind of knowledge plays, relatively, a much larger role than its mode in producing its beneficial effects. The intuition only compounds what in itself already has immense psychological power. For what the intuition compresses is no less than my detailed and concrete realization that I exist in God and that God exists through me, a unity which rivals (and in its way, usurps) the most exalted states envisaged by mystics and great religious figures. It is a rational translation of the ideal of *unio mystica*, in which the individual both *actualizes* his or her unity with God and becomes powerfully *aware* of it.

At this point I should like to pause and consider how Spinoza's Marrano background is here translated into his revolutionary new context, that of immanent reason. Like the Marranos, Spinoza is looking for an alternative road to salvation, in defiance of the one accepted in his established culture. But whereas Marranos sought it in a substitute *historical* religion ("The Law of Moses" replacing Christ's) Spinoza looked for it outside all historical religions. It is by the third kind of knowledge, a rational-intuitive procedure bound by no historical cult, Revelation, Election, Covenant etc., that philosophers are eventually supposed to be able to attain what the great mystics and religious aspirants have always been seeking misguidedly and inevitably failed to find, because they relied on superstitious beliefs and practices. As in their conceptions of God, they were aiming at something true and real but missing the actual reference of their concepts.

I think this dimension is crucial when trying to interpret the moral and metaphysical effects attributed to the third kind of knowledge. Spinoza was not a mystic, but he recognized in mysticism a misguided form of yearning and endeavor which, correctly transformed by reason and the third kind of knowledge and guided to its proper object, will become the rational philosopher's way of salvation, a reward as rare and high in achievement as that which mystics have been pretending to attain by irrational means. In other words, it will be a secular (and truly universal, as distinguished from the Catholic claim to universality) form of salvation.

But this secular salvation has also a metaphysical dimension, associated by Spinoza with eternity and immortality - and giving him some of his most notorious problems. Without removing them all, I think an adequate interpretation should distinguish between the above two concepts and view salvation, or the overcoming of finitude, as a state achieved within this life rather than after it. Whatever else it is, it enriches the philosopher's immanent, this-worldly existence and has no important meaning beyond it.

(b) Salvation and Immortality

Particular essences are eternal in the sense of supra-temporality. But in them essence does not involve existence. This means that they can either exist in a definite time and place, or not. In the latter case they exist logically as implied in God's attributes (E IIP8) and their ideas are contained in God's infinite idea,[15] but they do not have *duratio*. An essence will enter into the realm of duration when there are specific mechanistic (external) causes that will produce the thing of which it is the essence. The existence in duration of an essence is expressed in all the attributes simultaneously, as is its ceasing to endure. Hence the duration of the mind must end with that of the body. Minds cannot endure as separate entities.[16]

How then is immortality possible? To answer in a word: it is not possible. When the third kind of knowledge takes place, I know myself through my particular essence as it inheres in God. This essence is eternal, as is the idea by which I know it; and in the act of knowledge the eternal idea by which I know myself becomes identical with part of the complex idea which is my mind, so to this extent my mind gains eternity. But it gains this eternity within this life and not beyond it. Eternity is not sempiternity; it is a metaphysical state or quality, which does not signify indefinite existence, and which is here seen as penetrating into duration and as being attained and realized within it. In other words, the mind attains a form of eternity within this life and while the body, too, endures.

To clarify, let us distinguish in Spinoza between (1) eternity, (2) salvation, and (3) immortality. While every finite thing has an eternal side, nothing is immortal and only a small group of humans can attain salvation. Every finite thing has eternity by virtue of having an eternal essence and an idea reflecting it in the infinite intellect of God. But no finite thing is immortal, if by this we understand that it endures indefinitely in the realm of duration and external causes. No finite thing which comes into existence in duration can sustain this kind of existence indefinitely; at a certain point the external causes will overcome its conatus and destroy it.[17] The destruction will affect both its body and its mind, since a mind (*mens*) is constituted by the ideas of its body (and reflexively also of itself) as they, the body and the mind, exist in duration, not as they are from the standpoint of eternity.   Therefore *minds* die with their bodies; what remains is the eternal essence which had been there all along.[18]

We may say that particular essences are eternal while minds are perishable. Salvation consists in uniting the two, the perishable mind and the eternal essence, so that they become identical over a significant range.   According to Spinoza, the mind does not "have" ideas but *is* the complex of "its" ideas.   A true idea, however, is timeless and unique and is the same in all its occur- rences; therefore, the more true ideas I know, a larger part of my actual, or existential mind is constituted of timeless ingredients.   This is the cognitive basis of salvation in Spinoza, on which all the rest hinges; and it is an occurrence within this life and world, as eternity penetrates my actual existence and transforms its quality and direction.

Upon a certain reading of Spinoza, my eternal essence is modified by the knowledge I have gained during life - as if I enter life with one essence and exit with another.   But this reading is incoherent.   Nothing, by definition, can affect an eternal essence.   What can be affected by the third kind of knowledge is my actual, existential mind, when larger parts of it become identical with eternal ideas; but this achievement is attained within life and cannot affect the way "I" shall exist after death, since without my body there will be no "I" either - no individual *ego cogito* and no conatus to sustain.   There will only be an eternal particular essence existing regardless of time (as it did even before my birth).

Thus Spinoza keeps to his strict immanent philosophy even when offering a theory of salvation. The transcendent-religious idea of an afterlife, in which our existence will be modified in proportion to what we have done in this life, is foreign to his mind and fundamentally un-Spinozistic. His famous statement, that virtue is its own reward, also implies the same.   A Marrano of reason, Spinoza unites this-worldliness with a new way to salvation, which not only relies upon reason and knowledge rather than on religious cult, but also makes salvation an immanent affair, consummated within this world and life.

It is therefore not in immortality that metaphysical salvation consists, but in the realization of eternity within time.   The third kind of knowledge helps me overcome my finitude, not my mortality.   I am saved as long as I live.   I enjoy a state of timeless necessity in the midst of my duration, but when I die all will be over, except for an impersonal essence, or idea, existing in God's infinite intellect.   The mere existence of this idea is no comfort to me and does not signify my salvation; it is only a metaphysical prerequisite for it.   All things in the universe have such ideas, my dog, the Emperor Caligula, his horse, the bomb in Hiroshima.   What if I know that my idea, like that of Caligula's horse, is timeless?   Neither of us is thereby saved.   Salvation means that a timeless idea has become part of my actual, enduring mind.   And this can happen only while I endure.

Eternity in itself has no salvational significance.   What makes eternity count as salvation is its incursion into the individual's life *as a mortal and enduring thing.* It is the eternal affecting the temporal or realized in its domain. This alone, Spinoza believes, can make an existential difference and plausibly count as a secular mode of salvation - that "rare and difficult" reward Spinoza was seeking as philosopher and as the Marrano of Reason.

1. See my forthcoming book, *Spinoza and Other Heretics*, Vol 1, *The Marranos of Reason* (Princeton: Princeton University Press, 1989), Ch. 2. (The present paper, with slight revisions, is reprinted in Ch. 7 in that book).
2. The example of the proportion is at best a partial analogy which illustrates the intuitive and synoptic qualities of the third kind of knowledge (its working *uno intuito* - at a single glance) but misses some most essential ones. Above all, it is incompatible with the definition of the third kind of knowledge as given twice in the *Ethics* (IIP40S2 and VP25D), because knowledge in the example does not "proceed from the essence of some attribute of God" but is gained directly by a *particular* intuition. Moreover, intuitive knowledge occurs here spontaneously, whereas according to Spinoza's mature position it must arise from the second kind of knowledge (VP28 &D). And, as I mentioned in the text, the rarity and extreme difficulty *inherent* in the third kind of knowledge are incompatible with the commonplace kind of intuition to which the example refers.
   The example illustrates a shortcut scientific cognition which, bypassing deduction, provides a direct grasp analogous to that of axioms. But this in itself does not go beyond the boundaries of *ratio*. A mathematical genius capable of compressing a great many deductive steps into a single intuition will not thereby be in possession of the third kind of knowledge or enjoy a higher moral and metaphysical standpoint than his less talented colleagues, although he will certainly be a far superior scientist.
3. Bennett (1984), 357, 364-375. Bennett dismisses the last section of the *Ethics* in fierce language (it is an "unmitigated... disaster," "nonsense," "rubbish which causes others to write rubbish," and scholars like Pollock who take it seriously end up "babbling" and producing "valueless" material). Unfortunately it is Bennett's book - which otherwise offers many illuminating analyses - which comes out the loser; what it misses is not merely one chapter in Spinoza but a significant perspective for understanding the whole. I believe this shortcoming could have been avoided if Spinoza's aims about religion, the transformation of religious language and religious *emotions*, and ultimately his search for an alternative way to salvation, had been taken into account. (Bennett might then have used the argument he elsewhere borrows from Kripke (p. 366) and say that Spinoza - or Christianity, or Judaism, or this and that mystic or theologian - are speaking about the same thing, salvation, and participating in a meaningful (and to them, supremely important) discussion, even if some or all of them hold wrong theories about it.) In any event, this is a case in which the historical picture - Spinoza's Marrano background - could have helped in recognizing the importance which the issue of salvation has taken in Spinoza's systematic work *throughout*.
4. I mean *objectively* interiorized, that is, turned into a representation of what the thing's internal essence is.
5. This picture represents a change from TdIE where external causality is delegated to a much lower role. This change, raising the epistemic level of mechanical causation, parallels another: abolishing the immediacy of the third kind of knowledge and making it depend upon the products of *ratio*.
6. Incidentally, the idea that the universe has a "face," or human-like features, was certainly known to Spinoza from Jewish *Kabbalah*, where the universe is mystically structured on the lines of "Primordial Man" (*adam kadmon*). In accepting the metaphor Spinoza rejects its anthropomorphic implications: the only "face" the universe has is the

network of logical and mechanistic laws, without the slightest shred of teleology or any other human-like feature.

7. The attributes allow of no interaction, whereas the third kind of knowledge issues from the second as a necessary prerequisite. Also, officially no attribute is superior to the other, yet vertical knowledge through essence is supposed to give a deeper view than the horizontal mechanistic one.

8. Viewing natural laws as God's "immutable decrees" allows us to further develop this metaphor, even beyond Spinoza. Unlike the philosophers of his time, today we can conceive of sound natural science as liable to change; so using the metaphor of God's decrees one might say: the laws of nature are a fixed divine constitution which each scientific era interprets in its own way, subject to the ruling scientific paradigm; just as in religious tradition, the Bible is considered as God's immutable constitution which later generations are authorized to interpret in their own manner. This is not precisely Spinoza's position, but may be compatible with it.

9. When speaking of a "generative definition," Spinoza gives a technical or constructive example, taken from geometry; but what he is groping for is metaphysical generation: the authentic definition (essence) of a thing is equivalent to, and reached by, the network of causes by which it is generated. I see this intuition accompanying Spinoza from early on to the climax of the *Ethics*. Equally, when he says in TdIE that things are known either by their essence or by their proximate causes, he lays down the two approaches of which he will later stress the equivalence.

10. "Being of essence is nothing but that manner in which created things are comprehended in the attributes of God" (CM I/2, Curley (1985), 304). (Here the terms are defined to suit both tradition and Spinoza's innovation). Essences have being "outside the intellect" (*ibid*.). Every such "formal essence" has an idea by which it is "contained objectively" (= represented) in God's idea (later Spinoza will say more accurately: in God's "infinite intellect.") Formal essences exist even if the thing of which they are the essence does not. (See E IIP8; this is because the essence of particulars does not involve existence.) They neither exist of themselves nor are created, but "depend on the divine essence alone" (in which everything is contained, including the essences of non-existing things - *ibid*.) " So in this sense," Spinoza adds, "we agree with those who say that the essences of things are eternal."

11. That "which, being given, the thing is necessarily posited and which, being taken away, the thing is necessarily taken away" can be construed both as a logical essence and as a mechanistic process (or set of processes) which, conforming to the laws of nature, is a necessary and sufficient condition for the generation of the specific thing in question.

12. It is interesting to figure out how Spinoza would handle the phenomenon of unsettling philosophical truths. While his system *abounds* in them, it also states the principle that truth is the source of joy, not of suffering. There must be a moment of suffering in dispelling metaphysical illusion - which also explains the stubborn resistance it provokes. Freud, in many ways a disciple of Spinoza, knew this and accounted for it; so did Nietzsche. Spinoza lacks a theory explaining the mechanism of *passage* from comforting illusion to (at first) disquieting truth. But his theory, I think, can accommodate one. (In the opening of TdIE Spinoza himself describes a variety of such a passage).

13. See my *Spinoza and Other Heretics*, vol. 2, *The Adventures of Immanence*, (Princeton: Princeton University Press: 1989) ch. 2, 5.

14. Given the same body of scientific knowledge, there are three ways of relating to it. (1) A positivist, or a scientist uninterested in metaphysics, will try to avoid metaphysical interpretation altogether (although Spinoza will still attribute some metaphysical framework to him or her, possibly derived from the imagination). (2) A philosopher-scientist may interpret the same body of knowledge according to Spinoza's metaphysics but remain on

the level of ordinary rationality, or *ratio*, with its linear arguments and law-like explanations, understanding the relation of substance, attribute, mode, law, etc., or mind and body, emotion and cognition, in the same discursive way that governs his empirical science and is expounded in the "geometrical" layout of the *Ethics*. Finally (3) in the third kind of knowledge, the same things acquire a new, or higher interpretation when, through their particular essences, they are grasped as they are in God *and God too is now grasped only in and through them*. This adds new insight and a higher metaphysical interpretation to our knowledge of empirical particulars - *and it also makes us understand Spinoza's own metaphysics differently, since the preceding books of the Ethics are now grasped from the standpoint of book V.* In other words, metaphysical truths, too, are liberated now from their linear layout and grasped as the mutual system of ideas in which they actually exist. This new organization, or synthesis, of the same ingredients of knowledge allows a deeper peering into the texture of reality and the emotional response corresponding to it.

15. Or also: in the infinite intellect. Spinoza distinguishes here (IIP8) between ideas and essences. Essences are immutable entities existing logically as contained in the attribute. Ideas represent these essences *objective*, and depend upon their state. An essence which has no duration is represented as such, and an essence which does enter duration (or exists in that mode) is also represented *as such*. It follows that, on the theory implied in IIP8, essences are immutable but ideas are not.

Since ideas are the same as their objects, they must represent *objective* the fact that their object exists in duration or is a merely logical essence. But essences do not represent this difference within themselves. They are indifferent to existence: this is what distinguishes them from ideas.

Yet this theory cannot really work. It breaks down, I think, because it cannot sustain the parallelism between logical and mechanical particularization. If the sum total of transitive causes by which a thing is determined to exist and operate defines its uniqueness in being, and if this is supposed to be equivalent to its essence, then it cannot be that one of the equivalents (the first) includes the parameters of duration and the second (the essence) does not; for in this case they are not equivalents. Spinoza must either include durational parameters in the *essence*, or omit them from the causal explication, or else abandon the equivalence. He does not want to do the latter and he cannot, by definition, do the second; so it remains for him to include durational parameters in the essence - and do away with the distinction between essence and idea. And although this may raise problems for him elsewhere, I think it would be his most coherent solution.

16. As Spinoza says explicitly in V23D ("We do not attribute duration to it [the mind] except while the body endures." But then, his famous sentence, "it is time now to pass to those things which pertain to the mind's *duration* without relation to the body" (VP20), is clearly incoherent or intentionally misleading, because of the word "duration." On Spinoza's doctrine, the mind has duration while the body endures, and when the mind overcomes its finitude it gains a kind of eternity, not indefinite duration.

17. This is the difference between timelessness (eternity in Spinoza) and immortality. Immortality means indefinite existence *within time*. Moreover, it means indefinite *life*, since immortality can be attributed only to entities to which mortality, too, is logically attributable. In Spinozistic terms, the semantics of mortality and immortality can only apply to entities in the domain of duration and of external causes.

This also distinguishes immortality from sempiternity. The laws of nature (and the infinite mode they depend upon) are sempiternal; belonging to *natura naturata*, they determine its everlasting law-like structure. And like most intermediary stages they occupy a problematic position, for they have duration (indefinite duration), but are not themselves determined by external causes. Given the example of infinite modes, we may conclude that eternal essences are also, in their way, sempiternal, for at any moment in time they can be said to exist - however timelessly. Whatever the solution of this paradox (if it is a paradox), the sempiternal status applies to these essences regardless of whether their objects have entered the actual world of duration and external causality. But once they do, once an existing concrete thing expresses the essence in a definite time and place, it cannot sustain this existence indefinitely but, engendered by external causes which translate the essence "horizontally," and resisting, as *conatus,* as long as it can the assault of other external causes, it must eventually, by its ontological mode of being, succumb at a certain point and cease to exist in duration. At that point all that "remains" - or rather, is - of it is the eternal essence.

18. Of course, a particular essence, because it defines the individual's unique place in being, can and must include its life-history or career; but it expresses this from the standpoint of eternity, as a timeless implication of God (and one ontological "spot" in the eternal map of being).

DE L'ÉMOTION INTÉRIEURE CHEZ DESCARTES
À L'AFFECT ACTIF SPINOZISTE

J.- M. BEYSSADE
Université de Paris IV

I. Position du problème

Il existe dans l'*Ethique* (à quoi je me limiterai ici) une doctrine de l'affect actif. Cela signifie que l'affectivité (je traduirai *affectus* par *affects*) se répartit en deux genres. Il y a d'abord "les affects qui sont des passions" (IVP59, VP34), je dirai par convention les *affects passifs*. Le lecteur hâtif pourrait s'imaginer qu'ils couvrent tout le champ de la troisième partie, *de l'origine et de la nature des affects*, et comprendre ainsi la "définition générale des affects" qui termine l'appendice. Le début de cette définition dite générale exige pourtant un commentaire: "l'affect qu'on appelle *animi pathema*, passivité de l'âme, est une idée confuse" (II/203). La relative est ici déterminative et non explicative: ceux d'entre les affects qu'on appelle sentiments ou passions, *animi pathema* (expression qui se trouve, par exemple, chez Descartes dans les *Principes de la philosophie* IV, 190). Car il en existe aussi d'autres, "qui se rapportent à l'âme en tant qu'elle est active" (IIIP59). Spinoza les appelle des "actions" (IIID3Exp, IVApp§2) ou encore des "vertus" (IIIP55S, II/183/2-3, VP4S, II/283/26). Je les appellerai par convention *affects actifs*. Leur place logique a été réservée dès l'ouverture de la troisième partie, avec la définition *générale* des affects. L'explication précise en effet: "si par conséquent nous pouvons être cause adéquate de quelqu'une de ces affections, j'entends alors par affect une action; dans les autres cas, une passion."

La place n'est effectivement remplie qu'avec les deux dernières propositions de cette partie, 58 et 59. Le scolie de la proposition 57 souligne la transition: "voilà pour ce qui concerne les affects qui se rapportent à lui en tant qu'il est passif. Il me reste à ajouter quelques mots sur ceux qui se rapportent à l'homme en tant qu'il est actif." La proposition suivante s'appuie sur un fait, le fait de la raison ou de l'entendement ("l'âme conçoit certaines idées adéquates, d'après IIP40S2") pour affirmer qu'il y a, *dantur*, d'autres affects de joie et de désir, des affects *autres, alii*, "en plus de la joie et du désir qui sont des passions." Ces affects actifs (pour lesquels sont réservés les mots de *force d'âme, fortitudo*, avec les deux espèces de l'*animositas* et de la *generositas* - IIIP59S, IVP73S, VP41) jouent un rôle décisif dans l'équilibre des deux parties proprement morales. Dans la servitude, ils sont vaincus, subjugués ou éteints par les passions: ils "cèdent souvent à tout genre d'appétit sensuel" (IVP17S). Chez l'homme libre, ils prennent le dessus: en jouant entre les passions, ils conviennent ou s'accordent avec les passions joyeuses, utiles ou bonnes, pour juguler les passions tristes; et même, en jouant des passions, ils peuvent convertir toute passion, joie et même tristesse, en action ou affect actif.

Nous essayerons d'éclairer ensemble deux questions concernant cette doctrine des affects actifs: une question historique, une question systématique.

La question historique concerne son rapport à la théorie cartésienne des émotions intérieures. Car Spinoza, dans toute l'*Ethique*, ne cite nommément qu'un auteur, Descartes, et de cet auteur qu'un livre, les *Passions de l'âme* (IIIPref, VPref). Or cet ouvrage, après la définition des passions (I, 27 à 29) et l'analyse systématique des six passions primitives, ajoute à la fin de sa seconde partie un excursus de deux paragraphes, 147 et 148, consacré à ces "émotions intérieures qui ne sont excitées en l'âme que par l'âme même." A côté des passions au sens propre, où l'émotion corporelle cause dans l'âme une émotion passive ou passionnelle, "sensuelle ou sensitive" (à Chanut, 1 février 1647, AT IV, 602), à quoi il faut réserver le terme de sentiment, il y a aussi des émotions spirituelles sans cause physiologique, purement "intellectuelles ou raisonnables" (AT IV, 601). Devant la sévérité avec laquelle Spinoza critique la définition cartésienne de la passion, "plus occulte que toute qualité occulte" (VPref, II/279/24), nous nous demanderons si son silence sur la doctrine cartésienne de l'émotion intérieure ne suggérerait pas qu'il en a repris une bonne part dans sa doctrine de l'affect actif. Il faudrait alors revenir sur une thèse de F. Alquié dans son dernier livre: "pour Spinoza, tout sentiment n'est pas une passion. Descartes, au contraire,... appelle 'passions de l'âme' tous les états que Spinoza nomme ici 'sentiments.'"[1] Ou encore: "selon Descartes, tous les sentiments sont des 'passions de l'âme.' Au contraire Spinoza distingue avec soin les termes *affectus* et *passio*" (*ibid.*, p. 304).

La question systématique concerne la nature de la différence entre les passions et les affects actifs. En un mode fini comme l'homme, comment dissocier réellement l'activité et la passivité? L'*Ethique* semble parfois comporter un certain flottement. Tantôt les deux types d'affects sont distingués réellement ou mieux modalement, comme deux modes effectivement différents qui s'affrontent dans un champ de force soumis à des lois rigoureuses: "un affect ne peut être réduit ni ôté sinon par un affect contraire et plus fort que l'affect à réduire" (IVP7) et il s'agit de savoir si les "affects tirant leur origine de la raison ou excités par elle" (VP7) parviendront à contraindre "les affects qui leur sont contraires et qui ne sont point alimentés par leurs causes extérieures" à "s'accommoder de plus en plus à [eux] jusqu'à ce qu'ils ne [leur] soient plus contraires" (VP7D).

Mais parfois la différence s'estompe jusqu'à n'être plus qu'une différence de degré (ainsi la joie passive, qui est bonne et s'accorde avec la raison, "n'est pas une passion si ce n'est en tant que la puissance d'agir de l'homme n'est pas accrue à ce point que, *eo usque... ut*, il se conçoive lui-même et ses propres actions adéquatement" - IVP59D), voire une simple distinction de raison ("un affect qui est une passion est une idée confuse. Si donc nous formons de cet affect une idée claire et distincte, il n'y aura entre cette idée et l'affect lui-même, en tant qu'il se rapporte à l'âme seule, qu'une distinction de raison, *non nisi ratione distinguetur*, et ainsi l'affect cessera d'être une passion" - VP3D). Cette indécision entre passion et affect actif, qui est aussi transition ou conversion éthique, se laisse saisir sur un exemple privilégié. L'amour, qui a d'abord (IIIP11S) été défini à partir de la joie-passion (à laquelle il ajoute l'imagination d'une cause extérieure - IIIP13S), peut se substituer à la haine:

"la haine qui est entièrement vaincue par l'amour se change en amour, *in amorem transit*" (IIIP44). Or, dans le passage de la servitude à la liberté, Spinoza s'appuie sur cette conversion (d'un affect passif triste, la haine, en un affect joyeux mais toujours passif, l'amour) comme si elle était identique à la conversion des affects passifs en affects actifs: "Qui vit sous la conduite de la raison" s'efforce de compenser les affects tristes par "l'amour ou la générosité" (IVP46). La démonstration précise même: "l'amour, *c'est-à-dire, hoc est*, la générosité."

Nous avons ici, non pas une contradiction (car il y a bien un amour actif qui est justement générosité), mais une indifférenciation (entre le positif de l'amour, même passif, et l'activité généreuse). Elle est d'autant plus remarquable qu'elle s'opère à l'occasion de la générosité, qui impose presque la comparaison avec Descartes. Si différente dans les implications métaphysiques de sa définition, la générosité cartésienne est elle aussi, anthropologiquement, à double versant. C'est une passion dénombrée comme telle parmi les autres (*Passions de l'âme* II, 54, et III, 153-161) et étudiée dans son rapport au corps (III, 160); mais c'est aussi, comme passion de ce libre arbitre qui est en nous toujours actif, le "remède contre tous les dérèglements des passions" (II, 145, III, 156, 161). On retrouve la même indécision théorique: "on peut douter si la générosité et l'humilité, qui sont des vertus, peuvent aussi être des passions" (III, 160), mais, puisqu'on "peut exciter en soi la passion, et ensuite acquérir la vertu de générosité," vertu et passion réussissent ici, d'un verbe rare et curieux, à "*symboliser*" (III, 161).

Pour éclairer ces deux questions, historique et systématique, nous allons brièvement présenter: (1) la doctrine cartésienne de l'émotion intérieure, puis (2) la relation spinoziste entre raison et affect actif, et enfin (3) la transition opérée à la fin de l'*Ethique* de la passion à l'amour de Dieu comme affect actif prédominant.

II. La doctrine cartésienne de l'émotion intérieure

La doctrine cartésienne des deux affectivités s'est développée, depuis la publication des *Méditations métaphysiques* (où elle ne figure pas explicitement) jusqu'à son achèvement en 1649 dans les *Passions de l'âme* (dont la traduction latine posthume, en 1651, nous semble avoir fourni son lexique au *Court traité* d'abord directement, puis indirectement à l'*Ethique*). Dès les *Principia philosophiae* de 1644, l'originalité d'une "joie spirituelle" est affirmée: "lorsqu'on nous dit quelque nouvelle, l'âme juge premièrement si elle est bonne ou mauvaise; et la trouvant bonne, elle s'en réjouit en elle-même, d'une joie qui est purement intellectuelle, et tellement indépendante des émotions du corps, que les Stoïques n'ont pu la dénier à leur sage, bien qu'ils aient voulu qu'il fût exempt de toute passion" (*Principes de la philosophie* IV, 190, AT IX-2, 311). La traduction française des *Méditations*, en 1647, ajoutera "qui aime, qui hait" entre l'entendement et la volonté (AT IX-1, 27), comme pensées pures de l'âme seule, avant la frontière du *aussi*, "qui imagine aussi et qui sent," sentir auquel il faut rattacher les sentiments ou passions. Et la longue lettre à Chanut du

1 février 1647 approfondira, sur l'exemple des deux amours, ce que la correspondance avec Elizabeth avait établi de l'union substantielle, la fonction biologique des passions, et la satisfaction qu'elles procurent à l'âme une fois qu'elle les a "apprivoisées" (à Elisabeth, 1 septembre 1645, AT IV, 287).

Trois thèmes dominent cette doctrine cartésienne des deux affectivités.

D'abord, la différence modale, dans l'âme, entre les émotions intérieures et les passions, s'appuie sur la distinction réelle ou de substance entre l'âme et le corps. Des émotions "semblables" (*Passions* II, 147), amours haines, joies, tristesses, désirs, etc., peuvent être excitées ou bien par la mécanique corporelle, "l'agitation dont les esprits (animaux) meuvent la petite glande qui est au milieu du cerveau" (*Passions* II, 51), ou bien par les jugements de l'âme. L'émotion intérieure ("que ces seuls jugements excitent en l'âme" - *Passions* II, 79), par exemple, l'amour de Dieu, n'est ni une représentation intellectuelle (l'idée de Dieu) ni un jugement de valeur (juger que Dieu est souverainement aimable); elle est affective, et c'est un pur mouvement de volonté ("se joindre entièrement à lui de volonté" - à Chanut, 1 février 1647, AT IV, 609). "Et tous ces mouvements de la volonté auxquels consistent l'amour, la joie et la tristesse, et le désir, en tant que ce sont des pensées raisonnables, et non point des passions, se pourraient trouver en notre âme, encore qu'elle n'eût point de corps" (AT IV, 602). Pour l'âme cartésienne, réellement distincte du corps, la connaissance précède l'émotion que cette connaissance excite; et parmi les émotions intérieures, l'amour et la haine précèdent la joie et la tristesse (AT IV, 601-602).

Mais la passion est par nature donnée à l'âme en tant qu'elle est substantiellement unie au corps.[2]   La mécanique corporelle qui la produit est ordonnée au bien de ce corps (*Passions* II, 137). Et l'âme qui l'éprouve en elle est naturellement incitée par la passion "à consentir et contribuer aux actions qui peuvent servir à conserver le corps ou à le rendre en quelque façon plus parfait" (*ibid.*). Sous ce rapport, comme âme-du-composé ou forme substantielle de l'homme (pour Regius, janvier 1642, AT III, 503), je considère ce corps "comme une partie de moi-même, ou peut-être aussi comme le tout" (AT VII, 74; IX-1, 59) et tout se passe comme "si nous n'avions en nous que le corps ou qu'il fût notre meilleure partie" (*Passions* II, 139).   On peut reconstruire le mouvement passionnel sur le modèle d'une émotion intérieure, car le plus passionnel des désirs est aussi à sa façon une volonté. "Il n'y a en nous qu'une seule âme, et cette âme n'a en soi aucune diversité de parties: la même qui est sensitive est raisonnable, et tous ses appétits sont des volontés."[3]

Isolons, par exemple, dans la passion d'amour le moment cardio-vasculaire (je me joins de volonté au sang, comme aliment privilégié - *Passions* II, 107), moment à quoi se réduit le premier amour du foetus (pour le sang maternel - à Chanut, 1 février 1647, AT IV, 605) et qui accompagne ensuite tous les amours passionnels (*Passions* II, 107).   On proposera la reconstruction suivante:

(A) Majeure (implicite): je suis mon corps, son bien est le bien suprême unique.

(B) Mineure (expérience du foetus): or le sang (frais de la mère) convient au corps.

C) Conclusion (émotion): donc je me joins de volonté à ce sang (amour). On voit aussitôt que cette reconstruction a exigé deux prémisses. La majeure définit l'union substantielle en décrivant la situation initiale de l'enfant, parfaitement ignorant de la (seconde) vérité métaphysique essentielle pour la morale.[4] La mineure tient lieu ici de connaissance, et cette premiére expérience du plaisir correspond à la joie archaïque du foetus (*Passions* II, 94). Au regard du corps, la joie et la tristesse précèdent l'amour et la haine (*Passions* II, 137), ce qui est l'inverse pour les émotions intérieures. Et elles "tiennent le lieu de la connaissance": car l'âme n'est immédiatement avertie des choses qui nuisent au corps que par le sentiment qu'elle a de la douleur, lequel produit en elle premièrement la passion de la tristesse; et des choses utiles au corps que par quelque sorte de chatouillement, qui excite en elle de la joie.[5] La genèse, l'ordre, les définitions même (de la haine pour "ce qui cause cette douleur," de l'amour pour "ce qu'on croit être la cause" du chatouillement et de la joie)[6] s'inversent ainsi d'une forme d'affectivité â l'autre.

Et pourtant, en cette vie, ces deux affectivités s'accompagnent. Il n'est ni possible ni souhaitable de faire disparaître les passions, et Descartes s'est toujours vigoureusement défendu de ce projet qu'il prête aux stoïciens: l'*apatheia*, l'insensibilité, n'est pas son objectif.[7] Les passions sont toutes bonnes, ou presque toutes.[8] Elles sont "tellement utiles à cette vie, que notre âme n'aurait pas sujet de vouloir demeurer jointe à son corps un seul moment, si elle ne les pouvait ressentir" (AT IV, 538). Et, du point de vue moral, les plus grandes âmes (magnanimité ou générosité, deux noms pour une même chose - *Passions* II, 54) "ont des raisonnements si forts et si puissants que, bien qu'elles aient aussi des passions, et même souvent de plus violentes que celles du commun, leur raison demeure néanmoins toujours la maîtresse, et fait que les afflictions même leur servent, et contribuent à la parfaite félicité dont elles jouissent dès cette vie" (à Elisabeth, 18 mai 1645, AT IV, 202). Le problème n'est donc pas de substituer une forme d'affectivité à l'autre, mais de tirer au clair et de régler au mieux leur coexistence.

Le second thème concerne la solidarité naturelle entre les émotions intérieures et les passions "qui leur sont semblables" (même nom, même essence) et "dont elles diffèrent" pourtant (par leur causalité notamment - *Passions* II, 147). "Pour l'ordinaire, les deux amours se trouvent ensemble" (à Chanut, 1 février 1647, AT IV, 603). Le mouvement s'opère dans les deux sens. D'une part, quand l'âme forme en elle-même une émotion intérieure, par exemple, d'amour, "cet amour raisonnable est ordinairement accompagné de l'autre, qu'on peut nommer sensuelle et sensitive" (AT IV, 602): même l'amour de Dieu, intellectuel, peut "passer par l'imagination pour venir de l'entendement dans les sens," se redoublant ainsi ou se transformant en "la plus ravissante et la plus utile passion; et même... peut-être la plus forte" (AT IV, 607, 608). Notre libre arbitre, aussi inimaginable merveille à sa façon que l'infinité divine,[9] peut devenir dans la générosité objet d'une passion: la connaissance avec l'émotion qu'elle suscite se redouble en sentiment ("ceux qui ont cette

connaissance et ce sentiment d'eux-mêmes" - *Passions* III, 154). Réciproquement, quand l'âme unie au corps éprouve quelque passion, cela "la dispose à
cette autre pensée plus claire" (AT IV, 603) en quoi consiste l'émotion
intérieure correspondante. Non seulement l'analyse d'une passion y décèle
(entre autres) l'équivalent d'une émotion intérieure; mais surtout, comme l'âme
est une et sans parties, elle tend à éprouver au regard d'elle-même ce qu'elle
éprouve d'abord comme bon ou mauvais au regard du corps, valeur suprême
du composé.

C'est bien pour cela que, même lorsque la connaissance métaphysique a
détruit la fausse majeure (A) pour établir la majeure explicite (non-A): "le
corps n'est pas notre meilleure partie, il n'est que la moindre" (*Passions* II,
139), il reste que les passions positives (amour, joie, désir "accompagné d'amour
et ensuite d'espérance et de joie") sont, "considérées précisément en elles-
mêmes," "au regard de l'âme," comme "si nous n'avions point de corps,"
"incomparablement meilleures"[10] que les passions négatives (haine, tristesse,
désir "accompagné de haine, de crainte et de tristesse" - *Passions* II, 87). "Et
même souvent une fausse joie vaut mieux qu'une tristesse dont la cause est
vraie."[11]   Ce n'est pas seulement le fait de la passion qui est inéliminable, c'est
l'inégalité des passions au regard de l'âme.

"Bien que ces émotions de l'âme soient souvent jointes avec les passions
qui leur sont semblables, elles peuvent souvent aussi se rencontrer avec
d'autres, et même naître de celles qui leur sont contraires" (*Passions* II, 147):
la possibilité de briser cette solidarité est le troisième thème cartésien. La
dualité des substances explique suffisamment la coexistence des émotions
opposées, illustrée de façon un peu curieuse par l'exemple du veuf joyeux.[12]
Plus importante pour la morale est la capacité de l'âme à faire servir toutes les
passions, même tristes, "à augmenter sa joie" (*Passions* II, 148): "la sagesse est
principalement utile en ce point, qu'elle enseigne à s'en rendre tellement maître
et à les ménager avec tant d'adresse, que les maux qu'elles causent sont fort
supportables, et même qu'on tire de la joie de tous" (*Passions* III, 212). Deux
analyses aboutissent à ce résultat, sans que Descartes se soucie de les unifier:

(a) *L'amour de Dieu*, à partir de la première vérité métaphysique (la toute
puissance d'un Dieu aux perfections infinies): "lorsque nous élevons notre esprit
à le considérer tel qu'il est, nous nous trouvons naturellement si enclins à
l'aimer, que nous tirons même de la joie de nos afflictions, en pensant que sa
volonté s'exécute en ce que nous les recevons" (à Elisabeth, 15 septembre 1645,
AT IV, 291-292). Cette méditation remplit l'âme "d'une joie si extrême" et elle
se joint si "entièrement" à Dieu de volonté (la joie précéderait-elle l'amour?)
qu'elle "ne désire plus rien au monde, sinon que la volonté de Dieu soit faite"
(à Chanut, 1 février 1647, AT IV, 609). Même lorsqu'on en attend la mort ou
quelque autre mal, si par impossible on pouvait changer ce décret divin, on
n'en aurait pas la volonté. Cet amour pour un Dieu juste va au-delà de la
résignation à la fatalité, mais il n'annule pas l'inégalité des passions: "s'il ne
refuse point les maux ou les afflictions, parce qu'elles lui viennent de la
Providence divine, il refuse encore moins les biens ou les plaisirs licites dont
il peut jouir en cette vie, parce qu'ils en viennent aussi" (*ibid.*).

(b) *Le contentement intérieur*, rejoignant la considération du libre arbitre et *la générosité*: "elle se plait à sentir émouvoir en soi des passions, de quelle nature qu'elles soient, pourvu qu'elle en demeure maîtresse" (à Elisabeth, 6 octobre 1645, AT IV, 309). Parce que l'âme peut prendre ses distances d'avec le corps et l'union substantielle, elle peut faire l'épreuve de sa force dans la résistance aux passions. Tout comme, au niveau du corps, le chatouillement (excitation de fibres nerveuses qui ne sont pas brisées) produit d'abord la passion de joie par l'épreuve de la force physique, de cette perfection du corps qui fait le bien du composé,[13] de même l'âme forte ou généreuse éprouve sa perfection à être émue (à la surface) mais non troublée (en son intérieur) par des passions qui, même tristes, cessent d'être amères. Elle en devient pour ainsi dire spectatrice. "Nous avons du plaisir de les sentir exciter en nous, et ce plaisir est une joie intellectuelle qui peut aussi bien naître de la tristesse que toutes les autres passions."[14] L'émotion est ici à la fois sensible et raisonnable, indissociablement: sentir et se sentir, "se sentir émouvoir à toutes sortes de passions, même à la tristesse et à la haine" (*Passions* II, 94), et se sentir libre, "se sentir en soi-même une ferme et constante résolution de bien user de son libre arbitre" (*Passions* III, 153).

Opposées dans leur origine, les deux affectivités cartésiennes ont fini par se rejoindre et s'articuler dans la structure réflexive d'une conscience, sans que les figures de cette réunification soient vraiment systématisées.

III. Affect actif et raison

La doctrine des affects actifs rejette les bases métaphysiques du cartésianisme (dualité des substances entre l'âme et le corps, libre arbitre, union substantielle). Elle repose sur la fonction active de la raison dans les notions communes. Peut-elle éviter de réduire la différence entre les deux affectivités à une simple distinction logique, ou de raison?

Dans la chose singulière qui pense (*mens*, âme ou esprit), dans ses pensées (*cogitationes*), Spinoza distingue aussi soigneusement que Descartes deux modalités: cognitive ou représentative, l'idée au sens strict; et affective, l'*affectus* ayant ici pour forme propre, comme essence et comme définition, une variation en plus ou en moins de la puissance d'agir (E IIID3). Si l'affect implique toujours une idée, la réciproque n'est pas vraie (IIA3): l'affect ne se réduit pas à l'idée de son objet et si, logiquement, l'idée comme représentation d'objet est première, l'expérience effective fournit toujours ensemble de façon indivise une affection (l'idée) et son rapport à la puissance d'agir (dont la variation peut à la limite s'annuler).

Les affects assurément "naissent" (E VP4S) et "dépendent" (IIIP3) des idées, mais il ne faut pas isoler l'idée pour chercher comment l'affect s'y ajouterait ensuite: car l'affection est moins une cause efficiente ou génétique réelle qu'un moment abstraitement découpé dans l'affect, nommé avant elle dès la mise en place de l'imagination (IIP17). On peut appeler l'affect lui-même dans ce qu'il a de spécifique une idée, confuse quand l'affect est une passion, claire et distincte s'il est une action ou vertu. Mais c'est en un autre sens, large, du mot *idée*. "L'idée qui constitue la forme d'un affect affirme du corps quelque chose qui enveloppe effectivement plus ou moins de réalité qu'auparavant" (E IIIGenDefAffExp, G II/204/16-17). Plus ou moins de force d'exister, de puissance de penser et comprendre pour l'âme, d'aptitudes à agir, pâtir et réagir pour le corps.

Les affects qui sont des passions relèvent de l'imagination en un triple sens. Les idées auxquelles l'affect se rapporte sont inadéquates (par exemple, opinion sur ce qu'on croit être la cause d'un amour passionné). L'affect en sa forme constitutive est suscité de dehors par une cause extérieure: elle interfère avec ma propre essence, avec la force unitaire de mon *conatus*, pour déterminer un résultat mixte et confus, comme une conclusion où la part des deux facteurs interne et externe, des deux prémisses, ne se distingue pas (IIP28D). Enfin l'ordre de ces idées et de ces affects n'est pas l'ordre de l'entendement mais l'ordre des affections du corps, l'ordre commun de la nature qui est, rapporté à chaque mode fini, l'ordre des rencontres fortuites, du hasard et de la fortune (IIP29S).

Quand on accède à la Raison, la même structure se répète même si tous les termes changent. Il ne faut pas réduire la raison spinoziste à sa fonction cognitive, à des idées ou à des jugements, en face d'une affectivité toute passionnelle. On ne comprendrait plus "ce que peut la raison elle-même sur les affects" (E VPref, II/277/10): seule une force affective peut venir à bout d'un affect (IVP7) et si la raison du sage parvient à gouverner ses pulsions passionnelles, c'est que dès le début, chez les hommes "plus émus (*commoveantur*) par l'opinion que par la raison vraie," elle "excite des émotions, *commotiones*, dans l'âme."[15] L'ordre de l'*Ethique* veut que la raison soit étudiée comme "genre de connaissance" avant d'être explorée dans sa force affective. C'est pourquoi la théorie des notions communes (qui montre comment on forme des idées adéquates et comment on en déduit des conséquences nécessaires au contact des rencontres imaginatives, jusqu'à ce que l'idée de Dieu, qui est comme la plus haute et la plus universelle des notions communes, ouvre la voie à la procédure inverse, à la science intuitive ou troisième genre de connaissance) doit servir de modèle pour la théorie des affects actifs (où la raison comme principe éthique capte dans le dynamisme passionnel la force active du *conatus*, pour alimenter finalement l'amour de Dieu, comme "le plus constant de tous les affects" (VP20S), qui ouvre la voie à une éthique du troisième genre). La raison affirme donc, elle aussi, une triple spécificité. Un ensemble d'idées claires et distinctes, qui nous représente "dans leur vérité les choses telles qu'elles sont en elles-mêmes" (IIP44D - par exemple l'enchaînement nécessaire des causes et des effets). Un ensemble d'affects tous actifs et positifs, "qui tirent leur origine de la raison ou sont excités par elle" (VP7- des joies, des amours, des désirs sans excès qui sont "excités ou engendrés par des idées adéquates" - VP4S). Enfin un ordre entre ces idées (adéquates) et ces affects (actifs) qui est, sinon l'ordre de l'entendement, *ordo intellectus*, du moins un ordre valable pour l'entendement, *ordo ad intellectum* (VP10).

Une fois qu'on a restitué à la sphère isolée ou abstraite des connaissances sa dimension affective, on aboutit à une dualité. L'âme a deux parties et deux parties seulement (même si, d'une part, il y a trois genres de connaissance et si, d'autre part, le *conatus,* fondement des affects, est unique): l'entendement et l'imagination (VP40C). L'imagination avec ses idées inadéquates mais aussi ses passions. L'entendement avec les idées adéquates (où se regroupent second et troisième genres de connaissance) et ses affects (puisque le *conatus* se distingue selon cette division et devient "effort et désir de l'âme pour persévérer dans son être en tant qu'elle a des idées claires et distinctes" - IIIP9). On pressent comment les affects actifs pourront entretenir avec les passions le même rapport que les notions communes avec les images des choses. Et l'on voit pourquoi ils sont dits "se rapporter aussi à nous en tant que nous comprenons, autrement dit en tant que nous sommes actifs" (IIIP58D). En éliminant la dualité des substances, en ramenant la dualité affective à l'opposition entre des niveaux d'activité, Spinoza impose divers infléchissements à la doctrine cartésienne des émotions intérieures, dont nous signalerons deux.

(1) Il étend aux affects actifs ce que Descartes ne soutenait que des passions, et en tant qu'on les rapportait au bien du corps: que la joie et la tristesse précèdent l'amour et la haine, et qu'elles tiennent lieu de connaissance (du bien et du mal). F. Alquié avait remarqué que cette thèse, qui "annonce l'analyse Spinoziste,"[16] n'épuise pas la dérivation cartésienne. Les jugements fermes et déterminés de l'entendement, qui excitaient d'abord dans l'âme seule les émotions intérieures d'amour et de haine, sont réduits par Spinoza à des moments réflexifs seconds. Si la joie et la tristesse passionnelles sont, au sens large, des idées confuses, la connaissance (inadéquate) du bien et du mal sera seulement l'idée de l'idée. Le jugement de valeur ("ceci est bon ou utile") n'a qu'une distinction de raison avec le mouvement affectif qu'il redouble ("nous nous efforçons, voulons, appétons, désirons" - IIIP9S): ce qui revient identiquement à dire que "la fin n'est que l'appétit" (IVPref, II/207, D7), ou que "la connaissance du bon et du mauvais n'est que l'affect de la joie ou de la tristesse en tant que nous en avons conscience." (IVP8) Cette idée ne se distingue pas en réalité de l'affect lui-même, sinon par le seul concept, *revera non distinguitur, nisi solo conceptu* (IVP8D). Thèse étendue maintenant à "la connaissance vraie du bon et du mauvais" (IVP14), car "la fin ultime d'un homme qui est dirigé par la raison" se confond avec "le désir suprême par lequel il s'applique à gouverner tous les autres [désirs]" (IVApp§4). Dans la joie active, l'appétit s'explicite lui-même clairement et distinctement, et il se dédouble en désir conscient et en conscience vraie du bien suprême.

(2) L'âme cartésienne, réalité substantielle, peut éprouver, à son égard et pour son compte, toutes les émotions, positives et négatives: fondées sur des jugements vrais, il y a des tristesses et des haines intellectuelles, au même titre que des joies et des amours (à Chanut, 1 février 1647, AT IV, 601-602). Rien de tel chez Spinoza. L'être ici se confond avec l'agir, et la forme supérieure de l'affectivité se réduit au stade accompli de l'activité, lorsque l'individu s'élève à la causalité adéquate ou formelle. Spinoza part du corps et des affects passifs pour trouver le sens global de l'affect: certains seulement, qui sont déjà positifs et préparent un ressaisissement de sa propre activité, peuvent avoir un homologue actif. Pour Descartes les deux affectivités se répondent terme à

terme: à chaque fois, sous le même nom, on trouve une émotion intérieure et un sentiment ou passion.   Pour Spinoza, seuls la joie, l'amour, le désir se prêtent à ce dédoublement: les autres, tristesse, haine, etc., s'y refusent et restent inéluctablement enfermés dans la sphère de l'imagination (IIIP59D).

Concluons sur ce premier point que, tout en rejetant la majeure cartésienne (non A): "le corps n'est pas notre meilleure partie, il n'en est que la moindre," en revenant à une majeure explicite (A): "l'âme et le corps ne sont qu'un seul et même individu qui est conçu tantôt sous l'attribut de la pensée, tantôt sous celui de l'étendue" (IIP21S), Spinoza n'a pas rejeté l'opposition cartésienne des deux affectivités, qui semblait pourtant reposer sur cette base. Il a dû l'infléchir sur plusieurs points, mais il a conservé la dualité.   En un sens il l'a même accentuée: car il accepte, ce que Descartes refuse expressément, de parler de lutte, de *combats* entre les affects, et de reconduire ces combats à une diversité ou dualité de *parties* en l'âme.[17]

IV. L'amour de Dieu et la tristesse

Je n'essaierai pas, dans le dernier moment de cette communication, d'aborder dans son ensemble le passage spinoziste de la passion à l'action.   Je voudrais seulement contribuer à l'éclairer sur l'exemple particulier de l'amour de Dieu, tel qu'il entre en rapport (dans la première moitié de la cinquième partie) avec les affects passifs, et, plus particulièrement, avec les passions de tristesse.   Car il me semble que, sur ce point précis, Spinoza a retrouvé et systématisé la difficulté cartésienne: une fois soigneusement dissociées les deux affectivités, comment penser leur réunification requise par l'éthique en certains passages décisifs, quand la passion doit "symboliser" avec la vertu?

L'amour de Dieu, qui va se révéler ici le plus constant des "affects tirant leur origine de la Raison ou excités par elle" [VP7] et "tenir dans l'âme la plus grande place" (VP16, cf. VP20S) donne sa consistance définitive, parce qu'il ne peut pas être détruit (VP20S), au système hiérarchisé que la raison ébauche avant son exploitation, en "ordonnant et enchaînant les affections du corps suivant un ordre valable pour l'entendement" (VP10). L'amour de Dieu prolonge directement le rôle de la réflexion: il est la plus haute forme de ce remède que constitue la connaissance des affects passifs, "le plus excellent qui soit en notre pouvoir" (VP4S, II/283-284).   Car former d'une passion un concept clair et distinct, ce n'est pas seulement lui surajouter une idée adéquate et les affects actifs qui s'y rapportent, joie de comprendre, désirs sans excès, etc. "Elle cesse d'être une passion." (VP3) Son double réflexif l'attire en quelque sorte avec lui dans sa sphère d'activité.   L'amour de Dieu généralise cette procédure, puisqu'il est cause universelle et universellement connue de façon adéquate et parfaite.   En rattachant toutes choses à Dieu comme à leur cause, on fait entrer dans la sphère de l'activité rationnelle, sans exception possible, toutes les passions.   Elles sont comme reprises dans l'amour de Dieu, qu'elles contribuent à alimenter.   La tristesse elle-même "cesse d'être une passion, c'est-à-dire cesse d'être une tristesse; et ainsi, dans la mesure où nous connaissons que Dieu est cause de la tristesse, nous sommes joyeux." (VP18S) Nous retrouvons le point (indécidable?) où un affect triste est à la fois là, comme une tristesse et donc comme une passion, mais rattaché aussi à l'activité cognitive et affective, à la pensée adéquate et à l'amour actif de la causalité divine, et n'est donc plus une passion.

Conduite à fonctionner entre deux affectivités opposées, la distinction de raison proclamée dès le début et toujours maintenue entre idée de l'idée débouche sur un paradoxe logique. *Si l'on exclut tout changement réel*, la coexistence est impensable entre un affect passionnel (une idée confuse) et une idée de l'idée claire et distincte (une réflexion rationnelle, cognitive ou affective, sur cette passion). La majeure explicite (A): "l'idée de l'idée n'est rien d'autre que la forme de l'idée" (IIP21S), la distinction n'est que de raison (VP3), impose le choix entre deux consécutions opposées. Ou bien (B), mineure: "l'idée est inadéquate," c'est une opinion, une passion, une imagination. Et alors (C), conclusion: "l'idée de l'idée est inadéquate elle aussi," telle la conscience de ses sensations (IIP28), de soi-même (IIP29), telle la connaissance du mal et corrélativement du bien (IVP64, P68), telle enfin la haine qu'évoque l'objecteur pour un Dieu considéré comme cause de tristesse (VP18S). Ou bien (non C) est donné comme mineure: "l'idée de l'idée est claire et distincte," nous avons réflexivement une certitude rationnelle,[18] un affect actif. Et alors (non B) suit nécessairement comme conclusion: "l'idée n'est pas inadéquate," notre point de départ n'est pas une imagination ou une passion, l'affect repris dans un amour actif n'est pas une tristesse. *Mais ici le changement est réel.* Il y a un transit de l'affect passif à l'amour de Dieu qui modifie, comme tous les affects actifs rationnels nés de notions communes, son point d'application. Il desserre la contrainte passionnelle, l'étroitesse délirante (VP44S), du champ cognitif et sa prégnance affective. Pour parler comme Descartes, il "apprivoise" (AT IV, 287) la passion. Pour parler comme Spinoza il la contraint à "s'accommoder" (VP70) de plus en plus à lui, jusqu'à ce qu'elle ne lui soit plus contraire. L'insensé cesse d'être dès qu'il cesse de pâtir (VP42S), mais chez l'homme libre une passion triste, maîtrisée grâce au détour réflexif, ne cesse pas d'être, elle cesse d'être (seulement) une passion (VP3 et 18S).

Pour que la transformation effective échappe au paradoxe logique, il faut dégager une continuité entre imagination et entendement: entre idées générales, notions communes et idée de Dieu; entre rencontres passionnelles, joies rationnelles, et amour de Dieu. Si l'amour de Dieu doit finir par prédominer, c'est en tant que toutes les idées de l'imagination alimentent la connaissance adéquate de Dieu. Le Dieu de cet amour, qui n'est pas encore l'amour intellectuel du troisième genre, est la plus universelle des notions communes, et il est présenté comme tel: la force de l'affect renvoie "au grand nombre de causes par lesquelles les affections se rapportant *aux propriétés communes des choses ou à Dieu* sont alimentées" (VP20S). Mais penser à Dieu n'est pas l'aimer. Comment sans illusion être activement joyeux en pensant le rapport de Dieu à nos tristesses? Sans illusion des deux côtés: car le mal de la tristesse n'est pas et n'était pas illusion, si une mauvaise rencontre diminue ma puissance; et la joie qui nait de la rattacher à Dieu n'est pas et ne sera pas mensongère. Pour résoudre le problème, il faut qu'il y ait un élément de joie à produire ou à extraire de la tristesse, comme il y a une notion commune à extraire ou à former à partir de l'imagination, là où elle s'égare en idées générales et abstraites.   On pourrait rappeler qu'aucune chose ne nous rencontre, fût-ce pour nous diminuer, sans avoir quelque chose de commun avec nous (IVP29), et que jamais ce quelque chose n'est un terrain ou un théâtre inerte, mais toujours une affirmation commune, un bien et une joie. Sans renvoyer à ces trois propositions (IVPP29-31), Spinoza ressaisit avec Dieu, facteur universel de convenance, le principe d'une joie active opérant jusque dans les mauvaises rencontres.

Mais le transit n'est pas une conversion magique, un évanouissement de la tristesse.   La dichotomie affective n'est pas oubliée, au moment où l'affirmation d'une simple distinction de raison semble la gommer et permet en fait de reculer des frontières.   Le développement des idées adéquates et des affects actifs ne peut évidemment créer un autre individu à côté du premier ou à sa place: il déplace des équilibres.   Il ne fait pas disparaître les passions: "cette âme est active au plus haut point dont les idées adéquates constituent la plus grande partie, de façon, que, *tout en n'ayant pas moins d'idées in-adéquates que la première*, elle ait sa marque distinctive plutôt dans" les idées adéquates:[19] autant d'imaginations et de passions - Descartes ajouterait: et même souvent de plus violentes (à Elisabeth, 18 mai 1645, AT IV, 287).   A l'intérieur de l'imagination, un autre déplacement s'opère: même si les passions tristes subsistent, celui qui fait travailler ensemble amour et générosité réduit la haine, etc., à "occuper une très petite partie de l'imagination" (VP10S, II/288/11).

Reste la dernière étape: il ne suffit pas de former des pensées vraies, des affects actifs, de mobiliser les affects passifs de joie autour de la tristesse, affect primitif qui resterait inentamée dans sa pure factivité.   Il faut la mettre à contribution pour alimenter les joies actives.   Mais une fois posé avec la distinction de raison le principe de sa métamorphose, le caractère partiel et approché de cette conversion est établi (dès le corollaire - VP3C), et sans cesse rappelé.   Dans le second genre de connaissance, une notion commune ne rejoint jamais la singularité d'une essence (IIP37), et pas davantage la singularité d'un affect triste né d'une rencontre fortuite.   Dieu, le Dieu du second genre, n'y réussit pas davantage: il n'explique rien, sinon que tout est explicable.   On ne connait donc jamais un affect en particulier, sinon sous un certain aspect, et de mieux en mieux peut-être.   Par là jamais une tristesse ne sera absolument ôtés.   "Chacun a le pouvoir de se connaître clairement et distinctement, lui-même et ses affects, *sinon absolument, du moins en partie*, et de faire en conséquence qu'il ait moins à en pâtir" (VP4S).   "Si en effet les affects, en tant qu'ils sont des passions, *ne sont pas par là absolument ôtés*, il arrive du moins qu'elles constituent la moindre partie de l'âme" (VP20S, II/294/9-11).   On entend ainsi, à côté du langage des parties, un langage plus unitaire pour dire le même changement.   La passion triste subsiste, mais, si l'on ose dire, moins triste et moins passive.   L'âme en pâtit moins et elle n'en est pas tant afffectée.

Ainsi, sans paradoxe logique, l'amour de Dieu assure une rencontre entre les opposés (passion triste et affect actif) dès le second genre de connaissance et, si l'on peut dire, d'affectivité. Car on ne parle pas ici d'éternité, d'amour intellectuel ni de science intuitive: tout cela viendra ensuite et n'est pas requis pour ce premier niveau de la moralité et de la religion. L'amour (raisonnable ou rationnel) de Dieu, comme idée de l'idée,[20] relève assurément de l'âme "considérée en elle-même" et, en ce sens, "de l'âme seule" (VP20S, II/293/3-5): mais cette âme n'est que l'idée du corps existante en acte, prise dans la durée, en relation avec le corps et son existence. C'est donc bien sous le règne de la majeure: "l'âme et le corps sont une seule et même chose" que l'amour de Dieu réussit à relier à l'activité la passivité même de la tristesse, jusqu'aux frontières de la mort. "En tant qu'il se rapporte au corps, cet affect ne peut être détruit qu'avec le corps lui-même" (VP20S, II/293/1-2). Extraordinaire *fortitudo* à laquelle on donnerait volontiers pour emblème Judas dit le Fidèle, qui s'est mis à chanter au milieu des flammes tandis qu'on le croyait mort, et est mort en chantant l'hymne: "A toi, mon Dieu, j'offre mon âme" (lettre 76, à Burgh, IV/322).

V. Conclusions

Enonçons brièvement quelques conclusions sur les problèmes historiques et systématiques que soulève la théorie de l'affect actif.

1. Descartes, comme Spinoza, admet une dichotomie dans l'affectivité. Il faut ici en appeler de F. Alquié à F. Alquié lui-même. Car dans son *Rationalisme de Spinoza*, soucieux d'opposer les deux auteurs, il a méconnu les origines cartésiennes de l'affect actif, en prétendant que "selon Descartes tous les sentiments sont des passions."[21] Or, dans les notes de son *Descartes, Oeuvres philosophiques*, il avait (en gardant le même mot, malheureux à notre avis, de sentiment) fortement souligné que tout sentiment n'est pas une passion, que l'affectivité cartésienne se divise en deux espèces, "des sentiments intellectuels qui sont transparents à notre pensée: la réflexion nous les fait connaître de telle sorte que rien d'obscur ne demeure en eux" et "des senti-ments-passions, dont la cause est une action du corps" (III, 710, n. 2).

2. Mais surtout F. Alquié avait su saisir la filiation des deux doctrines sur ce point crucial du transit: "toute passion peut donc donner naissance à la joie, à une joie appartenant à l'esprit seul. Seulement ébauchée par Descartes, cette idée sera reprise et développée par Spinoza" (III, 1064, n. 1). La différence effective, réelle ou modale et non logique ou de point de vue, entre les deux affectivités n'empêche pas leur rencontre, leur convenance jusqu'au point (paradoxal!) où une joie active et réflexive se nourrit des tristesses passives.

3. Si Descartes appuie sur la distinction réelle des substances (âme, corps) la spécificité des émotions intérieures, Spinoza, qui part de l'unité de substance et pense d'abord les affects de l'âme sur le modèle des évènements corporels, ne sacrifie en rien l'originalité de l'affect actif. Distinction de raison, différence de degré finissent par se formuler dans le langage des parties de l'âme et de leur affrontement. Ce mouvement va si loin que, dans la seconde

moitié de l'*Ethique* V, on semble presque conclure, à l'inverse de la déduction cartésienne, de la distinction des affectivités à l'équivalent d'une distinction réelle ou de substance: elle oppose alors "ce qui concerne cette vie présente" (VP20S) et "l'éternité de l'âme" - même si, évidemment, les exigences du parallélisme interdisent d'écarter le corps, en son essence et l'idée éternelle qui en est donnée en Dieu (VPP22, 29, et 39).

4. Pour en rester à "cette vie présente," l'amour de Dieu permet d'unifier ce qui restait, chez Descartes, deux incarnations différentes de l'émotion intérieure active et joyeuse dans l'affectivité passionnelle. Le rapport cartésien est de volonté (divine) à volonté (humaine): ou contentement de soi dans la générosité (par quoi ma volonté tend à s'assurer dans la suffisance de son libre arbitre, en rejetant Dieu vers l'extérieur et la fatalité), ou consentement à la volonté divine (par quoi ma volonté tend à s'abandonner à une autre). Spinoza rejette le rapport de volonté à volonté, et substitue dans l'amour le contentement au consentement. Dans la mise en relation de Dieu et des tristesses, le cartésien consent: "que la volonté de Dieu soit faite" (à Chanut, 1 février 1647, AT IV, 609); le spinoziste est content de comprendre que sa causalité est exercée (VPP31 et 32).

5. Il faut attendre le troisième genre pour que soit tirée au clair l'identité des deux causalités ("avec l'accompagnement comme cause de l'idée de soi-même et conséquemment aussi de l'idée de Dieu" - VP32D), et que la réciprocité se substitue à l'unilatéralité:[22] au lieu que toutes les singularités (passionnelles) aillent alimenter, comme en s'y noyant, l'amour d'un Dieu sans affect, notion commune et la plus commune, le Dieu du troisième genre, "en tant qu'il s'aime lui-même, aime les hommes" (VP36C). Alors seulement nous procédons de Dieu vers "l'essence d'une même chose quelconque singulière" (IIP37 et VP36S), et "notre âme n'est pas affectée de la même manière" (VP36S). Mais ceci est sans doute obscur, peut-être douteux, et de toute façon, c'est une autre histoire.

1. F. Alquié, *Le rationalisme de Spinoza*, Paris: PUF, 1981, ch. xvii, §2, pp. 282-283 et n.
3. Rappelons que contrairement à Appuhn, Alquié traduit par *sentiments* le terme d'*affectus*.
2. A Elisabeth, 21 mai 1643, in Alquié, *Oeuvres philosophiques de Descartes*, III, 19, et notes; *Passions* II, 52 (Alquié, *Oeuvres*, III, 998 et note); *Entretien avec Burman*, AT V, 163.
3. *Passions* I, 47. Cf. Alquié, *Oeuvres* III, 990, note 1, pour la position du problème.
4. "La seconde chose, qu'il faut connaître, est la nature de notre âme, en tant qu'elle subsiste sans le corps, et est beaucoup plus noble que lui, et capable de jouir d'une infinité de contentements qui ne se trouvent point en cette vie." A Elisabeth, 15 septembre 1645, AT IV, 292. Cf. aussi *Principes de la philosophie* I, 71, *Entretien avec Burman*, AT V, 150.
5. *Ibid*. Cf. Alquié, *Oeuvres* III, 1052 et note 2.
6. *Passions* II, 137. Cf. Alquié, *Oeuvres* III, 1053, note 1.
7. A Elisabeth, 18 mai 1645, AT IV, 201-202. Cf. Alquié, *Oeuvres* III, 565, et note 2.
8. Cf. *Passions* III, 211; Alquié, *Oeuvres*, III, 1100, note 1; et à Chanut, 1 novembre 1646, AT IV, 538.
9. *Cogitationes privatae* AT X, 218, in *Olympiques*, Alquié, *Oeuvres* I, 63.

10. *Ibid*. Cf. *Passions* 141, 143.

11. *Passions* II, 142. Cf. Alquié, *Oeuvres* III, 1058 et note 1.

12. *Ibid*. Nous empruntons cette expression pittoresque à D. Kambouchner.

13. *Passions* II, 147. Cf. Alquié, *Oeuvres* III, 1025 et note 1, A. Matheron, *Dialectiques* 6(1974): 79-88 (repris in *Anthropologie et politique au xvii siècle*, Vrin, 1986.

14. *Passions* II, 147. Cf. Alquié, *Oeuvres* III, 1064 et note 1.

15. IVP17S, II/221/13-16. A la différence de Curley, nous croyons qu'il faut garder le même mot pour *commoveantur* (l. 14) et *commotiones* (l. 15), qui ne désigne pas le trouble, mais la motion émotive, cf. 279/7.

16. Descartes, *Oeuvres philosophiques*, ed. par F. Alquié, Paris: Garnier, III, 1053, n. 1, 1054, n. 3.

17. On opposera *Passions* à E VP20S et VP40C.

18. IIP43, dont la démonstration renvoie à IIP20 et le scolie à IIP21S.

19. VP20S, G II/293/31-35. Les idées qui relèvent de la vertu humaine sont les idées adéquates, celles qui sont inadéquates montrent sa faiblesse, et le sage se diagnostique, *dignoscatur*, à la prépondérance des premières.

20. Voir VP14 et P15, et PP3-4 et P18S pour justifier une formule qui n'est pas attestée dnas le texte.

21. Voir Alquié, *Le rationalisme*, p. 283 avec notes et p. 304.

22. VP17C versus VP36 et P36C.

COMMENTS ON J.-M. BEYSSADE, "DE L'ÉMOTION INTÉRIEURE CHEZ DESCARTES À L'AFFECT ACTIF SPINOZISTE"

MARGARET D. WILSON
Princeton University

It would be impossible to comment adequately on all the illuminating, deep, and provocative points in Professor Beyssade's extremely rich and original paper. Further, there's nothing in the paper that I'm inclined to dispute vigorously. Therefore I will simply attempt to express a few thoughts, first about Descartes's theory and then about Spinoza's, that relate more or less directly to Beyssade's exposition. My purpose will be to suggest the possibility of some qualifications of his viewpoint.

I. *Descartes.*

I basically accept Beyssade's account of Descartes's theory of the "interior emotions." I think it's worth noting, though, that *in certain respects* the concept is far from sharply delineated by Descartes.[1] It is true that the fact that these emotions are said to be caused by the soul, rather than the body, seems to provide a perfectly definite mark or criterion. But when one seeks to grasp its significance in application, the sense of definiteness tends to dissolve. Take Descartes's featured example of an interior emotion: the widower's secret relief or joy at the death of his wife. (*Passions* II, 147) One can easily understand how this might be the man's more persistent, as well as his more secret response: a response less tied than his grief to transient external physical circumstances, such as the funeral ceremony. But what sustains the idea that *this* emotional response - as opposed, for instance, to his limited compassion and pity - is caused "only by the soul itself"? Are we supposed to believe that his compassion is tied to the senses and imagination, while his relief is strictly an *intellectual* matter (now that she's gone he will be able to devote himself more fully to metaphysics and theology)? I suppose this is possible, but the moral I'm more inclined to draw from Descartes's example is that he himself had a rather weak grasp on the notion of an interior emotion - being able easily to conflate it with that of a *less transient* or *less public* state that ought nevertheless still to qualify as a passion, as depending partly on physical causes.

One of the few other theoretical clarifications Descartes provides of the distinction between passions and internal emotions has to do with the notion of representation. Thus he explains that in the *passion* of joy *impressions in the brain* represent a good to the soul as its own; while in the corresponding interior emotion - "purely intellectual joy" - the soul arouses the state in itself "whenever it enjoys a good which its *understanding* represents to it as its own." (*Passions* II, 91; emphasis added) This is really quite an obscure point of contrast, however. For one thing, while we know it's Descartes's view that the brain can in some sense "represent" corporeal things, and only corporeal things, how on earth could the brain represent even a corporeal thing "as the soul's own"?

The only further comment I want to make about the Cartesian theory has to do with Professor Beyssade's suggestion (p. 180) that the passions of love and hate are supposed to contrast with the corresponding interior emotions, in that joy and sadness *precede* the passional forms of love and hate, "taking the place of knowledge" (of good and evil). The reverse, he suggests, is true of love and hate as interior emotions: here joy and sadness *follow on* love and hate (which are presumed to "be founded on true judgments" (p. 184). It would be nice if this tidy contrast did emerge from the text; but as far as I can see it really does not. It seems to me that in *Passions* II, 139 Descartes allows for *cases* where joy and sadness precede the passions of love and hate, but treats as *primary* the situation where the *passions* of love and hate, "insofar as they relate to the soul," result from knowledge and precede joy and sorrow. Here again we find a blurring, rather than a precision, of the basis for distinguishing the passions (as bodily in origin) from the interior emotions (as having their source in the understanding). What this persistent blurring may tell us is that there was all along something specious in Descartes's attempt to found a meaningful distinction between types of affects on a simple metaphysical duality.

II. Spinoza

Although I do regard Descartes's conception of the interior emotions as rather poorly defined, I see no reason to dispute Beyssade's suggestion that it to some considerable degree prefigures and inspires Spinoza's notion of the active affects.[2] And I find both elegant and persuasive his account of how Descartes's distinction between emotions caused by the body, and emotions caused by "the soul itself," is transposed in Spinoza's monistic system to a distinction between affects tied to imagination, and affects that pertain to man "insofar as he understands."[3] It does not seem to me that this transposition in itself at all tends to undermine a genuine modal distinction between, say, the active and passive affects of joy. (And I take this to be Beyssade's conclusion as well, though one or two formulations in the earlier parts of his discussion may at first suggest the contrary.) I also agree with Beyssade that Spinoza does not very sharply and consistently distinguish - as it seems that he should - the vanquishment of sad passions by joyful passions from an increase in the *active* affects in relation to the passions in general.

I certainly agree further that VP3 and its Proof present the appearance of "paradox." Beyssade provides a fairly detailed treatment of issues raised by this Proposition, and I will concentrate my remaining comments upon them.

Perhaps it will be useful to have before us the actual Latin text of the Proposition and its Proof:

> *Affectus, qui passio est, desinit esse passio, simulatque ejus claram, & distinctam formamus ideam.*

DEMONSTRATIO: Affectus, qui passio est, idea est confusa (*per gener. Affect. Defin.*). Si itaque ipsius affectûs claram, & distinctam formemus ideam, haec idea ab ipso affectu, quatenus ad solam Mentem refertur, non nisi ratione distinguetur (*per Prop. 21, p. 2 cum ejusdem Schol.*); adeóque (*per Prop. 3, p. 3.*) affectus desinet esse passio. Q.E.D.

One problem presented by this Proposition - as Beyssade notes in passing - is how it is to be reconciled with IVP7 and its Corollary. For the latter seems to indicate that a given passion can only be overcome by a stronger and contrary affect that is on the same level as the originally given passion - i.e. the idea of a contrary bodily state. (*Affectus, quatenus ad Mentem refertur, nec coërceri, nec tolli potest, nisi per ideam Corporis affectionis contrariae, & fortioris affectione, quâ patimur.* (IVP7C)) VP3, however, seems to be saying that a mental state distinguished from the original passion only by a distinction of reason - an idea of that passion itself - is sufficient to free the mind from the passion.

Even more vexing, however, are the "paradoxes" internal to VP3D. Spinoza's argument might perhaps be rephrased in this way: A passion is a confused idea, whereas a mind is active insofar as it has distinct ideas. But the idea of an idea differs from the original idea only by a distinction of reason. Thus an idea of which we form a distinct idea "ceases to be a passion." It is clearly an underlying assumption of the argument that two ideas cannot be, respectively, distinct and confused, if they are distinguished from each other only by reason. One way of stating the central problem posed by the demonstration is, then, as follows: given all this, why should we not conclude that if an idea is confused in a mind, it is *impossible* for that mind to form a *distinct* idea *of it*? Spinoza's "paradoxical" position seems to be, though, that on the one hand we *can* form a distinct idea of a passion or confused idea, and this distinct idea will be distinguished only by reason from its object idea. On the other hand, no distinct idea can differ from a confused idea only by a distinction of reason. Therefore, we must suppose that the original confused idea ceases to be a confused idea (yet the distinct idea we formed of it is still an idea *of it*).

As I understand him, Beyssade in effect proposes that in order to make sense of Spinoza's position we need to keep two things in mind. First, this remedy for the passions is understood to pertain only to the "second kind of knowledge." Second, just as any confused, abstract ideas of imagination embody common natures that "can be conceived only adequately" (and that provide direct knowledge of the eternal and infinite essence of God), so even a passive state of sadness enfolds elements of the active affect of joy. Hence all affects, even the most passive, are capable of contributing to our intellectual love of God. Thus (I take it) the distinct understanding available to us with respect to the passions is in effect an eliciting from the passions of those *elements* which are in us just insofar as we are active (Cf. pp. 186-187). In their concrete individuality the passions remain passions, sadness remains sadness: the original affects are not actually *removed*. But what becomes (so to speak) uppermost in our minds with respect to them are just those distinctly conceived "elements" or "aspects" (p. 187) that nourish our active affect of intellectual love. (So, we may say, the claims of IVP7 and its Corollary are not after all undermined by VP3: a passion cannot be *restrained nor removed (coerceri nec tolli)* except by another affect; forming a distinct idea of a passion does not remove it, but rather, in effect, sublimates it.)

Although Beyssade does not belabor the textual support for his interpretation, I think he has in fact sensitively discerned and integrated a number of textual clues from the early Propositions of Part V. The result is a reading that does help to make pleasing sense of a substantial part of this text. I take Beyssade to be suggesting, however, that this reading shows us how to avoid the "logical paradox" originally presented by VP3. (Cf. p. 186: *Pour que la transformation effective échappe au paradoxe logique ...* ; and p. 187: *Ainsi, sans paradoxe logique ...*) Satisfying as his reading is in other ways, I'm very doubtful that it does succeed at *this* difficult (perhaps impossible) task.

In the first place, VP3 really does say that a passive affect of which we form a distinct idea "ceases to be a passion"; not merely that its passional aspect becomes less prominent in the mind. Beyssade himself stresses this point on (p. 185), but it is not clear to me that his reading does in the end preserve this strong claim. What worries me more, though, is that the logic of VP3 seems to me as obstinately paradoxical as ever, even in the light of his explication. For instance, if to form a distinct idea "of a passion" is really to conceive the common nature(s) inherent in the passion, it does not seem at all clear how the distinct idea of the passion can be "one and the same thing" as the passion itself (cf. IIP21S), or how it can be the case that the two are distinguished "only by reason." Yet this assumption must hold up in an intelligible way if the proof is to work at all.

I do not deny, then, that an interpretation along the lines proposed by Beyssade can help us make interesting sense of the general view that distinct understanding can relate a passion of sadness to intellectual love. I only suggest that this achievement may still leave us lacking a specific solution to the riddles of VP3.

1. See Curley (1988), p. 162, n. 13, for a similar, though less emphatic, judgment with respect to the treatment of this concept in the *Passions*. Curley indicates that Descartes does better in the Feb. 1, 1647 letter to Chanut (cited by Beyssade, and in n. 3, below).
2. At any rate, the two concepts are related sufficiently closely to support interesting detailed comparisons between them, as Beyssade's paper shows. I cannot go so far as to agree with his indication (p. 177) that Spinoza's failure to mention the interior emotions explicitly when he denounces Descartes's theory of the passions *suggests that Spinoza agreed with* a good part of the Cartesian concept of interior emotion. This omission might reflect nothing more than the fact that both Descartes and Spinoza deal so much more extensively with the passive affects. In any case, although the Cartesian "hypothesis more occult than any occult quality" that Spinoza castigates at the beginning of Part V is concerned specifically with the passions (and has to do with the pineal gland), his brief negative remarks on the Cartesian treatment of the affects at the beginning of Part III appear more general.

E. M. Curley, in the work alluded to in n. 1, proposes that Descartes's conception of the role of free will in judgment would render his account of interior emotions - which all rest on judgments of good and evil - a clear case of explanation by occult qualities in Spinoza's eyes.

3.   It's perhaps worth quoting in full a sentence from Descartes's letter to Chanut, February 1, 1647, which Beyssade partially quotes on (p. 180): "Mais pendant que nostre âme est jointe au corps, cette amour raisonnable est ordinairement accompagnée de l'autre, qu'on peut nommer sensuelle ou sensitive, & qui, comme i'ay sommairement dit de toutes les passions, appetits & sentimens, en la page 461 de mes Principes francois, *n'est autre chose qu'une pensée confuse* excitée en l'ame par quelque mouvement des nerfs, *laquelle la dispose à cette autre pensée plus claire en qui consiste l'amour raisonnable.*" (AT IV, 602-3, emphasis added.)

THE TWO FACES OF SPINOZA

AMELIE OKSENBERG RORTY
Radcliffe College and Mt. Holyoke College

"Nothing," says Spinoza, "can be destroyed except by an external cause" (IIIP4). And he adds: "An idea that excludes the existence of our body cannot be in our mind... The mind endeavors to think of those things that increase or assist the body's power of activity... and to think only of those things that affirm its power of activity" (IIIPP10, 12, 54). These upbeat passages are mystifying, and sometimes downright disturbing to us dark obsessive minds, prone to think of things that diminish our powers, prone to diminishing our powers precisely by thinking about what diminishes us, easily capable of thinking of a world that would, could and does exclude us. I want to try to make sense of the motifs expressed in these passages, reading them in such a way that they are not offensive to our sensibility, automatic grounds for distrusting the Spinozistic enterprise. Difficulties remain; but they are the ironies of all Stoics who speak with forked tongue. The optimism of the Stoic-enlightenment program of self improvement is Janus-faced with an equally familiar Stoic resignation in the face of necessity. The dynamic energy of conatus as the essence of individuals is revealed as mere partiality: conatus and the individual mind, the contrast between activity and passivity, the contrast between external and internal causes - all these are temporary and temporizing notions which the fully enlightened mind will recognize to be inadequate ideas. Necessary as they are, they are nevertheless merely perspectival. Individuals bent on self-improvement, perceiving themselves bounded by and opposed to the forces of similar individuals, mistake the ontological importance of their individuality and their activities. The Hobbesian strand that is woven through Spinozistic doctrine is visible only within middle-range opinion: it is not ontologically or epistemologically fundamental. Yet though it is partial and misleading, it remains among the phenomena to be explained. The enlightened will not eliminate but rather explain and understand the (necessitated) middle range talk of *conatus, activity and passivity, external and internal, individuals and relations*. Nevertheless, having questioned and even undermined the starting point of individuation, Spinoza returns the repressed: in Book V, (the ideas of) particular finite individuals are represented within eternity.

To understand the downbeat, ironic interpretation of Spinoza's two faced views, we need to take a detour, to contrast his views on the connection between knowledge and freedom with those of Descartes, to examine how his critique of Descartes' theory of the will sets the basis for his account of conatus. Against this background, Spinoza's irony emerges as sharply poised against his apparently remorseless and relentless optimism.

I

"You shall know the truth and it shall make you free" is the central - but ambiguous - motto of the Enlightenment. It is over the significance of this motto - on what is required to defend it - that Spinoza parts company with Descartes. The two sides of the Enlightenment - its attitudes towards the freedom and activity of the individual, and the role of knowledge in self-determination - are represented in the differences between Spinoza and Descartes. Their different conceptions of freedom carry correspondingly different views on the nature of knowledge, and radically different views on the identity and character of the individual mind.

Crudely, Descartes' represents that side of the Enlightenment that makes the will - its freedom from causal determination - the precondition for knowledge of the truth, while Spinoza represents that side of the Enlightenment which makes knowledge the precondition for the gradual progress towards active self-determination. Freedom is active self-determination through the rational realization of determinateness. An individual acts freely, from its own nature, only when determination is appropriated as self-determination, that is, when the mind acknowledges and absorbs as constitutive of its nature the determinative causal line that had seemed "external" to it. Because the appropriation of determining causes moves inadequate ideas towards greater adequacy, it transforms passivity into activity (IIID2; IIIP1). The movement towards knowledge - as the gradual process of articulating the determinants of an idea, its aetiology and preconditions - *is* the movement towards active self-determination.

For Descartes, the central example of knowledge is mathematics; the central mode of proof is the application of the law of noncontradiction in *reductio* arguments that require the unconditioned activity of the will to affirm, deny or doubt an idea. (Ironically, those writings which we take as centrally Cartesian are narrative, historical expositions.) For Spinoza, the model of knowledge is simultaneously genetic and analytic: the aetiology of an idea provides its history and its constitutive logical explanation. (Ironically, the geometrical mode of *The Ethics* would have been more appropriate for Descartes than for Spinoza.)

To understand the irony of Spinoza's optimism, let's examine Spinoza's disagreements with Descartes in a little more detail. Despite his insistence on the unity of the mind, Descartes presents (at least) an analytic distinction between the function of the mind in willing and understanding or entertaining an idea. Even though the will always operates on some particular content, it must be capable of entertaining an idea, and to affirm, deny or suspend judgment on that *same* idea. If every shift of propositional attitude were to reflect a shift of idea (or vice versa), there would be no continuity of thought or inquiry. The success of the method of doubt as a method of proof, particularly in *reductio* arguments, presupposes the identity of an idea through the vicissitudes of affirmation, negation and suspension of judgment. And *that* presupposes the separation of the functions of the understanding and the will, or as we might say, the independence of propositional attitudes from propositional contents.

The claim is strong: however variously congnitions or judgments may be formed, volitions are not causally determined at all. Of course the will can be inexorably inclined, and rationality can significantly coincide with inclination. But the will can only criticize its inclinations, if it is radically free. If this is an illusion, if all such critiques are merely higher level inclinations, then knowledge is an illusion.

Spinoza's attack on this view depends on his extreme particularism: there are no general powers or faculties of any kind. Volition, desire, understanding are not forces or capacities, but rather (particular) aspects of every individual act of thought (IIP48). Ontologically there are only particular *acts* of thinking, every detail of which is necessitated, causally determined. Adequate and inadequate ideas, truth and error alike are necessary, caused in all their details (IIP36). Before attacking Descartes' account of judgment, Spinoza issues a general warning, a warning that reveals his diagnosis of Descartes' fundamental error. He warns readers - he of course really means Cartesians - that they should not confuse ideas with images or words (IIP49S). It might seem otiose, even downright ridiculous to charge Descartes - of all people - with neglecting the distinction between images and ideas, still less between ideas and words. But Spinoza is not charging Descartes with reducing ideas to perceptions or images, as if Descartes had anachronistically made the mistake of accepting what we would call a picture theory of meaning. His charge is rather that Cartesians accept an inspection theory of thought and verification, that requires the will to scan the contents of the understanding, to determine whether they are well-formed, whether ideas are clearly and distinctly perceived.

From Spinoza's point of view, Descartes did not follow his best insights: in presenting thoughts as contents to be affirmed or denied, he failed to see the full significance of his view that the essence of mind is the *activity* of thinking. For all his recognition of the mind's essence as an activity, Descartes still thought of the mind as a substance which *has* thoughts. While he accepted a functionalist theory of passions in general and perceptions in particular, identifying them by their causal roles, Descartes held a representational theory of *ideas*, formally identifying them by their referential content.[1] Spinoza sees this as an unstable view: a functional-causal theory of perception cannot be integrated with a formal-referential theory of representation. On the best construal of a Cartesian theory, the content of any idea - adequate as well as inadequate ideas, clear and distinct ideas as well as confused perceptions - is given by its function in determining and being determined by other ideas.[2]

But for Spinoza, an individual mind is a finite mode which *is* the activity of its thinking. In having an idea, the mind does not have a possession which it is capable of examining. To think an idea is to *act*; to think of this or that idea is to act in this or that way. But if thinking is an *activity*, all thoughts, and not merely perceptions, are identified by their functional roles, by the ways they determine and are determined by other ideas. For Spinoza, every difference in conception makes a difference in attitude. Indeed the two are not distinct; to consider is to conceive; to conceive is to take an attitude, an attitude which must have been caused by previous thought. The causal history of the content of a thought - even of an erroneous thought - is identical with the causal history of the attitude towards it: they are co-determined (IIP49). The truth function of an idea - its being true or false - is a function of the way in which the mind conceives and connects it, rather than of its separable propositional content. An erroneous idea is an idea that is conceived in a mis-taking way, treated as isolated, fragmented incomplete. In thinking it, the mind is, in the several senses of the term, partial; it is fixed in a merely perspectival position. Images are not necessarily mental pictures: they are distinguished from ideas by their degree of partiality and abstraction, by their roles in the activity of thought. In thinking (of) them as incomplete fragments, abstractly and perspectivally, the mind focuses rather than expands: it over-estimates the separability and isolation of such ideas, almost as if it were engaged in idolatry on an *idolon*. (Sometimes indeed such images are so skimpy in expressing their determination - for instance, the idea of an unspecified winged horse - that we can't locate them within the system of ideas. That, I take it, is what Spinoza means by saying that such images are not even ideas: there is not enough of them there, for us to think with; they are not even proper images but empty phrases.)

Both parties have a great deal at stake. For Descartes, the possibility of a truthful science rests on the possibility of a rational mind forming an unconditioned independent, reflexive evaluation of its thoughts and desires. The two issues which are fundamentally at stake for Descartes - the possibility of a mathematically demonstrable science and that kind of intellectual reflection which can in principle assure every individual mind freedom from error - are interwoven. The latter is a condition for the former. Spinoza sees the Cartesian conditions as empty and arbitrary: rational evaluation is an activity with a particular content and context, with a particular aetiology in the chain of determination. It re-presents the structure of the real in just the same way as does every other act of thought. The will is not more rational because it is self-caused; it is only more rational if its affirmations are fixed by, and reflect the system of the world. The issue which is fundamentally at stake for Spinoza is the systematic rationality of the whole of nature, with human rationality assured by its being part of nature, explained by the very same laws that explain all other phenomena. All active logical determination is psychological determination: an agent's reasons are the causal determinants of his beliefs and actions. All psychological determination, properly understood, is logical determination: the causes of a belief are, when fully articulated in adequate ideas, its reasons.

II

What does all this have to do with the mysteriously affirmative passages with which we began?

Let's examine several stark cases, cases which on the face of it seem to present serious difficulties for Spinoza. First, as is natural, a physical case. An individual is, as we loosely say, dying of cancer. Superficially, this seems to present no problem for Spinozistic doctrine. The individual is overcome by a set of external forces more powerful than the force of her own conatus. Of course her conatus - her essence - combats the invasion. Indeed, that conatus is nothing more or less than the ways in which her body acts and reacts, the active organization of all the details of its activities, which, as things have it, are so constituted by their causal history and their place in the system of interactive individuals that they preserve the individual's ratio of motion and rest, in response to external forces as well as to its own internal dynamics. (IIP12) If the cancer wins, the individual is destroyed by forces more powerful than all those active in her self-preservation.

At a deeper level, however, there is a problem. The distinction between internal and external causes of determination is misleading and inadequate, narrowly perspectival. The details of an individual's nature are determined by its causal history and by its interaction with other individuals. Since an adequate cause contains all that is necessary to explain what follows from it, the necessary causes of an individual's determination are also constitutive of its determination. (IIIDD1,2) So regarded, the victory of the cancer is not a victory over the individual, but part of the life that constitutes its history. Because the individual is as much individuated, determined by her cancer as she is (as we would now say) by the genetic material she received from her parents, she is not destroyed by something *external* to her.

This might make it seem as if she had been destroyed by something within her. But properly described, she is not destroyed at all. To the extent that she has internalized her cancer - to the extent that it is also a determinant of her individuality - it expresses rather than destroys her. The cancer has reorganized the ratio of her body's motion and rest. If anything is destroyed, it is the physical object that was the object of the original inadequate idea of a body bounded to exclude a cancer that also determines it. (IIP36) But not even *that* is destroyed: for the inadequate idea of the individual, so bounded and defined, is explained and preserved in all its details, as necessary within the system of interactive ideas.

As is not surprising, we have drifted from the putatively purely physical case, to a physical case as intentionally identified. Everything that can be understood about physical conditions must be understood through their intentional descriptions. Inevitably we move from the problem of an individual body destroyed by cancer, to the problem of the diminution or destruction of a body intentionally identified by a description of its activities and their limits.

Cases of psychological invasion seem more perspicuous for revealing the force, and the irony of Spinoza's apparently remorseless optimism. Let's consider the case of an individual who is obsessed with, and crippled by a set of ideas that diminish her. She is suffering from an unrequited love of Spinoza, overcome by despair of understanding this labyrinthine mind, this system of ideas. This obsession jeopardizes her health: sleepless, she has lost her appetite, her inclination for her usual healthful pleasurable activities.

How can Spinoza's upbeat motto deal with this all too familiar case? Again, superficially, there is no problem. To the extent that her thoughts are invasive, she is, in a sense, suffering her thoughts without actively thinking them. The conatus of her individual mind will of course necessarily resist this invasion:

it will do - it consists in doing - whatever it can to preserve itself. (IIIPP6-9) Weaker minds may attempt evasive imaginative distraction; stronger ones become active and self-determined. Ironically, they will do this by accepting and absorbing the invasion, and in so doing transform the invasive ideas... and themselves as well. To the extent, and only to the extent, that the individual can come to think of herself as defined, rather than intruded upon, by her despairing attempts to understand Spinoza, does she become who she is. In actively thinking about Spinoza, she doesn't suffer, but is herself, thinking these thoughts. That she is likely to have perspectival and inadequate ideas about Spinoza does not affect the point. That she may continue to despair does not affect the point. As in the physical case, the destruction or diminution is transformed and redescribed, by a more adequate idea of her individuality, as in part constituted by her thinking these thoughts in this way. At best, her despair turns into joyful activity; at worst, she may only have the joy of being active in her despair, rather than suffering it passively. But in both cases, she no longer suffers an obsession because she has identified with the necessary and natural laws of the mind that are at work in her.

As in the case of truth and error, the difference between a positive and negative affect is not a difference in the affect itself, but in the functional role it plays, in the way a particular mind acts and reacts in expressing it. The sensation of physical pain is of course the hardest case: how can the suffering of such a sensation be transformed into an adequate idea, into an activity? In what could liberation from pain as a passive affect consist? The fortunate are sometimes - by virtue of their constitutions and the character of a particular pain - capable of taking a reflective attitude towards their condition. They can form an idea of their affect-idea, coming to see and to understand the patterned function of the salience of pain as focusing, rather than as expanding the mind. Pain just *is* the manifestation of a diminished conatus; it is the kind of affect whose perspectival, partial, and incomplete character resists expansion, absorbing its connections to other ideas. It is cold comfort, but perhaps comfort nevertheless, to recognize that in actively thinking the *idea of* the pain-affect, rather suffering the pain-affect, one realizes that it is just the sort of idea which standardly expresses the narrowing, rather than expansion, of an attentive understanding. To the extent that an individual mind can, in the middle of its pain, form an idea of its affect-idea - to the extent it can recognize the pattern immanent in pain-affects - it has moved to greater adequacy, by marking the interconnection between a particular pain-affect and other related ideas. Indeed the two are different ways of describing the same movement of the mind: to form an idea of an affect-idea just *is* to locate it within a nexus of related ideas, moving it towards (what might loosely be called) a common notion. When (with luck) the mind recognizes the necessary focalizing salience of pain, it sees its constitution expressed in a necessary pattern, one of the natural laws of the mind. It will still feel the pain as painful, but in recognizing the necessity of that feeling, its functional role in expressing the system of ideas, it becomes as active as is possible under the circumstances.

It sounds like an easy and cheap magic trick. Just wave your hand: all that is required for an individual to assure indestructibility is to brazen it out, and assert or claim as Her own, whatever it might be that could diminish or destroy her. It sounds for all the world like a child fighting off sleep by the power of a positive announcement that it has commanded sleep, indeed that it *is* sleep.

Things may be bad; but they are not quite so outrageously bad. In the first place, every movement towards a more adequate idea is also a movement towards a more active, more self-sustaining body. Whatever changes occur intellectually are registered physically; indeed only those increases in self-determination and power that occur physically have really occurred intellectually.

In the second place, the individual does not identify with the *general* laws of nature because those laws are nothing more than summaries of the immanent and particular relations obtaining among the individuals that constitute the system that is nature. Even common notions are universally exemplified particulars, their interconnections and structures rationally articulated (IIP3L2, 37-40). Since there is nothing there, In General, for her to become, in becoming herself, the individual doesn't become Mind in General, or Extension in General. The expansion of her identity is, so to say, outwards to include other particular individuals, rather than upwards to a single general abstraction. She cannot acquire a more adequate idea of her individuality by a formulaic phrase defining individuality as an affection or mode of substance. Particularity is preserved: coming to have more adequate ideas consists in absorbing as constitutive, the details of the individual ideas that determine an individual's system of ideas.

With this move - this absorption of determining ideas - the old distinctions between what is internal and what is external to a person's nature, between what is essential and what is accidental, between what is necessary and what is contingent, are shown to be inadequate. What had been seen as merely external and accidental - that there happened to be a copy of Spinoza's *Ethics* in her parents' library the long hard winter when they were snow-bound on the farm - turns out to be as essential to her individuation as anything else. Despite her despair, indeed including her despair and her inadequate understanding, Spinoza's writings have formed her outlook on the world. She is nothing if not a Spinozist. Her more adequate self-concept is not an abstract realization: it consists of and is expressed in the details of her psychological and intellectual functioning, as for instance, her becoming active in thinking of Spinoza rather than suffering thoughts of loving him.

III

Are we in the clear? Have we succeeded in defending Spinoza's upbeat optimism in such a way that it is no longer downright offensive? Not quite. There are still some problems. To see them more clearly, we need to give a summary account of how active conatus itself seems to undermine the very idea of individuality on which it rests.

An unreflective individual mind is a set of ideas of bodily modifications; a reflective individual mind is an increasingly adequate idea of a set of ideas of bodily modifications, so related that together, as a system, they have their own conatus, that is, they (happen to have necessarily) form(ed) a particular self-sustaining system of ideas. The conatus of an individual mind is its ideas, seen as actively endeavoring to become adequate, self-explanatory, self-determined. Whatever her conatus *can* do, what her essential nature can do, that it must do. It can do no other. The conatus of the individual mind, defined as desire along with the consciousness thereof, is not a single force or power, but is rather the set of ideas of the mind seen as active in their self-preservation and self-determination (IIIPP7-9). Desire as the essence of the mind is not a power over and above the mind's particular ideas: it just *is* the set of ideas actively endeavoring to move to greater adequacy, as self-explanatory (IIIDefAff1). That preservation takes place in a very straightforward and simple way: each inadequate idea is, as we might say, explanation-hungry for its determinants, to articulate their systematic inter-relation.

But there are difficulties. First, the complications of the physical picture. On the one hand, an individual body is identified by its maintaining a constant ratio of motion and rest. On the other hand, an individual must endeavor to increase its power to resist the force of opposing individuals who are, in *their* attempts at self-preservation, encroaching upon it. The interactive codetermination of individuals each bent on self-determination appears to require that each attempt to increase its relative power in order to have the necessary margin of power required to maintain itself. In a system of mutually determining individuals, each organized to preserve itself, simple self-preservation must move to expansive self-determination.

And so, too, the conatus of an individual mind appears to be necessarily unstable. Because the interaction of an individual with others modifies it in a way that can affect its functioning, self-preservation requires self-determination; and self-determination in turn requires self-expansion. On this middle range level, at any rate, Spinoza shares Hobbes' view that for the individual to retain its power, it must attempt to enlarge its sphere: even in cooperative situations, it needs a margin of power over other equally expansive individuals who are attempting to increase their self-determination in order to resist its encroachments on them. The power of an individual conatus is expressed in its attempt to appropriate and integrate an invading oppositional force. In cases of cooperation, the individual wants to secure, and set the terms and conditions for, the continuity of beneficial cooperation. Epistemologically, the mind endeavors to understand, and ontologically to absorb, the interconnected details of its determination. In moving to a more adequate idea, and to a more active realization of its nature, it expands its powers to overcome the limitations and partiality of its initial inadequate idea of itself. Ironically, a powerful conatus so transforms itself that the original limited individual technically expands/dies. (Shades of Nietzsche within Spinoza.)

It might be argued that an over-emphasis on the potential conflict between individuals neglects their cooperation, and sometimes even the identity of their directions.[3] Certainly individuals can stand in complementary, mutually supportive or enhancing relations; and sometimes indeed the direction of their forces, their interests, coincide. But each of these also present problems for individuation. As Hegel traces the cooperation that is hidden within opposition, so Rousseau traces the natural development from cooperation, to specialization and mutual need, to dependency, to the attempt at domination. Cooperative individuals are, when fully understood, mutually ingredient; as they become mutually dependent on their cooperation, they become mutually adaptive, each increasingly internally modified by its interaction with the other. Hegel's account of the absorption of conflict into inter-dependence, and Rousseau's account of the development of opposition from mutual dependence, tell the same story: the initial distinctness of individuals is overcome by the ways their interactions - whether cooperative, combative or (finally) identical - move to the mutual ingredience of what had been taken as distinct.

What is the criterion for the identity of an individual mind? In what sense is there a more adequate idea of the *same* individual, when every change in the set of ideas marks a change in the identity of the individual mind? The predecessor mind remains identical only in being fully contained, further empowered and realized within the successor mind, with more details of its ideas adequately explained. In actively thinking, the individual mind so transforms herself that it is no longer the same individual, there, to be preserved.

What is the relation between an individual mind (*de re*) and any given reflexive idea of that mind (*de dicto*)? An inadequate idea of the mind expands/dies outward: does the individual mind, which *is* the idea of a set of ideas thereby expand/die outward? The individual mind is finite; as an adequate idea in the mind of God - that is, as a necessary idea in the system of ideas - it is eternal. So it seems an individual mind cannot after all be an idea of a set of ideas, since it cannot be both finite (*de re*) and infinite (*de dicto*). This problem is, of course, an instance of the familiar vexed question about the relation between the idea of a bodily modification (i) and the idea of the idea of that modification (i.o.i). On the one hand, the two are extensionally identical because the idea of a set of ideas of a bodily modification cannot be *of* anything else than the idea of the original modification (or it could not be a more adequate idea of *that* modification). On the other hand, the two are distinguishable if not distinct (or it could be the case that one is adequate, the other not; and that they played different functional roles in the activity of thinking). Etienne Balibar has proposed that the distinction is a distinction of reason, between an idea as formally considered, and an idea as objectively considered.[4] Formally, ontologically, the idea of an idea (i.o.i) can only refer to that bodily modification to which the idea (i) itself refers. Objectively, psycho-logically however, an idea of an idea (i.o.i) might have a character and functions that are distinguishable, and different from its idea (i). Something like that must be right, if an idea of an idea (i.o.i) can play a distinctive intellectual function that is not reducible to, or identical with the intellectual function played by its idea (i). But this suggestion relocates our problem on another level: what are the criteria for determining the identity of an idea under its formal and its objective aspects? If, as Balibar argues, Spinoza is not committed to an indefinite regress of ideas of ideas of ideas..., then the problem about individuating ideas recurs as a problem of distinguishing the formal and objective aspect of any given set of ideas.

The problem about the individuation of ideas is replicated as a problem about the individuation of individuals. On the physical side, individuals are distinguished by all the particular details of the constitution of their bodies, their weight, height, eye color, gender, metabolism. But those differentiating details are themselves products of the interaction among individuals. Each has left traces of itself on the others; each *is* the tracery of all the others. On the intellectual or psychological side, individuals are distinguished by the particular set of partial, perspectival or inadequate ideas which happen to constitute a finite mind at any given time. But as these ideas become increasingly adequate, individuation is correspondingly diminished (IVP35). To the extent that two individuals have increasingly adequate ideas, they are decreasingly differentiated. This is not because they have identical general ideas, but because they come to have the same nexus of particular co-determining ideas.

But this is more of a notional or theoretical problem than it is a practical or immediate one. Since we find ourselves a long way from adequate ideas, a long way from having absorbed all the relevant determinants of individual minds, we have more than enough to distinguish them. As the movement to adequate ideas takes place gradually, incrementally, each individual expands from a different starting point. With the exception of the realization of common notions, the natural movement of expansion of different individuals moves in different directions, even when it involves mutual absorption. The details of the movement of two inter-active, mutually expansive minds to increased adequacy of their ideas will differ as the details of their history and location differ. To be sure, at the indefinite end, they will no longer be distinguishable, each having all absorbed all other individuals. But the trajectory of the movements towards adequacy will be as distinguishable as their histories and locations.

Put this way, it becomes clear why some individuals have greater difficulty in moving towards adequate ideas than others. By contrast to individuals whose causal histories and locations involve relatively simple, homogeneous, linear causal lines, individuals whose determination involves the coincidence of distinctive, heterogeneous and distant causal lines would naturally have greater difficulty integrating and systematically inter-connecting their determinants. As is evident for individual nation-states, the more complex and plural the determination, the more powerful - but also the more difficult - the active integration of mutually interactive particulars, each gradually realizing their immanent co-ingredience. But in diminishing their individuation, individuals do not diminish their individuality. Indeed individuality - that is, the power of an individual to preserve and determine itself - increases in direct proportion to the decrease of individuation, as the inadequate ideas that individuate are absorbed into the co-determinative system of adequate ideas.

IV

We have come full circle, to the differences between Descartes' and Spinoza's understanding of the connection between individual minds, knowledge and freedom. For Spinoza, as for Descartes, an individual's freedom is assured by its power to identify itself with its necessary and adequate ideas. And for Spinoza, as for Descartes, there are two stories of individuation. On the one hand, every detail of inadequate ideas differentiates individuals; and on the other hand, insofar as a mind has - or rather, *is* - a set of adequate ideas, it is not distinguished from any other adequately conceived mind. But although Descartes and Spinoza agree on these general formulae, they wholly disagree on their interpretation and significance. Descartes distinguishes individual minds in two quite different ways. On the one hand, since only contingent perceptions, bodily sensations and passions - all of them ideas caused in the mind by the action of the body - differentiate individual minds, and since these ideas are not essential to the identity or the existence of the mind, minds are not individuated by anything that is necessary or essential to them.[5] On the other hand, God created individual minds as distinct. And indeed, it is central to Descartes' version of the Enlightenment that individual minds are capable of autonomous acts of the will, capable of reflecting, doubting, knowing, independently of the actions of other individuals, or indeed in principle, of the conditions of the bodies to which they are attached. It is just in this that the freedom of the individual mind consists, that it can act independently of any causal determination, including the influence of contingent ideas that individuate it.

While Spinoza agrees with Descartes that individual minds are distinguished by their inadequate ideas, he holds that an individual mind's inadequate ideas are as essential and necessary to it as its adequate ideas: indeed they enter into the composition of its adequate ideas. Active self-determination is assured by identifying with, rather than detaching oneself from, the system of determining ideas.

V

We are now prepared to give a somewhat more adequate reading of our original, troubling quotations.

1. "Nothing can be destroyed except by an external cause." True enough: it is only insofar as an individual is defined as bounded, as excluding other individuals that it can be destroyed by them. But since the full explication of the details of every individual includes every other, there is nothing that is necessarily external to an individual. Although an individual is a finite mode of a substance, it follows from and is necessarily interactively defined by the system of individuals. Even the idea of finite modes, adequately conceived, is necessary and eternal in the mind of God.

BUT: The fuller explication of the quotation undermines its presuppositions. The idea of merely external causes is an inadequate idea: the expansive self-determination of individuals in a system of co-determination obliterates the distinction between internal and external causes.

2. "An idea that excludes the existence of our body cannot be in our mind." True enough: Trivially, no idea can exclude the existence of our body because ideas and bodies cannot exclude, or for that matter, include one another. More significantly, since every body is implicated in the full determination of every other, every adequate idea of every body is included in the full articulation of every other.

BUT: The fuller explication of the quotation undermines its presuppositions. For individual bodies naturally attempt and sometimes succeed in overcoming one another, in an opposition of forces. Since that very opposition acts to determine the nature of each body, an adequate idea of a body includes the idea of those bodies actively opposed to its own.

3. "The mind endeavors to think of those things which increase or assist the body's power of activity, and to think only of those things." True enough. The body's conatus is its activity in endeavoring self-preservation. There is an intellectual equivalent of all its endeavors. So it straightway - perhaps all too straightway - follows that the mind endeavors to think what conduces to the body's power of activity.

BUT: The fuller explication of the quotation undermines its presuppositions. For the mind can be forced to think what attempts to overcome the body, just exactly as the body can exist in an opposition of forces with other bodies. Indeed as the body can be overcome, so too the mind, inadequately conceived, can think of what overcomes the body or itself, even though it endeavors to think of those things, and only those things which enhance it. If it fails - and it might very well fail - it does so because it necessarily continued to have an inadequate idea of its own nature. But if it succeeds, it appropriated those things which it *had* thought of as destructive.

Of course, more adequately considered, there was never any serious problem in our passages. The upbeat passages only speak of the *endeavor* of individuals: they say nothing about the success of that endeavor. Whether the endeavor is successful depends upon the relative position of the individual and its history in relation to individuals around it. Some individual minds are so constituted that they are necessarily caused to think of themselves as capable of becoming self-determined, or at any rate increasingly self-determining. Others have no such idea. Some individuals are so constituted that they succeed in making some of their ideas more adequate. Others are so constituted that their modes of attempting to become more self-determining take other forms: they escape in fantasy, or remain conflicted. But in truth, the idea of the success or failure of individuals in their endeavors of self-preservation - indeed the idea of individuals as preserving themselves - is itself an inadequate idea. The original limited point with which we begin - Hobbesian individuals endeavoring to preserve themselves - is meant both to be undermined *and* to be affirmed. On the one hand, strictly speaking individuals as affections or modes of substance cannot be self-determining. Since only Substance can be self-determining, the idea of individuals as necessarily becoming self-determining is a (necessary) illusion.   And yet, substance is wholly expressed in the totality of its modes under each attribute.   Finite as they may be, individuals - taken together in their particularity, illusions of grandeur and all - are all the reality we've got.[6]

1. Cf. Calvin Normore, "Meaning and Objective Being: Descartes and his Sources," *Essays on Descartes' Meditations*, ed. Amelie Oksenberg Rorty. University of California Press, 1986.
2. Cf. Amelie Rorty, "Formal Traces in Cartesian Functional Explanations," *Canadian Journal of Philosophy*, Dec. (1984).
3. Yirmiyahu Yovel suggested this, at the Chicago Spinoza Conference, September, 1986.
4. Etienne Balibar made this suggestion at the Chicago Spinoza Conference, September, 1986.
5. Cf. "Cartesian Passions and the Union of Mind and Body," *Essays on Descartes' Meditations*, loc. cit.
6. I am grateful to David Lachterman, Genevieve Lloyd, Etienne Balibar, Yirmiyahu Yovel, Diane Steinberg and other participants at the Chicago Spinoza Conference, September 1986 for their searching questions and helpful suggestions.

THERAPEUTICS AND HERMENEUTICS

JOSÉ A. BENARDETE
Syracuse University

I

Although the protracted course of treatment prescribed by classical psychoanalysis has been less and less seen in recent decades, other more abbreviated forms of psychotherapy, notably, the behavior modification associated with B.F. Skinner have not been lacking to fill the gap. I myself have been undergoing Spinoza therapy, and while any such regimen fetched from the 17th century might be supposed to be about as relevant as the use of the horse-and-buggy on the modern highway, I have come to believe that it may yet prove serviceable in enabling us to cope with the psychopathology of everyday life. Scarcely more than anecdotal, the evidence for my belief is admittedly very exiguous, being confined to the use of myself as a *corpus vile* by way of informally testing the various "remedies for the affects" that are urged upon us by Spinoza. If I am thus to be seen as daring to practice medicine without a license, I am sufficiently encouraged by my results to anticipate the day when a Spinoza institute will be established to train and certify professionals and para-professionals in the accredited exercise of Spinoza therapy.

Verifying the efficacy of any such non-standard course of treatment must not be supposed to be any easier than comparable efforts to evaluate the performance of mainline psychoanalysis itself. To Spinoza, moreover, a special difficulty attaches from which Freud is altogether exempt. How precisely the therapist is to proceed along Freudian lines, we have a clear understanding today based by no means entirely on written records, seeing that the uninterrupted practice of psychoanalysis can always appeal in a pinch to an 'apostolic succession' that reaches back to its founder. In the case of Spinoza, there is presumably only the written record to go on, and that can hardly be said to provide us with anything like an effective manual of clinical practice. Generous enough at one point to allow that "Spinoza's psychology of the affects might be secure as a set of general theses," Jonathan Bennett wonders whether "the same might be true of the therapies" as well, confessing, however, that "I cannot work that line of thought out in detail, because the therapies are not well enough worked out by Spinoza to admit of such treatment." The operative word here is 'detail,' and it is just such an "absence of details" that Bennett deplores when he looks in vain to Stuart Hampshire's account of Spinoza therapy for what "specific things about his internal struggle" the patient is called upon to raise to consciousness. (Bennett (1984), 332, 348-49)

Therapeutics aside, there is indeed a more general tendency in Spinoza that Bennett shrewdly notices much earlier in his *Study* when he remarks on his "pleasure in starting at a dizzingly abstract level and moving in about two short steps down into the thick of everyday life" (*Ibid.*, p. 41), and it was thus perhaps to be expected that when it came to implementing his theoretical psychology in therapeutic terms, Spinoza would be found to be peculiarly unforthcoming. Negotiating the gap that separates theory from practice, vividly expressed above all in Gilbert Ryle's distinction between knowing-that and knowing-how, raises difficulties in any case. If Spinoza therapy is to be credited as a viable undertaking, it must transact the passage from mere theoretical psychology to practical know-how.   More through the spoken than the written word one expects such know-how to be informally transmitted from master to apprentice in a clinical setting, and one would dearly wish to find in Spinoza's correspondence some indication that he was actively engaged in that sort of praxis in the absence of which one might readily fear, with Bennett, that he was merely "arguing wildly that the acquisition...of some of his own principal character traits" can serve as "a sure route to freedom and happiness." (*Ibid.*, p. 347) It is not so much that Bennett doubts that freedom and happiness would in fact accrue to us as a result of our being so fortunate as to acquire the specific character traits of *animositas* and *generositas* - summed up as *fortitudo* - that are explicitly prescribed at E IIIP59S. Still less, I take it, is he querying Spinoza's character on a personal level. To the contrary, one has every right to suspect that if his so-called remedies for the affects have any efficacy at all, it is limited to the happy few who are like Spinoza himself in being least in need of them.

Precisely because I am one of those who are definitely excluded from that select society, at any rate for the foreseeable future, my own auto-therapeutic efforts to acquire *fortitudo* through the express use of those remedies can hardly fail to be instructive. It must be admitted, however, that my primary motivation in this undertaking has been less the desire to acquire *fortitudo*, let alone *beatitudo*, than to relieve myself of various forms of emotional distress. And even that is not quite right.   More fundamental still, speaking in an autobiographical vein, has been the purely scholarly effort to understand Spinoza on his own terms. In a word, hermeneutics, not therapeutics, always bearing in mind that *fortitudo* and *beatitudo* might - just possibly - come my way thereby as a welcome by-product of my textual studies. Put quite so nakedly, the order of my priorities can only be seen as objectionably risible, and if I derive comfort from the fact that most other Spinoza scholars are in the same embarrassing position, the exculpatory sentiment in which I am here indulging is almost certainly one that is to be frowned upon as unworthy, not least of all when it is viewed in Spinozistic terms.

A difficulty is raised, however, by my use of so moralistic an expression as 'unworthy' when it is above all characteristic of the Spinozistic conduct of life that it seeks to understand itself in therapeutic as opposed to moralistic terms. In fact we need not hesitate to register (1) as itself a cardinal maxim of Spinoza therapy:

(1) Replace moralistic by therapeutic considerations in the conduct of life.

If it should be objected that (1) is really only a meta-therapeutic injunction, a simplified version of (1) that meets the objection can be found in (2):

(2) In the conduct of life eschew moralistic considerations.

Notice that in Victorian times (2) might well have been felt to be much too vague to have any ready applicability while today, after Freud, in sharp contrast, it is almost second nature with us on the level of practical know-how. So much so that confronted with a Victorian puzzled by (2) we should know precisely how to proceed in explaining its uses to him on a case-by-case basis with the kind of richness of detail that we are entitled to demand of Spinoza therapy across the board. It goes almost without saying that anything like the clarity we enjoy in respect to (2) fails to be available to us in regard to the other, more positive tenets of Spinoza therapy, e.g., 'separating and joining' as Bennett designates the maxim implicit in VP2 that launches the therapeutic program of Part V. Here we are at last very much on our own with scarcely any further opportunity of falling back on Freud by way of eking out the meagerness of the text.

At the very outset a modal puzzle arises in connection with VP2 where we are assured that "if we separate emotions or affects from the thought of an external cause, and join them to other thoughts, then the Love or Hate toward the external cause is destroyed, as are the vacillations of mind arising from the affects." Why so? Well, as we learn from the demonstration, "what constitutes the form of Love, or Hate, is Joy, or Sadness, accompanied by the idea of an external cause (by Def Aff 6, 7). So if this is taken away, the form of Love or Hate is taken away at the same time. Hence these affects, and those arising from them, are destroyed." Quite apart from the general drift of the discussion, the last sentence here and above all the word 'hence' or 'therefore' (*adeoque*) explicitly commits Spinoza to the following principle involving *de re* modality.

(3) (x) if x is an instance of hate, then necessarily x is an instance of hate.

If querying (3) should seem altogether captious, one can only be surprised that (4), which is very much on a par with (3), appears to be denied immediately afterwards at VP3D, where again the role of '*adeoque*' should be noticed.

(4) (x) if x is an instance of passion, e.g., hate, then necessarily x is an instance of passion.

Because VP3 features the therapeutic technique of 'turning passions into actions,' it appears to allow for a case of hate, which is a passion, that ceases to be a case of hate even while continuing to exist only now as an action. Thus while being an instance of hate is seen to be an essential feature of any such instance according to VP2D, it proves to be only an accidental attribute of it according to VP3D.

Taken simply at face value, the trouble with VP2D is that, having insisted that every case of hate involves two components, namely (a) sadness and (b) the thought of an external cause, it fails to realize (as Bennett observes) that subtracting (b) from the total complex may still leave us with (a), and it is (a) even more than the total complex from which we are eager to be released. There is a further difficulty. Altogether absent from the demonstration, the notion of 'joining' figures only in the proposition itself where it guarantees that the distressful element, namely (a), does persist even after (b) has been separated from the complex. For it is precisely (a) that is to be joined to some new thought on being separated from the old one. This is not to say, however, that at this later stage (a) need remain distressful, assuming, of course, that being distressful may be only an accidental feature of (a). In the previous paragraph an inconsistency having been found to obtain as between VP3D and VP2D, that same inconsistency is now seen to infect VP2 on its own where (a) undergoes the following three events simultaneously: (1) being separated from the old thought, (2) being joined to a new one, and (3) being destroyed.

II

Although it is 'separating' not 'joining' that preponderates when VP2 and VP2D are taken together as a unit, the element of 'joining' acquires a new interest for us when we learn in VP4S that "the affect" is to be "separated from the thought of an external cause and joined to true thoughts." What sort of true thoughts does Spinoza have in mind here? Well, there may be various sorts but there is one in particular on which I propose to concentrate in my effort to implement 'separating and joining' as an effective piece of therapeutic know-how. This 'true thought' - whether it really is true will not be my concern - turns out to be pretty much the one that Spinoza expresses twice over at the end of Part III, first and succinctly in his "general definition of the affects" and again, but at some length, in the extended explanation that he appends to it. In brief, then, an affect which is called a passion (*passio animi*) is a confused idea by which the mind affirms of its body a greater or less power of acting than before. Not that the mind actually compares its body's present with its previous power of acting, for in that case the idea would presumably not be a confused one. Rather I take it that the passion itself somehow expresses in a confused way the fact that the body's power of acting is increased or diminished, aided or restrained. In its most uncompromising formulation, being in the psychological state of sadness just is identical with being confusedly aware that one's power of acting (= one's body's power of acting = one's mind's power of thinking = one's force of existing = one's conatus) suffers restraint precisely by being diminished.

Splendid rhetoric certainly, where the very essence of Spinoza shines at its brightest, though I should be embarrassed to be challenged to explain much less defend his thesis in plain terms. It will be enough, however, for us to enjoy the music here of high theory without looking too closely into it, seeing that my immediate purpose has to do not with theory but with practice, and our sophistication today prepares us to allow that a putative course of therapy, e.g., Freud's, might well prove effective even though the psychological theory sponsoring it should be independently found to be false or even worse than false, namely so confused as to lack a proper truth-value. Ultimately, of course, one would wish to achieve an integrated understanding of Spinoza on the level of theory as well as practice, Spinoza from above meeting Spinoza from below, and I am in fact undertaking to do just that in these pages, specifically by juxtaposing his general definition of the affects in their ontological import with the know-how presumed to be encapsulated in 'separating and joining.'

Recently characterized by Curley as a metaphysical moralist, in an effort to sum up his entire program in just two words, in that same vein Spinoza might still more radically be termed a metaphysical therapist, seeing that metaphysics and psychotherapy are quite properly felt to be even further removed from one another than metaphysics and morals. In either case, the two poles of Spinoza's enterprise are reflected in Pascal's distinction between the *esprit de géométrie* and the *esprit de finesse* where the former is to be understood broadly enough as to comprise all scientific, and the latter all humanistic, thinking. Although the *esprit de géométrie* of the *Ethics* is almost too literally advertised on its title page by the promise that ethics itself will be found therein to be *ordine geometrico demonstrata*, the *esprit de finesse* of the work is only fully displayed in the informal discussions of Parts III and IV, which can almost be read like a novel and where Spinoza is drawing on a rich humanistic tradition featuring such names as Ovid and Terence. Precisely how these two sorts of *esprit* are to be exercised more or less in conjunction, I am evidently committed to showing in this paper.

Suppose, then, that we address ourselves in something like novelistic fashion to a particular episode of suffering that touches us almost too closely as scholars. One has written a book and, reading a professional journal, one is now stung by the unjust criticism of a harsh review. In Spinoza's jargon one 'hates' the review, not to mention the reviewer, for hate just is distress or sadness accompanied by the thought of an external cause, in the present case the review itself. An affect will be said to be bad in our new therapeutic idiom only to the extent that it impedes the flow of clear thinking, and thus particularly to be noticed here is the extent to which one is obsessed by one's grievance and in consequence fixated on a single object to the exclusion of all others. The Freudian term is cathexis which his English translator, James Strachey, coined by way of conveying the notion of a military occupation that is implicit in the German *Besetzung*, as well as the Greek *katexein*. Rather like the incubus or succubus of medieval legend, one's passions involve a kind of military take-over of one's psyche by the enemy that is reminiscent of 'possession' by demons; and it is thus a happy accident scarcely supported by the Latin when Curley has Spinoza say that the affects are generally "excessive and *occupy* the mind in the consideration of only one object so much that it cannot think of others." (IVP44S) As a point of hermeneutics, this element of cathexis can probably be seen to be formally recognized in the general definition of the affects where a passion is said to be "a confused idea... which, when it is given, determines the Mind to think of this rather than that."

Cathected then to our grievance, how are we to cope with it? How break the cathexis? In the present instance it is to be assumed that we are to this extent already free of it, that we are to be found casting about, however blindly, for a remedy. In the extreme case, of course, where the fixation is complete, no such free play of the mind is available, and in IVP44S a person so cathected is, in effect, said to be clinically insane. Even in the more usual sort of case, however, merely resolving well in advance to apply the generic remedy, as I shall style it, for it is designed to supplement not replace any specific remedy for a specific passion, fails to provide any assurance that when the time comes and the remedy is called for one will be found in the pinch to have sufficient presence of mind to recall one's intention, let alone to execute it. In fact, achieving recall here in the very throes of passion turns out to be almost half the battle, and there were times when I positively despaired of ever being quick-witted enough or self-possessed enough - the failure could be seen to be one of either intelligence or character (a Spinozistic point) - to confront my ongoing passions with the generic remedy that I had been at such pains to formulate. For only after they had largely relaxed their hold on me, did I tardily recognize the opportunity that was no longer mine to seize, almost kicking myself in the process.

Doubtless itself a passion that is to be deplored when considered in isolation, this impulse of mine to punish myself for my amnesia I take to be on the whole a fairly salutary one, and indeed it is to be noticed that at IVP43 provision is in effect made for a kind of pain therapy which, on being viewed in the light of IVP54S, indicates how biblical, hairshirt morality can prove therapeutically valid when it comes at any rate to the vulgar. There is thus low-grade as well as high-grade therapy, and it was inevitably a source of some humiliation for me to realize that it might well be only the low-grade, biblical sort, which Spinoza characteristically dismisses with Nietzschean scorn, that might be applicable in my own case. Actually, it was a proper mix of the two, the cognitive sort as well as the hairshirt variety, to which I am indebted. For if my generic remedy will be seen to be designed in keeping with the former kind of therapy, the reiterated lashings of self-reproach that helped me to overcome my amnesia can only be subsumed under the latter.

III

Presupposing a kind of internal monitor that serves in effect as an early warning system, the generic remedy itself might now almost seem to be anti-climactic. At the outset one is called upon to abstract from the specific character of one's ongoing passion, e.g., a bout of envy, identifying it only as a case of sadness accompanied by the thought of an external cause. Then separating out the element of sadness from the total complex, one is instructed to join it to this line of reasoning. "Here is a case of sadness that afflicts me. But sadness is a confused idea by which the Mind affirms of its Body a lesser force of existing than before, indicating that the Body's power of acting (= the Mind's power of thinking) is at once diminished and subject to restraint. Therefore my power of acting is currently impeded." Conjuring with this syllogism like a charm, I was surprised by the frequent occasions when not only was the cathexis broken but the distress itself was dissolved even before I had quite completed the major premise, thereby rendering the projected conclusion of the argument false as well as otiose. More often perhaps, the distress persisted through to the end of the syllogism, and indeed well beyond it, only now very much (or at any rate somewhat) diminished in force.

On other occasions, alas, the incubus stubbornly refused to be exorcised, and reciting my ineffectual charm can only be likened, phenomenologically, to what happens when one drains a word of all meaning by mindlessly repeating it. To a greater or less extent I felt in these instances that the words of the syllogism simply ceased to serve me as a vehicle of actual reasoning, and merely going through the motions of reciting them in parrot fashion could prove too wearisome to endure.

It is the successful episodes, however, that I prefer to commemorate, though I am under no illusion that they provide anything but the most meager evidence in support of the hypothesis that the generic remedy is therapeutically effective. The present opportunity to collect further evidence pro or con the hypothesis I could hardly be expected to forego in this distinguished synod of Spinozists, and I am thus expressly inviting your participation in the conference-wide effort to test the hypothesis informally in the privacy of your closets. Indulging the hope that the results will be encouraging, I look forward to the day when the professional psychologist, and here I am thinking rather of those engaged in experimental than in clinical psychology, will undertake in 'double-blind' fashion with 'controls' etc., to measure the precise degree of effectiveness, or lack thereof, that may be assigned to the generic remedy vis-à-vis this or that form of emotional disorder. Any such vindication of Spinoza in empirical terms would, I fear, strike some of you as involving a radical betrayal of him on his own terms as a paradigmatic rationalist.

For my own part, before conceding the point I would need to understand much more clearly than I do what exactly is the role of scientific experiment in Spinoza's theory of knowledge, addressing especially Letter 6 in all its chemical detail. Almost equally obscure has been widely felt to be the purely rational component in his epistemology as featured on the highest level, in the intuitive knowledge of concrete particulars. As to what such knowledge might actually come to, the generic remedy is found to be highly suggestive at any rate in its abbreviated version when we proceed direct from the minor premise to the conclusion without engaging in a detour that involves the major premise. Merely omitting the major premise on a verbal or even sub-vocal level will not, of course, suffice, seeing that one may yet be tacitly relying on the universal premise in the fashion of any enthymeme. One is required rather to intuit directly that this instance of sadness just is - essentially - a case where my power of acting or my body's power of acting is diminished. Although there is plenty of room here for scepticism, one can readily appreciate perhaps for the first time the pull of rational intuition.

The issue comes down to this. Let it be granted that the major premise expresses a necessary, a priori truth. Rationality is only being exercised here, however, on the level of universals, though the term 'intuition,' recalling Aristotle's use of *noesis* in the last chapter of *Posterior Analytics*, can be employed with propriety to designate it. However problematical this universal sort of intuition may be, and the empiricist is eager to reject it along with the synthetic a priori, much more so is the particular or singular variety to which Spinoza appeals. A moderate version of it would allow us to dispense with the major premise of the generic syllogism only insofar as it is called upon to play an *occurrent* role in the cognitive episode. A dispositional role for the premise in the background will, however, be insisted on by this moderate version of singular intuition. While it is arguable that Spinoza would be content with the moderate version, the uncompromising version that dispenses altogether with the major premise is doubtless to be preferred when it comes to envisaging a form of ultra-rationalism with real teeth to it.

At the end of the preface to Part III, we learn that the affects of hate, anger, envy, etc., "follow from the same necessity and force (*virtus*) of nature as the *other* singular things." Any doubts one might have that an instance of sadness could count as a particular or singular thing ought thus to be allayed, and it is at any rate much harder to credit ourselves with a faculty of singular intuition into the essences of thick things like stones than in those of thin ones like sadness, which have the further advantage of satisfying Bennett's demand that "my body" should have "contained the thing in question." (*Ibid.*, p. 367)

There is also a metaphysical point to be made here. The essence of each thing is identified with its conatus, which in its turn is identified with its power to do anything whatever, either alone or with others (see IIIP7D). No wonder, then, that in intuiting the essence of an instance of sadness, the reality we are confronting should have to do expressly with a certain power of acting. If my formulation is felt to be self-servingly vague, the reason is not far to seek. I am merely gesturing toward ultimate issues in Spinoza in regard to which I am very unclear, and I am accordingly impatient to return to the relatively firm ground of therapeutic know-how. Even here, however, it is very much a metaphysical therapist with whom we have to deal. One has a distinct sense that in proceeding from the minor premise to the conclusion of the generic remedy, lingering along the way perhaps with the major premise, one is replacing the merely phenomenal (i.e., sadness as a confused idea) by the noumenal, seeing that the therapy proves to be accomplished precisely by plugging us into reality itself.

By no means gratuitous, my use here of the Kantian idiom is intended to enforce the suggestion that if Spinoza in effect identifies noumenal reality, in the small as well as in the large, with a power to act, which is neutral as between the attributes of thought and extension, the whole notion of power and causality assumes a peculiar urgency after David Hume. How Kant in particular can be seen to bear on this issue of a rational yet post-Humean intuition into power and causality, one can readily gather from my paper "The Deduction of Causality,"[1] where a framework is provided that allows for the recognition of the generic syllogism as being all of a piece with a whole battery of transcendental arguments.

IV

According to IVP53, "humility is not a virtue," which is pretty much to say that it "does not arise from reason." This anti-biblical sentiment is pursued at some length in the demonstration, where we are urged to recall that the affect of humility is

> a sadness which arises from the fact that a man considers his own lack of power. Moreover, insofar as a man knows himself by true reason, it is supposed that he understands his own essence, i.e., his own power. So if a man, in considering himself, perceives some lack of power of his, this is not because he understands himself, but because his power of acting is restrained.

That the whole discussion is immensely relevant to the generic remedy ought to be clear at once, though I confess to having been very slow to realize it, and even now I remain largely in a state of wonder over the irony of the situation. Having assumed that the generic syllogism takes us from a confused idea to one that is clear and distinct, the former being objectionably psychologistic, the latter admirably behavioristic in character, it now appears to be the case that one bad affect has merely been superseded by another; and the generic remedy comes to sight as a dubious piece of humility therapy.

If this result is unexpected, it is not as if there were no warning signals. Accompanied by the thought of an external cause, one's initial sadness presumably has that external item as its intentional object, helping ourselves to Brentano's idiom. Ostensibly saddened by (the thought of) that object, one is somehow invited by Spinoza to entertain the following suggestion. Surely what one really ought to be sad about is not so much the external object but rather the internal diminishment in one's power of acting that has, admittedly, been brought on by one's being cathected to the external object. Accordingly, a new intentional object for one's sadness emerges, and one thus comes to undergo the affect of humility from which in its turn one presumably wishes to be liberated. Although on the level of theory very little appears to have been gained, when it comes to actual praxis my clinical experience strongly suggests that in trading the one affect for the other one does in fact profit by the transaction.

There is even some reason to believe that the interplay of theory and practice, specifically in the form of hermeneutics and therapeutics respectively, can serve to advance us alternately now on the one front, now on the other; and indeed a more extended look at IVP53D, guided by the distinction between perceiving and conceiving - understood as involving the contrast between passivity and activity - that is drawn in IID3Exp is found to undermine my precipitate conclusion that the generic remedy is to be regarded as an exercise in humility. While it is true enough that "if a man in considering himself *perceives* some lack of power of his," he will undergo humility, "suppose that the man *conceives* his lack of power." What then? A mere distinction without a difference? Maybe so, but Spinoza expressly denies it, and it is here above all that we are challenged to translate a doctrine, in itself dizzingly abstract, into the thick of everyday life.

Arguably too generic in my approach, I am now prompted to engage a specific affect at close quarters in all its vivid specificity. An irresistible text is provided by IIIP32 which positively invites the following film script regarding an occasion of (what one would ordinarily suppose to be) gratuitous envy. Seated opposite one in a railway carriage, a man or woman is ostentatiously doting over (let us say) a rare Siamese cat, nuzzling it, etc. Spinoza's psychology now predicts that the more the person resembles oneself and the more idiosyncratic the object in which the person is taking delight, so much the more will one undergo distress, assuming of course - a sinister proviso - that no ready opportunity is afforded one to deprive the person of the object. As one of our moral heroes, Spinoza is standardly supposed to have risen above such unworthy sentiments, and yet here he appears to regard them as endemic to the human condition as much.

It must be admitted, however, that IIIP32, as well as other propositions in the vicinity, has inevitably a *ceteris paribus* clause tacitly attached it, which renders its application in any particular case less than perfectly straightforward. There is, correspondingly, an evident difficulty as to experimental design when it comes to verifying or falsifying IIIP32, though my own gloss on it will be seen to facilitate the undertaking by identifying two independent variables that can be controlled for fairly readily. Even so, there doubtless remain sufficient methodological difficulties to suggest Quinean misgivings as to the feasibility of testing whole theories on a sentence-by-sentence basis. One such sentence that does lend itself to being empirically confirmed or disconfirmed in *fairly* isolated fashion I take to be IIIP32, Quinean misgivings to the contrary notwithstanding.

Assuming now the truth of IIIP32, if only for the nonce, we want to know how we are to cope therapeutically with the episode in the railway carriage, in specific as well as generic terms. No mere example chosen at random, IIIP32 expresses a non-trivial, even shocking thesis of Spinoza's psychology, which convicts us post-Freudians of being much more moralistic than we suppose. It may be suggested that expressly conducting one's life under its auspices might well have practical consequences almost as far-reaching as those that devolve on the acceptance of the family romance as postulated by Freud in terms of a *ménage à trois*. The latter one might even undertake to explain as a special case of the former, on the ground that "if we imagine that someone," i.e., the father, "enjoys something," i.e., the mother, "that only one can possess, we," i.e., the son, "shall strive to bring it about that he does not possess it." The "motiveless malignity" of Iago (as Coleridge characterized it) might also be explained in terms of Desdemona's being an enjoyable object that only one, namely Othello (or is it Cassio?) can really possess.

At this point, fascinated by the implications of IIIP32, one may come even to welcome the kind of opportunity that is represented by the episode in the railway carriage, for "the Mind, as far as it can, strives to imagine those things that increase or aid the Body's power of acting" (IIIP12) and, though the episode itself appears to feature an occasion of distress, why should it not serve to activate so much rationality, in the course of one's achieving a clear and distinct idea of one's sadness, that on balance the occasion proves to be one of joy? The trick here is to exploit a qualifying phrase in the General Definition of the Affects where a passion is said to be "a confused idea by which the Mind affirms of its Body, *or some part of it*, a greater or lesser force of existing," i.e., power of acting, "than before."

In the case at hand, then, the sadness I undergo in the railway carriage may be presumed to involve only a part of my body, for otherwise the passion might be expected to be indeed disabling, and being rather very much on the *qui vive* in regard to all such challenges - the film script is being written by me - I proceed almost at once to address it with the following specific version of the generic remedy. "Here am I undergoing sadness of the IIIP32 or Iago variety. But sadness is a passion indicating that the body or a part of the body's power of acting is diminished. Therefore, the power of acting of my body or a part of my body is diminished." A new syllogism or immediate inference will now take me from the minor premise, "But I am actively aware that my power of acting in respect to at least part of my body is currently impeded," for the initial distress or sadness is presumed to remain largely undispelled by the exorcism, to the inevitable conclusion, "It is only in respect to part of my body that my power of acting is impeded." Combining now the conclusion of this second syllogism with its minor premise in order to construct a new minor premise of the form 'p & q' for a third argument, I am led to the further conclusion, "My power of acting while diminished in one respect is currently enhanced in another"; and in the most favored case, taken on balance, my power of acting will have increased, though the experience will be felt to have a bitter-sweet character. By no means an occasion of humility, this case will doubtless count as one where a "man conceives his lack of power" (in a certain respect). Suppose, however, that overall my power of acting has decreased, which is as much as to say that my sadness preponderates. Then Spinoza appears to be committed to the view that the minor premise of my second syllogism must be false, and I cannot be actively but only passively aware of my lack of power. Merely perceiving my lack of power, having failed in my effort to conceive it, I will doubtless abort the second syllogism in mid-career as well as undergo the affect of humility.

In the favored case, I am presumably to be understood as having succeeded in turning a passion into an action in accordance with VP3, and my undergoing a Iagoesque sentiment in these optimum circumstances even counts as a definite plus for me, on which I am entitled to congratulate myself. So at any rate, I am prepared to argue on the basis of IIP17S, IIP35S and IVP1S. A defect or limitation of my optical apparatus taken by itself in isolation, my visual representation of the sun as being only 200 ft. distant from me when I look up at it, is properly to be understood as the exercise of one of my powers or virtues when it is subsumed within the larger cognitive enterprise. All such perceptual illusions are in themselves to be classified as passions along with envy, hatred, etc., and the latter will thus be redeemed like the former by serving as mere components of larger cognitive activities. Far from being confined to a life of cloistered virtue, Spinoza's free man can be found on occasion to leap into the rough-and-tumble of the world, prepared even to undergo bad affects if overall they can be made to promote cognitivity into their own occurrence.

That, then, is what *fortitudo* and *animositas* finally come to, and though there are times in reading Part V when "it is hard not to see Spinoza as committed to offering sensory deprivation as an ideal" (Bennett (1984), 325), the effort probably ought to be made, bearing in mind that "our intellect would of course be more imperfect if our Mind were alone and did not understand anything except itself" (IVP18S, cf. also IIP29S).

1. In *The Philosophy of Immanuel Kant*, ed. by Richard Kennington, (Washington: 1985).

"A FREE MAN ALWAYS ACTS HONESTLY, NOT DECEPTIVELY": FREEDOM AND THE GOOD IN SPINOZA'S *ETHICS*

DON GARRETT
University of Utah

Spinoza devotes the last seven propositions of Part IV (PP67-73) of the *Ethics* to "the free man's temperament and manner of living."[1] Perhaps the most surprising and puzzling of these is IVP72, which asserts that:

(1) A free man always acts honestly, not deceptively.

The proposition is surprising because by this point in the *Ethics* Spinoza seems already committed to three other claims which are jointly incompatible with it:

(2) It is always good to act so as to best preserve one's own being.
(3) One can sometimes best preserve one's own being by acting deceptively, not honestly.
(4) It is never good to act contrary to the way in which the free man acts.

This paradox is so striking and fundamental that we can hardly claim to understand, much less evaluate, Spinoza's ethical views unless we know how - or whether - it can be resolved. In this paper, I will be concerned with three questions. First, which if any of (1)-(4) would he reject? Secondly, which of these propositions *ought* he reject, given the fundamental character of his system? Thirdly, to what extent can the resulting ethical theory be an adequate one? I will proceed by considering each of (1)-(4) in turn, describing and evaluating both the grounds for ascribing the claim to Spinoza and the ways in which its ascription to him might be denied. I will argue that Spinoza accepts (1)-(3), and that he would and should reject (4). I will conclude by considering the consistency and practical acceptability of the resulting ethical theory.

I

(1) *A free man always acts honestly, not deceptively.* The evidence for claiming that Spinoza accepts (1) appears at first sight to be incontrovertible: he explicitly asserts it as IVP72. But the simple fact that Spinoza *asserts* (1) does not by itself entail that he actually *accepts* it. To reach that conclusion, we require two additional suppositions: first, that he aims to act honestly, not deceptively, at IVP72; and secondly, that he accurately formulates - without, for example, inadvertent overstatement - the proposition that he intends. Either of these suppositions may be questioned.

With respect to the first supposition, the depth of Spinoza's commitment to honesty is precisely what is in question in the interpretation of IVP72; and to cite the proposition itself as evidence of that commitment would simply beg the question in this context. For suppose that Spinoza believes both of the following: (A) that he would always do best to preserve his own being, or maximize his own advantage; and (B) that he can best preserve his own being or maximize his own advantage by insincerely claiming that the free man always acts honestly. Under those circumstances, consistency would not only *permit* him to make such an insincere claim, it would positively *require* it of him. Indeed, in thus asserting (1) insincerely, Spinoza might not even intend to deceive the truly wise or free among his readers. He might be aiming merely to obtain the honesty of the credulous or to mollify the ignorant, perhaps secure in the knowledge that those who had fully understood the preceding propositions would recognize both the ironic falsehood of (1) and the self-interested grounds that compelled him, from consistency with his own principles, to assert it.

The possibility that Spinoza asserts (1) insincerely cannot, therefore, be dismissed without a hearing. Nevertheless, it is not ultimately convincing, for two main reasons. First, when we seriously consider the proposition's context in the *Ethics* as a whole, it soon becomes implausible that Spinoza should suppose an insincere assertion of (1) actually to serve any useful purpose. Its mere inclusion in the *Ethics* would be unlikely to increase the honesty of others with whom he might have dealings. Nor could it be supposed to play any significant role in warding off persecution from persons otherwise likely to be scandalized by the *Ethics*. For reassuring as (1) is, it is hardly enough to remove the sting from Spinoza's thoroughgoing determinism, his denial of a personal God, his mind-body identity theory, or his rejection of such Christian virtues as pity, humility, and repentance. At the same time, the *Ethics'* straightforwardness about these other doctrines would undermine any attempt to use (1) ironically.

The second main reason is perhaps even more fundamental. If Spinoza did not accept (1), then not only the proposition itself but also the *demonstration* of it must be insincere. To be sure, Spinoza wrote demonstrations in *Descartes'* **Principles of Philosophy** that he himself thought unsound - he must have thought them so, since he rejects some of their conclusions. But there is no internal or external evidence that he fails to take his own demonstration of (1) seriously. The demonstration contains nine explicit steps, the first of which is:

(i) We call a man free only insofar as he acts from the dictate of reason.

This is stated at IVP66S, and is a consequence of his definition of freedom as adequate self-determination [ID7] and his identification of human self-determination with acting from reason [IIIP1]. It directly entails:

(ii) If a free man did anything by deception, he would do it from the dictate of reason.

He then cites IVP24, which is a central claim of Part IV:

(iii) Acting absolutely from virtue is nothing else in us but acting, living, and preserving our being (these three signify the same thing) by the guidance of reason, from the foundation of seeking one's own advantage.

And from (ii) and (iii), he infers:

(iv) If a free man, insofar as he is free, did anything by deception, it would be a virtue to act deceptively.

This, I take it, means that if a free man, insofar as he is free, did anything by deception, then at least some kinds of deceptive actions would be virtues. So construed, it is a reasonable inference from (ii) and (iii), since (iii) identifies acting from virtue with acting by the guidance of reason. Also from (iii) he concludes:

(v) If it could be a virtue to act deceptively, then everyone would "be better advised" (*consultius esset*) to act deceptively to preserve his being.

This follows, given the additional but Spinozistic-sounding assumption that if one does something to preserve one's being "by the guidance of reason from the foundation of seeking one's own advantage," then one is "better advised" to do it. Next, he states:

(vi) If everyone would be better advised to act deceptively to preserve his being, then men would be better advised to agree only in words, and be contrary to one another in fact.

This claim depends only on the assumption that if one acts deceptively to preserve one's being, then one is agreeing with others only in words, and not in fact - a reasonable assumption, since whoever acts deceptively brings it about that others believe something that he himself does not believe or vice versa. Following this claim, he cites IVP31C, which states:

(vii) The more a thing agrees with our nature, the more useful, or better, it is for us, and conversely, the more a thing is useful to us, the more it agrees with our nature.

IVP31C is ultimately derived from two Spinozistic principles: that whatever pertains to a thing's nature tends to the preservation of its being, and that the same cause always produces the same effect. From (vii), in turn, he derives:

(viii) It is absurd that men would be better advised to agree only in words, and be contrary to one another in fact.

This inference requires only the plausible assumptions that (a) men are never "better advised" to pursue that which is not maximally useful to them, and that (b) "agreeing only in words while being contrary in fact" is a kind of "disagreement in nature" between two parties. Finally, then, from (iv), (v), (vi), and (viii), it follows that:

> (ix) A free man always acts honestly, not deceptively.

This is, of course, IVP72 - and (1) - itself. Complex as this demonstration may be, it appears to consist of premises and inferences that Spinoza would be likely to accept; it does not look like an attempt at a fraudulent proof. Thus, the first supposition - that Spinoza aims to act honestly at IVP72 - seems warranted.

What of the other supposition, namely that he accurately formulates the proposition he intends? It might be argued that (1) - though not intentionally dishonest - is something of an overstatement, describing as universal what is true of the free man only generally speaking, or in most cases. But Spinoza seems specifically to block this suggestion, while reinforcing the serious intent of his original Demonstration, in the Scholium to IVP72:

> Suppose someone now asks: what if a man could save himself from the present danger of death by treachery? Would not the principle of preserving his own being recommend, without qualification, that he be treacherous?

> The reply to this is the same. If reason should recommend that, it would recommend it to all men. And so reason would recommend, without qualification, that men should make agreements to join forces, and to have common laws only by deception - i.e., that they have no common laws. This is absurd.

Given the apparent sincerity of IVP72, the intent of this Scholium can only be to defend it from even the most plausible of the potential exceptions to it. Thus, I conclude that Spinoza means what he says when he claims that the free man always acts honestly, not deceptively, and that he means the claim to admit of no exceptions.

(2) *It is always good to act so as to best preserve one's own being.* IVD1 and IVD2 present the formal definitions of 'good' and 'evil':

> Definition 1: By good I shall understand what we certainly know to be useful to us.

> Definition 2: By evil, however, I shall understand what we certainly know prevents us from being masters of some good.

Since Spinoza identifies "one's own advantage" with "preserving one's being" (IVP20,S), however, he can also characterize good and evil in terms of self-preservation; and this is just what he does, citing IVD1 and IVD2 as support, at the outset of IVP8D: "We call good, or evil, what is useful to, or harmful to, preserving our being." (2) follows immediately.

Spinoza's commitment to (2) is thus both evident and fundamental. Since the good *is* the advantageous for Spinoza, and the advantageous *is* the preservation of one's own being, nothing can be better for oneself than self-preservation. To be sure, he also asserts that, "We know nothing to be certainly good or evil, except what really leads to understanding or what can prevent us from understanding" (IVP27). But the preservation of one's being is a logical prerequisite for having understanding; and this fact in itself prevents the preservation or increase of one's understanding from being a good that could *override* the preservation of one's being. Moreover, whatever leads to understanding, in Spinoza's view, by that very fact aids in the preservation of one's being, for two reasons. First, any maintenance or increase in understanding is a maintenance or increase in one's present power of action and the full realization of one's own nature, so that understanding literally *is* a preservation or amplification of one's own being. Secondly, precisely because it is the central element in one's active power and resources, maintaining or increasing one's present understanding also promotes the *future* preservation of one's being.

Spinoza also makes it clear that one's own good cannot be overridden by the good or advantage of any other being. For example, he offers a prospectus of his theory of the relation among different persons' interests at IVP18S:

> There are... many things outside us which are useful to us, and *on that account to be sought*. Of these, we can think of none more excellent than those that agree entirely with our nature. For if, for example, two individuals of entirely the same nature are joined to one another, they compose an individual twice as powerful as each one. To man, then, there is nothing more useful than man. Man, I say, can wish for nothing *more helpful to the preservation of his being* than that all should so agree in all things that the Minds and Bodies of all would compose, as it were, one Mind and one Body; that all should strive together, as far as they can, to preserve their being; and that all, together, should seek for themselves the common advantage of all. [emphasis added]

Here Spinoza characteristically emphasizes the extent to which the advantage of different individual persons can coincide. Nevertheless, he states that the interests of other individuals enter into one's own considerations only through their usefulness *to oneself*. This is just what one should expect, given his claim at IIIP20S that "no one, therefore, unless he is defeated by causes external, and contrary, to his nature, neglects to seek his own advantage, or preserve his being," and his claim at IVApp8 that "it is permissible for everyone to do, by the highest right of nature, what he judges will contribute to his advantage."[2]

Nor can the good or advantage of eternal things - such as "the idea that expresses the essence of this or that human Body, under a species of eternity" (VPP22-23), "the part of the Mind that is eternal" (VPP38-39), or even God himself - override one's own preservation as a good. For nothing can hinder or aid the preservation of an eternal being, nor can such beings have any potential objects of desire for themselves. Hence there is nothing for their "advantage" or "good" to consist in. To be sure, *an individual person* has an advantage in bringing it about that his present stock of eternal (and hence always-existing) ideas should remain as part of *his* mind, and also that it should come to be supplemented by other equally eternal and adequate ideas. But this is simply for that individual to increase his *own* knowledge, and not for him to benefit these eternal ideas. As we have seen, such an increase is not, for

Spinoza, incompatible with one's own advantage or preservation, but is instead precisely that in which one's own highest advantage and preservation consist.

Thus, the good, for Spinoza, is the advantageous; that which is most advantageous to oneself is one's own preservation; and the advantage of others cannot be ranked ahead of one's own as a good, even in the case of those beings that do have an "advantage." I conclude, therefore, that he is fully committed to (2), without exception.[3]

3. *One can sometimes best preserve one's own being by acting deceptively, not honestly.* Although Spinoza maintains that the greatest good - understanding - can be enjoyed equally by all (IVP36), he also holds that for the mind to be "equally capable of understanding many things," the body must be "equally capable of all the things which can follow from its nature" (IVP45S), so that the pursuit of understanding also requires intermediate goods to keep the body functioning properly. Thus he states at IVP39:

> Those things are good which bring about the preservation of the proportion of motion and rest the human Body's parts have to one another [i.e., continued life]; on the other hand, those things are evil which bring it about that the parts of the human Body have a different proportion of motion and rest to one another [i.e., death, as IVP39S indicates].

And again, at E IVApp27:

> The principal advantage which we derive from things outside us... lies in the preservation of our body. That is why those things are most useful to us which can feed and maintain it, so that all its parts can perform their function properly.

It seems an unmistakable fact, however, that circumstances can arise in which one's physical life can be preserved only by actions that would ordinarily be regarded as deceptive. Certainly there are cases in which successful competition for a limited supply of physical necessities will demand such actions. Moreover, there are also cases in which such actions are necessary to ward off an external danger - for example, when escape from immediate execution requires fraudulently offering one's guards a sum of money that one cannot actually command. Were it not for the Scholium to IVP72, it might be suggested that the abstractness of Spinoza's argument prevents him from noticing such cases. But the Scholium makes it clear that he has indeed noticed the possibility of such cases, and takes them seriously.

Given that he recognizes cases in which death can be avoided only by actions ordinarily deemed deceptive, then, Spinoza could deny (3) only by holding either (a) that preserving one's physical life in such cases does not constitute "*best preserving one's being,*" or (b) that preserving one's physical life in such cases does not constitute "*deception.*" Let us consider the first of these alternatives.

Spinoza makes several mitigating claims about physical death. He asserts that "a free man thinks of nothing less than of death" (IVP67); that "the more the Mind understands things... the less it fears death" (VP38; see also VP39-S); and that "death is less harmful to us, the greater the Mind's clear and distinct knowledge, and hence, the more the Mind loves God... [T]he human Mind can be of such a nature that the part of the Mind which we have shown perishes with the body... is of no moment in relation to what remains" (VP38S).

Upon examination, however, none of these remarks implies that one can ever best preserve one's being by actually choosing death over an alternative that involves continued life. The free man does not think of death, according to Spinoza, simply because he directly pursues the good rather than avoiding evil; hence the free man directly pursues the good of life, rather than being consumed with thoughts of death (IVP67D). The person with understanding has less fear of death because he is less subject to negative affects in general (VP38D). He is also less harmed by death, since, to the extent that a person gains knowledge, he brings it about that a greater and more important part of his mind consists of knowledge that is eternal. This means that a relatively smaller and far less significant portion of his mind is something that is absolutely destroyed by death (VP38D). As one gains in understanding, one begins to approximate, *as a limit*, a state in which one would be totally unaffected by death, or any other potential harm. But this limit could actually be reached only by an infinite being whose mind contained all knowledge and was not at all bound by imagination. Hence, Spinoza's doctrine does not entail that death could ever cease to be *of any harm at all for any finite human being*, who must remain a part of nature (IIIP4). On the contrary, death does constitute for us the end of at least *some* portion of the mind, even if the least important part, and hence constitutes a failure to preserve one's being completely. Moreover, death is the end of any prospect of further *increasing* one's understanding or that portion of one's mind that *is* eternal; indeed, it is the end of any prospect of *additional* gain at all. Thus, Spinoza writes at IVP21:

> No one can desire to be blessed, to act well and to live well, unless at the same time he desires to be, to act, and to live, i.e., to actually exist.

Hence, despite the *declining* importance of death to the wise man, any actual human being who acts, even deceptively, so as to save his physical life will always preserve his being better to at least some extent than one who does not.

The second approach to denying (3) would be to argue that no action can properly be regarded as *deceptive* if it is required to preserve one's being. Spinoza maintains, following Hobbes, that it is impossible completely to promise or contract away one's right of self-preservation, regardless of what one may say or do (TTP XVII; see also TP II-III). As a consequence, he holds that all compacts and promises should be understood to be operative only so long as they do not conflict with the preservation of one's being, since no compact or promise could possibly prevent one from pursuing the preservation of one's being. Because compacts and promises have this implicit limitation, it might be suggested, "violating" them for the sake of self-preservation is not, in Spinoza's view, really deception.

This suggestion is unsatisfactory, however, for several reasons. First, although Spinoza states explicitly (TTP XVI) that everyone has the right to break a promise when he judges that doing so will be advantageous (a minimal claim that follows from his assertion that 'right' and 'power' are co-extensive), he nevertheless characterizes such actions as practices of *deceit* (see also TP III, 17). And he does not give any indication that he is using the term 'deception'in any more restricted way in the *Ethics*. On the contrary, IVP72 and its Scholium strongly imply that he is speaking of deceit in the ordinary sense. For the reason why deception cannot be a virtue is said to be that it produces a circumstance in which persons do not agree in nature. And *every* case of deception in the ordinary sense - whether for self-preservation or not - is a case in which persons disagree in nature, since deception of any kind entails producing in others beliefs different from one's own.

Thus, although he does not assert (3) explicitly, Spinoza's position clearly commits him to it, and does so in such a way that he could hardly have been unaware of that commitment.

(4) *It is never good to act contrary to the way in which the free man acts*. In Part IV of the *Ethics*, Spinoza characterizes actions in four different ways, each *prima facie* relevant to ethics: he speaks (a) of "good" actions, or of those that achieve "a good"; (b) of actions performed "under the guidance of reason," or "from the dictate of reason"; (c) of actions performed "from virtue," or whose performance is "a virtue"; and (d) of actions that "a free man" would perform. Commentators generally treat the four characterizations as co-extensive. And this procedure appears to have some basis in the text. For according to IVP18S, "reason demands... that everyone... seek his own advantage... (and) preserve his own being as far as he can," i.e., do that which is good for him; (IVD1, IVP8D) while IVP66S states that "one who is led by reason... I call... a free man." These statements seem to imply that "good actions" and "actions of a free man" are both co-extensive with "actions performed from the dictate of reason," and hence that they are also co-extensive with each other - which entails (4). Virtue, in turn, enters in through IVP24 (cited in the demonstration of IVP72) which asserts that "acting absolutely from virtue is nothing else in us but acting, living, and preserving our being... by the guidance of reason, from the foundation of seeking one's own advantage."

But does Spinoza really intend *all* of these terms to be co-extensive? He devotes the Preface of Part IV to just two evaluative distinctions: "perfection and imperfection, good and evil." He begins by explaining the use of the term 'perfect' (*perfectus*, from *perficere*) in terms of its etymological sense of "completed" or "finished." Originally, he maintains, the term referred only to artifacts known or believed to be completed in the way intended by their authors. Under the influence of the false supposition that nature creates everything for a purpose, however, the term gradually came to refer more generally to the extent to which a thing, even a natural object, matches the generic "model" of its kind that each person forms on the basis of his own common experience.[4] Thus the term generally reflects only a "mode of thinking" rather than a real feature of the objects themselves, and is applied differently by different persons depending on the character of the "universal ideas" or models that they happen to have formed. 'Good,' in contrast, primarily expresses our desire for something; as he has already claimed at IIIP9S, we do not "desire anything because we judge it to be good; on the contrary, we judge something to be good because we strive for it, will it, want it, and desire it." Thus, it too reflects only a mode of thinking, and indicates "nothing positive in things, considered in themselves," since "Music is good for one who is *Melancholy*, bad for one who is mourning, and neither good nor bad to one who is deaf." It too is highly variable in its application, since what is judged to be good will depend on the judger's particular desires, which are often passions.

Spinoza's intent is to adapt these previously subjective predicates to designate objective practical *relations*. Thus he concludes near the end of the Preface:

> But though this is so, still we must retain these words. For because we desire to form an idea of man, as a model of human nature which we may look to, it will be useful to us to retain these same words with the meaning I have indicated. In what follows, therefore, I shall understand by good what we know certainly is a means by which we may approach nearer and nearer to the model of human nature that we set before ourselves. By evil, what we certainly know prevents us from becoming like that model. Next, we shall say that men are more perfect or imperfect, insofar as they approach more or less near to this model. (See also TdIE, 13, which is similar.)

Although the definitions of both pairs of terms employ the notion of a "model of human nature," they are by no means identical. The perfect/imperfect distinction, as defined here, applies only to persons, whereas the good/evil distinction applies to things of all kinds, including actions. Once we have the concept of perfection, of course, we can also speak of the actions that the perfect man would perform. But, although the point has apparently not been noted, even this latter concept need not be co-extensive with the concept of good actions. Someone is *perfect* to the extent that he presently *approximates* to the model or ideal; whereas something is *good* to the extent that it *aids us in becoming like* this model or ideal. *Prima facie*, there is no reason why an action that would be good for someone to perform, in this sense, should also be the action that the perfect man *would* perform - unless, perhaps, the agent in question were already perfect.

Consider an analogy. Suppose that our model or ideal were that of a person leading the characteristic life of the idle rich. Now, for someone who is already one of the idle rich, idle behavior would be "good" in the sense that it would help him to remain or become even more like the chosen model. For the poor man, however - who aspires to the model without having yet achieved it - idle behavior would be an "evil," likely to prevent him from obtaining the wealth needed to live the life of the idle rich; for him, in contrast, hard work would be a "good." The point is a simple one: when one has not yet achieved a certain kind of existence, the actions that one must perform in order to achieve it are not necessarily the actions that one will characteristically perform once one has achieved it.

After concluding his discussion of perfection and goodness in the Preface, Spinoza begins Part IV itself by offering formal, numbered definitions of 'good' and 'evil' (IVDD1-2), and goes on to use them frequently. Strikingly, however, despite the fact that by far the largest part of Part IV's Preface is devoted to a discussion of them, 'perfect' and its cognates do not occur at all in the Definitions, Axioms, Propositions or Demonstrations of Part IV, and they occur only four times, all in passing, in the Scholia (twice in IV 18S, once each in IVP45S and IVP58S). This omission is explicable, however. For the Preface defines "perfection" in terms of approximation to "the model that we set before ourselves," without actually specifying what that model is. The model itself is developed gradually throughout the course of Part IV, culminating in the portrait of the free man at IVP 67-72. (Presumably this initial lack of specificity about the model is also what accounts for the variation in the definition of "good," which is defined at IVD1 simply in terms of what is useful "to us," rather than in terms of what is useful for "approaching nearer to our model of human nature," as in the Preface.) Hence, we are to understand what human perfection is, and how the perfect man acts, in large measure at least, by understanding what the free man is, and how the free man acts. Freedom provides a specification of what human perfection actually consists in.

But for the same reason that the class of "good actions" need not be co-extensive with "actions of a perfect man," in Spinoza's sense, they also need not be co-extensive with "actions of a free man." Thus, I propose that we interpret Spinoza as holding *both* that the *ideal* or model free man would never act deceptively, *and* that deception may under some circumstances nevertheless be good for actual human beings who have not fully achieved this ideal. These circumstances will be the (generally rare) ones under which deception is genuinely necessary to preserve one's life or otherwise aid in the preservation of one's being.[5]

II

This proposed interpretation resolves the original paradox by rejecting (4). Before it can be accepted, however, it must be examined in greater detail. In particular, we must consider whether it is compatible with (a) IVP72 itself; (b) the Demonstration of IVP72; (c) the Scholium to IVP72; and (d) the remainder of Part IV.

IVP72 requires that the ideal free man would *never* act deceptively; but in discussing (3), we concluded that - for Spinoza - any actual human being *would* always best preserve his being by choosing an act of deception over death, if those were the only alternatives. Since the free man always does what is best to preserve his own being, we may appear to be involved in a contradiction that the mere rejection of (4) cannot resolve. In fact, however, what this shows is only that no actual human being is the ideal free man. But this consequence is just what we should expect, since the concept of a *completely* free man involves a contradiction. From a thing's being completely free, it follows that it is completely self-determined and utterly independent of external causes; on the other hand, from a thing's being a man, it follows that it is necessarily a part of nature and subject to external causes. Like the concept of the complete "agreement in nature" among persons that would result in a complete coinciding of interests and advantage (see note 2), or like the complete understanding that would make the whole of one's mind eternal so that death mattered not at all, the concept of the free man is the concept of a limit that can be approached but not completely attained by finite human beings.[6]

The final unattainability of these ideals does not completely undermine their cognitive value for Spinoza, however. For they can be used to convey at least two important things: first, that the presence of one characteristic can be fully explained through the presence of another characteristic; and second, that the former characteristic will - other things being equal - vary with the increase or decrease of the latter. Thus, the beneficiality of human beings to one another can be fully explained through their agreement in nature, and will tend to increase as that agreement increases. Lack of concern with death can be fully explained through the eternal part of the mind, and the mind will tend to have less fear of death as this part of the mind becomes a larger part of the whole. Similarly, a person's honesty (when it is a consequence of the endeavor to agree in nature with others) can be fully explained through his freedom, and his honesty will tend to increase along with his freedom, in Spinoza's view. For as a person becomes more free, he will lose the characteristic motives for dishonesty: he will forego the pursuit of temporary, competitive goods such as wealth, fame, and sensual pleasure; he will come to understand more clearly the value of society, friendship, and human aid, and the importance of honesty in procuring those goods; he will become more able to achieve goods by cooperative rather than deceptive means; and he will become less and less susceptible to harm. On the other hand, whenever deception is still required, it must be explained at least partly through the person's lack of freedom, including his dependence on external goods and his inability to achieve his ends by the more permanently beneficial means of producing agreement in nature between himself and others. Hence, those who are most free will also be most honest. Insofar as they are free, they will never deceive; though it will nevertheless remain true that, insofar as they are living, finite, human beings, they cannot be assured that they will never find it necessary to do so.

The proposed interpretation is thus compatible with IVP72; and it is also, I believe, compatible with its Demonstration. As we have seen, the demonstration seeks in effect to provide a *reductio ad absurdum* of the supposition that a free man could act deceptively *"insofar as he is free."* Insofar as he is free, Spinoza argues, the free man acts from the dictate of reason, hence virtuously, and hence does what he is "better advised" to do. But deception is an instance of persons failing to agree in nature, whereas what is best, or maximally useful, is that persons should agree in nature. Hence, he concludes, a free man cannot act deceptively insofar as he is free. The only difficulty here is with the meaning of the phrase 'be better advised' (*consultius esset*). The demonstration entails (via the simple conjunction of steps (vi) and (viii)) that one can never be "better advised" to act deceptively to preserve one's being. Hence, if we interpret "one is better advised to do x" as simply equivalent to "it would be good for one to do x," then it will follow that it can never be good to act deceptively, contrary to the proposed interpretation.

I see no reason to interpret the two expressions as equivalent, however. Indeed, if we do so, we threaten to invalidate Spinoza's inference from (vii) to (viii) (i.e., from the claim that things are best for us as they most agree with our nature, to the claim that it is absurd that men would be "better advised" to agree only in words and not in fact). For it is *not always good* to refrain from an action that will produce a less-than-optimal state of affairs - not unless the alternative of producing the optimal state instead is actually *within one's power*. More specifically, it need not be good for one to refrain from deception, even though it involves a lack of agreement in nature between persons, *if all* of one's actually-feasible alternatives *also* involve a lack of agreement in nature - such as competition for scarce life-saving goods - plus greater harms as well. (Compare, for example, IVP58S, which asserts that Shame, "though not a virtue," is still "a good" if the only alternative is conceived as that of being shameless through lack of desire to live honestly.) Hence, if the Demonstration is to be valid, we must understand "better advised to do x" as meaning something more like "*ideally* advised to do x." With that understanding, there is no conflict between the Demonstration and the proposed interpretation.

Before leaving IVP72, we must also consider its Scholium. There, as we have seen, Spinoza asks whether, if one faced a choice between death and treachery, the principle of preserving one's own being would not "recommend without qualification" that one be treacherous. His response is that "if reason should recommend that, it would recommend it to all men. And so reason would recommend, without qualification, that men should make agreements to join forces, and to have common laws only by deception," which he says is absurd. On the proposed interpretation, the principle of preserving one's own being *does* sometimes recommend treachery or deception - but it does *not* do so "without qualification." Specifically, it does not ever do so for the (ideal) free man, whose character is directly under discussion. To the perfectly free man, even death would be no harm whatever; rather, he would seek only to maximize the agreement in nature between himself and others. Similar considerations apply to the question of whether "*reason*" can recommend deception "without qualification." *Insofar as* one is guided by reason, one maximizes one's agreement in nature with others and cannot be harmed even by death, since the part of the mind involved in reason is eternal. In fact, since the free man's freedom *consists* in his having and acting on adequate ideas, the ideal of a life completely guided by reason is simply another way of formulating the ideal of the completely free man. Moreover, reason itself, because it can be common to everyone, must give the same counsel to all, as the Scholium implies. It therefore cannot dictate the preservation of one being *over* another. The fact that our necessary preference for our own being is *not* at the same time equally a preference for preserving the being of others, arises not from our common reason but rather (inevitably) from our passivity, finiteness, and hence lack of agreement in nature with others. If we were *perfectly* guided by reason, our good and the good of others would indeed *perfectly* coincide.

Finally, the proposed interpretation must be reconciled with the passages cited at the beginning of the present section [viz., IV 18S, IVD1, IVD8, IV 66S] which seemed jointly to suggest a commitment on Spinoza's part to (4). The key passage is the one at IVP18S, which reads in full:

> *Since reason demands nothing contrary to nature*, it demands that everyone love himself, seek his own advantage, what is really useful to him, want what will really lead man to a greater perfection, and absolutely, that everyone should strive to preserve his own being as far as he can. [emphasis added]

This seems to entail that, if deception is advantageous and hence good under some circumstances - as the proposed interpretation requires - then reason will demand deception; and since (by IVP66S and IVP72D) the free man does what reason dictates, it seems to follow that the free man will, after all, engage in deception. First, however, it must be noted *why* reason is said to demand that everyone seek his own advantage: because reason demands nothing contrary to nature. But for Spinoza, *nothing* occurs "contrary to nature," so that in this sense, everything whatever occurs by the "demand of reason." It is one thing to say that certain behavior is "demanded by reason" in this sense, and another to say that the behavior can be attributed entirely to one's *own exercise* of reason, or to reason as it is manifested in the agent himself. Secondly, it is quite compatible with the present interpretation that reason in each person *should* demand the preservation of that person's being, in the sense that whatever one does from the dictate of reason is, to that extent, conducive to one's own being. The present interpretation requires only that for those who are not governed entirely by reason - everyone at some time or another - some of the acts conducive to the preservation of one's being may not be *entirely* due to reason, or freedom. For both of these reasons, the passages cited need not entail a commitment to (4); hence the passages are compatible with the present interpretation.

The interpretation I have proposed and defended is thus compatible with everything Spinoza claims in the *Ethics*. It not only resolves the original paradox, it also provides the only resolution of that paradox that does not violate fundamental Spinozistic doctrines. Finally, it is strongly suggested by his account of perfection and the good in the Preface to Part IV. I therefore conclude that he both should and would have rejected (4) for the reasons suggested by that interpretation.

III

Consistency and Practical Acceptability. Of the various tests to which ethical theories can be submitted, two of the most fundamental are those of consistency and practical acceptability.   An adequate ethical theory must be internally consistent; and it must also be such that we can, upon critical reflection, eventually bring ourselves to accept the judgments of approval and disapproval that the theory makes of various actions and features of character.   Spinoza's ethical theory is, I believe, often thought to fail one or both of these tests - particularly with respect to IVP72.

I have already argued that Spinoza is guilty of no direct inconsistency in the case of the paradox considered, since he rejects the last of the four jointly inconsistent propositions.   Nor is his theory rendered inconsistent through its employment of such literally contradictory models as that of the "free man." For Spinoza intends his assertions about such models to be understood only as describing certain relationships between two or more variable characteristics - in the present case, freedom and honesty - of real individuals. (See TdIE, 57 for a discussion of the way in which formulations that verbally resemble dis- cussions of "fictions" can be used to state truths.) And although the completely free, reasonable, and virtuous man is a necessarily unreachable ideal, it is by no means unusual for an ethical theory to put forward an ideal that cannot, by the theory's own lights, be fully achieved by any actual person.   It is also not inconsistent to characterize as "good" some actions that are not regarded as completely "free," "reasonable," or "virtuous."   Spinoza aims, of course, to minimize the divergence between the "good" and the "perfect."   Nevertheless, some residual divergence is inevitable in his theory, as is evident most clearly in the case of choosing between death and deception.   But some such divergence is a potential feature of any ethical theory that places, as Spinoza's does, primary emphasis or value on features of character: in any such theory, the possibility exists, unless blocked by special features of the theory, that actions necessary to achieve the valued character should be different from those manifested by the valued character.   Although this is certainly a complication in an ethical theory, it is not a contradiction.

This complication does, however, pose some initial difficulty when we try to subject Spinoza's ethical theory to the test of practical acceptability. For we cannot determine whether we can accept a theory's judgments of approval and disapproval until we can determine what those judgments are; and it is not initially clear what actions and features of character Spinoza's theory does approve.   The *Ethics* avoids mere exhortation, aiming instead to state and demonstrate facts that will themselves be inherently motivating.   But *whose* motivation provides the test of "approval"?   On the one hand, we can speak of what the perfectly free man would be motivated to do by his knowledge (i.e., what actual persons would do *insofar* as they were motivated only by reason and not by features of their finiteness); *or* we can speak, on the other hand, of what even the most free and most knowledgeable of finite human beings would *actually* be motivated to do, given their finite knowledge and their finite situation.   The perfectly free man would never be motivated to deceive others or harm their interests; an actual, relatively-free individual, however, can at any time find himself in circumstances in which he *would* be necessarily motivated to deceive or otherwise harm others for his own advantage.   Should we think of Spinoza's ethical theory as "approving" the self-preserving deceptions of relatively free individuals, on the grounds that the theory pronounces those actions "good" for those individuals? Or should we rather think of such actions as outside the approval of the theory, on the grounds that they are - though predictable and even inevitable - due at least in part to our personal limitations and differences, and thus foreign to the very highest ethical ideals we can hold in common?

One way to resolve this interpretive dilemma is to ask what kinds of actions and features of character Spinoza or the Spinozist *himself* would approve. The affects that come closest to capturing ethical approval and disapproval are "favor" (*favor*, translated by Elwes as "approval," and by Shirley as "approbation") and "indignation" (*indignatio*).[7] The former is defined as "Love toward someone who has benefited another," while the latter is defined as "Hate toward someone who has done evil to another" (IIIDefAff19, 20). Given these terms, we can now ask what the Spinozistic attitude would be toward someone who, for example, employs deceptive means to preserve his own life at the expense of the lives of several innocent persons; or toward someone who, in the same circumstances, chooses to sacrifice his own life to save the others.

Let us consider first the person who chooses deception and self-preservation. It follows from IVP51S that the Spinozist's attitude toward him will not be one of indignation, for Spinoza there asserts that "Indignation, as we define it... is necessarily evil." (Certainly many critics will hold that the Spinozist's lack of indignation - in this case, and in general - by itself demonstrates that the theory cannot pass the test of practical acceptability. I am inclined to think, on the contrary, that the doctrine that indignation is always an evil is one of the theory's most attractive features.) But if the Spinozist will not respond with indignation, neither will he respond with favor. For favor is a species of love, which, in turn, is defined as "Joy with the accompanying idea of an external cause" (IIIP13S). Although the deceiver has benefited himself, he has also harmed others directly and harmed the institution of honesty as well. He will therefore not have produced much joy in the Spinozist. Nor will he himself have been the free or adequate cause of his own action, since to the *extent* that a person is free, he acts honestly and not deceptively. For each of these two reasons, he will not be the object of love or favor for his action. Rather, the Spinozistic attitude toward such a person will be that his action was a predictable phenomenon of nature, due in part to inevitable human weakness and deserving to be understood, but calling for neither indignation nor favor.

What, then, of the person who makes the opposite choice, sacrificing through honesty his own life for the sake of benefiting others? Once again the Spinozist will not respond with indignation, since it is an evil. Favor, on the other hand, "is not contrary to reason, but can agree with it and arise from it" (IVP51). Yet in the case of any actual self-sacrificing person, self-sacrifice cannot be due to the person's being so completely free that his own death does not matter to him at all. Any actual person who sacrifices his own life must therefore be failing to achieve his own advantage and the preservation of his own being. Hence the sacrifice must be the result of his being overcome by passions, such as pity, passionate love, fear of regret or punishment, or a misguided desire for fame or praise. For this reason, even though the action is beneficial to others, the person himself cannot be regarded as the free or adequate cause of the benefit. The Spinozist would therefore respond with little favor towards the agent, once again regarding his action instead only as an operation of nature - this time, perhaps, a more fortunate one - that results in innocent lives being saved. Thus on *neither* alternative would any actual person facing a choice between deception and death win Spinozistic favor. This is an example of a situation - that in which one can *benefit* others only by deceiving them is another - in which there simply can be no completely virtuous action to perform, because the situation itself involves a conflict that manifests ultimate lack of power.

The conclusion which seems to follow, namely that Spinoza would never approve of a person who sacrificed his own life to save the lives of innocent persons, may be taken by many to show that his ethics cannot, after all, pass the test of practical acceptability. However, it is somewhat misleading to conclude that *Spinoza* would not approve of such a person. For just as we must distinguish the *actions* of the ideal free man from those of even the most free of actual persons, so we must distinguish the ethical *reactions* of the ideal free man from those of even the most free actual persons. Insofar as Spinoza himself is governed by reason, he will neither approve nor disapprove of self-sacrifice. But insofar as he himself is a part of nature, and as such is subject to affects not entirely rational, it is quite possible that, through his imaginative fellow-feeling with others and the natural tendency to ascribe freedom to human actions whose causes we do not know in detail, Spinoza himself might feel some considerable favor or approval for a self-sacrificing individual - and perhaps even some indignation towards the person who preserves himself through deception.

Thus, if we find that we cannot fully bring ourselves to adopt the ethical attitudes that Spinoza claims one must adopt insofar as one is guided by reason alone, Spinoza might well agree that we cannot permanently and completely attain those attitudes. Any actual human being will be influenced in his ethical judgments not only by pure reason, but by his passions as well. Spinoza would add only that, as we come to gain understanding, we must then at least *begin* to approximate those reasonable attitudes more closely. This claim, if not obviously right, is at least not obviously wrong. Spinoza's *own* ethics at least, even if not also those of the Spinozistic perfectly free man, are arguably capable of passing the test of practical acceptability.

Conclusion. In this paper, I have argued that Spinoza does not contradict other doctrines in the *Ethics* when he claims that the free man always acts honestly, not deceptively. I believe that, in coming to understand the reasons why he can make this claim without contradiction, we gain a better appreciation of the character of his ethical theory in general, and of the considerations that are involved in assessing its practical acceptability. I have not shown that his ethical theory is consistent in all of its parts, nor that it is practically acceptable in all of its consequences, nor that it passes the other important tests to which an ethical theory might be subjected. A fortiori, I have not shown that it is true. I do hope at least to have suggested, however, that Spinoza's ethical theory has greater resources, and is of greater plausibility and philosophical interest, than is sometimes supposed.

1. All quotations are from Curley (1985), sometimes modified to incorporate corrections made in the second printing.

2. It may be noted that the passage cited from IVP18S mentions another kind of being in addition to individual persons: the "one Mind and one Body" that all persons who strive together can compose. Certainly the advantage of this composite being will be the overriding good *for that composite being*, just as the advantage of an individual human being overrides the advantage of any individual bodily organ *for that human being*. But this does not entail that the advantage of the composite being as a whole could, in a case of conflict, override the advantage of an individual part or member *for that part or member*. Spinoza clearly implies the contrary when discussing the advantage of parts of the human body at IVP60,D.

Steinberg, "Spinoza's Ethical Doctrine," *Journal of the History of Philosophy*, 22 (1984), 303-324, argues that the relations of organs to the whole body and to each other provide a model of how human beings can be so related that the true advantage of each must always completely coincide with the advantage of mankind as a whole, and hence also with that of every other human being. Unfortunately, however, these relations cannot provide the required model. The well-being of an organ, though intimately related to that of the body of which it is a part, does not completely coincide with it. The preservation of a particular body may require, for example, the non-preservation of one of its organs (as in cases of surgical removal); correlatively, the preservation of a particular organ may be a long-term harm to the body as a whole. The well-being of an organ also does not coincide completely with the well-being of any other individual organ - for example, when medical treatment needed to save one organ causes the death of another. Steinberg's conception does not explain why the advantage of an individual human being cannot similarly diverge from the advantage of another human being or from that of mankind as a whole - particularly in such crucial cases as a forced choice between dishonesty and death.

To be sure, Spinoza does hold that when human beings gain in understanding, they agree more closely in nature with one another (IVP35). And if human beings ever became *exactly* alike in nature, their advantages would then necessarily coincide completely (IVP31). But this ideal is only an approachable limit, not a completely attainable possibility. For as long as human beings remain finite parts of nature, they will always differ in at least *some* respects. Most importantly, perhaps, the specific "actual essence" of human being X will always be an endeavor to preserve the being of X, whereas the actual essence of human being Y will always be an endeavor to preserve the being of Y (IIIP7). One's own being, though greatly aided by other human beings of similar nature, does not literally entail and is not literally entailed by the being of any or all others. Hence, one's own good or preservation cannot be *identified* with the good or preservation of other persons or of mankind as a whole.

3. For a way of denying (2) based on a reading of IVDD1-2 that I reject, however, see note 5 below.

4. Even the term's most general and objective philosophical sense, in which it refers to a thing's degree of reality or being, is originally due to this same false supposition, combined with the tendency to think of all individuals in Nature as members of a single kind or genus. This is a sense that Spinoza has already employed at IP11S and IID6, and he regards his account of the "perfect man," described below, as a special case of this philosophically useful - though etymologically unfortunate - meaning of the term. (See also KV II, 4.) For

good discussions of Spinoza on moral language, see Edwin Curley, "Spinoza's Moral Philosophy," in Grene (1973), 354-376; and Bennett (1984), 289-299. However, Curley suggests taking "perfection" to be an absolute notion and "goodness" to be a matter of approximation; he otherwise draws no distinction between them (see especially p. 359). Bennett suggests that the notion of a "model of human nature" in the Preface to Part IV is a "relic" of an earlier period of composition, and plays no role in the body of Part IV.

5. Two paradoxes similar to the original one can be generated by replacing the term 'good' in (1)-(4) with 'a dictate of reason' and 'a virtue,' respectively. Since Spinoza equates "the free man's actions" with "actions done from the dictate of reason," (IVP66S and IVP72D) and further equates the latter with "actions done from virtue," (IVP24 and IVP72D) he cannot deny the resulting correlates of (4). Precisely because of their equivalence to the actions of the ideal free man, however, the requirements of virtue and reason cannot, in his view, exhaust the good or the self-preserving for finite human beings. Thus, he would reject the resulting correlates of (2). So, for example, where preserving one's own being requires deception, doing so will be neither a dictate of reason nor a virtue - though it is a personal good. (For what *may* be a weaker use of 'reason,' according to which reason "teaches" whatever is advantageous under the circumstances, see TP II, 17.)

It should also be noted that one might insist on treating the first person plural as essential to Spinoza's definitions of 'good' and 'evil.' On this interpretation, the "good" would be only that which we know to be useful to *all of us*. If a case should then arise in which the preservation of one's own being would conflict with the welfare of others, there would simply be no "good" thing to do. Although the text does not completely rule out this reading of his definitions, I do not believe that he intends it. However, if we do read the definitions in this way, then Spinoza must accept (4) but deny (2). For the "good" would then be restricted to that which reason could counsel all men jointly, so that good would become co-extensive with the perfect - at the expense of losing some of its connection to the preservation of one's *own* being.

6. Bennett (1984), 317, rightly suggests that we "might see the concept of the 'free man' as a theoretically convenient limiting case, like the concept of an 'ideal gas.'"

7. Although Spinoza also writes of "praise" (*laus*) and "blame" (*vituperium*), these are defined (IIIP29S) as "the Joy with which we imagine the action of another by which he has striven to please us," and as "the Sadness with which we are averse to his action," respectively. Favor and indignation are thus both more general in their scope and less tied to the imagination.

THÉORIE ET PRATIQUE DE LA LIBERTÉ
AU JOUR DE L'ONTOLOGIE SPINOZISTE:
NOTES POUR UNE DISCUSSION.

EMILIA GIANCOTTI
Université d'Urbino

J'ai dejà eu plusieurs fois l'occasion par le passé de m'interesser au thème de la liberté chez Spinoza,[1] et de tenter d'en proposer une lecture objective qui, sans pour autant ignorer les difficultés internes du système, s'appliquait de préférence à les resoudre en les rattachant à l'unité présumée de la théorie. Mon intention, dans la circonstance présente, est de procéder à une approche différente, en ce qu'il s'agira plutôt de vérifier, au cours de ce qui va suivre, si les difficultés internes peuvent aller jusqu'à compromettre tout fondement d'une théorie de la liberté en tant que principe régulateur d'une pratique réelle. Pour ce faire, il va d'abord falloir prendre comme point de départ la définition du concept de liberté, lequel pourra ensuite être confronté aux modalités d'exercice pratique de la liberté, de la part d'un sujet dont le statut ontologique est donné.

La première définition de la liberté, est celle que l'on trouve dans le *Court Traité*:

> La *vraie liberté* consiste uniquement en ce que la cause première, *sans être contrainte ni nécessitée par aucune autre chose*, par sa perfection seulement produit toute perfection; que *si*, par suite, *Dieu pouvait omettre de le faire, il ne serait pas parfait*; car pouvoir s'abstenir de bien faire ou de mettre de la perfection dans ce qu'il produit, cela ne peut avoir place en lui que par un défaut. Que *Dieu seul donc est l'unique cause libre*, cela n'est pas seulement évident par ce que nous avons dit, mais aussi parce qu'en dehors de lui n'existe aucune cause extérieure qui le contraigne ou le nécessite; ce qui n'a pas lieu dans les choses créées.[2]

Le pivot de cette définition est constitué par le binôme conceptuel indépendance/autonomie d'une part, et nécessité de l'autre: "sans être contrainte ni nécessitée par aucune autre chose... si... Dieu pouvait omettre de le faire, il ne serait pas parfait." Pivôt sur lequel s'articule également la définition de la *res libera* dans l'*Ethique*, où une veritable définition du concept de liberté n'apparait que dans la définition des modalités d'existence et d'action de la 'chose libre': "Cette chose est dite libre qui existe par la seule nécessité de sa nature et est déterminée par soi seule à agir."[3] C'est au reste la définition employée par Spinoza dans sa lettre à Schuller datée 1674 (Ep. 58), pour contester l'interprétation que E. W. de Tschirnhaus et lui-même avaient faite de son concept de liberté:

Je passe maintenant à cette définition de la liberté que votre ami dit être la mienne. Je ne sais d'ou il l'à tirée. J'appelle libre, quant'à moi, une chose qui est et agit par la seule nécessité de sa nature... Dieu, par exemple, existe librement bien que nécessairement parce qu'il existe par la seule nécessité de sa nature... Vous le voyez bien, je ne fais pas consister la liberté dans un libre décret mais dans une libre nécessité.[4]

La raison principale de ce désaccord, raison qui motive également l'incompréhension du concept spinoziste de la parte de ceux qui appartiennent encore au cadre théorique de la tradition cartésienne, réside dans le refus du libre-arbitre, refus que Spinoza - faisant preuve d'une rigueur et d'une cohérence extrêmes - applique également à la cause première, à Dieu. Cause première qui n'est libre que dans la mesure où tout y est contenu, rien ne pouvant se trouver hors d'elle pour en déterminer l'être ou l'agir. Sauf qu'elle n'est nullement libre d'être ni d'agir autrement que conformément aux lois de sa nature. L'exclusion de tout intellect et de toute volonté de l'essence de Dieu, et le changement de statut réductif de ceux-ci, passant d'attributs de Dieu à ses modes (infinis ou finis, peu import), relève d'un effort de transcription laïque, de depersonnalisation de l'absolu énergiquement accompli par Spinoza, encore qu'il n'ait pu éliminer toute trace résiduaire, héritage de la tradition judéo-chrétienne (mais la question n'est pas là).

Pour en revenir aux définitions initiales, on s'aperçoit - si l'on excepte, comme il se doit, les *Principia philosophiae cartesianae* et les *Cogitata metaphysica*[5] - que, d'un bout à l'autre de sa production philosophique, l'attitude de Spinoza face à cette question demeure inchangée.

Si indépendance/autonomie ontologique et nécessité intrinsèque de l'essence sont donc les conditions de la révélation de la liberté, seul est libre l'être dont semblabes conditions font partie de l'essence. Il n'y a par conséquent qu'une seule *res/causa libera* (E IP17C2): la substance absolument infinie, autrement dit: Dieu. Car seule la substance contient toutes le choses qui nécessairement découlent de son essence (E IPP15-16), et que rien ne saurait donc en déterminer l'existence ni l'action. Puissance infinie, elle se produit d'elle-même, tirant de l'unité de son être l'infinie multiplicité de ses modes qui - en tant que modes à elle propres - sont tous inhérents à son essence, qui est aussi son existence, de sort qu'ils n'ont sur elle aucun pouvoir coercitif.

Mais on sait que dans ses écrits, Spinoza traite abondamment de la liberté par rapport à l'homme, à l'essence duquel cependant n'appartient pas l'être de la substance (E IIP10), l'essence de l'homme étant quant à elle constituée de certaines modifications des attributs de Dieu (E IIP10C). Et, puisque les modes sont dans la substance, et sont conçus au moyen de la substance (E IDV), il est impossible que de l'essence de l'homme puissent faire partie les propriétés d'indipendance/autonomie ontologique et de nécessité intrinsèque de l'essence, que nous avons indiquées comme conditions de la manifestation de la liberté. S'il n'était que le fait de parler de la liberté humaine permet de s'attendre à une définition ou tout au moins en suppose une.

A ce propos, il me semble que le dernier chapitre de la II partie du *Court Traité* (II, xxvi, *De la liberté vraie*), offre une définition théorique de la liberté humaine très nette et qui ne se retrouve nulle part ailleurs sous une forme aussi complète:

> Par tout ce qui a été dit on peut bien aisément concevoir ce qu'est la liberté humaine (n.1: l'esclavage d'une chose consiste en ce qu'elle est soumise à des causes extérieures; la liberté, par contre, consiste à n'y être pas soumis mais à en être affranchi.); je la définis en disant qu'elle est une solide réalité qu'obtient notre entendement par son union immédiate avec Dieu pour produire en lui-même des idées et tirer de lui même des effets qui s'accordent avec sa nature, sans que ces effets soient soumis à aucunes causes extérieures par lesquelles ils puissent être altérés ou transformés. L'on voit aussi clairement par ce qui a été dit ce que sont les choses qui sont en notre pouvoir et ne sont soumises à aucune cause extérieure; en même temps que nous avons démontré la durée éternelle et constante de notre entendement, deja établie d'une autre façon; et enfin quelle sorte d'effets nous devons estimer plus haut que tous les autres.[6]

La liberté, dans cette définition, coïncide encore une fois avec une situation d'indépendance face aux causes extérieures, indépendance à laquelle peut parvenir notre intellect grâce à son 'union immédiate avec Dieu.' Cette union produit un double effet, l'un théorique et l'autre pratique. En effet, l'intellect acquiert - en vertue de cette union - le pouvoir de produire autant d'idées en soi que d'effets ou actions en dehors de soi, les unes et les autres en accord avec sa propre nature, et dans des conditions de sécurité, autrement dit sans devoir courir le risque d'exposer ses productions (théoriques et pratiques) au conditionnement des causes extérieures qui pourraient les transformer ou les modifier. Dans l'ensemble, donc, la liberté humaine, rendue possible par l'union privilégiée de l'intellect avec Dieu, intellect, dont les effets est-il dit un peu plus haut (p.193) "sont les plus excellents de tous et doivent aussi être estimés plus haut que tous les autres,"[7] consiste dans le fait de se rendre indépendante de toute cause extérieure.

L'intellect est le troisième genre de connaissance, "la connaissance claire... qui s'acquiert, *non par une conviction née de raisonnements*, mais par sentiment et jouissance de la chose elle-même et elle l'emporte de beaucoup sur les autres";[8] considérée supérieure à toute autre forme de connaissance, supérieure même à la raison, dont elle diffère par son caractère d'immédiateté, cette même connaissance prendra, dans l'*Ethique*, le nom de 'science intuitive.' Quoiqu'elle prenne part au processus d'acquisition de notre liberté, la raison, quant à elle, ne revêt cependant pas la même importance, étant celle-ci - si l'on en croit le texte - insuffisante. Parlant des passions et de la fonction que la raison assume dans le processus de libération de celles-ci, Spinoza note:

> je crois ainsi avoir suffisamment montré et prouvé qu'il n'appartient qu'a la Croyance Droite ou à la Raison de nous conduire à la connaissance du bien et du mal. Et aussi quand nous montrerons que la première et principale cause de toutes ces affections est la Connaissance, il apparaîtra clairement que, si nous usons bien de notre entendement et de notre Raison, nous ne tomberons jamais dans une de ces passions qui doivent être rejetées par nous. Je dis: notre entendement parce que *je pense que la Raison seule n'a pas le pouvoir de nous délivrer de toutes.*[9]

Et, plus clairement encore: "la Raison n'a pas le pouvoir de nous conduire à la santé de l'âme."[10] Ce salut, mieux: la libération des passions, consiste dans l'union immédiate avec Dieu et est du ressort de l'intellect.

Mais laissons momentanément de côté cet aspect de la question, sur lequel nous aurons l'occasion de revenir plus avant. Quant à nos définitions, l'*Ethique* confirme celle ayant trait à la liberté humaine relevée dans le *Court Traitè*, dans la mesure où la liberté y est identifiée au salut et à la béatitude et consiste "dans un Amour constant et éternel envers Dieu, ou dans l'Amour de Dieu envers les hommes."[11] D'autre part, plus l'esprit aimera Dieu, savoir: plus il jouira de la béatitude, plus grande en sera sa capacité d'entendement, autrement dit plus grande sera sa puissance sur les affects (E VP40D), et plus grande donc sa liberté. Dans cette définition, c'est encore dans l'indépendance par rapport à quelque chose d'autre que nous, et des effets que ce quelque chose d'autre peut produire sur nous, que se situe la véritable essence de la liberté. Cette indépendance est un produit de l'intelligence, et notre liberté sera d'autant plus grande que s'élevera notre degré de connaissance, le plus haut degré étant la connaissance de Dieu, de ses attributs et des actions conséquentes à la nécessité de sa nature. Dans cette intelligence - intelligence des diverses articulations de la réalité, mais à partir de Dieu, à partir donc de la totalité - réside notre bonheur, notre béatitude et notre liberté (E IVApp§4), car seule cette connaissance nous rachète de la dépendance des causes extérieures.

Avant de clarifier autant la signification que la portée de cette indépendance, revenons à l'individualisation de l'organe de production de cette même indépendance ou liberté. Confrontée au *Court Traitè*, la position adoptée dans l'*Ethique* est moins nette. En effet, malgré une distinction des trois genres de connaissance et donc une différenciation de la raison et de l'intellect, la IV et la V partie de l'*Ethique* assimilent fréquemment ou équiparent ces deux genres lorsq'il est question du thème de la liberté. Le passage auquel je viens de faire allusion (E IVApp§4) est un exemple précis de ce manque de distinction:

Il est donc utile avant tout dans la vie de perfectionner l'Entendement ou la Raison autant que nous pouvons; et en cela seul consiste la félicité suprême ou béatitude de l'homme; car la béatitude de l'homme n'est rien d'autre que le contentement intérieur lui-même, lequel naît de la connaissance intuitive de Dieu; et perfectionner l'Entendement n'est rien d'autre aussi que connaître Dieu et les attributs de Dieu et les actions qui suivent de la nécessité de sa nature. C'est pourquoi la fin ultime d'un homme qui est dirigé par la Raison, c'est-à-dire le Désir suprême par lequel il s'applique à gouverner tous les autres, est celui qui le porte à se concevoir adéquatement et à concevoir adéquatement toutes les choses pouvant être pour lui objects de connaissance claire.[12]

Dans ce passage, les deux niveaux de connaissance sont manifestement équiparés, car si c'est d'une part de la connaissance vraie que naissent aussi bien la liberté que l'indépendance qui en est l'essence, la raison tout comme l'intellect (ou science intuitive), sont également formes de connaissance vraie. D'autre part, dans un passage de E IVP68D, il y a cette nette affirmation: "J'ai dit que celui-là est libre qui est conduit par la seule Raison."[13] Au reste, les formules du genre *homo liber est qui ratione ducitur*, sont très fréquentes. Est-il licite de supposer à première vue qu'à l'un et à l'autre de ces genres correspondent des degrés ou formes de liberté différentes, et partant des formes différentes de vie?

D'un point de vue théorique, on peut concevoir sans peine deux formes différentes de liberté et de vie correspondant aux deux différentes modalités de la connaissance. Tout au plus s'agira-t-il d'établir en quoi consiste la différence. Sauf qu'auparavant il convient de se demander si - au jour de ce même point de vue théorique - la liberté humaine ainsi qu'elle a été définie est compatible avec la définition du statut ontologique du sujet de cette liberté. Une longue analyse n'est nullement nécessaire pour fournir une réponse négative à cette question. Alors que la définition de *res libera* évoquée plus haut s'applique à la substance, à l'homme par contre revient la seconde partie de cette même définition: "cette chose est dite nécessaire ou plutôt contrainte qui est determinée par une autre à exister et à produire quelque effet dans une condition certaine et déterminée."[14] Or, comme "l'essence de l'homme n'enveloppe pas l'existence nécessaire, c'est-à-dire il peut aussi bien se faire, suivant l'ordre de la Nature, que cet homme-ci ou celui-là existe, qu'il peut se faire qu'il n'existe pas,"[15] pour qu'un homme quelconque puisse exister il faut qu'une cause en détermine l'existence. Son essence est - on l'a vu - constituée de certaines modifications des attributs de Dieu, si bien que comme tous les modes il "est dans une autre chose, par le moyen de laquelle il est aussi conçu."[16] Et comme "toute chose qui est finie et a une existence déterminée, ne peut exister et être déterminée à produire cet effet par une autre cause qui est elle-même finie et a une existence déterminée..."[17] La dépendance ontologique formulée dans cette proposition contredit nettement l'indépendance des causes extérieures qui nous avait semblé fournir l'essence de la liberté humaine. Le fait de la dépendance ontologique de l'homme n'est pas modifiable; étant lui même l'un des infinis modes, tous nécessairement dérivés de la substance (E IP16), et dont l'essence comme l'existence sont - en vertu d'un acte de causalité immanente tout aussi nécessaire - production de la substance infinie, Dieu, l'essence de l'homme - dont fait partie la dépendance ontologique - n'est pas modifiable. Toute forme de liberté doit par conséquent se greffer sur ce fondement de la contrainte.

L'impossibilité de supprimer ce fondement apparaît de façon particulièrement nette dans les prèmieres propositions de la IV partie:

> Nous pâtissons en tant que nous sommes une partie de la Nature qui ne peut se concevoir par soi sans les autres parties;

> La force avec laquelle l'homme persévère dans l'existence est limitée et surpassée infiniment par la puissance des causes extérieures;

> Il est impossible que l'homme ne soit pas une partie de la Nature et ne puisse éprouver d'autres changements que ceux qui se peuvent connaître par sa seule nature et dont il est cause adéquate;

> Il suit de là que l'homme est nécessairement toujours soumis aux passions, suit l'ordre commun de la Nature et lui obéit, et s'y adapte autant que la nature des choses l'exige.[18]

Or c'est justement dans cette dépendance des causes extérieurs que consiste comme on le sait la servitude alors que, au contraire, la liberté, elle, consiste dans l'indépendance acquise par rapport à ces mêmes causes extérieures ainsi que par rapport aux effects que produit sur nous leur action.

La théorie de la liberté contredit donc le statut ontologique de l'homme, en vertu duquel celui-ci est déterminée par autre chose et soumis à l'action de causes extérieures, dont ne dépend pas seulement sa venue au monde, mais dont sont également tributaires les modalités de celle-ci ainsi que sa propre conservation. C'est en fait de la nature, des agents de sa génération que dépend, tout au moins en partie, la nature propre de l'homme: sa constitution. La structure composite du corps humains, en outre, le porte à avoir besoin de nombreux autres corps dont "il est continuellement comme régénéré."[19] La dépendance des causes extérieures est à la fois structurale et inéluctable. D'autre part, l'union essentielle du corps et de l'esprit - dont le fondement métaphisique réside dans l'unité de la substance et dans l'identité de l'ordre d'explication de ses attributs - est tel que l'esprit lui-même ne saurait se passer de tout rapport avec les causes extérieures. A partir des derniers postulats du petit traité de physique, la II partie de l'*Ethique* décrit la phénoménologie de cette dépendance, la genèse des affects au demuerant, ainsi que la sujétion à ceux-ci, supposant cette même dépendance. Polémiquant contre Descartes et les stoïciens (E IIIPref, E VPref), Spinoza ne reconnaît pas à l'esprit une absolue faculté de domination sur les affects. Il y a dans le chapitre conclusif de l'Appendice à la IV partie, la déclaration suivante:

> Mais la puissance de l'homme est extrêmement limitée et *infiniment surpassée par celle des causes extérieures; nous n'avons donc pas un pouvoir absolu d'adapter à notre usage les choses extérieures* (souligné par nous).

Malgré cette déclaration d'impuissance, le texte continue préparant ainsi le développement de la V partie:

> Nous supporterons, *toutefois*, d'une âme égale les événements contraires à ce qu'exige la considération de notre intérêt, *si nous avons conscience* de nous être acquittés de notre office, savons que notre puissance n'allait pas jusqu'à nous permettre de les éviter, et avons présente cette idée *que nous sommes une partie de la Nature entière dont nous suivons l'ordre.* Si nous connaissons cela clairement et distinctement, cette partie de nous que se définit par la connaissance claire, c'est-à-dire la partie la meilleure de nous, trouvera là un plein contentement et s'efforcera de pérseverer dans ce contentement...[20]

La prise de conscience de notre condition de dépendance, ainsi que le côté inéluctable de cette même condition, si elle ne nous fournit aucun moyen pour l'abolir, produit néanmoins un changement dans notre état d'âme qui, partant de l'inquiétude propre à qui méconnaît l'ordre nécessaire de la Nature, passe à une forme de satisfaction plénière qui augmente au fur et à mesure des progrés de l'intelligence.

Or c'est ici que réside, sinon la solution de la contradiction - qui apparait irréductible - du moins la réponse à la question concernant la signification de cette indépendance, à l'interieur de laquelle on a vu résider l'essence de la liberté. Il ne s'agit évidemment pas d'une indépendance réelle. Au reste, comment une partie pourrait-elle se soustraire au conditionnement du réseau de relations dont est formée et au moyen duquel s'exprime la totalité? Comment un corps pourrait-il se passer du rapport avec les autres corps et, conséquemment, comment un esprit pourrait-il se passer du systéme d'échanges sans lequel aucune science ne peut être produite? D'autre part, ce rapport structural est à l'origine de toutes les formes de dépendance, dépendances affectives, sociales et politiques comprises. Dans la mesure où la production des biens nécessaires à notre subsistance recquiert la coopération des autres hommes (concept clairement énoncé dans le chapitre V du *Traité théologico-politique*, G III/ 73/13-24), le rapport avec ceux-ci fait naître les affects qui, eux, naissent des idées des affections ou modifications auxquelles est sujet notre corps dans son rapport avec les autres corps; le système social lié à la coopération est un système de relations où chacun a une place donnée et dont la variation n'est pas indépendante du système, la sphère politique formalisant l'ensemble du système des dépendances. Et donc, si la réelle dépendance des causes extérieures ne peut être supprimée, l'indépendance dont il est question se doit d'être absolument autre, si bien que l'homme vit nécessairement une contradiction déchirante, partagé entre une condition de dépendance structurale et la tendance à rompre les limites de cette dépendance. La conviction, largement répandue parmi les hommes, se croyant dégagés de cette dépendance, autrement dit sujets d'une volonté libre, bref, cette idée courante que les hommes ont de la liberté est illusoire, dans la mesure où elle est le résultat d'une combinaison de connaissance et d'ignorance: connaissance des finalités de nos actions et ignorance des causes qui les déterminent. Cette idée de liberté produit toute la série des préjugés dénoncés par Spinoza dans l'Appendice à la I partie de l'*Ethique*.

Mais si maintenant l'indépendance avec laquelle s'identifie la liberté n'est pas réelle, quelle est la signification, la portée de cette liberté? Peut elle, malgré sa totale et exclusive appartenance à la sphère de la théorie, en d'autres termes au domaine de la connaissance et de l'intelligence du réel, avoir quelque efficacité pratique? Les deux réponses son liées l'une à l'autre, comme le sont pareillement les deux questions.

On sait qu'après avoir placé l'essence de l'esprit dans l'idée ou connaissance du corps, et après avoir décrit les modalités du rapport esprit/corps et les conséquences de cette union, Spinoza expose sa propre théorie de la connaissance, où il énonce les différents modes de connaissance accessibles à l'esprit en sa qualité d'idée du corps, étant lié à celle-ci par le même genre de rapport unissant une idée à son objet, en même temps qu'il clarifie la genèse de ces modes, leur nature et leurs contenus. C'est sur cette base que se fonde la déduction de notre condition 'd'agissant' ou 'd'agis,' d'hommes libres ou d'esclaves, selon que nous sommes ou ne sommes pas cause adéquate de quelque chose qui a lieu en nous ou en dehors de nous (E IIID2) et selon que nous avons ou n'avons pas connaissance adéquate de ce quelque chose (E IIIP1), et que se fonde également la déduction des affects, répartis à leur tour en actions ou passions inhérentes à notre double condition. La description de la formation de ces affects, analytique et convaincante, permet d'en donner une définition. Et il appert clairement de cette description que, parmi les affects, les passions se produisant en nous du fait que nous ne sommes que cause partielle des affections de notre corps, dont nous n'avons qu'une connaissance confuse, sont contraires à l'affirmation et à l'exercice de notre puissance individuelle, de notre conatus, dépendants que nous sommes des causes extérieures. Il s'agit d'un enchevêtrement complexe de dépendance: si, d'une part, les affects-passions se produisent en nous parce que nous ne sommes que cause partielle des affections de notre corps, desquelles nous n'avons qu'une idée confuse, dans la mesure où notre puissance individuelle (d'agir et de penser) résulte entravée par les causes extérieures, de l'autre, ces mêmes affects-passions limitent l'affirmation de notre puissance individuelle.

Inversement, les affects-actions, se produisant en nous du fait que nous sommes cause adéquate des affections de notre corps et que nous en avons une connaissance adéquate, outre à être expression de notre puissance individuelle, en favorisent également l'expansion.

Dès lors, il est évident que puissance d'agir, puissance de penser et affectivité sont étroitement liées et que, par conséquent, la détermination d'un degré quelconque ou d'une quelque forme d'indépendance ne saurait avoir lieu dans l'une seulement des sphères où s'exerce notre puissance individuelle. Conformément à la théorie de l'identité de l'ordre des idées et de l'ordre des choses (parallélisme), sur laquelle se fonde la théorie de l'esprit et de son union avec les corps, on ne peut que déduire que l'indépendance - qui constitue l'essence de notre liberté - concerne toutes les modalités de notre existence. E VP1 applique directement la théorie du parallélisme au rapport existant entre les idées des choses dans l'esprit et les affections du corps ou images dans le corps:

> Suivant que les pensées et les idées des choses sont ordonnées et enchaînées dans l'âme, les affections du Corps, c'est-à-dire les images des choses, sont corrélativement ordonnées et enchaînées dans le Corps.[21]

A ce point, et à vouloir répondre à la question de la signification et de la portée de la liberté humaine, il semble qu'il faille rectifier la formulation de cette même question, et s'interroger moins sur le sens et la portée d'une liberté qui ne fonctionne qu'a l'interieur de la théorie, s'attachant plutôt à la signification de l'indépendance telle quelle, et donc de la liberté, en conservant cependant les deux conditions théoriques fondamentales: la dépendance ontologique de l'être humain d'une part, et l'unité indivisible de la substance de l'autre, fondement métaphysique de l'unité-organicité des modes constitutifs de l'essence de l'homme, dont la puissance s'exprime indissolublement comme corps et comme esprit.

Qu'on me permette une citation personnelle; j'ai dit autre part ("La teoria dell'assolutismo in Hobbes e Spinoza," *op. cit.*, pp. 250-251) que l'anthropologie spinoziste peut être qualifiée de 'réelle et positive' en ce qu'elle identifie (et bien qu'elle considère la sujétion aux passions, autrement dit la servitude, comme l'inévitable conséquence de la condition ontologique de l'homme, de son être fini, et de sa structure composite formée de modes d'extension et de modes de pensée, et qu'elle décrive les modalités de cette sujétion avec l'objectivité appliquée d'ordinaire à la description des phénomènes naturels) l'essence de la singularité à sa puissance individuelle (le *conatus*) qui est un principe dynamique, indiquant par là même une possibilité d'évolution vers la rationalité et tant que connaissance et pratique de vie.

Je suis encore de l'avis que la clef pouvant fournir une réponse à la question initiale se trouve dans le concept de puissance individuelle, ce qui ne signifie pas pour autant qu'on en obtienne nécessairement la solution du problème.

Après avoir envisagé dans la IV partie les conditions de notre impuissance, de notre dépendance et de notre servitude - non sans avoir également fourni en cette occasion plusieurs indications lumineuses sur la possibilité d'echapper aux limites de cette même impuissance - la V partie s'attache à rendre compte de la "puissance de l'entendement ou de la liberté de l'homme." L'identification est nette, qu'il s'agisse d'intellect ou qu'il s'agisse de raison, dès qu'on aborde la question de la liberté humaine, le texte l'identifie à ces deux genres en tant que producteurs de connaissance vraie et adéquate de la réalité. Si l'on veut saisir correctement le sens de cette identification, il faut d'une part faire appel à ce qui a été dit précédemment sur le rapport esprit/corps, et relever d'autre part le contenu de cette connaissance vraie et adéquate. Pour ce qui est du premier point, on a dejà pu remarquer qu'il existe un lien constitutif entre la puissance d'agir du corps et la puissance d'agir de l'esprit, de sorte que les limites de l'une sont en même temps les limites de l'autre et, réciproquement, l'expansion de l'une implique l'expansion de l'autre. Spinoza ne semble pas craindre le paradoxe lorsqu'il déclare (alors qu'il avait précédemment annoncé qu'il allait passer à la question de la durée de l'esprit sans rapport avec le corps E VP20S):

> Qui a un corps possédant un très grand nombre d'aptitudes, la plus grande partie de son Ame est éternelle.[22]

Proposition qui se trouve être démontrée de la façon suivante:

> Qui a un Corps apte à faire un très grand nombre de choses, il est très peu dominé par les affects[23] qui sont mauvais (IVP38), c'est-à-dire par les affects (IVP30) qui sont contraires à notre nature; et ainsi (P10) il a le pouvoir d'ordonner et d'enchaîner les affections du Corps suivant un ordre valable pour l'entendement, et conséquemment de faire (P14) que toutes les affections du Corps se rapportent a l'idée de Dieu; par où il arrivera (P15) qu'il soit affecté envers Dieu de l'Amour qui (P16) doit occuper ou constituer la plus grande partie de l'Ame, et par suite il a une Ame (P33) dont la plus grande partie est éternelle.[24]

Ces deux passages confirment ce fait que si l'esprit parvient à une connaissance adéquate, le corps dont l'esprit est l'idée, est également cause adéquate des propres actions. Ce qui, appliqué à la liberté, signifie que si la liberté (de l'esprit) s'identifie à la connaissance adéquate de la réalité, cette connaissance implique que le corps de ce même esprit connaissant de façon adéquate, est cause adéquate des propres actions, et, par consequent, indépendant de toute cause extérieure, donc libre. Comment cette affirmation s'accomode-t-elle du statut ontologique de l'homme? Il se peut que la seconde partie de la démonstration (quoique ce passage ne soi pas le seul à permettre ce genre d'extrapolation) nous fournisse le fil d'Ariane qui nous permettra de trouver l'issue de cet apparent labyrinthe, comme cette même seconde partie pourrait bien également nous permettre de toucher au second but que nous nous étions fixé.

Que signifie, en effet, ordonner et enchaîner les affections du corps selon l'ordre de l'intellect en les rapportant à l'idée de Dieu, sinon prendre conscience de l'ordre nécessaire de la réalité dont nous sommes part intégrante et à laquelle nous ne pouvons nous soustraire? Comme il résulte du passage E IVApp§32 cité plus haut, le concept spinoziste de liberté s'explique donc, ce que l'on sait, dans la prise de conscience de la nécessité. Tel est le contenu des deux genres producteurs de connaissance vraie et adéquate. Mais - et il faut le souligner - cette conscience n'est que l'un des deux aspects d'un certain degré de développement de la puissance individuelle (conatus), laquelle, pour ce qui est de son côté physique et pratique, se manifeste dans la capacité d'être active par rapport au monde extérieur et, partant, de s'ériger au besoin contre le jeu des conditionnements exercés sur nous du fait de notre rapport avec les corps extérieurs.

Toutefois, la conscience à laquelle parviennent les deux genres de connaissance vraie et adéquate, en tant que conscience précisément de la nécessité, nous renvoie comme dans un miroir l'image de notre dépendance. De la même manière que la liberté divine n'abolit en rien la nécessité de la nature de Dieu et, par conséquent, de tout ce qui est dérivé de sa nature, la liberté humaine n'abolit pas le déterminisme; au contraire, elle naît de lui, s'accomplissant comme forme propre et conscience du déterminisme, mais se développant également à l'interieur comme tendance antagoniste, parce que tentative et effort de l'homme à se rendre indépendant des causes extérieures. Ceci est manifeste dans le procès qui conduit à la liberation des affects-passions:

> Si nous séparons une émotion ou un affect de l'Ame de la pensée d'une cause extérieure et la joignons à d'autres pensées, l'Amour et la Haine à l'egard de la cause extérieure sont détruits, de même que les fluctuations de l'Ame naissant de ces affects.[25]

Cette séparation d'une émotion ou affect de la pensée de la cause extérieure est une opération que l'esprit accomplit en union intrinsèque avec les corps, contre l'action des causes extérieures, tendant ainsi à en annuler les effets négatifs sur notre sensibilité. En ce sens, il me semble pouvoir dire que tout en étant conscience de la nécessité (et non possession illusoire d'une volonté libre), d'une nécessité qui s'affiche comme condition métaphysique donnée, par rapport a cette nécessité qu'elle reconnaît rationellement, la liberté ne se présente pas moins comme contradiction, comme tendance rationelle antagoniste au processus dont elle est elle-même issue. Reconnaissons toutefois que Spinoza n'accepterait pas notre conclusion et y répondrait comme il répondit jadis (dans l'épître 58 déjà citée) à l'objection de E.W. de Tschirnhaus:

> Pour ce qu'il dit encore 'que si nous étions contraints par des causes extérieures, nul ne pourrait acquérir l'état de vertu,' je ne sais de qui il tient que nous puissons avoir de la fermeté et de la constance non par une nécessité de notre destinée, mais seulement par un libre décret.[26]

En d'autres termes, Spinoza ne voyait aucune contradiction entre liberté individuelle et determinisme.

Je voudrais attirer encore l'attention sur deux points: le rapport raison/intellect dans le processus d'acquisition et de jouissance de la liberté, et les effets pratiques de la liberté en tant qu'affirmation du plus haut degré de la puissance individuelle (*conatus*) dans son ensemble organique formé de *potentia intelligendi* et *potentia agendi*.

Je vais être obligée de rappeler certains concepts assez connus, ce qui ne signifie pas pour autant qu'ils sont toujours très clairs. La raison équivaut, par définition, à la possession des notions communes et à l'idée adéquate des propriétés des choses (E IIP40S2), elle connaît les choses selon verité pour ce qu'elles sont en elles-mêmes et les considère donc comme nécessaires (E IIP41, 42). La science intuitive, dont l'organe est l'intellect, parvient au même résultat, encore que la procédure soit différente: l'intellect part de la connaissance adéquate de l'essence formelle des attributs de Dieu qu'il nous est donné de connaître (extension et pensée), pour parvenir à une connaissance adéquate de l'essence des choses (E IIP40S2). La science intuitive est une connaissance déductive de l'ensemble du réel et, en tant que telle, elle est connaissance de l'ordre nécessaire selon lequel tout ce qui est dérive de la substance. Les deux genres, donc, parviennent à la conscience de la nécessité, bien qu'ils saisissent cette même nécessité selon des points de vue différents. Néanmoins - et ceci pourrait être le critère distinctif de chacun de ces genres par rapport au thème de la liberté - alors que la raison joue quant à elle un rôle éminent dans le processus d'acquisition de la liberté et d'elaboration des normes pratiques d'une vie libre, autrement dit guidée par la raison, l'intellect, lui, s'identifie plutôt à la jouissance de cette même liberté: il est plus expression d'une possession permanente qu'acquisition sujette au risque, comme l'est fondamentalement la raison. Un passage de la V partie de l'*Ethique* me semble pouvoir autoriser cette hypothèse. En voici un extrait:

Par ce pouvoir (sc. rationis) d'ordonner et d'enchaîner correctement les affections du Corps nous pouvons faire en sorte de n'être pas aisément affectés d'affects mauvais. Car (P7) une plus grande force est requise pour réduire des affects ordonnés et enchaînés suivant un ordre valable pour l'entendement que si ils sont incertains et vagues.

Le mieux donc que nous puissions faire, tant que nous n'avons pas une connaissance parfaite de nos affects, est de concevoir une conduite droite de la vie, autrement dit des principes assurés de conduite, de les imprimer en notre mémoire et de les appliquer sans cesse aux choses particulières qui se rencontrent fréquemment dans la vie... si de plus nous ne perdions pas de vue qu'un contentement intérieur souverain naît de la conduite droite de la vie (IVP52) et que les hommes comme les autres êtres agissent par une nécessité de nature... Qui donc travaille à gouverner ses affects et ses appétits par le seul amour de la Liberté, il s'efforcera autant qu'il peut de connaître les vertues et leurs causes et de se donner la plénitude d'épanouissement qui naît de leur connaissance vraie... Et qui observera cette régle diligemment (cela n'est pas difficile) et s'exercera à la suivre, certes il pourra en un court espace de temps diriger ses actions suivant le commandement de la Raison.[27]

D'autre part, le troisième genre de connaissance engendre la plus haute satisfaction de l'esprit: "Le suprême effort de l'Ame et sa suprême vertu est de connaître les choses par le troisième genre de connaissance."[28] "De ce troisième genre de connaissance naît le contentement de l'Ame le plus élevé qu'il puisse y avoir."[29] Il est l'expression de la distance maximale d'avec la connaissance imaginative, et partant, de la plus grande distance qui soit des causes extérieures, ou, mieux encore, du plus haut niveau de contrôle des causes extérieures: l'aspiration à y accéder ne peut naître que du second genre (E VP28; Appuhn II/ 213/25-27).

Sans qu'il faille recourir à d'autres citations, la procédure - qui n'est autre qu'une technique de refoulement des affects-passions - à travers laquelle la raison (de ce qui en résulte du scolie cité et de la liste des remèdes contre les affects dans E VP20S) parvient non pas tant à une domination absolue qu'à une forme de maîtrise des affects-passions, cette procédure suggère que l'exercice de la liberté de la part de la raison s'applique essentiellement sur les choses qui existent actuellement dans la durée, sujets et sources des passions, et l'effort que fournit cette derniére à travers la connaissance vraie et adéquate avec laquelle elle se confond est double: d'un côté (théorie) elle ramène l'individualité et la singularité des choses existant dans la durée à leurs propriétés communes (amoindrissant les effets passionels de leur individualité specifique) et, d'autre part (pratique), elle élabore des normes communes de comportement qui, si suivies, permettent d'éviter les conséquences négatives d'un mode de vie individualiste. L'*homo liber, hoc est qui ratione ducitur*, agit dans la *civitas* (E

IVP73), au sein de laquelle il constate jour après jour l'immutabilité de sa condition ontologique, l'impossibilité de parvenir à une pleine indépendance des causes extérieures, faisant en sorte cependant de n'être dépendant de ces mêmes causes que dans ce qu'il ne peut éviter d'être en relations avec elles - et ce faisant les gouverne sans en être gouverné, grâce à l'elaboration de règles de vie directement issues de lui-même.

Cependant, Spinoza attribue au troisième genre de connaissance un pouvoir supérieur à celui de la raison sur les passions:

> La puissance de l'Ame se définit par la connaissance seule, son impuissance ou sa passion par la seule privation de connaissance, c'est-à-dire s'estime par ce que fait que les idées sont dites inadéquates. D'où suit que cette Ame est passive au plus haut point, dont les idées inadéquates constituent la plus grande partie, de façon que sa marque distinctive soit plutôt la passivité que l'activité qui est en elle; et au contraire cette Ame est active au plus haut point dont des idées adéquates constituent la plus grande partie, de façon que, tout en n'ayant pas moins d'idées adéquates que la première, elle ait sa marque distinctive plutôt dans des idées adéquates attestant son impuissance... Nous concevons facilement par la ce que peut sur les affects la connaissance claire et distincte, et principalement ce troisième genre de connaissance (voir a son sujet le Scolie de la IIP47) dont le principe est la connaissance même de Dieu; si en effet les affects, en tant qu'ils sont des passions, ne sont point par la absolument ôtés (voir P3 avec le Scolie de la P4), il arrive du moins qu'ils constituent la moindre partie de l'Ame (P14)...[30]

A partir de ce passage que, vu sa valeur récapitulative, j'ai préferé citer largement, le troisiéme genre de connaissance résulte posséder un pouvoir supérieur sur les passions (ce qui confirme ce qui avait été énoncé dans le *Court Traité*), mais non cependant au point de les éliminer complètement (à la difference du *Court Traité*, où l'indépendance des causes extérieures était au contraire affirmée). Ce qui confirme le fait que notre indépendance des causes extérieures peut être réduite et contrôlée mais ne peut être éliminée. La liberté n'élimine pas le déterminisme, même si elle s'affirme dans une tendance antagoniste à son égard. Le troisième genre de connaissance fournit l'instruments théorique le plus élevé pour pouvoir jouir de la liberté, mais l'elaboration des régles régissant la pratique de cette liberté est par contre du ressort de la raison.

Si l'on tient compte de l'extrême difficulté qu'il y a à parvenir à ce troisième genre de connaissance ainsi qu'à la satisfaction (*acquiescentia*) qui l'accompagne, l'objectif de la raison semble être un peu moins éloigné et moins difficilement réalisable, comme plus grande est également son efficacité pratique. Cette efficacité - on le sait assez, j'ai déjà eu l'occasion de le dire et je n'ai guère l'intention de le répeter ici - se relève dans le domaine politique outre que dans le domaine éthique. Mais les termes réels de sa manifestation sont ceux rendus possibles par la nécessité universelle.

Il me semble que l'on peut en tirer les conclusions suivantes:

1. pour ce qui est de sa définition générale, l'essence de la liberté réside dans l'indépendance ontologique qui implique l'absence de détermination provenant de l'extérieur, dans le respect de la nécessité intrinsèque à la nature de la *res libera;*

2. sous cette forme absolue, la liberté n'appartient qu'à la substance absolument infinie, Dieu;

3. l'identification de la liberté à l'independance restant acquise - identification ayant valeur générale - la liberté de l'homme - être ontologiquement dépendant en ce qu'il est par essence déterminé à l'existence et à l'action - s'accomplit dans la conscience de cette dépendance qui fait partie de l'ordre nécessaire en vertu duquel toutes les choses finies sont produites et dérivent de la substance infinie, comme elle s'accomplit également dans l'effort pratique visant à réduire l'ampleur de sa dépendance qui ne peut cependant pas être supprimée;

4. l'idée de la liberté humaine, dans le cadre d'un tel système qui fait de la nécessité le principe d'existence de la réalité, se pose en tant qu'idée régulatrice d'une pratique qui s'effectue dans la contradiction avec la dépendance naturelle;

5. le seul fondement théorique de cette liberté est une théorie de cette contradiction.

1. "Necessity and freedom - reflections on texts by Spinoza," Hessing (1977), pp. 90-107; "Liberté, démocratie et révolution chez Spinoza," *Tijdschrift voor de studie van de Verlichting*, 6de Jaargang (1978), 82-95; "Réalisme et utopie: limites des libertés politiques et perspective de libération dans la philosophie politique de Spinoza," C. De Deugd (1984), pp. 37-43; "La teoria dell'assolutismo in Hobbes e Spinoza," *Studia Spinozana* 1 (1985), 231-258.
2. (KV I,iv,5; *Oeuvres de Spinoza*, trad. et ann. par Ch. Appuhn, Paris, n. éd., 1928-29, I/75/31 - 76/11, souligné par nous) "Maar *de ware vrÿheid is alleen of niet anders als de eerste oorzaak*, de welke geenzins van iets anders geprangt of genoodzaakt word, en alleen door zÿne volmaaktheid oorzaak is van alle volmaaktheid. En dat dien volgende, zo God dit konde laten te doen, hÿ niet volmaakt zoude wezen: want het goet doen of volmaaktheid te konnen laten in het geene hÿ uÿtwerkt, en kan in hem geen plaats hebben, als door gebrek. Dat dan God alleen de enigste vrÿe oorzaak is, is niet alleen, uÿt het geene nu gezeid is, klaar, maar ook hier door, namentlÿk, dat er buÿten hem geene uÿtwendige oorzak is, die hem soude dwingen of noodzaaken; al het welk in de geschape dingen geen plaats heeft." (*Korte Verhandeling*, in Spinoza, *Korte geschriften*, bezorgd door F. Akkerman, H.G. Hubbeling, F. Mignini, M.J. Petry, N. en G. van Suchtelen, (Amsterdam:Wereldbibliotheek, 1982), 275-34/276-11).

3. E ID7; Appuhn, 1983r, I/ 21/8-10; souligné par nous. *Ea res libera dicitur, quae ex solâ suae naturae necessitate existit, et à se solâ ad agendum determinatur* (G II/46/8-9).

4. Appuhn, III/314/23 - 315/2. *Transeo igitur ad illam libertatis definitionem, quam meam esse ait; sed nescio, unde illam sumpserit. Ego eam rem liberam esse dico, quae ex solâ suae naturae necessitate existit, et agit... Ex gr. Deus, tametsi necessariò, liberè tamen existit, quia ex solâ suae naturae necessitate existit... Vides igitur me libertatem non in libero decreto; sed in liberâ necessitate ponere* (G IV/265/21-30).

5. A justification de cette affirmation, il peut suffire - je crois - de rappeler le passage suivant de la *Prefatio* aux *Principia philosophiae cartesianae*: *Animadverti tamen vel imprimis in his omnibus, nempe tàm in 1. et 2. Princip. partibus, ac fragmento tertiae, quàm in Cogitatis suis Metaphysicis Authorem nostrum meras Cartesii sententias, illarumque demonstrationes, prout in illius scriptis reperiuntur, aut quales ex fundamentis ab illo jactis per legitimam consequentiam deduci debebant, proposuisse. Cùm enim discipulum suam Cartesii Philosophiam docere promisisset, religio ipsi fuit, ab ejus sententiae latum unguem discedere, aut quid, quod ejus dogmatibus aut non responderet, aut contrarium esse, dictare. Quamobrem judicet nemo, illum hic, aut sua, aut tantùm ea, quae probat, docere. Quamvis enim quaedam vera judicet, quaedam de suis addita fateatur, multa tamen occurrunt, quae tamquam falsa rejicit, et à quibus longè diversam fovet sententiam. Cujus notae inter alia, ut ex multis unum tantùm in medium afferam, sunt, quae de voluntate habentur PP IP15S & CM II,12, quamvis satis magno molimine atque apparatu probata videantur: Neque enim eam distinctam ab Intellectu, multò minùs tali praeditam esse libertate existimat* (G I/131/23 - 132/5).

6. Appuhn, I/194/1-15. "Uÿt al dit geseÿde kan nu zeer licht begreepen worden, welke daar zÿ de menschelÿke *vryheid (*De slavernÿ van een zaake bestaat in onderworpen aan uÿtterlÿke oorzaaken; de vrÿheid daar en tegen, aan de zelve niet onderworpen, maar daar van bevrÿd te zÿn.), die ik dan aldus beschrÿf te zÿn: dat het nemelÿk is *een vaste wezentlÿkheid, de welke ons verstand door de onmiddelÿke vereeniginge met God verkrÿgt, om en in zich zelve | te konnen voort brengen denkbeelden, en buÿten zig zelve gevroghten met sÿn natuur wel overeen komende; zonder nochtans, dat noch sÿne gevroghten aan eenige uÿtterlyke oorzaaken onderworpen zÿn, om door de zelve te konnen of veranderd of verwisseld worden.* Soo blÿkt met eenen ook uÿt het geene gezeÿd is, welke daar zÿn de dingen die in onse magt en aan geen uÿterlyke oorzaaken onderworpen zÿn; gelÿk wÿ hier ook mede, en dat op een andere wÿze als te vooren, hebben bewezen de eeuwige en bestandige duuring van ons verstand; en dan eÿndelÿk, welke gevrochten het zÿn, die wÿ boven alle andere hebben te waarderen" (*op.cit.*, 382/7-26).

7. "Alle de gevrochte van het verstand, die met hem vereenigt zÿn, zÿn de aldervoortreffelÿkste, en moeten gewaardeert worden boven alle de andere" (*op.cit.*, 381/10-13).

8. II,ii,2 Appuhn, I/103/18-21. "Maar *klaare kennisse* noemen wÿ dat, 't welk niet en is door overtuÿging van reden, maar door een gevoelen en genieten van de zaake zelve, en gaat de andere verre te boven" (*op.cit.*, 298/27-299/2).

9. *Court Traité*, II, XIV,1; Appuhn, I/139/18 - 140/3. "So meen ik dan nu genoegzaam aangewezen, en betoogt te hebben, dat alleenlÿk het Waare *Geloov* of de Reeden dat geene is, het welk ons tot de kennisse van't goede en kwaade brengt. En zo wanneer wÿ zullen betoonen, dat de eerste en voornaamste oorzaak aller deser tochten is de *Kennissey*, zo zal klarlÿk blÿken, dat wÿ, ons verstand en reeden wel gebruÿkende, nooÿt in een van deze die van ons te verwerpen zÿn, zullen konnen komen te vallen. Ik zeg ons *Verstand*,

want ik niet en meÿne, dat de Reeden alleen maghtig is, ons van alle deze te bevrÿden: gelÿk wÿ dan zulks hier na op sÿn plaatze ook zullen bewÿsen" (*op.cit.*, 330/23 - 331/6).
10. *op. cit.*, II, XXII,1; Appuhn, I, 175/4-5. "de reeden geen magt heeft om ons tot onze welstand te brengen" (*op. cit.*, 364/3-5).
11. E VP36S; Appuhn II/ 225/29-30. ... *Ex his clare intelligimus, quâ in re nostra salus, seu beatitudo, seu Libertas consistit, nempe in constanti, et aeterno erga Deum Amore, sive in Amore Dei erga homines* (G II/303/2-4).
12. Appuhn II/147; souligné par nous. *In vitâ itaque apprimè utile est, intellectum, seu rationem, quantùm possumus, perficere, et in hoc uno summa hominis felicitas, seu beatitudo consistit; quippe beatitudo nihil aliud est, quàm ipsa animi acquiescentia, quae ex Dei intuitivâ cognitione oritur: at intellectum perficere nihil etiam aliud est, quàm Deum, Deique attributa, et actiones, quae ex ipsius naturae necessitate consequuntur, intelligere. Quare hominis, qui ratione ducitur, finis ultimus, hoc est, summa Cupiditas, quâ reliquas omnes moderari studet, est illa, quâ fertur ad se, resque omnes, quae sub ipsius intelligentiam cadere possunt, adaequatè concipiendum* (G II/267/2-13).
13. Appuhn II/ 133/29-30. *Illum liberum esse dixi, qui solâ ducitur ratione* (G II/261/15).
14. Appuhn I/21/10-12. *Necessaria autem, vel potiùs coacta [ea res dicitur], quae ab alio determinatur ad existendum, et operandum certâ, ac determinatâ ratione* (G II/46/10-12).
15. E IIA1; Appuhn I/117/27-30. *Hominis essentia non involvit necessariam existentiam, hoc est, ex naturae ordine, tam fieri potest, ut hic, et ille homo existat, quàm ut non existat* (G II/85/22-24).
16. E IDV; Appuhn I/19/20-21. *Per modum intelligo substantiae affectiones, sive id, quod in alio est, per quod etiam concipitur* (G II/45/20-21).
17. E IP28; Appuhn I/77/4-9. *Quodcunque singulare, sive quaevis res, quae finita est, et determinatam habet existentiam, non potest existere, nec ad operandum determinari, nisi ad existendum, et operandum determinetur ab aliâ causâ, quae etiam finita est, et determinatam habet existentiam...* (G II/69/2-6).
18. E IVPP2, 3, 4 et C; Appuhn II/17-21. *Nos eatenus patimur, quatenus Naturae sumus pars, quae per se absque aliis non potest concipi.; Vis, quâ homo in existendo perseverat, limitata est et à potentiâ causarum externarum infinitè superatur; Fieri non potest, ut homo non sit Naturae pars, et ut nullas possit pati mutationes, nisi, quae per solam suam naturam possint intelligi, quarumque adaequata sit causa.; Hinc sequitur, hominem necessariò passionibus esse semper obnoxium, communemque Naturae ordinem sequi, et eidem parere, seseque eidem, quantùm rerum natura exigit, accomodare* (G II/212/10-11, 19-20, 28-30; 213/31-33).
19. E IIPost.4; Appuhn I/157/25-26. *Corpus humanum indiget, ut conservetur, plurimis aliis corporibus, à quibus continuò quasi regeneratur* (G II/102/29-31).
20. E IVApp§32; Appuhn II/165/15-26. *Sed humana potentia admodùm limitata est, et à potentiâ causarum externarum infinitè superatur; atque adeò potestatem absolutam non habemus, res, quae extra nos sunt, ad nostrum usum aptandi. Attamen ea, quae nobis eveniunt contra id, quod nostrae utilitatis ratio postulat, aequo animo feremus, si conscii simus nos functos nostro ufficio fuisse, et potentiam, quam habemus, non potuisse se eò usque extendere, ut eadem vitare possemus, nosque partem totius naturae esse, cujus ordinem sequimur. Quod si clarè, et distinctè intelligamus, pars illa nostri, quae intelligentiâ definitur, hoc est, pars melior nostri in eo planè acquiescet, et in eâ acquiescentiâ perseverare conabitur...* (G II/276/5-17).

21. Appuhn II/175/2-5. *Prout cogitationes, rerumque ideae ordinantur, et concatenantur in Mente, ità corporis affectiones, seu rerum imagines ad amussim ordinantur, et concatenantur in Corpore* (G II/281/10-12).

22. E VP39; Appuhn II/231/9-10. *Qui Corpus ad plurima aptum habet, is Mentem habet, cujus maxima pars est aeterna* (G II/304/32-33).

23. Le terme *affection* employé par Ch. Appuhn dans sa traduction de l'*Ethique* a été remplacé par *affect*, plus à même de rendre compte de l'*affectus* latin.

24. E VP39D; Appuhn, *ibid./231/12-24*. *Qui Corpus ad plurima agendum aptum habet, is minimè affectibus, qui mali sunt, conflictatur (per Prop.38 p.4.), hoc est (per Prop.30 p.4.), affectibus, qui naturae nostrae sunt contrarii, atque adeò (per Prop.10 hujus) potestatem habet ordinandi, et concatenandi Corporis affectiones secundùm ordinem ad intellectum, et consequenter efficiendi (per Prop.14 hujus), ut omnes Corporis affectiones ad Dei ideam referantur, ex quò fiet (per Prop.15 hujus), ut erga Deum afficiatur Amore, qui (per Prop.16 hujus) Mentis maximam partem occupare, sive constituere debet, ac proinde (per Prop.33 hujus) Mentem habet, cujus maxima pars est aeterna* (G II/305/2-12).

25. E VP2; Appuhn II/175/19-23. *Si animi commotionem, seu affectum à causae externae cogitatione amoveamus, et aliis jungamus cogitationibus, tum Amor, seu Odium erga causam externam, ut et animi fluctuationes, quae ex his affectibus oriuntur, destruentur* (G II/281/23-26).

26. Appuhn III/317/19-24. *Quòd porrò statuit: quòd si à causis externis cogeremur, virtutis habitum acquirere possit nemo; Nescio, quis ipsi dixerit, non posse ex fatali necessitate; sed tantummodò ex libero Mentis decreto, fieri, ut firmato, et constanti simus animo* (G IV/267/32-35).

27. E VP10S; Appuhn II/189/11 - 193/24. *Hâc potestate rectè ordinandi, et concatenandi Corporis affectiones efficere possumus, ut non facilè malis affectibus afficiamur. Nam (per Prop.7 hujus) major vis requiritur ad Affectûs, secundùm ordinem ad intellectum ordinatos, et concatenatos coërcendum, quàm incertos, et vagos. Optimum igitur, quod efficere possumus, quamdiu nostrorum affectuum perfectam cognitionem non habemus, est rectam vivendi rationem, seu certa vitae dogmata concipere, eaque memoriae mandare, et rebus particularibus, in vitâ frequenter obviis, continuò applicare... et propterea [si etiam in promptu habuerimus] quòd ex rectâ vivendi ratione summa animi acquiescentia oriatur (per Prop. 52, p. 4), et quòd homines, ut reliqua, ex naturae necessitate agant... Qui itaque suos affectûs, et appetitûs ex solo Libertatis amore moderari studet, is, quantùm potest, nitetur, virtutes earumque causas noscere, et animum gaudio, quod ex earum verâ cognitione oritur, implere... Atque haec qui diligenter observabit (neque enim difficilia sunt), et exercebit, nae ille brevi temporis spatio actiones suas ex rationis imperio plerumque dirigere poterit"* (G II/287/20-289/13).

28. E VP25; Appuhn II/211/14-15. *Summum Mentis conatus, summaque virtus est res intelligere tertio cognitionis genere* (G II/296/22-23).

29. E VP27; Appuhn II/213/9-10. *Ex hôc tertio cognitionis genere summa, quae dari potest, Mentis acquiescentia oritur* (G II/297/12-13).

30. E VP20S; Appuhn II/203/26-205/18. *Mentis potentia solâ cognitione definitur; impotentia autem, seu passio à solâ cognitionis privatione, hoc est, ab eo, per quod ideae dicuntur inadaequatae, aestimatur; ex quo sequitur, Mentem illam maximè pati, cujus maximam partem ideae inadaequatae constituunt, ità ut magis per id, quod patitur, quàm per id, quod agit, dignoscatur; et illam contrà maximè agere, cujus maximam partem ideae adaequatae constituunt, ità ut, quamvis huic tot inadaequate ideae, quàm illi insint, magis tamen per illas,*

quae humanae virtuti tribuuntur, quàm per has, quae humanam impotentiam arguunt, dignoscatur... Ex his itaque facilè concipimus, quid clara, et distincta cognitio, et praecipuè tertium illud cognitionis genus (de quo vide Schol.Prop.47 p.2.), cujus fundamentum est ipsa Dei cognitio, in affectûs potest, quos nempe quatenus passiones sunt, si non absolutè tollit (vide Prop. 3 cum Schol.Prop. 4 hujus), saltem efficit, ut minimam Mentis partem constituant (vide Prop. 14 hujus)... (G II/293/25 - 294/11).

LE PROBLÈME DE L'ÉVOLUTION DE SPINOZA DU *TRAITÉ THÉOLOGICO-POLITIQUE* AU *TRAITÉ POLITIQUE*

ALEXANDRE MATHERON
Ecole Normale Supérieure
de Saint-Cloud

Je voudrais simplement ici apporter quelques compléments à l'interprétation que j'avais donnée jadis, dans *Individu et communauté chez Spinoza* (Matheron (1969), pp. 307-330) d'un fait qui, en un sens, n'est contesté par personne: Spinoza, dans le TTP, rend compte de la genèse de l'Etat en termes contractualistes, alors que, dans le *Traité politique,* il cesse de recourir au langage du contrat social. Cette évolution est-elle réelle ou apparente? A mon avis, elle est réelle: j'ai soutenu jadis, et je pense encore, que le langage du TTP doit être pris au sérieux et que sa disparition dans le TP correspond vraiment à l'émergence d'une doctrine nouvelle; j'ai caractérisé, et je caractérise encore, cette doctrine nouvelle comme consistant en une explication non-contractualiste de la genèse de l'Etat par le seul jeu, anarchique et aveugle, des rapports de forces tels qu'ils fonctionneraient spontanément à l'état de nature selon le mécanisme de l'imitation des sentiments. Mais l'on m'a fait des objections, et je voudrais y répondre.

Il faut tout d'abord éliminer les faux problèmes. Spinoza a toujours pensé que l'existence et la légitimité de la société politique découlent, en définitive, du consentement des sujets; si l'on veut appeler cela "contrat," il a donc toujours été contractualiste; mais il s'agit de savoir *comment* ce consentement est donné. De même, Spinoza a toujours pensé que le droit était identique à la puissance; si l'on veut appeler "contractualisme" la doctrine selon laquelle la conclusion d'une convention engendrerait par elle-même, à elle seule, indépendamment de toute fluctuation ultérieure des rapports de forces, une obligation irréversible, il n'a donc jamais été contractualiste; mais il s'agit de savoir *comment* se crée la puissance collective unifiée qui définit le droit du souverain. Ce que l'on peut appeler le contractualisme au moins apparent du TTP concerne donc, non pas le fondement de la légitimité de l'Etat, mais son mode de production: l'Etat, dans cet ouvrage, semble bien naître d'une décision collective, délibérée et concertée, qui romprait , comme chez Hobbes, avec la dynamique de l'état de nature pour créer de toutes pièces un rapport de forces nouveau. Le non-contractualisme que j'ai cru pouvoir attribuer au TP consiste au contraire à affirmer que la dynamique même de l'état de nature, grâce à l'imitation des sentiments, engendrerait d'elle-même, sans concertation aucune, la société politique. Et le problème est de savoir si Spinoza a réellement évolué de la première de ces deux positions à la seconde.

On peut donc contester la thèse de l'évolution de Spinoza de deux façons: ou bien en montrant qu'il s'en est tenu jusqu'à la fin à la première position, ou bien en montrant qu'il avait adhéré dès le début à la seconde.

I

La première façon de réfuter la thèse de l'évolution de Spinoza consiste à essayer de montrer que, dans le *Traité politique* lui-même, Spinoza, malgré les apparences, s'en tient encore au point de vue contractualiste du TTP. On recourt pour cela, soit à une argumentation positive, soit, en dernier ressort, à une argumentation négative. Mais ni l'une ni l'autre, à mon avis, n'est satisfaisante.

L'argumentation positive revient à dire que, si l'on examine attentivement les textes, on trouve à plusieurs reprises dans le TP l'affirmation *explicite*, quoique très discrète, d'une origine contractuelle de l'Etat. On ne s'interroge d'ailleurs pas sur les raisons d'une telle discrétion. Mais en réalité, les textes que l'on allègue, et qui sont de trois sortes, ne prouvent pas du tout ce que l'on veut leur faire prouver.

1 - On invoque le plus souvent le paragraphe 6 du chapitre IV, qui est le seul paragraphe de tout le TP où soit employé le mot *contractus*: "Le contrat, c'est-à-dire les lois par lesquelles la multitude transfère son droit à une assemblée ou à un homme, etc..." Mais si la multitude transfère *son droit*, au singulier (*suum jus*), c'est qu'il y a déjà *un* droit de la multitude en tant qu'entité collective, et non pas simplement une juxtaposition de droits naturels individuels. Et puisque le droit est identique à la puissance, ce droit de la multitude n'est pas autre chose que la puissance de cette même multitude. Or, nous le savons par le paragraphe 17 du chapitre II, le droit défini par la puissance de la multitude, *c'est*, très exactement, la souveraineté, ou l'Etat (*imperium*). Donc, manifestement, le contrat dont il est ici question n'est pas celui par lequel des individus vivant à l'état de nature conviendraient ensemble de sortir de cet état pour se constituer en société politique en se donnant un souverain: il y a *déjà*, par hypothèse, un souverain, à savoir la multitude elle-même, et par conséquent aussi un Etat démocratique. En fait, dans ce passage, Spinoza discute tout simplement un cas très classique et bien connu, que Grotius (à tort, selon lui) avait allégué pour justifier sa théorie d'un partage possible de la souveraineté: celui où un peuple souverain transfère à une assemblée aristocratique ou à un roi la souveraineté qu'il exerçait collectivement sur chacun de ses propres membres, mais après avoir établi au préalable un certain nombre de lois fondamentales que ce roi ou ce conseil s'engage pour sa part à respecter (d'où l'expression "*contractus, seu leges...*"). Le mot *contractus* renvoie donc ici, non pas à la genèse de la société politique en tant que telle, mais à l'un des modes de transformation possibles d'un Etat démocratique en un Etat non-démocratique. Et il ne figure nulle part ailleurs dans le TP. Quant au verbe *contrahere*, il y figure six fois (deux fois dans III, 14; deux fois dans III, 15; III, 6; VI, 33) mais il s'y applique uniquement à la conclusion des traités de paix entre Etats.

2 - On peut faire exactement la même remarque à propos de l'expression "transfert de droit," qui, elle aussi, est assez souvent invoquée en faveur de l'interprétation contractualiste. Remarquons d'ailleurs que, même si Spinoza l'appliquait vraiment à la genèse de la société politique en tant que telle, cela

ne prouverait encore rien: "transfert de droit" signifie "transfert de puissance," c'est-à-dire instauration d'un rapport de forces nouveau et relativement irréversible, et il n'est nullement nécessaire (bien que ce ne soit pas non plus impossible) qu'une telle instauration se fasse par contrat. Mais *en fait*, dans le TP, Spinoza n'applique *jamais* cette expression à la genèse de la société politique en tant que telle: sans doute pour éviter toute équivoque, il ne dit *jamais* (alors qu'il aurait très bien pu le dire, compte tenu de son langage) que les individus instituent l'Etat en transférant leurs droits naturels à un souverain. Le verbe *transférer*, qui figure 22 fois dans le TP, y désigne un transfert de souveraineté qui s'effectue d'un peuple (déjà constitué comme peuple) à une assemblée aristocratique ou à un roi (IV, 6, VII, 5, VIII, 3), d'un peuple à un roi (VII, 5), d'un peuple à un chef militaire qu'il autorise à recruter des mercenaires (VII, 17), d'un peuple à une assemblée aristocratique (deux fois dans VIII, 3), d'un peuple ou d'une assemblée aristocratique à un roi (VI, 8, VI, 14, VII, 2, VII, 5, VII, 23), d'une assemblée aristocratique à quelqu'un d'autre qu'elle (VIII, 17), d'une assemblée aristocratique à un monarque (VII, 9), ou enfin d'un monarque à un autre (cinq fois dans VII, 14; VII, 23); par ailleurs, il désigne une fois un transfert de droit effectué par l'Etat au profit d'un particulier (III, 3), et il apparaît une autre fois pour indiquer que le droit d'honorer Dieu est intransférable (VII, 26). Il n'est donc jamais possible de l'interpréter comme renvoyant à un éventuel "contrat social."

3 - Le dernier refuge de l'interprétation contractualiste du TP, c'est l'emploi du verbe *convenire* dans le paragraphe 13 du chapitre II: "*si duo simul conveniant, et vires jungant, etc...*" Ce passage, cette fois, concerne bien la genèse de la société politique. Et *convenire* entre autre sens, peut avoir celui de "conclure une convention." Dans ces conditions, au lieu de traduire ce début de phrase, comme on le fait habituellement, par "si deux individus s'accordent ensemble et joignent leurs forces" (en donnant un sens général et non-spécifiquement juridique au verbe "s'accorder"), on pourrait être tenté de le traduire par: "si deux individus *conviennent ensemble* de joindre leurs forces," au sens juridique strict qu'a le verbe *convenir* en français du 17ème siècle. Mais, s'il est vrai que *convenir* peut avoir ce dernier sens, encore faudrait-il savoir s'il l'a effectivement *dans le langage de Spinoza*; sinon, on commettrait une pétition de principe en prouvant le contractualisme du TP à partir d'une traduction qui ne s'imposerait qu'à la condition de l'avoir préalablement admis. Or, d'une part, lorsque Spinoza parle expressément du contrat social en termes juridiques, c'est-à-dire au chapitre XVI du TTP, il n'emploie pas *convenire*, mais *pacisci* (G III/191/28): mot qui ne figure nulle part dans le TP, pas plus d'ailleurs que le mot *pactum*. De autre part, dans le TP lui-même (où "contracter", on l'a vu, se dit habituellement *contrahere*), *aucune* des 19 autres occurrences de *convenire* n'a de sens spécifiquement juridique. Ce verbe, en dehors du passage litigieux (II, 13), signifie "se réunir en un même lieu" (IX, 3), "être conforme à..." (I, 4, VI, 2, VIII, 5, VIII, 7; deux fois dans VIII, 37; X, 1, X, 9), voter de la même façon (VIII, 25, IX, 6), s'entendre pour voter de la même façon (VI, 25), s'entendre entre sujets sur les conditions à imposer au roi que l'on projette d'élire (VII, 30), s'entendre entre alliés sur l'interprétation des clauses d'un

traité déjà conclu (III, 15), s'entendre pour commettre un crime (VII, 14, X, 2), vivre dans la concorde dans une société politique déjà constituée (II, 15, VII, 5). Enfin, dans le seul autre passage (en dehors de II, 13) où *convenire* soit utilisé pour rendre compte de la genèse de l'Etat, c'est-à-dire au paragraphe 1 du chapitre VI (*multitudinem... naturaliter convenire, et una veluti mente duci velle*), l'interprétation contractualiste de ce verbe est formellement exclue par l'adjonction de l'adverbe *naturaliter*: si les hommes "s'accordent naturellement" pour vivre en société politique, cela veut dire que, contrairement à ce que pensait Hobbes, ils n'ont pas besoin de l'artifice d'une convention pour parvenir à ce résultat.

L' argumentation positive ne tient donc pas: Spinoza, dans le TP, *ne dit nulle part* que la société politique est d'origine contractuelle; et le passage que je viens de citer tend déjà à suggérer le contraire. L'impression se renforce si l'on confronte ce passage avec la fin du même paragraphe 1 du chapitre VI, où Spinoza nous dit que "les hommes, par nature (*natura*), aspirent à la société civile." Elle se renforce davantage encore si l'on tient compte de deux des trois autres occurences de *naturaliter* dans le TP. "La société civile, déclare Spinoza, s'institue naturellement" (*naturaliter instituitur*) (III, 6). Et le paragraphe 25 du chapitre VII est encore plus précis: après avoir dit qu'à la mort d'un roi, si le peuple n'a établi aucune règle de succession au moment où il s'est donné une Monarchie, on retourne à l'état de nature, Spinoza ajoute: "et en conséquence, la souveraineté retourne naturellement à la multitude" (*et consequenter summa potestas ad multitudinem naturaliter redit*). Spinoza ne veut évidemment pas dire que l'état de nature, où il n'y a pas de *summa potestas,* est identique à une souveraineté populaire: ce qu'il veut dire, c'est que, lorsqu'un groupe d'hommes est retourné à l'état de nature, il en sort naturellement, spontanément, quasi-automatiquement, pour instaurer aussitôt (toutes choses égales d'ailleurs) une souveraineté démocratique, même si cette instauration reste informelle.

Cependant, objectera-t-on, cela ne prouve rien: pour Spinoza, tout est naturel, et par conséquent aussi les contrats; ne pourrait-on pas alors penser que *naturaliter convenire* signifie "conclure une convention qui, comme toutes choses dans la nature, est comprise dans le déterminisme universel"? Même si cela semble un peu bizarre, Spinoza, en tout cas, ne dit pas expressément le contraire. Et c'est ici qu'intervient l'argumentation négative en faveur du contractualisme du TP.

II

Cette argumentation négative revient à dire qu'il n'existe, dans le TP, *aucun* texte où soit indiqué sans ambiguïté le mode de production exact de la société politique en tant que telle, et que par conséquent l'explication par l'imitation des sentiments ne repose sur rien. D'où l'on conclut que, puisque Spinoza s'est déjà exprimé sur ce sujet et n'a entre-temps rien démenti, rien ne permet de supposer qu'il ait modifié ou dépassé, au moment où il écrit le TP, l'explication contractualiste proposée au chapitre XVI du TTP.

Je dois reconnaître avoir moi-même donné prise à cette objection dans *Individu et communauté chez Spinoza,* où je ne m'étais guère soucié de confirmer mon interprétation par des textes du TP: j'avais constaté dans ce Traité l'existence d'une lacune, et le recours au livre III de l'*Ethique* me semblait à la fois nécessaire et suffisant pour la combler (ce qui, du reste, est vrai *en soi*). Mais en réalité, *il y a bien,* dans le TP, des textes qui, *pris ensemble,* confirment mon interprétation tout en la simplifiant quelque peu. Ce qui est vrai, c'est qu'ils ne figurent pas dans le chapitre II, où ils auraient dû normalement trouver leur place: cela pose un problème que j'évoquerai en conclusion. Mais on les trouve *avant* et *après* le chapitre II. Et de leur confrontation, ainsi que de leur mise en rapport avec l'*Ethique,* on peut dégager trois sortes de considérations.

1 - Le passage déjà cité du paragraphe 1 du chapitre VI n'a pas seulement, en réalité, la signification négative à laquelle j'ai déjà fait allusion (non-nécessité d'un contrat). L'expression *naturaliter convenire,* si nous considérons l'usage qui en est fait par ailleurs dans l'*Ethique,* nous donne déjà, *par elle-même,* une indication positive sur la manière dont peut effectivement s'opérer une genèse non-contractuelle de l'Etat. Et, du même coup, l'on peut en dire autant des autres occurences déjà citées de *naturaliter* (III, 6, VII, 25) et de l'ablatif *natura* (VI,1). Dans le livre IV de l'*Ethique,* en effet, les propositions 32-34 nous apprennent que, dans la mesure où les hommes sont soumis aux passions, ils ne s'accordent pas nécessairement par nature et peuvent même s'opposer les uns aux autres; et l'un des exemples donnés dans la démonstration de la proposition 34 est celui de l'envie, à propos duquel Spinoza renvoie à E IIIP32: Pierre et Paul entreront en conflit, nous dit-il, si Pierre jouit d'une chose qu'un seul peut posséder et si Paul, par imitation de ses sentiments, aime à son tour cette chose et désire s'en emparer. Mais, dans le scolie qui suit, Spinoza précise: si Pierre et Paul se font du mal l'un à l'autre, ce n'est pas "en tant qu'ils s'accordent par nature *(quatenus natura conveniunt),* c'est-à-dire en tant qu'ils aiment les mêmes choses"; car, dans cette mesure, leurs amours respectifs, c'est-à-dire leurs joies respectives, se renforcent mutuellement par le mécanisme de l'imitation. S'ils se nuisent l'un à l'autre, ajoute Spinoza, c'est parce qu'ils sont en même temps supposés "diverger par nature" *(natura discrepare):* parce que le caractère monopolistique de la chose aimée, qui fait obstacle au sentiment de joie imité par Paul, transforme finalement l'imitation affective en son contraire en amenant Paul à s'attrister d'être privé de ce que Pierre se réjouit d'avoir. Donc, "l'accord naturel" dont il est ici question, c'est *l'imitation des sentiments* dans tous les cas, et dans les seuls cas, où rien n'empêche les sentiments imités de produire jusqu'au bout et sans contradiction tous leurs effets dans l'esprit de ceux qui les imitent. Et si l'on admet que le *naturaliter convenire* du TP a le même sens que le *natura convenire* de l'*Ethique* (ce qui est probable, puisque, dans le même paragraphe 1 du chapitre VI, Spinoza emploie *aussi* l'ablatif *natura* comme synonyme de *naturaliter),* il faut bien en conclure que, sous une forme ou sous une autre, le même mécanisme doit jouer dans la formation de l'Etat. Mais sous quelle forme? D'autres textes du TP permettent de le préciser.

2 - Nous trouvons en effet, au paragraphe 5 du chapitre I, un résumé très exact et très complet de toute la seconde moitié du livre III de l'*Ethique*, c'est-à-dire de la théorie des *passions interhumaines*, qui se déduit elle-même tout entière de la proposition 27, consacrée, précisément, à l'imitation des sentiments. Non seulement Spinoza s'y réfère expressément à l'*Ethique*, mais il en reprend telles quelles un certain nombre de formulations. Il indique d'abord, en reprenant les termes mêmes du scolie de la proposition 32, que c'est le même mécanisme d'imitation qui est à l'origine de la *pitié* (E IIIP27S) et de l'*envie* (E IIIP32). Il explique par ailleurs, à peu près dans les mêmes termes que dans l'*Ethique* (E IIIP31C&S), ce qu'est *l'ambition de domination,* qui est en son fond *intolérance:* vouloir dominer autrui, c'est essentiellement vouloir le contraindre à adopter nos propres valeurs, à aimer ce que nous aimons et à haïr ce que nous haïssons; mais l'emploi du verbe *glorietur* rappelle en même temps que cette intolérance a son origine dans *l'ambition de gloire* (E IIIPP29,30): si nous voulons convenir autrui à nos valeurs, c'est pour pouvoir faire son bonheur et nous réjouir de le réjouir (c'est-à-dire nous glorifier) sans être obligés pour cela de lui sacrifier nos propres désirs; ce que nous recherchons dans la lutte pour le pouvoir (et Spinoza, ici, reprend les termes mêmes d'E IV58S), c'est donc moins un véritable avantage personnel que la joie d'avoir mérité les éloges de nos semblables en éliminant l'adversaire qui, selon nous, tentait de les fourdoyer en leur imposant de fausses valeurs. Enfin, entre ces deux explications, l'allusion au conflit entre *miséricorde* et *vengeance* (avec prédominance de cette dernière) évoque brièvement les conséquences de ces quatre sentiments fondamentaux (E IIIPP33-44): alternance perpétuelle entre des cycles de réciprocité négative, où la haine appelle la haine, et des cycles de réciprocité positive qui s'amorcent toutefois plus difficilement. Donc, on le voit, tout est bien là.

Or, après ce résumé magistral, Spinoza nous dit, au paragraphe 7 de ce même chapitre I, que les causes et les fondements naturels de l'Etat doivent se déduire, non des enseignements de la raison, mais de la nature ou condition humaine commune - c'est-à-dire, très évidemment, de la nature ou condition des hommes soumis aux passions. Mais de quelles passions peut-il s'agir, sinon, très précisément, de celles dont il vient d'être question au paragraphe 5? Et de fait, ce paragraphe 5 permet déjà d'entrevoir la façon dont les choses se passent. De la pitié à l'envie, de l'ambition de gloire à l'ambition de domination, et inversement, le passage, dans les deux sens, est à la fois nécessaire et incessant. La pitié et l'ambition de gloire sont à l'origine de la sociabilité, l'ambition de domination et l'envie sont à l'origine de l'insociabilité, et ces deux groupes de passions sont inséparables. On comprend donc que les passions interhumaines, en raison même de la contradiction qui les traverse, puissent à la fois nous rendre l'état de nature insupportable et nous faire sortir spontanément de cet état. Comment cela exactement? Je l'avais expliqué autrefois par une inter-action de calculs individuels: si chacun forme le projet global d'utiliser à son profit la sociabilité naturelle de tous les autres pour se défendre contre l'insociabilité naturelle de chacun d'eux, la résultante de tous ces projets finira, après quelques tâtonnements, par engendrer, sans contrat aucun, un pouvoir collectif unifié. C'est là, je le pense encore, un processus *possible.* Mais il y a, dans le TP, un autre texte qui permet de tout expliquer plus simplement encore, sans faire appel au calcul, en recourant uniquement à l'imitation des sentiments. Mais il faut pour cela faire intervenir un sentiment supplémentaire qui n'est pas mentionné au chapitre I.

3 - Revenons en effet au paragraphe 1 du chapitre VI. Spinoza y déclare que, si les hommes s'accordent naturellement pour vivre en société politique, ce n'est pas sous la conduite de la raison, mais sous l'influence d'une passion commune: un espoir commun, une crainte commune, le désir de venger un dommage subi en commun; et tous les hommes, ajoute-t-il, craignent effectivement la solitude, qui leur ôte les moyens de se défendre et de se procurer les choses nécessaires à la vie. Or, pour justifier cette affirmation, *Spinoza renvoie au paragraphe 9 du chapitre III*, qui concerne, non pas la genèse de l'Etat, mais *les causes de sa dissolution:* l'Etat, est-il dit dans ce paragraphe 9, a d'autant moins de droit sur ses sujets qu'un plus grand nombre d'entre eux *s'indignent* de ses procédés et se coalisent par là-même contre lui. Et à la fin du paragraphe 4 du chapitre IV, le lien entre crainte commune et indignation est précisé: le souverain, nous dit Spinoza, perd sa souveraineté lorsque, par suite de ses exactions répétées (assassinats, spoliations, viols, etc.), la crainte qu'il inspirait à tous ses sujets *se change en indignation,* transformant ainsi l'état civil en état de guerre. L'indignation, nous le savons, est encore une autre forme d'imitation affective: c'est *la haine que nous éprouvons pour celui qui fait du mal à un être semblable à nous* (E IIIP27C1); et nous l'éprouvons par imitation des sentiments de la victime, avec une intensité d'autant plus grande que cette victime nous ressemble davantage. On comprend alors comment son intervention est nécessaire pour rendre possible une révolution. S'il y avait simplement crainte commune, c'est-à-dire si chacun, pour son compte personnel, craignait solitairement le tyran sans penser aux maux d'autrui (cf. la solitude sous le régime turc évoquée par Spinoza en VI, 4), rien ne se passerait: la haine envers le tyran resterait épisodique, car il ne tyrannise pas à chaque instant *chacun* de ses sujets; et, de toute façon, personne ne verrait le moyen de mettre fin à cette situation. Mais l'apparition de l'indignation vient tout changer: comme le tyran tyrannise toujours *quelqu'un* à n'importe quel instant, l'indignation que nous en éprouvons nous fait ressentir *en permanence* le caractère intolérable de son gouvernement; et l'indignation qu'éprouvent nos semblables contre le mal que nous fait le tyran, s'ils la manifestent quelque peu, nous apprend que *nous ne sommes pas seuls* en face de lui et qu'il est possible de nous unir pour le renverser. Or, si nous prenons au sérieux la référence à III, 9 donnée par Spinoza en VI, 1, il faut admettre que *l'indignation engendre l'Etat de la même façon, exactement, qu'elle cause les révolutions.* Et pour le comprendre, il suffit de remplacer, dans ce que nous venons de dire, la solitude initiale de chacun face au tyran par la solitude de l'état de nature, le tyran par l'ensemble de tous les individus en tant qu'agresseurs, et les sujets par l'ensemble de tous les individus considérés en tant que victimes.

Supposons en effet qu'un certain nombre d'individus juxtaposés, sans aucune expérience de la société politique, vivent à l'état de nature dans une région déterminée. Si l'un d'entre eux éprouve des difficultés à trouver sa subsistance, un ou plusieurs autres, par pitié ou ambition de gloire, lui viendront en aide; puis, si leur aide est efficace, leur pitié et leur ambition de gloire se changeront en ambition de domination et en envie, et ils commenceront à l'agresser; mais un certain nombre d'autres, jusque là témoins passifs, s'indigneront du mal qui lui est fait et seront disposé à le défendre. Et cela se produira plusieurs fois. Mais lui-même, pour les mêmes raisons, se trouvera à plusieurs reprises en position d'agresseur et suscitera à chaque fois l'indignation de plusieurs autres. Et lui-même, pour la même raison, s'indignera contre chaque agression dont il aura été témoin. Si bien qu'au bout d'un temps peut-être assez court, comme chacun est dans le même cas, chacun aura successive-ment provoqué l'indignation de chacun et considérera donc chacun comme un agresseur potentiel, chacun aura successivement bénéficié de l'indignation de chacun et considérera donc chacun comme un allié potentiel, et chacun, se trouvant sans cesse en état d'indignation contre quelqu'un, jugera cette situation intolérable et sera disposé en permanence à aider quiconque se fera agresser. Dès lors, chaque fois que deux individus entreront en conflit, chacun d'eux appellera à l'aide tous les autres; et chacun des autres, répondant à l'appel et imitant les sentiments de celui des deux adversaires qui sera *le plus semblable à lui,* s'indignera et entrera en lutte contre celui qui lui ressemblera le moins: contre celui dont les valeurs divergeront le plus d'avec les siennes, ou qui possédera *(de facto)* le plus de choses dont lui-même sera privé. Celui qui s'écartera le plus de la norme majoritaire sera donc écrasé et dissuadé de recommencer; ou, s'il ne l'est pas tout de suite, il le sera au terme du prochain conflit, car s'il récidive, ceux qui l'auront vaincu une première fois verront certainement grossir leurs rangs. Dans ces conditions, après un certain nombre de répétitions, un consensus finira par se dégager pour imposer des normes communes, pour réprimer massivement ceux qui les violeront et protéger massivement ceux qui les respecteront: il existera une *puissance collective de la multitude* qui assurera la sécurité des non-déviants; et par conséquent, par définition (Cf. II, 17), nous aurons, ne serait-ce que de façon informelle, une souveraineté et un Etat (un *imperium*). Après quoi, si des problèmes nouveaux surgissent, la situation pourra s'institutionnaliser sous une forme ou sous une autre.

On voit donc que, si nous nous en tenons strictement aux textes du TP, en admettant simplement que les mots qui y désignent des passions ont le même sens que dans l'*Ethique*, nous y trouvons tout ce qu'il nous faut pour rendre compte d'une genèse non-contractuelle de l'Etat: si la pitié et l'ambition de gloire sont à la racine de la sociabilité, si l'ambition de domination et l'envie sont à la racine de l'insociabilité, l'indignation (à défaut d'autre chose) suffit, à elle seule, à faire apparaître une force commune qui réprime l'insociabilité et protège la sociabilité. Mais alors, dira-t-on, si tout cela se déduit aussi directement du livre III de l'*Ethique*, comment se fait-il que Spinoza n'y ait pas immédiatement pensé? Est-il même vraisemblable qu'il n'y ait pas immédiate-ment pensé? Ne faudrait-il pas plutôt admettre que, même s'il avait de bonnes raisons de n'en rien dire, il avait déjà cette explication présente à l'esprit au moment où il écrivait le TP?

III

Nous arrivons alors à la seconde manière de contester la thèse de l'évolution de Spinoza. Elle consiste à dire que, dès l'époque du TTP, *Spinoza était* en possession de la doctrine du TP. L'argumentation, ici, ne peut pas être positive: les textes qui justifient l'explication par l'imitation des sentiments, déjà peu nombreux dans le TP, sont totalement absents du TTP. Mais il y a une argumentation négative, et elle est même très solide. Elle revient à affirmer que, dans la mesure où *il n'y a pas de contradiction entre le TTP et le TP,* rien ne prouve que le contractualisme du premier de ces deux ouvrages n'est pas simplement une version exotérique, ou encore une application particulière, du non-contractualisme du second.

Or, *il est vrai* qu'il n'y a pas de contradiction entre le TTP et le TP; je l'ai d'ailleurs toujours pensé, et même écrit (*Ibid.*, pp. 328-29). *Il est vrai* que la doctrine du TTP peut être considérée, d'une certaine façon, comme une version exotérique de celle du TP: lorsqu'on s'adresse, comme le fait Spinoza, à des lecteurs formés à l'école de Grotius et de Hobbes, on peut fort bien, pour s'adapter à leur langage, appeler "contrat" le consensus par lequel s'engendre et se réengendre l'Etat. *Il est vrai aussi* que, d'une autre façon, le contractualisme du TTP peut être considéré comme un cas particulier du non-contractualisme du TP. L'explication du TP, telle que j'ai cru pouvoir la restituer ici, vaut pour le cas le plus général, pour celui qui exige le minimum d'hypothèses: les individus qu'elle met en présence sont considérés abstraction faite de tout usage (même instrumental) de leur raison, abstraction faite de toute expérience antérieure de la vie en société politique, abstraction faite, à la limite, de tout souvenir; et elle revient à montrer que, même dans ce cas extrême, la société politique naîtra *de toute façon* du seul jeu de leurs passions. Mais il est évident que, si l'on réintroduit ce que l'on avait négligé par abstraction, les choses iront plus vite: plus les individus en présence seront capables, au début du processus, d'en anticiper les résultats, plus les étapes seront brûlées et les tâtonnements évités. A la limite, s'ils en anticipent avec précision le résultat final, c'est-à-dire la société politique elle-même, ils s'entendront sans doute, par quelque chose de plus ou moins analogue à un contrat, pour la créer ou la recréer immédiatement; et ce sera le cas, comme ce l'est dans la réalité, s'ils ont eux-mêmes *déjà vécu* en société politique et s'en souviennent - le processus se rapprochant d'autant plus du pur modèle contractuel qu'ils auront davantage appris à se servir de leur raison pour mieux satisfaire leurs passions (les mêmes, bien entendu). Je suis donc entièrement d'accord avec la démonstration de non-contradiction donnée par Douglas Den Uyl dans *Power, State and Freedom* (Den Uyl (1983), ch. III): mon interprétation fondée sur le TP convient pour un état de nature "absolu," qui n'aurait été précédé par rien, et elle explique ontologiquement *pourquoi*, d'une façon générale, il y a société politique; l'interprétation contractualiste (plus ou moins pure) convient pour un état de nature "intermédiaire," résultant de la décomposition d'une société politique donnée, et elle explique (plus ou moins approximativement) *comment*, historiquement, l'on passe d'une forme d'Etat à une autre.

Mais que prouve exactement cette démonstration? Ce qu'elle établit en toute rigueur, c'est que Spinoza, à l'époque de la rédaction du TP, interprétait rétrospectivement l'exposé du chapitre XVI du TTP comme une application particulière, formulée d'ailleurs en un langage un peu *ad hominem*, de la théorie plus générale dont il était alors en possession. Mais peut-on en conclure qu'il l'interprétait déjà de cette façon *au moment même où il rédigeait le TTP?* Aucun texte ne le suggère. Spinoza déclare bien, en ce chapitre XVI, que le transfert de puissance par lequel se constitue l'Etat peut s'opérer de deux façons; mais la différence qu'il indique *(vel vi, vel sponte,* G III/193/11) ne va pas au delà de celle qui existe entre le Commonwealth d'acquisition de Hobbes et son Commonwealth d'institution, tous deux contractuels. N'est-il donc pas vraisemblable de supposer, en l'absence d'indication contraire, que Spinoza, à cette époque, n'était pas encore parvenu à dépasser l'horizon du contractualisme en général?

Il faudrait, dira-t-on, définir un test qui puisse permettre d'en décider positivement. Or, ce test a été trouvé, et il me semble efficace. Il a été trouvé par un jeune chercheur français, Christian Lazzeri, qui l'a exposé dans une conférence encore inédite prononcée en décembre 1985 à Paris.[1] L'hypothèse de Lazzeri est la suivante: Spinoza, à l'époque du TTP, ne pouvait pas encore dépasser le point de vue contractualiste parce qu'il n'en avait pas encore les moyens théoriques; et il ne les avait pas parce que, au stade où il en était alors de la rédaction de l'*Ethique, il n'avait pas encore élaboré sa théorie de l'imitation des sentiments* telle qu'elle devait être finalement exposé au livre III à partir de la proposition 27. Ce qui le prouve, déclare Lazzeri, c'est que, dans un cas au moins, le texte même du TTP témoigne assez précisément de cette non-élaboration. L'exemple invoqué me paraît assez convaincant, et je crois même que l'on peut en donner encore un autre.

1 - Le texte sur lequel s'appuie Lazzeri se trouve dans le troisième alinéa du chapitre XVII du TTP (G III/203/21-26). Ce passage, en un sens, est l'homologue du paragraphe 5 du chapitre I du TP: on y trouve aussi une sorte de résumé des principales passions interhumaines. Mais, précisément, il est très différent de celui du TP, et *il n'évoque en rien le livre III de l'Ethique. L'ambition de domination* y est mentionnée, mais elle n'y est pas caractérisée comme étant essentiellement intolérance (ce qui est assez surprenant dans un ouvrage dont l'un des objectifs principaux est justement la lutte contre l'intolérance); son lien avec l'ambition de gloire n'est pas non plus indiqué, ni par conséquent son caractère non-utilitaire; elle n'est même pas présentée comme consistant particulièrement en un désir de dominer *les autres hommes:* Spinoza dit simplement que chacun veut toujours tout diriger à son gré *(omnia ex suo ingenio moderari vult),* choses et événements aussi bien qu'êtres humains; et l'allusion qui suit à *suum lucrum* semble bien suggérer que, pour le Spinoza du TTP comme pour Hobbes, l'ambitieux aspire à dominer ses semblables, non pour faire ce qu'il considère comme leur bonheur, mais pour les utiliser, au même titre que les autres choses, comme de simples moyens au service de ses intérêts. La

gloire, il est vrai, est également mentionnée; mais Spinoza déclare que, sous son influence, chacun "méprise ses égaux" *(aequales contemnit),* alors que la gloire au sens du livre III de l'*Ethique* nous amène au contraire à attacher une importante *exagérée* à l'opinion d'autrui; on peut donc penser que le mot "gloire" a ici, non pas son sens spinoziste (joie de réjouir autrui), mais le sens de Hobbes (joie de contempler notre propre puissance, celle-ci étant elle-même conçue de façon purement instrumentale): si nous nous croyons beaucoup plus puissant que les autres, alors, en effet, nous les mépriserons.   Enfin, l'envie   est mentionnée, mais sans que soit évoqué son lien nécessaire avec la pitié, sentiment dont il n'est même pas question ici. Il semble donc bien que Spinoza, à cette époque, expliquait encore les passions interhumaines à la manière de Hobbes.   Et dans ces conditions, effectivement, l'état de nature devait se caractériser, non par une insociable sociabilité, mais par une insociabilité pure et simple; il ne pouvait donc se dépasser de lui-même par le seul jeu de sa propre dynamique: il fallait bien, pour en sortir, une rupture radicale obtenue par une décision commune réfléchie et concertée, c'est-à-dire quelque chose d'analogue à un contrat.

2 - Peut-être pourrait-on aller plus loin encore. Si la doctrine de l'imitation des sentiments n'est pas encore élaborée à l'époque du TTP, cela ne vient-il pas de ce que le fondement même de toute la théorie des passions, c'est-à-dire la théorie du *conatus,* n'est elle-même pas encore au point?

On sait, à coup sûr, que cette théorie a évolué. Dans le *Court Traité* (KV,I, v,1), Spinoza parle de l'effort que fait chaque chose pour "persévérer dans son état" et "s'élever à un état meilleur" (G I/40/8-10): une formulation statique et une formulation dynamique sont juxtaposées sans que leur lien soit élucidé. Dans les *Cogitata Metaphysica* (CM I,6), il emploie indifféremment "conserver son être" (G I/248/5) et "persévérer dans son état" (G I/248/10-11), semblant ainsi donner à la première de ces deux formules une signification statique. Dans l'*Ethique,* au contraire, non seulement Spinoza a définitivement abandonné "persévérer dans son état" (qu'il maintient pour le principe d'inertie, mais non plus pour le *conatus)* au profit de "persévérer dans son être" (E IIIP6), mais il explique ensuite ce que cela veut dire exactement: notre *conatus* n'étant rien en dehors de notre essence actuelle (E IIIP7), "persévérer dans notre être" signifie non pas simplement "ne pas mourir," mais produire les effets qui se déduisent de notre nature; *conatus,* essence actualisée, productivité de l'être, puissance d'agir, tout cela devient identique (Cf. E IIIP7D).   On pourrait d'ailleurs peut être penser que, dans l'*Ethique* elle-même, la mise au point de la doctrine ne s'est pas faite du premier coup: je développerai ce point ailleurs. Mais ce qui est certain, c'est que l'évolution va dans le sens d'une assimilation progressive des deux notions d'auto-conservation et de dynamisme causal, l'une et l'autre s'identifiant finalement à celle d'actualisation des conséquences de notre essence.

Or, au chapitre XVI du TTP, Spinoza nous donne une formulation du *conatus* qui se situe à un stade *très archaïque* de cette évolution. Au cours de sa déduction du droit naturel, il déclare (G III/189/26-27) que chaque chose, autant qu'elle le peut, s'efforce de persévérer *dans son état (in suo statu):* c'est l'énoncé statique du *Court Traité* et celui des *Cogitata*. S'agit-il d'une inadvertance de langage? Non, sans doute, car ce qu'il dit aussitôt après va dans le même sens. S'agit-il d'un simple énoncé du principe d'inertie? Peut-être, mais alors le *conatus* humain en relève entièrement, car tout ce passage est précisément destiné à s'appliquer à l'homme; et ce qui suit fait intervenir la conscience et le calcul. Spinoza ajoute en effet: "et cela sans tenir aucun compte d'autrui, mais seulement de soi" (G III/189/27-28). C'est incompatible, à coup sûr, avec la doctrine de l'imitation des sentiments, qui nous apprendra au contraire que nous sommes affectés directement, immédiatement, antérieurement à tout calcul utilitaire, par ce qui affecte autrui. Mais c'est une conséquence assez logique de la conception statique du *conatus*: si l'effort pour nous conserver se réduit, comme chez Hobbes, au simple désir de ne pas mourir, et si tout le reste n'est que *moyen* en vue de cette fin, ce qu'éprouve autrui ne sera jamais rien pour nous, puisque sa vie n'est pas la nôtre; l'imitation des sentiments sera donc impossible.

On peut donc bien penser, avec Lazzeri, que le contractualisme du TTP a été pour Spinoza une sorte de pis-aller, dans la mesure où il n'avait pas encore les moyens de comprendre comment l'on pouvait sortir autrement de l'état de nature. Et s'il a pu ensuite acquérir ces moyens, peut être cela vient-il, comme le veut Negri, de ce que lui a appris entre temps l'écriture même du TTP: l'intolérance, la productivité de l'imagination dans le phénomène religieux, tout ce à quoi il s'était trouvé confronté au cours de la rédaction de cet ouvrage, il lui fallait tenter d'en élaborer le concept. D'où la rédaction finale du livre III de l'*Ethique*, qui à son tour a rendu possible le non-contractualisme plus global et plus radical du TP.

* * *

Reste une dernière question: pourquoi Spinoza, au terme de cette évolution, n'a-t-il pas exposé en clair la conception à laquelle il était finalement arrivé? Pourquoi n'en a-t-il rien dit au chapitre II du TP, où la question de la genèse de l'Etat aurait dû trouver sa place? Pourquoi n'y fait-il que des allusions qui ne nous permettent de la dégager qu'en procédant à des recoupements? Cela vient, je crois, de ce que Spinoza était gêné. En effet, nous l'avons vu, l'explication de la genèse de l'Etat est d'autant plus simple et d'autant plus générale, elle requiert d'autant moins d'hypothèses, elle fait d'autant moins intervenir le calcul, que l'on fait jouer un plus grand rôle à *l'indignation*. Or, selon Spinoza, l'indignation est *nécessairement mauvaise* (E IVP51S). Elle n'est même pas indirectement bonne, comme la honte et le repentir: même chez les hommes passionnés, la pitié et l'ambition de gloire, jointes à un peu de calcul, *pourraient*, à elles seules, produire exactement les mêmes effets socialement utiles. Mais, *en fait*, la pitié et l'ambition de gloire se prolongent *nécessairement* en haine pour celui qui fait du mal à ceux auxquels nous nous identifions, et leurs effets en sont décuplés avec un prix très lourd payer. Il n'y aura jamais d'Etat, si parfait soit-il, sans répression, si réduite soit-elle, ni de répression sans une indignation collective au moins abstraite contre les non-conformistes en général.

Il faut donc bien admettre, bon gré mal gré, qu'il y a quelque chose de foncièrement mauvais à la racine même de l'Etat, corollaire nécessaire de ses effets bénéfiques: le même mal, en définitive, qu'à la racine des révolutions. Et sans doute Spinoza l'a-t-il admis de mauvais gré. Ce n'était pas là une aporie théorique, mais la constatation d'une réalité désagréable à laquelle il a sans doute préféré ne pas trop penser.

1. Christian Lazzeri est l'auteur d'une thèse encore inédite, soutenue en 1985, sur *Anthropologie, pouvoir et droit naturel à l'âge classique: Essai sur Hobbes et Spinoza.* Il a publié plusieurs articles sur la philosophie politique à l'âge classique, dont deux sur Spinoza: "Les lois de l'obéissance: sur la théorie spinoziste des transferts de droit," *Les études philosophiques*, (1987), n°4; "L'économique et le politique chez Hobbes et Spinoza," *Studia Spinozana*, 3 (1988).

INDIVIDUAL AND COMMUNITY IN
SPINOZA'S SOCIAL PSYCHOLOGY

LEE C. RICE
Marquette University

This study does not aim to provide a general outline of Spinoza's social psychology, but rather to focus upon the concept of an 'individual' as this concept is developed in his physics and psychology and extended into his treatment of political community. One particular view of Spinoza's method and psychology (typified by Matheron, Zac, and Sacksteder) sees the claim that the state is an individual as a univocal consequence of Spinoza's methodology. This extension of Spinoza's ontologico-physical model of individuation from the *Ethica* to his political theory is rife with political and sociological consequences. I shall argue that such an extension is wholly erroneous: it is based upon a misreading of critical passages in the *Ethica*, and ignores the fact that many of its consequences are explicitly rejected by Spinoza in his own political theory. In the first part I examine what I call the 'literalist' interpretation of societal individuation. In the second part, I propose what I call a 'metaphorical' interpretation, based in part upon suggestions by McShea and Den Uyl, and try to provide an extended defense of it by an examination of relevant passages from the *Ethica*. Finally, in the third part I examine consequences of the two interpretations; and argue that Spinoza explicitly accepts the consequences of the metaphorical view.

1. The Literalist View of Political Order

Following E IIP13 Spinoza introduces a series of lemmas and definitions intended to clarify his notion of individuation. The first two pairs of axioms, together with the intervening first three lemmas, running from G II/97/20 to 99/22, are concerned with the simplest bodies (*corpora simplicissima*). Contrary to Matheron's suggestion,[1] these 'simplest bodies' are not marked by their number of parts, but rather by homogeneity of force or matter.[2] The section running from G II/99/23 to 101/24, comprising a definition, yet another axiom, and lemmas 5-7, deals with bodies composed of parts which are similar but in relative motion one to another. In L7S (G II/101/25-102/18) and through the six postulates following it, Spinoza deals with composite bodies whose parts are dissimilar (heterogeneous and in relative motion). We may follow Hampshire (1962, 71-72) in translating 'motion and rest' as 'energy.' Then parts of an individual are homogeneous if and only if the quantum of energy predicated of them is constant; otherwise heterogeneous, in which case they are interchanging energy within an individual which itself may maintain a uniform and constant quantum. This is the basic model which underlies what Bennett happily calls Spinoza's "field metaphysic."[3]

Using Spinoza's method of composition for individuals, we can construct higher and higher orders of individuals, each individuated by fixed and internal relations among the individuals which are its components. The higher we ascend the more determinate are the internal relations among the proper parts: the higher the composite, the more it is immune to loss of identity ("disindividuation") through external forces. If we carry this transformation through an actual infinity of embedded hierarchies of individuals, we arrive at the *facies totius universi*, which changes an infinite number of ways without loss of identity.[4] Matheron summarizes these lemmas by noting that (physical) individuals are for Spinoza relatively closed systems,[5] related to the hierarchy of individuals by their respective degrees of integration.[6] There is, however, no reason to follow Matheron (1969, 53-54) in suggesting that the notion of infinity here is only that of a limit concept. I would suggest that, when Spinoza intimates that we must proceed *ad infinitum*, he means no less than what he says.

Spinoza's account of individuation is hardly the model of clarity for extensions beyond physics. Indeed, I suspect that he introduces it in *Ethica II*, which deals with the flip side of his psychophysical parallelism, precisely because he is without a model to explain its workings in the area of mental events.[7] To extend the account to sociology or political theory is even chancier. While Spinoza tells us that it is the relatedness of components which constitute an individual (which 'individuate' it), his physical model provides no obvious means for extending the notion of individuation to cognitive or social models in general.

One approach, that of Matheron, is to regard one of the next levels up in the hierarchy of individuation mentioned in E II as that of political society itself. I shall hereafter refer to this as a literalist interpretation of the state as individual. Seen in this light, the passage to civil society is of a piece with the passage from substance to human individuation.[8] This interpretation has the advantage of removing any notion of historicity from the talk of social contract in the first political tractate, and of explaining the more ingrained naturalism which emerges in the second. Matheron's suggestion that Spinoza would have been better off renouncing all talk of a social contract from the start suggests that he (Matheron) seeks a literal ontology of civil society, a uniform extension of the *Ethica*, within the political writings.[9] This literal interpretation is implemented by interpreting the relation of *corpora simplicissima* to more complex individuals ("organisms") as exactly parallel to the relation of individuals to civil society as to a larger hierarchical individual (1969, 301-302).

The general model of civil society which emerges from such an interpretation is summarized by Matheron as follows:

> *La conception spinoziste de la structure de l'Etat apparaît ainsi en toute clarté. L'Etat est un système de mouvements qui, fonctionnant en cycle fermé, se produit et se reproduit lui-même en permanence. Les individus répartis sur le territoire, armés ou désarmés, éprouvent des désirs dont l'orientation et les limites sont déterminées par le régime de la propriété.* (1969, 346)

The transition which is made from physical to political individual occurs via a univocal interpretation of law ("physical" and "civil"), and the relations which unite lower-order individuals within the unity of the state are here conceived of a piece with the physico-chemical relations outlined by Spinoza in E IIP13:

> *Nous pouvons même préciser d'avantage. La définition spinoziste de l'individualité, en effet, comporte deux termes: d'une part, le nombre et la nature des éléments composants; d'autre part, la loi selon laquelle ils se communiquent mutuellement leurs mouvements. Le premier terme, ce sont les institutions territoriales qui le recouvrent: tel est la **societas**, ou ensemble des groupes humains qui habitent le pays et lui donnent son aspect extérieur; **societas** qui existerait tout aussi bien à létat de nature, même si son fonctionnement rede-venait alors anarchique, car il y aurait toujours une population et un sol.* (1969, 347).

Under such an interpretation, there is in fact no difference between positive and physical law.[10]

Although Matheron does not lean explicitly toward a panpsychist interpretation of Spinoza, his interpretation of the state as individual accords well with any interpretation which sees a mysterious living force permeating all levels of individuation. Under such an interpretation, which is that of Sylvain Zac, *conatus* itself is literally extended to the level of the state as individual:

> *La société est une association de **conatus**, dans ce qu'il y a en eux de positif et non en tant qu'ils sont contrariés les uns par les autres. Or, ce qu'il y a de positif dans les **conatus** malgré la diversité des natures individuelles, c'est la vie de Dieu qui reste toujours la même.* (19, 225-226).

History here emerges as a science on a footing with physics, for the laws by which individuals, *all* individuals including the state itself, are formed and develop are the laws of nature themselves. Indeed, like Marx, Spinoza can be interpreted as viewing history as a higher science, insofar as it deals with hierarchically higher levels of individuation in nature.[11]

What Zac above describes as a "living force" can be characterized less mystically, but with equal literalness of extension from physics to political philosophy, as "communal order"; and it is so described by Sacksteder:

> Whatever its limitations with respect to some more complex natural order, any political order is a simple whole formed from parts which are complex so far as they depend on that whole. By the contractual device, dependence on wayward individuals' rights is relinquished to a rule determined by the unified power of the multitude. This unity in turn defines wrong-doing and justice. Enforcement of these may be transferred to a highest political authority, though that body yet remains limited by the public power and by possible indignation among the citizens. (15, 209).

Note that Sacksteder, unlike Matheron and most other commentators, makes room for the possibility of a literal interpretation of the social contract within the literalist model itself. This is accomplished by inverting the dependence relationships among the models. Whereas both Matheron and Zac, correctly, as I shall shortly argue, try to establish the primacy of the physical model, and derive political consequences by its literal extension to the communal level of social life, Sacksteder sees the communal order of political life as Spinoza's primary paradigm.[12]

Speaking of the state as a unit whole (Sacksteder), a quasi-living organism (Zac), or a higher-order individual (Matheron) places Spinoza's political thought at the beginning of a tradition leading to Hegel and eventually to Marx's communalism. This is not to say that all of the consequences of such communalism for the nonautonomy of the individual will follow from the adoption of such a model in Spinoza; for, as we shall see, Matheron explicitly tries to sidestep some of them. In what follows, I will examine, and partially defend, an interpretation which sees Spinoza's political philosophy as radically individualistic and more exactly as a precursor of contemporary libertarianism.

2. The Metaphorical Interpretation

What I call the metaphorical interpretation insists that the state has no ontological status as an individual, but functions only as an historical aggregate in the loosest sense of that term. This interpretation is aptly summarized by McShea:

> Spinoza holds the individualist view of man on several counts besides that of his involvement in the thought of his time. His metaphysics is nominalist, at least in intent, so that "society" or "mankind," for instance, cannot for him be anything but collective nouns that point to numerous concrete individual relations. (10, 67)

Spinoza's nominalism is a central metaphysical component of the radical individualism which he espouses in moral theory - an individualism which can be easily, but mistakenly, identified with egoism.[13] Spinoza argues that men who are naturally enemies, cannot lead a solitary life,[14] since it is not possible to sustain life without mutual assistance.[15]

The communal unities, however, are the products of perceived utilities,[16] and based upon a limited principle of self-defense:

> Quia homines, uti diximus, magis affectu quam ratione ducuntur, sequitur multitudinem non ex rationis ductu, sed ex communi aliquo affectu naturaliter convenire et una veluti mente duci velle... Cum autem solitudinis metus omnibus hominibus insit, quia nemo in solitudine vires habet ut sese defendere et quae ad vitam necessaria sunt comparare possit, sequitur statum civilem homines natura appetere, nec fieri posse ut homines eundem unquam penitus dissolvant. (TP VI, 1).

Clearly the emergence of political or other community follows from the passional nature of human existence. There is an ambiguity, however, in paraphrasing this as the claim that "the state is a product of nature."[17] What is a product of (human) nature is the proposition (idea) that there exist political communities; but there is no political community (or aggregate thereof) of which it can be said that it (they) is (are) a product of human nature. Note the phrase *una veluti mente* in Spinoza's argument: what is produced is not an individual mind (or the corporeal correlate thereof), but an aggregate whose members may, on occasion and depending upon environing conditions, operate in a more or less unified manner.[18]

This interpretation of Spinoza's political philosophy is characterized by Den Uyl as "methodological individualism."[19] The emergence of political communities within the framework of methodological individualism is explained by appeal to the laws of individual psychology (specifically, those explicitated by Spinoza in E III and E IV). Indeed,as human beings aggregate their forces, driven by individual passional causes, generalizations on these laws of individual behavior can be constructed. Matheron refers to these as *relations interhumaines directes*, but fails to notice that they are at the order of statistical, rather than nomological, generalizations.[20]

Den Uyl in fact has two arguments to support his claim that states are not ontological individuals for Spinoza. The first of these rests upon his analysis of the state of nature itself:

> Nonetheless, institutions are not emergent individuals - that is, super-individuals which have arisen out of the larger mass of individuals in society. To claim that there are such super-individuals is to advocate something which contradicts the thesis of the omnipresence of the state of nature, since such individuals would also have to be found, at least theoretically, in the state of nature. (1983, 70)

While this argument is based on Spinoza's political theory, the second looks to his ontology:

> The fact that one person rules does not imply that the effects of his ruling are singular. The proper way to view either the *civitas* or its government is not as an individual, but rather as an organized set of relations. Unity in Spinoza's political thought is a matter of harmony, not of individuation. (1983, 80)

Both Den Uyl and Matheron are in agreement in seeing Spinoza's notions of individuation and order as paradigmatically ontological and derivatively political or sociological (against Sacksteder's claim that they are primarily sociopolitical). The second argument, accordingly, must bear the heat of the battle between Den Uyl and Matheron; since, if it failed, the first argument would imply only that Den Uyl's reading of the state of nature was similarly defective.

The key issue, then, is that of barring the move from "an organized set of relations" to individuation in the ontological sense.

> ...the author in Chapter IV believes that he is able to conclude that the state is not "an individual, but rather... an organized set of relations" (p.80). But what is an individual, according to the definition given after Proposition 13 of Book II of the *Ethics*, if not precisely "an organized set of relations"? What the author has proven... is that the state is not an individual in the "substantialist" sense given this word by non-spinozists, nor is it an individual in the anthropomorphic sense. That indeed suffices on the whole to make impossible the "totalitarian" interpretation of Spinoza's political theory.[21]

What must be shown is that not every organized set of relations is constitutive of an individual from the ontological perspective.

There are two characterizations of individuation in the *Ethica*, the first of which we have already examined in the lemmas and definitions following E IIP13. Yet another is given by Spinoza in E IIDef7:

> By singular things I understand those things which are finite and have a determinate existence. If several individuals come together in a single action in such a manner that they are all simultaneously the cause of a single effect, I consider all of them to that extent as one singular thing.[22]

Mugnier-Pollet argues that these two conceptions of individuation are quite different,[23] and tries to show that both conceptions are present, in different functions, at the level of political community.[24] Spinoza is not, however, offering two concepts of individuation here, but rather clarifying a single concept. Real external relations for Spinoza are uniquely reducible to causal interactions,[25] and any real set of organized relations must by nature be causal.

Den Uyl's approach to separating nonindividuating from individuating causal relations is by way of a distinction between *per se* and *ad aliud* powers, using the analogy of a group of men pushing a boulder:

> ...the power exerted by the men upon the boulder may be regarded as a single power *relative to* the task at hand and to the nature of the boulder. The power is thus not a *per se* power, but rather a power *ad aliud*. Individuals are, strictly speaking, *per se* powers. They have a specific *conatus* urging them toward their own self-preservation. (1983, 71-72)

This is more the description of a possible answer than an argument, since the distinction between the two types of power is not based directly on any text in Spinoza; and both Mugnier-Pollet and Matheron regard the state itself as having a *conatus*, contrary to Den Uyl's claim that it does not.[26] We need, not a description, but a set of criteria for distinguishing the conditions under which individuals constitute only an aggregate from those under which they are causally constitutive of an individual in the proper (non-metaphorical) sense of that term. *Conatus* is clearly a key here, but we cannot speak of the *conatus* of an individual without first identifying the individual; and the criteria for identification in the *Ethica* are provided only in the context of Spinoza's emergent physics.[27]

Spinoza provides an example, from which a criterion may be extracted, in Ep32. Oldenburg has requested an explanation of the relations which hold among the various parts of nature, and Spinoza asks him to consider a small worm (we would say "microbe") living in the blood, in much the same way as each man inhabits the universe. It would regard each particle as a whole rather than as a part, and its knowledge of the laws governing these particulate interactions would not enable it to see in what manner these laws are consequences of still more general laws governing the nature of blood.[28]

Spinoza here is *not* denying that the worm is an individual, but he is affirming that it is also (and quite consistently) constitutive of a higher order individual (the bloodstream itself), which in turn is constitutive of yet an higher individual (the organism). The criterion for identifying levels of individuation here is not, as Sacksteder suggests (cf. (16), 34-37, and (15), 207-208), simplicity or complexity (however these are characterized), but rather the extent to which activity at *lower* levels is *deducible* (Spinoza says "follows from") laws at *higher* levels. The key which makes individual chemical compounds components of yet higher individual compounds is the as-yet-unborn (in Spinoza's time) molecular bonding theory,[29] and the key to the individuation of the worm or microbe within the bloodstream, as that of the bloodstream within the individual organism, is molecular chemistry itself, which provides the necessary reduction schemata by which laws of higher-order individuals imply those for individuals of lower orders.   The converse of the claim that higher-order laws imply lower-order ones is that lower-order predicates (or "modes") are the definienda of higher-order modes or predicates.

The key concept here is that of a scientific law, or rather a hierarchy of laws which are related deductively so as to produce reduction schemata for the objects which fall under these laws. This might provide some meaning for the ill-defined notion of "organicism" which seems to linger in the thought of both Matheron and Sacksteder. A complex may be said to be "more than the sum of its parts," and thus an individual from an ontological perspective, if and only if the laws governing those parts are a subset of the implication class of the laws governing the complex whole. If this subset relation does not hold, then the complex is a logical individual.[30]

To claim that one or more individuals ("subjects" or citizens) figure as real parts of another complex individual (the state), we need laws (historical or political: not generalizations, but nomologically universal claims) which imply the laws of passional activity operative at the atomistic or individualistic human level. There are no such laws to be found in Spinoza's political writings, for the very good reason that he did not believe that they exist; and there are no such laws even today, for the very good reason that he was correct:

> But that men should surrender, or be forced to surrender, the right which they hold from nature, and should bind themselves to pursue a definite rule of life, is dependent upon human volition. Although I fully concede that all things are determined to exist and to act in a fixed and definite way by universal laws of nature, I still add that laws of the second type depend upon the will of men (TTP IV, 2-3).

The phrase *ex placito hominum* here refers to an aggregate, what Den Uyl would call causal relations *ad aliud*. Generalizations about political communities and the relations of individuals which enter into these are based upon certain psychological laws of human interaction. Even if there were "laws of politics" (and I doubt that there are, and am sure that Spinoza doubted their existence as well), the laws of human psychology would not be reducible to them, or deducible from them. In the following section, I shall examine some of the general consequences of this situation for Spinoza's view of the place of the social sciences in human knowledge.

3. Models, Consequences, and Questions

It is important not to overstate the differences between the rejected literalist model and the metaphorical model which I have defended and some-what expanded. In both models the status of individuals, or even of subindi-viduals, which exist within a larger hierarchical whole is real and not illusory: the individual is not somehow "swallowed up in the whole" in either model. Return to Spinoza's example of the worm/microbe in the bloodstream. The reality of that microbe *as an individual* is in no way compromised by Spinoza's insistence that it is part of a larger individual. The distinction which Spinoza makes is not between illusion and reality, but rather between levels of necessary inter-dependence which are deducible from causal laws. The microbe is "meta-physically correct" in describing itself as an individual, and in the expression of its own conatus for its own self-preservation. It would be "metaphysically incorrect" in trying to provide causal explanations for all events at its own level in terms of laws for that level. This is the import of Spinoza's claim that "it would not see in what manner these laws were consequences of still more general laws governing the nature of blood" (Ep32).

Even if the literalist interpretation were correct, a human being in civil society would be no less an individual for its being part of a hierarchically superior whole. A micro-explanation of the interactions of the microbe with its environment would appeal to basic laws of cellular interaction, and would also be correct as far as it went. The cellular interactions which occur at the microbe's level, however, are consequences of still more general laws for the whole (Spinoza says the "bloodstream") of which the microbe is a part. That bloodstream is itself a part of a larger individual, the human being, and its laws are deducible from those higher laws of physiology.

If we look at the human being, however, in relation to civil society, no such deductive hierarchy of laws obtains. If we wish to explain the social interactions of one person or group with another, we must appeal to the laws of human passional interaction (this is *Ethica* III and IV), but these laws are not deducible from some higher set of "socio-political laws." Spinoza's discussions in the two political tractates follow exactly the reverse order from the one which would be expected from the literalist model. In explaining (really "describing," since we are dealing here with statistical generalizations only) social or political trends, Spinoza appeals to basic laws of human psychological interaction; but he never attempts to explain the psychological interactions by appeal to higher politico-social frameworks.

How decisive is this argument? Could not a proponent of the literalist interpretation simply claim that Spinoza deferred from making any such explanations because the actual laws were not at hand? This suggestion is hardly a convincing one. The laws of physical interaction were not at hand when Spinoza wrote Part II of the *Ethica*, but he still felt it a methodological requirement to provide a general outline of the types of laws required following E IIP13. In short, Spinoza's method did not require him to be omniscient regarding the future growth of the inventory of scientific laws, but he clearly realized that it did require him to provide structural descriptions as place holders for the laws not yet explicitated.

There is a second consideration which also weighs heavily in favor of the metaphorical interpretation, and that is the method of composition for individuals made explicit following E IIP13. Spinoza suggests that a hierarchically higher individual will have as its subindividuals entities which are *diverse in nature and operation*.[31] I suspect that this is also the key to the stratification of levels which underlies Spinoza's model. If we have laws which explain interactions among individuals of type A, and other laws which explain interactions among individuals of type B, laws which explain A(-)B interactions will be stratified at an higher level than A-laws or B-laws.

Return to the pseudo-individual which the state is, an individual which Spinoza cautiously characterizes as *sometimes* acting *una veluti mente*. Of what subindividuals is such an individual composed? Quite clearly, its component parts are human beings: individuals of one and only one type. Given the fact that we are not dealing with stratified laws which bind individuals of different types, the resultant collection of human beings has all the unity of a heap of stones; and the laws which correctly describe the interactions among them are of one level only. There is no diversity here, and consequently no integration, and no higher order integrating laws.

The interpretation which sees man in civil society like the microbe in the blood is a metaphor, certainly a useful one in formulating political or social generalizations, but a dangerously misleading one if charged with any ontological weight. Paradoxically, the literalist interpretation can have explanatory power only insofar as it is rooted in passional nature itself.[32] To the extent that citizens view themselves as parts of an higher social individual, to that same extent their self-perception becomes a self-fulfilling prophecy; but it is rooted, as Spinoza says (TTP IV), in the will and not in the nature of the state as individual. To say that it is rooted in the will is not to claim that it is less necessitated, for Spinoza is a determinist at all levels of explanation. It is, however, to claim that the laws which explain the efficacy of the state as individual are laws of individual human volition (one is almost tempted to say "imaginational illusion"), rather than the laws of politics or sociology.

One easy consequence of the metaphorical interpretation here defended is that history, politics, and sociology are not sciences at all in the spinozistic sense (i.e., deductive systems of necessary laws). Psychology (or some spinozistic version of an as-yet-undiscovered "utopian psychology") is a science because it deals with the necessary connections among the human passions. The student of psychology is on the track of necessary laws of human action and interaction. The student of history, or politics, or sociology utilizes the laws of psychology in the applied context of empirical data formulated as historical and social trends.[33] The descriptions and recommendations which Spinoza provides of and for political orders do not operate at the level of necessary laws of nature, but rather at the level of empirical generalizations based upon limited knowledge of the laws of human psychology and even more limited knowledge of the historicocultural facts related to the evolution of particular societies.[34] There is no paradox in the claim that the arch-rationalist in science should argue for a modest empiricism in social studies, for such a modest empiricism is itself the necessary consequence of Spinoza's metaphysical rationalism. The best state for Spinoza is the minimal state precisely because the extent to which we, as human individuals, can control the state and use it to our best collective utility, is severely limited both by our knowledge and by our power. Seen in this perspective, Spinoza is not a precursor of either Marx or Hegel. There is no intelligibility to history itself, and no underlying structure of nomological connections by which such an intelligibility could arise. The "iron laws" of history are neither iron (since they describe at best trends) nor laws in the fundamental sense of that term (since their operation depends upon the consent of the governed).

Two problems emerge from my analysis of literalist and metaphorical models and defense of the latter. I cannot resolve them here,[35] they should be addressed and articulated. My suggestions for their resolution are tentative and provisional only.

First, if the state itself is not a super-individual whose members are individual persons, what in fact is the next individual upward in the hierarchy of individuation described by Spinoza following E IIP13? He clearly insists that the levels of individuation proceed upward to infinity. We know that the series comes to a halt at the *facies totius universi*, and that one intermediate stage is that of human individuals; but what comes after this intermediate stage? The structural requirements are two. First, the new super-individual must be heterogeneous: it must be composed of individuals of diverse natures. Secondly, the laws describing the new type of super-individual must be necessary laws (not merely empirical generalizations) among whose deductive consequences would be the laws of human psychology themselves.

I would hesitatingly suggest that the above two requirements can be met by the contemporary concept of an "ecosystem." Such ecosystems, as described by population biology and environmental physics, are partially closed systems. While ecology as a science is hardly a fully developed system as of this writing, the laws which are being articulated appear also to meet the spinozistic requirement of full generality (= necessity) and rigor. The requirement of heterogeneity of subindividuals is quite clearly and elegantly met by the diversity of ecological substrata (some organic, many purely inorganic) within an ecosystem. The need for further super-individuals in the hierarchy is also met. The collection of ecosystems themselves form a larger system which we could call the "planetary system," and which is again relatively independent for the purpose of establishing causal laws. Independence here requires what the physicist or population biologist would describe as relative closedness from a theoretical perspective. The planetary system itself figures as one type of component in a larger super-individual of diverse components; so the general spinozistic requirement of diversity and integration is also met. A full defense of this suggestion would require greater articulation of the developing discipline of ecology, and extensive analysis of the text of Spinoza.

The second problem is not so easily handled. In developing Spinoza's concept of "individual" (and withholding literal application of the term to the state), I have taken a Goodmanian turn: the individuals are just those which a theory characterizes as such among its own primitives.[36] Spinozism is saved from the pure formalism of Goodman's analysis[37] by the requirements which it places on theory status: a theory must contain necessary laws which are universal, and which can in principle be connected deductively to higher-order and lower-order theories. So Spinoza, like Goodman, "ontologizes" individuals by appeal to theories; but, unlike Goodman, he legitimizes theories by appeal to their integration within larger families of theories. For each sortal type of individual, there is a theory (containing necessary laws) which describes its activities; and for each theory there exists a super-theory which has as one subset of its consequence class the set of postulates or primitive laws of the sub-theory.

Quite clearly the "ultimate super-theory" for Spinoza is that which describes nomologically the *facies totius universi*: we would perhaps not be too much off the mark by calling it "cosmology." To describe laws as 'necessary' is to mark their place *within a theory*: they describe certain invariant relations among the primitives or individuals of the theory itself. The problem is this - is the hierarchy of theories itself necessary?

This problem can be further articulated as follows. Within each theory (or at each hierarchical level of individuation) the laws are necessary because of the invariant relations which they describe among individuals. In addition to the hierarchy of theories, however, we could talk about a set of metatheoretical statements (again arranged hierarchically) which describes the relations of particular theories to sub-theories and super-theories. Does Spinoza believe that such a hierarchy of metatheories is also necessary? Do the statements which it contains describing subordination and integration of theories hold necessarily?

Spinoza himself never addressed this problem, and perhaps it is good that he did not do so; for even its analysis lies beyond any techniques which were available to him. The problem is in fact equivalent to the question of grounding iterated modalities within a system of monomodal statements or laws. Granted that a scientific law is necessary, is it necessarily necessary? A negative answer to this question entails the position that, while each level of the hierarchy of theories or individuals is wholly necessary and deterministic, the hierarchy itself is a contingent one. Laws are necessary because they are subsumed as deductive consequences of still higher orders of laws, but propositions claiming this subsumability are themselves not necessary.

I doubt that Spinoza would be sympathetic to the notion of 'contingent necessity,' but I know of nothing in his system which is logically opposed to it. It should be noted that, although the problem becomes more visible in my own articulation of the metaphorical interpretation, it is no less present for the literalist interpretation. One way out of the problem would be to deny the meaning of iterated modalities. For Spinoza this would amount to the claim that modalities have meaning only intra-systematically, and cannot be iterated among distinct systems. I am uncertain both about the consequences of such a proposal for Spinoza's system generally, and about the means by which such a claim could be supported within the text of Spinoza. The most I can here conclude is that it deserves some further attention by students of Spinoza.

Robert McShea argues that Spinoza can be credited with three distinct achievements:

> ...the conversion of a great metaphysical tradition into a philosophy of science, the creation of a naturalistic ethics, and the reconciliation of the claims of individual freedom and social peace through an analysis of the nature of political power. (10, 197)

If my analysis and defense of the metaphorical model are correct, then the third of these achievements is a derivative of the second; and Spinoza's analysis of power and *conatus* pervades all three. In one limited sense, a genuine spinozistic individual is greater than the sum of its parts (has more *conatus* than the sum of its conative elements). The state, however, is not a genuine spinozistic individual, and exemplifies the situation where an individual is far less than the sum of its parts. It is on the basis of this insight that Spinoza preserves the natural right or power of human persons within civil society,[38] and evades the twin difficulties of totalitarianism and the metaphysical reification of social aggregates.

References

Quotations from Spinoza are from the Van Vloten and Land edition, which was checked against the Gebhardt edition. English translations are my own. I have profited from the translations of Samuel Shirley (Baruch Spinoza, *The Ethics and Selected Letters*. Indianapolis: Hackett, 1982), Charles Appuhn (*Benoit de Spinoza, L'Ethique* (Paris: Vrin, 1977), and Curley (1985).

(1) Bidney, David. *The Psychology and Ethics of Spinoza* (NY: Russell & Russell, 1962).

(2) Commers, Ronald. "Marx's Concept of Justice and the Two Traditions in European Political Thought," *Philosophica* 33 (1984), 107-130.

(3) De Deugd, C., ed. *Spinoza's Political and Theological Thought* (Amsterdam: North-Holland, 1984).

(4) Frankena, William K. "Spinoza's New Morality: Notes on Book IV," in Mandelbaum and Freeman (1975), 85-100.

(5) Giancotti, E. "Man as a Part of Nature," in (18), 85-96.

(6) Harris, E. E. "Spinoza's Treatment of Natural Law," in (3), 63-72.

(7) Jarrett, Charles E. "Materialism," *Philosophy Research Archives*, No. 1459 (1982).

(8) Klever, W. N. A. "Power: Conditional and Unconditional," in (3), 95-106.

(9) McShea, Robert J. "Spinoza, Human Nature, and History," in Mandelbaum and Freeman (1975), 101-116.

(10) McShea, Robert J. "Spinoza on Power," *Inquiry* I#12 (Spring, 1969), 133-143.

(11) Mugnier-Pollet, Lucien. *La philosophie politique de Spinoza* (Paris: Vrin, 1976)

(12) Rice, Lee C. "Emotion, Appetition, and Conatus in Spinoza," *Revue Internationale de Philosophie*, (1977), 101-116.

(13) Rice, Lee C. "Spinoza on Individuation," in Mandelbaum and Freeman (1975), 195-214.

(14) Rousset, Bernard. "Eléments et hypothèses pour une analyse des rédactions successives de *Ethique IV*," *Cahiers Spinoza* 5 (1984-85), 129-146.

(15) Sacksteder, W. "Communal Orders in Spinoza," in (3), 206-213.

(16) Sacksteder, W. "Spinoza on Part and Whole: The Worm's Eye View," *Southwest Journal of Philosophy* 11 (1980), 25-40.

(17) Wartofsky, M. W. "Nature, Number, and Individuals: Motive and Method in Spinoza's Philosophy," *Inquiry* 20 (1977), 457-479.

(18) Wetlesen, Jon, ed. *Spinoza's Philosophy of Man* (Oslo: Universitetsforlaget, 1978).

(19) Zac, Sylvain. *L'idée de vie dans la philosophie de Spinoza* (Paris: PUF, 1963).

1. Matheron (1969), 51: *Le corpus simplicissimum, en un sens, vérifie déjà la définition de l'individualité. Le nombre de ses parties est égal à 1.*

2. Works not on the list of frequently cited secondary sources in the prefatory material will be cited by their number on the list of references at the end of this article. Cf. (13) for a general discussion of these lemmas. McKeon (1928, 16-24) provides a discussion of the methodological importance of the distinction between homogeneous and heterogeneous individuals. Finally, Spinoza's Letter 13 to Oldenburg (1663) provides a summary of his disagreements with Boyle on the question of individuating the components of a chemical compound.

3. Bennett (1984), 93: "If I am right that Spinoza espoused the field metaphysic... then he could say that the relation of particular extended things to the one extended substance is enormously like the relation of a subject to its predicate, or (to move out of Curley's linguistic idiom) the relation of a property to its possessor)."

4. E IIL7S: *Et si sic porro in infinitum pergamus, facile concipiemus, totam naturam unum esse individuum, cujus partes, hoc est omnia corpora, infinitis modis variant, absque ulla totius individui mutatione.*

5. Matheron (1969), 43: *Tout individu physique est un système de mouvements et de repos qui, abstraction faite des perturbations d'origine externe, fonctionne en cycle fermè.*

6. Ibid., 57: *Mais elle dépend aussi, en second lieu, de son degré d'intégration.*

7. An interpretation also suggested by Bennett's discussion, (1984), 49-51.

8. (1969), 289: *Passage de l'état de nature à la société politique, celle-ci découlant de celui-là comme l'individualité humaine découlait de la substance.*

9. (1969), 313: *Ne vaudrait-il pas mieux, dans ces conditions, renoncer au mythe d'origine et, dans la reconstruction de la société politique à partir de l'état de nature, ne faire intervenir que les motivations passionnelles de la vie interhumaine telle qu'elle se déroule tous les jours et sous nos yeux?*

10. Ibid., 348: *Aucune différence, par conséquent, entre lois juridiques et lois physiques: les unes comme les autres sont les règles uniformes par lesquelles s'exprime la vie d'une essence individuelle.*

11. (19), 227: *La vraie thèse de Spinoza est que la société politique, coalition de forces matérielles et spirituelles, unifié par les lois générales, comporte des attributs analogues à ceux d'une personne.*

12. (15), 208: "The political order must be taken as a kind of prototype of communal orders more generally. Perhaps more than any other, unless nature itself or biological organisms, a political order is easily identified a by a prevailing unity, according to Spinoza's principles. The state or the commonwealth is a single power which constitutes the corporate body of any political order. By that criterion, it is a unit whole."

13. Cf. Bennett (1984), 299-307, which is based upon a misunderstanding of Spinoza's nominalism. My critique of this position, and defense of this nominalism, may be found in Rice (1985), 244-245. A discussion of this nominalism as it relates to Spinoza's

epistemology will be found in G. H. R. Parkinson, *Spinoza's Theory of Knowledge*, (Oxford: Clarendon Press, 1954), 129-134.

14. Cf. TP VIII, 12: *Sunt enim homines, ut diximus, natura hostes; ita ut, quamvis legibus copulentur adstringanturque, retineant tamen naturam.*

15. E IVP58S: *Sed omnes revera, quatenus ex affectibus, qui passiones sunt, in nobis ingenerantur..., nec ullius usus essent, si homines facile duci possent, ut ex sola rationis dictamine viverent, ut jam paucis ostendam.*

16. Cf. E IVApp12: *Hominibus apprime utile est, consuetudines jungere, seseque iis vinculis astringere...*

17. On this point see Jean Préposiet, *Spinoza et la liberté des hommes*, (Paris: Gallimard, 1967), 220-222.

18. Den Uyl (1983), 71: "Spinoza does not think of social unity as something organic, but simply as the effective organization of individual powers."

19. (1983), 67: "More precisely, methodological individualism would hold that, *in principle*, explanations of social events are reducible to explanations of the relationships between individual agents, and that any 'social laws' are reducible to laws of human psychology." The position is further defined by May Brodbeck, "Methodological Individualism," *Philosophical Analysis and History*, William Dray, ed., NY, (1966), 319-332. (Cited by Den Uyl (1983), 138)).

20. (1969), 151: *Le problême que doit résoudre ici Spinoza, c'est celui-là même qui se posait à Hobbes: comment faire dériver des passions simples les passions proprement humaines?* Note, however, that much of this problem is already resolved by Spinoza in E IV, rather than in the political tractates proper.

21. From my translation of Matheron's review of Den Uyl (1983), which appears in *Studia Spinozana* I (1985), 422-426.

22. E IID7: *Per res singulares intelligo res, quae finitae sunt, et determinatam habent existentiam, Quod si plura individua in una actione ita concurrunt, ut omnia simul unius effectus sint causa, eadem omnia eatenus ut unam rem singularem considero.*

23. (11), 145: *L'union est ici définie formellement comme une relation fixe entre des éléments composants et elle fonde l'existence d'un individu. Mais un autre texte du même livre présentait une détermination cette fois dynamique de l'union.*

24. (11), 145: *Or, ces deux conceptions de l'union se retrouvent, à peine estompées, dans la description de la vie politique.*

25. E IP36: *Nihil existit ex cujus natura aliquis affectus non sequatur.*

26. Cf. Matheron (1969), 348-349, and (11), 143-144.

27. Indeed the concept of conatus is not introduced definitionally in the *Ethica* because it is already available from other (non-spinozist) sources: for bodies it is equivalent to the newtonian *vis inertiae*. Confer (17, 245-247). For a more detailed examination of the transfer of the physical model to psychosociology; cf. (12), 110-113.

28. *nec scire posset, quomodo partes omnes ab universali natura sanguinis moderantur, et invicem, prout universalis natura sanguinis exigit se accomodare...*

29. Spinoza does anticipate the requirements which such a theory would have to meet to provide a reduction of chemistry to physics. Cf. his Ep11 to Oldenburg, which deals with experiments which he and Robert Boyle were both undertaking with salts of nitre.

30. In Goodman's sense. The square root of 2, the Eiffel Tower, and an old shoe constitute a logical individual. Indeed, there are relations which hold between them (even which hold uniquely between them). Cf. Nelson Goodman, "Seven Strictures on Similarity," in *Problems and Projects* (Indianapolis: Hackett, 1982), 437-446.

31. E IIP13L7S: *His itaque videmus, qua ratione individuum compositum possit multis modis affici, ejus nihilominus natura servata... Quod si jam aliud concipiamus, ex pluribus diversae naturae individuis compositum, idem pluribus aliis modis posse affici reperiemus, ipsius nihilominus natura servata.*

32. Cf. (10), 136: "Most men live completely within a social microcosm whose conventions are for them laws of nature. Conventions are often functional and not necessarily irrational; they often prescribe precisely what would be suggested by an informed intellect, but they are not rationally understood by those subject to them and so society is almost always out of human control. If the social microcosm fails to adapt to its environment, or if some inner dynamic of change erodes or renders inappropriate the customary routine, there will be social disorder and weakness and individual psychic disorientation."

33. Cf. TP I,4: *Cum igitur animum ad politicam applicuerim, nihil quod novum vel inauditum est, sed tantum ea quae cum praxi optime conveniunt, certa et indubitata ratione demonstrare, et ex ipsa humanae naturae conditione deducere intendi; et ut ea quae ad hanc scientiam spectant eadem animi libertate, qua res mathematicas solemus, inquirerem, sedulo curavi humanas actiones non ridere, non lugere, neque detestari, sed intelligere...*

34. Cf. Jacques de Visscher, "Y a-t-il du volontarisme dans la penseé politique de Spinoza?" in (3), 228: *Spinoza, illuminé par la vraie connaissance, ne fait que constater ce qui est raisonnable ou pas. Ces descriptions de l'Etat libre ne sont que des descriptions conditionnelles; c'est-a-dire que les conditions de cet Etat raisonnable doivent être comprises dans le sens de la métaphysique spéculative qu'il nous fournit dans l'**Ethique**, son oeuvre majeure.*

35. In fact their lack of resolution here is not so much due to lack of space as to want of ideas. Both these problems deserve more serious attention than they have hitherto been given in the literature.

36. Cf. Nelson Goodman, *Of Mind and Other Matters* (Cambridge: Harvard UP, 1984), 66-71.

37. A charge partially answered also by Catherine Z. Elgin, *With Reference to Reference* (Indianapolis: Hackett, 1983), 97-103.

38. Cf. Ep50: *Quantum ad politicam spectat, discrimen inter me et Hobbesium, de quo interrogas, in hoc consistit, quod ego naturale jus semper sartum tectum conservo, quodque supremo magistratu in qualibet urbe non plus in subditos juris, quam juxta mensuram potestatis, qua subditum superat, competere statuo, quod in statu naturali semper locum habet.*

NEGRI ON SPINOZA'S POLITICAL AND LEGAL PHILOSOPHY

MANFRED WALTHER
University of Hanover

1. Introductory Remarks

Antonio Negri, former professor of public law at the University of Padua, while imprisoned and accused of being one of the spiritual leaders of the autonomous left in Italy and their terrorism, wrote a book on Spinoza in 1979 entitled: *The Wild Anomaly: Baruch Spinoza's Outline of a Free Society.*[1] Published in 1981, the book was immediately translated into French[2] and into German[3] only one year later. The French translation is prefaced by comments on Negri by three of the leading figures in French Spinoza scholarship, to whom Negri had referred, both positively and critically: Gilles Deleuze (Deleuze (1968)), Pierre Macherey (Macherey (1979)) and Alexandre Matheron (Matheron (1969)). Immediately, a keen discussion arose in most of the west European countries; in the Netherlands, for example, a review of the book by Wim Klever in a weekly newspaper provoked a long debate by the readers, many of the participants not being philosophers at all; all of them were passionately engaged in the debate. One can trace the influence of Negri's book in many of the papers presented at the various Spinoza congresses in 1982, the 350th anniversary of his birthday. What are the peculiarities of this Spinoza interpretation that evoked such an echo, unparalleled in recent Spinoza research? The only historical parallel which comes to my mind is the echo evoked by Jacobi in 1787 when he stated that Lessing had confessed to him that he was a spinozist, causing an uproar in the spiritual world in Germany for decades.

2. Outlines of Negri's Interpretation

What Spinoza shows, according to Negri, is that "the history of metaphysics includes radical alternatives."[4] Given the fact that even modern times can only be properly understood through the complex way of metaphysics (*ibid.*), the *dominant* form of modern philosophy from the very beginning takes a completely different course. With the breakthrough of the productive forces of man that organize and acquire the world for the first time in history, this main stream philosophy immediately occupies itself with justifying the domestication of those newly arisen productive forces through definite mechanisms of domination erected on private acquisition instead of collective liberation. This dominating line of modern thought, which in the field of political philosophy is represented by the line Hobbes-Rousseau-Hegel, like the empiricism that forms its complement, is in fact fundamentally dualistic. In political philosophy that means dualism of society and the state, in precisely the form that these thinkers postulate the state as something higher and more substantial *vis à vis* society, a state which is the only possible institution - in form of the supreme power -

to synthesize the supposedly self-exploding bourgeois society: in Hobbes in the form of a sovereign power that has been made juridically independent of the citizens-subjects; in Rousseau in the form of the *volonté générale* being played off against the *volonté de tous* and in Hegel in the form of the reality of the moral idea vis à vis a society that explodes itself.

If, according to Negri, the dominant line of modern philosophy is thus organized as an expression of the unleashing of the productive forces - and as its recantation at the same time - Spinoza's philosophy is sharply contrasted with this line that is victorious in the first instance: "Spinoza is an anomaly" (p. 9). He doesn't belong to this line of thought although he "was too often cooked in that sticky 'democratic' soup of normative Hobbesian transcendentalism, Rousseauist general will and Hegelian *Aufhebung*."[5] He is the founder of a "non-mystified form of democracy." His philosophy is modern beyond any doubt, in so far as it is a philosophy of the productive forces, too. But it insists on the one-dimensionality of the productive world constitution of man as a process in which the productivity of being expresses itself - without any dualism, without any teleology. Teleology is, according to Negri, constitutive of ideological bourgeois thought in all of its parts. Spinoza's criticism of all teleology, of all transcendence of being vis à vis the real world, this negativity of his philosophy, is nothing but the necessary complement of its pure positivity, i.e. of conceiving the productivity of being in all its forms, from physics via psychology to politics and finally, to ethics. Here this means: the more complex the composition of being becomes, the more its productivity increases: with man as the subject (*Subjekt*), a factor appears that completely produces and acquires the world itself, i.e. man conceived as *erste Natur* (first nature) creates himself as *zweite Natur* (secondary nature), without any reference to transcendence and teleology. Here it comes out clearly why Negri says that his book would not have been possible without the Spinoza monograph written by Deleuze (Note 3 to Ch. 9).

If the second nature is entirely the result of the productivity of the human subject (subjectivity) - or, to be more precise, as the result of the productivity of being itself on the complexity level of subjectivity - then one understands why Negri comprehends, on the one hand, Spinoza's political theory, which is a theory of collective emancipation, as a strict continuation of his ontology, and on the other hand why he states, that "The true politics of Spinoza are his metaphysics."[6] For Spinoza's political philosophy is not designed as a voluntaristic and normativistic theory of legitimation, but as the strict application of the conditions that are exposed in his general ontology and, especially, in his doctrine of the *conatus* in *Ethics* III. The process of the productivity of being is continued in the collective *practice* of the political: political theory is thus nothing but an analysis. And so, political knowledge is, like all knowledge, "nothing else than the continuous analysis of this forward movement, of this weaving, of this continuous accumulation of being."[7]

Thus, the fundamental relevance of Spinoza consists in his being "the founder of modern materialism in its highest form, and in doing so, he determines the actual surroundings of modern and contemporary philosophical speculation - a philosophy of the worldly and determined being and of an atheism as the negation of every preestablished order for human action and for the constitution of being."[8]

At the very end of his book he himself raises an important objection: after such a long period when the capitalist fettering of the productive forces was dominant - is it really possible then to form links once again to a period of development and to a philosophy that originated in the period when everything seemed to be historically open?

Negri puts this question by quoting Walter Benjamin, and in his answer he also goes along with Benjamin: Negri's thesis of Spinoza's actuality for the present rests on a hypothesis: "namely on the knowledge (sic!) that the development of the bourgeois culture has not completely distorted the history of its origins."[9] Spinoza's actuality that really becomes recognizable only after the crisis of the dominant answer given at the starting point of modern times - it was, so to speak, not contemporary with its own presence - Spinoza's actuality consists of his representing, as nobody else does, the alternative philosophy of the early bourgeois development - although not without any forerunner and not without any successor. The line Hobbes-Rousseau-Hegel is juxtaposed by the other line from Machiavelli via Spinoza to Marx.

3. The Three Main Theses of the Book

I will take a second step and try to elaborate the main theses Negri develops in his interpretation of Spinoza - as far as I see them. There are three of them. Let me say, beforehand, that there are two peculiarities that characterize Negri's book which make an exact report on the content of his book a really difficult task:

First, there is an overwhelming richness of allusions to the historical context and development of European thought before and after Spinoza; and Negri knows a great deal about the political, economic and religious configurations in the Netherlands in the 17th Century; his book is also rich in interpretative findings in all of Spinoza's texts - and Negri treats them all extensively, including the correspondence.

Second, the way he expresses himself and his views has caused me extraordinary difficulties. Some passages read more like a hymn on being than like an analytical philosophical text - but a hymn whose material consists of highly speculative terms. So I am not sure that I have genuinely understood his argument everywhere.[10]

{3.1} With a materialist thinker, and with an historian of philosophical thought, it appears rather strange that he postulates that the spirit of a philosophy does not belong to its own time. Negri explains in what sense he means this by expounding his first thesis:

> Spinoza's thought has a necessary but not sufficient condition of possibility in the two-fold anomaly of the economic, political and spiritual situation of the Netherlands in 17th Century Europe on the one hand, and in the anomaly of the Marrano mentality (*mentalité*) of his ethnic group, on the other hand. So

there is a determinate *fundamentum in re* for this philosophy, although Spinoza rises above this given context in so far as his thought is anomalous even in relation to this anomalous context.

{3.1.1} *The Republic of the United Netherlands*, in the early prime of its commercial capitalism and in its political structure, which shows many early modern features, is - notwithstanding the social structure that was still completely corporate, guild-dominated - nevertheless an exceptional phenomenon in its own time, as many contemporaries, among them the English Ambassador in the Netherlands, Sir William Temple, have observed. In the Netherlands the process of modernization does not follow one of the later dominant patterns of parliamentarism (as in England) or of bureaucratic and military centralization of the state (as in France, and later, in other parts of the Continent), but it is the result of a kind of direct path from the Netherlands' medieval political structure to modernity - this structure, in many respects not being typical for the other countries in the Middle Ages.

{3.1.2} With regard to the history of mentalities, Spinoza as a Marrano,[11] i.e., a member of the Jewish group that had been forced to become Catholics in Spain, but clandestinely continued to practice their old faith, and thus continually accused of crypto-judaism, a group that had migrated from Spain via Portugal and France to the Netherlands at the end of the 16th Century - Spinoza as a Marrano represents a quite extraordinary type of Europeans who, on the basis of their experience with the competing and mutually destructive claims to absoluteness of the positive religions (Judaism, Catholicism and Protestantism) had developed something like a *Weltanschauung* beyond all positive religions. To this extent they, especially some members of the Amsterdam Jewish community, represent a kind of proto-enlightenment in early modern Europe.

This twofold anomaly, the "wildness" (*Wildheit*) of the social structure and the political constitution of the Netherlands and of the mentality history of the Marranos in the Netherlands, are not sufficient reasons for explaining Spinoza's anomalous thought, but they are the general conditions of possibility for a philosophy that overcomes the traditional medieval world view, as well as for its finding itself at a distance from the philosophy of poetic subjectivity of modern times with state absolutism as its political complement.

In radicalising current tendencies of his own society and spiritual heritage, Spinoza goes far beyond this context. But he is, nevertheless, indebted to this same context.

{3.2} For Negri, Spinoza's philosophy in its mature shape (*Gestalt*) is a materialistic theory of the world. It is at the same time opposed to the dominant tendencies in contemporary philosophy, insofar as it insists on the possibility of the radical self-liberation and emancipation of mankind. This constellation - the opposition to his own time of Spinoza's central concept of philosophy as a metaphysics and politics of collective emancipation - has made its mark on nearly all the subsequent expositions of his philosophy. Hence Negri's second thesis:

> "There are two Spinozas" who fight with each other nearly continuously, and that
> pattern of his philosophy that is more closely related to the philosophical and
> ideological inheritance of the past has left its traces even in the mature form of his
> philosophy. Spinoza's first philosophy (Spinoza I, so to speak), which dominates the
> early expositions of his thought, is that philosophy of the crisis of his time that links
> up with the Renaissance and the millenarian features of those who formed the
> "Spinoza circle." Although the concept of the infinitely active and dynamic substance
> is present from the very beginning, Spinoza's philosophy is still neo-platonic; especially
> the speculations on the attributes and the doctrine of the parallelism of extension and
> thought reveal the emanationist features of this early elaboration of Spinoza's
> metaphysics. There is a permanent struggle in Spinoza which gives his philosophy that
> ultimate tension which is the genuine sign of his trying to escape inherited
> transcendentalism and to expound and unfold the metaphysics of the self-producing
> being in and through all stages of reality.

The breakthrough of his mature materialistic philosophy (Spinoza II) occurred
in the period after 1672 when he turned to improving the first version of the
Ethics. It is especially in the third and fourth books of the *Ethics* that Spinoza
is mostly on his own, when he elaborates the concept of conatus and its specific
concretisation (*Konkretisierung*) in men. Although there is a certain reversal in
the fifth book of the *Ethics*, where many passages of the first draft have survived
and Spinoza tends to give an ascetic ethical doctrine of liberation, the *Tractatus
Politicus* picks up just those doctrines of the third and fourth books that are
the closest metaphysical exposition of his mature philosophy. Although in the
parts of that *Tractatus* devoted to the analysis of the various forms of
government Spinoza falls back into what Negri calls the standard form of
political theory of his time, even there one can see the subversive power of his
general political ontology at work.

{3.3} Negri stresses, as others have done before,[12] the inner relation,
even the linking of Spinoza's metaphysics with his political theory. It is with
respect to the theory of State and law that the continuing importance of Spinoza
exists. This is Negri's third thesis:

> that Spinoza is the first to criticize the state-absolutist juridical paradigm in
> Hobbes, not from the traditional teleological natural-law-position, but from a
> radical democratic and ontological position which stresses the dynamic and
> spontaneous power of the multitude as the very agent of politics. He thus
> outlines the fundamental alternative political theory over against the juridical
> ideology of the higher dignity of the state.

This twofold opposition to traditional thought as well as to the ideological
version of early modern thought explains why Spinoza was a lone thinker not
only in his own century but in the 18th Century as well. The motto at the
beginning of Negri's book is a sentence from Voltaire: *Je ne connais que Spinoza
qui ait bien raisonné; mais personne ne peut le lire.* I know none but Spinoza who
has argued well, but nobody can read him.

It is mainly because of this ontologico-political structure of Spinoza's thought that Negri holds Spinoza to be relevant for contemporary philosophical reflection and systematic theory: "Spinoza lives as the alternative: today this alternative is real and topical. Spinoza's analytics of the filled space and of the open time is on the way to becoming the ethics of liberation, in all dimensions which this examination creates and prepares."[13]

4 Critical Remarks

In all three topics Negri has inspired or at least pushed forward scholarly research. I would like to comment on the first and the second thesis only very briefly because the first doesn't concern the philosophical problems, meaning here the systematic problems, of his doctrine, and because the second is dealt with explicitly by Matheron with reference to Spinoza's political philosophy.

{4.1} Some remarks on the anomaly of the "context of discovery" for Spinoza's philosophy. Here I will only comment on the first aspect, i.e. Dutch society in relation to early modern Europe. As far as I can see, Negri is correct in stating that the situation was anomalous.

In the economy, not only did the Netherlands develop an immense commercial capitalism, as is widely known, but we can unambiguously identify the beginning of an industrial capitalism, indicated by its "ability to modernize the agricultural sector and to develop an efficient and productive manufacturing sector centered around textiles and shipbuilding."[14] Thus, the Dutch provinces, and especially Holland, could be classified among the most 'industrialized' countries of the Seventeenth Century.[15] Nevertheless - and this may be called the anomaly of the Netherlands in the economic sector - it was not here but in England that industrial capitalism asserted itself: quite a lot of conditions[16] were lacking, and thus the Netherlands, that seemed to be at the top of the economic modernization process, fell back in the following century.

The political situation was, at any rate, at least as complicated as the economic one.[17] Whereas the nation building process, which is one of the indicators of political modernization, in other countries was mainly the result of the activity of a more or less centralized, more or less bureaucratic and more or less militant *state*, in the Netherlands the main forces to create a homogeneous nation were located in *society* itself, especially in the upper classes of the big towns. And although the formal constitutional structure in the Netherlands was still mainly medieval - there was no direct participation of the citizens either on the local or on the provincial or on the federal levels of the Dutch "Republic" - and the class assemblies were theoretically subordinate to a governor of the king of Spain, a governor that did not exist of a king who was no longer acknowledged - there were strong and effective tendencies inherent in Dutch society towards transforming the corporate liber*ties* into general political liber*ty*. Thus in the Netherlands one can see in the Seventeenth Century a process of social and political integration not inaugurated by the State but by the social forces themselves, and the trend was to democracy in an egalitarian sense. The outstanding degree to which religious and ideological toleration were real in the Netherlands may be taken as a clear sign of this tendency indicated by a great number of newspapers and a flood of pamphlets on nearly all political topics. So, although political power was in the hands of some patrician families of the big towns (because the clergy as the first rank no longer existed and the aristocracy was weak or culturally and economically integrated in the bourgeoisie) there was no country where democratic principles were as deeply rooted as in the Netherlands.

So I think Negri is right again in perceiving Spinoza's political theory as rooted in the economic and political anomaly of the Netherlands as compared with the way in which the modernization process developed in other countries. But it is a matter of fact that this anomalous path to modernity declined in the Eighteenth Century, economically as well as politically, and was taken up again only in the Nineteenth Century as a kind of "import" from those countries that had followed different lines of development.

{4.2} Although Negri is correct in his observation that the dynamism of substance, its world constituting power (*potentia*), is most clearly developed in the third and fourth books of the *Ethics* and in the basic reflections of the *Tractatus Politicus*, his statement that there is not only an inner tension, but an inner division into two different philosophies in Spinoza, doesn't deserve much confidence. Negri himself gives evidence of the arbitrariness of his hypothesis in showing that Spinoza, when elaborating his "materialist" philosophy (Spinoza II), often refers to those parts of his earlier work that belong, according to Negri, to the pre-mature phase (Spinoza I).[18] But the hypothesis is necessary for Negri to make Spinoza appear a materialist: It is only in separating the religious and intellectual features from the exposition of Spinoza's philosophy that Negri can "demonstrate" that Spinoza was a materialist philosopher.[19] So it is the interpreter's preconception, his *Vorverständnis*, that is at work when Negri produces Spinoza's inner biography as a drama. Negri's immense knowledge of all the relevant late medieval and early modern traditions and trends of thought give this drama a colorful background so that one often forgets that one is just at a performance.

{4.3} The most exciting thesis in Negri's work is the strict confrontation of Spinoza's theory of state and law based on the ontological productivity of the multitude as the very agent of politics, with the main line of political theory from Hobbes via Rousseau and Kant to Hegel who contrast the state with society and thus give it a specific dignity and legitimacy. I will restrict myself in this context to discussing the stated opposition of Spinoza's theory of State and law to Hobbes'.

{4.3.1} Before starting to discuss Negri on Spinoza's political and legal philosophy, I would like, in passing, to draw your attention to an aspect of the influence of Spinoza's political philosophy which has not yet found the interest it deserves: the influence he had during the founding period of the Constitution of the United States. As Guiseppa Saccaro Battisti[20] has shown, there were three books of Spinoza's in Thomas Jefferson's library - the *Opera Posthuma, the Tractatus Theologico-politicus*, which Jefferson himself "ordered from Paris in 1792" (Saccaro Battisti, p. 1), and the English translation of that same work dating from 1789.[21]   Besides the reflections on the different forms of government or constitution in the *Tractatus Politicus*, especially on a federalist form of the state, which Signora Saccaro Battisti mentions, special attention has to be given to Spinoza's theory of *civil religion* (*religio civilis*) as the secular complement of positive religion. While positive religion, because of its inherent particularism, divides people, civil religion is, according to Spinoza in the TTP, the necessary medium of political integration on the level of imagination - imagination being the level on which collective political thought is effective. The religious pluralism of the founding period of the United States demanded such a unifying religiously founded common belief, and as far as I can see, it is Spinoza's theory of civil religion that inspired the Founding Fathers, especially Jefferson, to push forward this concept. As far as I can see, nobody has, up to now, tried to trace Spinoza's influence on this debate around the Federalist Papers.

{4.3.2}   It is, of course, true that the ontological foundation of political theory in Spinoza is the most outstanding feature that distinguishes his political philosophy from the nominalism, constructivism, and thus, the arbitrariness of Hobbes' political thought, even if one considers that Hobbes' voluntarism is a kind of rational voluntarism. But at the very moment when one articulates such a thesis, one hesitates, because of the fact that in Hobbes we can identify another line of reasoning that runs in a kind of parallelism through nearly all of his political theory:

(a)   We start with the observation that political theory in Hobbes is just the application of his general concept of "matter in motion" to the field of collective, i.e., political action.   From this it follows that political theory has to be elaborated as a kind of physics of collective action in building "that great Leviathan."

(b)   We then go to the passage at the end of *Leviathan* xiii, where Hobbes resumes his analysis of the antagonism of the state of nature:

> And thus much for the ill condition, which man by mere nature is actually placed in; though with a possibility to come out of it, consisting partly in the passions [*affectus*, in Spinoza's language], partly in his reason. (*English Works*, ed. Molesorth, III, 115-116).

(c)   We end with the unfolding of the competing efforts of the sovereign, on the one hand, and of the subjects, on the other hand, to unfold their respective requirements and plans of life - with the unambiguous establishment of a right of resistance on the part of the subjects in case the sovereign fails to fulfill the aims of the state.

So there is a kind of physics of political power in Hobbes which enabled Spinoza consequently to develop his political philosophy as a "geometry of the intersubjective affective *conatus* of the masses."

{4.3.3}   But, on the other hand, there is this entry of *right reason* as a kind of *Deus ex machina*, which directs people to renounce the exercise of their unlimited right to everything, resulting in their irreversibly transferring their rights to the sovereign (with the exception, it is true, of the ultimate right of resistance if "life and liberty" are endangered). What takes place in Hobbes here is the abstraction of an autonomous juridical sphere - an abstraction from the struggles immanent in society, an abstraction meant to calm down or to suppress this antagonism from above, from a region of fundamentally legitimated power and force on behalf of the state.

And Spinoza puts his finger on precisely these features of Hobbes' theory as an arbitrary vanishing from society itself, presupposing a faculty of reasonable self-conduct and self-discipline which is completely fictitious, given the real constitution of the political agents as it is presupposed in Hobbes himself. What follows from this, according to Spinoza, is that one has to demonstrate the possibility of the emergence of political reason *inside* this struggle and without abstraction from the general rules of human behavior. From this it follows that there is no transfer of power on behalf of the individuals at all. The emergence of the state has to be explained from the natural condition of mankind alone, as a kind of *Lernprozess* in the light of the experience everybody acquires when trying to live according to his own right, without taking the power and forces of the others into account. But at no time in this process did any individual ever renounce the expression and exercise of his own power. It is only by a power superior to his that he is restricted - and thus restricts himself. That means that the state is not located *vis à vis* society and its members, but is an institution that develops solely in society itself and remains indissolubly connected to society. This is because it is only by consent of the citizens that peace can be obtained which is not a mere absence of war but the true mediation between the interests of the masses and their power and the interest and power of those who govern. If consent to, or at least acceptance of, the imperatives of those who govern is what constitutes the power and strength of government, any separation of a juridically, and thus legitimately, autonomous sphere of the state from society is simply ontologically impossible, given that "the right of government of the supreme power is nothing else but the right of nature itself, which is not determined by the power of a single person but by the multitude guided as by one mind" (TP III, 2, beginning). So finally, it is true that Spinoza's political theory is an alternative to the mainstream of modern political thought, conceptually separating state and society and legitimating oppression from above as being the will of the subjects themselves.

{4.3.4} As is widely known, Hobbes is viewed as the founder of modern legal positivism. Although there are elements in his theory of state and law that show his indebtedness to the natural law tradition, it is beyond doubt that natural laws have a completely different status in Hobbes when compared with the natural law tradition: they are no longer ontologically or de-ontologically preexisting obligations, but they are the very product of the constructive human reason; and their validity inside the state rests on the presupposition that they form a part of the sovereign's will - although this is clearly presented as a legal fiction in Hobbes. But it is true, again, that all the laws of the state are said to be valid only because they are related to the will of the sovereign. And in this respect Hobbes can be said to be the founder of legal positivism in the special form of validity positivism.

I use this term "validity positivism" (*Geltungspositivismus*) to compare Hobbes' political philosophy with that of Spinoza once more - now in the field of legal theory. Spinoza insists on *effectiveness* as a decisive defining element of the concept of law, and from this he infers that what is true with the laws of nature in general has to be true with the laws of the state as well: every law that really is a law is effective - in general. Now, as the effectiveness of a law in the state is dependent not only on the will and power of the sovereign, but on the will and power of the multitude as well, which surpasses every group of ruling men by far, it is the interaction of these two powers that constitutes and defines a law. From this it follows that law is never identical with the imperatives given by the government or with the law in the books, but that law is always "law in life," i.e. the vector of the diverse acting forces in society. That is what I call the "sociological positivism" of law. In the light of this fully developed concept of law, the "validity positivism" which is commonly identified with legal positivism, is only half the truth: it is a juridically bisected positivism - and that is why it is ideological, and the ruling legal positivism can correctly be identified as the juridical version of the bourgeois political ideology, as Negri states.

Let me add the remark that the radically modern features of Spinoza's philosophy of society, state and law, are nowhere more apparent than where he gives a theory of the genesis of normativity: as norms have no ontological or de-ontological pre-existence, they have to be understood as the very product of human interaction. In the light of this reasoning one can clearly see the originally normative features even in Hobbes, who has not completely conquered the normativist - that is: the idealist - tradition in political philosophy.

{4.4} Some final remarks on Spinoza as a materialist:
Negri tends to interpret Spinoza as being more voluntaristic and - if this equation holds true - more idealistic than Spinoza really is, even in the part where Negri sees him at the climax of the materialistic thought. Negri writes: *Das existente Politische ist absolut kontradiktorisch zur konstitutiven Notwendigkeit. Weil es nämlich zufällig ist. Es ist die Negation des Seins* (234). Translated: "The existing political is absolutely contradictory to constitutive necessity. Because it is contingent. It is the negation of (the) being." What he means is that the existing political structure Spinoza has in mind in the Netherlands and elsewhere is, for him, not the ultimate development and expression of that struggle for liberty that is, as an expression of the infinite power of being, immanent in the multitude as a political subject, or *as the* political subject itself. But in what sense can something really existing be called contingent without denying Spinoza's doctrine of universal necessity? Here I find in Negri something that reminds me of Hegel's talk of *faule Wirklichkeit*, and that means opening a gap between what is and what ought to be. This is possible only when one takes men indeed to be an *imperium in imperio*, i.e., when one exclusively regards the place of the human subject *vis à vis* nature as a whole. And this is, as far as I can see, the way Negri can make Spinoza a philosopher of the revolution and

of the future - not only in the sense that the historical time for Spinoza's philosophy is one that is still to come, but in the sense that he ontologically opens the space for further human emancipation *vis à vis* nature and its necessity. So, notwithstanding Negri's continuous affirmation that Spinoza is a - or *the* - materialist thinker of early modern times, in the end his Spinoza looks very much like an idealist thinker in this respect.

1. Negri, *L'anomalia selvaggia: Saggio su potere e potenza in Baruch Spinoza.* Milano: Feltrinelli, 1981.
2. Idem: *L'anomalie sauvage: Puissance et pouvoir chez Spinoza.* Traduit de l'italien par François Matheron. Préfaces de Gilles Deleuze, Pierre Macherey et Alexandre Matheron. Paris: Presses Universitaires de France, 1982. (Pratiques théoriques.)
3. Idem: *Die wilde Anomalie: Baruch Spinozas Entwurf einer freien Gesellschaft.* Translated from the Italian by Werner Raith. Berlin: Wagenbach, 1982.
4. *daß die Geschichte der Metaphysik radikale Alternativen einschließt* (p.10). All page references are to the German translation (note 3).
5. *Dennoch wurde Spinoza viel zu oft in der klebrigen 'demokratischen' Suppe aus normativem Transzendentalismus, Rousseauschem Gemeinwillen und Hegelscher Aufhebung gekocht* (p. 10).
6. *Die wahre Politik Spinoza ist seine Metaphysik* (p. 243).
7. *...nichts anderes als fortwährende Analytik dieses Fortschreitens, dieses Webens, dieser fortwährenden Anhäufung des Seins* (p. 256).
8. Spinoza *begründet den modernen Materialismus in seiner höchsten Form und bestimmt damit dem eigentlichen Umkreis der modernen und zeitgenössischen philosophischen Spekulation - einer Philosophie des weltlichen und bestimmten Seins und eines Atheismus als Verneinung jeglicher vorgegebenen Ordnung für das menschliche Handeln und für die Konstitution des Seins* (p. 9).
9. *nämlich der Erkenntnis, daß die Entwicklung der bürgerlichen Kultur die Geschichte ihrer Ursprünge nicht völlig entstellt hat* (p. 256).
10. The difficulties increase if one has to refer to a translation and is not able to read the original Italian text. As far as the German translation is concerned, these difficulties are multiplied by the fact that this translation is full of mistakes - some of them severely darkening Negri's arguments. So, for instance, the Italian term *giusnaturalismo* is rendered as *Rechtsnaturalismus* instead of *Naturrechtsdenken* which is, in German, quite the opposite of *Rechtsnaturalismus* (naturalistic realism). In many cases I was able to solve the problem by consulting the French translation, which is to be preferred to the German edition. But sometimes the darkness seems to be inherent in Negri's text itself.
11. The "detection" of the specific Marrano mentality as the most important biographical context for Spinoza's philosophy still owes much to the works of Carl Gebhardt. Cf. above all, his "Das Marranenproblem," *Die Schriften des Uriel da Costa*, mit Einl., Übertr. u. Regesten hg. von Carl Gebhardt, Amsterdam... : Carl Winter..., 1922 (Biblioteca Spinozana, 2), pp. V-XL. As one of the most recent and most penetrating studies on this subject, cf. Yirmiahu Yovel, "Marrano patterns in Spinoza," in Giancotti (1985), 461-85.
12. Especially Matheron and Konrad Hecker with his voluminous study *Gesellschaftliche Wirklichkeit und Vernunft in der Philosophie Spinozas: Untersuchungen über die immanente Systematik der Gesellschaftsphilosophie Spinozas im Zusammenhang seines philosophischen Gesamtwerks und zum Problem ihres ideologischen Sinngehalts.* Regensburg: Kommissionsverlag Buchh. Pustet, 1975. Hecker's book is immensely rich in comments on earlier Spinoza literature.

13. *Spinoza lebt als Alternative: Heute ist diese Alternative real und aktuell. Spinoza's Analytik des erfüllten Raumes und der offenen Zeit ist im Begriff, zur Ethik der Befreiung zu werden, in allen Dimensionen, die diese Untersuchung schafft und vorbereitet* (p. 243).

14. Stefan Breuer, in his review of G. Slicher van Bath, *Dutch Capitalism and World Capitalism: Capitalisme hollandais et capitalisme mondial* (Cambridge: Cambridge University Press; Paris: Editions de la maison des sciences de l'homme, 1982). The review was published in *Studia Spinozana* 1 (1985), 430-432.

15. G. Slicher van Bath, in *Dutch Capitalism,* p. 26.

16. See the studies of van Bath, Boyer and de Vries in *Dutch Capitalism* and the account given by Breuer (see note 14).

17. In the following remarks I mainly rely on the interpretation recently given by Heinz Schilling, especially in his "Die Geschichte der nördlichen Niederlande und die Modernisierungstheorie," *Geschichte und Gesellschaft* 8 (1982), 475-517, as well as in his "Der libertär-radikale Republikanismus in der frühen Neuzeit," *Geschichte und Gesellschaft* 10 (1984), 498-533.

For the development of political theories before and after the Dutch Revolution, cf. Richard Saage, *Herrschaft, Toleranz, Widerstand: Studien zur politischen Theorie der Niederländischen und der Englischen Revolution,* Vorw. v. Walter Euchner (Frankfurt am Main: Suhrkamp, 1982).

18. Alexandre Matheron, in his introduction to the French translation of Negri's book (13-17), was the first to draw attention to the fact that Spinoza, when demonstrating propositions in the "mature" books 3 and 4 of the *Ethics,* often refers to propositions which, according to Negri belong to Spinoza I. Matheron's methodological reflections concerning the validity of Negri's approach are convincing. Cf. the elaborated version of the same text: Alexandre Matheron, "'L'anomalie sauvage' d'Antonio Negri," *Cahiers Spinoza* 4 (1982-83), 39-60.

19. For the refutation of the hermeneutical premises underlying the idealist and the materialist interpretations of Spinoza, cf. Manfred Walther, *Metaphysik als Antitheologie: Die Philosophie Spinozas im Zusammenhang der religionsphilosophischen Problematik* (Hamburg: Meiner, 1971), pp. 97-101.

20. Guiseppa Saccaro Battisti, "Some Spinozan Political ideas in the Mazzei-Mably dispute." Unpubl. paper, Spinoza conference Wolfenbüttel, Sept. 1982.

21. See the preface to this translation, with an editorial note by Wim Klever, in *Studia Spinozana* 2 (1986), 351-353.

FORTUNE ET THÉORIE DE L'HISTOIRE

PIERRE-FRANÇOIS MOREAU
Université de Paris IV

"Si les hommes pouvaient régler toutes leurs affaires suivant un dessein arrêté, ou encore si la fortune leur était toujours favorable, ils ne seraient jamais prisonniers de la superstition."[1] La première phrase du *Tractatus theologico-politicus* nous jette d'emblée dans l'*expérience* de la condition humaine, et la première condition de cette expérience, condition à la fois constitutive de ses structures et première ou presque dans sa perception, c'est sa variabilité temporelle. Spinoza précisera un peu plus loin la trame de cette variabilité: épisodes de prospérité, épisodes d'adversité, retours de fortune. Si on peut parler de pessimisme, en un certain sens, ou de constatations désabusées, il faut se hâter d'ajouter que ce pessimisme ou cette absence d'illusion ne concerne que la forme (la stabilité d'une situation donnée) et non le contenu des situations (le malheur n'est pas plus sûr que le bonheur). La dimension de l'expérience désignée par ce terme de fortune comporte trois caractères, effectivement formels:

- elle est variable dans le temps;
- elle est répétitive (dans la vie d'un individu, et d'un individu à l'autre - comme tout ce qui est enregistré sous la rubrique "expérience")
- elle est indépendante de nous: chacun des moments s'impose à nous sans que nous l'ayons choisi; la fortune, c'est l'expression du fait que nous ne pouvons pas régler nos affaires suivant un dessein une fois arrêté: autrement dit que nos affaires ne sont pas *nos* affaires. Autant dire que la première figure de l'histoire, c'est le hasard historique, en tant qu'il pèse sur nous et nous empêche d'accorder complètement nos desseins et notre action.

Une seconde condition de l'expérience apparait dans le même texte: cette variabilité historique, loin d'être insignifiante, produit au contraire l'essentiel des conduites humaines; si la fortune n'existait pas, il n'y aurait pas de superstition; il n'y en aurait pas non plus si cette fortune était toujours favorable. Mais il est de l'essence de la fortune de n'être pas *toujours* quelque chose. Cependant cette subordonnée initiale introduit une lueur d'espérance, une ultime possibilité, non réalisée à ce jour, de changement: si un jour se constituent - peu importe comment pour l'instant - des conditions de vie qui font reculer les effets de la variabilité de la fortune, alors la superstition reculera aussi. On peut dire que tout un pan du TTP et, plus tard, du TP, est un développement de cette subordonnée.

Enfin troisième condition de l'expérience: une des preuves les plus fortes de l'irrationalité des hommes, c'est qu'ils cherchent la raison là où elle n'est pas. Ils cherchent l'intention dans le hasard et, puisqu'ils savent bien que ce n'est pas *leur* intention, ils supposent que c'est celle d'un autre. Ils souhaitent trouver un contenu sous sa forme et, ainsi, la méconnaissent. Autrement dit, un des aspects de leur domination par la fortune, c'est qu'ils refusent, lorsqu'ils en font l'expérience, de s'en tenir à la stricte fortune. Ils essaient d'expliquer les choses qui leur échappent (qui échappent et à leur maitrise et à leur compréhension) en y cherchant une *intention historique*;[2] ils ont donc une tendance spontanée à anthropomorphiser l'histoire, comme ils anthropomorphisent la nature. A bien lire cette préface du TTP, on se rendra compte qu'elle est parfaitement parallèle aux textes comme l'appendice de la Première Partie de l'*Ethique*, qui expliquent l'illusion finaliste à l'égard des choses naturelles. Pour la même raison qu'il y a un finalisme "dans l'espace," il y a un finalisme "dans le temps"; il est non moins nécessaire, puisqu'il s'enracine à la fois dans l'expérience et dans l'interprétation spontanée de l'expérience. Il prend la forme élémentaire de la croyance aux signes et aux présages (équivalents pour l'histoire de ce que sont les miracles pour la nature), mais ces formes et ces matériaux imaginaires simples peuvent se combiner jusqu'à constituer une théorie de l'Election ou de la Providence.

Cette théorie de la fortune joue un rôle-clef dans le système spinoziste et notamment dans les secteurs de ce système qui reprennent et repensent la tradition classique de la lecture de la vie humaine. On en retiendra ici trois aspects: l'héritage critique de la rhétorique classique; la description des structures de l'expérience; les matériaux pour une théorie de l'histoire.[3]

I

Le TTP ne présuppose pas, pour le lecteur, la connaissance du système. Pourtant, Spinoza y procède bien par démonstrations rationnelles; mais ces démonstrations s'appuient sur un espace de rationalité commun, qu'il peut légitimement supposer acquis chez le lecteur cultivé de son temps. Cet espace est double: il est constitué d'une part de réflexions sur la vie et la société, que tout un chacun peut faire lui-même ou bien hériter d'une tradition anonyme à force d'être répétée; d'autre part d'une culture moyenne assez aisément identifiable, plutôt latine que grecque, fondée sur des exemples historiques et littéraires plutôt que sur la connaissance des grands systèmes philosophiques, mais où une sorte de sagesse commune fournit les moyens de théoriser les leçons du livre du monde. Une culture rhétorique non pas parce qu'elle ne comprendrait que des orateurs, mais parce que poètes et historiens, par exemple, y sont assez volontiers enrôlés dans un schéma rhétorique.[4] Dans le cas de Spinoza: Térence, Tacite, Quinte-Curce particulièrement.

Or la Préface du TTP s'appuie précisément sur l'un de ces auteurs pour confirmer ce qu'elle avance concernant les rapports entre revers de fortune /crainte et espoir/ superstition. Deux références explicites à Quinte-Curce permettent d'établir qu'Alexandre ne tomba dans la superstition que lorsqu'il conçut des craintes sur la fortune (une page plus loin, une troisième citation du même auteur marquera les liens entre superstition et gouvernement de la multitude).[5] On peut donc s'attendre à trouver cette théorie commune de la fortune dans l'*Histoire d'Alexandre le Grand*. Il n'est pas inutile de rappeler qu'au XVIIe siècle, Quinte-Curce jouit, chez les auteurs qui se rattachent à une tradition critique ou sceptique, d'une réputation d'ennemi de la superstition, et ce d'autant plus qu'il traite une matière qui s'y prêtait largement.[6] On ne peut donc s'étonner que Spinoza l'ait choisi comme médiateur entre son lecteur et lui pour introduire préphilosophiquement ses thèses: il était sûr de rencontrer un accord au moins vague comme base de la discusssion; reste à savoir ce que recouvre cet argumentaire et ce lexique et les choix que le traitement philosophique proprement dit va y opérer.

Limitons-nous au livre V, le premier cité ici. Il raconte les événements qui suivent la bataille d'Arbèles; la reddition de Babylone, la prise de Suse, et, du côté perse, la fuite de Darius, la trahison des chefs Bactriens, enfin la série d'intrigues qui mènent à l'arrestation et à la mort du Grand Roi (les derniers chapitres, qui racontent l'assassinat lui-même, manquent). Ce qui est remarquable, c'est que le terme de *fortune*, s'il apparait souvent dans le texte, indique beaucoup plus souvent ce qui arrive aux Perses qu'aux Grecs, quand il n'est pas directement placé dans la bouche de Darius. Dans le §4, que cite Spinoza, il n'est pas dit explicitement qu'Alexandre doute de la fortune, mais les lignes qui précèdent (fin du §3) soulignent nettement l'opposition entre deux séquences historiques: l'une (au passé) où tout semblait permis à Alexandre (*invictus ante eam diem fuerat, nihil frustra ausus*), l'autre, au présent, où il semble se heurter à des obstacles, où son bonheur jusqu'ici constant semble pris au piège (*tunc haesitabat deprehensa felicitas*). Et c'est alors qu'ayant dû reculer de trente stades, avant de trouver un guide qui lui permettra de contourner et d'encercler les troupes ennemies, il se met à consulter les devins par esprit de superstition. Donc, s'il n'y a pas le mot, il y a bien les caractères que l'on associe avec l'idée de fortune; il ne manque même pas l'idée courante que l'excès du revers met en rage qui en est victime: car l'armée d'Alexandre n'est pas simplement tenue en échec, elle a été coincée dans un défilé où ses soldats ont dû mourir sans même pouvoir rendre les coups, situation la plus misérable pour des hommes courageux.[7] A l'insolence du bonheur passé répond donc le supplément de malheur qui rend impuissant au moment du revers. Cette idée des excès opposés se lie au thème des *ludibria fortunae*, les ironies ou les moqueries par lesquelles est frappée l'imagination humaine.[8]

Passons maintenant du côté de Darius. Vaincu, il est normal qu'il médite plus sur la fortune que le vainqueur, et effectivement on le voit au début et à la fin du livre opposer sa grandeur passée, et celle de ses ancêtres, à ses épreuves présentes. Mais une autre façon de parler apparaît: il parle de *sa* fortune et dit à ses compagnons: "vous avez préféré vous attacher à ma fortune plutôt qu'à celle du vainqueur" (V, 8). La fortune n'est plus alors la répartition abstraite des biens et des maux, elle désigne la série de biens et de maux attachés à chacun, et même la série *prévisible* - à tel point qu'on pourrait traduire par le sort ou le destin, et non plus par le hasard.[9] Ici, ce n'est plus la variabilité, mais au contraire la constance individuelle qui est mise en relief. L'extrême de cette constance, c'est l'intention qui destine un homme à une fin: à ce stade la Fortune n'a plus qu'à recevoir un nom pour être considérée comme une personne, qu'il faut ménager de peur de l'irriter. Ainsi, au livre précédent, la mère du Grand Roi, recevant la nouvelle, d'ailleurs fausse, de la victoire, "garda la même attitude: Pas une parole ne lui échappa; elle ne changea pas de couleur, sa physionomie resta la même, sans doute pour ne pas irriter la fortune par une joie prématurée."[10]

La notion commune de *fortuna* livrée au lecteur par Quinte-Curce a donc trois niveaux:

- la variabilité des affaires humaines; la crainte et la superstition où, on doit le constater, les revers jettent les hommes; leur oubli relatif lors du retour de la prospérité;
- la série de ce qui arrive à un individu; l'idée que cette série lui constitue un destin;
- enfin la personnalisation de l'intention qui est sous ces hauts et ces bas - personnalisation au moins rhétorique sous la plume de l'historien, mais qu'il n'hésite pas à attribuer à ses personnages comme croyance réelle.

Peut-on affirmer qu'on a là le champ sémantique total de ce que le terme évoque à un lecteur du XVIIe siècle? Il faudrait sans doute ajouter encore un quatrième sens, qu'on peut lire chez Machiavel, et qui n'est pas très éloigné de ce qu'on désigne maintenant par conjoncture: la fortune comme *occasio* et non plus seulement *casus*. Plutôt une possibilité d'être actif à l'égard de l'histoire que le fait constaté qu'on la subit. C'est en tout cas sur ce cercle de significations que Spinoza va commencer son analyse de l'expérience.

II

Lorsque Spinoza analyse des données de l'expérience humaine, il fait référence, indissociablement, à ce que chacun peut voir en lui-même, à ce qu'il peut observer chez les autres, à ce qu'il hérite de déjà constitué dans une culture classique, aussi bien comme maximes que comme *exempla*. C'est un type d'écriture auquel il a recours en fait assez souvent (début du *Traité de la réforme de l'entendement*, lettres, scolies et appendices de l'*Ethique*, etc.), qui a d'autres contraintes que la déduction géométrique, et joue un rôle différent, tout aussi nécessaire, mais qui prend le lecteur sous un autre regard.

Que dit-il, à ce niveau, dans ce regard, concernant la fortune? Deux choses épistémologiquement essentielles:

- "cela, j'estime que nul ne l'ignore" (thèse A);
- "tout en croyant que la plupart s'ignorent eux-mêmes" (thèse B).[11]

On peut dire que ces deux thèses encadrent tout l'usage spinoziste de l'expérience. A la différence de la géométrie, c'est du toujours déjà su; quand on commence à discuter avec quelqu'un, il n'a peut-être jamais entendu parler des lois mathématiques (ou construites sur le modèle des mathématiques) qu'on va lui démontrer; ce n'est pas gênant s'il connaît et accepte la règle du jeu; en revanche, il a forcément entendu parler de, et réfléchi lui-même à, ce qu'enseigne l'expérience (ici: les lois de la fortune; mais ce pourrait être aussi: que l'amoureux revient vers la coquette malgré ses serments, que l'ivrogne ou la bavarde parlent malgré leur volonté, que nul n'est si vigilant qu'il ne sommeille parfois, que les jeunes gens si l'on n'y prend garde sont attirés par la mode et les prestiges de l'étranger, que la loyauté mène souvent les conseillers à leur perte ...) Et ce savoir n'est pas une illusion; pour Spinoza l'expérience ne trompe pas. Pourtant les gens sont trompés (*Quamvis centies fallat, ibid.*); pourquoi? *d'une part* parce qu'ils greffent sur l'expérience toutes sortes d'idéologies ou de mythologies qui en sont l'interprétation, la prolongation artificieuses; *d'autre part* parce qu'ils n'en tirent pas les leçons et, notamment qu'ils n'appliquent pas à leur propre cas ce qu'ils voient chez autrui, ou bien qu'ils n'appliquent pas dans l'adversité les maximes qu'ils élaborent dans le calme; les conditions de l'expérience font qu'elle est opaque à ses propres leçons. D'où ce paradoxe: de ces leçons chacun n'ignore rien, sauf qu'il s'ignore lui-même. Lorsque Spinoza dit qu'aux jours de prospérité chacun est plein de sagesse, il est à peine ironique: les propositions où se formule cette sagesse (celles du néo-stoïcisme, pour fixer les idées) sont peut-être exactes, mais elles ne tiennent pas compte de l'*enracinement* des situations humaines et sont donc de simples *dictamina* qu'on aura du mal à appliquer dans des situations, nullement impossibles à prévoir, où la raison est submergée.

Dès lors, comment traiter les leçons de l'expérience dans ce double contexte de savoir ignorant? En triant ce qui est leçon proprement dite (*experientia docet...*) et mythologie: on observera donc que l'usage spinozien du terme fortune le réduit au maximum à ses aspects formels, énumérés tout à l'heure; pas de référence à la fortune individuelle et moins encore à sa personnalisation. Egalement en modifiant la théorie commune pour lui faire intégrer ouvertement les aspects qu'elle rend opaques: donc la Préface insiste sur le caractère universel des réactions de peur et d'espoir, et sur les apparentes exceptions que constituent les périodes stables. On pourrait dire que la théorie commune de la fortune dégage deux types de périodes et, dans ses formes les plus cultivées, les caractérise par la présence ou l'absence d'une idéologie (la superstition) et de son enracinement affectif (la peur et l'espoir); et que Spinoza greffe sur elle une théorie critique de la fortune qui repère *deux* idéologies et non pas une seule: la superstition dans les périodes troublées, l'illusion d'en demeurer à l'abri, dans les moments d'assurance. Le savoir inaugural du TTP, le minimum nécessaire pour discuter rationnellement mais non géométriquement avec le lecteur, réside dans l'application de la seconde de ces théories sur la première.

Est-ce là tout? Non, si l'on se tourne vers le système dans l'ordre de ses raisons. Car on trouvera là une troisième théorie, où la fortune est cette fois au bout du raisonnement et non au départ: on peut *démontrer*, à partir des livres I et II de l'*Ethique* que nécessairement notre propre vie nous échappe, que nous sommes soumis à des lois, physiques et psychologiques, que nous ne maitrisons pas, que nous sommes affrontés, par notre corps, à un ordre de rencontres extérieures dont certaines nous nuisent et certaines nous sont utiles. Mais cette théorie-là n'est pas présente dans le TTP, encore qu'elle n'y soit nullement contredite: ce qu'ailleurs Spinoza démontre à partir des prémisses du système, ici il le montre à partir du noyau vrai du toujours-déjà-su ou le rappelle à partir de la culture rhétorique qui l'a enregistré, mis en forme et condensé depuis longtemps.

III

Si maintenant on applique la troisième théorie à la deuxième, il faudra dire qu'il n'y a pas de contingence historique en dernière instance. Le système démontre la pleine nécessité de ce qui survient dans chaque vie humaine. Mais il y a une contingence *pour nous*: il y a de l'inattendu, et précisément là où nous le désirons le moins. La fortune désigne les conséquences hasardeuses de cette absence de hasard. Les lois nécessaires qui régissent les choses naturelles, y compris les actions humaines, ne marquent pas une intention; mais notre ignorance de ces lois, et notre incapacité à en déduire les événements singuliers fait que d'une part nous les vivons sous la forme d'un hasard temporel et répétitif, d'autre part que nous sommes tentés de les assigner à une Volonté ou à une Ironie qui nous dépasse - afin de croire saisir ce qu'en fait nous ne saisissons pas. C'est en ce point que s'enracine la tendance naturelle à sacraliser l'Histoire.[12]

En construisant sa théorie critique de la fortune, Spinoza extrait de la théorie courante ce qu'elle a de positif (et qui est une négation: celle de la certitude quant aux événements singuliers); il en retranche ce qui pourrait donner prise à une élaboration théologique. Faut-il alors penser que le dernier mot de sa philosophie de l'histoire est négatif? Qu'il se contente de séculariser l'histoire sainte et de refuser ou de dissoudre les diverses philosophies de la Providence? La méditation sur la fortune aboutirait alors a réaffirmer simplement la vanité et l'absence de sens des conduites humaines: tous les empires périssent, la nature humaine, étant éternelle, engendre éternellement les mêmes effets, on ne sort donc jamais d'une histoire cyclique faite de barbarie, civilisation, décadence.[13]

Ce n'est peut-être pas si simple: la théorie affirme l'existence d'une base anthropologique éternelle de l'histoire, mais peut-être n'en connaissons-nous pas encore tous les effets possibles. On peut tirer de la nature humaine un petit nombre de traits fixes qui expliquent suffisamment l'espace de variations dans lequel surviennent succès et catastrophes des individus et des sociétés. Il existe donc, malgré la variété des individus, et le caractère irréductible de l'*ingenium* de chacun, une description possible de l'espèce humaine et de ses comportements, qui correspond à des motifs constants.

Mais ces motifs, nous les connaissons toujours sous une forme déjà socialisée: il n'existe pas d'individus vivant réellement à l'état de nature et, d'un autre côté, la nature ne crée pas de peuples, ce sont les lois et les moeurs qui le font. Donc même si la psychologie individuelle est à la base supposée de l'histoire, celle-ci se déroule ensuite dans une trame où les effets de cette psychologie sont toujours imbriqués à l'acquis des moeurs et des lois, qui forment les hommes dès leur plus tendre enfance.

Qu'en est-il dès lors des effets de la fortune? Sont-ils immuables? Ils le sont dans la mesure où la fortune est immuablement variable; ils le sont même si cette variabilité inclut, par un hasard qui n'est pas impossible, une longue période de stabilité individuelle; car, on l'a vu, l'individu sera peut-être alors éloigné provisoirement de la superstition, mais il n'en arrachera pas les racines, perpétuellement reproduites par les appareils idéologiques mis en place pendant les périodes de peur et d'insécurité. Mais que se passera-t-il si, par une suite de circonstances initialement dues au hasard, une société tout entière vient à jouir de la sécurité? Alors non seulement la superstition reculera, mais on verra, à long terme, s'installer des institutions aptes à la faire reculer encore plus, ou à développer la civilisation et le commerce qui la feront reculer. On échappera ainsi, en partie du moins, au jeu inéluctable de la peur, de l'espoir et de leurs conséquences, tout cela non pas sur la base d'une mystérieuse disparition de la nature humaine, ou d'un rachat de la corruption, mais au contraire par le même jeu des mêmes lois nécessaires dans d'autres conditions. La production de ces conditions est bien originairement l'oeuvre de la même contingence-pour-nous; elles sont ensuite reproduites par les effets qu'elles ont engendrés, la civilisation, la raison, et même le regard philosophique sur la société qui conduit, dans la Hollande du XVIIe siècle, à la lutte pour la liberté de conscience.

En ce point on peut conclure: la théorie critique de la fortune élaborée dans le TTP est *aussi* un moyen d'échapper collectivement aux aléas de la fortune. Elle fait partie de la stratégie qui permettra, sans ignorer les cycles de l'histoire, de sortir de l'histoire cyclique.

1. G III/5. Traduction Appuhn (Garnier-Flammarion) II, 20.
2. "Si en effet, pendant qu'ils sont dans l'état de crainte, il se produit un incident qui leur rappelle un bien ou un mal passé, ils pensent que c'est l'annonce d'une issue heureuse ou malheureuse ..." *ibid.*
3. Sur d'autres aspects de ce problème de la fortune, qui ne seront pas abordés ici, on doit se reporter au remarquable article de F. Mignini: "Theology as the work and instrument of Fortune" dans les Actes du colloque d'Amsterdam de 1982, *Spinoza's political and theological thought*, Amsterdam (1984) 127-136.
4. Sur ces questions on ne peut que renvoyer aux travaux d'Akkerman et Zweerman.
5. Quinte-Curce: livre V §4; livre VII §7; livre IV §10; les citations seront empruntées à la traduction Crépin (Garnier) parfois modifiées.
6. Bayle note, à l'article Quinte-Curce: "l'auteur a eu même la sagesse d'aller au-devant du reproche de crédulité qu'il avait à craindre" et il cite La Mothe Le Vayer (*Jugement des principaux historiens*): "Pour faire voir bien clairement avec quelle circonspection cet historien a toujours traité les choses dont on se pouvait défier, je mettrai ici les termes dont il accompagne la narration de ce chien qui se laissa couper les membres pièce à pièce au royaume du Sophite, plutôt que de démordre et lâcher la prise du lion: *equidem*, dit-il, *plura transcribo quam credo. Nam nec affirmare sustineo quibus dubito, nec subducere quae accepi.*"
7. *Nec id miserrimum fortibus viris erat, sed quod inulti, quod ferarum ritu, velut in fovea deprehensi caederentur. Ira igitur in rabiem versa...* (V,3).
8. Exemples IV, 16; V, 12 (Darius enchainé avec des chaines d'or).
9. Il faudrait tenir compte aussi de fortune au sens de "mauvaise fortune, infortune," par exemple dans le cas des Grecs torturés par les Perses (V,5).
10. *Praecoci gaudio verita irritare fortunam* (IV, 15).
11. *Atque haec neminem ignorare existimo, quamvis plerosque se ipsos ignorare credam,* G III/5.

12. C'est à limiter cette tendance que sont *en fait* consacrées les équivalences énoncées au chapitre III du TTP, et notamment celle qui définit la fortune comme le "gouvernement de Dieu en tant qu'il gouverne les choses humaines par des causes extérieures et inattendues" et ce gouvernement lui-même par "l'ordre fixe et immuable de la nature, autrement dit l'enchaînement des choses naturelles" (G III/45-6; Appuhn p. 71).

13. Sur ces questions, et en particulier sur l'importance accordée par Spinoza à l'époque même où il écrit, voir les ouvrages récents d'A. Tosel et E. Balibar; sur la théorie de l'histoire, Matheron (1971).

Y-A-T-IL UNE PHILOSOPHIE
DU PROGRÈS HISTORIQUE CHEZ SPINOZA?

ANDRE TOSEL
Université de Nice

1. Pour tous les commentateurs qui jadis abordaient la philosophie de Spinoza par la seule *Ethique* une telle question paraîtrait absurde et sans objet, tant pour eux l'*Ethique* se réduisait à une théorie de la connaissance atemporelle et à une théorie de la modération des passions débouchant sur une mystique laïque de la libération intellectuelle et sur une conquête de l'éternité, exclusive d'une prise en compte positive de la durée.[1] L'orientation récente de la recherche française centrée davantage sur les rapports du procès éthique de libération et de la politique ont proposé l'idée d'une théorie spinozienne de l'histoire; mais en ce cas, la démarche partait du livre qui a été pensé par Spinoza comme l'introduction à sa philosophie, le *Traité théologico-politique*.[2]

   Ce faisant, la recherche spécialisée retrouvait à sa manière une thématique qui lui était antérieure, et qui en quelque sorte lui donnait ses fondements et justifications. Il s'agit de la thématique du procès historique comme passage d'une forme de vie et de pensée inférieure à une forme de vie et de pensée supérieure. Thématique qui bien avant les philosophies de l'histoire de la fin du XVIIIème siècle avait été celle d'un puissant mouvement d'idées qui avait vu converger les spéculations et recherches sur l'histoire de la terre, de la vie sur la terre, sur la chronologie de l'histoire humaine, sur l'histoire des nations, celle de leurs moeurs, religions, formes d'organisations politiques, sur le passage de la nature à l'humanité, sur la transition ou progrès de l'humanité barbare à l'humanité civilisée, sur le progrès de la connaissance depuis les mythes, fables, langages symboliques jusqu'aux à la pensée scientifique, aux langages conceptuels, et cela dans le cadre de la querelle des Anciens et des Modernes.[3] Spinoza surtout dans le TTP, se présente comme un protagoniste, un de ces héros des temps modernes, qui aux côté de F. Bacon et de T. Hobbes ont pris parti pour affirmer la possibilité de l'*advancement of learning*, pour soutenir la nécessité de sortir des premiers temps de l'humanité où la "vie de l'homme est alors solitaire, besogneuse, pénible, quasi-animale et brève."[4]

   2. Le TTP en effet rend possible un accès à l'histoire: par la destruction de l'histoire sacrée, par la critique de la Bible et de la religion révélée, par la démystification des oeuvres, sans validité théorique, de la théologie juive et chrétienne, Spinoza fait apparaître la théocratie hébraïque comme produit d'un mode d'organisation de la vie et de la pensée rude et barbare. La théocratie représente comme un passé qui ne peut être un modèle pour le présent, et qui doit être définitivement remplacé par un Etat libéral-démocratique, défenseur des sciences et des arts, promoteur des puissances délivrées des *conatus* humains, eux-mêmes capables de multiplier les échanges et d'approprier de manière élargie tous les corps naturels dont ils ont besoins.[5]

   Tout en développant une théorie de la puissance de la Nature-Dieu qui exclut l'origine créée de l'univers, tout en rendant possible une explication causale des processus de formation des corps naturels au sein de l'étendue, le

TTP, par sa théorie des lois, rend possible une explication causale de l'histoire des hommes en terme de passions, et il introduit la perspective d'une transition d'une forme de vie dominée par les passions tristes, les guerres de religion, la faible expansivité des forces humaines au sein d'un bloc théologico-politique, à une autre forme de vie généralisant les passions joyeuses, assurant la participation du plus grand nombre possible, permettant par la liberté de penser une promotion de l'*intellectus* et par la démocratie celle des *conatus*. Si rien n'est dit sur l'origine et la formation de l'univers, sur celle de la terre et de la vie, le cadre épistémologique d'une explication causale, immanente et laïque, est construit, et il permet une théorie de l'histoire des sociétés organisées autour de l'idée d'une conquête des degrés de puissance physique et logique. La théocratie hébraïque figure comme emblème d'une origine où se rejoignent faible capacité intellectuelle, faible développement des puissances des corps humains, domination de la superstition. Du même coup l'histoire sacrée perd sa sacralité: nulle valeur originaire n'est attribuée à cet Ancien Peuple et à cette ancienne Loi, pas plus qu'aux anciens peuples en général. Moïse perd son statut de législateur modèle. Le TTP conquiert simultanément la dimension des longues durées historiques puisqu'il critique l'attribution des livres de la Bible à un seul auteur et élargit la chronologie biblique, cadre de l'histoire alors reconnue. Ainsi se trouve confortée l'idée d'une primitivité des moeurs, des mythes, des langues des Anciens Peuples qui cessent d'être des modèles à imiter et deviennent les antagonistes des Modernes. Les Hébreux relèvent des premiers Temps où l'entendement avait forgé peu d'instruments, où la vie passionnelle avec ses cycles répétitifs dominait, prise dans une impuissance fondamentale, non encore à même de promouvoir l'industrie, la navigation, les arts, les machines, la médecine.

Dans le TTP la durée cesse d'être le phénomène de l'éternel, elle cesse d'être orientée par des Idées atemporelles auxquelles les phénomènes devraient plus ou moins participer, elle cesse de se référer à des Normes auxquelles il faudrait revenir comme à une origine bienfaisante mais perdue, pour annuler par cet effort de retour le pouvoir de dispersion temporelle. La durée obtient une consistance spécifique. C'est en elle que l'on accède aux vérités et que se détermine ce qui pour l'espèce représente son bien propre, son utile spécifique. Le temps des Prophètes, des Législateurs sacrés est fini, et avec lui celui de la superstition, de l'étroitesse de formes sociales vouées à la reproduction difficile d'individus faiblement développés. L'usage de la raison par l'intervention des sciences, l'usage du langage appelé à devenir conceptuel et à perdre sa dimension mythique ou fabuleuse, témoignent de ce que peut une série de tentatives, d'accumulation d'expériences, de mises au point de méthodes. Raison et langage sont de ce point de vue des acquis, produits de transformations. La société elle-même est susceptible de se transformer: elle ne tient plus sa signification d'une incarnation du sens de l'histoire universelle dans une histoire particulière, celle du peuple hébreu. Elle la tient d'elle-même, de son organisation interne, de sa capacité à aménager les rapports des individus passionnés qui la composent de manière à ce que ces rapports permettent le meilleur essor de leurs forces et aptitudes, l'essor des sciences et de la philosophie, au sein d'une libre opinion publique. De ce point de vue, manifeste d'une philosophie de la libération de *l'intellectus* et du *conatus*, le TTP s'inscrit délibérément comme acteur dans ce procès du transition de la barbarie à la civilisation, d'une vie sociale étroite et dominée par la superstition à une vie sociale plus riche, ouverte à la pratique élargie de la connaissance. Le TTP se pense comme instrument de progrès dans l'aménagement de la vie passionnelle et dans l'émergence d'une possibilité, la vie de la raison.[6]

3. Peut-on dire que cela suffit pour autoriser l'attribution à Spinoza d'une philosophie du progrès historique? Une telle philosophie, lorsqu'elle se systématise à la fin du XVIIIème siècle, avec par exemple Condorcet, unit dans une structure conceptuelle forte des thèses (avec des variantes contradictoires certes) que l'on peut formuler de la manière suivante:

> Thèse 1 - Le réel est intelligible et rationnel comme processus orienté vers une fin. Non seulement on a la possibilité d'une explication rationnelle des éléments irrationnels en leur efficace et nécessité - passions, intérêts, conflits, contradictions - mais on a la capacité de montrer que par ces mécanismes se produit l'avènement d'une raison substantielle unissant intérêt général, reconnaissance réciproque, universel concret et maîtrise de la nature.

> Thèse 2 - Cette fin qui est la vie de la raison, la raison comme fin, s'inscrit dans une structure téléologique: elle s'anticipe dans une origine et s'atteint au sein d'un procès qui est à la fois caractérisé par des moments critiques, et par des étapes où capacités, connaissances, habiletés s'accumulent. Périodes, âges, s'enchaînent dans une nécessité qui est garantie par la dynamique même du procès. Mis en mouvement, ce procès est irréversible, linéaire.

> Thèse 3 - Cette raison a pour noyau la connaissance scientifique et technique. C'est le progrès de cette dernière qui conditionne la possibilité de réaliser des valeurs éthiques, politiques ou juridiques, c'est-à-dire les autres progrès.

Nulle part Spinoza ne représente comme Condorcet un "tableau historique des progrès de l'esprit humain." Nulle part il ne formule une question comme celle qui tourmente Kant et à laquelle ce dernier répond, positivement sur le plan pratique (le progrès comme devoir moral), et négativement sur le plan théorique "déterminant" (il n'y a pas de savoir démontré du progrès, car la civilisation, le progrès des sciences, des arts sert la recherche de l'utile mais dans l'élément du conflit d'intérêts égoïstes et il ne se confond pas avec la moralisation). Spinoza ne pose même pas la question "Le genre humain est-il en progrès constant"? (Cf. "Conflit des facultés"). Mais la problématique du TTP - une théorie de l'histoire pensant la possibilité d'une promotion des entendements et des forces des *conatus* selon la transition barbarie-civilisation, superstition-raison-demeure présente dans les autres textes majeurs, l'*Ethique*, et le *Traité politique*. Selon quelles modalités? Sous quelles formes Spinoza pense-t-il alors le devenir de l'entendement, celui de la force productive des hommes, celui des formes d'association et d'organisation politique?

4. On ne peut en effet méconnaître que la dimension du processus accumulatif et linéairement orienté caractérise le procès de la connaissance, celui

des modes de vie - éthique - et celui du procès de la vie politique. On ne peut méconnaître que ces progrès constituent une durée organisée par la tension entre deux pôles, entre lesquels s'opère bien une transition qui n'est pas simplement logique, mais effective en sa durée même.

Commençons par la première de ces progressions, celle de la connaissance. l'*Ethique* ne renie pas le *Traité de la réforme de l'entendement*. Comme ce dernier elle affirme à la fois la logicité ou éternité de l'idée vraie ou adéquate et la temporalisation spécifique du procès de la connaissance. La *vis nativa* de l'entendement affirme la positivité de ses premières idées vraies au sein même de la prison de la *perceptio ex auditu aut ex aliquo signo*, dans celle de la *perceptio ab experientia vaga*. Ces premières formes de connaissance ne sont pas simplement "l'autre" de la vraie connaissance, elles sont premières dans la durée et il y a bien progrès de la connaissance lorsque émerge, se stabilise, se reproduit de manière élargie la *perceptio ubi essentia rei ex alio re concluditur*. Si les forces de connaissance peuvent être considérées comme autant de manières de se rapporter au même objet et si elles se hiérarchisent dans un espace logique, il y a genèse de la raison, développement de la *vis nativa* de l'*intellectus*. Il faut prendre au sérieux l'analogie avec le progrès de l'instrumentation technique: la connaissance vraie forme ses idées qui pour elles sont autant d'idées nouvelles permettant d'approprier peu à peu ce qui jusqu'ici était inconnu. Une technique empirique, mise en échec, laisse place à une technique rationnelle, vérifiée, et il faut alors abandonner les anciennes certitudes de la tradition, des mythes et représentations symboliques, de la simple empirie. Il faut pouvoir multiplier en quantité, dans une durée intensive, les nouvelles certitudes de la *perceptio per solam essentiam*, qui sont jusqu'ici peu nombreuses.[7]
"De même que les hommes, au début à l'aide d'instruments innés et bien qu'avec peine et d'une manière imparfaite, ont pu faire certaines choses très faciles, et après avoir fait celles-ci, en ont fait d'autres plus difficiles avec moins de peine et plus de perfection et ainsi s'élèvant par degrés des travaux les plus simples aux instruments et des instruments revenant à d'autres oeuvres et instruments, en arrivèrent à pouvoir accomplir beaucoup de choses, et de très difficiles, de même l'entendement par sa puissance innée se forme des instruments intellectuels à l'aide desquels il acquiert d'autres forces pour d'autres oeuvres intellectuelles, et grâce à ces oeuvres, il se forme d'autres instruments, c'est-à-dire le pouvoir de pousser l'investigation plus avant; ainsi il avance par degré jusqu'à ce qu'il ait atteint le comble de la sagesse" (¶ 32, p. 37).

L'arrachement à la simple expérience et aux préjugés de la tradition théologique et politique est bien un nouveau départ pour une "science" qui se constitue ainsi un avenir indéfini dans la connaissance des *essentiae*. S'ouvre l'histoire au sens plein du savoir, le savoir comme histoire, comme accumulation d'idées vraies, comme progression effective. L'*Ethique*, lorsqu'elle analyse la *transitio* de l'*imaginatio*, ou connaissance du premier genre, à la *ratio* ou connaissance du second genre, prolonge la même thèse. Il ne s'agit pas du passage de la nature à la culture, mais celui d'une culture grossière de notre *mens* à une culture promouvant par les notions communes les idées adéquates. On pourrait ici montrer que cette transition rend possible une histoire du langage commun qui de métaphorique peut devenir réellement conceptuel. Le langage commun, de même que les imaginations, dépendent de la puissance conditionnante des autres corps sur le nôtre, en ce que cette action est l'objet privilégié de l'imagination. Voilà pourquoi avant que l'entendement puisse produire de manière plus continue et élargie ses idées à partir d'autres idées, se produit la masse confuse et inconstante des images, et des idées de ces images ou imaginations qui reflètent les changements intervenus dans notre corps sous l'action des autres corps. C'est dans cette occurrence de la "fortune" que se forment les termes transcendantaux (être, chose, quelque chose) et les notions universelles (homme, cheval, chien) qui n'ont rien à voir avec les concepts adéquats. Les mots sont bien une partie de l'imagination, et nous commençons par construire beaucoup de nos concepts en rapport à la manière dont ces mots se composent vaguement dans la mémoire selon une disposition donnée du corps.

La naissance du langage scientifique exige une critique de ces "verba": beaucoup de concepts reçoivent des *nomina negativa* (infini, incorporel) en raison des confusions du langage commun.[8] Il faut pouvoir distinguer de manière dynamique entre les images des choses et d'autre part les idées et concepts de l'esprit, et contrôler le processus par lequel le sens "vulgaire" de quelques termes philosophiques se transforme en sens "savant." Il faut de même "distinguer entre les idées et les mots par lesquels nous désignons les choses." Or, la nature de la pensée implique que "l'idée ne consiste ni dans l'image de quelque chose ni dans les mots. L'essence des mots et des images est constituée par les seuls mouvements corporels qui n'enveloppent en aucune façon le concept de la pensée" (E IIP49S). La pensée progresse donc à partir de la connaissance du sens commun, des notions avec lesquels le *vulgus* entend expliquer la nature, pour dépasser la simple indication des états du corps et pour fixer la nature des choses.

De ce point de vue la redéfinition des concepts comme ceux de substance, attributs, mode - "qui ne peuvent pas s'acquérir par l'imagination, mais par l'entendement seul" - représente de droit une étape décisive dans le développement de la raison. Qu'il y ait un développement progressif, on en a la preuve a contrario en ce que l'imagination désigne un mode de connaissance où domine la fluctuation permanente, où il est impossible de s'orienter, de former des projets à long terme, où les cycles d'idées confuses empêchent la détermination des connaissances de notre propre corps, des autres corps, et celle de l'âme même. Connaître réellement c'est cesser d'être la proie d'un ordre commun de la nature et approprier l'ordre et la connexion des choses par celui des idées. L'imagination n'a pas d'histoire interne, la raison en a une; elle est un commencement de la vie intellectuelle où l'esprit demeure affecté par l'idée qui représente l'affection des corps étrangers sur le nôtre. En son procès au contraire la raison signifie sortie de cette confusion, réorganisation de notre rapport aux corps extérieurs et au nôtre propre, elle est "ordre" et ordre de marche, accumulation d'idées par lesquelles se produit l'appropriation théorique de la nature, de notre nature propre, avec progrès simultané dans la compréhension de l'universel et du singulier, avec conquête de la compléxité.[9]

On peut souligner cette historicité interne qui est celle d'un commencement surmonté, d'un piétinement sur place interrompu, d'un chaos stochastique modifié en ordre de marche, en la précisant par recours à la théorie des "notions communes." Si la raison progresse en déterminant "ce qui est commun à toutes choses et se trouve pareillement dans la partie et le tout", elle est appropriation des relations de convenance entre tous les corps, entre les corps et le corps humain (E IIPP38,39). Elle est un système ouvert découvrant les appartenances, elle est instance de communication orientée sur un élargissement dont la limite est reculée à l'infini. L'éternité des relations découvertes connote leur teneur épistémique, mais n'annule en rien leur découverte progressive. Par la raison la durée est constitution de systèmes relationnels de communication toujours plus intensément activés. Cette histoire est ainsi celle d'une appropriation des choses et d'une constitution de notre puissancc logique, dans la complexité dynamique de ses relations constitutives.

Il y a plus encore. La science intuitivc radicalise cette histoire de la connaissance, elle dynamise la connaissance comme histoire. La déduction des notions communes a certes son historicité intrinsèque; elle construit par les notions communes l'essence nécessaire ouverte de l'être en tant qu'il est régi par des enchaînements causaux infinis et éternels. Mais la science intuitive est elle aussi procès, déduction métaphysique en ce qu'elle va de la connaissance de l'essence nécessaire de l'être (les attributs) à l'essence des choses singulières, laquelle inclut l'existence *sub specie aeternitatis*. Malgré l'éternité de son objet, elle a bien lieu dans la durée. Comme tclle, cllc élargit indéfiniment le savoir général des choses, et procède à la conquêtc dc la complexité propre aux *res singulares*. Elle est progrès intensif et extensif dans la connaissance indéfiniment ouverte de ces *res*. "Plus nous comprenons les choses singulières, plus nous connaissons Dieu" (E VP24).

Loin d'être détachement ascétique du mondc ct de ses éléments, tous pris dans leur procès propre, la *Scientia intuitiva* est approche progressive de la totalité en ses éléments, et elle s'enrichit de l'infinité ouverte de ces *res singulares* saisie elle-même au sein de la richesse la plus ample possible des rapports avec le monde. La science intuitive, loin d'être une intuition unique de la totalité donnée *una simul* est appropriation des *res singulares* sur la base de leur position dans le système des relations d'appartenancc. Elle a donc une carrière, un avenir. Elle est sa reproductibilité élargie propre.

5. La connaissance-progrès se révèlc êtrc l'autrc face du procès éthique lui-même, du procès d'éthicisation de l'individualité humaine elle-même. La théorie des genres de connaissance est la face intellectuelle de la théorie des modes d'effectuation du désir et de la vie des affects. A la polarité *Imaginatio-Ratio* correspond, en raison du parallélisme des attributs de la pensée et de l'étendue, la polarité *Passio/Actio*. Ce qui restait abstraction logique se concrétise avec la prise en compte du corps, du *conatus*, de ses affections passives et de ses actions! S'il y a progrès de la connaissance dans la transition de la connaissance du premier genre à celles de second et troisièmc genres, il y a progrès éthique depuis la vie dominée par les passions (et les passions tristes) jusqu'à la vie sous la conduite de la raison où nous agissons commc cause adéquate. Les états que

l'homme franchit pour parvenir à la production d'idées vraies se réciproquent avec les états qu'il franchit dans la détermination de son utile propre, de ce qui est pour lui le bien. Action et idée, causation et conception sont données comme une seule et même chose. La transition éthique est le chemin de la servitude à la liberté, et l'on peut parler de transition de mode de vie à un autre qui est réellement un progrès.

La vie du premier genre - la servitude - est dominée - en ce qui concerne le mode humain fini - par la dépendance des causes extérieures. Le *conatus* s'y exprime à un bas degré de puissance, dans une oscillation qui est en fait un chaos stationnaire; la causalité *in alio* domine quasi absolument, à la différence infinitésimale près de ce minimum de positivité qu'est toute essence singulière. Avec la vie du second genre, dans la condition de dépendance, s'esquisse une genèse du "conatus", de sa capacité de causalité adéquate d'action. Dans l'*in alio* se développe une sphère de relations pratiques dont est responsable la causalité *in se*. Par un progrès qui est une technique de gradualisation, l'essence humaine s'approprie la nature extérieure, la sienne propre. S'opère un procès d'éthicisation qui est procès de substantialisation relative pour le mode, dans les limites modales. L'homme libre est celui qui peut à la fois guider le procès de reproduction de son individualité corporelle, se subjectiviser, tout en s'appropriant de manière élargie les corps extérieurs dont son propre corps a besoin pour son expansion. La vie selon la raison est à la fois expansivité positive du corps, appropriation (et non domination idéaliste ou prométhéenne) de la nature en ses éléments, constitution de réseaux de reconnaissance et de communauté avec tous ceux qui obéissent aux mêmes lois internes rationnelles et raisonnables. Elle se définit comme possibilité d'une histoire individuelle en communauté avec les autres, nos semblables, et ce au sortir des cycles répétitifs de l'impuissance propre à la vie passionnelle, et à sa fluctuation propre. De ce point de vue la vie dans la servitude définit un passé par lequel le *conatus* a commencé et qui dure comme un passif dont il faut se libérer. La vie de liberté définit un présent qui peut se construire un avenir, en ce que l'alternance des cycles des passions fixant notre *conatus* peut céder la place à un chemin vers notre perfection. De ce même point de vue l'*Ethique* serait la codification de cette transition, et elle assumerait sa fonction de partage historique entre la préhistoire encore présente de notre effort pour nous conserver et son histoire possible. Cette conscience d'une historicité est revendiquée discrètement par Spinoza qui s'attribue le mérite d'être le premier à avoir compris la dynamique et la morphologie de notre *conatus* et d'avoir rendu ainsi possible la conquête d'une individualité libre, développant une raison capable de gouverner nos passions pour en faire le matériau d'une expansion.[10]

Dans l'inversion graduelle des polarités de la *causa in alio* et la *causa in se*, se produit comme un *exemplar naturae humanae*, le procès-progrès de la constitution de la libre individualité. Le déplacement du régime constitutif de la modalité de l'homme va tendanciellement de l'être dans l'autre et par l'autre vers l'être par soi. La transition éthique humaine de la servitude à la liberté, ce progrès qui s'opère dans la durée et ouvre une histoire de la modalité humaine, est expression de la pulsation ontologique qui détermine le procès du réel à se reproduire pour soi, éternellement, en un enchaînement d'êtres plus ou moins causés par un autre, plus ou moins capables de se substantialiser, de s'éthiciser.

L'*Ethique* présente ainsi une histoire abstraite des formes de l'individualité humaine. Mais il ne s'agit pas d'une typologie méta-historique valable en tous temps et tous lieux. Il s'agit d'une axiomatique de la libération dont la méta-historicité se réciproque avec l'historicité. Le progrès du procès d'éthicisation détermine une durée humaine où le procès ontologique s'exprime comme procès de la liberté, histoire de la libération. La typologie des formes d'individualité - l'ignorant, l'homme libre-sage - est une grammaire méta-historique du traitement de la durée humaine, comme histoire-transition de la servitude à la liberté.[11]

Ainsi au sein d'une ontologie causale, rigoureusement critique du finalisme transcendant de la pensée antique et médiévale (E IApp), par le biais de la destruction de tout anthropomorphisme, lequel transpose les fins de l'homme superstitieux au plan de la nature, l'*Ethique* présente une théorie du progrès d'éthicisation, laissant place à une finalité interne, et immanente au développement du *conatus* humain. Sans que soit oubliée la critique de l'illusion axiologique - il ne saurait y avoir de Bien et de Perfection en soi - l'*Ethique* thématise la validité objective du point de vue de la modalité humaine. Sur la base du jeu des mécanismes causaux de la servitude, il est possible de former le "modèle d'une nature humaine supérieure," *exemplar naturae humanae*.[12] L'*Ethique* est *transitio*, une *transitio* qu'il faut stabiliser, que l'on peut stabiliser dans le sens de l'action et de l'actif, de la conception toujours plus adéquate, de la causation interne toujours plus puissante. Pour nous, les hommes, la productivité anonyme de la puissance se projette comme transition pour ce "nous," ce *nos*, comme possibilité d'une réalisation. *Nos, posse a minore ad perfectionem transire.*

La vie de la raison est donc progrès dans la constitution d'un *nos* qui s'approprie les corps de la nature, sans mythe de domination, et qui tend à s'élargir. Les notions communes, en particulier, se déterminent, sur le plan pratique, comme schémas d'appropriation des corps dont nous avons besoin pour nous conserver et simultanément comme schémas de communication, producteurs de relations communautaires. Tendanciellement la vie selon la raison est une vie qui multiplie les relations de convenance avec les autres choses, les communications avec ces autres choses qui nous sont les plus communes et qui sont les autres hommes. La nature humaine supérieure est construction progressive d'un *nos* élargi, d'une communauté ouverte. Cette vie n'est pas idéal transcendant - pur devoir - elle exprime un accord nécessaire, issu de la puissance en expansion de notre nature en ce qu'elle recherche l'utile propre et se perfectionne en sortant des cycles statiques et répétitifs de la servitude. Le progrès est celui de la communauté avec les choses et les hommes, de la communication. On peut ici parler d'une histoire de la vie de la raison et d'elle seule comme mécanisme d'accumulation de rationalité, d'appropriation non possessive des choses naturelles, de constitution de réseaux de communication impliquant tendanciellement la rationalité du plus grand nombre d'*alter ego* possibles.[13]

6. Cependant, le processus éthique ne concerne que l'histoire pure des formes de l'individualité humaine, l'histoire-modèle. Le même texte qui énonce que l'homme qui vit de la vie de la raison est un dieu pour l'homme corrige: "Il est rare que les hommes vivent sous la conduite de la raison" (E IVP35S). Dans le présent, "l'homme est nécessairement toujours soumis aux passions, suit l'ordre commun de la nature et lui obéit, et s'y adapte autant que la nature des choses l'exige."[14] Le processus éthique émerge sur le terrain de l'organisation passionnelle des hommes, qui est servitude, et qui soit être désormais considéré comme ordre social et politique. Celui-ci semble alors annuler ou limiter comme une histoire possible ou pure - *exemplar* - le processus d'éthicisation. Si la politique est une organisation immanente des hommes passionnels, elle reste dans la servitude; et celle-ci ne peut plus être dite étape, période initiale d'une progrès-procès de libération. Elle devient condition générale dont ne peut sortir qu'une minorité. Si le concret de la vie humaine est celui de la servitude des passions, ce concret se détermine comme politique, puisque les hommes passionnels "ne peuvent passer la vie dans la solitude et à la plupart agrée fort cette définition que l'homme est un animal sociable, et en effet les choses se sont disposées de telle sorte que de la société commune naissent beaucoup plus d'avantages que d'inconvénients" (E IVP35S).

Et pourtant tout se passe comme si la pulsation ontologique entre "l'être causé dans un autre" et "l'être cause en soi" se réfléchissait, certes affaiblie, mais réelle, dans l'ordre politique. La grande transition pure ou axiologique des formes de vie, la transition éthique qui est rare et difficile, qui est un *posse*, s'anticipe ou s'esquisse sans nulle prédétermination dans une quasi-transition intérieure à la politique même, définie d'abord comme ordre de coexistence dans la servitude d'hommes passionnels, pourtant condamnés à la perpétuelle fluctuation stationnaire des cycles passionnels répétitifs, voués à la constance de l'inconstance. Dans l'ordre politique, effet et forme d'aménagement de la servitude de la *multitudo* passionnelle (*multitudo* qui est alors *vulgus*), se produit, dans ce qui semble intransitif, une transition intra-passionnelle qui n'exclut pas les rechutes dans les cycles (puissance supérieure - puissance inférieure), mais qui les neutralise. Le *Traité politique* ne renie pas ce que semblait énoncer le *Traité théologico-politique* lorsque celui-ci présentait la séquence théocratie-Etat libéral-démocratique comme le schéma d'évolution tendancielle des passions du corps politique au sein de l'opposition Barbarie/ Civilisation. Le *Nos* qui est alors celui de la *multitudo* ignorante, lorsqu'il recherche son utile propre, au milieu des oppositions mutuelles et de leurs surdéterminations imaginaires, ne peut pas ne pas exprimer sa puissance. Cette multitude est conduite à faire de la paix et de la sécurité un objectif majeur; elle laisse se produire dans son système relationnel des conduites un système d'institutions qui doivent produire paix et sécurité, mais en tenant constamment son autorité du consensus de la *multitudo*. L'individuation propre de l'Etat est un problème permanent, problème dynamique puisque il s'agit d'obtenir de la part de l'appareil d'Etat des décisions qui puissent être consenties par la *multitudo*, en ce qu'elles ne lèsent pas directement la représentation plus ou moins imaginaire que cette *multitudo* en ses membres se fait de son intérêt. Dans ces conditions, la *multitudo* obéit, et l'obéissance produit la paix et la sécurité. Sécurité des individus donnant leur consensus et obéissant, stabilité d'institutions qui garantissent cette sécurité et ne prenant jamais de décisions qui soulèvent la désobéissance, telle est la mécanique qui aménage concrètement la servitude des hommes passionnels en cité.

> Ce qui est le meilleur régime (*status*) pour tout Etat, on le connaît facilement en considérant la fin de la société civile: cette fin n'est rien d'autre que la paix et la sécurité de la vie. Par la suite, le meilleur Etat est celui dont les hommes passent leur vie dans la concorde et dont les lois ne sont jamais transgressées. En effet, il est certain que les séditions, les guerres et le mépris ou la transgression de la légalité doivent être imputés non pas tant à la méchanceté des sujets qu'au mauvais régime de l'Etat. Les hommes en effet ne naissent pas aptes à la vie en société, ils le deviennent.[15]

Le mécanisme politique décisif est celui par lequel la multitude accorde - en le laissant se constituer - la puissance à un appareil d'Etat, et cela à chaque instant. Ce mécanisme repose à son tour, en retour, sur la capacité de cette institution à inspirer à chaque individu assez de crainte et d'espoir (donc assez de possibilités de vivre selon son désir de l'utile tel qu'il se le représente) pour que tous raccordent majoritairement à l'appareil d'Etat l'usage de leur puissance associée à l'instant suivant.

Il semblerait que ce mécanisme ait pour effet de stabiliser les menaces de guerre civile permanente liées aux "abus" de l'appareil d'Etat et aux "désobéissances" des citoyens. On serait loin de toute transition si ce mécanisme n'était que celui d'une régulation continue. Or, tel n'est pas le cas. Ce mécanisme se reproduit, s'autorègle, si de fait les régimes organisent la tendance immanente de la démocratisation par un élargissement maximal du corps des citoyens et par le maintien d'une sphère de libre communication. Le *Traité politique*, en analysant les mécanismes causaux de la reproduction de l'équilibre entre institutions et multitude forme des modèles de réalisation de cet équilibre. Exemples analogues à ceux du progrès éthique.

Ces modèles sont inégalement puissants, selon leur teneur plus ou moins grande en démocratie. La démocratie est dite de toutes les formes d'imperium, *omnino absolutum*, totalement absolue (*Traité politique*, XI, 1, p.80). Absolu en ce que le pouvoir en entier est dans les mains de tous les citoyens et que la *multitudo* devenue peuple, *populus*, est libre, puisqu'elle obéit à elle-même, source de la loi et sujet de cette même loi. L'absoluité ici se fonde sur la communauté du vouloir, librement formée de tous. Cette communauté n'est pas rationnelle au sens strict, mais elle produit des effets qui sont ceux de la raison: elle rend possible une obéissance à la loi comme telle; et en tant que sphère d'une libre opinion publique, elle rend possible l'apparition des sciences et de la philosophie. Dans les processus de la démocratisation, et de la libre communication des jugements, il devient possible d'indiquer à l'appareil d'Etat les possibilités de changement devenues nécessaires (lois, institutions). La tendance à la démocratisation comme forme immanente optimale de résolution du problème politique tient lieu de transition et de progrès historique. Cette démocratisation progressive peut conduire à ordonner les régimes (monarchie, aristocratie, démocratie), tout comme elle peut transformer de l'intérieur chacun de ces modèles pour que fonctionne le meilleur des régimes. Celui-ci produit alors des effets que la raison valide et universalise, car il s'agit de l'aptitude à respecter la loi à laquelle on participe comme fin en soi. La quasi transition ou le quasi progrès démocratique est une tendance objective de la politique qui rend possible la vie de la raison et que celle-ci interprète comme une transition intérieure à la servitude passionnelle lui permettant de produire comme l'antichambre de la transition proprement éthique. Il n'y a pas de loi de passage nécessaire à la démocratie par la monarchie et l'aristocratie; il y a une loi tendancielle de démocratisation comme *exemplar naturae politicae.* Si tel n'était pas le cas, on ne comprendrait pas que Spinoza ajoute en fait à la paix et à la sécurité comme oeuvre de l'Etat le meilleur, la garantie de la vraie vie humaine. "Quand nous disons que l'Etat le meilleur est celui où les hommes vivent dans la concorde, j'entends qu'ils vivent d'une vie proprement humaine, d'une vie qui ne se définit point par la circulation du sang et l'accomplissement des autres fonctions communes à tous les animaux, mais principalement par la raison qui est la vraie vie de l'Ame."[16]

Il n'y a pas de philosophie du progrès historique en politique comme ordre de succession d'étapes ou d'âges, selon une loi nécessaire. Il y a une théorie du progrès politique comme démocratisation, et cette théorie est énoncé d'un problème et d'une ligne tendancielle de résolution. Le progrès en politique, sur la base acquise de la sécularisation (Dieu est sorti de l'horizon du TP; la fonction de l'autorité ecclésiastique s'est réduite), consiste dans la perte de transcendance de l'appareil d'Etat, dans une circulation de plus en plus organique entre appareil d'Etat et base constituée par la Multitude, en élargissement de la base de masse de l'Etat, en pénétration du *populus* dans les institutions, en progression de l'automatisme législatif, en extension des procédures conscientes de discussion des intérêts. Tous ces mécanismes de la transition démocratique obtiennent de la *Multitudo* ce que la raison vise, paix, sécurité, vie de libre discussion, possibilité de la vie de la raison elle-même. Dans la servitude, la tendance à la démocratisation réalise une quasi action par laquelle l'Etat, le Peuple, conquièrent une quasi causalité adéquate.

Les passions du corps politique peuvent ainsi produire une quasi action adéquate de l'Etat. L'analyse causale du *Traité politique* est un programme de transformation visant à produire un système complexe de décisions collectives où les citoyens passionnels s'auto-déterminent, devenant un peu mieux cause adéquate de la gestion de leur force collective. Le système autorégulé des passions se transforme par son mécanisme même en système de la liberté politique, lequel prépare l'expansion de la libération éthique: dès lors celle-ci peut interpréter celle-là sans céder à l'imaginaire finaliste, comme son antichambre, son milieu. Les modèles du *Traité Politique* sont des opérateurs de transition démocratique, elle-même condition de la transition éthique.[17]

7. Que conclure de cet examen? Quelle réponse donner à notre question initiale? Nous dirons qu'il n'y a pas chez Spinoza de philosophie du progrès

historique au sens fort défini en 3, mais une théorie d'un progrès-problème qui est un possible objectif causalement produit.

Point 1. L'ontologie spinozienne de la production, développe un rationalisme du mouvement qui interdit de projeter la catégorie de progrès, comme celle de bon et de mauvais, et comme toutes les notions axiologiques, au plan de la substance. Si ces notions ont un sens relationnel et relatif, quoiqu'objectif, c'est au niveau des modes et particulièrement au niveau du *nos* humain. La substance comme puissance infinie qui se cause par soi en causant l'infinité de ses modes, nous y compris, n'est pas Histoire, Progrès, puisqu'elle s'exprime tout aussi bien dans des processus non irréversibles, non cumulatifs selon une infinité de modes. L'attribution du maximum de puissance causale à la substance et à elle seule, exclut que celle-ci soit interprétée selon des catégories qui n'ont de sens qu'au niveau des modes. La substance n'est pas histoire, elle n'a pas d'histoire, puisqu'elle est ce en quoi et par qui il y a progrès historique et régression, cycles, processus divers. L'histoire alors est locale et modale. Mais précisément, parce que le mode est mode de la substance, la puissance de la substance s'exprime plus ou moins en ses modes. La possibilité de la transition éthique ne peut pas ne pas nous apparaître à nous, le "nos" humain, lorsque nous sommes munis de la connaissance de notre nature au sein de la nature, comme expression éminente de la substance, comme procès de substantialisation possible. Si la substance n'est pas seulement histoire, l'histoire elle est de la substance, elle est en elle et par elle. Le progrès comme nécessité éthique est conquête de substantialité. L'histoire qui ne peut être que locale et modale apparaît néanmoins comme un cas particulier et éminent de la puissance de certains modes, de leur transformabilité et de leur productivité. La substance comme Individu total, où se produit et se joue la modalité universelle y compris la modalité historique, ne change pas. Elle continue à demeurer une et la même, selon une modalité difficile à préciser d'ailleurs, dans et par la transformation incessante de ses formes (y compris la forme-progrès). "Toute la nature est un seul individu dont les parties, c'est-à-dire tous les corps varient d'une infinité de modes, sans aucun changement de l'Individu total" (E IIL7S). La catégorie de progrès cumulatif indéfini réglé par une fin est inutilisable comme celle de durée pour expliquer la causalité de la substance. De ce point de vue, il serait spinozien d'inclure comme un chapitre de l'appendice du livre I de l'*Ethique* l'idée de Progrès comme être de raison, fiction issue de la projection de notre désir, c'est-à-dire hypostase d'une modalité de l'expérience humaine.

L'efficacité du procès d'éthicisation ne doit pas être transposée et projetée en tant que loi de la substance, comme si celle-ci visait et avait pour but le progrès historique, et se limitait à cette seule fin.

Mais la réalité - qui est aussi *posse* où se réalise le *nos* humain - du progrès éthique a pour nous sa validité objective: le processus d'éthicisation a plus de substantialité pour nous que n'importe quel autre processus, parce qu'il exprime notre nature en sa puissance propre, supérieure à d'autres natures. Le processus-progrès éthique doté de son historicité propre - dépend du degré de complexité élevé du corps humain et des modalités sous lesquelles celui-ci est nécessité à

se conserver en augmentant sa capacité d'appropriation. Il dépend simultanément de la haute complexité de l'âme de l'homme qui peut penser par concepts
adéquats et devenir cause adéquate. Le progrès éthique est donc inscrit dans
la nature d'une chose singulière complexe, relativement puissante, comme
l'homme, union d'un corps composé de nombreux autres corps complexes et
d'une âme correspondante. Si les autres choses ont leur perfection, cette
perfection implique pour beaucoup d'entre elles leur appropriation par le corps
humain, leur insertion dans le *nos* humain, dont la perfection propre inclut sous
beaucoup d'aspects une puissance supérieure. "Il vaut beaucoup mieux considérer
les actions des hommes que celles des bêtes," car "ce qui est humain est plus
digne de notre connaissance."[18] Mais cela ne saurait faire oublier l'égalitarisme
ontologique: on ne saurait classer dans une hiérarchie univoque les êtres et
développer "l'illusion progressiste" qui ferait du progrès humain la fin de la
nature, et des être de la nature des matériaux définis par leur appropriation
humaine. L'objectivité relationnelle du progrès pour le *nos* humain doit
s'affirmer en simultané avec la critique de cette illusion progressiste. (Tout serait
fait pour notre domination indéfinie, tous les êtres seraient préordonnés à notre
"usus" illimité comme pouvoir d'user et d'abuser, et seraient les moyens de notre
domination sur la nature).

8. *Point 2.* Le progrès éthique doit être désolidarisé de "l'illusion
progressiste" qui est un fantasme de maîtrise solidaire d'une interprétation
imaginaire de ce qu'est la vraie puissance. L'histoire-modèle du procès (progrès)
d'éthicisation doit être comprise sans être mystifiée par la thèse des pouvoirs
illimités du seul progrès scientifique et technique. Le fantasme progressiste de
maîtrise doit être dissocié de la conception adéquate du progrès éthique. Sur
le plan théorique, le progrès n'est pas domination, conception idéaliste de son
objet. Il est appropriation théorique du réel découvert, respecté et utilisé selon
ses rapports de convenance et de communauté. Le maître est toujours celui
qui a besoin d'un esclave, or la liberté est fin de la servitude. L'*intellectus* n'est
pas despote. Il est ami de ses objets, même de ceux qu'il doit approprier.
Autant dire que Spinoza ne développe pas une idée faustienne du progrès de
la connaissance qui en ferait une expression démiurgique. A ce propos il
convient de revenir sur les modalités et les formes de ce progrès.

Il ne saurait signifier une prise de congé définitive de l'imagination, un
passage sans reste à un âge de la raison qui serait accessible directement.
L'imagination est à la fois une condition originaire à laquelle toute *mens* est
soumise et un état dans lequel l'esprit peut s'enfermer à tout jamais. Il faut
donc distinguer ce qui dans la connaissance du premier genre représente un
commencement, un recommencement obligé, et ce qui peut faire d'elle l'horizon
indépassable de la confusion. L'âme ne peut pas ne pas avoir des idées confuses
parce qu'elle est âme d'un corps qui ne peut pas ne pas être affecté par les corps
extérieurs, et parce qu'elle reflète ces relations de dépendance. La servitude est
forme radicale d'une situation de dépendance, l'homme n'est pas empire dans
un empire, mais partie de quelque chose d'autre, son esprit ne peut être conçu
par soi mais par un autre. Ce serait pure imagination que de se représenter
un esprit qui n'aurait plus à refléter les images des affections des corps sur le

sien. De ce point de vue l'imagination désigne la relation originaire qui nous lie aux corps, au corps qui est le nôtre, et par laquelle nous sommes donnés à nous-mêmes comme un autre dans une altérité fondamentale. Vivre dans l'imagination, par contre c'est ne jamais délivrer la force innée de l'entendement par laquelle nous concevons adéquatement notre relation de dépendance et sommes cause d'idées adéquates. On ne sort pas *stricto sensu* de l'imagination, on rectifie les imaginations en limitant la limitation qu'elles constituent, en inversant tendanciellement la proportion entre idées confuses et mutilés et idées adéquates, en transformant le rapport immédiat, subi, causé, aux corps extérieurs, à notre corps, à notre esprit, en formant une idée adéquate de notre esprit, de notre corps, des corps de la nature, en découvrant leurs relations de convenance et en pensant leur singularité. Tout se joue dans la transition comme graduation en acte, comme élargissement des idées adéquates. Mais si l'on développe ces idées on ne supprime pas l'imagination en tant que rapport théorique passif par lequel nous sommes donnés à nous mêmes, et donnés au monde dans l'altérité. Ce monde, on peut seulement l'aménager, y construire une sphère d'idées adéquates. Si le progrès signifiait abandon complet d'un âge de l'imagination, il serait un mythe. La raison est liée dialectiquement à une imagination qu'elle doit critiquer, limiter, recouvrir d'une zone expansive de connaissances, mais non éliminer. Une idée rationnelle de la raison fait du progrès théorique une tension dialectique permanente assignant à l'imagination une condition de donné; elle permet une appropriation de cette nature d'abord subie en nous comme notre relation à notre corps en tant qu'il est causé et affecté par les autres corps. (Cf. E III).

Le progrès de l'imagination à la raison doit être pensée sans illusion progressiste. Il ne signifie donc pas disparition du premier terme pour autant que celui-ci désigne une condition originaire de commencement qui peut être modifiée, non supprimée. Un rationalisme raisonnable connaît ses conditions de possibilité, d'exercice, et ses limites. Voilà pourquoi on ne doit pas imaginer l'entrée définitive et totale dans un âge de raison auquel nous accéderions spontanément. Chaque esprit doit toujours développer ses idées vraies, accroître leur capital sur la base de cette condition originaire qui est liée à la nature de l'âme comme idée d'un corps existant en acte. La raison doit se souvenir de la difficulté et de la modestie de ses débuts - une idée vraie - elle doit lutter en permanence pour se reproduire: les chaînes causales dont elle forme le modèle se forgent dans la conjoncture mouvante des fluctuations de l'imagination réfléchissant les affections du corps.[19] Elles sont menacées d'interruption, de destruction; car notre corps en dépit de sa puissance peut toujours rencontrer un corps plus fort, et notre âme malgré sa supériorité peut être contrainte à interrompre son effort de conception provisoirement ou définitivement. Le progrès n'est pas garanti, sinon par illusion rétrospective lorsque nous appuyant sur les chaînes causales reconstruites nous les projetons comme devant se prolonger indéfiniment, en oubliant que l'âme est idée du corps et qu'il n'est donné dans la Nature aucune chose singulière qu'il n'en soit donnée une autre plus puissante et plus forte. "Mais si une chose quelconque est donnée, une autre plus puissante par laquelle le première peut être détruite est donnée."[20]

Il importe donc de démystifier la raison dans son exercice, et de ne pas oublier que la transition est tâche à reproduire en chaque occurrence, à chaque instant de notre existence.

Il y a davantage. Pour des raisons naturelles - liées à la fois à des conditions internes et externes difficiles à préciser - l'égalité ontologique des âmes comme modes finis de la même substance, et comme citoyens de la même nature supérieure,[21] se réciproque d'une inégalité dans la capacité de concevoir et de progresser. La nature humaine ne doit pas être confondue avec l'idée générale d'homme: elle existe concrètement dans la multiplicité d'individus, de corps et d'âmes individuelles qui actualisent des degrés inégaux de puissance physique et intellectuelle. Le progrès est donc affecté d'une loi d'inégal développement. Il est précaire, fragile, reproductible dans une tension qui réduit ce qu'il y a d'erreur dans les idées inadéquates sans pouvoir supprimer la dépendance de l'altérité. Ce progrès n'est pas le fait de tous. L'espèce humaine est affectée d'une division, certes transformable, mais réelle, entre la multitude et la petite élite des hommes libres-sages. Ni universel, ni irrésistible, davantage caractérisé par une transition-tension dans la gradualisation des pouvoirs de l'*intellectus* que par une transition-arrachement définitif à la dépendance de l'imagination, le progrès se révèle comme non universel de fait. Il se produit sans intention ni garantie. Il apparaît alors comme une possibilité liée à la conjoncture et à la dépendance de la conjoncture. La fortune est le visage de l'histoire comme possible.

On pourrait faire la même analyse pour le versant physique-affectif du progrès éthique. Ce qui a été dit de l'imagination vaut pour la servitude passionnelle. La transition éthique comme vie de la raison est bien une possibilité ontologique et une réalité. Mais il est significatif que Spinoza consacre le meilleur des son effort non pas à exalter la transition éthique, à la fétichiser, mais à analyser les mécanismes de sa réalisation, les formes de sa consolidation, les limites qui l'affectent. "Il est impossible que l'homme ne soit pas une partie de la nature et ne puisse éprouver d'autres changements que ceux qui se peuvent connaître par sa seule nature et dont il est cause adéquate." Il suit de là que "l'homme est nécessairement toujours soumis aux passions (*passionnibus esse semper obnoxium*), suit l'ordre commun de la Nature, et lui obéit, et s'y accomode autant que la nature des choses l'exige." (E IVP4&C) Tout le problème est de déterminer le mécanisme par lequel, dans la servitude passionnelle, la liberté, comme cause interne, se forme.

La domination sur les passions, la stratégie d'utilisation des passions joyeuses pour les transformer en vraies actions implique une très délicate opération de filtrage et de déconstruction de l'apport des causes extérieures. Le processus éthique est maîtrise des affects par leur connaissance adéquate et par réplication de la connaissance en capacité d'agir. Il peut s'aider de la représentation d'un progrès (comme accumulation des relations de convenance), mais il doit se réeffectuer au coup par coup. Il n'est que tendanciellement cumulatif; il est privé de la garantie de sa poursuite, puisque cette accumulation est liée à une effectuation conjoncturale (l'ordre commun de la nature). Le progrès éthique n'est ni régulier, ni assuré: il est heurté, stochastique, menacé d'interruption, de régression. Notre *conatus* lorsqu'il devient davantage cause adéquate, demeure dans un équilibre instable, exposé aux défis et démentis de la conjoncture, c'est-à-dire de son appartenance au monde des corps extérieurs. Passions tristes et passions joyeuses, *Passio* et *Actio*, sont en concurrence permanente, et se renversent les unes dans les autres: le progrès éthique est tendanciellement orienté, mais il n'existe que dans la dialectique de transitions contraires, de transitions qui inversent la grande transition passivité-activité. Il y a une menace permanente d'effacement de la grande transition dans les fluctuations. En ce sens la "fluctuation de l'âme" n'est pas une passion parmi les autres, elle est la marque de la servitude passionnelle.[22]

Cela explique pourquoi la loi de l'inégal développement des esprits est immédiatement loi de l'inégal développement des *conatus*. Cet inégal développement fait du progrès éthique une tendance objective mais suspendue à des formes aléatoires, décalées, non universelles, de réalisation. Parcequ'il y a concurrence dans la transition éthique entre actif et passif, la vie de la raison comme recherche de relations d'appartenance dans l'utile propre et de réseaux de communication est concurrencée dynamiquement par la socialisation passionnelle, laquelle est intrinsèquement insociable. La transition éthique-progrès se réalise comme compétition, conflit incessant entre ce que les hommes découvrent de leur être commun et ce qu'ils perçoivent comme les faisant différer. De l'intérieur, la transition éthique est menacée par son autre; et le progrès éthique est de manière immanente menacé d'être réabsorbé dans ce qui est la forme concrète de la vie passionnelle de la multitude, la vie politique.

> Les hommes peuvent différer en nature en tant qu'ils sont dominés par des affects qui sont des passions, et dans la même mesure le même homme est changeant et inconstant (E IIIP33).

> En tant que les hommes sont dominés par des affects qui sont des passions, ils peuvent être contraires les uns aux autres (E IIIP34).

Oui, décidément l'espèce est de manière permanente contraire à elle-même, elle est menacée de brisure entre masse et élite de la sagesse. L'inégalité intellectuelle est simultanément inégalité éthique au sein de la même condition d'égalité modale (le *nos* humain avec sa supériorité relative). De par sa dynamique même le procès d'éthicisation révèle non pas tant son étrangeté au procès de socialisation et de politisation que sa complémentarité dialectique. L'inégal développement éthique comme forme concrète d'existence rappelle l'appastenance de ce progrès à la dynamique à la dynamique de la vie passionnelle de la multitude, à la vie politique.

9. *Point 3*. Il n'est donc pas question de rêver à un inévitable progrès théorique ou scientifique qui se renverserait en inévitable progrès éthique, à fortiori juridico-politique. Le processus d'éthicisation est inévitablement inséré dans la politique, il est en décalage permanent avec la vie politique qui est fondamentalement passionnelle, même si les passions sont aménagées dans des formes de socialisation conflictuelle. Il est menacé par les oscillations, les

transitions négatives ou inverses qui caractérisent les passions du corps politique (désobéissance des citoyens, arbitraire de l'appareil d'Etat avec son autonomisation, incapacité à reproduire la paix et la sécurité minimales). L'ordre commun de la nature pour le *nos* humain s'identifie à la politique, considérée dans sa relation différentielle avec l'éthique. La vie de la raison n'est pas un Etat dans l'Etat, tout comme la vie passionnelle politique n'est pas non plus un Etat dans l'Etat, même si en elle, contre elle, agit la raison en tant que découverte et pratique de relations communautaires.

Cela signifie que le procès-progrès éthique, ce possible objectif, conjonctural, aléatoire, tendanciellement cumulatif, continue à agir au sein de la vie politique. La situation n'est pas désespérée, car l'ordre politique demeure parcouru par la tendance à la démocratisation, même s'il est massivement dominé par la recherche objective des mécanismes de stabilisation des fluctuations des passions du corps politique. Si un progrès historique de la barbarie à la civilisation ne peut revêtir l'aspect d'une loi nécessaire, si la séquence monarchie-aristocratie-démocratie n'est qu'un modèle hypothétique, il reste bien place pour un quasi progrès politique. Les rapports du progrès d'éthicisation et du progrès politique sont donc en définitive l'objet essentiel de la philosophie. En effet ils sont de fait un objet privilégié de la *Scientia intuitiva*. Si celle-ci consiste à déduire les essences singulières des attributs, si elle est accumulation de la connaissance de choses singulières, il faut bien voir que pour le *nos* humain les choses singulières les plus importantes sont les autres hommes saisis dans leur tension éthique.

Il faut ici mettre en rapport le Livre V et le Livre IV. "Plus nous connaissons les choses singulières, plus nous connaissons Dieu" (VP24). "Il n'est pas donné dans la nature aucune chose singulière qui soit plus utile à l'homme qu'un homme vivant sous la conduite de la raison" (IVP35C1). Mais comme ces *res singulares* sont rares, et quelles vivent avec cet autre *res singulares* qui est la masse des hommes qui ne peuvent se passer de la société (IVP35S), il suit que le vrai problème éthique est éthico-politique, puisqu'il n'est pas donné de processus d'éthicisation achevé pour la totalité du genre humain, mais que la vie éthique se construit au sein de la singularité de la vie politique, en débat avec elle. Tout le problème est de savoir ce que peut le procès politique et comment il s'articule au procès éthique. Le politique est-il susceptible d'un progrès interne qui ne le rende pas incompatible avec le procès éthique? Si le politique produit de lui-même sans l'avoir voulu, ni visé, des effets éthiques que la raison valide, si la raison n'a pas à se penser comme fin de la politique, de son point de vue à elle est décisive la compréhension de la politique, dans le sens de sa compatibilité, de son usage pour le procès éthique. Le *Traité politique*, oeuvre de la science intuitive, ne se résout pas dans une séparation radicale entre éthique et politique. Il ne faut pas confondre éthique et moralisme. Mais la raison, la vie éthique se doit de comprendre la politique en son autonomie pour déterminer ce qui dans cette autonomie crée des conditions d'une poursuite de la vie éthique. Elle se doit de former les modèles qui permettent de consolider la paix et sécurité. Le progrès démocratique, la démocratisation comme problème permanent et toujours ouvert, sont compris par la raison à la fois comme tendance interne de la mécanique politique passionnelle et comme élément qui en elle rend possible le procès d'éthicisation. Si le politique ignore l'éthique, celle-ci ignore pas celui-là, et comprend la tension interne qui anime la politique pour objectivement la faire progresser - sans qu'elle le veuille - dans le sens du progrès éthique. Le *Traité politique* se veut assimilable par les Politiciens réalistes lesquels peuvent produire leur ouvrage - paix et sécurité - sans se soucier de la vie éthique ni de son progrès. Mais le philosophe sait que l'intelligence autonome de la vie politique fait apparaître en quoi celle-ci produit de fait des conditions pour le progrès éthique (coopération, paix, sécurité, liberté de penser, expansion des réseaux de communication).

Le progrès politique est tendance interne à l'ordre politique et cette tendance est prise en charge par le procès éthique comme une condition de sa réalisation. Il n'est pas indifférent que la *Civitas* s'ouvre à la plus grande masse possible, unifie administration et consensus, sécurité et obéissance. Il n'est pas indifférent que la *Civitas* se développe en libre république ou qu'elle se corrompe. Il n'est pas indifférent de déterminer d'abord, de promouvoir ensuite, les mécanismes qui permettent à tout régime de favoriser dans l'élément du consensus les conditions de la vraie vie. La science intuitive pense la radicale autonomie de la politique pour y déceler les formes d'un progrès immanent dans les stratégies d'échange, de communication. Le progrès éthique, cette tendance immanente à la réalisation de soi, prend en charge la tendance à la démocratie immanente à la stabilisation de l'ordre politique pour déterminer cet ordre et le construire comme progrès politique. Si le progrès politique s'identifie de manière réaliste à la tendance à la démocratisation (passionnelle, elle aussi), si sa configuration est fragile et tend à disparaître dans les cycles des passions du corps politique, il n'est pas rien. Il est lui aussi une tendance à consolider sur la base même de ses prémisses causales.

Spinoza, ainsi, reste fidèle à ce qu'il affirmait depuis le *Traité de la réforme de l'entendement*. Mais ce qui était objectif du philosophe se révèle désormais tendance effective du *nos* humain en débat avec la tendance contraire. "Telle est la fin vers laquelle je tends, acquérir une telle nature supérieure et travailler à ce que beaucoup d'autres l'acquièrent avec moi. En effet, cela aussi appartient à mon bonheur de m'appliquer à ce que beaucoup d'autres comprennent ce que je comprends, afin que leur entendement et leurs désirs s'accordent parfaitement avec mon entendement et mes désirs. Afin que cela se fasse, il est nécessaire d'avoir de la Nature une connaissance suffisante pour l'acquisition de cette nature humaine supérieure; puis il est nécessaire de former une société telle qu'elle doit être, afin que le plus grand nombre d'homme arrivent aussi facilement et sûrement qu'il se peut à ce but."[23]

1. On peut songer au célèbre livre de L. Brunschvicg, *Spinoza et ses contemporains,* (Paris: P.U.F., 1932).
2. Le tournant décisif a été constitué par le livre devenu classique de A. Matheron, *Individu et communauté selon Spinoza* (Paris: Minuit, 1961) Depuis ont paru, dans la

même orientation, les ouvrages de A. Negri, *L'anomalia selvaggia* (Milano: Feltrinelli, 1981), et E. Balibar, *Spinoza et la politique* (Paris: P.U.F., 1985).

3. Au sein d'une vaste littérature, on peut citer E. Cassirer, *La philosophie des Lumières*; F. Manuel, *The Eighteenth Century Confronts the Gods* (Cambridge, Mass: 1959); C. G. Gillispie, *Genesis and Geology* (Cambridge, Mass: 1951); F. C. Haber, *The Age of the World: Moses to Darwin* (Baltimore: 1966); R. V Sampson, *Progress in the Age of Reason*, (London: 1956). Et plus récemment P. Rossi, *Immagini della scienza* (Roma: Riuniti, 1977), et du même *I Segni del Tempo. Storia della terra e Storia delle nazioni da Hooke a Vico* (Milano: Feltrinelli, 1979).

4. T. Hobbes, *Léviathan*, trad. de F. Tricaud (Paris: Sirey, 1971), ch. xiii, p.125.

5. Spinoza, *Traité théologico-politique*. Sur les Hébreux qui, ennemis des sciences et de la philosophie, n'ont pas excellé sur les autres nations par la science et la piété, voir ch. III (Van Vloten II, p. 122). Sur leur organisation politique: elle a permis d'assurer sécurité et paix, mais dans des conditions de faible développement des forces productives des conatus; elle ne saurait être imitée car elle ne convient pas à une nation civilisée qui encourage les sciences, le commerce, l'économie; voir ch. XVIII (Van Vloten II, p.288): *Deinde talis imperii forma iis forsan tanquam utilis esse posset qui sibi solis adsque externo commercio vivere, seseque intra suos limites claudere, et a reliquo orbe segregari velint, ut minime iis, quibus necesse est cum aliis commercium habere; quapropter talis imperii forma paucissimi tantum ex usu esse potest.*

6. Sur la dimension "progressiste" du TTP, voir les travaux décisifs de Leo Strauss, en particulier *Spinoza's Critique of Religion* (New York: Schocken, 1965) (la première édition allemande date de 1930). Je me permets de renvoyer à A. Tosel, *Spinoza ou le crépuscule de la servitude* (Paris: Aubier, 1984). Voir aussi, bien entendu, le livre de Matheron cité qui est le premier à avoir pensé ensemble théorie de l'histoire et théorie de la politique chez Spinoza.

7. Spinoza, *Traité de la réforme de l'entendement*, ed. A. Koyré, (Paris: Vrin, 1951) ¶19, p. 17 et ¶22, p. 21 (*perpauca fuerunt*).

8. E IIP40S1. Les notions communes sont formées par rupture avec le procès par lequel se forment les transcendantaux et les notions générales. Voir les remarques pertinentes de P. Rossi, *I segni del Tempo*, pp. 240-246.

9. E IIP16&C2. Voir aussi IIP29C. "L'âme humaine toutes les fois qu'elle perçoit les choses selon l'ordre commun de la nature n'a ni d'elle-même, ni de son propre corps, ni des corps extérieurs une connaissance adéquate, mais seulement une connaissance confuse et mutilée." Thème décisif que celui de la constance de l'inconstance de l'imagination qui constitue comme une impossibilité à sortir de l'immédiateté et d'inaugurer le savoir comme histoire. N'est-ce-pas là la manière dont à la fin même de l'*Ethique* Spinoza (E V42S) définit l'ignorant par opposition au Sage? "L'ignorant outre qu'il est de beaucoup de manières agité (agitatur) par les causes extérieures et ne possède jamais le vrai contentement intérieur, vit dans une quasi inconscience de lui-même, de Dieu, des choses, et sitôt qu'il cesse de pâtir, il cesse aussitôt d'être." La raison est intrinsèquement son histoire.

10. E III. Il s'agit de l'introduction de III "certes n'ont pas manqué les hommes éminents (au labeur et à l'industrie desquels nous devons beaucoup) pour écrire sur la conduite droite de la vie beaucoup de belles choses, et donner aux mortels des conseils pleins de prudence; mais quant à déterminer la nature et les forces des affects, et ce que peut l'âme de son côté pour gouverner, nul que je sache ne l'a fait." *Nemo quod sciam determinavit.* La même conscience de singularité épocale transparaît dans la Préface du Livre V. Nul n'a pu avant Spinoza traiter de "la puissance de la raison," montrer "ce que peut la *Ratio* sur les affects, et ensuite ce qu'est la liberté de l'âme ou Béatitude; par où nous verrons combien le sage a plus de puissance que l'ignorant."

11. Nous nous permettons de renvoyer à A. Tosel, "Quelques remarques pour une interprétation de "l'*Ethique*," in Giancotti (1985), pp. 143-171. Dans une perspective voisine voir Paolo Cristofolini, "Esse sui juris e scienza politica," in *Studia Spinozana* 1(1985), 53-71; Emilia Giancotti, "Necessity and Freedom in the philosophy of Spinoza" in Hessing (1977).

12. Dès le livre II, la détermination éthique du *On* ontologique de la substance en *nous* humaine se précise, avec la détermination de la transition. Le court texte qui ouvre ce livre précise que au sein de "l'explication des choses qui ont dû suivre nécessairement de l'essence de Dieu, et qui sont une infinité, il ne sera expliqué seulement que ce qui peut nous conduire comme par la main à la connaissance de l'âme humaine et de sa béatitude supérieure." *Transeo ad... ea quae nos ad Mentis humanae, ejusque summae beatitudinis cognitionem quasi manu ducere possunt.* A rapprocher du célèbre texte de la Préface du Livre IV: bien que les termes de bon et de mauvais n'expliquent rien de positif dans les choses considérées en elles-mêmes, chacune étant en elle-même parfaite, "cependant il nous faut conserver ces vocables. Désirant en effet former une idée de l'homme qui soit comme un modèle de la nature humaine placé devant nos yeux il nous sera utile de conserver ces vocables dans le sens que j'ai dit."

13. E IVP35C1,2&S "Dans la mesure où les hommes vivent sous la direction de la raison, ils s'accordent toujours nécessairement par nature." "Il n'est donné dans la nature aucune chose singulière qui soit plus utile à l'homme qu'un homme vivant sous la conduite de la raison." "L'homme est un dieu pour l'homme." Voir aussi E IVApp25,26.

14. E IIIP4C. La servitude radicalise comme forme de vie un des éléments de la condition ontologique de base, qu'énoncent les propositions 2, 3, 4 du Livre III. "Nous pâtissons en tant que nous sommes une partie de la Nature qui ne peut se concevoir par soi sans les autres parties." "La force avec laquelle l'homme persévère dans l'existence est surpassée infiniment par la puissance des causes extérieures." "Il est impossible que l'homme ne soit pas une partie de la Nature et ne puisse éprouver d'autres changements que ceux qui peuvent se connaître par sa seule nature et dont il est cause adéquate." L'appendice du Livre IV, §32, rappelle cette structure de base.

15. *Traité politique*, V, 2, Van Vloten II, 23. Voir E. Balibar, *Spinoza et la politique*, 3, pp. 72-90.

16. *sed quae maxime Ratione, vera Mentis vita definitur.* *Traité politique*, V, 5, p. 23. C'est là ce que conteste aujourd'hui A. Matheron dans son article "Etat et Mortalité selon Spinoza," in Giancotti (1985). Pour Matheron, qui modifie l'interprétation donnée dans son ouvrage de 1961, il y a radicale séparation entre politique et éthique. Que la politique ait des effets que l'éthique valide n'autorise pas à finaliser la politique comme service de l'éthique. La lecture que donne Matheron tend à exclure l'idée même d'un progrès intra-passionnel (dans la servitude), qui soit possible pour la majorité des hommes, *obnoxi passionnibus*. Nous estimons au contraire que le Matheron 1969 est plus près de Spinoza que le Matheron 1985.

17. *Traité politique* III, 7. Ce texte évoque une hypothèse que l'on jugerait impossible dans le TP, qui part de la "commune nature humaine." C'est l'hypothèse d'une Cité fondée sur la raison et dirigée par elle. "17.Cette Cité est la plus puissante et relève le plus d'elle-même (*sui Juris*). Le droit de la cité en effet est défini par la puissance de la masse qui est conduite en quelque sorte par une même pensée, et cette union des âmes ne peut se concevoir en aucune façon si la Cité ne tend éminemment au but que la saine raison enseigne à tous les hommes leur être utile d'atteindre." La cité de la servitude peut produire ce que la raison enseigne.

18. E IIP17S. "Les imaginations de l'âme considérées en elles-mêmes ne contiennent aucune erreur. L'âme n'est pas dans l'erreur parce qu'elle imagine mais elle est dans l'erreur, en tant qu'elle est considérée comme privée d'une idée qui exclut l'existence de ces choses qu'elle imagine comme lui étant présentes."

19. Fragilité du début de la raison: elle a commencé son progrès effectivement lorsqu'il a été possible d'enchaîner quelques idées vraies. C'est la mathématique qui a permis cette délivrance. Le genre humain serait demeuré dans l'illusion finaliste et la superstition théologico-politique "si la mathématique, occupée non des fins mais seulement des essences et des propriétés des figures n'avaient fait luire devant les hommes une autre mesure de vérité" (E IApp.).

20. E IVA, ouverture auquel correspond le chapitre de fermeture du même livre.

21. E IIP13S. "Plus un corps est apte comparativement aux autres à agir et à pâtir de plusieurs façons à la fois, plus l'âme de ce corps est apte comparativement aux autres à percevoir plusieurs choses à la fois; et plus les actions d'un corps dépendent de lui seul et moins il y a d'autres corps qui concourent avec lui dans l'action, plus l'âme de ce corps est apte à connaître distinctement. Par là nous pouvons connaître la supériorité d'une âme sur les autres." Si l'âme humaine diffère des autres et l'emporte sur les autres, les âmes humaines diffèrent entre elles d'une moindre différence certes, mais d'une différence réelle.

22. E IIIP17&S ("Cet état de l'âme qui naît de deux affections s'appelle fluctuation de l'âme; il est à l'égard des affects ce que le doute est à l'égard de l'imagination").

23. *Traité de la réforme de l'entendement*, ¶13, p. 13. Pour tout ceci voir l'article de P. Cristofolini, cité à la note 11. On retrouve le même thème en E VP20&D: l'amour envers Dieu - *Amor erga deum* - contient un principe interne d'universalisation. Cet amour est "d'autant plus alimenté que nous imaginons plus d'hommes joints à Dieu par le même lien d'amour." Il est commun à tous les hommes et nous désirons que tous en jouissent. *Omnibus hominibus commune est et omnes ut eadem gaudeant cupimus.*

SPINOZA, LA FIN DE L'HISTOIRE ET LA RUSE DE LA RAISON

P. MACHEREY
Universite de Paris I

Le titre de ce travail le suggère assez clairement: il y sera encore question, sous un aspect singulier, du rapport de Spinoza à Hegel. Disons rapidement pour commencer ce qu'on peut attendre d'un tel rapprochement: on ne cherchera pas, lisant Spinoza dans Hegel, ou Hegel dans Spinoza, à poursuivre la chimère d'un Hegel spinoziste ou d'un Spinoza hégélien; mais il s'agira seulement de lire Spinoza et Hegel ensemble, c'est-à-dire l'un avec l'autre mais aussi l'un contre l'autre, de manière à dégager les éléments éventuels de divergence tels qu'ils apparaissent à travers leur convergence même. De façon extrêmement sommaire, le caractère de cette relation pourrait être exprimé de la façon suivante: sans doute Spinoza et Hegel parlent-ils de la même chose - et c'est pourquoi s'établit entre eux une réelle communauté - mais ils en parlent différemment, et peut-être même de manière opposée - et c'est pourquoi, s'il n'est pas permis d'assimiler purement et simplement leurs positions philosophiques, il n'est pas possible non plus de les séparer absolument.

Cette hypothèse très générale sera mise en ici à l'épreuve de la confrontation entre deux textes bien connus, dont la signification est certainement cruciale pour leur auteurs: le début du *Traité politique* et la Préface des *Principes de la philosophie du droit*. En effet, si l'on procède à une lecture parallèle de ces deux textes, en les considérant selon une perspective sans doute assez cavalière, on y trouve trois thèmes, solidaires entre eux, à propos desquels on peut se demander si vraiment Spinoza et Hegel leur appliquent un traitement comparable: l'appel au réalisme politique, la fin de l'histoire, et la ruse de la raison.

D'abord le réalisme politique. Entamant une réflexion philosophique sur le droit, Spinoza et Hegel subordonnent la rationalité de leur démarche à un présupposé critique qui est le suivant: il faut que soit écartée de cette réflexion toute spéculation concernant ce qui doit être, c'est-à-dire le possible, et que l'essence du droit soit ramenée à sa réalité effective. Toute la question est alors de savoir si, à travers cet appel au réel, Spinoza et Hegel visent un même concept de réalité: prendre l'Etat tel qu'il est, ou les Etats tels qu'ils sont, pour en découvrir la raison spécifique, est-ce adopter les préceptes d'un positivisme avant la lettre, ou bien est-ce admettre le présupposé d'une rationalité immanente, qui maintient l'idéalité de son objet? En d'autres termes: connaître la réalité du politique, est-ce la réduire à ses phénomènes, ou bien est-ce dégager la finalité qui est en elle et qui permet de la comprendre telle qu'elle est en soi?

Cet appel au réalisme débouche sur l'affirmation d'une fin de l'histoire, qui en constitue en fait le présupposé. Chez Hegel, ce thème est énoncé, proclamé, de manière éclatante: on ne philosophe que sur ce qui est, c'est-à-dire aussi sur ce qui a été, c'est-à-dire sur l'accompli; c'est pourquoi la rationalité effective est celle qui, s'astreignant à ne peindre son gris que sur du gris, se situe elle-même au terme des processus réels qu'elle récupère dans la pensée en en dégageant rétrospectivement la logique interne. Il est surprenant de retrouver cette suggestion, sous une forme atténuée il est vrai, dans le texte de Spinoza: en effet, lorsque celui-ci se déclare

> tout à fait persuadé que l'expérience a fait voir tous les genres d'organisation sociale qui peuvent être conçus en vue d'organiser la concorde entre les hommes, en même temps que les moyens par lesquels la multitude doit être dirigée, c'est-à-dire être contenue dans des limites déterminées (TP I, 3),

il développe apparemment la même hypothèse, d'après laquelle l'expérience, qu'on peut ici assimiler à l'histoire réelle des hommes, ayant donné tout ce qu'on peut attendre d'elle, il ne reste plus qu'à prendre en compte ses résultats pour en extraire les principaux enseignements en les totalisant. Le problème est ici le suivant: les concepts d'histoire à l'oeuvre chez Spinoza et chez Hegel sont-ils comparables? Entre la représentation de celle-ci comme un processus orienté, conduisant à la révélation finale d'une rationalité qu'il porte en lui depuis le début, et sa réduction à une succession d'expériences ou n'interviennent apparemment que l'occasion et le hasard, la différence est manifeste. Remarquons que la question posée ici s'apparente à la précédente: la réalité est-elle ou non soumise à des fins qui en conditionnent la compréhension? Dans quel sens est-il alors permis de parler d'une fin de l'histoire?

Enfin, Spinoza appuie son exigence de mesurer le droit par le fait, selon les enseignements de l'expérience, sur la nécessité de prendre les hommes tels qu'ils sont (*ut sunt*), au lieu de substituer une nature humaine fictive (*humana natura quae nullibi est*) à celle qui existe en fait nécessairement (*ea quae revera est*) (TP I, 1). Ici le réalisme politique se double apparemment d'un réalisme anthropologique; les sociétés sont telles que l'expérience nous les présente, et il est vain de chercher à les imaginer autrement, parce que les individus qu'elles rassemblent sont dirigés dans leur conduite, non par un idéal *dictamen rationis* qui résoudrait tous les problèmes du pouvoir politique en évacuant la nécessité de ce pouvoir même, selon la logique de l'utopie, mais par la puissance de leurs affects, en tant que celle-ci coïncide spontanément, donc avant toute réflexion, avec leur conatus, c'est-à-dire leur tendance native à persévérer dans leur être. En ce sens la rationalité politique, si elle existe, doit passer par le mécanisme de penchants naturels instinctifs, qui constitue le contenu de sa réflexion, et délimite le terrain de son intervention. Or, ce thème recoupe une idée qui, si elle n'est pas explicitement formulée dans la Préface des *Principes de la philosophie de droit*, est sous-jacente à toute la pensée politique de Hegel; celle de la ruse de la raison, d'après laquelle la raison ne se manifeste dans l'histoire que par l'intermédiaire des passions humaines qui sont l'instrument de son opération; ainsi, ce que Hegel appelle dans la Préface de la *Phénoménologie* *"le monstrueux travail de l'histoire mondiale"* (*das ungeheure Arbeit der Weltge-schichte*) n'est-il rien d'autre que l'explication de la reconnaissance qui s'effectue primitivement au niveau des expériences de la conscience. Toute la difficulté de la théorie hégélienne tient à la métaphore de la "ruse" (*die List der Vernunft*), qui semble surimposer le schéma de la finalité externe, la raison s'ajustant aux éléments spontanés qu'elle détourne à son profit, sur celui de la finalité interne, d'après laquelle les affects humains ne sont pas seulement les instruments dont se sert la raison mais les formes actuelles de son effectuation. On peut alors se demander duquel de ces deux modèles de référence - le premier maintenant une discontinuité entre la raison et les passions humaines, dont elle réfléchit le rapport comme un rapport extérieur, et le second supposant au contraire une identité essentielle, au niveau au moins de leur contenu, entre ce qui est immédiatement donné aux consciences et l'ordre immanent qui aimante leurs mouvements - se rapproche le plus l'*emendatio* que Spinoza fait subir à la raison juridique: jusqu'à quel point, selon cette *emendatio*, la raison peut elle s'incarner dans la société, et identifier en elle ses propres fins?

Mais est-il possible, suivant Spinoza, de parler de fins de la raison? Soumettre la rectitude d'une pensée adéquate, parvenant à une complète compréhension de son objet, au préalable d'une théodicée rationnelle, celle-ci donnant sa base à une philosophie de l'histoire, n'est-ce pas réintroduire dans la science un préjugé téléologique qui en dément la rigueur démonstrative, strictement génétique et causale? Ce qui est ici en question, c'est le rapport entre la philosophie et la politique, en tant que celui-ci est lié au statut même de la connaissance vraie: si comprendre l'existence sociale des hommes c'est ramener celle-ci à ses conditions nécessaires, cela ne signifie-t-il pas que la réflexion sur le droit n'est possible qu'à la condition d'être renfermée dans d'étroites limites, en dehors desquelles, sinon contre lesquelles, le projet de libération propre au philosophe doit être maintenu? Or Hegel n'affirme-t-il pas lui-même la nécessité pour la pure pensée, une fois qu'elle a traversé tous les stades de son effectuation de se replier "dans la figure d'un royaume intellectuel" (*in Gestalt eines intellektuellen Reichs*)?

On le voit, la relation qui passe entre la pensée de Spinoza et celle de Hegel est autrement complexe que celle d'une identité abstraite ou que celle d'une irréductible différence: elle ne peut être appréhendée que comme un échange, à travers lequel les positions de l'un et de l'autre se correspondent et se répondent, sans pourtant jamais se confondre. C'est pourquoi une lecture simultanée de leurs discours peut être féconde.

Maintenant il faut revenir plus précisément sur les trois thèmes qui viennent d'être superficiellement répertoriés, pour tenter d'appréhender le contenu de cet échange, c'est-à-dire pour en mesurer les enjeux philosophiques.

Le Réalisme Politique

Sur ce point, on partira de Hegel, pour pouvoir ensuite, à la lumière de sa réflexion sur ce qui est effectivement réel (*wirklich*), relire le texte de Spinoza. D'après Hegel, la réalité (*Wirklichleit*) est intrinsèquement rationnelle dans la mesure où elle est l'oeuvre (*Werk*) de la raison, c'est-à-dire le produit de son travail: ainsi peut-on dire que la raison s'effectue dans le monde, dans des formes qui sont d'ailleurs très diverses, allant de l'*Erscheinung* empirique à l'*Offen-barung* idéale, c'est-à-dire de la réalisation au sens strict à l'incarnation. Dans quelle mesure l'histoire peut-elle être considérée comme une telle oeuvre rationnelle? Dans la mesure où, considérée dans son ensemble , comme histoire universelle, et dépouillée de l'enveloppe factuelle relevant de la pure contingence de l'événement qui définit la *Realität* au sens strict, c'est-à-dire le détail de ce qui est arrivé, elle révèle son noyau mystique, contenu substantiel éternellement présent (*das Ewige, das gegenwärtig ist*) qui constitue sa loi immanente. En ce sens, le refus de transgresser les limites du monde tel qu'il est, au nom d'une transcendance illusoire parce que nécessairement subjective, coïncide pour Hegel avec la reconnaissance du fait que la raison est effectivement présente dans ce monde ci (*diesseits* et non *jenseits*, selon une alternative qui se transmettra dans la pensée philosophique allemande jusqu'au jeune Marx), parce que le monde est le produit du travail qu'accomplit l'Esprit, en tant qu'Esprit du monde (*Weltgeist*), pour s'effectuer lui-même nécessairement.

En ce sens, l'Etat, qui est la forme historique la plus accomplie du droit, représente aussi par excellence pour Hegel l'Esprit objectif (*der objektive Geist*), l'Esprit tel qu'il s'est lui-même objectivé dans le monde sous sa figure la plus parfaite, telle qu'aucune autre ne soit rationnellement pensable qui puisse idéalement, au sens où l'idéal s'opposerait au réel au lieu de s'effectuer en lui, lui être substituée. C'est pourquoi, faire sa paix avec la réalité, ce n'est rien d'autre que se réconcilier avec le présent, "reconnaître la raison comme la rose dans la croix du présent," "réconciliation que procure la philosophie à ceux à qui est apparue un jour l'exigence intérieure d'obtenir et de maintenir la liberté subjective au sein de ce qui est substantiel et de placer cette liberté non dans ce qui est particulier et contingent, mais dans ce qui est en et pour soi."[1] En d'autres termes, - Hegel utilise cette expression dans la Préface à ses *Leçons sur la philosophie de l'histoire* - la raison est "l'Hermès qui guide effectivement les peuples," au long de cette procession qui les conduit à assumer tour à tour, chacun selon son rang et selon son temps, leur destination spirituelle, celle-ci étant de représenter adéquatement, dans les limites imparties à leurs situations respectives, une seule et même réalité qui confère à leur existence sa substance spirituelle. Toute la question est alors de savoir si l'histoire, ramenée à sa norme rationnelle, est *Vorstellung* ou *Darstellung*, représentation du présent à travers des intermédiaires qui l'en maintiennent dans une certaine mesure séparée, ou présentation effective, qui intègre absolument la raison dans les limites de l'histoire universelle, au point d'identifier complètement ses fins avec celles de cette dernière.

Le réalisme politique revendiqué par Spinoza s'inscrit dans un contexte théorique apparemment très différent, puisqu'il se présente dès le départ comme un réalisme de l'expérience, qui cherche ses premières références dans la pratique. Dans la perspective ainsi ouverte, il est vain de chercher hors de l'expérience un modèle politique, à propos duquel il faudrait se demander ensuite comment le mettre en pratique: le droit, quelle que soit sa forme, a toujours été élaboré dans l'usage, de manière complétement empirique, par l'intervention des *Politici*; ce sont ceux-ci qui ont mis au point les procédures les mieux adaptées aux affects des hommes, procédures dont l'efficacité permet de mesurer le degré de cette adaptation: c'est pourquoi, s'ils ne connaissent pas à proprement parler la nature de l'Etat, ils sont ceux qui s'y connaissent le mieux en fait de droit, car "du fait qu'ils ont disposé de plus d'expérience, ils n'ont rien enseigné qui s'écartât de l'usage" (TP I, 2). Or, il n'y a pas d'autre voie en politique que celle qui est ainsi montrée dans les fait, et qui conduit, pour comprendre la réalité du droit, à prendre en compte l'expérience qui en est donnée: toute l'expérience, mais rien que l'expérience. Dans quelle mesure est-il possible de parler ici d'empirisme? Spinoza invalide la démarche qui consiste à évaluer l'expérience au nom de principes extérieurs qui en disqualifieraient les phénomènes en les ramenant au rang de simples apparences: les principes d'une connaissance adéquate doivent au contraire être inhérents à l'expérience, en ce sens qu'ils sont donnés en elle, ou qu'ils s'accordent avec elle. Mais cela ne signifie pas que ces principes, qui sont donnés dans l'expérience, soient données par l'expérience, car si celle-ci, dans ses limites, revèle tous les effets dont est susceptible la nature politique de l'homme, elle ne montre pas directement les causes de ces effets, et on peut même considérer qu'elle est organisée de manière à dissimuler ces causes, ou à en différer la manifestation. Connaître dans les limites de l'expérience, c'est donc raisonner sur les objets de l'expérience, de manière à en comprendre la véritable nature: or, cette explication relève de la même exigence démonstrative que toutes les autres formes de connaissance rationnelle, que l'object de celles-ci soit ou non immédiatement donné dans l'expérience. Même si, dans le *Traité politique,* ses arguments ne sont pas formellement rangés selon le modèle déductif strict mis en oeuvre dans l'*Ethique,* l'objectif de Spinoza reste celui d'une *Politica more geometrico demonstrata,* c'est-à-dire, d'une politique nécessaire.

Qu'est-ce qui constitue le point de départ de cette démonstration? C'est l'homme réel, c'est-à-dire la pratique effective des rapports humains: ces expressions peuvent paraître anachroniques, et pourtant l'idée qu'elles véhiculent est bien comprise sous le concept de nature humaine tel qu'il est formulé par Spinoza. A partir d'une prise en compte des affects et de leur libre jeu spontané, indépendamment de la prise de conscience et du jugement rationnel dont ils peuvent faire ultérieurement l'objet, il s'agit donc de dégager la logique des actions humaines, en tant que celles-ci dérivent d'une "nature" qui est la source réelle de tout droit. Un lien nécessaire est ainsi posé entre l'anthropologie et la politique: il s'agit à la fois de conclure à partir des expériences de vie en société les lois communes qui s'en dégagent, et de démontrer la validité de ces expériences à partir des lois nécessaires qui les dirigent. Ainsi, les hommes, qui font de la politique sans le savoir, par là-même font du droit, en ce sens qu'ils font le droit, et, par leur actes, confèrent à celui-ci le seul type de légitimité dont il soit susceptible. Mais, le principe essentiel du naturalisme politique de Spinoza étant que la nature fonde le droit, cela ne signifie pas que celui-ci découle de celle-là comme d'une base qui lui préexisterait de manière indépendante et cela ne signifie donc pas non plus que l'anthropologie conditionnerait l'étude de la politique comme une forme de connaissance indépendante: Spinoza veut dire au contraire que la nature est imprégnée de droit, qu'elle est déjà le droit lui-même selon sa constitution essentielle qui, tout en maintenant les caractères spécifiques du droit social, ancre ceux-ci au plus profond du droit de la nature, et en circonscrit strictement le champ d'exercice. Pas plus que l'homme lui-même, la société n'est *tanquam imperium in imperio*, mais elle est soumise aussi, en tant que *pars naturae*, aux lois communes qui commandent la réalité toute entière. Plutôt que de dire que le droit dérive de la nature, il faut donc dire qu'il est complètement immergé en elle, et c'est pourquoi il ne constitue ses propres figures (*species*) que dans les limites qui lui sont imposées par l'expérience.

La position de Spinoza ne se ramène donc pas à un simple pragmatisme. Elle n'est pas non plus assimilable à une sorte de positivisme avant la lettre. Pourtant ce dernier rapprochement s'impose comme de lui-même à la lecture des première pages du *Traité politique,* et si le concept de science auquel est lié la politique spinoziste semble évoquer prémonitoirement des schémas de pensée qui seront explicitement au centre de la spéculation philosophique dans la première moitié du XIXème siècle, plutôt que chez Hegel, avec sa tentative d'une déduction complètement rationnelle du droit comme effectuation médiatisée de l'Esprit, c'est chez Comte, en tant que celui-ci pose aussi la réduction du droit au fait et fait de cette réduction la condition d'une rigueur théorique authentique, qu'il faudrait chercher les indices d'une telle communauté. Comte écrit par exemple, dans le premier texte où il a défini les concepts fondamentaux de la politique positive:

> L'administration et l'improbation des phénomènes doivent être bannies avec une égale sévérité de toute science positive, parce que chaque préoccupation de ce genre a pour effet direct et inévitable d'empêcher ou d'altérer l'examen; les astronomes, les physiciens, les chimistes et les physiologistes n'admirent ni ne blâment leurs phénomènes respectifs, ils les observent, quoique ces phénomènes puissent donner une ample matière aux considérations de l'un et l'autre genre, comme il y a beaucoup d'exemples; les savants laissent avec raison de tels effets aux artistes, dans le domaine desquels ils tombent réellement; il doit en être sous ce rapport dans la politique comme dans les autres sciences.   Seulement cette réserve y est beaucoup plus nécessaire, précisément parce qu'elle y est plus difficile, et qu'elle altère l'examen plus profondément, attendu que dans cette science les phénomènes touchent aux passions de bien plus près que dans toute autre.[2]

A première lecture, on pourrait croire que ce texte a été directement inspiré par la lecture de Spinoza.   Pourtant, il est évident que Comte, s'il avait eu connaissance de la référence spinozienne, l'aurait énergiquement récusée, au nom de son refus radical de la démarche métaphysique.   C'est précisément alors que la confrontation de Comte et de Spinoza prend son sens, au moment ou elle met en évidence l'irréductible divergence qui les oppose. Pour Comte, la politique est une science comme les autres, dans la mesure où, ayant préalablement circonscrit le niveau d'études où elle se situe, celui des phénomènes proprement humains, elle parvient à formuler les lois nécessaires auxquelles ceux-ci obéissent spécifiquement, les lois naturelles de l'histoire, soumises à un principe de progression rationnelle dont le développement semble dépendre davantage d'un "dessein de la nature," au sens de Kant, que d'une "ruse de la raison," au sens de Hegel. Or, pour Comte, une telle étude suppose qu'on ait complètement renoncé à chercher les causes de ces enchaînements, pour s'en tenir aux relations nécessaires qui s'établissement au niveau de leurs effets.

Spinoza au contraire affirme avec insistance que la science politique véritable, comme toute connaissance adéquate, s'appuie sur une compréhension complète de ses phénomènes, qui les fait connaître tels qu'ils sont en eux-mêmes, c'est-à-dire tels qu'ils sont produits réellement par leurs causes. C'est pourquoi cette connaissance prend la forme d'une "déduction":

> j'ai seulement cherché à démontrer rigoureusement *(certa et indubitata ratione demonstrare)* les choses qui s'accordent le mieux avec la pratique, et à les déduire de la condition de l'humaine nature telle qu'elle est en elle-même *(ex ipsa humanae conditione deducere)* (TP I, 4).

On retrouve ici l'idée d'un fondement anthropologique du droit: si les sociétés sont ce qu'elles sont, c'est-à-dire régies par des lois qui décident du juste et de l'injuste, c'est parce que passe en elles quelque chose qui appartient d'abord à la nature des hommes; cette chose est la puissance. La puissance, c'est ce qui détermine toutes les choses de la nature à exister et à agir: la société, qui est aussi une chose naturelle, n'a de puissance que pour autant que celle-ci lui a été communiquée par les individus qui la composent, en lesquels elle a sa source. Ceci ne signifie pas que, selon, une perspective mécanique, Spinoza cherche à constituer la réalité sociale complexe par une construction abstraite, en agençant ces éléments simples qui seraient les hommes dans cette totalité organisée que serait l'ordre politique: en effet, les sociétés, tout comme les êtres qu'elles rassemblent, sont des individus; réciproquement, les agents sociaux, ou si l'on veut les sujets politiques, ne sont des individus que pour autant qu'ils sont eux mêmes organisés comme des systèmes complexes, rassemblant encore d'autres éléments, en des sortes de communautés corporelles et mentales, qu'on peut se représenter à leur tour comme étant déjà des espèces de sociétés.

Tout ceci découle de la notion très particulière d'individualité développée par la philosophie spinoziste: cette notion n'est jamais assimilable à celle d'entités élémentaires, atomes physiques ou psychiques, qui donneraient son terme absolu à une analyse de la réalité. C'est ce point qui oppose parti-culièrement cette philosophie au mécanisme des anciens. Spinoza pense toujours l'individu synthétiquement, comme le résultat d'un mouvement de totalisation qui a commencé bien avant lui et se poursuit au delà de ses propres limites. C'est précisément ce que signifie la définition de l'individu comme *pars naturae*, définition qui, remarquons le, s'applique aussi bien à l'être humain singulier qu'au corps social considéré dans sa spécificité: *pars*, non au sens d'une partie en soi indécomposable, suivant la logique d'une démarche strictement analytique, mais au sens d'une détermination qui trouve elle-même son principe dans l'existence du tout auquel elle appartient solidairement, et dont elle ne peut être que provisoirement et relativement détachée. C'est pourquoi la forme par excellence de réalisation de la puissance individuelle est le *conatus*, effort pour persévérer dans son être, qui, loin d'isoler les unes des autres les choses finies, *tanquam imperia in imperio*, les rattache au contraire nécessairement, par l'intermédiaire de leurs rapports mutuels, à la nature dont elles ne sont que les "parties." Car ce qui définit les choses finies, c'est qu'elles ne sont pas en elles et par elles-mêmes, et c'est pourquoi le *conatus* qui délimite la puissance de ces choses ne trouve pas son principe dans leur seule essence, puisqu'il ne se conclut pas de leur définition: "d'où il suit que la puissance des choses naturelles, qui les fait agir et opérer, ne peut être une autre puissance que celle même de Dieu qui est éternelle" (TP II, 2). C'est la puissance de la nature considéré dans son ensemble qui se poursuit dans l'existence des choses individuelles et se communique à tout ce qu'elles font; et c'est la raison pour laquelle elles peuvent aussi transmettre cette puissance à d'autres configurations dans lesquelles elles entrent elles-mêmes comme des éléments constituants, qui persistent à affirmer leur puissance jusque dans la dynamique de leur fusion.

En ce sens, on peut dire que le réalisme politique de Spinoza est d'abord un naturalisme, à condition d'épurer ce terme de toute référence pragmatiste ou empiriste. Naturalisme doit évidemment s'entendre ici au sens de la nature absolue, ou de la substance divine, qui, parce qu'elle produit tous ses effets en elle-même, constitue aussi le principe de toute existence et de toute puissance. S'il y a des sociétés, et si les hommes peuvent réaliser dans l'ordre qu'elles définissent la part d'éternité qui leur revient, c'est-à-dire parviennent à être libres, c'est parce qu'elles incorporent ou informent, c'est-à-dire, il n'y a pas de meilleur mot, individualisent, à leur manière, la puissance globale qui appartient à la nature tout entière: c'est cette puissance qui constitue leur cause ultime, à partir de laquelle elles peuvent être expliquées adéquatement. Arrivé à ce point, on peut se demander si la divergence qui oppose Spinoza à Hegel ne s'estompe pas quelque peu: que les sociétés et les hommes qu'elles font vivre ensemble soient les produits d'une nature absolument première, ou les réalisations d'un Esprit qui est à la recherche de lui-même à travers l'ensemble de ses déterminations, il reste que le droit est justiciable d'une logique dont le développement coïncide exactement avec celui d'une ontologie, et de ce point de vue, les "réalismes" de Spinoza et de Hegel, qu'il s'agisse d'un réalisme de l'expérience ou d'un réalisme de l'effectivité, peuvent sembler très proches. Sans doute, le fait que Spinoza pense la nature comme substance, alors que Hegel définit au contraire l'Esprit comme sujet, maintient entre eux une irréductible différence, celle qui sépare un ordre rigoureux des causes d'un ordre absolu des fins. L'étude du thème de la fin de l'histoire devrait permettre de mettre au jour les présupposés qui sont en jeu dans cette dernière alternative.

La Fin de L'Histoire

Pour commencer, essayons cette fois de caractériser la position de Spinoza. De quelle manière le thème de la fin de l'histoire s'inscrit-il dans son texte? Préalablement à la déduction du droit, Spinoza affirme: toutes ses formes sont effectivement réalisées dans la pratique, et il est difficilement croyable que nous puissions concevoir quelque chose qui soit d'usage dans la société commune, et que l'occasion ou le hasard n'ait fourni, ou que les hommes, dans la mesure où ils sont attentifs aux affaires communes, et prennent soin de leur sécurité, n'aient point vu" (TP I, 3).

On peut donc considérer que l'expérience a déjà montré - Spinoza écrit bien: *ostendisse*, et non: *ostendere* - tout ce qu'il est possible d'attendre du droit en matière d'organisation sociale: il ne reste donc plus qu'à récapituler les éléments présentés dans cette expérience sous une forme dispersée, comme s'ils relevaient de l'occasion et du hasard, cest-à-dire qu'il ne reste plus qu'à les totaliser en en effectuant la synthèse rationnelle. Démarche, on peut le dire très classique, consistant à soustraire l'objet qu'elle considère aux conditions contingentes de la durée, pour ne prendre en compte que l'ordre immuable, et donc intransformable, qui constitue sa vérité. De façon comparable, dans le chapitre du *traité Théologico-politique* consacré aux miracles, Spinoza confirme, en s'appuyant sur le texte même de la Bible, cette position rationnelle en vertu de laquelle l'ordre des choses ne peut être fondamentalement modifié, parce qu'il ne peut entrer en contradiction avec lui-même:

A propos de la nature en général, l'Ecriture affirme en plusieurs endroits qu'elle conserve un ordre fixe et immuable (Ps. 148:6, Jer. 31:35-36). En outre, le philosophe en son Ecclésiaste (1:10) enseigne de la manière la plus claire que rien de nouveau n'arrive dans la nature; et (1:11-12), développant cette même idée, il dit que, bien qu'arrive parfois quelque chose qui semble nouveau, cela pourtant n'est pas quelque chose de vraiment nouveau, mais est arrivé dans des siècles fort antérieurs bien qu'il n'en demeure aucune mémoire: car, comme il le dit lui-même, il n'est aucune mémoire des choses anciennes chez ceux qui vivent aujourd'hui, et de même aussi la mémoire des choses d'aujourd'hui n'existera plus pour ceux qui viendront plus tard. Puis (3:11) il dit que Dieu a ordonné toutes choses comme il convient en leur temps, et (3:14) il dit qu'il sait que, quoi que Dieu fasse, c'est pour l'éternité, sans que quelque chose puisse y être ajouté ou retranché. Tout cela enseigne de la manière la plus claire que la nature conserve un ordre fixe et immuable, que Dieu a été le même pour tous les temps, que nous les connaissions ou non, et enfin que les miracles n'apparaissent comme quelque chose de nouveau qu'à raison de l'ignorance des hommes," (TTP vi, §§67-68, G III/95).

De la même manière, prétendre que l'ordre politique puisse être radicalement changé, n'est-ce pas engager sa créance en d'impossibles miracles, tout, dans ce domaine comme dans les autres, étant déjà arrivé?

Si Spinoza s'installe au point de vue d'une histoire qui est finie - remarquons d'ailleurs que, si nous en restons à ce qui vient d'être dit, elle était finie dès le départ, et en fait n'a jamais eu lieu, l'ordre véritable étant par définition sans histoire - c'est donc pour des motifs apparemment opposés à ceux qui inspirent Hegel: le raisonnement de Spinoza ne prend nullement en compte une dialectique de l'innovation, appuyée sur le travail du négatif, mais développe au contraire toutes les conséquences de ce que nous avons déjà appelé son réalisme politique. Rien de nouveau sous le soleil: les formes sociales, si elle ont été réellement inventées, l'ont été dans une époque tellement reculée que la mémoire s'en est dissipée, et c'est pourquoi il ne reste plus qu'à les admettre telles qu'elles se présentent aujourd'hui, sans prétendre y ajouter ni retrancher quoi que ce soit, comme si elles valaient pour l'éternité. Toutefois, il apparaît aussitôt que ces formulations ne doivent pas non plus être prises à la lettre, car il n'est pas davantage possible de ramener la théorie politique à un simple enregistrement de l'état de fait: l'expérience ne délivre de véritables enseignements que si elle est considérée *sub specie aeternitatis*, donc dégagée des circonstances accidentelles qui lui confèrent sa situation temporelle singulière. Aussi bien, pour Spinoza, il s'agit, en analysant les différentes sortes de structures sociales, c'est-à-dire les régimes politiques, de replacer ceux-ci dans le cadre de cette déduction générale qui les fait dériver d'une nature commune. Or, cette démarche n'est elle-même possible qu'à travers la prise en considération des formes optimales dans lesquelles s'effectue l'organisation essentielle du pouvoir politique: "Maintenant que nous avons traité du droit de chaque forme d'organisation sociale en général, il est temps que nous traitions du meilleur régime adapté à chaque Etat" (TP V, 1). Il est clair que l'ordre politique, dans les conditions auxquelles il est ainsi présenté, correspond à quelque chose de parfaitement inédit en regard de l'existence actuelle de la société, et Spinoza remarque lui-même:

> Bien que, à ce que je sache, aucun Etat n'ait été institué d'après toutes les conditions que nous avons énoncées, nous pourrions cependant faire voir aussi, en nous appuyant sur l'expérience elle-même, que cette forme-ci d'Etat monarchique est le meilleur, si nous voulions prendre en considération les causes de la conservation de chaque Etat, tant qu'il n'est pas retourné à la barbarie, et de son renversement." (TP VII, 30)

Il suffit, semble-t-il que la démarche théorique ne contredise pas l'expérience pour se trouver du même coup en parfait accord avec elle: mais cela signifie aussi que, pour comprendre la raison substantielle des phénomènes, dans le domaine politique comme dans tous les autres, on s'écarte de leur réalité factuelle, en leur appliquant des principes, qui, sans être nécessairement d'une autre ordre, restent pourtant inaperçus à leur niveau.

On peut donc dire que Spinoza ne se résigne pas passivement à un état de fait, ne serait-ce que parce que l'actualité dans laquelle celui-ci s'incarne est par définition précaire et condamnée tôt ou tard à se défaire: les événements qui ont agité la Hollande en 1672 viennent d'ailleurs d'en donner un témoignage éclatant, et sans aucun doute ce sont eux qui ont donné à la réflexion du *Traité politique* son incitation initiale, voire son premier objet. Il n'est donc pas question de nier que l'histoire soit le lieu de constants changements, et qu'elle soit hantée par une dynamique qui tend de manière quasiment permanente à en déstabiliser les figures apparentes. L'objectif d'une pensée théorique, appuyée sur des démonstrations, est en quelque sorte de remonter ce mouvement en sens inverse, en ramenant la société, toute société, à son principe, qui n'a d'ailleurs rien à voir avec une origine historique. Mais il serait parfaitement inconséquent de supposer que cette déduction, qui s'effectue d'une certaine manière a priori, puisse renoncer à voir ses objets réalisés dans la pratique, et qu'elle se satisfasse d'en donner la présentation scientifique, pour le simple plaisir de comprendre (bien que Spinoza fasse explicitement référence à ce dernier argument: TP I, 4). Spinoza s'est évertué dès le début de son traité à établir l'identité nécessaire de la théorie et de la pratique, et on ne saurait admettre que cette identité soit elle-même seulement "théorique": le fait que la théorie et la pratique ne se contredisent pas est le signe, mais non le fondement de leur accord. Sans doute n'est-il pas permis de lire le *Traité politique* comme un discours adressé au Prince, ou comme un manuel du militant, ni même comme un traité d'instruction civique à l'usage des bons citoyens: car il n'est rien d'autre au fond qu'une réflexion philosophique sur le meilleur, ou le moins mauvais, usage que peut faire le sage de l'état social, dont de toutes façons il ne peut se déprendre, dans la perspective de libération qui le définit. Mais cette réflexion, pour théorique et philosophique qu'elle soit, ne saurait évidemment se couper de toute perspective de réalisation pratique, étant entendu que celle-ci ne dépend en dernière instance des décisions et des bonnes intentions de qui que ce soit: admettre que la forme optimale convenant à chaque sorte de régime politique pourrait n'exister qu'en idée, ce serait illogiquement cantonner la pensée théorique dans la considération d'un pur possible, complètement coupé des conditions de son effectuation. Au contraire, envisager comme réalisable, pour autant que les circonstances extérieures s'y prêtent, la structure sociale qui garantirait autant que possible la paix civile, et assurerait du même coup les condition les plus favorables à la liberté de penser, c'est retirer à cette structure le caractère irrationnel d'un possible idéal, réservé aux rêveries subjectives qui constituent spécifiquement l'univers de la fable (TP I, 5).

Rien de nouveau sous le soleil: cette considération vaut donc pour les causes qui déterminent le droit des sociétés, dont la nécessité est éternelle, mais en aucun cas pour leur effets, qui sont au contraire en transformation incessante. Sans doute les hommes sont ils toujours les mêmes, en ce sens que, en tous lieux et en tous temps, ils sont nécessairement conduits par leurs affects: mais ceux-ci les entraînent dans des formes d'associations toujours nouvelles, qui ne relèvent jamais de configurations exactement identiques. Et c'est pourquoi, si tout sans doute n'est pas possible dans l'histoire, où il est de toutes façons exclu que se produise quelque chose d'en soi contradictoire, car on ne fera jamais manger d'herbe à des tables, il reste que tout ce qui peut se conclure des principes fondamentaux, c'est-à-dire des causes réelles du droit, doit un jour ou l'autre arriver: au moins cette éventualité ne peut-elle être définitivement écartée. L'histoire n'est donc jamais finie, mais elle poursuit toujours au delà de ses formes actuelles, un mouvement de production qui, s'il n'altère en rien ses conditions essentielles, varie indéfiniment les formes dans lesquelles elles se réalisent. Le "réalisme" se Spinoza le conduit à la considération d'une histoire ouverte, pour laquelle le moment présent, quel qu'il soit, n'a jamais que le caractère relatif d'une manifestation occasionnelle, et non celui d'une expression absolue. L'histoire est sans fin, et sans fins, parce qu'elle dépend nécessairement de causes qui agissent toujours en elle, quelles que soient les conjonctures qui fixent le contexte de leur intervention: c'est pourquoi d'ailleurs, dans les pires moments de cette histoire, ceux dans lesquels la puissance civile

dégénère en une contrainte arbitraire qui dénie le droit lui-même, il reste
néanmoins possible, pourvu qu'on revienne aux causes réelles du droit, de penser
à être libre, de penser la liberté, sur un mode qui n'est pas seulement celui d'une
idée sans contenu. Eternel optimisme du sage.

Penser le droit, si ce n'est donc penser l'histoire en tant que telle, n'est
pas non plus penser sans elle ou contre elle: mais c'est nécessairement penser
dans l'histoire, dans l'horizon où ses successives expériences se poursuivent, *ad
infinitum*. Pourtant, si l'histoire n'est pas absente de la réflexion théorique de
Spinoza, c'est dans la mesure où elle est envisagée dans son rapport avec la
puissance illimitée de la nature, en l'absence donc de tout présupposé
téléologique. Ici encore, entre la pensée de Spinoza et celle de Hegel, se
découvre un motif de divergence apparemment radical. Du point de vue de
Spinoza, la déduction rationnelle du droit ne peut en aucune manière coïncider
avec la révélation d'une progression rationnelle, qui disposerait les formes
historiques de sa réalisation au long d'une ligne continue, orientée par sa propre
dynamique interne dans un sens unique et uniformément ascendant. Certes, il
est possible de sérier les formes de l'Etat, mais cet ordre prend, dans le *Traité
politique* la forme d'une typologie, d'un répertoire de structures à l'intérieur
duquel il semble n'y avoir qu'à choisir, à chaque moment, celle qui est le mieux
adaptée à ses exigences spécifiques, étant entendu que ce choix ne relève pas
de décisions individuelles qui au contraire le présupposent toujours. Dans la
mesure où Spinoza s'est engagé dans une réflexion sur la logique de l'histoire,
celle-ci s'est limitée à la constatation de la dérive monarchique qui obsède toutes
les formes de sociétés, et qui, restreignant peu à peu les assises de leur pouvoir,
rend plus en plus précaires les conditions de leur perpétuation (TP VIII, 12).
S'il est possible de réfléchir l'histoire universelle, c'est dans la perspective d'un
cycle revenant indéfiniment sur lui-même, et non dans celle d'une tendance
progressive qui se dirigerait vers l'idéal d'une société de droit intrinsèquement
rationnelle, qu'elle incarnerait au terme de son mouvement.

Ici encore, on peut voir une occurrence du réalisme politique de Spinoza:
le philosophe ramène toutes les sortes de sociétés à des principes communs,
qui sont ceux de la nature, mais il renonce à privilégier absolument telle ou telle
structure de pouvoir, et à constituer celle-ci en paradigme universel, qui
constituerait la forme unique vers laquelle tendrait chaque Etat, quelles que
soient les conjonctures qui président à leur formation. S'il y a une essence du
social, dont l'explication complète relève de la connaissance adéquate du déterminisme universel, il n'y a pas une essence de la société qui préexisterait à
l'ensemble de ses manifestations, s'incarnerait en elles, de manière à parvenir,
traversant toute l'histoire, à sa plus parfaite réalisation. La véritable sagesse
est de ne jamais se laisser surprendre par les modifications auxquelles la société
est exposée en permanence, et de parvenir à identifier, à chaque moment, le type
spécifique de régime social auquel on a affaire, de manière à comprendre en
quoi il s'accorde avec les fondements naturels du droit, et à déduire en
conséquence tout ce qu'on peut en attendre dans la pratique, en envisageant
les améliorations éventuelles qui pourraient lui être apportées pour lui assurer
un maximum de stabilité, et garantir ainsi, autant que faire se peut, la paix civile.

Cette évaluation comparée procède de ce qu'on peut appeler un scepticisme historique, dans la mesure où elle limite étroitement les espérances, mais du même coup aussi les craintes, qu'on peut attacher à telle ou telle situation: si elles se valent toutes, c'est parce que, malgré leur hétérogénéité, elles expriment de manière toujours différente ce même fond commun dont elles dépendent, et qui n'est pas même le droit, en tant que, dans une perspective artificialiste ou formaliste, sa spécificité serait irréductible, mais la nature et ses lois universelles. Car l'horizon ultime du droit, pour Spinoza, n'est pas l'histoire mais la nature: et ce point évidemment l'oppose à Hegel, puisque celui-ci ramène au contraire l'organisation de toutes les sociétés à un principe essentiellement spirituel qui, s'il s'effectue dans des figures historiquement diverses, obéit néanmoins à une logique de développement interne; et c'est cette logique qui engendre les figures du droit comme les moments successifs d'une unique série qui trouve son commencement véritable dans sa fin: l'Etat rationnel.

Pourtant, ici encore, reconnaitre l'opposition radicale qui s'élève entre les points de vue de Spinoza et de Hegel, ce ne peut être seulement les renvoyer dos-à-dos, en prenant simplement acte de leur désaccord: car celui-ci n'a de sens que sur la base d'une entente implicite; et c'est celle-ci qui permet d'identifier dans leurs discours respectifs l'existence de certains enjeux, voire de certains objets, communs. Si on reconsidère la philosophie hégélienne de l'histoire à la lumière du raisonnement de Spinoza, tel que les grandes lignes viennent d'en être reconstituées, on s'aperçoit que ses enseignements sont moins simples, et surtout moins simplistes, que ceux auxquels on la ramène d'ordinaire. Si Hegel avait réellement formé l'idée que la rationalité de l'histoire ne peut être dégagée que sous la condition que celle-ci ait effectivement atteint son terme absolu, celui-ci coïncidant avec le moment où se situe la réflexion de Hegel, et s'instituant dans la forme supposée indépassable de l'Etat prussien, il est clair que sa doctrine dépendrait d'une présupposé injustifiable, démentant la rigueur de son organisation interne et, à la limite, mettant le système en contradiction avec lui-même. Aussi bien Hegel n'a-t-il jamais dit cela: c'est en vain qu'on chercherait dans toute son oeuvre, à l'exception de quelques formules métaphoriques, une spéculation sur le moment terminal de l'histoire. Ceci se comprend si on réfléchit attentivement à ce que signifie pour lui la notion de "présent." Hegel rapporte celle-ci à l'éternité *(das Ewige das gegenwärtig ist)* du concept et à l'identité à soi de l'esprit qui demeure toujours auprès de lui-même, et non à l'actualité empirique de tel ou tel moment temporel *(die Gegenwart als Jetzt)*, qui n'en est que la forme extérieure finie. Si l'histoire est le lieu d'une Aufhebung qui la dirige vers un maximum de rationalité, c'est parce que la vérité infinie du concept qui la hante continûment ne passe pas en elle, mais persiste à travers toutes ses transformations. C'est pourquoi la philosophie ne considère jamais que le présent: c'est celui-ci qui donne son sens au passé, en en faisant l'objet d'une *Erinnerung* qui littéralement l'intègre à la réalité effective de l'Esprit tel qu'il est maintenant, du point de vue de laquelle la perspective d'un avenir possible relève d'un devoir-être *(sollen)* irrationnel. Revenant, dans ses *Leçons sur la philosophie de la religion*, sur la nécessaire réconciliation de l'esprit et de la réalité, en reprenant la fameuse formule de la Préface des *Principes de la Philosophie du Droit*, "reconnaitre la raison comme la rose dans la croix du présent," Hegel réfute les conceptions mystiques du droit qui en replacent l'idéal dans une origine perdue ou dans un avenir espéré, Paradis passé ou futur, de toutes les façons absent (alors que la pensée authentique ne s'applique qu'à ce qui est présent):

> Cette théorie détermine son idéal comme passé ou futur. Il est nécessaire qu'elle se pose et elle exprime ainsi le vrai en et pour soi, mais le défaut est précisément cette détermination de passé ou de futur. Elle en fait quelque chose qui n'est pas présent et lui donne ainsi immédiatement une détermination finie. Ce qui est en et pour soi est l'infini: toutefois, ainsi réfléchi, il se trouve pour nous en état de finité. La réflexion sépare avec raison ces deux choses; elle a toutefois le défaut de s'en tenir à l'abstraction et exige cependant que ce qui est en et pour soi doive apparaitre aussi dans le monde de la contingence extérieure. La raison assigne sa sphère au hasard, au libre arbitre, mais en sachant que dans ce monde extrêmement confus en apparence la vérité se trouve cependant. L'état idéal est une chose sacrée, mais cet état n'est pas réalisé; si l'on se représente par sa réalisation les complications du droit et de la politique, les circonstances qui se présentent ainsi que la multiplication des besoins humains doivent être conformes tous à l'Idée; il se trouve ici un terrain qui ne saurait être adéquat à l'idéal mais qui doit exister cependant et où l'Idée substantielle est partout réelle et présente. Ce que l'existence a d'absurde et de trouble ne constitue pas à lui seul le présent. Cette existence présente n'est qu'un côté, et ne comprend pas la totalité qui appartient au présent. Ce qui détermine l'idéal peut exister, mais on n'a pas encore reconnu que l'Idée est réellement présente parce qu'on ne l'observe qu'avec la conscience finie. Il est difficile de reconnaitre la réalité à travers l'écorce du substantiel, et parce qu'on trouve difficilement l'idéal dans la réalité on le place dans le passé ou dans l'avenir. C'est un labeur possible de reconnaitre à travers cette écorce le noyau de la réalité - pour cueillir la rose dans la croix du présent, il faut se charger soi-même de la croix.[3]

S'il y a une philosophie de l'histoire, c'est, pour Hegel parce que la raison se trouve partout "présente" dans l'histoire, et non seulement dans tel ou tel de ses moments finis, abusivement privilégié par rapport à tous les autres, et arbitrairement identifié avec son terme absolu. En ce sens, c'est toujours, pour la philosophie, la fin de l'histoire, dans la mesure où celle-ci, en chacun de ses moments, doit être réfléchie de manière récurrente à partir de son état actuel, de manière à révéler les conditions rationnelles qui rendent celui-ci nécessaire. Et si Hegel représente l'Etat comme la forme accomplie de l'Esprit objectif, il faut justement comprendre que, du même coup, celle-ci ne coïncide jamais tout à fait avec la réalisation de l'Esprit absolu, qui relève de tout autres conditions. L'Etat est éternel, précisément parce que l'idée qui est en lui ne s'identifie jamais complètement avec ses réalisations circonstancielles, mais se trouve irrésistiblement amenée à "dépasser" ces réalisations, la vérité qui la hante la poussant à chercher sans cesse, au delà des limites d'une actualité historique, les conditions de son accomplissement. Ainsi, pour Hegel comme pour Spinoza, si la raison rencontre l'histoire, c'est dans la mesure où elle n'est pas tout à fait du même ordre qu'elle, et se maintient, par rapport à ses manifestations singulières, dans une constante réserve. C'est précisément ce qui permet de dire que la raison "ruse" avec l'histoire, car celle-ci n'est pour elle qu'un instrument occasionnel.

La Ruse de la Raison

L'étude de ce dernier thème va nous permettre de revenir encore une fois sur le rapport entre nature et raison tel qu'il est instauré par le droit. On peut dire que la démarche de Hegel est dialectique dans la mesure où elle parvient à réconcilier ces deux termes en maintenant jusqu'au bout leur contradiction: la raison s'effectue dans le droit contre la nature, mais en même temps elle exploite les éléments qui lui sont fournis par la nature pour les détourner à ses propres fins. "Les passions se réalisent suivant leur détermination naturelle, mais elles produisent l'édifice de la société humaine, dans laquelle elle ont conféré au droit et à l'ordre le pouvoir contre elles-mêmes."[4] Spinoza veut-il dire autre chose lorsqu'il reprend à son compte la définition de l'homme comme "animal social" (TP II, 15)? Incontestablement, cette dernière formule signifie pour lui que le droit, fondé en nature, est, sinon du même ordre, du moins en rapport de continuité avec la nature: la société n'étant après tout que la continuation de la nature par d'autres moyens. Or, pour Hegel, si le droit s'appuie sur la nature, c'est dans la mesure où il est aussi en rupture avec elle, et c'est bien ce que signifie la métaphore de la ruse, qui fait implicitement référence à une négativité dont on chercherait en vain la trace dans le texte de Spinoza.

Pour Hegel, la genèse du droit s'appuie sur le développement d'une contradiction qui, en dernière instance, se ramène à celle du singulier et de l'universel: dans leur conduite empirique, les hommes sont conduits par la recherche de leurs intérêts particuliers, et il faut en même temps que leurs actes s'inscrivent dans le cadre défini par la loi, qui pose au contraire la prééminence du bien général commun. Pour que la raison s'effectue objectivement dans le monde du droit, il faut qu'elle reprenne à son compte cette contradiction, et qu'elle la développe jusqu'à son terme: c'est-à-dire s'intègre au rapport naturel qui s'instaure spontanément entre les hommes, à travers le libre jeu de ce qu'ils croient être leurs intérêts, de manière à contrôler ce rapport et à le diriger; tout se passe alors comme si elle manipulait les passions humaines comme un matériau, de manière à les soumettre à ses propres fins. Or ce retournement n'est possible que parce que la raison introduit, ou fait apparaitre, entre les termes extrêmes qu'elle réconcilie, des médiations. Dans le contexte de l'histoire universelle, ces médiations sont les peuples qui participent à la fois du singulier, par les caractères spécifiques qui les différencient entre eux, et de l'universel, par l'esprit commun qu'ils élaborent, et qui les autorise à revendiquer, quand le moment en est venu pour eux, la fonction de représenter l'Esprit universel sur la scène de l'histoire: en effet, pour Hegel, l'histoire est comme un théâtre sur lequel la raison s'incarne dans des personnages, les peuples, qui entrent et sortent de scène suivant les exigences de leur rôle. Si les peuples sont les "acteurs" de l'histoire, c'est précisément en raison de cette situation intermédiaire qu'ils occupent entre la nature et la raison: la vie d'un peuple n'est rien d'autre que le développement de cette contradiction, développement fécond, puisqu'il porte en lui la promesse d'un dépassement, jusqu'au moment où un autre peuple prend la relève dans l'accomplissement de la même mission, qui est la réalisation de l'état de droit, et la rationalisation des rapports humains.

Ceci signifie que, pour Hegel, la matière effective de l'histoire est donnée dans l'existence des peuples, et non dans celle des individus: ou plutôt: l'existence des individus n'y est impliquée que dans la mesure où elle est déjà informée par la configuration culturelle collective à l'intérieur de laquelle elle s'inscrit et qui lui préexiste nécessairement. C'est pourquoi Hegel ne donne pas au droit un fondement anthropologique, pas davantage qu'il ne développe une vision humaniste de l'histoire. En effet, il pense que l'histoire, considérée dans son mouvement objectif, n'entretient pas un rapport direct avec l'existence des individus, et ne peut donc être expliquée à partir d'elle. Si l'histoire est possible, c'est parce qu'elle travaille non sur les hommes eux mêmes, mais sur des rapports humains déjà constitués, qu'elle transforme progressivement, en jouant sur leurs conflits internes, de manière à leur conférer la structure rationnelle de l'Etat. Ce point est essentiel, car il permet de comprendre pourquoi Hegel s'oppose radicalement à Rousseau, à qui il impute la conception inverse, qui tend à déduire l'esprit du droit, défini, à tort selon lui, comme "volonté générale," à partir des décisions arbitraires des individus. Car le reproche fondamental que fait Hegel aux théories du contrat social, c'est qu'elle substituent au fondement juridique rationnel de l'Etat un fondement psychologique irrationnel.

On peut légitimement se demander où Spinoza se situe lui-même dans cette discussion, lorsqu'il entreprend de déduire les formes de l'organisation sociale à partir de la nature humaine: tend-il à réduire le juridique à l'anthropologique, ou bien s'appuie-t-il sur une conception de la nature dont les réquisits rationnels invalident au contraire une telle réduction? On a commencé à répondre à cette question, au début de cet exposé, en dégageant les caractères originaux du concept d'individualité tel qu'il est exploité par Spinoza. Dans la mesure où l'individu est *pars naturae*, il n'y a pas d'existence individuelle en soi, dont les limites seraient fixées et définies une fois pour toutes, mais il n'y a que des ensembles individualisés, qui se forment et se diluent à l'intérieur de totalités plus vastes qui les déterminent. Or, ce raisonnement, qui s'applique d'abord aux êtres humains singuliers, vaut aussi pour les peuples: la conception spinoziste de l'histoire ne reconnait pas l'existence privilégiée aux peuples - à l'exception peut-être des Hébreux: mais ceux-ci ne sont-ils pas plutôt, à travers leur rêve d'élection, un "anti-peuple"? - et en tout cas ne leur reconnait pas une fonction nécessaire de médiation entre le singulier et l'universel, puisqu'elle prétend au contraire expliquer directement les formes relatives d'organisation instaurées par le droit à partir de la nature humaine telle qu'elle s'incarne immédiatement dans les affects individuels. Si l'on peut parler d'une ruse de la raison chez Spinoza, c'est à propos précisément de cette démarche, qui consiste à retrouver, derrière toutes les motivations et les conduites collectives, la détermination nécessaire, parce que strictement causale, des passions, celles-ci exprimant la puissance de la nature en l'homme, en tout homme, quelle que soit sa situation historique. Mais la nature qui agit en l'homme n'est pas non plus sa nature, en ce sens qu'elle lui appartiendrait exclusivement, et le détacherait artificiellement de tous les autres êtres, humains ou non, auxquels il est au contraire objectivement lié par le fait qu'il appartient à la même nature qu'eux.

Lorsque Spinoza parle de l'homme comme d'un animal social, il ne tend donc nullement à affirmer un primat de l'anthropologique sur le politique, parce qu'il s'appuie sur un concept de la nature humaine qui interdit de penser un tel primat. En effet, qu'est-ce qui est naturel dans les hommes? Spinoza le répète inlassablement: ce sont leurs affects, en tant que ceux-ci jouent spontanément, et les conduisent, sans même qu'ils en aient conscience. Ces affects sont les mêmes, et sont soumis aux mêmes lois, qu'ils soient rapportés aux individus, d'après le *jus naturae*, ou aux relations collectives qu'ils nouent à l'intérieur de l'organisation sociale, selon le *jus civile*: c'est précisément l'identité de ces affects qui fonde la nécessité du droit, selon un ordre objectif naturel qui n'est réductible à aucune convention artificielle. Mais sur quoi est fondée cette communauté des affects qui conditionne la vie sociale des hommes? Sur la nature même de ces affects, qui se présente d'emblée comme une nature commune, et, on peut le dire, communautaire. Sur ce point, il n'est pas indispensable de se reporter au détail des démonstrations qu'enchaîne le livre III de l'*Ethique;* il suffit de se reporter au bref résumé que Spinoza en présente lui-même au début du *Traité politique,* car, malgré son caractère schématique, il en dégage très bien l'esprit essentiel. Le propre des désirs humains, c'est qu'ils ne se développent pas à partir du rapport singulier à soi de l'individu considéré comme une entité autonome, comme un "sujet," pour la bonne raison que ce rapport est illusoire et n'a aucune réalité du point de vue de la nature; mais ils se constituent immédiatement à travers le rapport à autrui qui donne à la nature humaine le contexte objectif de son développement. Non seulement les hommes sont en proie à un certain nombre de passions élémentaires, qui leur font envisager pour eux-mêmes un mode de vie adapté à leurs aspiration, à la mesure de leurs craintes et de leurs espérances, mais ils sont poussés en même temps à désirer (*appetere*) que les autres hommes vivent aussi selon leur propre idée: d'où l'esprit de compétition et les conflits qui coïncident nécessairement pour les hommes avec la libre réalisation de leurs désirs, c'est-à-dire avec la manifestation, l'expression de la puissance qui est en eux, en tant que *partes naturae.*

En ce sens, on peut parler, d'après Spinoza, d'une socialisation spontanée des affects humains, qui fait que les individus n'existent et ne prennent conscience d'eux-mêmes que sur le fond des relations réciproques qui s'établiment entre eux et les autres, et qui d'emblée les fait communiquer. Que ces relations soient imaginaires n'altère en rien leur caractère de nécessité, qui est au contraire renforcé par le fait qu'elles sont subies plutôt qu'elle ne sont voulues en vertu d'une décision rationnelle. Cette théorie relationnelle des affects présente le désir (*appetitus*), en tant qu'il dérive directement de la tendance naturelle de l'individu à persévérer dans son être (*conatus*), comme ayant naturellement la force du désir de l'autre, aux deux sens que peut prendre cette expression: il n'y a pas d'abord mon désir, et d'un autre côté le désir d'autrui, d'où résulterait ensuite leur confrontation; mais autrui se trouve immédiatement impliqué dans mon propre désir, qui est aussi à la fois mien et sien, parce qu'il n'est pas la propriété d'un sujet particulier, enfermé dans les limites de sa singularité. C'est pourquoi la doctrine de Spinoza ne rentre pas du tout dans le cadre de ce qu'on a appelé les théories de l'individualisme possessif: car, selon lui, l'individu ne peut vouloir pour soi-même sans du même coup vouloir aussi pour les autres, et c'est pourquoi ses actes s'inscrivent à l'intérieur d'un réseau de rapports préétablis qui le lient nécessairement aux autres hommes; ce sont pas ces rapports qui constituent l'horizon de son enviroinment, à l'intérieur duquel il faudra bien qu'il trouve les conditions de sa libération. Ainsi, agir à son idée *(ex suo ingenio)*, en suivant les indications qui sont complètement commandées par ce système de relations imaginaires, d'où résultent les conflits des hommes, ce n'est pas être libre, mais c'est au contraire s'exposer à assumer tout le poids de contrainte qui résulte de l'enchaînement causal des affects et transforme le fait de vivre selon son propre droit *(esse sui juris)* en celui d'être soumis, on dirait aussi bien d'être aliéné, au droit d'autrui *(esse alterius juris)*. Tout ceci fait irrésistiblement penser à la dialectique de l'Anerkennung que Hegel a mise à la base du rapport entre les consciences dans sa *Phénoménologie de l'esprit*.

Cette analyse est cruciale, parce que c'est elle qui établit la continuité fondamentale de la nature et du droit. Non seulement les hommes, du fait qu'ils se soumettent à un droit qui n'est plus seulement celui de la nature mais celui de la société, ne quittent pas la nature humaine pour en prendre une autre toute différente (TP IV, 4), mais on peut dire que les formes immédiates de leur existence, dans la mesure où elles sont complètement déterminées par les lois de la nature, sont déjà marquées par le droit, ou si l'on peut dire en puissance de droit, dans la mesure où, comme on vient de le voir, elles prennent place dans le système des relations imaginaires qui créent d'emblée entre les individus une sorte de société naturelle, même si celle-ci prend la forme déréglée d'une société sauvage. C'est pourquoi entrer en société, ce n'est jamais abandonner définitivement l'état de nature, parce que c'est dans celui-ci que en dernière instance sont donnés les éléments ou les matériaux à partir desquels se constitue la vie sociale des hommes. Sur ce point, Spinoza est aussi éloigné des positions de Rousseau que de celles de Hobbes. Rousseau critique Hobbes pour avoir, sans même s'en rendre compte, projeté à l'intérieur de sa description de l'état de nature les conditions de la société sous la forme de la compétition permanente entre les individus; et c'est pourquoi, de son côté, il définit l'homme à l'état de nature comme étant totalement seul et oisif. Mais, cette critique étant faite, il est parfaitement d'accord avec Hobbes pour établir une discontinuité entre l'état de nature et l'état de société, et il reproche seulement à Hobbes d'avoir atténué le caractère radical de cette discontinuité: lui-même interprète cette rupture comme le passage d'un mode de vie solitaire à un mode de vie collectif, alors que Hobbes la représente à travers la conversion d'une sociabilité instinctuelle et conflictuelle, pratiquement invivable, en un état rationnel, fondé sur le calcul des intérêts, et supposant un strict contrôle, voire la mise entre parenthèses, des passions naturelles. Ainsi, malgré les divergences très considérables qui les opposent, Hobbes et Rousseau sont néanmoins d'accord pour admettre que l'homme social n'est pas le même que l'homme naturel.   Or, c'est sur ce point que précisément Spinoza adopte une position différente: selon lui, non seulement, du fait qu'il vit en société, l'homme ne change pas de nature, mais ce sont fondamentalement des mêmes causes qui dirigent sa conduite dans l'état de nature et dans l'état de société, qu'il est de toutes façons impossible de séparer radicalement.

Arrivés à ce point, nous voyons la formule: "l'homme est un animal social" s'enrichir de nouveaux sens: elle signifie que les hommes sont naturellement plongés dans le droit, qui n'est donc pas le résultat d'une construction artificielle résultat d'un calcul rationnel ou d'un engagement volontaire, comme le représentent toutes les doctrines contractualistes; et on comprend alors que, dans le *Traité politique*, Spinoza ait complètement renoncé à faire référence à un pacte social. Lorsque Spinoza écrit: *Homines... civiles non nascuntur, sed fiunt.* (TP V, 2), c'est précisément pour faire comprendre que les hommes sont façonnés par le droit qui leur est imposé, exactement comme Hegel montre que toutes les représentations de la conscience individuelle sont d'emblée informées par un conditionnement culturel, objectivement incarné dans l'esprit d'un temps, et qui détermine leur existence historique.   Ainsi, pourrait-on dire, nul ne peut sauter par dessus le droit de son temps.   Pour Spinoza, cela signifie que la tentation de sortir de l'état de société et de vivre dans la solitude est vaine, parce qu'aucun homme, qu'il soit libre ou asservi, ne peut aimer ni rechercher la solitude:

> Du fait que la crainte de la solitude obsède tous les hommes, parce que nul n'a les forces, dans la solitude, d'assurer sa protection et de se procurer les choses nécessaires à la vie, il s'ensuit que les hommes désirent par nature l'état de société *(statum civilem homines natura appetere)* et qu'il est impossible que les hommes suppriment jamais tout à fait cet état. (TP VI, 1)

On l'a dit, on ne sort pas vraiment de la nature pour vivre en société: réciproquement, on ne peut jamais quitter tout à fait la société pour retourner à la nature, parce que c'est la nature même des hommes, telle qu'elle joue à travers le libre enchainement de leurs affects, qui les incline spontanément les uns vers les autres, ou si l'on peut dire, qui les incline les uns aux autres, sans qu'ils puissent jamais se défaire de ce penchant qui ne se ramène pas à une simple représentation de leur conscience mais s'inscrit dans le système de la nature.   S'il est possible, à propos de Spinoza, de parler d'un naturalisme politique, c'est donc, plutôt qu'au sens d'un effort pour rapporter le politique au naturel, comme une superstructure à une infrastructure, à celui au contraire d'une tentative pour penser l'un et l'autre au même niveau, comme deux déterminations simultanées et solidaires, qui nouent inextricablement leurs effets à l'intérieur du réseau de relations collectives qui rassemble tendanciellement tous les individus à l'intérieur de la nature considérée dans son ensemble.   Si l'ordre politique dépend des conditions d'une nature, c'est donc aussi parce que l'ordre de la nature est, au sens le plus général, politique.

Ici encore, on voit les positions de Spinoza et de Hegel se rapprocher à travers la divergence même qui les oppose. Sans doute, l'un rapporte le droit à la nature et l'autre à l'esprit: mais, dans les deux cas, c'est pour conférer au droit le maximum d'objectivité et de nécessité, sans pour autant lui accorder un caractère absolu, détaché de ses conditions de possibilité historiques. Qu'est-ce que cela signifie que le droit soit un système objectif et nécessaire? Cela signifie qu'il ne se ramène pas aux décisions subjectives des individus, qui ne se forment au contraire que sur fond de droit et dans le cadre préétabli que celui-ci leur impose. Cela signifie aussi que sa rationalité ne se ramène pas au fait que les hommes subordonnent leur conduite aux enseignements de la raison, ce qui, ou bien dépend de l'existence du droit lui-même, puisqu'on pense plus librement dans une société mieux ordonnée, ou bien relève de tout autres conditions, puisqu'il ne faut pas confondre les problèmes de l'Esprit absolu avec ceux de l'Esprit objectif. Sur ce point, à partir de prémisses qui paraissent fondamentalement différentes, Spinoza et Hegel parviennent à des conclusions très voisines, ce qui est confirmé par le fait qu'ils s'opposent identiquement aux théories contractualistes du droit. Pour l'un comme pour l'autre, il faut bien que la raison ruse avec le droit, c'est-à-dire à la fois qu'elle se serve du droit comme d'un instrument dans sa lutte pour conquérir les conditions d'une vie authentiquement libre, et aussi qu'elle prenne le droit comme il est déjà pour en réajuster le fonctionnement, de manière à ce que leurs intérêts respectifs soient accordés, et que l'existence humaine devienne tout simplement vivable. Or, ceci ne dépend ni des intentions ni même des actes d'aucun individu, ou d'aucun groupe d'individus, qui, par lui-même et pour lui-même, déciderait ce qui est bon pour tous les autres, et du même coup, sans même parvenir à supprimer le droit, ne ferait que ramener celui-ci aux conditions de son irrationalité native. Spinoza et Hegel s'accordent donc sur ce point fonda-mental: le droit est un procès sans sujet.

1. Préface des *Principes de la philosophie du droit*, trad. Derathé, (Paris: Vrin, 1975), p. 58.
2. *Plan des travaux scientifiques nécessaires en vue de réorganiser la société*, 1ère Ed. 1822.
3. Glockner XV, p. 293, cité d'après la traduction française de Gibelin, Vrin éd., t. II, p. 32).
4. *La raison dans l'histoire*, Préface aux *Leçons sur la philosophie de l'histoire*, trad. Papaioannou, Paris (1965), 107.

Spinoza and the *Three Imposters*

RICHARD POPKIN
Washington University

Much has been written about the fact that Spinozistic ideas were spread in the early 18th century through the underground work, *Les trois imposteurs, ou l'Esprit de M. Spinosa*, which was first printed in 1719.[1] There is a good deal of research going on presently in Europe and the United States on the origins and dissemination of this work, and its possible relation to Spinoza's circle.[2] What I wish to deal with today is where Spinoza himself fitted in the historical development of the work. I shall try to show that an early formulation of at least chapter three of *Les trois imposteurs, Ce que signifie le mot religion. Comment & pourquoi il s'en est introduit un si grand nombre dans le monde. Toutes les religions sont l'ouvrage de la politique...*, existed in some form by 1656. This formulation was known to Henry Oldenburg, later Spinoza's friend and correspondent, and probably to Queen Christina who had just abdicated as ruler of Sweden. Oldenburg communicated what he knew to Adam Boreel, the leader of the Dutch Collegiants, the non-sectarian creedless group which took Spinoza in after his excommunication. Oldenburg begged Boreel, a renowned theologian of the time, to refute the terrible thesis that Moses, Jesus and Mohammed were imposters who created religions for political reasons. Boreel worked for five years writings an immense answer, which exists in manuscript form. Spinoza, I shall try to show, was also writing an answer of a different kind at the same time, while he was living with the Collegiants in Amsterdam and Rijnsburg, an answer that appears in the *Tractatus Theologico-politicus*.

Next I will suggest that the *Trois imposteurs* grew from an advanced form of Hobbes' political evaluation of religion, to a more psychological, sociological and philosophical analysis of the three main Western revealed religions by incorporating parts of the French translations of the *Tractatus*, and portions of the *Ethics* into the text. The text we now have is thus properly entitled *L'Esprit de M. Spinosa* in that it develops a part of Spinoza's view. Spinoza's own role in this transformation is still unknown.

Before beginning on this excursion into the underside of late seventeenth century intellectual history, let me clarify some confusion concerning the topic. First, there are two works which circulated in manuscript from 1680–95 to the late Enlightenment, *De Tribus Impostoribus* and *Les trois imposteurs*. They are quite different. The first is shorter and deals with some details of Biblical criticism. It claims to have been written by the secretary of Frederick II in the Middle Ages.[3] The second has two titles, *Les trois imposteurs*, and *L'Esprit de M. Spinosa*, and sometimes both. It is often bound with *La vie de M. Spinosa*, attributed to one Jean-Maximilien Lucas, the so-called "oldest biography of Spinoza."[4] There are dozens, hundreds of manuscripts of the French text, varying in content. There is a basic content that is approximately the same in all of the manuscripts I have seen. Then there are additional parts, including chapters drawn from the writings of Pierre Charron and Gabriel Naudé, that appear in some of the manuscripts. The manuscripts can be found all over Western and Central Europe, and in the United States and Canada.[5] The French text was printed and suppressed in 1719,[6] and later reprinted several times in the eighteenth century. I will deal only with the French text. The text always contains a criticism of Descartes, and some lines from Hobbes' *Leviathan* of 1651, which sets a lower limit on when it could have been written in the present form.

Second, there are several manuscript traditions.[7] The list given by Ira Wade misleadingly suggests the manuscripts must all be eighteenth century ones, and the text also. Wade's list is mostly taken from eighteenth century collections in France. There are a large number of manuscripts in Holland which do not fit with Wade's classifications. The list given by Dunin-Borkowski of manuscripts of *L'Esprit de M. Spinosa* contains mainly ones in German and Austrian libraries. The manuscripts can be grouped by title, by whether they include the five chapters from Charron and Naudé, by whether they include various front matter giving a bogus history of the work, by whether they include a letter of 1695, and other features. Some younger scholars are working on this, and hopefully will sort out all of the manuscripts presently available, and give us a plausible history of their origins and dissemination. As of the moment I would adjudge one of the six manuscripts in the Herzog August Bibliothek in Wolfenbuttel as the best text, though it must be a copy of another text. My reasons for saying this will be discussed elsewhere.

Now on to our story. Henry Oldenburg, who at the time was a tutor to a young nobleman at Oxford, wrote a letter in April 1656 to his friend, Adam Boreel who was then in London. Oldenburg told Boreel the sad news that "religion falls into contempt, the raillery of the profane grows sharper, and the hearts of those who fear God are crucified." He then added,

> What I shall say next is of great concern to you. Two problems were mentioned lately, in the solution of which I seek your assistance. The first is that the whole story of the Creation seems to have been composed in order to introduce the Sabbath, and that from motives of merely political prudence. For to what purpose (says the objector) is the fatiguing labor of so many days assigned to Almighty God, when all things submit to his bidding in a single instant? It seems that that very prudent legislator and ruler, Moses, concocted the whole story on purpose, so that (when he had gained acceptance of it in the minds of his people) one certain day should be set aside on which they should solemnly and publicly worship that invisible Deity; and so that whatever Moses himself should say proceeded from that same Deity they would observe with great humility and reverence. The other problem is that Moses certainly encouraged and excited his people to obey him and to be brave in war by hopes and promises of acquiring rich booty, and ample possessions, and that the man Christ, being more prudent than Moses, enticed his people by the hope of eternal life and happiness though aware that the soul seriously contemplating eternity would scarcely savor what is vile and low. But, Mohammed, cunning in all things, enlisted all men with the good things of this world as well as of the next, and so became their master, and extended the limits of his empire much more widely than did any legislator before or after him. You see what licence this critic adopts out of love of reasoning.

I earnestly beseech you to stop his mouth and to stretch out a helping hand to me, struggling here.

Oldenburg then urged that they correspond about these views and "that these letters should not be made public." But the answer must depend

upon the solid establishment of that first pillar of all true religion, that is to say the existence of God and his care for human concerns, and upon the certainty of divine revelation. Surely all religion totters and falls when that is undermined or overthrown. You, my dear friend, will easily perceive my purpose and because of your love of God and of religion will not hesitate to fight on their behalf.[8]

The two problems Oldenburg stated appear in chapter three of *Les trois imposteurs* (though, of course, Oldenburg's letter was written in Latin and *Les trois imposteurs* in French.)[9]

Boreel, at the time was the leader of what Kolawkowski has labelled *Chrétiens sans église*.[10] He was an Oxford graduate, and *a* or *the* leading Dutch Hebraist. He had worked with two of Spinoza's teachers, Rabbis Jacob Judah Leon and Menasseh ben Israel, on the Hebrew vocalized edition of the *Mishna* of 1646. He was a central figure among the Millenarian non-confessional thinkers in Holland and England, involved with Mennonites, Quakers, Jews and such chiliasts as John Dury, Samuel Hartlib, Jan Amos Comenius and Peter Serrarius. In 1655-56, when Menasseh ben Israel was negotiating with Cromwell for the readmission of the Jews to England, Boreel was in London, and entertained Menasseh along with Robert Boyle and Oldenburg. Boreel raised problems that may have led to the disintegration of the negotiations. He left London shortly after receiving Oldenburg's letter, and set to work in Amsterdam on answering the challenge to revealed religion. Boreel was in Amsterdam when Spinoza was excommunicated, and no doubt knew of his reception into the small Collegiant group on the outskirts of the city. The Collegiants were often called the "Borellists" after their leader.[11]

By the beginning of 1657 Boreel had completed part of his answer. Oldenburg was very pleased that Boreel was arguing "that the origin of religion is truly divine and that God appoints no one but himself to be the legislator for the whole human race."[12] The correspondence of Oldenburg and of Samuel Hartlib indicates Boreel's progress in writing his tome entitled *Jesus Christ Universi humani Generis Legislator*.[13] Oldenburg had added more to Boreel's task by telling him about, and maybe sending him a copy of, Bodin's *Colloquium Heptaplomares*, which Oldenburg had learned about in Paris.[14] Boreel finished his work in 1661, and was in failing health. A copy was made by Spinoza's patron, Peter Serrarius, at the behest of Robert Boyle.[15] I found this copy in the Royal Society's collection of Boyle papers. It had apparently gotten out of order, and is bound haphazardly in three volumes.[16] Francis Mercurius Van Helmont also had a copy, which was copied by Henry More, who used it in his theological works, and considered it one of the most important works of the century.[17]

No study has yet been made of Boreel's opus. A quick review of it indicates that at least one of its aspects is that it is a refutation of the three imposters thesis mentioned by Oldenburg. Boreel insisted true religion is of divine origin and that Jesus was and is the Divine Legislator of the human race. The work is an enormous philosophical and theological attack on atheism, religious scepticism, deism, paganism, Judaism and Mohammedanism.

In the period 1656-61, Boreel was in close contact with several people who we know knew and talked to Spinoza - the Millenarian Peter Serrarius, who apparently introduced Spinoza to the Quaker leader, William Ames, and to the Quaker missionaries in Amsterdam. Boreel was also in close contact with Spinoza's friend, Peter Balling. In addition, Boreel had learned Portuguese and Spanish in order to work with various Amsterdam rabbis on the Hebrew edition and Spanish translation of the *Mishna*.[18] Perhaps evidence of a close link with Spinoza is that in 1661, Balling, who spoke Spanish, went to see Spinoza at Rijnsburg on behalf of the Amsterdam philosophical group that was interested in his ideas. Spinoza had just completed the treatise on the improvement of the understanding, which he showed Balling. Then, or immediately thereafter, Balling wrote *Light on the Candlestick*, a statement of the rational basis of religious mysticism. The short work uses many of Spinoza's terms and ideas. Balling wrote this in Dutch. Boreel did the Latin translation of the work, and the Quaker, Benjamin Furly did the English. The work became a widely disseminated statement of rational mysticism, based on Spinoza's epistemology.[19]

So, Boreel presumably knew what Spinoza was doing. Boreel was a close friend of Henry Oldenburg, who visited Spinoza in Rijnsburg in 1661, and formed a life-long intellectual relationship with him. Presumably, since Oldenburg was *au courant* about Boreel's work refuting the three imposters theory, and was so anxious to receive and use Boreel's answer, he would have discussed the matter with Spinoza when they met. Boreel must have known Spinoza through the Collegiants. He may have known him earlier through his associations with at least two of Spinoza's teachers, Menasseh ben Israel and Jacob Judah Leon. Boreel continued working with the Amsterdam rabbis on editing and translating ancient Jewish texts until his death.

And, presumably, Spinoza should have heard of what Boreel was working on, either from Boreel himself, or from the various Collegiant and non-conformist figures he was in contact with. Spinoza's discussions in the *Tractatus* indicate that he, too, was considering the three imposters theory and offering a quite different resolution to it.

Besides what is in Oldenburg's letter to Boreel in April 1656, other items indicate that the theory was circulating that religion was a political institution created by political leaders in order to control societies. Machiavelli, Charron, Naudé, Hobbes, and others offered this analysis of the origin of pagan religion and false Judeo-Christian movements.[20] Most European writers, including Spinoza, thought it was obvious to every intelligent European that Mohammed was an imposter, who had created the Islamic religion for personal and political ends.[21] Queen Christina is reported to have said around 1656 that Moses was just an imposter, who used the crossing of the Red Sea, to take political control of the Jews.[22] She was also desperate to obtain a copy of the supposedly existing manuscript of *Les trois imposteurs*.[23] Perhaps her offer of $1,000,000 for the manuscript led someone to write it. J.P. Marana, in the oft-printed *Letters writ by a Turkish Spy in Paris*, covering events from 1637-82, indicates that the three imposters theory began circulating in Paris around 1656.[24] Hobbes, in *Leviathan*, analyzed how non-revealed religions of Greece, Rome and elsewhere, developed as ways of running political societies. Although Hobbes specifically exempted Judaism and Christianity from his analysis, since they got their authority from God,[25] it is possible to see how someone could, (and in chapter three of *Les trois imposteurs* did) extend his analysis to the roles of Moses and Jesus. Uriel da Costa, in the text of his that we have, which may have been written before his death in 1640 or 1647, asserted that all religions are man-made for human purposes, and proclaimed, "Don't be a Jew or a Christian! Be a Man!"[26]

So I think we can say that the three imposters theory was in the air. It is, of course, a basic ground for rejecting Judaism and Christianity, and for accounting for the power of these religions.

Spinoza, in his examination of how Judaism began, and what Jesus added to it, discussed various elements of the three imposters theory, and then offered a solution which makes Moses a benign or even beneficent imposter, and Jesus no imposter at all, since he was not a lawgiver, a view that was pretty far removed from Boreel's.

Spinoza's picture of Judaism beginning as the result of the ancient Hebrews escaping from the Egyptian political world, and finding themselves with no laws, in a state of nature in the desert, led to seeing Moses' role as very helpful and constructive. He organized the escaping Hebrews into a political society by asserting that the laws he imposed on them came from God.

In the fifth chapter of the *Tractatus* Spinoza developed this interpretation clearly and forcefully. Having distinguished divine law that governs all of nature from ceremonial law that regulates human behavior in special circumstances, Spinoza showed how Jewish ceremonial law began. The laws enunciated by Moses, covering moral, sanitary and ceremonial behavior

> appear not as doctrines universal to all men, but as commands especially adapted to the understanding and character of the Hebrew people, and as having reference only to the welfare of the kingdom.[27]

The Mosaic commandments are not given as prophecies. They are given solely in Moses' capacity as a lawgiver and judge. Moses did this because of the need of the Hebrews, in their circumstances, to have a legal system imposed on them. This is said in contrast to Jesus' role, which Spinoza described as follows:

> Christ, as I have said, was sent into the world, not to preserve the state, nor to lay down laws, but solely to teach the universal moral law, so we can easily understand that He wished in nowise to do away with the law of Moses inasmuch as He introduced no new laws of his own. His sole care was to teach moral doctrines, and distinguish them from the laws of the state (Elwes, 70-71; G III/70-71).

(Here Spinoza sided with the Christian Judaizers like John Dury, Henry Jessey and Anna Maria von Schurmann, who insisted that the Mosiac law, especially the Fourth Commandment, was not abrogated by Christianity.)[28]

Moses' and Jesus' roles are carefully distinguished. Moses instituted or made laws for the Hebrews in their circumstances and within the compass of their understanding. Jesus made no laws, and just taught morality to everyone, without affecting the laws of the state. Moses' case is then examined in the light of what the Jews were like when they escaped from Egypt: "they were entirely unfit to frame a wise code of laws and to keep the sovereign power vested in the community; they were all uncultivated and sunk in a wretched slavery" (Elwes, 75; G III/75). They were no longer bound by any national laws, and desperately needed a lawgiver and a ruler. They were in a state of nature, unable to reason their way out of it by holding a constitutional convention.

Spinoza then explained that because of Jewish incompetence and Moses' virtues, the latter

> made laws and ordained them for the people, taking the greatest care that they should be obeyed willingly and not through fear, being specially induced to adopt this course by the obstinate nature of the Jews, who would not have submitted to be ruled solely by contract... Moses therefore, by his virtue and the Divine command, introduced a religion, so that people might do their duty from devotion rather than fear (Elwes, 75; G III/75).

So religion was made the basis for the Mosaic legal system which covered practically all possible human behavior because the Jewish people were in no position to govern themselves. What they ate, how they worked, how they clothed themselves, how they shaved, and so on, were made part of ceremonial law, whose force was that it was supposed to have been told to Moses by God.

Spinoza concluded the section about this by pointing out that Jewish ceremonial laws have nothing to do with blessedness, but have "reference merely to the government of the Jews, and merely temporal advantages" (Elwes, 76; G III/76). Spinoza next expressed his doubts that Christian ceremonial activities had any more status. They did not lead to blessedness, probably were not instituted by Jesus and his Apostles, and functioned only to preserve Christian societies.

In this analysis Spinoza did not make Moses or Jesus villains, as *Les trois imposteurs* does, imposing laws for their own benefit and aggrandizement. Rather, Moses did what was necessary to constitute a Hebrew state, when the Jews had fallen back into the state of nature.

> After their liberation from the intolerable bondage of the Egyptians, they were bound by no covenant to any man; and therefore, every man entered into his natural right and was free to retain it or give it up, and transfer it to another. Being then in the state of nature, they followed the advice of Moses, in whom they chiefly trusted, and decided to transfer their right to no human being, but only to God... This promise, or transference of right to God, was effected in the same manner as we have conceived it to have been in ordinary societies, when men agree to divest themselves of their

natural rights (Elwes, 218-219; G III/205).

Moses was given the complete right to consult God and interpret His commands. He established the Hebrew theocracy which served to keep the community functioning for centuries. (Spinoza claimed that this sort of theocratic commonwealth can no longer be set up, because "God, however, has revealed through his Apostles that the covenant of God is no longer written in ink, or on tables of stone, but with the Spirit of God in the fleshy tables of the heart" (Elwes, 237; G III/221). Hence, Spinoza's lengthy examination of the Hebrew theocracy and commonwealth was not just to show that Moses was a benign, beneficent imposter, *but* also to warn that the Hebrew commonwealth could not be reconstituted again, as various seventeenth century Millenarians were trying to do.)

Spinoza took up the specific case mentioned in Oldenburg's letter to Boreel of 1656, the role of the ordinance of the Sabbath. The point at which the ancient Hebrews had transferred all their rights to Moses, and given him absolute authority was when they had so yielded up their natural rights, that "the ordinance of the Sabbath had received the force of law" (Elwes, 71; G III/71). Spinoza, unlike Boreel, had answered the problems raised in the Oldenburg letter, the basic themes of *Les trois imposteurs*, by showing how and why Moses saved the Jews in their then existing anarchic condition, and by insisting that Jesus was not a law-giver, but was a moral teacher. Boreel could argue for the divine authority of the Bible, and of Moses' role, and that Jesus was the lawgiver of the human race. Both Spinoza and Boreel had offered divergent answers to Oldenburg's problems. Spinoza's, by putting the development of religious ceremonial law into human contexts, and into human causal sequences, made the process natural rather than supernatural. The next step of the irreligious thinkers was to make the process malign rather than benign, as occurs in *Les trois imposteurs*.

And so, what does Spinoza have to do with the work that emerges in the underground world of the late eighteenth century, *Les trois imposteurs ou L'Esprit de M. Spinosa*? The work circulated widely in manuscripts and was published several times. If Spinoza had lived in the world of the literary agent, he or his heirs could have collected much money in the form of royalties. A sizeable part of the text of *Les trois imposteurs* is either word for word, or obvious paraphrase, from the French translation of the *Tractatus*, which appeared in 1678.[29] Dr. Silvia Berti of Milan has found that a large part of chapter two of *Les trois imposteurs* is a translation of the Appendix of Book I of Spinoza's *Ethics* into French. (Berti, pp. 31-32. This would be the first known appearance of any part of the *Ethics* in French.) If Spinoza was not a participant in the composition of *Les trois imposteurs*, then its authors had to have access to the *Ethics*, either after it was published in 1677, or in the manuscript form that was in existence by 1675. If the text was taken from the published version, Spinoza by then had passed from the scene and could not have been involved. If this was the case, then the portions of the *Ethics* translated into French were done independently of Spinoza.

The little we know of the preparation of the French translation of *Tractatus* allows for two possibilities, one that Spinoza was involved with the translator and maybe with his more seditious efforts at disseminating Spinoza's views about organized religion, or the other, that the French translation, both as an undertaking, and as a publication, postdates Spinoza, and that he knew nothing about it. If the second is the case, then Spinoza would have had nothing to do with the way his writings were used in the final composition of *Les trois imposteurs*.

The first possibility is intriguing and deserves some investigations. The French translation is attributed to a M. Saint-Glain, a Huguenot refugee.[30] *La vie de M. Spinosa*, often published with, or copied with, *Les trois imposteurs ou L'Esprit de M. Spinosa*, is attributed to Jean-Maximilien Lucas, also a Huguenot refugee. The information naming Saint-Glain comes from Charles Saint-Evremond and Pierre Desmaizeaux, both of whom learned this, they say, from one Doctor Henri Morelli, a friend of Spinoza's.[31] Morelli, according to Saint-Evremond's biographical note on him, was an Egyptian Jew, Henriquez Morales, who received his medical training in Italy and Holland.[32] He became a good friend of Spinoza's, and became Saint-Evremond's doctor. He later became the doctor of the great Parisian courtesan, Ninon de l'Enclos, and then the doctor of the Countess of Sandwich in England, the daughter of the notorious Earl of Rochester. Bayle's editor, Desmaizeaux, knew Morelli in England, and around 1710-12 asked him for information about Spinoza's meeting with the Prince of Condé in 1673.[33] Morelli's data, as presented by Desmaizeaux, in notes in his edition of Bayle's letters in the *Oeuvres diverses*, involved Spinoza's having met the Prince, having spent some time with him, and having been offered 1,000 écus to become Condé's house philosopher at Chantilly. Morelli claimed Spinoza was seriously tempted, and that he discussed the matter several times with Morelli. Spinoza, we are told, finally decided that Condé, with all of his power, could not guarantee Spinoza's safety amongst the Catholic bigots in France. So Spinoza stayed in Holland (*ibid.* 7).

Morelli gave the impression that he was close to Spinoza in the latter's last years. Only Morelli knew who the French translator was. Other data indicate that from 1670, when Spinoza met Saint-Evremond, and 1672, when he met the French military commander, Col. J. B. Stouppe, the former French Protestant pastor in London, Spinoza seems to have entered into the circle of the *libertin* Protestant entourage around the Prince of Condé, many of whom stayed in Holland after the French invasion. Saint-Glain was apparently one of these people. So Spinoza may have known him, and been a party to planning a French edition of the *Tractatus*, with all three of its catchy false titles, *La clef du sanctuaire*, *Traité des cérémonies superstitieuses des Juifs tant anciens que modernes*, and *Réflexions curieuse d'un esprit désintéressé sur les matiéres les plus importantes au salut tant public que particulier*.[34] The French translation became of great importance in the dispersion of Spinoza's ideas, and was still being read over a century later. Tom Paine cited it in his *Age of Reason* which he wrote in 1793 in Paris.[35] Hegel referred to it in a comment to the 1802 editor of Spinoza's *Opera*.[36] Saint-Glain might have been involved in extending the influence and impact of Spinoza's most irreligious ideas, perhaps even as an author or co-author of *Les trois imposteurs* with Spinoza's knowledge and acquiescence.

At the present time we know very little about Spinoza's relations with the Condé circle, and little about when and why the French translation of the *Tractatus* was made. A speculative possibility is that, as Spinoza realized that the bigots would scream if he published the *Ethics*, he arranged, while alive and of sound mind, for the *Opera Posthuma* and the French translation of the *Tractatus*, and the Dutch edition of his works, plus the most provocative use of his ideas in *Les trois imposteurs*. If there is anything to this speculation, which future research may confirm, modify or reject, then *Les trois imposteurs* might deserve its other title, *L'Esprit de M. Spinosa.*

On the other hand, as far as we presently know, Spinoza played no part in arranging for the posthumous dissemination of his work beyond having some role in planning the *Opera Posthuma*, and its Dutch edition. Then, what should we say of Spinoza's role in the history of the development of the text of *Les trois imposteurs*? I hope that the material presented here has shown (a) that Spinoza was aware of the core statement of the three imposters theory, as reported by Oldenburg to Boreel in 1656, (b) that the *Tractatus* is in part an attempt to offer a benign solution, to wit, that Moses instituted the Hebrew religion to rescue the escapees from Egypt from the anarchy of the state of nature, and he made it acceptable by contending that the religion he was instituting was of divine origin. Jesus was not an imposter, since contrary to Boreel, he was not a law-giver and he instituted no new laws or ceremonies. He only stated clearly the moral law that all rational men would accept on the basis of reason. Mohammed, on the other hand, as Spinoza told Jacob Ostens, was not a true Prophet:

> it clearly follows from my principles that he was an imposter, seeing that he entirely took away that freedom which Universal Religion, revealed by the natural and prophetic light, allows, and which I have shown ought to be fully allowed,[37]

(c) that Spinoza, in developing his theory of how religions arise and why they persist and are accepted, presented what was taken over, in Spinoza's own words, as the principal theory of *Les trois imposteurs*. Spinoza, willingly or unknowingly, supplied the theoretical side of the work.

Still, in emphasizing only the critique of religion, *Les trois imposteurs* pretty much ignored Spinoza's positive theology, though Spinoza's definition of God appears, and ignored Spinoza's positive theory of the role of religion in a human world. The thesis of *Les trois imposteurs* is the irreligious side of Spinoza. The more spiritual and more practical sides are ignored. Spinoza is not mentioned in the text, only in one of the main versions of the title. Perhaps the author or authors thought that in so distilling Spinoza's ideas, they were presenting the true *esprit de M. Spinosa.* One way or another, the three imposter theme plays a significant role in Spinoza's own presentation of his theory, and willingly or not, he provided the basis for the finished product. And the finished product circulated so widely through the Republic of Letters in so many clandestine copies that it is still to be reckoned with in evaluating Spinoza's influence on the Age of Reason. Perhaps in a decade or two we may be able to trace the whole history of the work from the 1656 version to the finished product, its dispersion and its influence. For it spread through the Old and New Worlds and was being issued as atheist propaganda even at the middle of the 19th century.[38] The view expressed in it counters the acceptance in some historical sense of the Judaeo-Christian tradition; *L'esprit de M. Spinosa* helped to develop the secular mentality of the late 18th century, while the actual metaphysics of Spinoza helped underwrite a new naturalistic view of the world.

1. See for example, Margaret C. Jacob, *The Radical Enlightenment: Pantheists, Freemasons and Republicans* (London: Allan & Unwin, 1981) and Paul Vernière, *Spinoza et la pensée française avant la Revolution* (Paris: Presses Universitaires de France, 1982).
2. This is being looked into by Margaret Jacob and myself in the United States, by a project directed by Olivier Bloch in France, and now by an international group involving Jeroom Vercruysse, Bloch, Canzanini, Paganini, myself and others, who are planning a bibliography of clandestine literature of the period.
3. Cf. the text of *Traité des trois imposteurs*, edited by Pierre Rétat, (Saint-Etienne; Universités de la Région Rhone-Alpes, 1973), 147. At the present time this is the most available text, a reprint of the 1777 one. Dr. Silvia Berti is bringing out an edition of the first printed text, that of 1719.
4. See Abraham Wolf, *The Oldest Biography of Spinoza* (New York: Dial Press, 1928).
5. I have examined copies in Germany, Austria, The Netherlands, France and England, as well as copies at Harvard, Cornell and the University of British Columbia. No complete inventory exists, and it is hoped that the new project being organized by Bloch, Canzanini, Paganini, Vercruysse and others will accomplish this.
6. The only known copy of the 1719 printing is at the University of California, Los Angeles. It was discovered by Silvia Berti in 1985 in the Abraham Wolf collection there, and is now being republished in Italy and the Netherlands.
7. Ira O. Wade, *The Clandestine Organization and Diffusion of Philosophic Ideas in France from 1710-1750* (Princeton: Princeton University Press, 1938) esp. ch. 2; and S. von Dunin Borkowski, "Zur Textgeschichte und Textkritik der altestenen Lebensbeschreibung Benedikt Despinosas," *Archiv für Geschichte der Philosophie* 18 (1904), 1-34.
8. Henry Oldenburg, *The Correspondence of Henry Oldenburg*, ed. and tr. by A. Rupert Hall & Marie Boas Hall, (Madison and Milwaukee: University of Wisconsin Press 1965), I, 89-92.
9. *Les trois imposteurs*, Rétat edition, ch. 3, esp. pp. 38-78.
10. Leszek Kolakowski, *Chrétiens sans église* (Paris: NRF Gallimard, 1969). Boreel is discussed on pp. 197-199 and 243.
11. Cf. Richard H. Popkin, "Some Aspects of Jewish Christian Relations in Holland and England in the 17th Century," in Jan van den Berg and Ernestine van der Wall, *Jewish Christian Relations in the 17th Century* (The Hague: Martinus Nijhoff, forthcoming); and "The Lost Tribes and the Caraites," *Journal of Jewish Studies* 37 (1986), 213-227.
12. Oldenburg, *Correspondence*, Jan. 24, 1656-57, I, 115-116.
13. For the revelant references, see R. H. Popkin, "Could Spinoza have known Bodin's *Colloquium Heptplomares*?", *Philosophia* 16 (1986) 309, and notes 19-22.
14. *Ibid.*, 309-310.

15. *Ibid.*, 313n22. The details about the making of the copy, and its large cost, appear in Oldenburg's letters to Robert Boyle from 16-18 June 1665 to 16 January 1665-66 in *Correspondence*, Vols. II and III.

16. It is in volumes 12, 13 and 15 of Boyle's papers, located at the Royal Society. It seems to be several presentations of Boreel's case, in various forms. It is to be hoped that a study will be made of it soon.

17. Cf. Henry More, *The Theological Works of the Most Pious and Learned Henry More*, (London 1708), "Preface to the Reader," iv-v. More said he saw Van Helmont's copy at Ragley Hall, the home of Lady Anne Conway, and copied some of it.

18. Cf. Popkin, "Some Aspects of Jewish Christian Relations," and *The Earliest Publication of Spinoza?, The Hebrew Translation of Margaret Fell's **Loving Salutation to the Seed of Abraham*** (Assen, Van Gorcum, 1987), Intro.

19. On this see R. H. Popkin, "Spinoza's Relations with the Quakers in Amsterdam," *Quaker History* 70 (1984), 27; and Michael J. Petry, "Behmenism and Spinozism in the Religious Culture of the Netherlands, 1600-1730," in Karlfried Grinder and Wilhelm Schmidt-Biggemann, *Spinoza in der Frühzeit seiner Religiosen Wirkung, Wolfenbüttler Studien zur Aufklarung*, 12:112.

20. This theory is discussed in Niccolo Machiavelli's *Discourses on Livy*, in Pierre Charron's *Les Trois Veritez*, Gabriel Naudé's *Considérations sur des Coups d'Etat*, and Thomas Hobbes' *Leviathan*.

21. Spinoza said this in his letter to Jacob Ostens, February 1671, Ep. 43, Gebhardt, IV, 225-226.

22. Cf. Urbain Chevereaux, *La Génie de la Reine Christine*, Paris (1655), 36.

23. Cf. Gilles Menage, *Menagiana*, Paris (1754), IV, 397-98.

24. J.P. Marana, *Letters Writ by a Turkish Spy in Paris*, (London: 1723), letter of the 30th of the 7th Moon of the Year 1656, V, iii, 130. This volume first appeared in English in 1692, and is probably not by Marana, who wrote the initial volumes in Italian, and published them in French.

25. Thomas Hobbes, *De Homine*, XIV.

26. Uriel da Costa, *A Specimen of a Human Life*, New York, Bergman Publishers, 1967, where the translation of this passage is given as "He who pretends to be neither of these [Jew or Christian] and only calls himself a man, is far preferable," p. 43.

27. Benedictus de Spinoza, *Tractatus Theologico-Politicus*, Elwes ed., (New York: Dover, 1955), V, 70; G III/70.

28. David Katz is publishing a study of the Sabbath observers in England, the Traskites, and those around Henry Jessey. John Dury, Anna Maria von Schurman and others argued that the Fourth Commandment had not been abrogated by Jesus. Dury, in an unpublished essay in the Hartlib Papers argued that one could be a true and believing Christian and a fully observant Jew, which would mean that no Jewish laws had been abrogated by Jesus, which seems to be implied in Spinoza's discussion of Jesus as a non-lawgiver.

29. Cf. Silvia Berti, "'La Vie et l'Esprit de Spinosa'(1719) e la prima traduzione francese dell' Ethica," *Rivista Storica Italiana*, 98 (1986) 31ff.

30. On what is known about M. Saint-Glain, see the new edition of K.O. Meinsma, *Spinoza et son cercle* (Paris: Vrin, 1983), 6-7 and notes on this section.

31. See Pierre Bayle, *Lettres*, ed. by Pierre Desmaizeux, Amsterdam (1729), I, 143.

32. What we know about Morelli appears in Charles Saint-Evremond, *Oeuvres de Monsieur de St. Evremond*, ed. by Pierre Desmaizeux (Amsterdam: 1726), V, 274-275, and the notes by Desmaizeaux in Pierre Bayle's *Oeuvres diverses*, IV, Amsterdam (1729), IV, 872.

33. Desmaizeaux, *Lettres de Bayle*, notes to a letter from 1706. The "letter" is actually just a portion of the review of Colerus' *Vie de M. Spinosa* in the *Memoires de Trevoux*. On Desmaizeaux's attempt to unravel the story about Spinoza and the Prince of Condé, see R. H. Popkin, "Serendipity at the Clark: Spinoza and the Prince of Condé," *The Clark Newsletter* 10 (1986), 4-7.

34. The three French titles sometime appear in the same volume. Various places of publication are given - Leiden for *La Clef du Sanctuaire*, Amsterdam for *Cérémonies superstitieuses*, and Cologne for *Réflexions curieuses*. All are dated 1678.

35. Thomas Paine, *The Age of Reason*, in *The Writings of Thomas Paine*, ed. by Moncure Daniel Conway, New York and London, G.P. Putnam's Sons, 1891, 273.

36. See the introductory material of the 1802 edition of Spinoza's *Opera*, ed. by Paulus, the first publication of the works since 1677. It was in the French translation of the *Tractatus* that the footnotes to the text first appeared. They were added in Latin, from a handwritten copy at the University of Leiden in the 1802 Jena edition.

37. Spinoza's letter to Jacob Ostens, G IV/226; Wolf, 226.

38. *The Three Imposters*, tr. (with notes and illustrations) from the French edition of this work, published at Amsterdam 1776, published by J. Myles, Dundee, 1844, and republished by G. Vale, New York, 1846. Myles said he was reissuing it at a very cheap price so that working class people could obtain it.

SCHELLING AND SPINOZA: SPINOZISM AND DIALECTIC

ERROL E. HARRIS
Northwestern University

I

The transition from the Critical Philosophy of Kant to the Absolute (or Objective) Idealism of Hegel proceeded through the work of Fichte and Schelling, and is liable to be misconceived, if indeed it can be made intelligible at all, without their intervention. In the hands of the British Idealists of the nineteenth and early twentieth centuries, this transition was obscured by their aversion to the Philosophy of Nature, their consequent neglect of what Hegel had written on that subject, and their almost total disregard of the early Schelling. Influenced by Hegel's criticism of Kant, they eschewed subjective idealism, but they took Hegel to be advocating a doctrine that simply objectified the subjective content of individual experience in a way which, if adopted, generated insuperable difficulties concerning the finite nature of the self and its relation to the transcendental ego. This is a problem latent in Fichte's *Wissenshaftslehre*, but one which Schelling was at least well on the way to overcoming, and which no longer existed for Hegel. But because of their neglect of the Philosophy of Nature, it reemerged in the metaphysics of T.H. Green and F.H. Bradley, and later in the Phenomenology of Husserl.[1] Yet even when notice was taken of the intervening stages of development (e.g., by Josiah Royce), the part played in the conversion of Schelling from his early close adherence to Fichtean Transcendental Idealism by the influence of Spinoza remained largely unnoticed. To draw attention to the intrinsic Spinozism of the early Schelling is, therefore, what I propose to do in this paper.

Kant's critical Idealism left the real world, as the realm of things in themselves, beyond the reach of human theoretical knowledge. We could, in his view, perceive only appearances (*phenomena*); and our natural science was the result of bringing the manifold of sense *a priori* under the schematized categories of the understanding, which were themselves specific forms of the synthetic unity of apperception, the focus of which was the transcendental ego. Fichte saw that the postulation of things in themselves beyond the sphere of possible knowledge was itself as much an act of the Ego as any organization under the categories of empirically given data, so that for him the phenomenal world was simply the dialectical result of the Ego's own activity, positing itself in opposition to a non-Ego, as it necessarily must in order to have an object on which to exercise its subjective activity. Any metaphysical or ontological theory of the natural world, as an existent, or collection of existents, prior to, or independent of the transcendental Ego, he therefore castigated as dogmatism, the paradigm case of which was, he maintained, the system of Spinoza. That, he held, was the only consistent alternative to his own.

The epistemological grounds for this position seemed unchallengeable and the difficulties confronting its alternative insuperable. To maintain, as Locke had done, the existence of a world external to our consciousness, external bodies, that, through their physical and physiological effects upon our sense organs could give rise to 'ideas' (*Vorstellungen* for Kant and his successors), had proved self-defeating. Locke himself was forced to confess that we could know only our own ideas, so that any external world, and any process of causation, should inevitably have been inaccessible to our knowledge. Consequently, Locke's successors, Berkeley and Hume, seeking to make his theory consistent, became committed to a subjectivism, from which not only was escape precluded but all possibility of objective scientific knowledge seemed to have been banished. Kant professed to restore this possibility by giving the word 'objectivity' a new sense (through his 'Copernican revolution'), subjectively founded upon the *a priori* synthesis of the understanding, by means of the categories. Spinoza, on the other hand, had asserted the unity of the subjective and the objective, apparently at the cost of reducing human self-consciouness (and thus any transcendental ego) to a finite idea within the divine intellect - much as Alice, through the looking glass, was relegated by the Red King to the status of something in somebody else's dream.

This, at least, was Fichte's view of Spinoza's position.[2] He conceded that Spinoza admitted an empirical ego, which was 'I' for itself, but which related to the absolute Ego (that is, Spinoza's God) as one idea to a series of ideas. Pure consciousness, Fichte says, was always denied by Spinoza. Then later, in the same paragraph, he alleges that Spinoza separated pure from empirical consciousness, assigning the first to God and the second to a modification of Substance. But Spinoza's God, according to Fichte, never becomes aware of Himself, because (he says) pure consciousness never attains to consciousness. This cryptic statement is left unexplained. But Fichte's main accusation against Spinoza is that he oversteps the limits of his own awareness and enters a realm inaccessible to reason by postulating a part-whole relation between the human mind and the divine intellect, so that his system, though entirely consistent and irrefutable, is so only because, by exceeding the limits of human knowledge, it is also incapable of proof. The postulation of the existence of God, and man's relation to the *Deus-sive-Substantia-sive-Natura*, is simply the consequence of the necessary urge to achieve the highest possible unity in human knowledge. Fichte thus follows Kant faithfully in attributing the belief in God's existence (Spinoza's along with all other) under whatever conception of divinity, to a practical requirement rather than to theoretical cogency.

Kant considered direct knowledge of the nature of the transcendental subject to be unattainable, because it would involve bringing the ego under the very categories to which it was necessarily prior, both logically and ontologically. This was, for him, the paralogism of pure reason, committed by traditional metaphysics in its attempts to characterize the self (or soul) as a simple substance. The empirical self, as a stream of concious states (*Vorstellungen*), experienced in inner sense, on the other hand, was knowable, but only as phenomenal object, never as subject. The empirical self is a natural product, subject to the laws of Nature, and (for Kant) our knowledge of Nature, objective science, is constituted by the transcendental synthesis spontaneously effected by the synthetic unity of apperception, through subsumption of phenomena under the schematized categories. But this knowledge is only of appearances, the reality of which is attributed to things in themselves, that are unknowable. But for Fichte there are no things in themselves. The fundamental reality is the Ego; and the whole world of Nature is subordinated to the constitutive theoretical activity and the practical demands of the transcendental subject. Accordingly, the Ego becomes absolute, and the embrace of transcendental subjectivity infinite, replacing what for Spinoza was Substance-or-God-or-Nature. In fact, in his later work (written in 1810), *Die Wissenschaftslehre im Allgemeinen Umriss*, Fichte himself equates the Ego with God, although earlier he had admitted that it is the same ego to which Descartes had referred in *cogito ergo sum;* i.e., the finite self. Precisely how are these two conceptions of the Ego, finite and absolute, to be distinguished and related? The unanswerable question for the dogmatic realist had always been: How can ideas of an external world get into the mind? Consciousness is a self-illuminating self-awareness; physical and physiological effects are not. What process of transition could ever convert the latter into the former? The only acceptable course seemed to be to abandon realism altogether and to submit, with Fichte, to an inescapable subjective idealism, harboring its own unrecognized, yet insoluble problem of the relation between the natural (or empirical) self and the transcendental ego.

When we turn from Fichte to Hegel, however, we find realism and idealism reconciled, the existence of Nature, in its own right, as 'the Idea in the form of other-being,' affirmed, and the question how knowledge of the world can get into the mind answered in the declaration that 'the mind is the truth of Nature' - or Nature come to consciousness of itself as the human mind. For Hegel, Nature is the self-manifestation of the Idea as the real external world. 'The external world is in itself (*an sich*) the truth,' he writes, 'for the truth is actual and must exist.' (*Enzyklopadie*, 38, *Zusatz*). Through Nature, the Idea develops in a series of dialectical forms, physical, chemical and organic, which, in the highest stage of organism, bring it to consciousness of itself in the minds of human beings. They, on the one hand, are products of Nature, and on the other hand, constitute the level at which the Idea, immanent throughout the dialectical process, rises to self-consciousness.

It is only natural to ask how Hegel succeeded in arriving at this position from the apparently inescapable circle of the pure activity of Fichte's transcendental ego. The answer, of course, is to be found in Schelling's *Ideen zu eine Philosophie der Natur* and the works immediately succeeding. Schelling was quite clearly aware of the problems set by Locke's realism, as his discussion in the Introduction to the *Ideen* plainly shows. But he is equally aware that Nature - organic Nature, especially - could not properly be disposed of simply as a creation of the activity, theoretical and practical, of the self-conscious Ego, however free and independent that activity might be. To work out a solution to his problem he sought fresh inspiration from Spinoza. But before we

investigate this Spinozistic element in his thought, we must return briefly to Kant
to trace the germ of Schelling's ideas in the *Critique of Judgement*.

Kant had already drawn attention, in the *Critique of Teleological Judgement*,
to the problematical character of organization as a natural phenomenon. With
unerring insight he saw that purposiveness and wholeness were inseparably
connected. 'It is requisite,' he writes,

> to a thing as natural end [or purpose] first that the parts (as regards their existence
> and their form) are possible through their relation to the whole. For, consequently,
> the thing itself is an end conceived under a concept or an idea which must determine
> *a priori* everything that is contained in it (*Kritik der Urteilskraft*, §63).

If the thing is simply thought of as possible under these conditions, it is only
an artifact. But if it is to be related to a purpose in itself as a natural product,
without the intervention of an extraneous rational cause (e.g., human or divine
intention), the second condition must be fulfilled that parts and whole are
mutually ends and means, for only so is it possible that the idea of the whole
should determine, and be determined by, the form and connection of all the
parts. Each, then, is mutually cause and effect of the other(s), and only then
is the thing an organized and self-organizing being such as may be called a
natural end.

There is considerable affinity between this characterization of teleology and
what Spinoza writes about whole and part in the 32nd Letter (to Oldenburg),
where he insists upon the adaptation of the parts to one another in determining
the nature and identity of the whole, which, again, by its overall configuration
determines the interrelation and reciprocal changes among the parts; so that it
would not be inappropriate to describe them as mutually means and ends. There
is no evidence that Kant had this letter in mind, but it is not improbable that
Schelling (who, as we shall presently see, builds on Kant's position) was
influenced by it. Now, according to Kant, observation of Nature, as brought
under the categories of the understanding, yields only mechanical laws, by which
this mutual teleology cannot be explained. There are no *a priori* grounds in the
idea of Nature, as a complex of observed objects, for the belief that they serve
one another as means and ends. Nor can we discover this from experience.
To conceive natural things as teleological organisms (a notion as indispensable
to biology as mechanism is to physics), we must impose upon our experience
of them, not just categories of the understanding, but an idea of reason, which
is not constitutively valid, but only regulative. To be constitutive, the idea must
be the necessary condition, not only of our representation of the thing as
organized (on the analogy of our own purposive action), but of its very existence.

The effect, however, of Fichte's replacement of things in themselves by the
Ego, as the original source of our sense experience, was to make Kant's
distinction between phenomena and noumena, and so between constitutive and
regulative ideas, purely relative to the dialectical level at which the subject was
operating. Ideas of reason could thus be conditions of objective knowledge just
as well as, or even better than, concepts of the understanding. Schelling

concluded, in consequence, that objectivity and subjectivity were merely two aspects of the same reality, which was itself neither, or both; just as the Attributes of Extension and Thought for Spinoza were two alternative aspects of Substance, which was itself neither or both. Organization thus becomes, for Schelling, clear evidence of the coordinate reality of Nature, equal and opposite, to that of the conscious experience of the knowing subject, because organization, and the organic (teleological) activity of living natural things could not be the mere projection of the self-consciousness of the ego upon its self-posited object. This realization seems to have sent him back to Spinoza, who, he says, (in the Introduction to *Ideen*) was the first to recognize the identity of subject and object.

Organism implies, and is in itself, a whole, determined in structure and function by a holistic principle (which Schelling calls *Begriff,* concept), and this holism cannot be regarded merely as imposed upon the object by our minds, because our minds are compelled, by the very nature and possibility of the object, to recognize the immanence in it of the concept (or principle of organization) as the condition of its being. The phenomena of physical nature, obeying the laws of mechanics, might well be no more than the subjection of phenomena to the ordering categories of the understanding (although this is not Schelling's final view), but an organism is self-subsistent and self-maintaining, through its own life and activity, and its organs can be what they are, and function as they do, only because they are subject to the organizing principle (*der Begriff*) of the whole, in a way that the categories do not and cannot require. It must therefore be an independent manifestation of the concept or idea. This, in effect, is Spinoza's doctrine as set out in the epistle to which reference has already been made, and in the Scholium to EIIP13, and L7. Although Schelling here makes no comparison with Spinoza, he comes to the conclusion that the Idea manifests itself indifferently in two coordinate ways, as organic Nature (for he subsequently finds, like Spinoza, that all Nature is ultimately organic - cf. Spinoza's account of *facies totius universi* and his assertion that all bodies are *animata*), and as subjective experience. This corresponds to Spinoza's Substance expressing its essence under the two attributes of Extension and Thought.

On the one hand, then, Fichte is vindicated, so far as his *Wissenschaftslehre* goes; but this needs, in Schelling's view, to be supplemented, on the other hand, by a *Naturlehre,* to do justice to the objective aspect of the real. The Ego is the original act of cognition, in itself indifferently subjective and objective (for Schelling), from which the ideal world is subjectively generated (as in Fichte's philosophy), but which equally manifests itself in a world of Nature, rising (through a series of 'potencies') to the level of organism where it gives rise to consciousness and reason in mankind.

The metaphysical background of Schelling's *Naturphilosophie* is set out, not always in quite the same terms, in a number of works subsequent to the *Ideen.* The general outline of the system seems to have been taking shape in his mind when he wrote that book, but he seems not to have felt sure about it until later, when he came to write *Darstellung meines Systems der Philosophie,* although it also appears, with certain minor differences, in *Von der Weltseele* and in *Bruno*. He never seems to have been able to make it quite unambiguous or clear-cut, never as systematic or coherent as Spinoza's, but with very definite parallels to Spinoza's ideas.

II

In Schelling's system, as in Hegel's, the ultimately real is the Absolute, corresponding to Spinoza's Substance. Schelling gives different descriptions of it and gives it different names in different contexts. Sometimes it is the Indifference-point, sometimes pure Identity; at other times it is the Infinite, or 'sheer Absoluteness'; then again he calls it Absolute Knowing, or the absolute Act of Cognition, and likewise the unity of the Absolute-real and the Absolute-ideal. Sometimes Schelling seems to identify this with the Idea, but sometimes the Idea appears to be put on a slightly lower level in the hierarchy of the real, and it is never quite clear whether it is the same as 'the Essence' or alternatively what he calls 'the Form.' Essence and Form are, however, the two opposites into which absolute Identity differentiates itself, and he seems to have had Spinoza's attributes of Thought and Extension in mind and their identity in Substance, although the exact correspondences remain vague. Essence suggests the category of universality, and Form that of particularity, but both are still held to present ideal and real aspects, both are at once objective and subjective. The latter (Form) is the projection of the former in the realm of appearance to constitute what Schelling calls relative objectivity, as opposed to relative subjectivity, both uniting in the indifference of absolute Identity.

Form is the realm of embodiment (*Einbildung*), or objectification, of the infinite in the finite, and is primarily differentiated into relative identity, relative difference (or opposition), and the unity of these - the identity of identity and non-identity. There is, presumably, a similar differentiation of Essence, but we are told little about it, though it ostensibly constitutes the ideal sphere set out in detail in Schelling's *System des Transcendentalen Idealismus*. Thus there are three major unities: 'that in which the essence is embodied absolutely in the form, that in which the form is absolutely in the essence, and that in which both these absolutenesses are again one absoluteness.'[3]

So the three potencies are generated, exemplified at various levels (but never systematically expounded by Schelling) as thing, concept and idea, or intuition, concept and idea, or real, ideal and the identity of the two, or finite, infinite and eternal, or Nature, Mind and the Absolute (indifferent or neutral Identity). Schelling flits from one to another of these diverse methods of expressing the triadic structure of his Absolute in a rather confusing manner, so that it is difficult to say just how they are all to be included in one system. Nor is it clear whether the absolute act of cognition (also called absolute knowing) is the Absolute itself, or only the second of the three major unities. At times he refers to it as if it were the latter, but at other times he seems to be insisting that this is the original and primordial unity from which the other two emerge.

It was left to Hegel to weld all these representations of the Absolute and its dialectical self-differentiation into a single coherent whole by means of one consistent principle. But it was Schelling who first came to see that Fichte's transcendental Ego was really the Absolute (for Hegel, absolute Idea) which objectifies or differentiates itself, on the one hand, as the system of Nature, through which its dialectical development brings it to consciousness in the human mind, and, on the other hand, as mind (or spirit, *Geist*), in a parallel system identical with the first in ideal content.

III

Spinoza anticipated all this when, at an early stage in the *Tractatus de Intellectus Emendatione*, he realized that adequate knowledge can only be generated (or deduced) from the idea of the most perfect being, that this is the most perfect method; and that the perfect being, God, expresses its essence in the attributes of extension and thought, which are identical in Substance. This Substance-or-Nature-or-God, he saw, was immanent in all the modes into which, under each attribute, it differentiates itself (or, as he puts it in E IP16: infinite things proceed from it in infinite ways). Of these modes, the human body and its mind are each one, under corresponding attributes, identical with each other as *idea* and *ideatum*.

When Schelling tells us that the Philosophy of Nature is one essential aspect of the whole of Philosophy, he may well be using the word 'Nature' in Spinoza's sense of *Substantia-sive-Deus*. In fact, Schelling's thinking is so closely molded on Spinoza's that Spinozistic terminology is frequently appropriate, and is often used by Schelling himself, to give it expression, as when he refers to the absolute act of cognition as *natura naturans*, and to the natural world, 'the mere body or symbol thereof,' as *natura naturata*.

It must be borne in mind that Schelling never really expounds his metaphysics in systematic fashion, so that one can hardly demonstrate any clear and systematic parallel between his theory and Spinoza's; but I shall give examples of the echoes of Spinoza's thoughts as they occur from time to time in Schelling's writings, and shall point out latent applications of Spinoza's ideas in Schelling's more poetic and often somewhat fantastic speculations.

Throughout *Von der Weltseele*, in which he insists on the organic character of Nature, Schelling stresses the immanence of the whole in every part, both in general and in detail, saying at one point that the highest aim of science is to reveal the ubiquitous presence of God in all things. God, he says, is the One in the totality, in whom all things live and have their being. Although one cannot point specifically to Spinoza as the source of this sentiment, the whole passage is Spinozistic in tone and Spinozism is its most likely inspiration. A little further on, Schelling quotes Spinoza directly as saying 'the more we know of things, the more we know of God,' supporting his own conviction that those who seek 'the science of the eternal' should do so by way of physics.[4]

When we turn to *Darstellung meines Systems*, where the exposition is as systematic as Schelling ever succeeds in making it, the evidence of Spinoza's influence is more copious. He begins by declaring Reason to be absolute and indifferent to all subjectivity or objectivity. He asserts that all philosophy proceeds from the standpoint of reason, and treats things, therefore, as they are in themselves, and not otherwise. As such, he says, they are essentially infinite, and the fundamental law of reason being A = A, it posits absolute Identity, which is the absolutely infinite. This is clearly, Spinoza's God, defined precisely in these terms in E ID6.

Schelling proceeds immediately to give a Spinozistic proof of this absolute Infinity, to the effect that there can be nothing to limit it either internal or external to itself, because it is all-inclusive and self-identical. The absolute Identity, he asserts, does not emerge or proceed out of itself, and true philosophy consists in proving this - namely, that all things in themselves are infinite and are the absolute Identity itself (in short, it is all-inclusive). Only Spinoza, he says, among previous philosophers, had recognized this truth, although even he (Schelling contends) did not carry through the proof completely, nor state it with sufficient clarity to prevent misunderstanding.[5]

Schelling proceeds to tell us that there is a primordial knowledge of the absolute Identity, posited with the proposition, A = A; and, because there is nothing external to the absolute Identity, this knowledge is in the absolute Identity itself. But it does not follow immediately from its essence, from which only its being follows. The knowledge, therefore, belongs to the form of its being, and that is as original as the being itself. Thus there is an original knowledge of the absolute Identity belonging to the form of its being - that is, Schelling avers, an attribute of the absolute Identity itself (*ibid.*, §17).

It is fairly obvious that what he has in mind here again is Spinoza's Substance with its attribute of Thought, the infinite modes of which are the infinite intellect and the idea of God. Also, he is remembering Spinoza's doctrine that, because Substance is *causa sui*, its essence immediately involves existence. Spinoza says that an attribute is what the intellect perceives as the essence of Substance, and Schelling seems to be trying to convey something of the sort by saying that the original knowledge of the absolute Identity belongs to the form of its being and is posited with it as following immediately from it, just as the infinite modes follow immediately from the attributes of Spinoza's Substance. For Schelling, essence is the dialectical opposite of form, but just what he means by form is far from clear. It does, however, seem in some contexts to be akin to what Spinoza calls Extension.

In §31 Schelling says that the absolute Identity *is* [exists] only under the form of indifference of the subjective and the objective (and thus also of Knowing and Being). He speaks of this indifference as 'qualitative' maintaining that there is no qualitative difference between the subjective and the objective, and that they can be differentiated only quantitatively. This is probably a reflection of Fichte's assertion that contradictory opposites can be reconciled when treated as mutual complements.[6]

Further, when Schelling uses the word '*Differenz*,' as he does here in the negative, what he means is complementarity rather than (or as well as) difference. So if absolute Identity exists only under the form of 'indifference' of Knowing and Being, the indication is that these two complementary opposites are united in it much as Thought and Extension are united in Substance for Spinoza.

Schelling goes on to explain that the absolute Identity is the universe, and *vice versa*, because it is only as universe, and can be treated in accordance with essence and form only under limitation (*Erschrankung*) - again reminiscent of Fichte (not to say Spinoza, for whom Substance, considered under its attributes, is perceived under limitation, as modified, or affected by finite modes). It follows that it is the same in essence in every part, and so is indivisible (§§ 33-34). Spinoza, it will be remembered, insists that the essence of Substance, as expressed in each attribute, is indivisible, for much the same reason.

Then, Schelling continues, no limited individual has the ground of its being in itself, for all are equal in essence (the absolute Identity is the same in each) and the being of every limited individual derives from the Absolute. Here again we have pure Spinoza. Next we are told, almost in Spinoza's own words, that every individual thing is determined by another individual thing, and that by another, *ad infinitum*, the reason being that the existence of none is determined by itself, and the absolute Identity encompasses the ground of the totality (§§ 35-36). In other words, only Substance is in itself and is conceived through itself, while its finite modes are all in it and are conceived through one or other of its attributes, each being an effect of a finite cause, itself similarly the effect of another finite cause, and so on *ad infinitum*.

So Spinozan is §38 that one is tempted to quote it *in toto*:

> *Every individual being is, as such, a determinate form of the being of the absolute Identity, but not its being itself, which is only in the totality.*
>
> For every individual and finite being is posited through a quantitative difference of subjectivity and objectivity, which again is determined by another individual being, that is, through another determinate quantitative difference of subjectivity and objectivity. Now, however, subjectivity and objectivity as such is form of the being of the absolute Identity, the determinate quantitative difference of both, therefore, is a determinate form of the being of the absolute Identity, but for just that reason not its being *itself*, which is only in the quantitative indifference of subjectivity and objectivity, i.e., only in the totality. So the statement can also be expressed thus: Every individual being is determined by the absolute Identity not insofar as it is absolutely, but insofar as it is under the form of a determinate quantitative difference of A and B [subjectivity and objectivity], which difference, again, is determined in the like manner, and so on *in infinitum*.

With the substitution of a few Spinozan terms for Schelling's (e.g., Thought and Extension for subjective and objective, finite mode for individual thing, Substance for absolute Identity), this passage could almost have come straight out of the *Ethics*. Spinoza, when he discusses space, time and number (or quantity), as he does in the twelfth letter (on the Infinite), as well as in the *Korte Verhandling* and the *Ethics*, insists that quantitative division is conceivable only in terms of finite modes. And here Schelling is echoing very closely the Spinozan doctrine. In the remark appended to §44, Schelling expressly states that his 'A and B' (subjectivity and objectivity) are precisely Spinoza's attributes, Thought and Extension, except that, so he says, 'we never think of them as merely *idealiter* (as one generally at least understands Spinoza), but *realiter*.' Whether one generally understands Spinoza as identifying the attributes only ideally (which is questionable), Spinoza himself is quite clear that they are really, substantially, one and the same.

In §53, Schelling tells us that, through the absolute Identity, subjectivity and objectivity are immediately posited as being, or as real; just as Spinoza tells us that, from eternal things (i.e., from Substance and its attributes), eternal and infinite modes follow immediately (E IPP21-23). And just as Spinoza asserts that, from the necessity of the divine nature, infinite things follow in infinite ways (E IP16), Schelling proceeds to 'deduce' from his absolute Identity and his two 'attributes,' A and B, the two fundamental attractive and repulsive forces which for him together constitute matter, and thence the entire physical world (as he deduces the ideal world from the absolute identity of the Ego in the *System of Transcendental Idealism*). Similarly, for Spinoza, the infinite mode, Motion-and-Rest, follows immediately from the attribute of Extension, and from that again the *facies totius universi*. Schelling also speaks in Spinozan language of gravity striving to maintain physical bodies in being, indicating the identity of A and B. According to him, light is the ideal or inner aspect, while gravity is the real, or outer aspect, of matter as such; thus to say that gravity strives to maintain bodies in being, is much the same as what Spinoza maintains when he says that everything, so far as it is in itself, strives to preserve itself in its own being, and that this *conatus* is its own essence (E IIIPP6,7).

From what Spinoza writes in the 32nd Letter, it is clear that he conceived *facies totius universi* as a universal organic whole, made up (at different levels of 'perfection') of subordinate organisms; and that is exactly how Schelling conceives Nature, both in *Von der Weltseele* and in *System der transcendentalen Idealismus* (Teil III, ii, D 4). He could as well have gotten the idea from Leibniz, but the source in Leibniz is surely Spinoza. In the *System of Transcendental Idealism*, Schelling defines freedom exactly as Spinoza does: the absolute act of the will is free, simply because it is determined by the necessity of its own nature. However, Schelling's argument here is as much Kantian as Spinozan, although there can be little doubt that the influence of Spinoza persists.

In *Bruno*, in an extraordinary amalgam of Plato's *Timaeus* and Spinoza's *Ethics,* an account is given of the relation of soul and body, which is in all essentials Spinozan. The universe is said to be a vast immortal animal, so well ordered that it can never die. Organisms, we have already seen from *Ideen* and *Weltseele*, are unified and organized in accordance with a principle identified by Schelling as the Concept. So the universe unites a vast multiplicity in the same way as, in a living animal, each individual organ is both distinguished from and united with every other, each having, as it were, its own soul, yet all bound together in the unity of the whole. The soul is the concept, and that of which it is the concept is the body. Thus all things are, each in its own degree, animate, and the soul (or mind) of each, being the idea of its body, contains only what is expressed in the particular thing of which it is the idea. Schelling's reasoning, demonstrating how the body can contain within its concept the possibility of and relation to innumerable other things is much vaguer and looser than Spinoza's, but the general doctrine is the same.[7]

IV

It is hardly necessary to give further instances to show that Schelling's speculation is saturated with the thought of Spinoza. But what, you may now ask, is the historical and philosophical significance of this fact?

As was observed earlier, the problem set for Western philosophy in the seventeenth century, by Descartes and Locke, each in his own peculiar way, was: How do ideas of the external world get into the human mind? Reflection on this question led all their immediate successors, except Spinoza, into an incurable subjectivism, liable to the most serious objections.

Spinoza was the one philosopher of the era who recognized that ideas of an external world did not, and did not need to, get into the mind, that the mind and physical things were not entities of the same order, related in space and by causation, but were two different aspects of the same thing. Ideas, for him, were simply the self-awareness of the bodies whose minds they constituted, and the more complex and organically self-complete those bodies were, the more adequate and comprehensive were their ideas. Both bodies and the minds were ranged in an ascending scale of 'perfection' culminating in an all-encompassing whole, or infinite mode, that was the direct outcome of the necessary nature of an absolutely infinite Substance.

Thus, by relating everything to the whole, to what he appropriately called 'the most perfect being,' Spinoza avoided a causal-representative theory of perception and knowledge, which leads either to a realism, and a theory of knowledge, that, if it can be framed by the human mind, must be false, and if it were true could not be humanly known; or to an idealism, which has (by implication) to equate the human mind, or make it privy, to the divine, and is prone to a solipsism that contradicts itself and fails to resolve the problem originally posed of how a finite member in an environing world can become aware of that world and of its own relation to it.

It was only when Schelling, who was very well aware of the original problem, recognized that Spinoza, in unifying Thought and Extension in Substance, had pointed the way to a solution, that he and then Hegel were able to develop a dialectical conception of the universe, which was at once both realistic and idealistic, and could account satisfactorily for human perception and knowledge. The key influence in all this was Spinoza's. Little wonder that Hegel called him the philosopher's philosopher and declared that the first essential step in philosophizing was to be a Spinozist.[8]

Schelling's position is, in a way, nearer to Spinoza than Hegel's, although it is less clear and more ambivalent, for he envisages Nature as the coordinate objective counterpart of knowledge, differentiated from it within an Absolute which is, as he calls it (among other epithets), 'the indifference point' neutral between objectivity and subjectivity. He never satisfactorily makes clear the dialectical relation between nature and mind. Nevertheless, in Schelling's speculative system, there is an implicit dialectic, vaguely following Fichte's dialectic of antitheses, and proceeding by way of the three potencies (again never very clearly explained) of infinite, finite, and eternal, etc. Through these potencies, represented at successive levels (of which Schelling's various accounts are rather confused and his deduction often far-fetched) Nature, on the one hand, and cognition, on the other, develop towards absolute Identity; yet this takes us back to the original act of cognition, of self-consciousness in the Ego, whose position in the general scheme, as related to its own self-objectification as Nature and human experience, remains ambiguous.

It was left to Hegel to weld all this into a coherent and dialectically consequent system. His Absolute is no mere indifference point, nor a blank unity, but is a definite, absolute whole, which would not (and could not) be a whole if it were not the unification of an infinity of differences (as Spinoza's Substance depends for its absolute infinity on the possession of infinite attributes). And just as the attributes, for Spinoza, are 'powers' and his Substance dynamically active, so Hegel's absolute Idea is an 'infinite restlessness' perpetually differentiating itself as the organizing principle (or Concept) of the universal whole, specifying itself in avatars of dialectical forms constituting Nature and Mind. These range from space and time (united as motion) up to organism, in which the Concept, immanent throughout the process, comes to consciousness of itself in human experience. That develops through its own appropriate scale of forms to absolute knowing, or philosophical knowledge (*Wissenschaft*), culminating in the absolute Idea. Thus an objective realism is intelligibly reconciled with an absolute idealism, and the problem set by the reflective understanding, from which Schelling begins in the *Ideen zu einer Philosophie der Natur*, is solved.

It is no wild conjecture to suggest that in all this Hegel followed the lead of Spinoza, with his account of the gamut of increasingly complex and individualized bodies up to the *facies totius universi*, under Extension, mirrored under Thought by their increasingly intelligent minds, in the order and connection of ideas. Schelling, with whom I have been primarily concerned in this paper, thought constantly in Spinozan terms, and Fichte, whom he closely followed, was hardly less influenced by Spinoza, recognizing Spinoza's system as the only consistent alternative to his own, and constructing the *Wissenschaftslehre* always with one eye on Spinoza, while he kept the other steadily on Kant.

There can be no dispute about the dialectical character of the thought of these three thinkers. Overlooking what Plato and the ancients had to say about Dialectic, and regarding Kant as providing, as it were, negative suggestions about the place and function of dialectic in philosophy, one could say that Fichte was the initiator of the dialectical method, Schelling its somewhat confused, if also inspired developer, and Hegel its consummate master. But Kant's contribution is greater than this ordering implies; for he it was who, in the *Critique of Judgement*, recognized the importance of holism and its implication of teleology;

and, as I have argued repeatedly elsewhere, the specification of every genuine whole, and the structure of every genuine system, is dialectical.[9]

Equally, there should be no dispute about the holistic character of Spinoza's system, and I have persistently contended that he is a dialectical thinker, although the dialectical structure of his thought is obscured by the geometrical cast of his exposition. This contention, when it has not been simply disregarded, has been hotly disputed and denied. Yet it seems clear that all the major dialectical thinkers of German Idealism have, in one way or another, formed their thought on a Spinozistic model, while strenuously resisting the kind of empirical naturalism so often attributed to Spinoza.

It would hardly be proper for me to repeat here what I have written in *Salvation from Despair* and have argued at length elsewhere. The kernel of the argument has been that a dialectical system (and every genuine system, as I say, is dialectical) is determined throughout by an organizing principle, which specifies itself in a scale of forms, related as distinct and complementary instantiations of the holistic principle in progressive degrees of adequacy.

Spinoza gives repeated evidence that he conceived God-or-Substance-or-Nature in just this way, although he tends to set out the system from the top down rather than from the bottom up (as Hegel mainly prefers to do). The scale, in Spinoza's presentation, runs from Substance to attribute, from attribute to infinite modes, thence to finite modes, and so through the entire range of body-minds from the most complex down to the very simplest. He maintains that all things are determined by the necessity of the divine nature; but it is clear that not all forms of necessity are the same. There is mathematical necessity, physical (causal) necessity, psychological necessity (determined by passion), and rational necessity (determination solely by the nature of the agent). Each of these is an exemplification of the divine nature, but as we proceed through the series each form is a more adequate manifestation of that nature, until finally we reach the free creative action of God (exemplified in a lesser degree by the free action of the reasonable man).

In partial association with this scale of forms, there is that displayed in human knowledge. In the TdIE there are four: hearsay, vague experience, inference from the essence of one thing to the essence of another, and finally that wherein a thing is perceived through its essence alone, or through its proximate cause. In the *Ethics* there are three: *imaginatio, ratio,* and *scientia intuitiva.* Here, again, the scale satisfies the conditions I have required for a dialectical series. The continuous range of individual bodies with their correspondingly competent minds, increasing progressively in wholeness and self-dependence, and so increasingly manifesting the self-sufficiency, each under its appropriate attribute, of the infinite mode, and so of Substance itself, has already been noticed. Thus it is entirely fitting for Spinoza to declare, toward the end of the first Part of the *Ethics:*

> Non defuit materia ad omnia, ex summo nimirum ad infimum perfectionis gradum, creanda...

in effect, there was no lack of material for the creation of a complete system of forms in every grade of perfection - what I have claimed to be a dialectical system.

1. Cf. my article, 'The Problem of Self-constitution in Idealism and Phenomenology', *Idealistic Studies* 7 (1977), 1- 27.

2. Cf. J.G. Fichte, *Grundlage der gesamten Wissenschaftslehre (1794)* (Hamburg: (1956)), pp. 20-21.

3. *Ideen zu einer Philosophie der Natur*, Introd., *Zusatz*, *Sammtliche Werke*, II (Stuttgart: (1857)), p. 64.

4. *Von der Weltseele*, *Sammtliche Werke*, IV, 378.

5. Cf. *op cit.*, §§1-14, *Sammtliche Werke*, IV, 114-120.

6. *Grundlage der gesamten Wissenschaftslehre*, Erste Teil, #3.

7. Cf. *op. cit.*, *Sammtliche Werke*, IV 278ff.   The parallel with Spinoza is recognized by Michael Vater in his translation of *Bruno* in footnote 68.

8. Cf. *Lectures on the History of Philosophy*, London, 1896, reprinted, 1955, 1963, 1968; tr. E.S. Haldane and Frances H. Simson, III, 257.

9.   Cf. *The Foundations of Metaphysics in Science*, (London: G.Allen and Unwin, 1965, reprinted by The University Press of America, Lanham, MD., 1983). Part IV; *Formal, Transcendental and Dialectical Thinking* (Albany, NY: SUNY Press, 1987). Pt. III; *The Reality of Time* (Albany, NY: SUNY Press, 1988), 102ff., 133-145.

PIERRE MACHEREY'S *HEGEL OU SPINOZA*

GEORGE L. KLINE
Bryn Mawr College

In this rich and stimulating book[1] Pierre Macherey displays an impressive mastery of the difficult philosophical systems of both Spinoza and Hegel. However, his sympathies appear to lie one-sidedly with the former, and this results in certain controversial claims and (to me at least) unconvincing interpretations. Most of Macherey's criticisms of Hegel's own Spinoza-*Deutung* are well taken. Yet Errol Harris, whose sympathy for Spinoza is at least as deep as Macherey's and whose sympathy for Hegel is deeper than Macherey's, has recently formulated many of the same objections to Hegel's misinterpretations of Spinoza's position.[2]

I

Hegel is indeed wrong in regarding Spinoza's Substance as "dead and rigid" (*tot und starr*).[3] And Macherey is right - as is Harris - to respond to this charge by emphasizing the "life," activity, and dynamism of that Substance (110, 113, 119). But responsibility for Hegel's misinterpretation must be laid at least partly at Spinoza's own terminological door: when he characterizes God or Substance as *res extensa* (E IIP2; quoted at 129) - an expression which Hegel renders accurately as *ausgedehnte Sache* (e.g., *Vorlesungen*, XIX, 387) - Spinoza's use of the past passive participle misleadingly suggests passivity and inertness. Spinoza seemed unable to break with Cartesian terminology and continued to clothe a radical doctrine in traditional language. He might better have called God or Substance a *res extendens* on the model of the present active participles *res cogitans* and *natura naturans*. Spinoza's Substance, in its activity of self-determination, its self-determin*ing* activity, is not only a think*ing* but also an extend*ing* entity: self-think*ing* and self-extend*ing*.

Spinoza's position stands in sharpest contrast to the dualism of the Cartesian ontology, which is not only a dualism of mind and matter but also a dualism of the active and the passive. For Descartes only minds (the Divine Mind absolutely, and human minds relatively) are active. Matter, extension, is wholly passive. It is not only created and preserved, it is also made to be extended - created and sustained as a multitude of *res extensae* - by God, the uniquely active *Res Cogitans*. If Spinoza's God or Substance were to assume a Cartesian voice, it surely would *not* say *Sum Res Cogitans Resque Extensa* but rather, *Naturo, cogito, et extendo, id est, sum Res Naturans, Cogitans, et Extendens.*

II

To translate Spinoza's term *intellectus* by *Verstand*, as Hegel standardly does, is highly misleading (cf. *Vorlesungen*, XIX, 377, 380, 381, 384-86, 388, 389, 391,

395). Only occasionally does he translate it as *Intellekt* (cf. ibid., 382), though he usually translates *intellectualis* as *intellektuell* (cf. ibid., 405). Naturally, he renders Spinoza's *ratio* as *Vernunft*, e.g., at E IIP44 (ibid., 404). But this introduces the invidious distinction between a superior *Vernunft* and an inferior *Verstand*, which has no counterpart whatever in Spinoza, for whom *intellectus* and *ratio* stand at the same (high) epistemological and ontological level, often being equated, as in the expression *intellectum sive rationem* (IVApp§4).

It would, I think, have been useful if Macherey had paused to criticize this usage, since it tends to support his interesting claim that Hegel assimilates Spinoza to Kant on many crucial points (cf. 105, 226-47). Macherey might also have noted that in the Lectures on the History of Philosophy Hegel places his discussion of Spinoza under the general heading *Verstandes-Metaphysik,* which is often a code-word for Kant's philosophy.[4] It is unfortunate that Macherey and the French translators of Spinoza's works whom he quotes have been content to render *intellectus* as *entendement* (cf. 57, 59, 60, 82, 99, 105, 106, 108, 109, 162, 183, 193, etc.), although they render *intellectualis* as *intellectuel* (e.g., 197, 247). Surely the noun *intellect* is also available to French translators! Since *ratio* is rendered as *raison*, Macherey, perhaps *malgré lui*, introduces what I take to be a quasi-Hegelian ranking of *raison* above *entendement* (108) which has no counterpart in Spinoza. There is no term or concept in Spinoza's philosophy that stands to *intellectus/ratio* as *Verstand/entendement* stands to *Vernunft/raison*. In epistemological discussions Spinoza tends to use *intellectus* (sometimes *intellectio*) and to contrast it with *imaginatio*. Typically, he makes an invidious distinction between what is (adequately) present *in intellectu* and what is (inadequately) present *in imaginatione* (e.g., TdIE, §89; for the contrast of *intellectio* and *imaginatio* see ibid., §§87, 90). In ethical and political discussions he tends to use *ratio* and to contrast it with *affectus, cupiditas*, etc. A conspicuous exception to this general rule is the phrase *humana potentia ad coërcendos affectus in solo **intellectu** consistit* (VP42D, emphasis added). He could equally well have said *in sola **ratione** consistit*. Perhaps the use of *intellectus* was influenced by the repeated use of the expression *Amor Dei intellectualis* in E V. More typical is Spinoza's contrast between acting *ex solo ductu **rationis*** and acting *sola **cupiditate** ductus* and his claim that the [*multitudo*] *non **ratione**, sed **solis affectibus** gubernatur* (TTP, XVII; G III/203/19, emphasis added).[5]

In sum, Hegel's contrast of *Vernunft* and *Verstand*, like Macherey's contrast of *raison* and *entendement* (e.g., 108), as applied to Spinoza, is unfortunate and misleading.

III

Macherey's discussion of the vexed question of the *infinita attributa* is, in the end, mostly on the right track. But along the way he permits himself a number of what appear to be distracting, even misleading, formulations. Though Spinoza himself was scrupulously careful never to use the expression *infinitas [n.] attributorum*, Macherey repeatedly uses the expression *infinité d'attributs*, both in quoting French translations of Spinoza's works and when speaking *in propria persona*. (For the former cases, see 113, 155; for the latter, 104-106, 119, 120, 122, 123, 132, 134-36, 157.) Similar expressions, similarly objectionable, include *multiplicité, pluralité*, and *diversité infinie* as applied to the attributes (35, 122, 206).[6] Machery also quotes without critical comment Hegel's reference to the *unendliche Vielheit* (accurately translated as *multiplicité infinie*) of the attributes (WdL, II, 165; quoted at 133).

Surely a *Vielheit, pluralité*, or *diversité* of attributes would be countable, subject to numerical expression. Yet in several passages Macherey takes a much more reasonable position, citing with approval Gueroult's claim that the *infinité d'attributs* involves no *numération* (cf. 120, 126, 130, 132, 222-23).[7] Macherey's clearest and most welcome statement on this matter is that *l'infini n'est pas un nombre* (123). Yet the inconsistency of both Macherey and Gueroult on this key question remains troubling. Gueroult rightly declares that *l'infini et le nombre s'excluent* (Gueroult (1968), I, 517). But he dilutes this admirable assertion with the problematic claim that *les expressions numériques peuvent, malgré leur impropriété, être utilisées pour signifier la pluralité concrète des attributs telle que l'entendement la conçoit* (Gueroult (1968) I, 1959).[8]

There is a roughly parallel inconsistency in Hegel's treatment of the *infinita attributa*. Alongside his talk about the *unendliche Vielheit*, there is an occasional recognition (not noticed by Macherey) that the term *unendlich* as applied to the attributes is to be taken in the sense of 'inclusive' or 'exhaustive' like the "present, completed infinity" of the circle. In Hegel's words: *positiv, wie ein Kreis vollendete gegenwärtige Unendlichkeit in sich ist* (Vorlesungen, XIX, 387).[9]

Macherey's expression *tous les attributs* is decidedly preferable to his *infinité d'attributs* (cf. 122, 124, 131). My own view is that the term *infinitum* as applied to Substance means 'perfect without limitation' - what I have elsewhere called *infinitum I* - and that the term *infinita* [neuter pl.] as applied to the *attributa* means 'all without exception' - what I have called *infinita II* - and has nothing to do with multiplicity, number, or counting.[10]

My own interpretation of ID6 - an interpretation with which, I suspect, Macherey might have a certain sympathy - could be formulated as follows: "By God I understand a being absolutely perfect without limitation, that is, a Substance consisting of all the attributes without exception, each of which expresses an essence eternal and perfect without limitation" (*Per Deum intelligo ens absolutê infinitum [I], hoc est, substantiam constantem infinitis [II] attributis, quorum unumquodque aeternam et infinitam [I] essentiam exprimit*).[11]

IV

Much of what Macherey has to say about negativity, positivity, and the (reconciling) "negation of the negation" is both informative and helpful. But it strikes me as misleading to introduce the expression *omnis determinatio est negatio* simply as *la thèse bien connue* (102) and to repeat it several times (137, 141, and passim), failing to inform the reader until almost sixty pages later (at

158) that Spinoza himself in fact *never* used the expression in this universalizing form.[12] Even when the qualification is finally entered, it seems to me to be rather half-hearted: *Revenons maintenant*, Macherey writes, *à la formule **omnis determinatio est negatio** et voyons quelle est sa signification pour Spinoza lui-même. Elle [sic] apparaît dans la lettre 50 à J. Jellis...* (158).

But of course the *omnis* formulation does not appear in that letter, or in any other text from Spinoza's hand. Macherey is aware of this fact, but he puts the point with curious indecisiveness: *Littéralement, elle [sic] s'y écrit: **determinatio negatio est**...* (loc. cit.). Fair enough! But then why not say flatly, and at the first mention of the *omnis* formulation (102), that this formula is Hegel's, not Spinoza's? What Macherey eventually informs the reader is accurate enough, but comes very late in his account:

> *d'une incidente qui renvoie à un contexte bien particulier... [Hegel] a fait une proposition générale, qui prend une signification universelle, par l'adjonction d'un petit mot qui change tout et qui confond beaucoup de choses: **omnis**.* (158)

It would also have been helpful to point out that the *omnis* formulation, which Hegel included in only one of the works which he himself prepared for publication, namely, the second, extensively revised edition of the first part of the *Wissenschaft der Logik* (completed in 1831, published posthumously in 1833), did not occur in the first edition of that same work (published in 1812).[13] A possible partial explanation for this curious fact is that when he was preparing the first edition of the *Logic* Hegel was more familiar than he was later with the details of Spinoza's texts, having recently collaborated with Paulus in the preparation of the *Opera quae supersunt omnia* (Jena, 1802, 1803).[14]

According to notes taken by Hegel's student, H. G. Hotho, editor of the *Lectures on Aesthetics* (vol. X) in the first edition of Hegel's *Werke*, Hegel had used the *omnis* formulation in his Berlin lectures on the history of philosophy as early as 1823-1824.[15]

The *omnis* formulation is linked to the broader question of the role of negativity in Spinoza's philosophy. As Harris has pointed out, for Spinoza it is only determination *ab extra* that is a kind of negation.[16] In other words, although the other-determination of the modes does indeed involve negation, the *self*-determination of Substance is wholly positive.

Macherey quotes the well-known passage in which Spinoza complains that such entirely positive properties of Substance as its being *increatum, independens, infinitum* have to be expressed by negative terms, because their contraries (viz., *creatum, dependens, finitum*) arose first in the development of human language and *nomina positiva usurparunt* (TdIE, §89; quoted at 177-78). But Macherey fails to make clear that Substance for Spinoza is something wholly positive or affirmative, that negation or privation is only a partial and provisional aspect of reality. In other words, as Hegel shrewdly observed, Spinoza conceives *das Negative* as only a *verschwindendes Moment*, i.e., a "vanishing phase or aspect" of the positive (*Vorlesungen*, XIX, 410).

V

Macherey seems to me to draw too sharp a distinction between Hegel's teleological system and Spinoza's anti-teleological one, and to assimilate Hegel's teleology too intimately to the principle of the "[reconciling] negation of the negation." (See esp. the final section of his book, entitled *La téléologie*, 248-60.) Macherey's impatience with what he calls variously *l'illusion finaliste* (70, 83, 190), *le préjugé de finalité* (196), and *l'illusion d'un ordre finalisé* (221) is evident. (Parallel strictures are to be found at 21, 23, 93, 182, 190, 209, 215-19, 222, 252, and 256-59.)

According to Macherey, Spinoza élimine la conception d'un sujet intentionnel (257). But is this "elimination" complete and unqualified? What about Spinoza's references to ordinary human intentions in such passages as *homo ex eo, quod vitae domesticae commoda imaginatus est, **appetitum habuit aedificandi domum*** and *ut ad exemplar humanae naturae, quod **nobis proponimus**, magis magisque accedamus* (IVPref, G II/207, 208; emphasis added). And what about the celebrated *conatus... in suo esse perseverare* (IIIP7), which is said to characterize all finite things? Macherey quotes both IIIP6 and IIIP7 (210), noting that it is eternally of the essence of *les choses singulières* to have a *tendance immanente à persévérer dans leur être* (212). But he appears not to notice the tension between this claim and his denial of purpose or intentionality in Spinoza's philosophy. On this point I would agree with one of Macherey's recent critics, who writes:

> Persévérer, c'est aussi bien augmenter sa puissance d'agir, s'accroître dans son être. Cette opération... semble bien indiquer un minimum de "réflexivité," disons-le brutalement: un agir **de soi, en soi, par soi, pour soi**... Le principe de finalité n'est que la figure imaginative du principe de **raison interne**.[17]

Such a "principle of internal [cause or] reason" (*causa sive ratio*) is what (in the case of Substance) I would call a principle of total self-determination and self-necessitation, and (in the case of the modes) a principle of partial self-determination and partial self-necessitation, hence of partial other-determination and other-necessitation. More simply put, this is a principle of freedom - absolute and relative freedom, respectively.[18] Such a principle seems much closer to Hegel's principle or concept of purpose and purposive activity than Macherey would allow (cf. the discussion of *Zweck, das Zweckmässige, Zweckmässigkeit*, and *Selbstzweck* in WdL II, 391-93, 396-405, 411-412, and 478-83).

VI

I am unable to take seriously Macherey's apparently quite serious claim that, because Spinoza refused, and Hegel accepted, a professorship at Heidelberg (and later, in Hegel's case, at Berlin), the Hegelian system *s'enseigne à des élèves, de haut en bas*, whereas the Spinozistic system *se transmet à des disciples, à égalité* (9). The words *élève* and *disciple* strike me as inappropriate in *both* cases. Why not 'students' or even 'junior colleagues'? I call Macherey's attention to the words with which Hegel closed his series of lectures on the history of philosophy, expressing his appreciation for the intellectual and spiritual support and companionship of his students and his hope that their intellectual and spiritual bond would continue into the future. Here are Hegel's words, the Latin equivalents of which, it seems to me, Spinoza might well have spoken to the small circle of friends and sympathizers who had been working through a draft of the Ethics under his gidance:

> *Für Ihre Aufmerksamkeit, die Sie mir bei diesem Versuch* [viz., the attempt, referred to earlier in this passage, to place before the students' minds the series of intellectual and cultural shapes which philosophy has taken in the course of its development, and the connection of these shapes with one another] *bewiesen haben, habe ich Ihnen meinen Dank abzustatten; er* [viz., this attempt] *ist mir ebenso durch Sie zur höheren Befriedigung geworden. Und vergnüglich ist es mir gewesen, in diesem* **geistigen Zusammenleben mit Ihnen** *gestanden zu haben: und nicht gestanden* **zu haben,** *sondern, wie ich hoffe,* **ein geistiges Band mit einander geknüpft zu haben, das** *zwischen uns* **bleiben möge!** *Ich wünsche Ihnen, recht wohl zu leben.* (*Vorlesungen*, XIX, 691-92; emphasis modified).

On a related point, I take Macherey quite seriously, although I am unclear as to the shape of the alternative he would propose to the Hegelian *conception évolutive* of the history of philosophy (258). Macherey claims that, once the Hegelian conception has been discarded, *le rapport réel des philosophies n'est plus seulement mesurable par leur degré d'intégration hiérarchique; il n'est plus non plus réductible à une lignée chronologique qui les dispose l'une par rapport à l'autre dans un ordre de succession irréversible* (258-59). The proposed non-Hegelian history of philosophy will be marked by a *lutte de tendances qui ne porte pas en elle-même la promesse de sa résolution. Ou encore: unité de contraires, mais sans la négation de la négation* (259). In such a timeless or trans-historical philosophical *agon* it will turn out that Spinoza, whose philosophy constitutes *la véritable alternative à la philosophie hégélienne* (13), and who *avait très bien compris Hegel"* [!] (259), *réfute Hegel, objectivement* (13) - on such points as the role of negativity, the (reconciling) negation of the negation, hierarchy, and teleology.

Taken together with Macherey's rather cryptic comments which appear to favor not only a *dialectique sans téléologie* (13) but also a *dialectique matérialiste* and an *histoire... matérielle* (of philosophic thought) (259), all of this leaves one reader with many more questions than answers. To begin with: 'materialist' or 'material' in just what sense(s) of these notoriously equivocal terms? Elsewhere I have distinguished seven distinct senses of the term *materiell* as used by Marx. Only two of them would appear to be relevant in the present context--what I have called 'material 1a' (= 'technological') and what I have called 'material 4' (= 'economic').[19] But a historical dialectic grounded in, or focussed on, either technological or economic factors would surely be "developmental," cumulative, and - in some sense - irreversible. It would also be *reductionist* in a sense that Hegel's dialectic is not; but that is a story for another occasion.

Macherey appears to want to purge away all three of the essential characteristics of Hegel's dialectical presentation of the history of philosophy:

(diachronic) development, accumulation (of adequacy, of truth), and irreversibility. Just what, if anything, would be left of either the history or the philosophy after such a purging is difficult for me to imagine.

1. Pierre Macherey, *Hegel ou Spinoza*, Paris: François Maspero, 1979, 261 pp.
2. See Errol E. Harris, "The Concept of Substance in Spinoza and Hegel," in Giancotti (1985), 51-70.
3. *Wissenschaft der Logik*, ed. Georg Lasson, Hamburg: Meiner, 1934, 1967, I, 250, 337; *Vorlesungen über die Geschichte der Philosophie* in *Sämtliche Werke*, ed Hermann Glockner, Stuttgart: Frommann, 1928, XIX, 377, 379 (quoted by Macherey at 152 and 154), 382. Cf. also Macherey 99, 113. Hereafter references to the works of Hegel and Spinoza, as well as to Macherey's book, will be inserted in parentheses in the text, the first two with standard sigla, the latter with page number only.
4. The Table of Contents, under the general heading *Neuere Philosophie*, includes a *Zweiter Abschnitt* with the heading *Periode des denkenden Verstandes*, Ch. 1 of which is entitled *Verstandes-Metaphysik*. Curiously, in the text of this volume the title of Ch. 1 appears in the blander form *Periode der Metaphysik*.
5. Cf. my essay, "Absolute and Relative Senses of *liberum* and *libertas* in Spinoza" in Giancotti (1985), esp. Sec. III (266-73).
6. There is a serious slip (either in the French translation which Macherey quotes or in his quoting of that translation) in the rendering of ID6Exp. The expression *in suo genere tantum infinitum* is mistranslated as **indéfinis** *seulement en leur genre* (98, my emphasis) The shift from singular to plural is perhaps justified; the substitution of *indéfini* for *infini* surely is not. Charles Appuhn renders the expression accurately as *infini seulement dans son genre* (Spinoza, *Oeuvres*, Paris: Flammarion, 1965, III, 21).
7. H. H. Joachim was, so far as I know, the first to make this point with full clarity and consistency. "The true infinite," he wrote in 1901, "cannot have its nature expressed in number... at all. - If we will endeavor to enumerate God's Attributes, we shall find that no number can exhaust them: but this indicates no indefiniteness in God, but simply the absurdity of conceiving him under 'modes of imagination'" (Joachim [1901], 41). Cf. my paper, "On the Infinity of Spinoza's Attributes" in Hessing (1977), esp. 345-46.
8. The French translators quoted by Macherey (113) misleadingly render *constantem infinitis attributis* (ID6) as *consistant en une infinité d'attributs*.
9. Interesting variants of these expressions occur in the second edition (1844) of Hegel's *Werke* (which, like the first edition of the early 1830s upon which Glockner's *Jubiläumsausgabe* of 1928 is based, draws primarily from student notes and only in part from Hegel's own lecture notes): *unbestimmten Vielen* rather than *unendlich viele* and *die vollkommene Unendlichkeit* rather than *vollendete gegenwärtige Unendlichkeit* (cf. XV, 343).
10. See "On the Infinity of Spinoza's Attributes," esp. pp. 342-45.
11. Cf. ibid., 344 for an alternative interpretation of *absolutê*. Hegel, despite his tendentious talk about the *unendliche Vielheit* of the attributes, translates ID6 quite untendentiously: *Gott ist das absolut unendliche Wesen oder die Substanz, die aus unendlichen Attributen besteht, deren jedes eine ewige und unendliche Wesenheit... ausdrückt* (*Vorlesungen*, XIX, 383).
12. In Macherey's book both the title page of Pt. IV and the running heads of that entire part (143-259) carry the *omnis* formulation.
13. In the *Vorlesungen* the Latin version is given without any reference to its source, except for Spinoza's name. Hegel introduces it quite matter-of-factly: *In Rücksicht des Bestimmten hat Spinoza so den Satz aufgestellt:* **Omnis determinatio est negatio.** (*Vorlesungen*, XIX,

376) Similarly in the *Logic*: *Die Bestimmtheit ist die Negation als affirmativ gesetzt, ist der Satz des Spinoza: Omnis determinatio est negatio.* (WdL, I, 100)

Engels is even more cavalier than Hegel in attributing the *omnis* formulation to Spinoza and no less cavalier than the Hegel of the *Wissenschaft der Logik*, 2nd ed., in offering no source for his "quotation." He writes: *Schon Spinoza sagt: Omnis determinatio est negatio, jede. . .Bestimmung ist zugleich eine Negation* (Friedrich Engels, *Herrn Eugen Dührings Umwälzung der Wissenschaft* [1878] in *Marx-Engels-Werke*, [East] Berlin: Dietz, 1968, XX, 132).

Marx, in an earlier text, had been more careful, putting simply *determinatio est negatio*, but also failing to give any source (cf. *Grundrisse* [1857-1858], [East] Berlin: Dietz, 1953, 12).

14. See Hans-Christian Lucas, "Hegel et l'édition de Spinoza par Paulus" (tr. by Pierre Garniron), *Cahiers Spinoza* 4 (1983): 127-38. Hegel himself declared: *ich habe auch Anteil an dieser Ausgabe durch Vergleichung von französischen Uebersetzungen* (*Vorlesungen*, XIX, 371).

15. See Pierre Garniron, "Hegel: deux leçons sur Spinoza," *Cahiers Spinoza* 4 (1983): 96.

16. Harris, "The Concept of Substance in Spinoza and Hegel," 64.

17. Stanislas Breton, "Hegel ou Spinoza. Réflexions sur l'enjeu d'une alternative," *Cahiers Spinoza* 4 (1983): 73, emphasis added.

18. Cf. my "Absolute and Relative Senses of *liberum* and *libertas* in Spinoza," esp. 266-75 and 279.

19. See my paper, "The Myth of Marx's Materialism" in *Philosophical Sovietology*, ed. Helmut Dahm, Thomas J. Blakeley, and George L. Kline, Dordrecht and Boston: Reidel, 1988, esp. Sec. II (159-69). What I call 'material 1' (= 'physical', 'spatio-temporal') does not seem relevant here, although, puzzlingly, Macherey refers at one point to a *dialectique de la substance* as a *dialectique matérielle* (209, emphasis added). This suggests that he may have tacitly accepted the highly controversial Plekhanov-Deborin interpretation of Spinoza's metaphysics of substance as a *materialist* ontology.

SPINOZISM AND SPINOZISTIC STUDIES
IN THE NETHERLANDS SINCE WORLD WAR II

H. G. HUBBELING
Groningen University

In this paper I shall try to give a survey of Spinozism and Spinozistic studies in the Netherlands since World War II. I shall also try to give more than only a *bibliographie raisonnée*. This would certainly occur if I tried to give a complete enumeration of all the works published on Spinoza during this period. I do not have to do this, for we have excellent bibliographies that cover the period.[1] Especially I want to mention the bibliography written by Van der Werf, Siebrand and Westerveen.[2] Siebrand had the brilliant idea of giving an alphabetical list of works written on Spinoza and then to give a survey in a systematic order. The study is published in the well-known series of *Mededelingen vanwege het Spinozahuis*. It is unavoidable that a paper like this looks a little bit like a *bibliographie raisonnée*, but I have tried to give more background information, so that the reader will receive an impression of the main trends of Spinozism and of the main topics of Spinozistic studies in the Netherlands.

As one of the few Dutch philosophers who has attracted international attention, Spinoza has always been studied and discussed on a relatively large scale in the Netherlands. Dutch Hegelians have very often incorporated Spinoza in their philosophy. He was also studied extensively in Marxist circles and among freethinkers, etc. There were even two Spinoza societies in the Netherlands before World War II. The oldest one was situated in Rijnsburg, where Spinoza lived for part of his life and where the house where he lived still exists. This house was bought by the society, which was and is open to everyone who is interested in Spinoza. Officially it did not favor any interpretation of Spinoza, but perhaps it must be said that it still had a rationalistic flavor because its dominant members, W. Meyer and W. G. van der Tak, both secretaries, gave a rationalistic interpretation of Spinoza. But it must be explicitly stated that other interpretations of Spinoza were also heard in the papers read at the Society.[3] Further the organization of the society was democratic. The meeting of the members took the final decisions.

The other society owned the house in the Hague, where Spinoza died in 1677. This was not a society in the ordinary sense, but a foundation. It did not have a democratic structure, for a board of directors took the decisions with no responsibility to its members. Nobody could even become a member of this society; one could only support it by a yearly gift. In this society the mystical interpretation of Spinoza was dominant. During the war, however, this society received a dubious reputation, because its chairman, J. H. Carp, became a National Socialist. After the war he was accused by van der Tak, the secretary of the other Spinoza society, of "giving away the house into the hands of the Germans." After the war the foundation was dissolved and its properties were administered by a committee of three men. In the beginning of the 70s the house and other properties were given to the Rijnsburg society that in turn gave it to *Monumentenzorg Den Haag* which in cooperation with the Rijnsburg society restored the building. One room is devoted to Spinoza study. Now the situation is that in the Rijnsburg house Spinoza's original library can be seen and can be consulted, whereas in The Hague house modern literature on Spinoza is collected and a study room for consulting it is available. It goes without saying that the society keeps its neutral and open attitude in that one need not be an adherent of Spinoza's philosophy in order to become a member and that all possible interpretations of Spinoza may be heard in the society.

In 1977, G. van Suchtelen, the present secretary, in cooperation with C. Roelofsz, corrected the accusation against Carp. Although he was a National Socialist and as such is to be blamed for having cooperated with the Germans, he took pains to keep the house out of the hands of the occupier. In the beginning the Germans did not take measures against the two Spinoza societies, although Spinoza was a Jew. He had had a positive influence on German Idealism and this the Germans evaluated positively. But they did forbid freemasonry and in its archives they discovered that freemasonry had given donations to one of the Spinoza societies. So they took over the two houses and sent the two libraries to Germany, where they were rediscovered after the war and sent back to the Netherlands. Carp, however, managed to keep the house in The Hague out of the hands of the Germans. The building was given to a foundation that would educate the higher officials of the Dutch National Socialist movement. But this foundation was only a fake and served as a cover. It did not fulfill its supposed function. In this way the building could be prevented from being ruined by the German army. The house in Rijnsburg remained inhabited by the custodian and his family. Two Jews hid themselves there during the occupation.[4]

Perhaps I may insert a little anecdote with respect to the house in The Hague. In the beginning of the 70's the administrative board of the dissolved foundation decided that they would give away the house and the properties that belonged to it. They thought that the best way to do this was to give it to the Rijnsburg society. The board of this society agreed with one exception, *viz.* its chairman, J. J. von Schmid. He even resigned as a chairman, when the other members of the board tried to force him to the decision to accept the gift which was only to the advantage of the society and the study of Spinoza. And what was the reason for this stubborn refusal? Its recent history and geographic situation! For it had been used as a brothel until the foundation bought it and it still lies in an area where many brothels flourish. As is so often the case, in The Hague the older parts of the city have declined in their social status. In contradiction to Von Schmid, the rest of the board evidently saw the house in a Spinozistic way, i.e. in itself, not in its relations to the other houses, and they saw it in the present not in the past!

The Rijnsburg society has always been, and still is to the present day, a center of Spinoza studies. I hardly know of any other philosophical or intellectual society that covers such a broad spectrum in its membership. You may meet ultra-religious orthodox people, Jews, Christians, Mohammedans, but also vehement atheists. In politics, too, all kinds of trends are represented and

Spinozism itself is present in all shades of interpretation. It has become a club of friends, where people of all kinds of profession meet each other. The philosophers form only a minority among the members, although the papers read are on a high level, as a look in the well-known series mentioned above may reveal, for this series consists mainly of papers read during the meetings of the society. The advantage of the study of Spinoza is that not only professional philosophers can find something to their liking. Also historians, jurists and medical doctors can study Spinoza fruitfully. Even non-intellectual people are represented and some of them did contribute considerably to the study of Spinoza. So some of our members played a role in discovering that a certain house in Voorburg was a house where Spinoza may have lived; others collected material for Spinoza's biography, again others for the history of Spinoza's tomb, etc. You do not have to be a professional philosopher in order to do this. Now the society is flourishing after the meagre years shortly after the war.[5]

We also changed the style of our meetings. Formerly there was a fashionable dinner at the end of the meeting. The participants bought a stately new suit for it, etc. It was always very impressive, but the number of participants was only small, of course. Now we have an informal lunch between the two papers and the number of participants has increased four times! And, of course, such an informal lunch is good for promoting lively personal and intellectual contacts.

Besides the society there are two centers for the study of Spinoza, *viz.* at the universities of Groningen and Rotterdam. In the study of Spinoza after the war we can distinguish three periods. Shortly after the war there was not much interest in Spinoza in the world. The dominant philosophies were existentialism and phenomenology on the continent, and analytical philosophy in England and the USA. The dominant philosophy in the Netherlands during that time was certainly existentialism, although there was more interest in logical empiricism and similar movements in the Netherlands than, e.g., in France and Germany. This is typical for the history of Dutch philosophy. Dutch philosophers have very often mediated between the various cultures. There was also a relatively great interest in Spinoza, but Spinozism was by no means dominant. This is also the case for the later periods, when there has been more interest in Spinoza. Still Spinozism has never been the dominant philosophy in the Netherlands. As was also the case elsewhere in the world, there was a revival of interest in the 60's and this revival still continues. But perhaps we may say that there is a shift of interest. In the 60s and early 70s the interest in Spinoza was predominantly systematic, in contradistinction to the great German works before 1933, which were more historical. But perhaps we might say that by the end of the 70s, a great wave of new, purely historical works appeared, and at least it is the policy of our society to promote the study of Spinoza's philosophy in relation to its Dutch and Jewish background. Another characteristic of our policy is to give younger scholars a chance! I think that it is necessary for understanding an author that one studies his direct environment. He always discusses something with people around him, so it is necessary to study this environment. Ironically, I myself started with a dissertation on Spinoza[6] that was predominantly systematic, because I thought that it could be fruitful to study Spinoza's argumentation, the role some key concepts played in his system, the tension between Spinoza's deductive method and his nominalism, etc. But even then I could not avoid making at least some historical remarks! Another facet characteristic of the Spinoza revival after the war is an interest in Spinoza's ideas on law, the state, tolerance, etc. In the following I mention some of the main topics that have been studied in the last forty years without explicitly stating in what period a certain work was written. That can, of course, easily be inferred by looking at the year of publication.

In the first place, I think, *the preparing of a new Dutch translation* of the complete works of Spinoza is important. The society took the initiative for this translation and supports it. Three volumes have appeared and another three will follow. We even intend to give a translation of the *Hebrew Grammar*, a work that has not yet been translated into Dutch. Also an illuminating commentary is added to the translations. The following works have appeared: the *Correspondence*, the *Ethics*, the work on Descartes together with the *Metaphysical Thoughts*, the *Short Treatise*, the works *On the Rainbow* and *The Calculus of Chances*, and the *Treatise on the Improvement of the Understanding*.[7] The work is not only a translation. By its commentary it is also a contribution to Spinoza scholarship. Besides, the works that have been written in Dutch (some letters, the *Short Treatise* and the works on the rainbow and the calculus of chances) are a new edition. Akkerman has shown that the Gebhardt edition, despite all its merits, is insufficient and unreliable from a modern philologist's point of view.[8] Therefore the Dutch parts in the new translation are a step forward. But also in the Latin part some improvements of the text are given.

Of course, there has always been much *criticism* of Spinoza. The main objection was put forward by Bierens de Haan, who belonged to a former generation, but was schooled in Dutch philosophy. He saw himself as a man who synthesized Spinoza and Hegel, but he considered himself more a Spinozist than a Hegelian. But Spinoza's philosophy was too static in his eyes. History did not play a decisive role in it. Spinoza thinks too much in fixed patterns. J. van der Bend showed in some studies that Bierens de Haan came to his Spinozistic viewpoint only gradually. Originally he belonged more to the school of the English empiricists, *viz.* Shaftesbury. He also introduced esthetical elements into Spinoza's philosophy.[9]

Van Os had the same criticism; he added the concept of life as a dominant concept into Spinoza's philosophy. He has the great merit of introducing Whitehead into the Netherlands at a relatively early stage and he combined elements of process philosophy with Spinoza.[10] This is, in my view, a promising enterprise in view of the fact that Whitehead had a great admiration for Spinoza. There is a great structural similarity between Whitehead's and Spinoza's doctrines of God, immortality, etc. The differences lie in the organic character of Whitehead's philosophy (which is also stressed by Van Os) and the esthetical elements in Whitehead's philosophy, which are apparently lacking in Spinoza. Still some esthetical principles that play a great role in Whitehead (e.g. unity in variety) can also be found in Spinoza, without his having indicated these principles as esthetical.[11]

Brunt showed that Spinoza's *theory of physics* is completely dated. He was too little of an empiricist to be able to be fruitful in the progress of science.[12] By the way, there is, as is well-known, a defence and reevaluation of Spinoza from the side of systems theory. Van der Hoeven has shown that Spinoza was heavily dependent on Descartes in his theories of physics. He was even less empirical than Descartes, but he improved on him in some of the demonstrations.[13]

There was also criticism of the way Spinoza presented *his ideas in the TTP*. Here Den Tex followed Strauss' theories of the double meaning in the *TTP*.[14] This was vehemently contradicted by Harris and others.[15] Spinoza received a critical defence from an unexpected side. Mönnich came from another direction, because he is more interested in claiming the independence of theology and in his view the relevance of philosophy for spiritual matters is only marginal.[16] But it remains remarkable that Spinoza's philosophy is able to arouse so much interest even among orthodox Christians in the Netherlands, despite the vehement criticism he meets there. We will come back to this point later on.

In the *doctrine of the state and in political philosophy* the relation with Hobbes and Machiavelli has been much discussed. On the whole the Dutch scholars tend to emphasize the differences between Spinoza on the one hand and Hobbes and Machiavelli on the other. They emphasize that Spinoza has a Hobbesian and Machiavellian starting point, but that despite this framework Spinoza tries to defend a democratic and liberal state wtith all the liberties granted to the subjects. This we do not find in the two other authors.[17] A different position has been taken by Klever. He introduced the new thoughts of Antonio Negri into the Netherlands and roused thus a vehement discussion.[18]

On the whole there were only a few studies of Spinoza's *anthropology*, fewer than could be expected in a time in which anthropology took so central a place. Van Peursen, a man internationally well-known for his anthropological studies and who, by the way, had personal contacts with Sartre and Wittgenstein(!), gave a study on the place of finitude in Spinoza. He discusses the problem of the possible and the real. Is everything that is possible to be realized one day? Or is a kind of selection to be made? According to Van Peursen we get into troubles here, because we introduce the Leibnizian idea of possible worlds into Spinoza's philosophy and the latter is incompatible with that idea.[19]

J. J. Groen is of the opinion that Spinoza was a great forerunner of the new psycho-physical approaches in medicine. The exact parallelism between the world of thinking and the world of matter (extension) leads to many conclusions that anticipate modern discoverings, *viz.* that physical troubles immediately have their phychical counterparts and *vice versa*. There are, of course, differences. Modern medicine has not yet fully discovered what kind of link there is between the two worlds (that of thinking and that of the body), whereas Spinoza 'solves' this problem with his doctrine of parallelism and denying any direct influence of one world on the other. The contact is established by the substance! Groen also points out that Spinoza is a forerunner of Freud. Of course, we do not find Freud's theory of the unconscious fully developed by Spinoza. But he also points out that once we are better conscious of our passions and know what really troubles us, we are no longer driven by our passions.[20]

Spinoza as a *mystical thinker* was also a theme in Dutch studies after the war, but less than before the war when we had the flourishing 'mystical' society in The Hague. Boasson was the scholar who defended this approach,[21] but there were others who stood close to this view point, as e.g., Frenkel.[22] The latter was a clear representative of rationalistic mysticism with a strong emphasis on the concept of Necessity. He emphasizes that there is a double kind of necessity in Spinoza, a necessity in the series of events in time and a necessity of the eternal world of God. Despite the fact that the third way of knowledge plays its role in Frenkel's interpretation, he is much more rationalistic than Boasson. By the way, Frenkel was also a philosopher of The Hague society. I myself defended the thesis that Spinoza's philosophy had definitely a mystical structure, but on his whole system based on the theory of parallelism of thinking and matter and on his whole axiomatic method. This thesis aroused some discussion.[23]

There has been much discussion on Spinoza's *method*. De Dijn introduced the theories of Gueroult into the Netherlands. According to him, Spinoza was strongly influenced by Hobbes and through him by Euclid. Spinoza's theory of definitions and axioms is constructivistic and genetic, i.e., if we want to know what a thing is we must study the way it emerges in the world or, if we have to do with mathematical objects, the way it is to be constructed. If we study an eternal object, e.g., God, then it is necessary to find the most fundamental elements and with the help of these one can construct the concept of God. As a consequence of this approach, Spinoza's axiomatic method is more than only an instrument. It is the way in which Spinoza's system has been necessarily built up. It could not be done otherwise.[24] Against De Dijn I defended the thesis that Spinoza uses the axiomatic method in a relatively modern way and at least he is modern in this point, that we can build up our system as we like it. Spinoza himself built up his system in various ways! What is a proposition in one system can become an axiom in another system and *vice versa*.

This discussion is revealing also in another point. De Dijn is strongly influenced by French structuralism and I myself by logical empiricism and modern logic. Now we see Spinoza with different eyes and a different Spinoza emerges in our interpretations! De Dijn's Spinoza looks more like a structuralist and mine more like a modern logical empiricist, of course, a logical empiricist that permits metaphysics![25] Also, Klever is preparing a more extended paper on Spinoza's logical approach in which it will be shown that Spinoza is very modern in the handling of the axioms.[26] By the way, in the Netherlands there has always been a strong division between the southern part and the Dutch speaking part of Belgium on the one hand and the northern part of the Netherlands on the other hand. The first is always strongly influenced by France, the latter by Germany and England. De Dijn and I also discussed the question as to whether we may ascribe consciousness and self consciousness to God (the substance).[27]

De Deugd emphasizes the value of the first way of knowledge in Spinoza.[28] Of course, he does not claim that Spinoza is an empiricist. But the system that arises from the second way of knowledge is a general system that is valid for everything whatsoever. It needs a concrete filling in. And for this filling in the first way of knowledge is much more important than the third way. Zweerman emphasizes the rhetorical elements in Spinoza's approach. Also Akkerman had already called attention to this fact.[29] Zweerman analysed Spinoza's introduction to the *Treatise on the Improvement of the Human Understanding*. In this he made also use of the methods of modern reception theory. Siebrand did this already before him.[30] Until now reception theory has been used much more in literary criticism and literary theories than in the study of the history of philosophy. Now Zweerman shows that the introduction to the *Treatise* has an inclusion structure in that the first part corresponds to the sixth, the second to the fifth and the third to the fourth. He also indicates the importance of the so called focalisators (i.e., here the narrating persons, who introduce themselves with 'I') and of the famous open gaps of the reception theory. Between the third and the fourth part there is a breach in Spinoza's tone. First he speaks rather autobiographically, but then he speaks in a more sophisticated tone, in which the final goal of the philosophical way of living is shown. But now, certain stages are left out in this philosophical way and they must be filled in by the reader.[31] Meerloo introduced certain aspects of the theory of rhetoric already in the earlier stage. His view is that Spinoza wrote in order to communicate with people and that therefore his ways of reasoning differ from book to book and even from passage to passage. The presuppositions that were taken for granted by the people with whom Spinoza wanted to communicate were always taken into account by him.[32] Further, Spinoza can certainly be considered a forerunner of modern methods of interpretation. Spinoza showed something of this in his book on Descartes, where he tries to give a genuine interpretation of Cartesian philosophy but at the same time improves the proofs and the way of reasoning of Descartes himself.[33]

Several studies appeared on Spinoza's contemporaries in their relation to our philosopher. L. Thijssen-Schoute discussed several details of Lodewyk Meyer's life and his important work in the field of theater and language. As a philosopher he is disappointing, according to Thijssen-Schoute. He remains a Cartesian and his influence on Spinoza can be neglected. On the other hand we do not discover much influence of Spinoza on him. But they were good friends.[34] Jarig Jelles, the author of the introduction to Spinoza's *Opera Posthuma*, an introduction which was translated into Latin by Meyer, gave a synthesis of Meyer and Spinoza. He gave a Christian interpretation of Spinoza, but Jelles' Christian belief had stong moralistic overtones. His Christology resembles that of Spinoza, but there are reasons to believe that Spinoza took this over from Jelles rather than the other way round, for in Jelles' system they form much more a genuine part than in that of Spinoza.[35]

The first man to publish in a more or less Spinozistic way was Spinoza's friend Koerbagh, but there were also some differences between the two. Koerbagh is less of a scholar. His main purpose was to enlighten the ordinary

people so that they no longer are the slaves of the Calvinistic ministry.[36]
Another disciple of Spinoza was Pieter Balling. He was less a theologian than
Jarig Jelles. According to Balling all knowledge of God rests on a direct
intuitive knowledge, whereas Jelles developed a cosmological argument for God's
existence. Balling was a man of the 'inner light,' a doctrine of the Collegiants.[37]
Another book that has appeared in Spinozistic circles was *The Life of Philopater*.
It consisted of two volumes. In this book different materialistic interpretations
of Spinoza are given.[38]

A very interesting discussion has been held between the Spinozist Van
Leenhof and the Cartesian Wittich. They both indicated correctly where the
differences in the starting point are. Descartes uses the *via eminentiae* in the
developing of God's properties. Therefore we need not ascribe extension to
God. We may say that God possesses the properties of extension *in an eminent
way*. According to Van Leenhof, who follows Spinoza, God cannot produce
something outside himself, for God rejoices in his own perfection. As nothing
can be produced from nothing (*nihil ex nihilo*), there is no creation in the
ordinary Christian sense. Because God is perfect, everything occurs necessarily and it is impossible that there would be no world. Contradicting Van
Leenhof, Wittich defends the possibility of a creation from nothing. This is
unintelligible, but not everything that is unintelligible is false. Finite beings
cannot create from nothing but God can. This discussion is interesting and has
been overlooked by the schoolarly world until now.[39]

There is also interest in Bredenburg, a man who opposed Spinoza, but
challenged him with his own weapons. At last he constructed an ontological
argument by himself which gave his thinking a strong Spinozistic flavour. As
he was also a biblical believer, he tried to defend the possibility of a double
truth: for theology and not for philosophy something can be true and *vice
versa*.[40] Of course, Bredenburg was accused of hypocrisy during his lifetime,
but he was defended by Bayle. The latter was also studied in this period. He
was certainly a faithful Christian. His scepticism referred only to his philsophy
and not to his belief. His interpretation of Spinoza, however, was very bad and
was not congenial to the spirit of the great philosopher.[41]

New studies on the great Dutch physico-theologian Nieuwentijt show that
it was through the empirical method that he showed the weak points in Spinoza's
philosophy. He already had a very modern concept of mathematics, carefully
distinguishing between pure and applied mathematics. Spinoza's geometrical
method is only valid within pure mathematics, but thus it says nothing about
the real world. Here we need empirical knowledge besides mathematics. New
studies showed that there was much interest in Spinoza's philosophy in the
Netherlands up to the time of Nieuwentijt. It was not the Calvinist ministers
who drove Spinoza's philosophy from the Dutch scene, but Nieuwentijt.[42]

There are also new studies on Van den Enden, Spinoza's teacher in Latin.
It has been shown that he remained a faithful Catholic despite his modernistic
tendencies, that he was a great inventor in technical matters and that probably
Spinoza played the role of a slave in one of his performances of Terentius![43]
New studies in archives demonstrate that Spinoza was a less obscure figure than

was thought before. His name appeared as a witness in many legal acts and these witnesses were always well-known, reliable persons. There are also studies on Coornhert, a great defender of religious tolerance,[44] on Christian sects that are influenced by Spinoza,[45] on Colerus,[46] Spinoza's biographer, on the relation of Spinoza and Leibniz,[47] on the relation of Spinoza and De la Court,[48] the discovery of Spinoza by Nieuhoff,[49] on Spinoza's doctrine of immortality.[50] But we cannot go into all the details here.

Spinoza's relevance for literature has also been discussed. There appeared works on Spinoza and the movement of the 1880s,[51] on Spinoza's influence on Goethe,[52] on Wordsworth,[53] and others. Also the traditional studies on Spinoza and Hegel appeared.[54] It is interesting that Klever, who started as a Hegelian and defended the superiority of Hegel's dialectics over Spinoza's axiomatic method, became more and more impressed not only by Spinoza's axiomatic method but also by the content of Spinoza's philosophy, especially his political philosophy. He was not the only one who was 'converted' in the direction of Spinoza's thinking without becoming, however, an 'orthodox' Spinozist.

In the movement of *freethinking* and *atheism* Spinoza was seen as an important forerunner who has contributed to the development of a modern atheistic world view. Also in the circles of the *labor movement* and *Marxism* Spinoza was widely read.[55] T. de Vries wrote an important work on Spinoza based on historical materialism. He placed Spinoza as a man between the classes. Spinoza's sympathy was with the working class, but in his day the laborers were still under the influence of the orthodox Calvinistic ministry. So his ideas were more to the taste of the progressive, liberal bourgeoisie.[56] Steenbakkers got his interest in Spinoza from the study of Althusser. Later he became strongly critical of Althusser, but his sympathy for Spinoza remained. Being a good philologist, he is now preparing, together with Akkerman, a new critical edition of Spinoza's *Ethica*.[57] There were also Marxists who were of the opinion that a kind of Spinozistic belief should be added to the doctrines of historical and dialectical materialism.

There were also *liberal protestants* who were strongly influenced by Spinoza. As a matter of fact the revival of Spinozistic studies in the Netherlands in the 19th century came from a Calvinistic Spinozist, J. H. Scholten.[58] He had a great influence on Van Vloten[59] and Meyer,[60] who were both originally students in theology with Scholten. They continued their scholarship, however, by leaving theology completely and by defending a naturalistic kind of Spinozism. Scholten himself thought that the main concepts of Spinozism were compatible with the Calvinistic variant of Christianity. At least they both teach a strong determinism. Scholten did not teach an orthodox form of Christianity, but he managed to keep as close to the biblical doctrines as they are compatible with modern science and critical exegesis.[61]

As we said before, Orthodox Christianity always had an interest in Spinoza too. New studies appeared on Gunning, a great admirer of Spinoza, although he was an orthodox Christian. He especially admired Spinoza's attitude in life, his unity of thinking and moral behaviour. He criticized Spinoza because the concept of a person was lacking in Spinoza. Spinoza's thinking is only rationalistic. But besides rational thinking a man needs direct intuition. One sees that Gunning challenges Spinoza using Spinoza's methods! By intuition we see the relevance of being a person. In other Christians the dominant place of God is positively evaluated.[62]

Akkerman stimulated the study of the *Latin* of Spinoza. He also showed that Gebhardt did not follow the right editorial principles. He showed that the *Opera Posthuma* and the Dutch translation were independent sources, a fact that was recognized by Gebhardt too. Contrary to Gebhardt, however, Akkerman showed that the Dutch translation did not go back to an earlier stage. Gebhardt also did not evaluate the Dutch translation correctly. Further Akkerman made it plausible that Balling was the first translator of the first two parts of Spinoza's *Ethics*.[63]

There was also a study on Spinoza's *Hebrew Grammar* in which the Jewish sources for this grammar were indicated. Spinoza is less original than it was believed before, but therefore also less extravagant.[64]

Our society has further good connections with the *International Constantin Brunner Society* (die Internationale Constantin Brunner Gesellschaft), which is devoted to the study and promotion of the thoughts of Constantin Brunner, a Neo-Spinozist, who died in The Hague, having left Germany because of the Nazis.

This paper tries to give a survey of Spinoza study in the Netherlands. For many scholars Spinoza is only an interesting object of study. For many others Spinoza means more, however. I do not believe that anyone of us is an 'orthodox' Spinozist, but his person and philosophy give more than purely intellectual enjoyment. He also gives us something for our view of life. Above we have seen already the 'conversion' of Klever. But he was not the only one. I myself have developed in a Spinozistic direction too. A few years ago I studied the relation of God to the eternal logical laws. Are they created by God as Descartes thought? Or are they true independently of God and is God thus submitted to them, as Leibniz thought? Both solutions are unsatisfactory. I thought the best solution is that they are in some way an emanation from God and after some reflection I discovered that this is Spinoza's solution.[65] Also my logical reconstructivism is Spinozistic as this is the way Spinoza writes about Descartes: giving his viewpoint, but improving the argumentation.

But there are more: Mrs. Gokkel, a dentist, has found much support in Spinoza's philosophy for her personal life, but she also designed some lines for the relation of body and thinking which are strongly inspired by Spinoza.[66] Also Groen is of the opinion that Spinoza's philosophy is relevant to modern life.[67] Modern man cannot live without some spiritual background and as the importance of the churches is waning - Groen and I say this with deep regret - Spinoza's philosophy can often fill the gap.

Of course, nobody can follow Spinoza blindly. His philosophy has its merits and insufficiencies. But he is a philosopher worth studying. In the Netherlands this is done with a feeling of some congeniality.

1. J. Préposiet, *Bibliographie spinoziste. Répertoire alphabétique- Registre systématique- Textes et documents: Biographies de Lucas et de Colerus, article 'Spinoza' du Dictionnaire de Bayle, inventaire de la bibliothèque de Spinoza, etc.*, Paris, 1973; J. Wetlesen, *A Spinoza Bibliography. Particularly on the Period 1940-1967*, Oslo, 1968 (Reprint: Oslo, 1971).

2. Th. van der Werf, H. Siebrand and C. Westerveen, *A Spinoza Bibliography 1971-1983* (Mededelingen vanwege het Spinozahuis XLVI), Leiden, 1984. In the following the series will be abbreviated by M followed by the number of the series. The credit for continuing the work and looking after the final draft goes of Van der Werf.

3. G. van Suchtelen, "Waarheid en verdichtsels omtrent het Spinozahuis. Een causerie," *Bzzlletin* 13 (1984), 36-42.

4. G. van Suchtelen (ed.), *Spinoza's sterfhuis aan de Paviljoensgracht. Levensbericht van een Haags monument 1646-1977*, Den Haag, 1977; idem, "The Spinoza houses at Rijnsburg and The Hague," in Hessing (1978), 475-478; C. Roelofsz, "Het Spinnnozahuis te 's-Gravenhage 1646-1977," *Algemeen Nederlands Tijdschrift voor Wijsbegeerte* 69 (1977), 26-32.

5. G. van Suchtelen, "Découverte d'une maison Spinoza à Voorburg?" *Bulletin d'Association des Amis de Spinoza* 13 (1984), 1-2.

6. H. G. Hubbeling, *Spinoza's Methodology*, Assen, 1964, 2nd ed. 1967.

7. *Werken van B. de Spinoza*. Uitgave onder auspiciën van de Vereniging Het Spinozahuis. Amsterdam:

Vol 1: Briefwisseling. Vertaald uit het Latijn en uitgegeven naar de bronnen alsmede van een inleiding en van verklarende en tekstkritische aantekeningen voorzien door F. Akkerman, H. G. Hubbeling en A. G. Westerbrink, 1977;

Vol 2: Ethica. Uit het Latijn vertaald en van verklarende aantekeningen voorzien door Nico van Suchtelen. Nieuwe uitgave, herzien en ingeleid door G. van Suchtelen, 1979;

Vol 3: Korte Geschriften. Bezorgd door F. Akkerman, H. G. Hubbeling, F. Mignini, M. J. Petry, en N. en G. van Suchtelen, 1982.

8. F. Akkerman, "L'édition de Gebhardt de l'Ethique de Spinoza et ses sources" (*Raison présente*, 43 (1977): 37-51; idem, "Vers une meilleure édition de la correspondance de Spinoza?" *Revue internationale de philosophie* 31 (1977), 4-26; idem, *Studies in the Posthumous Works of Spinoza. On Style, Earliest Translation and Reception, Earliest and Modern Editions of Some Texts*, Diss. Groningen, 1980.

9. J. G. van der Bend, *Dr. J. D. Bierens de Haan en Spinoza* (M 24), Leiden, 1968; idem, *Het spinozisme van dr. J. D. Bierens de Haan*, Diss. Groningen, 1970; idem, "Dr. J. D. Bierens de Haan," *Amersfoortse Stemmen* 57 (1976), 83-88.

10. C. H. van Os, *Tijd, maat en getal naar aanleiding van Spinoza's brief over het oneindige* (M 7), Leiden 1946; idem, "Over de philosophie van A. N. Whitehead" (*Synthèse*, 1939).

11. H. G. Hubbeling, "Whitehead and Spinoza," in H. Holz and E. Wolf-Gazo, ed., *Whitehead und der Prozessbegriff/Whitehead and The Idea of Process*, Proceedings of the First International Whitehead-Symposium 1981, Freiburg, 1984, 375-385.

12. N. A. Brunt, *De wiskundige denkwijze in Spinoza's philosophie en de moderne natuurkunde* (M 12), Leiden, 1955.

13. P. van der Hoeven, *De cartesiaanse fysica in het denken van Spinoza* (M 30), Leiden, 1973; idem, "Over Spinoza's interpretatie van de cartesiaanse fysica, en de betekenis daarvan voor het systeem der Ethica," *Tijdschrift voor Filosofie* 35 (1973), 27-86; idem, "The Significance of Cartesian Physics for Spinoza's Theory of Knowledge," in J. G. van der Bend, ed., *Spinoza on Knowing, Being and Freedom*, Proceedings of the Spinoza symposium at the International School of Philosophy in the Netherlands, Leusden, September 1973, Assen, 1974, 114-125. Cf. H. G. Hubbeling, "Van der Hoeven als interpreet van Descartes en Spinoza," *L'esprit de géometrie, l'esprit de finesse*, Groningen, 1977, 20-27.

14. J. den Tex, *Spinoza over de tolerantie* (M 23), Leiden, 1967.

15. E. E. Harris, *Is there an esoteric doctrine in the T.T.P.?* (M 38), Leiden 1978. Cf. also the discussion at the end of Den Tex' work (see note 14).

16. C. W. Mönnich, *De verhouding van theologie en wijsbegeerte in het Tractatus Theologico-Politicus* (M 15), Leiden, 1958.

17. J. J. Boasson, *De rechtsidee en de vrijheidsidee bij Spinoza* (M 8), Leiden, 1949; B. H. Kazemier, *De staat bij Spinoza en Hobbes* (M 10), Leiden, 1951; Th. de Vries, *Spinoza als staatkundig denker* (M 20), Leiden, 1963; G. A. van der Wal, *Politieke vrijheid en demokratie bij Spinoza* (M 41),Leiden, 1980.

18. Benedictus de Spinoza, *Hoofdstukken uit De politieke verhandeling*, ingeleid, vertaald en van commentaar voorzien door W. N. A. Klever, Meppel, 1985; W. N. A. Klever, "Spinoza's filosofie als radicale inspiratiebron voor Italiaans kamerlid en terrorist Negri" (*NRC Handelsblad* 24 -12 -1983).

19. C. A. van Peursen, *Eindigheid bij Spinoza* (M 37), Leiden, 1977. Van Peursen wrote also on the problem of truth in Spinoza: "Spinoza: veritas norma sui et falsi," *Wijsgerig Perspectief op Maatschappij en Wetenschap*, 18 (1977/78), 69-72; idem, "La critère de la vérité chez Spinoza,"*Revue de métaphysique et de morale* 83 (1978), 518-525.

20. J. J. Groen, *Ethica en ethologie. Spinoza's leer der affecten en de moderne psychobiologie* (M 29), Leiden, 1972; idem, "Spinoza: Philosopher and Prophet" (J. G. van der Bend, ed., *Spinoza on Knowing, Being & Freedom* 69-81); idem, Spinoza als voorloper der moderne psychobiologie en psychosomatische geneeskunde" (*Wijsgerig perspectief op Maatschappij en Wetenschap* 18 (1977-78), 114-132); idem, "Spinoza's theory of affects and modern psychobiology" (J. Wetlesen, ed., *Spinoza's Philosophy of Man*. Proceedings of the Scandinavian Spinoza Symposium 1977, Oslo, 1978, 97-118).

21. J. J. Boasson, *Ratio en Beatitudo in Spinoza's wijsbegeerte* (M 19), Leiden, 1963.

22. H. S. Frenkel, *De noodwendigheid van het Spinozisme* (M 22), Leiden, 1965.

23. H. G. Hubbeling, *Logica en ervaring in Spinoza's en Ruusbroecs mystiek* (M 31), Leiden, 1973; idem, "Logic and experience in Spinoza's mysticism," in J. G. van den Bend, *Spinoza on Knowing, Being and Freedom* 126-143); idem, "The logical and experiential roots of Spinoza's mysticism - an answer to Jon Wetlesen," in Hessing (1978), 323-329; J. Wetlesen, "Body awareness as a gateway to eternity: a note on the mysticism of Spinoza and its affinity to Buddhist meditation," in Hessing (1978), 479-494.

24. H. de Dijn, *De epistemologie van Spinoza*, Diss., Leuven, 1971; idem, "Spinoza's geometrische methode van denken," *Tijdschrift voor Filosofie* 35 (1973), 707-765; idem, "Historical Remarks on Spinoza's Theory of Definition," *Spinoza on Knowing, Being and Freedom*, 41-50; *Methode en waarheid bij Spinoza* (M 35), Leiden, 1975; idem, "Opnieuw over de geometrische methode bij Spinoza," *Algemeen Nederlands Tijdschrift voor Wijsbegeerte* 70 (1978), 18-28.

25. H. G. Hubbeling, "La méthode axiomatique de Spinoza et la définition du concept de Dieu," *Raison présente* 43 (1977), 25-36; idem, "The development of Spinoza's axiomatic (geometric) method. The reconstructed geometric proof of the second letter of Spinoza's correspondence and its relation to earlier and later versions," *Revue internationale de philosophie* 31 (1977), 53-68; idem, "Spinoza's axiomatische methode en zijn definitie van God," *Algemeen Nederlands Tijdschrift voor Wijsbegeerte* 70 (1978), 18-28.

26. "Axioms in Spinoza's Science and Philosophy of Science," *Studia Spinozana* 2 (1986), 171-195. Cf. further: W. N. A. Klever, "Spinoza's methodebegrip" *Algemeen Nederlands Tijdschrift voor Wijsbegeerte* 74 (1982), 28-49); idem, *De methodologische functie van de Godsidee* (M 48), Leiden, 1985.

27. H. de Dijn, "De God van Spinoza is geen persoonlijke God," *Algemeen Nederlands Tijdschrist voor Wijsbegeerte*. 70 (1978), 47-51; H. G. Hubbeling, "Heeft de God van Spinoza (zelf) bewustzijn?" *ibid.*, 70 (1978), 38-46.

28. C. de Deugd, *The Significance of Spinoza's First Kind of Knowledge*, Diss., Assen, 1966.

29. F. Akkerman, *Spinoza's tekort aan woorden. Humanistische aspecten van zijn schrijverschap* (M 36), Leiden, 1977; idem, "Le caractère rhétorique du *Traité théologico politique*," in *Spinoza entre Lumière et Romantisme, Les Cahiers de Fontenay*, 36-38, (1985), 381-190.

30. H. J. Siebrand, *Logica, rationaliteit en intuïtie. Methodologische perspektieven op de Ethica Spinozae*, M. A. Thesis, Groningen, 1980; idem, "On the early Reception of Spinoza's *Tractatus theologico-politicus* in the Context of Cartesianism," in C. de Deugd, ed., *Spinoza's Political and Theological Thought*. International Symposium under the Auspices of the Royal Netherlands Academy of Arts and Sciences Commemorating the 350th Anniversary of the Birth of Spinoza, Amsterdam 24-27 November 1982, Amsterdam, 1984, 214-225. Siebrand is writing a dissertation on the early reception of Spinoza's philosophy in the Netherlands.

31. T. F. Zweerman, *Spinoza's inleiding tot de filosofie. Een vertaling en structuuranalyse van de inleiding der Tractatus de intellectus emendatione; benevens een commentaar bij deze tekst*, Diss. Leuven, 1983; idem, "Op de drempel. Aantekeningen bij de aanhef van Spinoza's Vertoog over de zuivering van het verstand," *Wijsgerig Perspectief op Maatschappij en Wetenschap* 17 (1976/778), 133-150). Zweerman also discussed French structuralism in its relation to Spinoza: *Spinoza en de hedendaagse kritiek op het humanisme als ideologie*, (M 34), Leiden, 1975.

32. J. A. M. Meerloo, *spinoza en het probleem der communicatie* (M 28), Leiden 1972.

33. H. G. Hubbeling, "Spinoza comme précurseur du reconstructivisme logique dans son livre sur Descartes," *Studia Leibnitiana* 12(1980), 88-95. See also the works mentioned in note 13.

34. C. L. Thijssen-Schoute, *Lodewijk Meyer en diens verhouding tot Descartes en Spinoza* (M 11), Leiden, 1954; idem, *Nederlands cartesianisme*, Amsterdam 1954, 380-398, 419-426.

35. F. Akkerman and H. G. Hubbeling, "The Preface to Spinoza's Posthumous Works, 1677, and its author Jarig Jelles. (c. 1619/20-1683);" *Lias* 6 (1979), 103-173. H. G. Hubbeling, "Zur frühen Spinozarezeption in den Niederlanden," in K. Gründer and W. Schmidt-Biggemann, *Spinoza in der Frühzeit seiner religiösen Wirkung*. Wolfenbütteler Studien zur Aufklärung, XII, 149-180 (on Jelles:158-162).

36. H. G. Hubbeling, *o.c.*, 152-155; H. Vandenbossche, *Spinozisme en kritiek bij Koerbagh*, Brussels, 1974; idem, *Adriaan Koerbagh en Spinoza* (M 39), Leiden 1978; idem, "Le spinozisme d'Adriaan Koerbagh:une première analyse" *Bulletin de l'Association des Amis de Spinoza* 1 (1979), 15-36.

37. H. G. Hubbeling, *o.c.*, 155-158.

38. H. G. Hubbeling, *o.c.*, 162-165; idem, "Philopater. A Dutch Materialistic Interpretation of Spinoza in the Seventeenth Century," in Giancotti (1985), 489-514.

39. H. G. Hubbeling, *o.c.*, 167-168; cf. also H. Vandenbossche, *Frederik van Leenhof*, Brussels, 1974.

40. H. G. Hubbeling, *o.c.*, 169-171.

41. H. G. Hubbeling, *o.c.*, 171-173. J. Goossens, *Bayle en Spinoza* (M 17), Leiden, 1960.

42. H. G. Hubbeling, *o.c.*, 173-175. M. J. Petry, *Nieuwentijt's criticism of Spinoza* (M 40), Leiden, 1979.

43. J. V. Meininger and G. van Suchtelen, *Liever met wercken, als met woorden. De levensreis van doctor Franciscus Van den Enden. Leermeester van Spinoza, complotteur tegen Lodewijk de Veertiende*, Weesp, 1980; F. Akkerman, *Spinoza's tekort aan woorden. Humanistische apecten van zijn schrijverschap* (M 36), Leiden, 1977, 9.

44. J. J. von Schmid, *Coornhert en Spinoza* (M 14), Leiden, 1956.

45. G. C. van Niftrik, *Spinoza en de sectariers van zijn tijd (M 18), Leiden, 1962.*

46.　　H. G. Hubbeling, "Johannes Colerus, Verteidiger der christlichen Wahrheit und ehrlicher Bekämpfer Spinozas," G. Kurtz, ed., *Düsseldorf in der deutschen Geistesgeschichte (1750-1850)*, Dusseldorf, 1984, 67-78.

47.　　H. G. Hubbeling, "The Understanding of Nature in Renaissance Philosophy, Leibniz and Spinoza," in A. Heinekamp, ed., *Leibniz et la Renaissance*. Colloque à Domaine de Seillac (France), 17-21 juin 1981, Wiesbaden, 1983, 210-220.

48.　　H. W. Blom, *Spinoza en De la Court* (M42), Leiden, 1981.

49.　　H. J. Siebrand, "Nieuhoff et la réforme romantique du spinozisme, in *Spinoza entre Lumière et Romantisme*, 327-338; idem, "Tussen stelkunst en levenskunst. Bernard Nieuhoff over het Spinozisme," *Bulletin* 13 (1984), 11-15.

50.　　K. Hammacher, *Spinoza und die Frage nach der Unsterblichkeit* (M 43), Leiden, 1981.

51.　　R. van Brakell Buys, *De wijsheid van Spinoza en de schoonheid der Tachtigers* (M 16), Leiden, 1959; R. Henrard, *De spinozistische achtergrond van de Beweging van tachtig* (M 32), Leiden, 1974 idem, *Wijsheidsgestalten in dichterwoord. Onderzoek naar de invloed van Spinoza op de Nederlandse literatuur*, Assen, 1977.

52.　　W. G. van der Tak, *Spinozistische gedachten in Goethes Faust* (M 9), Leiden, 1950; Th.C. van Stockum, *Goethe en Spinoza* (M 13), Leiden, 1956.

53.　　C. de Deugd, *Wordsworth en Spinoza* (M 25), Leiden, 1969.

54.　　M. Gysens-Gosselin, *Hegel en Spinoza* (M 27), Leiden 1971; W. N. A. Klever, *Dialektiek contra axiomatiek. Een confrontatie tussen Spinoza en Hegel onder methodologisch opzicht* (M 33), Leiden, 1974; H. C. Lucas, *Spinoza in Hegels Logik* (M 45), Leiden, 1982.

55.　　For Marx's own reception of Spinoza, see E. E. Schrader, *Substanz und Begriff. Zur Spinoza-Rezeption Marxens* (M 47), Leiden, 1985.

56.　　T. de Vries, *Baruch de Spinoza in Selbstzeugnissen und Bilddokumenten*, Reinbek bei Hamburg, 1970 (reprints in 1981 and 1983); idem, *Spinoza, beeldenstormer en wereldbouwer*, Amsterdam 1972 (reprint 1976).

57.　　P. Steenbakkers, *Over kennis en ideologie bij Louis Althusser. Een materialistische kritiek*, Groningen, 1982.

58.　　H. G. Hubbeling, "Calvinistisch Spinozisme: J. H. Scholten," *Bzzletin* 13 (1984), 16-19, 23; idem, "Synthetisch modernisme: J. H. Scholten als wijsgeer en theoloog," *Nederlands Theologisch Tijdschrift* 16 (1961), 107-142.

59.　　G. van Suchtelen, "Le spinozisme de Jan van Vloten ou le romantisme d'un penseur naturaliste" *Spinoza entre Lumière et Romantisme*, 339-348; idem, "Het Spinozisme van Jan van Vloten. De romantische aard van een naturalist," *Bulletin* 13 (1984), 20-23.

60.　　W. G. van der Tak, "Willem Meijer, de vrijdenker-spinozist," *Bzzletin* 13 (1984), 33-35.

61.　　See also C. Bouman, *Het zondebergip bij Spinoza en Scholten. Een vergelijking*, Thesis, Utrecht, 1982.

62.　　A. de Lange, *J. H. Gunning jr. en het Spinoza-standbeeld* (M 44), Leiden, 1982.

63.　　F. Akkerman, *Studies in the Posthumous Works of Spinoza*, Groningen, 1980; idem, "J. H. Glazemaker, an early translator of Spinoza," *Spinoza's political and theological thought*, 23-29.

64.　　A. J. Klijnsmit, *Spinoza and Grammatical Tradition* (M 49), Leiden, 1986; idem, "Spinoza over taal," *Studia Rosenthaliana* 19 (1985), 1-38.

65.　　H. G. Hubbeling, *Spinoza*, Freiburg/München, 1978, 61.

66.　　In a paper that is not yet published.

67.　　J. J. Groen, "Spinoza: Philosopher and Prophet," *Spinoza on Knowing, Geing and Freedom*, 69-81.

Proper Name Index

References to philosophical or religious movements bearing the name of an individual, e.g., Cartesianism, Christianity, etc., are listed with those to the individual after whom they are named.

Subject Index

English and French terms are indexed together (along with the occasional Latin or Greek term), with the English term given priority and the French equivalent given in parentheses, in cases where both an English term and a French equivalent rate an index entry.

(the) Absolute, 360, 364-368, 370

action (activité), 2, 9, 11, 41, 43, 44, 47-49, 51, 53, 58, 59, 61, 70, 71, 75, 83, 92, 93, 94, 100, 102, 104, 107, 110, 114, 117, 118, 125, 127, 134, 137, 140-142, 147, 148, 150, 151, 153, 155, 161, 176-179, 182-184, 186-189, 192-194, 196-207, 211, 217, 219, 223, 225-230, 232, 234-236, 238, 239-244, 246, 247, 249-253, 263, 276, 277, 279, 288, 290, 291, 293, 298, 302, 303, 310-313, 316, 318, 320, 326, 332, 359, 361-363, 370, 371, 373, 377

affect, 49, 52, 58, 59, 66, 83, 102, 117, 152, 161, 162, 169-171, 176-178, 182-189, 191-194, 201, 203, 209-213, 216-220, 227, 235, 236, 242, 245-252, 256, 257, 269, 284, 310, 311, 318-321, 324, 326, 329, 330, 332, 338, 343-346, 374, 392

affect actif, affects-actions, 176-178, 182, 186, 188, 191, 247

affects-passions, 247, 249, 251

anthropomorphiser, 299, 313

apatheia, 180

appetite, appetitus, 41, 47-50, 52, 55, 100, 200, 343

atomisme, 60

attribute (attribut), 1-16, 23-26, 29-31, 32, 34-38, 42, 47, 51, 53, 54, 63, 65-76, 77-81, 87-90, 97-99, 101, 105, 106, 109, 110, 118, 119, 126, 127, 140-146, 148, 159-165, 170, 172-174, 185, 208, 211, 216, 240-243, 245, 250, 283, 290, 310, 311, 322, 363-368, 370, 371, 375, 379

autonomie, 68, 239, 240, 322, 323

béatitude, 242, 243, 324, 325

blame, 51, 238

body (corps), 1, 15, 19, 25, 28, 29, 43, 47-50, 54, 55, 58-61, 63-67, 74, 76, 77, 79-81, 82-86, 88-93, 96-100, 104, 111, 121-123, 125, 127, 131, 132, 141, 144, 146, 148-150, 154, 162, 163, 165-167, 170, 171, 173, 174, 178-185, 188, 189, 191, 192, 195, 196, 200, 202, 203, 206-208, 212, 214-216, 218, 219, 222, 225-227, 237, 238, 244-251, 271, 273, 284, 285, 302, 306, 307, 310-324, 326, 334, 360, 363, 365, 368-371, 385, 390, 392

cause, 6, 14, 15, 18, 23, 32, 40-56, 58-67, 69-76, 77-79, 82, 86, 87, 88, 91, 95, 102, 107, 111, 114-118, 120, 121, 128, 131-133, 136-140, 142-146, 159-168, 170, 172-175, 176, 177, 180-183, 185, 186, 188, 189, 191, 196-200, 205-207, 211-214, 216, 217, 223, 225, 235-237, 239-244, 246, 247, 249-252, 263, 264, 268, 276-278, 280, 304, 311, 312, 314, 316-321, 324, 325, 335, 332, 334, 335, 337-339, 346, 345, 353, 362, 367, 369, 371

causa sui, 71, 137, 140, 366

cause adéquate, 176, 244, 246, 247, 249, 311, 316, 318, 320, 321, 325

causes intérieures, 61, 196

external cause (cause extérieure), 14, 15, 115, 137, 177, 183, 196, 206, 211-214, 217, 235, 239, 241, 242, 244-247

final cause (cause finale), 40-45, 47, 48, 51, 59, 62, 65, 77-79, 246, 313, 328, 330, 377

immanent cause (cause immanente), 69, 70, 160, 244

proximate cause, 86, 87, 136-140, 142-144, 371